ISBN 978-0-483-62370-5
PIBN 10165876

THE

# WESTMINSTER REVIEW.

*JANUARY TO JUNE*
*(INCLUSIVE)*
1900.

---

"Truth can never be confirmed enough,
Though doubts did ever sleep."
SHAKSPEARE.

aḥrḥeitšliebe zeigt ſich darin, daß man überall das Gute zu finden und zu ſchätzen weiß.
GŌTHE.

---

VOL. CLIII.

NEW YORK:
THE LEONARD SCOTT PUBLICATION COMPANY,
7 & 9 WARREN STREET.
MDCCCC.

# THE
# WESTMINSTER REVIEW.

### VOL. CLIII. No. 1.—JANUARY 1900.

## THE CARNAGE IN SOUTH AFRICA.

"In some quarters the idea is put forward that the Government ought to have issued an ultimatum to President Kruger—an ultimatum which would have certainly been rejected, and which must have led to war. Sir, I do not propose to discuss such a contingency as that. A war in South Africa would be one of the most serious wars that could possibly be waged. It would be in the nature of a civil war. It would be a long war, a bitter war, and a costly war ; and it would leave behind it the embers of a strife which I believe generations would hardly be long enough to extinguish. To go to war with President Kruger, in order to force upon him reforms in the internal affairs of his State, in which Secretaries of State, standing in this place, have repudiated all right of interference—that would be a course of action as immoral as it would have been unwise."

THIS prophecy, uttered by Mr. Chamberlain in the House of Commons on May 8, 1895, has already been fulfilled to a large extent. Soon three months will have elapsed since that immoral and unwise war began. It has been a bitterer war already than he himself, no doubt, imagined. He miscalculated the power of resistance shown by the inhabitants of two Commonwealths, in the spirit of the Swiss of old, against an aggression which has been described as a Capitalists' War, an Exchange War, a Gold Gamblers' War. The remainder of the prophet's forecast will come true in due time. All sensible friends of progress will regret that ; but they know on whose shoulders the responsibility lies.

I do not say this from the point of view attributed to those who are nicknamed Little Englanders because they maintain principles formerly asserted in the strongest manner by the Colonial Secretary himself. I hold that this country, if acting on the proper lines of public justice—which includes faith being kept in regard to treaties solemnly concluded, even with a weak people—has a great and noble mission to accomplish. For this reason, among others, I should have been sorry to see England weakened at home by dis-

ruption ; and whatever I have been able to do in the way of helping
to counteract such a movement, has—I may, perhaps, be allowed
to state here—been once acknowledged in public meeting by
Mr. Chamberlain in very honouring terms.

If I have any other title to free speech on the present occasion,
it is this. I do not go with the maxim : "My country, right or
wrong!" No; I have opposed the Governments of my own
country when it was a question of the rights of Italians, Hun-
garians, or Poles, against unjust oppression. If Switzerland, which
once belonged to us, and whose inhabitants are, by two-thirds,
German in race and speech, were to-morrow attacked by Germany,
I would stigmatise such a deed as a shameless crime. I would not
say that it must be seen through. So, I think I may claim the
right of free criticism when I see a land which has become my
second home, involved, through an immoral war, in grave perils
predicted by Mr. Chamberlain himself.

The difficulties of such criticism I know only too well. For
many years past I have been astonished over and over again to
find, in conversation with highly educated men, with public writers,
and politicians of note, a most egregious ignorance of the simplest
facts connected with Transvaal affairs. Up to the recent complica-
tion, how few there were who had even a notion of two different
treaties having been concluded, one of which was superseded by the
other. None of those I spoke to—and they were many—had ever
read the text of those treaties. Yet they were men who had to
enlighten public opinion! It is such tiresome work to "potter over
Blue-books," as Mr. Disraeli said, under whose Government the
South African Republic was lawlessly destroyed. The Press, I am
sorry to say from much personal experience, in but too many cases
fostered the continuance of this strange ignorance, either by wilful
misrepresentation or by its own lack of distinct knowledge.

At this moment, such is the heat of unjust passion against a
people defending its independence against baseless claims of suzerainty, that the war which the Boers have been craftily forced into
is even styled a "revolt." Do those who use that word realise the
consequences? Or have they, perchance, already those cruel court-
martial procedures in view, which generally follow the overthrow
of a revolt?

A revolt, forsooth! The suzerainty, which did exist from 1881
to 1884, was formally abolished by the new Treaty of that latter
year. For that very purpose the Transvaal Deputation had come
to London in 1883; and after prolonged negotiations Lord Derby
granted their demand. With his own hand he struck out all the
suzerainty clauses both in the Preamble and in the several paragraphs
of the Pretoria Convention of 1881. The new Treaty of 1884,
which does not contain a syllable about suzerainty, he declared

to be " in substitution for the Convention of Pretoria." No sophistry, no deliberate falsehood, will alter that plain fact.

As late as the time of the criminal Jameson Raid, Mr. Chamberlain, in an official despatch, declared the South African Republic to be " a foreign State, a foreign Power, with which Her Majesty is at peace and in treaty relations." Can a foreign State, a foreign Power, be in revolt against another foreign Power? The idea is too absurd to be discussed for a single moment.

How did the Governments of other countries act in that matter? In February 1895, Baron Marschall von Bieberstein, the Foreign Secretary of Germany, declared both to Sir Edward Malet, the English Ambassador at Berlin, and to the Government in London through Count Hatzfeld, that " German interests demanded *the continuance of the Transvaal as an* INDEPENDENT STATE, *as defined by the Treaty of* 1884, and the maintenance of the *status quo* with reference to the railways and the harbour of Delagoa Bay."

This declaration was made eleven months before the Rhodes-Jameson Raid. In the midst of that abominable act of land-piracy, which the Poet Laureate fervently sang, but which was branded as a crime by an English Court of Justice, Mr. Chamberlain found it advisable to acknowledge the South African Republic as a foreign Power. Yet now that war into which the Transvaal people have been driven by an interference in their internal affairs, which Conservative and Liberal State Secretaries had repudiated as a wrong ever since 1884; that bitter and costly war which Mr. Chamberlain said generations would hardly be long enough to extinguish; that war is suddenly to be changed into a "Boer Revolt" against a non-existent suzerainty!

It is a significant fact that, since the German Emperor paid his private visit here, a communication has been sent round, after all, to the various foreign Governments intimating that this country is in "a state of war" with the two South African Republics. This was a very necessary act, considering that England could not otherwise exercise that right of search which she has recently used at sea during the present hostilities. Foreign Powers would not tolerate a different conduct. Let it be noted here that the Governments of Pretoria and Bloemfontein have acted, in this matter, quite correctly from the beginning. They, already in October last, issued their proclamation of "a state of war." Even as President Kruger had Treaty right on his side, when refusing to submit to the suzerainty claim which was craftily maintained down to the last moment of the negotiations, by the false use of the term "Conventions" in the plural, so he also acted in full accordance with international law when declaring that between his country and his Orange Free State ally on the one hand, and England on the other, there was now a state of war.

The rather belated similar declaration, which has now been made here, was a sad blow to those who went by the theory of a Boer " revolt." So they tried to recover lost ground by pointing to the fact of the United States Government having acknowledged the Southern Confederates as belligerents, whilst yet maintaining that they were " rebels." A moment's reflection will show how hollow this would-be comparison is. In the interest of England herself it would have been far better not to bring those days of a tremendous struggle to mind.

It is the custom now to speak of an Anglo-Saxon Alliance. Mr. Chamberlain has continually dwelt upon it, even going to the extent of wrongly announcing a new Triple Alliance between the three Germanic races on this and on the other side of the Atlantic. Of the plain fact that the Low German or Dutch-speaking Boers also belong to the Germanic race—President Kruger being even the descendant of a German, as not a few other people of the Transvaal, of the Orange Free State, and of the Cape Colony are—he took no heed. However, let that pass. Protests loud enough were raised at once by those who were to be drawn into the new Triple Alliance. In America, more especially, the idea of " either a present or a prospective alliance " was absolutely rejected in the severest terms.

Every one in England must remember into what stress of difficulties the United States—the " Disunited States," as they were sneeringly called—had been brought by the virtual support given to the Slaveholders' League by the then governing classes of this country. The destruction of the great Transatlantic Republic was their distinct wish and aim. Palmerston, Russell, Gladstone, were at one in that desire. Pirate ships were fitted out here with the evident knowledge of the authorities.

When the war was over, Lord John Russell, wishing to obtain introductions to distinguished men in the United States for his son, Lord Amberley—" lest that son should meet there manifestations of ill-will on account of his father "—applied to a prominent English writer, who had always stood true to the American Union cause and was well acquainted with its leaders. Dining in the house of that friend of mine, Lord John Russell was first subjected by him to a severe cross-examination on the question of the *Alabama*. Driven into a corner, the Foreign Secretary of England had finally to avow that he had really been quite aware of the character of the *Alabama* when it left port. After this pitiful confession and an expression of repentance, the desired introductions were given to Lord John Russell.

Now, it was partly owing to the harassing pressure put upon the Government at Washington by the English Government, partly to humanitarian considerations, that the United States finally acknow-

ledged the rebel Slaveholders' League as a belligerent body.    But
rebels the so-called Confederates were.    They tried to secede from,
and to dismember, a country of which, constitutionally, their States
were as much an integral part as the Principality of Wales and the
Kingdoms of Scotland and Ireland are integral parts of the United
Kingdom.

Rebels, the people of the South African Republic, acknowledged
as a foreign Power by England herself, or of the Orange Free
State, another independent State, are not.    The expression " revolt "
does, therefore, not apply to them.    They rightfully wage war.

Much has been said by those who misrepresent the status of the
South African Commonwealths, about the evil designs shown by the
Government at Pretoria through its vast armaments since 1884—
that is, before the Jameson Raid.    Was that not, it is asked, clear
proof of aggressive Boer intentions ?

According to the official report of Major White, who made his
inspection in the interest of this country, there were no vast
armaments in the Transvaal at that early time.    An alleged recent
letter of General Joubert is, however, quoted to the contrary.    In
it he says, or is made to say, that Major White was purposely not
shown everything.    It is difficult to know whether that letter of
Joubert is genuine.    But supposing it were : has a people which
had been unjustly put under foreign dominion for four years, and
which at last recovered its independence, at least to some extent, in
fair fight, and afterwards by negotiation—has such a people, being
a " foreign Power " since 1884, no right to arm itself in order not
to fall once more under the yoke of another foreign Power ? Why
is the fact of the South African Republic having been lawlessly
overrun and destroyed from 1877–81, never alluded to in those discussions ?    Would Englishmen, if they had been conquered by
France, then been restored, after a fight, to partial independence
under French suzerainty, and finally been acknowledged as a foreign
Power, though under an irksome treaty obligation—would they
consider themselves disentitled from armaments in view of future
new dangers ?

If the Government at Pretoria made such armaments since 1884,
the subsequent Jameson Raid proved that they were right and wise.
The present war shows their wisdom once more.

The whole population of the allied South African Republics,
which have to stand or to fall together, is not more than that of a
second-rate English town.    Was it, then, to be expected that in
presence of the largest Power of the world, they, with the experience
of their former subjection to conquest, would stand forth wholly
naked for any fresh aggression to come upon them ?    Is this the
proper notion of chivalry ?

As it is, the peasant militia of those Commonwealths, though in possession of good artillery and guns, have no Lancers, no swords, no bayonets even, and can consequently be easily treated to " cold steel " at close quarters. Still, even in this condition, they give a great deal to do to their enemies, and will yet give them a great deal more to do for some time to come. Here a sad outlook opens up. No one could more deplore it than the writer of these present remarks, which, harshly as they may grate on the ears of men misled by want of knowledge or by passion, are only made in the cause of truth, of justice, and of what he holds to be the best interests of England herself.

Foreign Powers hostile to this country, such as Russia and France, eagerly watch the continuance of this war. They see that mighty England will soon have more than one-half of her regular army engaged in a struggle with the tiny population of the Transvaal and of the Orange Free State. They know that, small as the number of that army, as fixed by Parliament, is, it could not even be completed by recruiting. They see that in the militia there has also been a dwindling away of numbers. They are surprised by observing the necessity of using sea-forces, England's strongest arm, hundreds of miles away inland—both men and material. They remember the extraordinary advice given to officers by Lord Wolseley in his " Soldier's Pocket-Book," and they draw therefrom an obvious conclusion as to the disproportionate loss of officers, which decapitates an army, as it were. They probably ask themselves whether, under these circumstances, England will be compelled, or whether her popular classes will be willing, to militarise her institutions on the Continental system ? Perchance her worst enemies may already ponder over the question whether, if she is yet more deeply engaged in South Africa, this would not be the opportunity for striking a blow at her—say, in Asia.

Be that as it may, and whatever be the issue of this immoral and unwise war, England's forces will for a long time to come be engaged in South Africa to such an extent as to cripple her power, if her citizens are not inclined to become soldiers, one and all. Even if victorious in this present struggle, she would have a new Ireland upon her hands ; which would mean free leave for Russian and perhaps French designs. Such will be to all appearance, in the opinion of one who claims to be a well-wisher of England, the inevitable and sad results of this frivolously fostered carnage.

KARL BLIND

# A PLEA FOR FINLAND.[1]

At a time when the public mind in England has been inflamed by a war-fever generated by the aggressive spirit of Jingoism it is probable that the struggle of heroic little Finland for the preservation of her autonomy has not attracted the attention it deserves. The great Powers of Europe must unhappily be regarded as rather the enemies than the friends of liberty. Militarism has rendered this inevitable. The case of Finland is an illustration of the indifference of at least one great Empire to the principles of justice which ought to regulate its relations with a people who had by the greatest self-sacrifice won the right to the internal management of their own affairs. There is a grim irony in the fact that, only three months before the Peace Conference promoted by the present Czar commenced its meritorious task of trying to substitute arbitration for the sword, the same sovereign deliberately broke the solemn promise made by his predecessors and by himself to uphold the fundamental laws of Finland.

The story of Finland's shameful betrayal by a crowned head, so recently as February 1899, is clearly and eloquently told in the pamphlet *Pour la Finlande*, by M. René Puaux, which has been published by the well-known Paris firm of P. V. Stock. In an interesting preface to the pamphlet, M. Anatole France well describes the cause of Finland as a cause which ought to interest every nation, " if it be true that there is a human solidarity."

The history of Finland is, indeed, exceedingly interesting, and not inglorious unless the love of freedom and the passionate devotion of a people to their national ideals are to be treated with indifference and distain in these days when the vile and, one would imagine, the obsolete theory that " Might is Right " has been advocated not only by a section of the English Press, but by Cabinet Ministers, with brazen effrontery.

The early inhabitants of Finland apparently lived in separate little communities, each independent of the other. Their religion was a deification of the elemental forces of Nature. In this respect they resembled most of the Scandinavian races.

In 1157 Christianity was introduced into the country by Erik

---

[1] *Pour la Finlande.* Par Réne Puaux. Avec une Préface d'Anatole France, de l'Académie Française. Paris : P. V. Stock.

Jeddvardssen, King of Sweden, better known as St. Erik, and by Henry, Bishop of Upsala, an Englishman by birth. King Erik, being called away to attend to the affairs of his own country, left the Bishop of Upsala behind him to complete the task of converting and civilising the Finns, and in 1158 this pious prelate sealed his faith with his blood. Since then St. Henry has been the patron saint of Finland. Until 1209 the country was partly independent, when Thomas, another bishop of English' birth, came to supplement the missionary work of St. Henry, and, according to some accounts, nearly succeeded in handing over Finland to the Pope. After a series of sanguinary conflicts, the Christian faith finally obtained a lasting foothold in the country, and in 1284 Finland, colonised by the Swedes, was mentioned in official documents as the apanage of the Swedish Crown. Sixty years later we find the Finns recognised as the equals of the Swedes. The inhabitants had cast off the yoke of slavery, and each of the large provinces of Finland had a separate code of legislation. By this time Russia had appeared upon the scene as the rival of Sweden in the struggle to dominate the fate of Finland. In 1362 the Swedish Government recognised the political rights of the Finns to the extent of granting to the Chief Justice, the Bishop, and a dozen representatives of the peasantry, the privilege of taking part in the election of the King of Sweden. About this time agriculture and other useful arts were introduced into Finland. Russian aggression had for the time been checked, and for a short period Finland enjoyed prosperity and progressed with marvellous rapidity. In the wars against the Russians the Finns had displayed heroic bravery.

It is recorded that the Finnish leader, Knut Posse, maintained a successful siege for six weeks in the Castle of Viborg against 60,000 Russian soldiers. In 1496 the Russians resumed their barbarous attacks on the country, which they devastated with fire and sword. The Swedes were driven out of Finland, and a treaty of peace was concluded with the Russians by the envoys of the Bishop of Abo, who had then supreme authority in the country, and also of Knut Posse, on behalf of the Finns. The peace lasted up to the time when Gustavus Vasa ascended the throne of Sweden. He, of course, as a conqueror by profession, kept his eyes on Finland, and thought it his duty to interfere in the affairs of that country. A comparative peace, however, reigned, broken only by occasional conflicts with Russia. Under the successors of Gustavus Vasa Finland was sometimes dependent on the Swedish Crown, but at other times it was practically free. Under King Johan III. the title of Grand Duchy was assigned to Finland. Whenever the country found a period of repose, wonderful efforts were made by the inhabitants to develop its material and intellectual resources. Under the Governor, P⸱r Brahe the Younger (1637–54), Finland for the first time had a University—

the University of Abo. Printing was introduced; the Bible was translated into Finnish, and the first Finnish Grammar made its appearance.

Unfortunately, this bright spell of prosperity was not destined to last long. A contingent of troops from Finland was required by Sweden, and many young Finlanders, who might have signalised themselves by the cultivation of the arts of peace, perished fighting bravely in Poland or Denmark. A succession of wars had almost ruined the country, and when the Treaty of Saint-Germain opened a perspective of peace and happiness, fresh misfortunes decimated the population.

Peter the Great cast envious eyes on Finland, and sought to wrest the country from the Swedes. To his ambitious designs the Finns owed a renewal of their sufferings. Charles XII., when he came to the Swedish throne, brought war in his train. The people of Finland were forced to leave their country in thousands for military service in the Baltic Provinces, and the Russians took advantage of the country's unprotected condition to ravage it in their usual ruthless fashion. Resistance, which, under the circumstances, was ineffectual, only led to a Russian occupation of eight years. The Russians carried off 20,000 of the inhabitants to sell the most of them as slaves in Persia. By the Peace of Nystad, in 1721, the province of Wiborg was ceded to Russia as the price of peace. Then once more came a golden era during which "the war-drum throbbed no longer." The Finns were not slow in making good use of their opportunities. A Parliamentary régime was introduced. The Swedish Codes were translated into Finnish, and the finances of the country were regulated so as to lay the foundation for the commercial prosperity of Finland. This was Finland's happy period, the age of liberty, the " Frihetstiden."

In 1741 " ravening politics," to use the perhaps unwise phrase of the late Poet Laureate (for no wise man can afford to "scorn" politics), led to a recrudescence of war. The new political leaders of Finland in 1741 entered into a secret alliance with France against Russia with a view to supporting Elizabeth, the rival of Ivan VI. Elizabeth, having triumphed, ascended the Russian throne and declared war against Sweden. The Finns, who were willing to aid her when she was at war with Russia, refused to join her against Sweden. The result was a Russian military invasion. Once more desolation reigned in this ill-fated country. In 1743, by the Treaty of Abo, Russia gained a fresh portion of Finnish territory.

Again there was peace, and deathless Finland, arising like the Phœnix from her ashes, marched resolutely along the path of progress. To quote the beautiful language of M. René Puaux, " those alternatives of death and resurrection are the most profound characteristics of her nature. Just as in her climate the six long months of winter seem for ever to destroy every hope of fresh germination, though a few fine days suffice to make the flowers bloom and the fields teem with golden grain, so it is with her national life. ' Never vanquished': such has been her motto, and yet never has any people experienced such hardships at the hands of Nature and of man."

Gustavus III. gave the Finns the fundamental laws which they still justly claim as their national heritage. He built canals in the country and encouraged science and art.

Towards the close of the eighteenth century, when Gustavus IV. refused to take part in a coalition of Continental Powers, the Czar, Alexander I., then an ally of Napoleon, invaded Finland. The Swedish monarch was too much occupied with a war against Norway to send troops to help the Finns, who, after a gallant struggle, had to yield, and in 1809 a treaty was solemnly entered into and concluded between the Czar and the people of Finland.

The terms of the Treaty of Fredriksham are memorable, especially its sixth article, whereby the Czar declares that he has resolved to govern the inhabitants of the country he had taken possession of so as to allow them "the spontaneous exercise of their religion, their rights of property, and their privileges." The King of Sweden is made a party to this treaty to the extent of declaring himself freed from the duty, which he would otherwise have held sacred, of making reservations in favour of his former subjects. The treaty made with the Finns by Alexander I. was as much dictated by self-interest as by a sense of justice. The Czar had reason to anticipate an alliance between Napoleon and Sweden, and by annexing Finland to Russia he was able to prevent the passage of an invading army north-ward into Russia. When opening the Diet at Borga, in 1809, the Czar promised to maintain the fundamental laws of Finland. He con-firmed this promise by his manifesto, which is still known as " the Great Charter " of Finland. The political organisation of the Grand Duchy of Finland, in accordance with the " Form of Government " of 1772 and the Act of Union of 1789, declares that the monarch is to govern the country according to law, and not to interfere with the life, honour, liberty, or property of any subject unless in virtue of a legal condemnation; that every subject is to be tried by the tribunal to which his case is assigned by the general law; that the monarch cannot create any new law, or abolish any old law, save by the consent of the Estates; and that the Estates cannot alter the laws save with the consent of the monarch. The Act of Union pre-scribes that the offices of the country are to be open only to citizens resident in the country, and that the nation has the imprescriptible right to deliberate and confer with the monarch as to whatever was necessary for the maintenance of the State. Thus it will be seen that, while the power of government belongs to the monarch alone, he is responsible for his proper exercise of it to God and to the country. The Emperor Alexander III. extended the right of legal initiative to the Diet of Finland. The Emperor was to be assisted in his task by the Governor-General of Finland, whom he was to select, and by the Senate, composed of twenty members and divided into a juridical and administrative section.

Such was the Constitution of Finland, under which the country progressed " by leaps and bounds." It is true that the reaction in Europe after the Treaty of Vienna made itself felt in Finland, and we find that for fifty years no Diet was convoked. However, when in 1863 Alexander II. convoked the Diet of Finland, he declared his desire to be " useful " to Finland, and five years later a new law was passed, fixing a period of five years at most for the convocation of the national assembly, and declaring that no fundamental law could be created, amended, interpreted, or revoked, save on the proposal of the Emperor and Grand Duke, and with the consent of all the Estates. Alexander II. gave his consent to this law, and solemnly affixed his signature to it.

The Budget of Finland for 1898-1900 shows a considerable surplus of revenue over expenditure. The country's prosperity was a fact patent to all. It had about 1050 schools of all kinds. It had given, moreover, to the world poets, painters, sculptors, and explorers. The names of Runeberg and Johani Abo may not be as familiar as those of Shakespeare or Browning, but, nevertheless, they are eminent poets. As an explorer certainly Nordenskiöld has won a world-wide reputation.

It has been the unenviable task of the present Czar of Russia, Nicholas II., to strike a blow at the autonomy of Finland, and that in the teeth of his own promise on ascending the throne in 1894 to "ratify and confirm expressly the religion, the fundamental laws, rights and privileges " of the country. The enemies of Finland had plotted against her liberties, and they succeeded. On February 15, 1899, Nicholas II. issued a manifesto, the effect of which was to deprive Finland of self-government. By reserving to himself the power of deciding what were Imperial and what were local questions the Czar can exercise autocratic authority, so that the old Constitution of Finland is virtually wiped out.

In vain were appeals made by the Senate, and afterwards by the whole nation, to reconsider this matter, and to spare the political rights which the Finns had purchased so dearly. Russia, the ruthless destroyer of Polish liberty, was not likely to have mercy on Finland. And now the people of this northern land have shown their sense of the foul wrong done to them by going into national mourning.

In many respects the case of Finland resembles that of Ireland. Indeed, the fate of Ireland has, if possible, been worse. It was not through the rivalries of two strong nations that the Irish people suffered. They were the victims of a war of extermination. We have seen how in the early years of the eighteenth century Russia sent the Finns to be sold as slaves in Persia. Cromwell drove the Irish into slavery in like manner, unless he had already put them cruelly to the sword. As the Irish put it, he sent them to "Hell or Connaught." Finland, at least, had a Constitution, the advantages of which she enjoyed for the best part of a century. Not so Ireland. From 1782 down to 1800 she had a Parliament of her own, and that only a sectarian Parliament. The Act of Union, of which mention is made in Finland's history, gave her a measure of freedom and a field for self-development. The Irish Act of Union was a convenient mode of strangling a nation's liberties. To-day, disarmed, impoverished, over-taxed, Ireland appeals to the "dominant partner"—or rather to her hereditary tyrant—for the restoration of her legislature—for the modicum of political independence called Home Rule. Finland and Ireland should, therefore, be bound by kindred sympathies, for they are fellow-sufferers. It were well for humanity if these two great Powers, England and Russia, which both aim at material aggrandisement, strove to show the world they were truly civilised by securing the inalienable right of self-government to the struggling nationalities which groan under their oppressive sway.

D. F. HANNIGAN.

# OTTOMAN PROVINCIAL GOVERNMENT.

ALL Turkey is divided into "vilayets," or provinces, governed by a
"Vali," or governor, in "Merkez-i-vilayet." The "vilayet" comprises "sandjak," "kaza," "nahiyeh," or department, district,
commune—being each of first or second class, and the "kaza"
being also of third class. This hierarchy of departments, &c., is
often overruled by geographical contiguity. Besides the familiar
administrations civil—of justice, financial, military, of police, of public
instruction, local, of census—Turkey has her special arrangements
for "evkaf" (charitable bequests) and "tapoo" (explained later).
The Vali oversees all but matters of justice and the military
administration.

I. In every "Merkez-i-vilayet" or "Vilayet-merkezi," the epony-
mous residential town of the Vali, there is a Council of Administration ("mejlis-i-idâré"), with a "qâdi" (judge) and "mufti" (sort of
religious judge), presided over by Vali, who also gives a list out of
which the councillors—Christian and Mussulman, city notables—are
chosen by the people. Of these members one is *procureur-général.*

In *civil* administration, the Minister of the Interior sends to the
various Valis his orders. These each Vali opens, sends to his chief
secretary, who hands to the secretary, called "mumâïz." The latter
sends copies of each order to the under-governors ("mutesarif,"
"kaïmakam," and "mudir") of the vilayet. Each vilayet's *Official
Gazette* is censured by this chief secretary.

In *justice* administration, the "Merkez-i-vilayet" has its Civil
Permissive Court ("Bidayet-i-huqûq") of first instance; its Permissive Penal Court of first instance; its courts of appeal ("istinâf")
and of commerce ("tijârat"). [The only Court of Cassation is in
the capital.]

The *finance* administration is under the "defterdâr" (registrar).
Second to him in control in his bureau is the "muhasebejy"
(accountant). The "defterdâr" alone authorises employés' salaries
to be paid out of the "caisse," where are deposited the imposts, &c.
of the whole "Merkez-i-vilayet."

*Military* administration is under the Commandant (military)
Pasha, ranking as "mushîr" (marshal) whenever the "Merkez-i-
vilayet" is also "Merkez-i-ordu" (centre for troops).

*Gendarmerie and police* are administered by a pasha of gendarmerie, called " Alaï bey," in the " Merkez-i-vilayet," which has both gendarmerie and police.

A Council of Education, with honorary members, looks after *instruction.* The president (" ma'arif mudiri,") has his secretary and oversees all schools both of vilayet and of " Merkez-i-vilayet." The president is sent from Constantinople.

Government does not interfere with *local* or *oppidan* administration, with its local assembly, local rate-collectors (sergeants), and night watchmen—local assembly being elected on same lines as " mejlis-i-daré."

In one chamber of the bicameral *census* bureau sits the " nufûs me'moory " (census chief), while in the other clerks enter the " hamidiyyé "—papers of origin, determining claim to passports and liability to military service.

The *charitable bequests* (" evkâf ") bureau has its (turbaned) " hoja " (*lit.* master), called " mudir," and clerks.

" *Tapoo* " is the most peculiarly Turkish bureau. All land is inalienably Government property. " Tapoo " transfers land. Transference to dead holder's heirs is " naql." Transference to proposed holder (under Government) by living actual holder (under Government) is " feragh." For " naql " no judge need be present. For " feragh " a judge (" hakim ") must be at hand to examine all papers, &c. The " Tapoo " bureau has its " me'moor " and clerks.

So much for the " Merkez-i-vilayet." I now pass to the " Sandjak-merkezi " or " Merkez-i-sandjak."

II. Here, in *civil* government, the president is the " mutesarif " (governor of sandjak), assisted by a " mufti " and " qâdi," besides " tahrirât mudiri," answering, in Sandjak, to the chief secretary in vilayet council.

In Sandjak *justice,* besides much that is an adumbration of vilayet justice, we have, specially, the " mustantiq " (interrogator or *juge d'instruction*), who is, however, the *procureur-général* of the " Merkez-i-vilayet " (to which ordinarily lies an appeal from Sandjak justice), under another name.

In Sandjak *finance* the " mal-mudiri " answers to the vilayet " defterdâr," and " sanduk-ermini " to the vilayet *caissier.*

In things *military* the vilayet commandant pasha is, in the Sandjak, only " kaïmakan " (colonel), with his staff.

The Sandjak *police* bureau comprises one commissary, one officer of gendarmerie, and horse and foot.

*Instruction* in the Sandjak is represented, in each case, by one primary (" rooshdeea ") school, two teachers, and a porter, payable by the Sandjak " mal-mudiri."

The local, census, charitable bequests, and *tapoo* bureaus of the Sanjak are mere miniatures of those in the " Merkez-i-vilayet."

III. Administration of " kaza " (called also " kaïmakamlik ').

The " Merkez-i-kaza " *civil* court president is a " kaïmakan " ; this court has a " tahrirât kâtibi " (clerk), instead of " tahrirât mudiri " (overseer), as in the Sandjak court (civil). The " kaza " has a council-chamber and secretarial bureau (" tahrirât odasy ").

In the " kaza " the *military* head is " binbashi " (*lit.* " head of 1000 ").

The other bureaus approximate, in miniature, to those of the " Merkez-i-sandjak."

IV. The government of the " nahiyé " or commune. This is the smallest administration. In the " Merkez-i-nahiyé " are a " mudir," " qadi-naïbi " (judge-substitute), and one " gizer " or " mookhtar " —common to " nahiyé," " kaza," " sandjak," and " vilayet "—a collector of taxes on land, houses, polls, and property other than real. Again. in every commune there is, in places where there is no " mudir," a sort of local government county council, called " Ikhtiyâr mejlisi " (*lit.* choice council), and dealing with the commune's *own* administration. The judge-substitute is appointed by the judge (" qâdi "), and can give from twenty-four hours' to one week's imprisonment, besides, like our registrar, controlling marriage-papers.

Thus far the commune or " nahiyé."

I add provisions, &c., common to " vilayet," " sandjak," " kaza," (and " nahiyé ") :

(*a*) The only Court of Cassation for all Turkey is in Constantinople.

(β) The judge for " vilayet," " sandjak," and " kaza," as also the " vali," " mutesarif," and " kaïmakam," comes from Constantinople. " Nahiyé " has its " judge-substitute."

(γ) All contributions are collected by the " gizeer " or " mookhtar," appointed for and by the people of each quarter, and collecting (as mentioned under " nahiyé ") alone or with the assistance of gendarmerie.

(δ) Conscription is by lot. Conscription is according to " terteeb evvel " (first arrangement), when a soldier is made *at once*, or according to " terteeb sâni " (second arrangement), when a soldier is made only *when and if wanted.*

Unless previously called up, soldiers are drafted into the reserve, called " redeef," in three years' time.

(ε) " Sergeants " look after bad meat offered for sale, see to fires, collect Government shop-rents and municipality fines.

(ζ) From the capital comes the municipality doctor for " vilayet," " sandjak " and " kaza." He is paid by the municipality ; sees to the hospital, if there is one ; attends the poor, and supervises the meat, vegetables, fruit, &c., unfit for human food, that is often exposed for sale.

The above sketch gives a kind of map of the Ottoman provincial government. In this *esquisse* all appears well arranged. Each employé's appointed place is marked on the sketch. Up to now, however, I have only given the official machinery of provincial government in briefest outline. The following description will show how "official" is all that I have written so far, how corrupt are the employés, what ignorance prevails, how little the provincials in Turkey experience of clean-handedness—conscientious duty, pity— among the men in office and all their subalterns. Indeed, the meaning of "duty," that Roman law conception, was not bequeathed by the dying Eastern Empire to its living Turkish successor. That successor "conveys"; does right ungentle spiriting; is brusque— nay, hard. Money is so tight everywhere. A remnant there is of such as do justly and right—a remnant of some 1 per cent. Vice springs from ignorance, and here ignorance is crass. A remnant, more` enlightened and less vicious, is at the mercy of the calumniating majority. So the instructed perforce ·fall into line with the mass. And when the better sort so fall into line, *corruptio optimi pessima*. Once corrupted, the educated few are more sly and subtle in parrying the law's awards.

All malpractices in official Turkey rise from jobbery and bribery. These two sources spring from Yildiz. In Turco-Arabic they have their own names, "Iltimûs" and "Rushwa" respectively. Now, of these two, the greater is bribery. Defined, "Iltimûs" is (a) a man's undue protection of his *entourage* at the expense of all outsiders; (β) a man's utilising his own influence on a second individual as a means of protecting his own (the first man's) *entourage*. Similarly, "rushwa" is taking a bribe from Government employés, (a) to "place" a man in the Government; or, (β) to do for other than reasons of public good what should be done only *pro bono publico;* or, (γ) "to make the worse appear the better reason."

In the Penal Code, a bribe (as above) is "rushwat"; the giver of "rushwat" is "râshi"; the receiver of "rushwat" is "murteshi"; the go-between in "rushwat" is "râïsh."

To these three the Penal Code awards the same severe penalty. No two of this trinity can successfully go to law with the third, nor any one with another. They are thus *officially* protected, as the following story—a fact—proves. A rich Egyptian went to Con- stantinople to receive a decoration through the son of the late Osman Bey, a celebrated chamberlain of the Sultan. So many hundred pounds paid, he was at last told the day of the decoration's arrival, against which he bespoke a banquet. Company came, but no decoration. Chagrined, the Egyptian brought to trial the son of Osman Bey. Jevdet Pasha, the then Minister of Justice, sent for and explained to the Egyptian that he would be proceeded against under the laws dealing with bribery. As the Egyptian, duly terrified, was leaving, the pasha's assistant, who had been present at the interview, followed, and promised to have the affair hushed up for a "consideration." The "consideration" was then shared between Jevdet Pasha and his assistant, and the incident closed.

Thus, bribery in Turkey is fairly universal, from Grand Vizier to sweeper on the civil side; from marshal to sergeant on the military; from Sheik-il-Islâm to Imâm of the quarter on the "hoja" side; from Minister of Justice down to usher on the justice side. The "murteshi" is *hic et ubique*.

Promotion comes neither from the east nor from the west—from bribery only; and that in one of two ways: either the Sultan's *entourage* is paid for promotion, or the person to be promoted is a *protégé* of that *entourage*.

Let us consider the Vali who receives his "place," or vilayet, on the "bribe-down" system. As soon as he is installed in his "Merkez-i-vilayet" the Vali starts recouping himself for his losses in place-hunting. (i.) He has brought with him from Constantinople his "men." These he puts into good places, vacated compulsorily by their old holders. (ii.) He has come from the capital with no suite. Good places are held or vacated by the "old gang" as they pay, or are niggardly towards, the new governor (Vali). But the end is not yet. The Vali, who has spent so much on securing his governorship, must spend more to keep it. The Sultan's favourites have a Vali dismissed unless he fees them, or if a would-be Vali fees them better. Besides, the existing Vali must peculate, so as to tide over the interval of time at Constantinople which he must, later, spend between losing one and gaining another place. [Else, when *en rétraite*, he must borrow from Jews or Armenians on high usury. I knew an Armenian at Constantinople, in 1891, who "accommodated" the old Vali of Erzeroum—dismissed, and then drawing the tithe of his official *working* salary, £20 per mensem, for £200 (Turkish).]

Take now the Vali who owes his place to his being a *protégé* of the Sultan's creatures. These gentry are sent by this Vali one-half or three-quarters of what clings to his Excellency's hands.

Places are kept or resigned in favour of better places on a monetary sliding scale.

The mudir is appointed by the Grand Vizier, who is subject to bribes from candidates for the mudir's place and to pressure from the Padishah's (Sultan's) favourites. The Vali can press the mutesarif and kaïmakam, and the second of these the third, &c., to appoint creatures to a place.

The private paper ordering an appointment of a creature to a place is put inside an official letter, and is known as "pussula." The conclusion of the whole matter is told in a sentence. Whatever the air played at Yildiz, to that dance the great officials and Ministers.

Each in his place of residence, the Vali, the mutesarif, and the kaïmakam, are demigods. Each is attended by six horsemen, with drawn swords; salutation being exacted from all, when each passes by, under high pains and penalties.

Some say the Sultan cannot know of the prevailing corruption! He happens, in fact, to be an accomplice. Witness the concessions and privileges he grants. His motto is, "Après moi le déluge." Profoundly selfish, he neglects the empire's good. In his lifetime to have peace and quiet is his sole thought, his one wish.

Sublime Porte to-day there is none, except in name. Its some-time influence has been transferred absolutely to Yildiz, the all-in-all. H.I.M. 'Abdu'l Hamid has another old motto in his mind: "Divide et impera." To-day he makes one favourite, to-morrow another. Thus envy is aroused fresh every morning against each successive upstart. So, himself, he lives in security, while each of his creatures is against the other.

A word on those who turn jugment to wormwood, the judges so called.

We have seen that for the three great divisions of the body politic, "Merkez-i-vilayet," "Merkez-i-sandjak," "Merkez-i-kaza," the judges come from Constantinople, whence hail also the presidents of "Merkez-i-vilayet" courts generally. The bribes paid for these appointments are divided among the Sheikh-il-Islâm, the Chief Minister of Justice, and the Assistant Minister of Justice.

The men appointed to do justice are *protégés*, and the *protégés* fee their protectors, who in turn are Imperial *protégés*. If, in the process, those suffer to whom "justice" is dealt out, so much the worse for them. Justice is bought and sold on reasonable terms, from 3s. 4d. (1 medjidié) per job. To dream of justice absolute, undiluted, in such a course of proceeding, is naturally to dream of Paradise in hell.

A judge is employed in the provinces for three years. He must then return to the capital and stay there idle for three years. Thus, triennial spells of enforced leisure presuppose triennial periods of active work with fingers lighter than their hands are clean. They have to live, these judges, through three years' "play," and during those three years also buy themselves a new post, probably more lucrative, in each individual case. I have mentioned as a low figure for perverting justice the legal 3s. 4d. But in the lowest are yet lower depths.

Within the last few years at Tarsus, once "no mean city," a "qâdi" (judge) was walking to court. A local gardener wished him to do something for him at court, but pathetically declared, in the hearing of my Turkish informant, that he had not even a "medjidié." "Then," said the judge, "send to my house from your garden some 'aubergine' (euilé issé, benim evimé, bir az patlajâı gueunder)."

That city on the Cydnus has fallen somewhat from the estate she held in the days of Cleopatra, or even of St. Paul. Of the courts of justice employés not 1 per cent. knows what is meant by "law" or "justice." Some 1 per 1000 has a diploma from the elementary schools. Search far and wide through the Turkish provinces, you will find no lawyer holding an upper or lower school certificate. (The distinction between barristers and solicitors is unknown in European, Asiatic, or African Turkey.) Most have only passed through the so-called primary schools, in no way comparable to those of Europe generally.

Such are the advocates. Where, then, do I place the people, their clients? Like Daniel O'Connell, "between the devil and the deep sea"—the devil of corrupt judges and the deep sea of ignorant grasping lawyers. True, the capital has a few advocates holding diplomas from schools of law. But these favoured beings are not enough to supply the demand of the metropolis, and so do not go to the provinces. One has read that formerly the law in France was in evil case. Better were it then, it is written, for one charged with hiding in his handkerchief, *e.g.*, a cathedral purloined, to agree with his adversary quickly out of court on any money terms than face the charge and the corrupt judges. So in Turkey. Accused of stealing—on his head, Mount Ararat; in his pocket, Galata Tower —any Ottoman subject had better to-day buy off his prosecutor than appear before his country's tribunals.

Coming now to military bribe-eating, I shall have to deal in some technical details:

(i.) Privates have their "rations" or "sizings" "scanted."

(ii.) Men of the legal age for serving in the army are, for a douceur, let off service.

(iii.) Money changes hands illegally at the time of what is called "bedelût-i-askeriyya," or "exchange(s) of military service."

(iv.) At times of reserve mobilisation "bakhsheesh" is the order of the day.

I proceed to comment briefly on each of the above.

(i.) Certain officers are in charge of the stores for "rations." These are monetarily influenced by one of the Government contractors to make him *the* Government contractor. (Such corruptly chosen contractor may, of course, have tendered at a higher figure than the rejected ones.) By this arrangement both officers in charge and contractor that is favoured gain alike. Next, both the said officers, of the one part, and the said favoured contractor, of the other, agree together to change the quality of "rations" contracted for for another, inferior, quality—*e.g.*, fresh butter changed for rancid. This for the privates. The officers are also allotted "rations," which they do not take, but receive, in lieu thereof, exchange-money at generous rates from the contractors.

Again, the officers filch somewhat of the privates' daily bread, and keep the difference themselves.

(ii.) Next I take the case of provincial military officers saving from military service men liable to such service. Let the former be AA, and the latter BB. AA take aside BB who are anxious to accommodate AA. AA "coach" privately BB in (false) reasons for exemption from service. Later, in public, AA listen to and accept as valid the said reasons. For instance, paying malingerers among BB find doctors attached to the army most willing to write for men reports suggested by AA. And these reports excuse from service in the army those men. *Contra*, men really legally exempt, but not paying the medical fee extra-legal, are forcibly made soldiers.

(iii.) The red-tape worm thrives in Turkey. So many papers have to be filled up before an exemption certificate is granted, and so much time is purposely wasted by officers looking for their douceurs, that the poor shiftless folk of the provinces are at their wits' end. They cannot lose day after day, going and coming to and from the Government bureaus. "'Tis deeper, sweeter," better far, and wiser, to pay the douceur, and be quit of the waste and ruin of time—time wanted for the plough, the harrow, the rickyard.

(iv.) The day has come, I suppose, for mobilising the "redeef" (reserves), or "mustahfiz" (territorial army, *landwehr*, *landtruppen*). It is a gala for the officers, who are all radiant. The hour of gain has sounded, and the glad news is echoed afar and anear. But the poor folk—what of them? Their knell has rung. Bent in sorrow, the "masses" brood over the coming breaking up of homes and famine of children. The officers first take a consideration from members of the "redeef" or "mustahfiz" anxious to escape service; for these a loophole is discovered. Money finds its way, too, from old members of the "redeef" wishful to find substitutes. This process takes at least three forms : (*a*) the substitute proposed as an exchange is declared unacceptable first of all, but later, when the officers' palms are suitably treated, acceptable ; (*β*) the substitute is held good and proper, but red-tapeism sets in, and is only cured by an adequate fee ; (*γ*) the substitute passes the officers as *primâ facie* acceptable. At the barracks, however, he is found to be drunken, &c. &c., and is rejected contumeliously. Another substitute and another fee have now to be found.

And now I shall broach a secret. Turkish Mussulmans detest being soldiers. They had rather see their children in the arms of 'Azrael (the angel of death) than in the "'askar-ojaghi" (*lit.* "foyer militaire "). A man-child is born to a Turk. His first thought, generally, is not, Will it live? but, How can it escape military service? This point was considered according to experimental studies by a "Young Turk," Tarsusi-zâdé Munif, in the Geneva paper *Hakikât* (*Truths*) in 1896. [This "Young Turk" published later in Cairo, Egypt, the *Osmanli* and *Yildiz*.] Munif Effendi traces the hatred of serving in the army to the misery reigning in the "'askar-ojaghi." He gives the original of the following accurate translation. The original was from a young soldier to his father, a mountain sheep-master:

"My dear Father,—I ask after your condition and health. If you inquire after my state—thank God, I am alive; but, myself, I know not in what plight I am. I have seen that the ''askar-ojaghi' was all along exactly what they said it was. Our uncle Durnush used to say they made folk wretched in the ''askar ojaghi.' I used not to believe him, but our uncle Durnush's word was true after all. They do not give enough to fill a man's belly. We have never had a day when we slept after eating enough. Ah! where is our warm coat? *Here* we make our clothes of sacking—did we not see corn put in it when we went to the towns?—why, that's the sacking of which we make our clothes! The tears in our clothes we patch with sacking. They say they give soldiers monthly pay, but there's no pay we've seen. In short, we're very wretched, my father. Boots we've none—half hungry, half full! Ah, in father's house we had never seen such things. For pity's sake, father mine, sell a few sheep and send me a little money. The money I brought is finished."

In most countries priestly office excuses army service. "There are no monks in Islâm," says the *Qúrân*. But there are softas in Islâm. Softas study the Arabic scholastic books in schools called 'medressés." For these students, arrived at military age, there was formerly an annual examination by a "mumaïz" from Constantinople. Every year, at a fixed time, the softas are registered, and it is seen whether they are to be found in the "medressés." [The "mumaïz" is a "hoja" (turbaned).] He examined each softa of the age of twenty-one, continuing to examine him for several years after he was twenty-one. A different "mumaïz" went to each "Merkez-i-vilayet," whither, as to a centre, came all the softas from the whole "vilayet" (including "sandjak," "kaza," &c.). Failing to pass, a softa at once became a soldier. But he generally passed. The "mumaïz," tithing each softa, gave each beforehand (in writing) the questions to be set and the answers to be sent in. Said questions were then learned off, together with their answers— examinations "passed"—and army service duly excused accordingly. This useful "examination" has been remitted by the Sultan for the last seven years, and military service is also excused. The reason is this. Some seven years ago two shiploads of softas were expelled from Stamboul. I saw them, packed as close as sardines, in the two Turkish steamers standing out between Seraglio Point ("Serai Boorunu") and Dolma Baghtché Palace, as I was coming from one of the Isles of the Princes. The softas were annoyed at the expulsion and prepared for revolution. So, true to himself, the

Sultan, to secure peace and quiet, let them off both examination and service in the army.

## POLICE.

The best gamekeeper is an old poacher. This is a British motto. Turkish, is the idea of recruiting the police and gendarmerie out of the ranks of pickpockets, swindlers, and assassins. *Similia similibus curantur.* The "Three R's" disqualify for the force. This is like "Not corrupt enough for the New York police." The Turkish police are so seldom and so ill paid, that they will accept even tobacco-money to let a man off. Even an assassin can go scot-free for the slightest payment in cash.

In the provincial villages, when the "tahsildar," an employé of the Finance Department, with an escort of cavalry, collects taxes, strange things are enacted. The horsemen forcibly bait their steeds on the people's barley, using their straw for litter. The peasants' chickens are killed and bees smothered, to feast on the pullets and honey. From misery and poverty, if any cannot pay, their oxen, donkeys, quilts, mattresses, pots, and kettles are sold at bankrupt-stock rates, to pay the Government taxes. Those who have nothing to sell, the "tahsildar" and his escort, chaining their legs, drive with blows of whips—the drivers mounted and the driven afoot—in troops before them to the town prisons. To believe the roughness of the cavalry one must see it; and to see it for any length of time one must have a heart of stone.

## MUNICIPALITY.

Terms are strictly cash for an appointment as president of a municipality. The receiver is the Vali. The municipality president is a domestic of the Vali, mutesarif, or kaïmakam, each of which three acts at his own sweet will as regards the municipality and its revenues. Thus, even in the largest Turkish towns, two men abreast cannot pass along the narrow, dirty streets. The Governor's privy purse has taken all the available funds. The "fiscus" has, in fact, swallowed the "ærarium." Now the municipality revenues are often not small.

Again, the weights and measures (*e.g.,* the "arshi," or *mètre,* and "dirhem," or drachm) of the sellers are deficient; but the sellers pay the "charshi aghalar," or (municipality) market sergeants, who wink at the deficiency. Similarly, dough is sold for bread, as the former weighs more.

Failing to arrange with the "charshi aghalar," the sellers with light weights put themselves in accord with the municipality authorities themselves. This is more direct and equally easy to do.

The street-sweepers are paid by the municipality, not for street-sweeping, but for acting as grooms and stablemen at the Vali's.

At all events, that is what they do.   The Vali's horses are also sometimes supported out of municipal rates, which are eked out to keep up that Governor's country-house as well.   On the Sultan's birth- and accession-days the Vali spends the municipal funds on illuminations (" qandil-gejesi ") and on feasting in his own house. He thus gains credit with those at headquarters at the expense of the municipality.   In this action he is imitated by the presidents of municipalities, mutesarifs, and kaïmakams.

### FINANCE.

Finance offers a fair field to the light-fingered " defterdâr," " muhasebeji," " mal-mudiri," " mal-me'mouri," and " sandook-emini." Peculation in the case of these comptrollers is called by a special name, " *Ikhtilâs*," as it is not (directly, at least) at the expense of the people.   The last mentioned, " sandook-emini," must always be an accomplice of the other four in " *Ikhtilâs*," which I proceed to explain.

" Ikhtilâs " is theft by enployés from the public treasury revenues. The thieves here are Finance employés, those of the Post (" postes et télégraphes "), and those of the Customs, together with all officers in general who have the handling of money.

For metropolitan " ikhtilâs " there is a special civil court at Constantinople (being part of the Council of State) ; for that committed in the provinces the administrative council of the Merkez-i-vilayet is the court of first instance, whence the case can be transferred to the capital.

The cleanness of the caissier's (or " sandook-emini's ") hands, in general, may be estimated by the number of trials for " ikhtilâs " now and always *sub judice* in whatever vilayet you may examine. Often two or three " caissiers " and as many " mal-mudiris " are under trial at the same time in Provincial Turkey.   Apparently, fear of detection does not deter from peculation the Finance emoloyés, conscious as they are that they err in company, and that the judges have generally " the silver-quinsy "—that disease most incident to men of law and the Bench.

A pretty sight and an instructive is to find before one in one vilayet men actually condemned in another and forbidden employment for ever in the Government!   Specially colossal are the " pickings " of the " mal-me'mouri."

### INSTRUCTION.

As it is the most backward thing in the Ottoman provinces, so I have reserved Instruction for the close of this article.   The provincials pay all Public Instruction taxes, which go direct to the

Minister at Stamboul. From this Minister of Education, after a small expenditure on the Constantinople schools, the rest flows to Yildiz Serai. In the Turkish " mudirlik," or sphere of mayor's jurisdiction, there are no primary schools. The " rooshdeea " (primary) schools in the " sandjak " and "kaza " have been mentioned in their place. The " Merkez-i-vilayet," also, has its preparative schools. Nothing, however, is taught in them, as the Sultan's blackest of " bêtes noires " is education. This he began to destroy as soon as he learned that the students were against his peculiar mode of autocracy. Students become atheists, his Imperial Majesty has discovered. He has, therefore, appointed as present Minister of Education that ablest " Vitruvius of ruin," Zuhdi Pasha. This Minister of Education and Instruction can scarcely speak Turkish. On a par with his knowledge of his mother tongue is his acquaintance with geography. A French artist, on coming to Constantinople from Paris, went to see Zuhdi. The Pasha, knowing no French, asked the Frenchman, through his interpreter, whence he came. " From Paris," he replied. " Ask him," said the Pasha to his dragoman, " if he touched at Japan *en route* " !

On becoming Minister, Zuhdi spoiled the whole programme of the schools, which was before less miserable than it is to-day. In lieu of lay lessons he substituted religious teaching and reading of *Qúrán*. All this piety had not prevented him, when Finance Minister, from " thieving like a skilful player."

H. H. JOHNSON.

# CO-EDUCATION.

AMONG the many and varied necessary means whereby progress may be secured to humanity in its onward march towards perfection, the educating together of boys and girls, young men and young women, is, at this particular time, one of the most important.

There are nowadays a good many people who are, more or less consciously and intelligently, working in the helping on of evolution. On all sides we see men and women serving on, or anxious to serve on, such bodies as School Boards, Parish, District, and County Councils, Boards of Guardians, &c. &c.; but they are considerably handicapped in their work from having been for the most part reared under a system of sex isolation. They are not accustomed to working together, they do not feel natural and at ease with one another. When acting together as Poor-law Guardians, for instance, there is a certain amount of awkwardness and embarrassment felt when what are called "delicate questions" arise for discussion and settlement. Had they been brought up together and taught to regard all Nature's operations of whatever nature as natural, simple, and necessary matters of daily life, to be treated with no more shamefacedness or diffidence than any other natural incident, their work, in whatever direction, would be much more effective.

The constant association of boys and girls together under adult influence in habitual and unconscious companionship is Nature's indication of the right method of education. From the cradle to the grave, whether we recognise it or not, the whole of life is an unbroken course of education. In every moment of our lives we are educating, in the right direction or the wrong, our bodies, our minds, our wills, and some one or more of the many instruments we all possess. And Nature indicates that the two sexes should be educated together throughout life. It occasionally happens that a boy and a girl are actually born together, and a closer and more intimate companionship than the pre-natal one of such a case can hardly be imagined. Male and female children are brought up together in the nursery for several years; they have their meals together, they play together, they learn their first lessons together. After the school and college life is over they come together again, they marry, and then live together until they die. It is only during the school life that the first line of hard and fast separation is drawn, just at the time when the faculties are beginning to awake and to brighten; the time when impressions come thickest, and when the mind is most sensitive to and retentive of them; the time when habits and ideas are formed most readily and strongly and are indelibly impressed upon the consciousness for life; this is the time which is selected for isolating the boy and the girl who have been growing up together and who will in a few years' time be living in an even more intimate relationship as the husband or wife of some other woman or man.

It is somewhat singular that the school should have become the place for separation in its most rigid form. For in no other department or occupation in life are boys and girls under greater control or more careful supervision; the instructor's whole attention is rivetted on the class during school-hours, at the end of which the isolation is, for the time, at an end. In the case of an ordinary Board school the boys and girls are then free to mix together again. But the damage has been done, the cleavage has begun, the mystery and division of sex has, unconsciously at first, become part and parcel of the growing child-nature.

Who would dream of despatching a valuable ship to a distant port without having first provided its captain with a chart, whereon were marked each reef, rock, or shallow which lay in his course? And yet the vast majority of parents do not scruple to send out upon the sea of life children who are in utter ignorance of the terrible risks and dangers before them, till it is a very wonder that the moral shipwrecks among us are so few. The remedy for this evil will be found in co-education and in proper physiological instruction. The former, having broken down the mystery and barrier of sex, will allow the latter to be imparted freely and naturally. A doctor was once talking about the education of his little son to a schoolmaster, and he asserted that when the boy was a little older he intended instructing him in the facts of reproduction and its allied details, in order that the boy might be duly warned of the snares and pitfalls to be encountered in later life. In after years the schoolmaster inquired whether the expressed intention had been carried out; the doctor in reply assured him that when the time had arrived he felt absolutely unable to talk to his boy upon the subject; and the boy was left, consequently, to find out his information on this most vital point for himself, by any chance or haphazard, and with probably many a sad tumble and disaster. Had this medical man been brought up in a mixed school, receiving there in a legitimate manner his knowledge on the subject in question, and completing his studies in classes containing medical students of both sexes, he would have had no more difficulty in imparting to his son a knowledge of the reproductive function than in telling him of the details connected with nutrition.

Co-education. too, in conjunction with proper physiological instruction and real, true, unperverted knowledge on questions relating to sex, would cause the extinction of those evil practices which are sapping the vitality and corrupting the morals of the youth of this generation.  Having been brought up in the knowledge that their bodies must be kept sacred to the purposes of reproduction and that the consequences of disregarding such information would be disastrous, boys and girls would be unlikely to tamper and experiment with themselves.  Owing to the defectiveness of their own upbringing the great majority of parents, like the doctor just alluded to, are unable or unwilling to instruct their children in this most important question.  Some parents avowedly prefer the innocence of ignorance to the innocence of knowledge.  To such I would say: There can be no such thing as complete ignorance of this subject. From maidservants or from schoolfellows, from literature or from casually overheard words, children are bound to acquire knowledge in this direction.  We get proof of this from all sides.  The chaste maiden who becomes insane, although she may have been brought up with the greatest possible care and in the utmost apparent seclusion, evinces a complete knowledge of the facts and actions of reproduction, together with the vulgar vocabulary appertaining to the same.  Nature, of course, supplies the reproductive instinct, but it did not provide her with the vocabulary.  Therefore, seeing that such knowledge is bound to be obtained somehow, how much wiser would it not be that such a maiden should be given proper, legitimate instruction instead of being allowed to acquire vicious information, and that she should possess the dry, cold, scientific terms instead of their vulgar equivalents ?

"Few boys," says the head-master of a large school, "ever remain a month in any school, public or private, without learning all the salient points in the physical relations of the sexes.  There are two very grave evils in this unlicensed instruction: first, the lessons are learned surreptitiously ; second, the knowledge is gained from the vicious experiences of the corrupted older boys, and the traditions handed down by them."

Would it not be better, then, that this inevitable knowledge should arrive in a wholesome way, with every point carefully explained, so that there could be no possibility of the misunderstanding or the misuse of such knowledge ?  As Maudsley says :

"The best education would seem to be that which was directed to teach man to understand himself, and to understand the nature which surrounded him, and of which he is a part and a product ; so as to enable him, as its conscious minister and interpreter, to bring himself into harmony with nature in his thoughts and actions; and so to promote the progressing evolution of nature through him, its conscious self."

How can boys and girls bring themselves into harmony with Nature in their thoughts and actions if they are kept in utter ignorance of what the laws and procedure of Nature are? It is a logical and inevitable conclusion that, in this helpless ignorance, those laws must often be violated. And yet the remedy is so simple and so easily applied. There are, for instance, such books as Ellis Ethelmer's *Baby Buds*, and *The Human Flower*, which tell in exquisitely delicate language truths which it is imperative that every child should be made familiar with. Let them, then, receive as full instruction as possible at the right time, before any perverted knowledge has attained access to their minds. When the new, strange sensations are experienced which the time of puberty brings, let the children thoroughly understand what is happening, so that they may know what natural laws are working in them, and obey and intelligently help in their operations; thus becoming the masters of those laws and, in the end, masters of their own environment and development. To quote Maudsley again:

"It would seem indispensable to a right training of the mind of every child, that it should be instructed in the knowledge of the nature of the world in which it has been placed and of which it is a part. . . . The constitution of the human body and mind, and of the relations of body and mind to their environment, are subjects on which a vast amount of knowledge has been formulated in the various natural sciences. It is strange, when we think of it, that any education which leaves a man ignorant of these things should be deemed an education at all; marvellous that intelligent men should be content to go through their lives knowing little more of them than savages."

The early and continuous system of co-education is most necessary; the boys and girls should first become accustomed to each other's society in the preparatory school, and from that continue together until, and including, university life. There would naturally be a certain amount of risk attached to the throwing together of young men and women who had hitherto been educated on the old isolated system, although, at the same time, it would be possible, with a judicious exercise of supervision and regulation, to guard against any undesirable incidents, and to make such impossible as the students become familiarised with their new environment. The Oberlin College in America was started in this way. The young men and women attended the same classes, they had their meals together, and were allowed to call upon each other in their respective rooms. This system has been found to work admirably.

In the method of education which is here advocated, combined with instruction in physiology and its kindred subjects, lie the only solution of all those social problems of the day which are primarily based upon sex relationship. It should be quite understood, too, that the principle of co-education must be extended to all the relationships of life; that the sex barrier must be completely broken down once and for ever, so that the children of the future shall be free from this unnatural restraint and infliction. These children on arriving at maturity will then understand the meaning and necessity of the differentiation into sexes. Sex relationship will contain no mystery for them. They will see that it is based upon the continuation of the species, that the attraction which man has for woman and woman for man exists for purposes of reproduction, for without this attraction the race would die out. Possessing this wholesome knowledge, the people of the future will gradually free themselves from the perverted and abnormal sexuality which is so prevalent among us at the present time; self-restraint and moderation will have utterly changed the whole aspect of social life. Seductions and outrages will die out, divorces will become incidents of very rare occurrence, and unhappy and unsuitable marriages will become the exception instead of, as to-day, the rule. Women will not accept the first offer of marriage which they receive, for their early and familiar association with men will enable them to estimate character and disposition more correctly, and to judge whether the closer relationship of marriage would be happy and suitable. Above all, young people would not fall into the mistake, so common now, of confounding sexual attraction with love.

When this healthy natural view of sex relationship has been developed it will naturally follow that prostitution will cease to exist. The two most important factors in this question are the physiologic and the economic. I have tried to show how the solution of its moral aspect will be found in co-education and in instruction in sexual relationship and duties. Its economic aspect cannot, of course, be dealt with now ; it will be sufficient to say that, the ideas of men having become revolutionised in this respect, all those women who have adopted prostitution from economic necessity—and I believe that the proportion is something like 85 per cent.—will be totally unable to live as heretofore, and will be obliged to find some other means of support.

Under the present system of education the members of the two sexes represent two opposed camps which are supposed to have nothing in common, and this deep, strong line of demarcation, once drawn, persists through life and can never be wholly erased. Ingrained in the minds of men and women is a feeling of differentiation, of separation, of aloofness. This early bias is extremely difficult to eradicate. Men nowadays are continually exhibiting jealousy of the women who appear to them to be encroaching on their own particular domain in professional and public work, and the majority of women hitherto seem to have acquiesced in this notion and to be loth to make attempts in directions where they know they will find opposition. Girls and boys, having worked side by side at the same occupations during their early years, will fall easily and naturally in later life into the custom of entering the same trades and professions.

Allusion has been made to the fact that in America great advantage has been derived from an arrangement by which men should have a part in the teaching of girls, and women in the teaching of boys. The good results which flow from this method can be explained by the statement of the fact that each boy and girl has in him or herself respectively feminine and masculine qualities. It is well known that a woman will bear a son who will reproduce traits and characteristics which distinguished her father, although they did not appear outwardly in herself; and that a man may become the father of a daughter who will reproduce traits and characteristics which were especially noticeable in his mother; consequently this woman must have had lying dormant in her the particular masculine qualities which she had passed on to her son after having inherited them herself from her father; the man also transmitted his mother's feminine qualities to his daughter, though he had never given any evidence of their possession. As, then, we each possess qualities which are usually considered distinctive of the opposite sex, it naturally follows that in the cultivation and development of those qualities teachers of the corresponding sex should be employed. The perfectly developed, well-balanced character consists of the harmonious blending of the various masculine and feminine qualities, for the indication of sex goes no deeper than the body, the clothing of the individuality; the real individual, the ego, is neither male nor female. Therefore, in a mixed school there should be mixed teachers, there should be a head-master and head-mistress, both possessing equal authority. If a boy be educated solely by men his feminine qualities, such as gentleness, sympathy, delicacy of feeling, considerateness, self-abnegation, may remain dormant; and the girl educated solely by women may not have developed in her the latent masculine qualities of boldness, firmness, determination, magnanimity, and chivalry.

Among other incidental advantages of the mixed school system are the opportunities of educating together brothers and sisters who are so greatly attached to each other that it would be undesirable to separate them. Boys are found to acquire much more social culture and polish from the refining influence of the girls than they can obtain under the old *régime.* The girls broaden out, and they develop much more self-reliance, besides benefiting considerably in other ways. Mixed schools are noted for the good order which obtains: the boys are naturally unwilling to run the risk of being reproved or punished before the girls, and the latter maintain their best behaviour for similar reasons.

Besides the co-educating of boys and girls, they should also be encouraged to play together. This is needed to complete the breaking down of the barrier of sex. There should no longer be particular toys exclusively appertaining to one particular sex. As the members

f each sex have a common stake and interest in the sterner matters
f life and should aid each other and participate in the serious work
hich has to be done on arrival at maturity, so, in childhood and
outh, should they share in the same pleasures, play the same games
ther, using the same toys.

The Society for Promoting the Co-education of Boys and Girls
will, so soon as it is in a position to do so, establish a school in
which the principles which it puts forward will be adopted. This
school will also serve as an object-lesson and be open to the inspection of all those interested in questions of education and of social
reform.

Children will be taken at a tender age and trained upon somewhat
similar lines to those indicated until they shall have attained to the
age and capability to strike out for themselves their own paths in
life.

One feature of the educational system which will be adopted in
the proposed school will be the absence of competition of every sort.
The girls and boys will be taught to be more on the alert to render
help to others than to seek their own gain and advantage ; for it
seems desirable that the amount of competition now existing among
us should receive a larger leaven of altruism. It is also thought
that the advent into the world of a number of open-eyed, broad-
minded, fearless, honourable, pure, altruistic men and women will do
much towards the evolution of the race, towards raising mankind
from its present level nearer the possibility of perfection, in which
direction it is so slowly and painfully climbing.

JOHN ABLETT.

# THE TRANSFIGURED THEOLOGY OF
# "PARADISE LOST."

DR. JOHNSON, in his *Life of Milton*, defines poetry as "the art of uniting pleasure with truth by calling imagination to the help of reason." This definition, though faulty when applied to some kinds of poetical composition—for example, the purely lyrical—does admirably describe the aim and spirit of Milton's poetry, and especially of *Paradise Lost*. Undoubtedly one of the chief attractions which the subject of this poem had for Milton was the basis of absolute truth which he supposed it to supply. He thought he was building upon the solid ground of literal fact. He confidently believed that the plain and brief story which he drew from the Bible would never lose credit. He was filled with the magnificent hope of handing down to posterity, in a new and glorifying dress, truths of eternal significance and of universal interest. Two hundred years, and especially the last fifty years, have brought Milton's posterity to a different point of view. What he supposed to be divine revelation turns out to be human invention. What he regarded as solemn truth we regard as fanciful myth. Hence, looking at *Paradise Lost* from the theological or philosophical standpoint, we must say, "Seldom, if ever, has so sublime a plan met with so complete a reversal." Milton's great design was "to justify the ways of God to men," but this design is now baulked by a previous question : "What *are* the ways of God to men ? Are they such as the poet believed them to be?" And upon this follows another question: "Is this mighty epic, hitherto regarded as one of the great masterpieces of English literature and one of the sublimest productions of human genius, henceforth valueless for those who do not accept its Biblical and theological basis ? Is it to be regarded as only a *tour-de-force*, stupendous but irrelevant, a relic of the activity of a splendid mind, but a thing out of relation to our present needs and interests?" This seems to be the opinion of many liberal thinkers—not that they say so in words, but they say so in deeds. They persistently neglect *Paradise Lost*. They put it on a high shelf in their libraries, with other books that they consider antiquated, there to accumulate dust.

I believe this is one of those exaggerations which naturally occur in periods of reaction, but are modified by time. It must, of course, be conceded that *Paradise Lost* can never occupy the same kind of place as it did formerly, when men put it beside the Bible and regarded it almost as a new scripture of the true faith. To take a long leap forward, let it be granted that the time will come when no one will read this poem except as a child reads a fairy-tale, enjoying what there is to be enjoyed and not critical about impossibilities because they are not supposed to be taken seriously. But even then, will not *Paradise Lost* live as one of the sublimest of fairy-tales for adults? The anti-theological feeling which it now provokes in some minds will be impossible, because its theology will be dead, and there will be nothing to disturb the full enjoyment of its plot, its splendid imaginative pictures, the majestic roll of its verse, its abounding pearls of beautiful speech and noble wisdom.

But the theology of *Paradise Lost* is not yet dead. We may talk of it as dead in an abstract way as much as we please, meaning that we can see no rationality in it, and that in our opinion modern thought has given it its mortal wound. But practically it is a long time dying—it still shows a good deal of vitality—it is still able to marshal strong social forces and the power of majorities against those who dare to impugn it. Hence the serious purpose and method of *Paradise Lost* have a claim upon our attention at the present time. It may, indeed, be doubted whether this aspect of the poem ever has been or ever will be so interesting and important to lovers of truth and workers for human progress as now, when old and new thoughts are struggling so vigorously together. For I hope to show that *Paradise Lost* is itself one of the best correctives of the theology on which it is based; that it is a magnificent winding-sheet for the creed it was meant to vivify; that it is a monument which crushes with its massive splendour the dry bones of a system it was meant to enshrine for men's reverence.

To prove this will not be to belittle Milton's greatness; on the contrary, it will show most conspicuously how much greater he was than his creed. There are stories of men who have entered upon a searching study of a book or a system with a view to demolish or convert the author, but have found *their own ideas* demolished and have confessed *themselves* converted. This is invariably a sign of a just and honourable spirit. But there are also instances, less frequently noticed, of men who have set out to advocate ideas which they supposed themselves to hold as very truth, but in the process have entirely *changed* them, thus giving the impartial onlooker a higher standard by which to gauge the meanness and poverty of the originals. This is what Milton has done, and it is equally a proof of a just and honourable spirit. This unconscious transformation of ideas was easy and natural in Milton because he was primarily a poet, and only secondarily a theologian. His treatise of *Christian*

*Doctrine*, first made known to the world in 1825, shows how exact a Biblical student and how close a theological reasoner he could be. But in writing *Paradise Lost* his supreme aim and impulse was poetic. This is shown most plainly by the fact that the story of the Fall was only one of many themes which he had pondered over for his great effort, and that some of these were non-Biblical. The Arthurian legends tempted him very strongly; he made elaborate historical studies for the sake of mastering them; and he abandoned them only because in the Biblical stories he thought he had facts and not mere legends—facts, too, of deeper meaning and more universal significance. It was the ambition of his life to write a great poem, and having chosen a Biblical subject, he could not but treat it with poetic freedom. But it was an act of marvellous daring, and nothing but the poet's earnestness on behalf of the fundamental ideas of the traditional Christian system, nothing but the genius he lavished upon them, could have disguised from critics from that day to this the unfavourable light in which he unconsciously placed them. It is an interesting and significant fact that one of the most gifted and earnest of his contemporaries, Andrew Marvell, himself a poet and Milton's friend, had the gravest fears regarding the great singer's attempt. At first the very plan of the poem seemed to him to involve an awful peril. He says:

> "The argument
> Held me awhile misdoubting his intent,
> That he would ruin (for I saw him strong)
> The sacred truths to fable and old song."

Even when he was constrained to own the plan allowable, he still had fears for his friend:

> "Through that wide field how he his way should find,
> O'er which lame faith leads understanding blind;
> Lest he'd perplex the things he would explain
> And what was easy he should render vain.
>   Or if a work so infinite he spanned,
> Jealous I was that some less skilful hand
> Might hence presume the whole creation's day
> To change in scenes and show it in a play."

The result, however, removed all his apprehensions and won his enthusiastic admiration.

> "Pardon me, mighty poet, nor despise
> My causeless, yet not impious, surmise.
> But I am now convinced, and none will dare
> Within thy labours to pretend a share.
> Thou hast not missed one thought that could be fit,
> And all that was improper dost omit.
>   *       *       *       *

That majesty which through thy work doth reign
Draws the devout, deterring the profane ;
And things divine thou treat'st of in such state
As them preserves, and thee inviolate."

Addison shows both the same sense of the difficulties of Milton's undertaking and the same admiration of his mastery over them :

" It was easier for Homer and Virgil to dash the Truth with Fiction, as they were in no danger of offending the Religion of their Country by it. But as for Milton he had not only a very few Circumstances upon which to raise his Poem, but was also obliged to proceed with the greatest Caution in everything that he added out of his own Invention. And, indeed, notwithstanding all the Restraints he was under, he has filled his Story with so many surprising Incidents, which bear so close an Analogy with what is delivered in Holy Writ, that it is capable of pleasing the most delicate Reader, without giving Offence to the most scrupulous." [1]

There is a passage in Matthew Arnold's *Essay on Milton* which has a similar tone—with a significant difference :

" Justice is not at present done, in my opinion, to Milton's management of the inevitable matter of a Puritan epic, a matter full of difficulties for a poet. Justice is not done to the *architectonics*, as Goethe would have called them, of *Paradise Lost ;* in these, too, the power of Milton's art is remarkable. But this may be a proposition which requires discussion and development for establishing it, and they are impossible on an occasion like the present." [2]

It is precisely the proposition here made that I propose to discuss and develop.

The most obvious and yet the most telling criticisms upon the Bible story of the Fall, when interpreted in the traditional way, are these—that the whole account is miserably meagre for so stupendous an event ; and that the *causes* of the catastrophe and the way in which it took place are altogether trivial and unintelligible. That the whole race of mankind should be ruined by a serpent enticing with a fruit, and that the whole incident should be explained in a single page of print, is so incongruous as to be ridiculous the moment it is thought about without implicit faith in Biblical authority. Now, in *Paradise Lost* the theme is at least treated with fulness and dignity. The length of the poem is worthy of the issues. The crisis is elaborately led up to. There is a serious attempt to make the causes clear and show them to be sufficient. Bravely is the question of divine justice wrestled with. If Milton fails, as he does fail theologically, a hundred times greater is the failure of the literal theologian who sticks to Genesis.

But even if the poet is held to have succeeded, all the new resources which he employs in aid of his attempt are themselves so many unconscious criticisms upon the Bible story.

*Paradise Lost* has twelve Books, but the fatal fruit is not tasted

<hr>

[1] *Spectator,* No. 267.    [2] *Essays in Criticism,* Second Series, p. 63.

till the ninth Book. A general glance at the contents of the preceding eight Books will at once give an insight into Milton's methods, and a more detailed examination will show how splendidly he built upon his false foundation. The first two Books describe the rallying of Satan and his host after their fall from heaven, their meeting in council, and their debate as to future operations, their decision to plot against mankind as a revenge upon the Deity, and Satan's setting forth on a reconnoitring expedition. The third Book takes us to heaven and shows us the Father and the Son watching Satan—they foresee what is going to happen, and the redemption of mankind by the Son is soon agreed upon. Meanwhile, Satan has made his way first to the sun (where the angel Uriel fails to identify him) and then to the earth. In Book IV. Satan leaps over the bounds of Paradise, overhears Adam and Eve talking, learns from this conversation about the Tree of Knowledge, and forms his plan. Uriel, however, comes down to earth on a sunbeam and warns Gabriel, who is in charge of Eden, that there is an intruder. Night comes on and Adam and Eve retire to rest. Gabriel sets guards over their bower, and goes his rounds through the garden. In spite of these measures, Satan sits at Eve's ear and causes her to dream that she is being tempted. He is caught in the act, but defies the angels and is allowed to escape. In the next Book Eve, with troubled mind, relates her dream to Adam. He consoles her, urging that a dream is in itself no wrong. However, Raphael is sent from heaven to warn them that they must be obedient. He relates the history of the war in heaven, and tells them of the danger which has come to them in consequence. Books VI., VII., and VIII. contain further explanations by Raphael. Adam and Eve learn enough to understand thoroughly their position and its perils. In Book IX. Satan enters Paradise by an underground stream and appears in the form of a mist. He takes up his abode in the body of a serpent. Eve proposes to go about her work alone, urging as a reason (a strange one, surely, for so ideal a personage) that the usual exchange of affectionate glances hinders work. Adam reluctantly consents. Satan tempts her with the forbidden fruit and she eats. Adam eats also, his motive being (and here is one of Milton's noblest additions to the bare original) pure affection and the resolve to share his beloved companion's fate.

The only special feature of the last three Books which need be mentioned is the vision which the angel Michael shows to Adam before dismissing him from Eden. This is the offspring of Milton's pity. How could he leave Adam and Eve and their posterity in ignorance of the future deliverance? That would have been an altogether repulsive conclusion to the great epic. Milton cannot let Adam depart from Paradise without a knowledge of the coming of the Son of God and the whole significance of that event.

Already this brief outline shows us the Biblical story transformed. But only by looking at a few of the chief points carefully can we realise how Milton's imagination glorified the theology on which he built, and how mean and poor it looks when stripped of his poetic adornments.

In the first place, the figure of Satan in *Paradise Lost* bears some fit proportion to the events which in Genesis are attributed to a mere serpent. The whole episode of the war in heaven and the expulsion of the fiends, especially the picture we have of the personalities of the rebel leaders—all this is not only a marvellous poetic creation, it also gives much-needed balance to a theological system. It provides something like an adequate cause for the ruin of mankind. But to feel the majesty of it in Milton's poem is to feel also the lack of majesty in the Genesis story. There is nothing whatever in the Biblical story to suggest that the word serpent was meant in any but a plain and literal sense—it signifies just a paltry snake. The identification of this snake with a mighty spirit of evil, Satan or the Devil, came later; and it came just because the story, when taken seriously as the basis of a theology, would have been a sheer mockery without such identification. No *Biblical* writer read the new interpretation into the word serpent. This was the work of the systematising theologians. It was they who identified "the most subtle of all the beasts of the field" with the Devil who tempted Jesus and the Satan who (we are told in Revelations) fell from heaven. From time to time attempts were made to present his personality and history in some clearer and fuller form. But when Milton approached his subject he found ample ground not yet occupied. One cannot resist the impression that he must have felt very keenly the curtness of the story of the Fall. The whole record must have seemed to him too incomplete and trivial for the stupendous issues involved. And, though he could at times deny as stoutly as any one the right of the human mind to speculate in matters of religion beyond the bounds of the Biblical revelation, yet in this matter we see him impelled with irresistible force beyond those bounds. In any case, he deliberately aims at giving a full vision of events (as he imagined them) which preceded and led up to the temptation in Eden; and this is the boldest, the most original, and the largest part of his poem.

But in describing Satan and the other fiends there were many difficulties and dangers. Such beings must, of course, be represented as very wicked, but if painted with black alone they would have no *interest* for the reader. The mind refuses to dwell on any picture of an entirely revolting creature. Therefore Milton had to give his fiends a certain *attractiveness* and *charm*. Then, again, he had to give them each an individuality. Their wickedness and their powers of dazzling weak human spirits must be different—otherwise they would be but a dull and monotonous company. Then, lastly, they must have superhuman characteristics, such as might naturally be supposed to belong to former occupants of heaven. Milton fulfils all these conditions in a most marvellous way. His imaginative power is nowhere more admirably displayed. But poetic art is one thing; Biblical theology is another thing. So long as people wished to be convinced of the truth of the orthodox scheme, such art as Milton's was gladly accepted as an ally and was allowed a good deal of freedom. But when doubts arise the liberties taken by art may strengthen the adverse evidence. Thus, in the present instance is it not clear that, if Milton's splendid imagination is needed to give meaning and reality to the story of the Fall, the poet, though from his own point of view the Bible's advocate, may appear from another point of view its unconscious critic!

Perhaps nowhere does Milton's art come so nobly into conflict with his theology as in his portrayal of Satan's affection and pity for the innocent creatures whom he is about to ensnare. A merely brutal enemy of mankind would have repelled every reader; but consider how far the poet goes in his desire to make the devil a being in whom we can take a real interest, and his deeds such as we can conceive as morally possible. In the fourth Book Satan, beholding Adam and Eve, speaks thus:

> "O Hell! what do mine eyes with grief behold?
> Into our room of bliss thus high advanced
> Creatures of other mould—Earth-born perhaps,
> Not spirits, yet to Heavenly spirits bright
> Little inferior—whom my thoughts pursue
> With wonder, and could love, so lively shines
> In them divine resemblance, and such grace
> The hand that formed them on their shape hath poured.
> Ah! gentle pair, ye little think how nigh
> Your change approaches, when all these delights
> Will vanish, and deliver ye to woe—
> More woe, the more your taste is now of joy;
> Happy, but for so happy ill secured
> Long to continue, and this high seat, your Heaven,
> Ill fenced for Heaven to keep out such a foe
> As now is entered; yet no purposed foe
> To you, whom I could pity thus forlorn,
> Though I unpitied. League with you I seek,
> And mutual amity, so strait, so close,
> That I with you must dwell, or you with me,
> Henceforth. My dwelling, haply, may not please,
> Like this fair Paradise, your sense; yet such
> Accept your Maker's work; he gave it me,
> Which I as freely give. Hell shall unfold,
> To entertain you two, her widest gates,
> And send forth all her kings; there will be room,
> Not like these narrow limits, to receive
> Your numerous offspring; if no better place,
> Thank him who puts me, loath, to this revenge

On you, who wrong me not, for him who wronged.
And, should I at your harmless innocence
Melt, as I do, yet public reason just—
Honour and empire with revenge enlarged
By conquering this new World—compels me now
To do what else, though damned, I should abhor."

Such a passage as this makes us feel that Milton's Satan would not have been altogether bad company after all. He could not help himself, poor fellow! Milton does, indeed, scorn this plea in the lines which follow:

> "So spake the fiend, and with necessity,
> The tyrant's plea, excused his devilish deeds."

But in Genesis not even necessity is pleaded. No reason of any kind is given for the temptation. If the snake had tried to give one, it could certainly have found nothing better than that of the poet's Satan. And as for pity, not even Jehovah pities Adam and Eve in Genesis. He has only jealousy—jealousy of the wisdom their disobedience had given them.

It is, indeed, the manifest injustice done by the primitive Hebrew Deity that leads Milton to make numerous palliatives. This is the reason why he weaves the story of the Redemption into the very tissue of the story of the Fall. The reader is told the whole scheme of Redemption before the Fall has occurred—and told it in the most vivid and moving way. This is truly a noble touch of poetic insight and tenderness, but it only mitigates, it does not remove, the essential harshness of the story. We feel still that Adam and Eve suffer a cruel fate. And when we go back to Genesis we of course feel it doubly.

Eve's dream is a more original and subtle device for justifying the ways of God to men. Milton had to face the contradiction that, though Adam and Eve did not know what evil was, and though in strict justice *conscious wrong-doing* alone deserves punishment, yet they were punished with terrible severity. So he takes us into the shadow-land of dreams, which is or is not a land of knowledge according to circumstances and especially according to your definition of knowledge. Here he gives Eve a dim ideal rehearsal of the fatal temptation, clearly intending it to be a definite and merciful forewarning. A noble gloss, whose partial success only makes more evident the failure of Genesis to solve the problem dealt with.

Lastly, there is Raphael's mission, which occupies so large a portion of the poem. This has, in part, the same purpose as Eve's dream. Here are the instructions which the angel receives from the Deity:

" ' Raphael,' said he, ' thou hear'st what stir c Earth ly, they
Satan, from Hell 'scaped through the darksome Gulf, rally b
Hath raised in Paradise, and how disturbed fulfils al
This night the human pair ; how he designs power
In them at once to ruin all mankind. ing ;
Go, therefore, half this day, as friend with friend, be
Converse with Adam, in what bower or shade
Thou find'st him from the heat of noon retired
To respite his day-labour with repast
Or with repose ; and such discourse bring on
As may advise him of his happy state—
Happiness in his power left free to will,
Left to his own free will, his will though free
Yet mutable. Whence warn him to beware
He swerve not, too secure ; tell him withal
His danger, and from whom ; what enemy,
Late fallen himself from Heaven, is plotting now
The fall of others from like state of bliss.
By violence ? no, for that shall be withstood ;
But by deceit and lies. This let him know,
Lest wilfully transgressing, he pretend
Surprisal, unadmonished, unforewarned.' " [1]

These lines are followed by the very significant words :

" So spake the Eternal Father and fulfilled
All justice."

Then where, we ask, is the justice of the Genesis story, which
has no Raphael ? What could more conclusively prove its injustice
than the fact implied by Milton that Raphael's important mission,
though nothing but an invention of his own, was required for the
fulfilment of justice ? Could anything show more clearly that
the poet felt the utter inadequacy of the outline he had to fill in,
and that he could not have regarded it as true had not Biblical
authority been a religious postulate of his time ?

A study of *Paradise Lost* on these lines must make it valuable in
two ways. By many persons, perhaps by most, the poem has been
read more as an exposition of theology than as a work of poetic
imagination. They have accepted Milton's story as a legitimate
version of the traditional scheme of doctrine. They have regarded
it almost as a new version of the Bible record, designed only to
make the essential teaching of the ancient Scriptures more intelligible and acceptable to the modern mind. But what do we discover
when we put aside preconceptions ? We do indeed find the original
elements of the orthodox theology in the poem, but nowhere do
they so clearly show their insufficiency. The quantity and richness
of Milton's adornments are a measure of the poverty of the Bible
story. And for any reader who has an open and unprejudiced mind,
nothing is better calculated to free the soul from the bonds of a false
theory of man's nature and his redemption than a study of Milton's

[1] Book V. lines 224 *ff.*

enlargements upon the traditional view and a consideration of their significance. In this, as in every instance of the kind, we see that a man of genius and transparent honesty cannot touch a theme without making the truth clearer—though the truth served may be of a kind which he least suspects, and his manner of serving it may be least known to himself. Andrew Marvell's fear for Milton—

> " That he would ruin (for I saw him strong)
> The sacred truths to fable and old song "—

was justified. Milton has ruined the Genesis fable—for theology. But this result is from our modern point of view no calamity, but the contrary. The recognition of it is even the essential condition of an intelligent appreciation of the splendid poetic structure for which Milton used the Biblical fragments. But this brings us to the second point. *Paradise Lost* itself cannot be fully enjoyed by this age of science and Biblical criticism except from the point of view here indicated. It must be read as Homer, or Virgil, or Dante, or Shakespeare is read. It must be read as a poem and not as a theology. Only when you feel yourself absolutely free to doubt any of its episodes as history, can you properly enjoy them as poetry, as the creation of man's thought and imagination.

This great work of art is at present much neglected, especially by those who have given up the old theology. Probably the chief reason (next to the flood of present-day literature and newspapers) is this—that the reader of the poem feels that he is expected to believe its main story as a truth of religion, and the instructed mind now resents that expectation. But the time is coming (for a large number of people the time has already come) when such expectation and such resentment will both have become impossible, and when it will be as natural and easy to discuss the plot of *Paradise Lost* as that of *King Lear* or *Macbeth*. To reach this position is to cease to be disturbed by any question as to the historical validity or non-validity of the original fable, and to be free to enjoy the way in which it is treated. From this point of view *Paradise Lost* is seen to be the revelation of a master mind struggling heroically with a theme not altogether tractable even in his hands, but ennobling it with the splendid riches of his imagination, and throwing broadcast pearls of wise and beautiful speech which are admirable and helpful for all time.

H. RAWLINGS.

# AGNOSTICISM IN ITS RELATION TO MODERN UNITARIANISM.

THE term "Modern Unitarianism" has been used in the title of this paper because Unitarianism, as we now know it, is a somewhat recent development of a mode of religious thought once much more nearly allied to that of the more orthodox forms of Dissent. It is indeed so modern in its methods that any one meeting with it for the first time in its present garb might almost fancy he saw in it an offshoot of Agnosticism, so untrammelled is it by its religious equipment, so free to accept or reject according to the dictates of individual judgment. But a more intimate acquaintance with it would not fail to show that a great gulf separates the two, since modern Unitarianism claims to be, no less than any of its orthodox neighbours, *religion*. The Agnostic, confronted by this claim urged on behalf of a position bearing so much outward resemblance to his own, feels tempted to institute an inquiry into the grounds on which it is based. The result of that investigation, so far as this is contained in the following pages, tends to show that this attitude, assumed by the Unitarian with respect to the form of faith he professes, is one which is not logically tenable, *unless he is prepared to shift the ground on which he seeks to establish it, and, to some extent, to retrace his footsteps.*

We have found that Unitarianism differs from Agnosticism in that it claims to be a religion, and if we ask ourselves how it differs from other forms of religion, the answer must be that it claims to be a religion freed from the fetters of creed and dogma. If, therefore, the Agnostic is to make good his contention that modern Unitarianism rests on an unsound basis, it must be partly on the ground that religion without any definite creed cannot rightly be called religion at all, unless we are prepared to limit its meaning to Matthew Arnold's well-known definition of it as "morality touched by emotion." For present purposes, however, this definition is outside the mark. It may be true that the religious attitude of mind is never quite independent of an emotional element; but it is also true that there is, especially at the present day, a good deal of "morality touched by emotion" which does not come under the heading of religion, and which is inspired by other than religious aims.

It is only when we consider religion in its more technical sense, as a system of faith and worship, that we find ourselves in doubt as to whether Unitarianism has a right to sail under its colours. Taken in this sense, religion must be said to imply the recognition of a revelation imparted to mankind by the Supreme Power of the universe—a revelation both of the nature of that Power and of the relations possible between that Power and humanity. Any form of the Christian religion which does not imply some such recognition must be meaningless, and the Unitarian will no doubt readily admit that his religion is dependent on revelation, but on revelation taken in a very enlarged sense. This revelation imposes upon him no definite system of belief; it cannot be restricted within the limits of a creed; it comes to the man not from without, but from within; it leaves him free to follow the guidance of heart, conscience, and intellect combined, believing that this guidance constitutes in itself the revelation of God to man. Dr. Martineau maintains that:

"If revealed religion is an immediate divine knowledge, it is strictly personal and individual, and must be born anew in every mind. . . . The secret of God is with the pure in heart, taken one by one. . . . It is through the human experiences of the conscience and affections, that the living God comes to apprehension and communion with us." [1]

To the individual Unitarian revelation may mean either more or less than this, but the point to be emphasised is the freedom which characterises the Unitarian use of one of the pillars of orthodoxy, a freedom which goes near to undermining it altogether.

There is much that is attractive in the tolerance and liberality of thought implied by this theory of revelation. It embraces within its ample folds men of divers creeds and countries, in fact it may almost be said to include men of no faith at all, and herein lies its weakness. If revelation be left to the mercy of individual interpretation, at what point are we to draw the line, and say, Here revelation ceases and ideas of purely human origin begin? The orthodox Christian would no doubt draw it at the Unitarian, and the Unitarian would, in his turn, draw it at the Agnostic. The Agnostic also might not prove unwilling to avail himself of this convenient theory and put in his claim to a revelation of the Unknowableness of the Ultimate Power of the universe. Thus we see that the idea of a Divine Revelation, divorced from any central authority external to that of the individual judgment, cannot long maintain its unaided position, but becomes chaotic, "without form, and void."

Putting aside this question of revelation, about which there has always been, since the Reformation, great difference of opinion even among the orthodox—some holding that it is imparted through a

1 *The Seat of Authority in Religion.*

Church, others that it is enshrined in the pages of a Book—we have to inquire farther into the tenets of Unitarianism before seeing how it stands with regard to Agnosticism. It is not necessary to dwell upon the attitude taken by Unitarianism with respect to the Founder of Christianity. All are sufficiently familiar with the fact that He is regarded by Unitarians not as God, but as man, and sharing man's limitations, and it needs no further elucidation. But this is merely its negative side, and what we have to consider in connection with the subject in hand is not the ground that has been relinquished, but that upon which the stand is still made. The "spirit that evermore denies" is not the one that founds a new form of Christianity.

Modern Unitarianism admits of such infinite variety of interpretation that it is by no means an easy task to present a clear idea of it, and still less to state it with brevity. At the outset we are met by a seeming contradiction, for it is difficult to reconcile the avowed rejection of creed with such statements as the following, which are fairly representative of many others to be found in Unitarian literature.

We read :

"The word 'Unitarian' properly and originally applies to one who holds the unipersonality of God, and consequently the unmixed humanity of Jesus Christ."

And again :

"The Unitarians are believers in one God—one Spirit, one Power, one Life, pervading, sustaining, guiding all that is." [1]

In considering such passages as these the bewildered Agnostic is fain to ask : If belief in one God does not constitute a religious creed, why should belief in a Trinity be dignified or disparaged (according to the individual outlook) by that appellation ?

There is a large quantity of Unitarian literature now in the market, and most of the writers, especially of the smaller publications, tracts, &c., seem to adopt the defensive attitude, evidently recognising the fact that they are members of a Church militant. But their defence is in the main directed against those who are more orthodox than themselves, and but few seem to realise that their most dangerous opponents lie on the opposite side of the camp. One writer at least, however, has made a direct excursion on this side by a publication entitled *A Unitarian's Answer to the Pleas of Agnosticism.*[2] The writer of this does ample justice to the moral attitude, if it may be so described, of the genuine Agnostic, as distinct from that of the merely irreligious or callous person who

[1] *H. W. Crosskey, his Life and Work.* By R. A. Armstrong.
[2] L. P. Jacks, M.A. McQuaker Trust Lectures. No. 15.

has no right so to designate himself. But when he proceeds to demolish the Agnostic position, we find that his method resolves itself into an attack upon the philosophy of Mr. Herbert Spencer, apparently taking it for granted that every Agnostic must be pledged to support that system. This idea by no means represents the true state of the case. Professor Huxley, who is the founder of the term "Agnosticism," joyfully admits that he has " Hume and Kant " on his side ; but, so far as can be gathered from his writings, he claimed for himself an independent position, quite the reverse to that of one who had sat at the feet of Mr. Spencer, and evolved his "Agnosticism " out of the latter's philosophy. Mr. Spencer's contribution to philosophy is said to be valuable mainly in its relation to Sociology ; and, so far as it concerns Agnosticism, it is more positive in its assertions than any philosophy of the genuine Agnostic type could possibly be. This difference in outlook seems emphasised by the following words of Huxley, to be found in the essay, *Agnosticism and Christianity*,[1] where he says : " I do not very much care to speak of anything as ' unknowable,' " and adds, " I confess that, long ago, I once or twice made this mistake, even to the waste of a capital ' U.' " That the two thinkers may have had much in common does not alter the fact that Agnosticism must stand or fall by its own merits, which are not necessarily identical with those of Spencerian philosophy.

The Unitarian Essay in question concludes with the expression of the writer's conviction that Mr. Spencer's " Ultimate Reality," declared by him to be unknowable, should be regarded as the union of " matter and mind ; " and that he " conceives of God, philosophically, as the bringing together of thought and things."

It is no surprise to find that the greatest and probably most representative book of modern Unitarianism, Dr. Martineau's *Seat of Authority in Religion*, is largely a philosophical work, much of which can be discussed only upon its own grounds, which do not come within the province of this paper. But we also find that it contains passages which verge on the borders of religious dogma, and, despite their philosophical guise, it is impossible not to recognise here and there its familiar features. In this book the basis for any kind of "authority" which is "external to personal reason and conscience and spiritual instinct " is swept away, and for it is substituted the individual judgment of mind and conscience. The keynote of this position is sounded in the preface, where we read that

" We never acknowledge [authority] till that which speaks to us from another and a higher strikes home and wakes the echoes in ourselves, and is thereby instantly transferred from external attestion to self-evidence. And this response it is which makes the moral intuitions, . . . more than egoistic phenomena, and . . . invests them with true authority."

[1] *Agnosticism.* Collected Essays. Vol. V.

And, again, in the following passage, where the writer says that

"the tests by which we distinguish the fictitious from the real, the wrong from the right, the unlovely from the beautiful, the profane from the sacred, are to be found within and not without, in the methods of just thought, the instincts of pure conscience, and the aspirations of unclouded reason. These are the living powers which constitute our affinity with God, and render what to Him is eternally true and good, true and good to us as well."

The weak part of this position has already been dwelt upon, in connection with the Unitarian theory of revelation; and the difficulty of claiming that it affords a basis for any form of faith definite enough to be described as a religion is sufficiently obvious. There are, as might be expected, many points throughout this work, and especially in the first half of it, which touch directly or indirectly on the subject in hand, but space will not admit of their being taken up here. Like other Unitarian theologians, Dr. Martineau, in undermining all the supports of orthodox Christianity, often runs the risk of cutting the ground from under his own feet, and we repeatedly find ourselves confronted with the problem: Amid this waste of error, who is to be the supreme arbiter as to the point at which the boundary line may be drawn, and where we may say with confidence that human error ceases and divine truth begins?

The second half of the book consists mainly of a critical inquiry into the origin and development of theories which either formed part of the original soil in which the "Gospel of Jesus Christ" took root, or have sprung up around it since. This examination is undertaken in that scientific and impartial spirit with which the Agnostic has no quarrel.

"The scientific theologian," observes Huxley, "admits the Agnostic principle, however widely his results may differ from those reached by the majority of Agnostics."[1]

There is one fallacy from which many Unitarian theologians seem scarcely less exempt than are those who work on less scientific and more orthodox lines. Like the latter, they often start by assuming their main thesis—*i.e.*, the existence of a Supreme Being, of God.

"Religion," says one writer, "is the conscious, willing attitude of submission and service of the soul to the will of the Supreme Power. Here are assumed only God, the Soul, and the Universe, with the necessary relations which link all these together."[2]

Though this assumption may hold good in their dealings with the

[1] *Agnosticism and Christianity.* Collected Essays. Vol. V.
[2] *Religion and Modern Thought.* T. W. Freckelton.

orthodox, it is the very point they have to establish in maintaining their position against the assaults of those who are less orthodox than themselves. If the Unitarian wishes to assume the scientific attitude with regard to his theology, he must be prepared to pay the price thereof, and first establish his main thesis. The Agnostic, who has no accepted definition of the term, God, and who is unprepared to take for granted the moral government of a universe in which, as Huxley wrote, " ignorance is punished just as severely as wilful wrong," and against the " moral indifference " of which " the conscience of man revolted,"[1] asks at once—What do you *mean* by *God?* Or, to reduce the question to more answerable limits— Is the God of modern Unitarianism to be regarded as akin to the personal Deity of orthodox theology, or only as another name for the Unknown Ultimate Power of the universe, invested, however, with moral attributes which it is difficult for the non-Platonic mind to conceive of apart from personality?

This question of personality in the religious conceptions of forces outside and above humanity marks an important point in the evolution of religion. Primitive theology is wholly anthropomorphic, but in its progressive stages the anthropomorphism is less clearly defined, and the number, also, of deities and demons, objects of worship or propitiation, diminishes; until in the case of religion of high moral type, such as the Jewish, we come to only two powers of any recognised importance: the creative and omnipotent God, beneficent and moral, of the universe, termed respectively by the earliest Biblical writers Jahveh and Elohim; and Satan, typifying the rebellious power of evil. Christian theology, with its doctrine of the Trinity, and, in the Romish form, with still further amplifications, has shown some tendency to revert to a cruder stage in religious evolution, though in the main the idea of the Christian Trinity has not been plurality of deities, but different manifestations of the same deity. In our own times the number has been again reduced, and the Devil is no longer taken very seriously, even by the orthodox. The tendency of modern times is, in short, to shelve the Devil, a fate which has overtaken many other mythological personages once occupying very different situations. The conception of the Supreme Being has, on the other hand, steadily grown in grandeur, and is less typical of physical than of moral supremacy. Advanced religious thought no longer regards God as the exclusive Deity of one religion, or still less, as in early Jewish times, of one nation, but as the prime moral agent of the universe.

Is the Christian conception of the " enduring Power, not ourselves, which makes for righteousness " as the *Universal Father*, doomed to share the fate of the personifications, in ruder forms, of the

[1] *Evolution and Ethics.* Collected Essays Vol. IX.

deities of earlier ages? Such a question as this the future alone can answer, but the Agnostic is justified in asking the Unitarian theologian to what extent this particular idea of personality still attaches itself to his conception of Deity? Mr. Herbert Spencer writes that

"if we wish to see whither [evolution in theology] tends, we have but to observe how there has been thus far a decreasing concreteness of the consciousness to which the religious sentiment is related, to infer that hereafter this concreteness will further diminish; leaving behind a substance of consciousness for which there is no adequate form, but which is none the less persistent and powerful." [1]

Is the Agnostic justified in the opinion that this "substance of consciousness for which there is no adequate form" is to some extent a very fair definition of the God of modern Unitarianism in its most advanced stage? It is not easy to obtain a definite, and still less an unanimous, reply to such a question as this from its literature. On the contrary, we find the word "God" used in so many senses, and with such unending diversities of definition, that the brain positively reels in the effort to reduce this intellectual chaos to cosmos. Did space admit of it many instances of this ambiguity might be given, and those who wish to convince themselves of it have only to dip into the literature referred to above. Enough has been said upon this point here, and it is needless, in bringing this important review of modern Unitarianism to a conclusion, to comment further upon the vagueness of outlook implied by its definitions of the Supreme Power. The difficulty of doing justice to Unitarian methods of thought is enhanced by the fact noted by a member of its clergy that,

"having no dogmatic standards, no creeds or church formularies, one Unitarian is not entitled to pledge himself for the theological opinions of another." [2]

But the inquirer cannot be blind to the fact that the position of the Unitarian theologian involves him in incongruity. He rejects the basis of authoritative dogma and revelation, but what has he to show instead of it that may not be used respectively in defence of Agnosticism and of orthodoxy? Paradoxical as this may sound, it must be borne in mind that while with one hand the Unitarian sweeps away the dogma of sect, Church, or Bible, with the other he sets up something very like the dogma of the individual in its place; and where, if not in religious dogma, are we to seek for the origins of all the orthodoxies? It is, therefore, no surprise to find that if we ignore the strictly philosophical side of Unitarianism (which can never satisfy the religious craving of humanity, or even be understood by more than a very small and cultured minority),

---

[1] *The Study of Sociology.*    [2] McQuaker Trust Lectures.

and confine ourselves to the simpler forms of its theology, with its doctrine of the Unipersonality and the Fatherhood of God, we are forced to the conclusion that it rests on something that bears a suspicious resemblance to the old-fashioned basis of creed and dogma which it has presumably discarded.

The history of Agnosticism is a much simpler affair, and has been graphically described by the late Professor Huxley in a passage to be found in the essay bearing this name. This is familiar to many readers and need not be repeated here, but it is necessary for the purposes of our argument to quote a later passage in the same essay where he writes :

"Agnostics have no creed ; and, by the nature of the case, cannot have any. Agnosticism, in fact, is not a creed, but a method, the essence of which lies in the rigorous application of a single principle. . . . Positively the principle may be expressed : In matters of the intellect, follow your reason so far as it will take you, without regard to any other consideration. And negatively : In matters of the intellect do not pretend that conclusions are certain which are not demonstrated or demonstrable. That," he concludes, "I take to be the Agnostic faith, which if a man keep whole and undefiled, he shall not be ashamed to look the universe in the face, whatever the future may have in store for him." [1]

It is curious to find almost the same words used in relation to Unitarianism :

"The Unitarians," writes one of their late divines, "are characterised by the method they employ to gain religious truth, more emphatically than by any system of doctrines whatever." "How vain," he exclaims, "are authoritative creeds !" [2]

Another Unitarian theologian writes :

"Unitarian Christianity . . . is in closest alliance with the most advanced thought of our time. On questions of history, of criticism, of science, of philosophy, its sole rule of judgment is the free and untrammelled application of reason and perfect openness of mind to all new thought and scholarship, which the wider outlook of our time presents." [3]

The similarity, both of ideas and language, is most striking, and it is the absence of creed, emphasised alike by Agnostic and Unitarian, which sounds the one true note of harmony between the two. But this point, which constitutes the strength of the intellectual position of the former, constitutes in no less a degree the weakness of that of the latter. The *raison d'être* of Unitarianism is not, in the first place, scientific or social, or philosophic or philanthropic, but *religious*, and it must therefore ultimately stand or fall by the test that applied to it in common with religious systems—*i.e.*, what it has to tell the world about religion. If any credit can ever justly attach itself to

---

[1] *Agnosticism.* Collected Essays by T. H. Huxley. Vol. V.
[2] *Wm. H. Crosskey, LL.D., F.G.S., his Life and Work.* [3] *Ibid.*

such a position as that of " no creed," it is a credit which pertains only to the Agnostic or the Freethinker; to the man, in short, whose convictions keep him outside of any religious sect. Such a position has nothing in common with the religious basis upon which every Christian Church, whether Unitarian or Trinitarian, must rest.

So far from Agnosticism and Unitarianism being, as it is sometimes thought, more or less in accord, there is, on the contrary, a special reason why the two should occupy antagonistic intellectual positions, and this antagonism is not unrecognised by Unitarians themselves, one of whom wrote :

" We scorn to say that we who minister in the Free Churches of England are not agnostics and atheists. It would be like saying we are not thieves and liars." [1]

And another contends that

" between the agnostic philosophy and religion there is a real antagonism, because a blank unknowable cannot be an object of reverence." [2]

In spite, then, of the celebrated controversy between the great exponent of Agnosticism and the representative of the orthodoxy of the Established Church of England (known by the irreverent as the " Gadarene Pig " controversy), the result of this seemed to show that the decisive battle between science and religion was not to be fought by these combatants, the position of each being so unmistakably beyond the other's range that they could not hope to arrive at anything like a mutual understanding. Sooner or later both champions had to recognise the fact that they were fighting, not each other, but the air, and that an obstacle divided them which was not to be penetrated by shafts aimed from either side. Dr. Wace fell back upon his entrenchments of faith, and Professor Huxley on his of science, and neither could dislodge the other from his position.

It is pregnant with interest to think what different results might have ensued had the contest taken place between the Agnostic and a champion of unorthodox religion, unhampered by the restrictions of authoritative dogma and special revelation. A Huxley pitted against a Martineau would have meant intellectual warfare worthy the regard of gods and men. Such a controversy would have had in it the elements of civil war in religion, each side fighting, as it were, on and for his own ground, and each claiming for himself the position secured to him by scientific and philosophical investigation. Huxley, it is true, states that " with scientific theology Agnosticism has no quarrel "; but when he goes on to say that the Agnostic " can wish for nothing more urgently than that the scientific theologian should not only be at perfect liberty to thresh out the matter in his own

[1] *Wm. H. Crosskey, his Life and Work.*
[2] *A Unitarian's Answer to the Pleas of Agnosticism.*

fashion, but that he should, if he can, find flaws in the Agnostic position,"[1] we feel sure that he was burning to find himself in the arena with a foeman of that ilk, worthy his steel. But this was not to be; and, if the encounter is ever to take place, it must be between other combatants. The fact remains that the respective attitudes of Unitarianism and Agnosticism are incompatible, and that the former, in trying to share much of the ground proper to the latter, exposes itself to the risk of being dislodged by its neighbour.

"I," says in effect the modern Unitarian, "occupy a unique religious position; one that is independent of creed, unaffected by the march of science, or the unmasking of error and superstition. Science is for me the voice of God, unfolding to man the secrets of the universe in which He is the Supreme Power; and, though discarding the ordinary channels of revelation, I claim for myself a revelation of that Power which reveals Him to me as a Being with whom I can enter into relationship, and who is an object no less of love than of worship."

This claim to read the secret of the universe, to represent scientific religion, is one which has yet to be made good as regarded from the Agnostic's standpoint, especially as it is partly based on the grounds which he himself occupies. It is needless to say that no such claim has ever been urged on behalf of Agnosticism.

"No two people agree," wrote Huxley, "as to what is meant by the term 'religion:' but if it means, as I think it ought to mean, simply the reverence and love for the ethical ideal, and the desire to realise that ideal in life, which every man ought to feel—then I say Agnosticism has no more to do with it than it has to do with music or painting. If, on the other hand, religion means theology, then, in my judgment, Agnosticism can be said to be a stage in its evolution, only as death may be said to be the final stage in the evolution of life."[2]

Here we touch again upon that divergence between the two modes of thought, Agnostic and Unitarian, which formed the starting-point of our inquiry with them. It will be remembered that in spite of their apparent similarity, they parted company so soon as one asserted its claim to be regarded as religion, taking the word in the technical—*i.e.*, the theological—sense. Whether or no I have been successful in the attempt to establish my main contention—which is, that the basis on which modern Unitarianism seeks to establish itself is one which can afford no logical support to any form of faith sufficiently definite to pass as religion—is a point which will probably be decided on the lines on which religious questions usually are decided—*i.e.*, in accordance with the *previous* convictions of any given individual. The claim of modern Unitarianism to be regarded as religion founded on scientific principles cannot be fully considered without facing the larger question: Are these the real or only the assumed bases of any form of religion,.

---

[1] *Agnosticism and Christianity.*          [2] *Ibid.*

even if it be of such an advanced type as the one we are now considering? The Agnostic is disposed to accept the latter alternative, and to record his conviction that the real basis of Unitarianism, no less than Trinitarianism, is the "faith" which is "the assurance of things hoped for, the proving of things not seen." If this be so, it may perhaps be said of it: "The stone which the builders rejected is become the head of the corner."

At the risk of incurring the charge of inconsistency, I am going to conclude with the avowal that, in spite of intellectual disagreement, there is no religious body with whom the Agnostic is so much in moral sympathy as the Unitarian. I believe that time will prove, and is, indeed, already proving, that Unitarians are attempting the impossible; but that does not prevent recognition of the fact that they are in pursuit of a noble ideal—that of setting up a rational form of the Christian religion. They yield to none in their fervour for a religious basis to morality, but at the same time they are determined to relinquish everything in religion which they feel to be irreconcilable with the knowledge gleaned by the human intellect in its march through "fresh woods and pastures new." They desire to secure for themselves a religious position which will enable them to welcome knowledge, not defy it. In this respect they must be said to place themselves in opposition to St. Paul, when he asks, "Hath not God made foolish the wisdom of this world?" and contends that "God chose the foolish things of the world, that he might put to shame them that are wise." They want to know God by wisdom, not by foolishness; by intellect, not by emotion.

I think it may also be justly said that nowhere do we find a religious sect more free from the taint of other-worldliness; more ready to do good for its own sake, "hoping for nothing again;" or whose ideals are less biassed by self-interest, by ulterior hopes of reward or dread of punishment. Theoretically, their position may be untenable; practically, they share no less in that spirit of universal love and tolerance of all save evil which characterised the Founder of Christianity, than those who take the orthodox view of His supernatural credentials. It is, however, not because of the miraculous side of Christianity, but in spite of it, that the modern Unitarian is, in the ethical sense, a Christian.

E. M. S.

# AN EDUCATED MATERNITY.

In this era of reason and time of higher education, that reveals the world's need, no more positive proof of the trend of the progressive thought of the age exists than is exemplified in the acknowledged fact that the true spirit of philanthropic effort recognises the necessity of not only alleviating the evils we have, but the urgent obligation to seek for and discover their cause, that ultimately a cure may be effected, whereby the whole race will be benefited.

Men for ages have sought diligently for the fabled "Spring of perpetual youth," "the alchemist's stone," or hoped by other or imaginary means to obtain their desires, while the minds of the more unselfish reformers have pondered long and reasoned earnestly over visionary and Utopian schemes—based on the division of wealth, co-operative methods, and the thousand other vague dreams that have, from time immemorial, charmed the minds and hearts of those great souls who have laboured for the public good and the longed-for millennium.

To us, who view the results of these various schemes, the world at large has been little helped by their attempted fulfilment. Humanity is to-day much the same as in the past, and the reason is not hard to find, for society itself is unchanged. If we look for any betterment of the river of humanity, for any hope of lessening its contamination by the foul streams of criminality which flow into it, we must understand that it can only be accomplished—not by any small dams, constructed with infinite care and at enormous expense, intended merely to confine the impure waters and to prevent as far as possible their escape—but the innumerable springs, the tiny rivulets, which, by their combined impurities, unite to form these polluted streams of humanity: these must not only be confined, but purified, and kept pure, that the danger of their contaminating and polluting influence need no longer be a menace to the welfare of the race.

In other words, the world recognises to-day, as never before, the necessity of not restricting and curbing, but seeks the absolute cure for the continual increase of crime, striving to accomplish on moral grounds the prevention of the propagation of criminals.

While the philanthropic spirit that now so generously supports our public charities, our orphan homes, reformatories, insane asylums, and homes for incurables, is most commendable—as is also the innumerable methods by which humanitarians seek to not only alleviate the miserable condition of our corrupt flotsam and jetsam, but to turn them from paths of suffering, sin, and degradation—still, if we are honest with ourselves, we must admit that the formula by which the great problem must be worked out, to find a correct and satisfactory answer to the query, " What shall be done for fallen humanity ? " still confronts us, and will until the laws governing crime and criminals is understood and acted upon.

The philanthropist must learn to recognise that his generosity comes too late, and can only alleviate, while helpless to prevent, the ever-widening influence of these corrupt and defective specimens of the human family who " increase and multiply," not only a curse to themselves, but a menace to society at large : festering sores on the body politic that it is idle to poultice and doctor without recognising the bad blood that, by the immutable laws of heredity, must continue to occasion other inflictions—the disease being driven in at one point, being as surely followed by an eruption at another—until the impurity of the vital fluid is acknowledged as the source of the manifestation and the cause removed.

How can this be done ? has been and is being asked, and innumerable answers have been given, all with more or less reasonableness and truth, but lacking in the one great essential, practical application.

" As the twig is bent the tree's inclined " is an old saying, but the copy-books of the future will go back still further, and speak of the character of the parent tree as being the still greater influence to be considered in reckoning the little twig's propensity to be either straight or crooked.

Such an accepted authority on heredity as Helen H. Gardner has stated that " We all follow the line of least resistance," and it follows that prenatal conditions are the real factors that must be considered in any practical plans for the future betterment of the race.

It is not enough to endow a ward in an asylum, build a reformatory, or rest content at having disposed of the degenerate—finally, as we hope, having once secured him behind the prison bars—we must go back of that and educate mothers, that the constantly increasing degenerate tendencies of criminal motherhood may be stamped out.

But how ? is again the very pertinent question. This is a subject of such momentous potentialities, such divine possibilities, such supreme importance, that we must not expect to find a speedy panacea, for the disease has become chronic, and the ailment from long continuance deep-seated. We must rest content to rely upon the slow and sure cure—education.

It is idle to contend that the lower classes are ready for the education they must ultimately receive to enable them to secure moral and physical health. First, it is necessary to teach the teachers, to educate the mothers blessed by more fortunate tendencies and environments, who are—in spite of an ever-widening sphere under improved conditions—still, as women, in absolute ignorance; as a sex regarding their obligations and responsibilities little above the condition that prevailed in the dark ages; having no higher idea of their own immense powers and importance as mothers of the. race than their degraded, ignorant sisters of the submerged world.

Most closely and justly bound up *in solido* with this sublime problem of the betterment of the race, woman stands by natural law its greatest exponent, and one who must, by her own active participation in the reproduction of the race, be the fountain-head, the absolute source of the human tide, and as such an instrument for the great future weal or woe of the human family.

It must be admitted that, although the statistics of birth prove that, in America at least, woman is not shirking to any appreciable degree the duties of maternity, and the consequent labours, the care, education, and rearing of the young—obligations laid upon her by Nature—still it is undoubtedly true that her work is done imperfectly, ignorantly, often most unwillingly, in a haphazard way, that leads to the inevitable result to be expected from inexperience, incompetence, and blind, unreasoning ignorance.

The belief prevails that the perfection or imperfection of offspring is the arbitrary edict of a Divine Providence that complacently decrees that one child shall be blessed with all the good gifts in life, be born approximately perfect, while another shall be cursed with " all the ills that flesh is heir to," be a cripple, deaf, dumb, blind, and idiotic, for no other reason than that it is God's will, a fiat of the Infinite, which the finite mind must neither question or try to explain, but accept, and in all humility bow to the inevitable.

In this age of enlightenment we must refuse to sanction such a monstrous blasphemy, such an absurd contradiction of the immutable and absolute laws of cause and effect, by which the whole world and " the innumerable worlds beyond our ken " are as divinely controlled and regulated.

In Nature it is law, not chance, and in mankind we see the selfsame laws at work, by which, consciously or unconsciously, the ultimate end, be it good or evil, is attained.

Women of the greatest intelligence and highest education must first be taught their responsibilities, and made to recognise the unpalatable truth that until they have learned their own lesson they will not be able to explain the subject to others and show them the way.

To-day we know by natural law, from whose effect mankind is no more exempt than the lowest of the brute creation, we know that a child can be well born if the laws governing reproduction are understood and obeyed. We know that effect is the natural sequence of cause, and that the mental, moral, and physical attributes of our children, their health, temperament, and sex, are only decrees of the Infinite in so much as they are the absolute result of obeyed or broken law.

When the women of the world are enlightened as to their own divinely ordained powers, the truth will be recognised that every child born has the right to demand health as its inalienable birth-right, and to be *well born ;* and the parents responsible for having forced into being an imperfect creature, a defective—either mentally, morally, or physically—have committed a crime, not only against their own progeny, but against society itself—a crime that will be no longer palliated or excused by criminal ignorance.

To the unbiassed judge, who views the facts dispassionately as he finds them, will come the conviction that women, as a class, know but little of themselves. Their minds are being freed from the narrow limits formerly fixed by an absurd sex-bias as " woman's sphere," and with her enlightened mind has come a wider horizon, and the old fetters that held captive the sex are broken ; but her emancipa-tion has not come, and will not come until her education is complete.

This education of the future must begin at the beginning with body, and not as is now attempted at the end, with mind.

To this end our women must be first emancipated from the doctor. At present not one woman in ten is physically able to do her duty as woman and wife, still less is she able to fulfil the much greater physical requirements of mother. Study the sex in every walk of life, and the truth will be admitted : she is handicapped, not by any lack of talent, but by a lack of constitution. When men recognise the incalculable benefit to the woman, and through her to his children and himself, he will not only encourage a " masculine education," but will insist upon it.

Honoré de Balzac, the great French writer, asserts in his *Physiologie du Mariage, Méditation Onze :* " A woman who has received a masculine education possesses the most brilliant and fertile qualities with which to secure, not only her own happiness, but her husband's as well."

While we recognise all that the entrance to college being opened to women means, we still more rejoice that to-day the door to the gymnasium has been unlocked and that the bars to the *campus* have been taken down, and that the road to health is no longer obstructed by the old scarecrows that once threatened all women with excom-munication from their sex who dared to aspire to athletic sports or other " unwomanly " exercises tending to develop and promote a sadly lacking physical soundness.

To-day the world has awakened to the absurdity of considering weakness and inefficiency as necessarily synonymous with feminity, and too late it recognises what incalculable detriment, as a whole, the inferior development of women has entailed upon the race.

Grant Allen states, for the male ethicists—of whom he was one—"that they will not rest content until they have vindicated the rights of all children to a sound father and a sound mother; and furthermore, that it will be their purpose to combat vices that bring about impaired vitality, and to put the relation of the sexes and the production of children on a sound and wholesome basis."

This wholesome basis must rest upon not only a mental but a physical foundation. It is idle to expect sound, perfect, well-born progeny from mothers who, at the present time, are yet without a realisation of what the word health really means. This is a sweeping statement to make, but one that can be easily substantiated. As a woman it has been my privilege to study women closely for a number of years, and from the testimony thus gathered, in answer to personally put questions, I have come to the conclusion that the real cause of the inferior position woman occupies to-day is due, not to any insuperable obstacle of lighter weight brain, but to her inferior physical condition. Not a condition forced upon her because born a female, but arising from the erroneous methods and false and pernicious ideas of what should constitute a feminine education. To the absurd notion that developed muscles and bodily vigour were male attributes, and that the "womanly woman" had no use for either, is due the pitiful creation we see, and has resulted in making women the petty, dressed-up puppets upon whom the latest monstrosities in "fashionable gowns" are displayed. Educate the woman in her youth to be comfortable, to have the joy of feeling physically sound from head to foot, and she will no longer be enslaved, in mind and body, by the "false gods" she now blindly and ignorantly follows.

The great imitative tendencies of the poor and lower classes are recognised by all who have come into touch with the submerged world. A lady related at the recent Congress of Mothers how she had told the denizens of Five Points that a good, cheap soup could be made of tomatoes, and had added by way of emphasis, that this tomato soup was a favourite one at the governatorial mansion. "Every grocer in the neighbourhood had an immediate demand for canned tomatoes," she states, "for none were so poor, or so low down in the human scale, that they did not have a desire to at once partake of 'Governor's soup.'"

This unconscious imitativeness being innate, we see in it a hopeful sign, and an augury, that with the education of the upper classes in bodily strength and health, and their enlightenment as women regarding the laws of maternity, and the obligations and rights of the unborn, will come an ultimate age of reason for the submerged mothers, who will most gladly follow the lead of their more fortunate sisters, when the laws of reproduction and their criminal neglect of them is understood and explained.    The criminal mother does not wilfully curse her progeny, but brings into being the degenerate because she knows no better, because she is untaught and in ignorance of the most vital truths that not only affect herself, but the future, for all time.

Professor Drummond, in his work, *The Ascent of Man,* comes to the exalted conclusion : " It is not too much to say that the one motive of organic nature was to make mothers.    Even on its physical side, this was the most stupendous task evolution ever undertook."

It was Emerson, I think, who aptly said, " It is idle to ask of the loom that weaves huckaback why it did not turn out cashmere."    It is also as absurd to expect the huckaback to become cashmere by any course of reformation and subsequent treatment.

The biblical saying, " A good tree bringeth forth good fruit," is exemplified before our eyes every day, as well as the fallacy of hoping '' to gather grapes of thorns and figs of thistles."    But men continue to marry physically imperfect women, and hope by some unexplained and mysterious workings of Providence to have sound and perfect progeny.    Content with a pretty face, and accepting an impaired nervous organisation, undeveloped muscles, aches and pains, as feminine concomitants, they go blindly forward, without a realisation that the rights of future generations demand an educated maternity, that will stop to reckon consequences before thoughtlessly transmitting a diseased body, an impaired mind, and the hopeless existence of the soul that has been sinned against—not blessed—by its forced and unasked being.

All thought on the subject of maternity comes back to the inevitable truth, that the rights of progeny *must* be respected.    The humanitarians of our time, who have societies for the prevention of cruelty to animals, and who scorn to see a maimed animal suffer, permit —nay, insist by law—that the maimed and incurable human body must not be relieved from its agony except by an often delayed long-prayed-for death.    What is commendable and humane for the lowest beast is a crime to man, under the law that insists that the malformed monstrosity and the incurable victim of a necessarily fatal ailment or accident must be forced to live out its last moment of agony, to die by inches, until death, more kind than man, releases the imprisoned soul from its imperfect shell.

Is it not this same unreasoning voice that reiterates the old cry, " Increase and multiply," without taking note of the hideous result due to imperfect creation—the sure result of ignorant, defective, and criminal reproduction ?    A crime, the most heinous in all the annals of the world's corrupt practices, and one that not alone curses the present, but that is the most awful menace to all future progress, as is exemplified in the descendants of *one* criminal mother.    We may well accept, in the light of known and verified cases, the old Presbyterian doctrine of infants "being born to be damned," for we see generation after generation of degenerates following out to the last step the criminal path to the gallows, or to a final bed in the Potter's Field, while most diligently adding to the population a horde of pre-ordained imperfects, who, like themselves, continue to " increase and multiply."

Reason rejects the thought that it is either right or necessary for women, even the highest and noblest, to jeopardise their own health, or endanger the happiness of the home and the children they have, by continual child-bearing, and in the coming era of education and maternal enlightenment they will not be permitted, on moral grounds, to immolate themselves (by following the dogma that she is the greatest woman who has had the greatest number of children), or encouraged to commit the inevitable wrong of bringing more children into the world than their physical condition will allow them to properly bear, and more than their impoverished mates can hope or expect to support.

"Man's duty to the future is fulfilled," says an eminent English writer, "not by the superabundance of his descendants, but by the excellence of their inherited qualities and proclivities, mental and physical, to which end—even in the absence of pecuniary conditions —there is due to each child an individuality of solicitude and guidance which cannot, from its very nature, be bestowed upon an indiscriminate number. Woman equally with man has a specified duty to herself, and is not—any more than he—to be considered merely in the light of a ' producer of children,' as has been done, with continual misery to herself and inevitable detriment to the race."

To the reasoning mind, an ignorant, forced maternity is no more honourable than is the compulsory enlistment of the conscript. The true education for the highest enlightenment of women must begin at the foundation, and consist of a rational curriculum that will teach the sex their manifest destiny as mothers of the race—an education that will lead to development not only along scientific lines, but a development and growth mental, moral, and physical, and that will not only show them their new powers as factors in the business world, their rights as citizens under the law, the justice of equal pay for equal work, but the diviner and more sublime destiny bestowed upon them alone by Nature, to be consummated by an intelligent, educated, purposed maternity.

An educated maternity will teach woman *her obligations* as well as her *rights*, and by her participation in the betterment of her off-spring, doing her whole duty to the child and herself, as she sees it and knows it, we may hope for the ultimate advancement of the whole human family, a lifting of the race to a higher and nobler destiny.

Olive Schreiner has said with truth : "He who stands by the side of woman cannot help her, she must help herself"; and many years ago Mrs. Farnham uttered the prophetic words, of which we even now see the promised fulfilment : "Woman will grow into fitness for the sublime work which Nature has given her to do, and man, through his help and persuasion, will spontaneously assume the relation of co-operator in it. Finding that Nature intends his highest good, and that of his species, through the emancipation and development of woman into the fulness of her powers, he will gratefully seek his own profit and happiness in harmonising himself with this method ; he will honour it as Nature's method, and woman as its chief executor."

As we view this new era of enlightened womanhood, we realise that the greatest boon to humanity, and the generations yet to come, will be found in a broader, higher, nobler recognition of the sublime possibilities of an educated maternity, an education that will fit woman for any position in life, and will enable her to perfectly and consciously perform her duty, not only to herself as a reasoning, responsible being, but to fulfil to the uttermost the sublime task trusted to her alone as mother of the human family.

ALICE LEE MOQUÉ,
Washington D. C., U.S.A.

# SUPERSTITIONS OF THE SCOT.

BELIEF in the supernatural seems to be absorbed from the climate of Caledonia. Superstition is the shadow of the Scot, and frequently plays him fantastic tricks. Mingling with the mists of the mountains, and hovering with fluttering wing over moorland and homestead, it is ingrained with his nature, greatly colouring and controlling his thoughts and actions. The general diffusion of superstition throughout Scotland, with its terrible influences on the native mind, is attributable to various causes. The circumstances and surroundings of the people are provocative of dark and gloomy hallucinations. Occupying an insular and isolated situation, with a social system suppressive of originality and progress, and bitterly opposed to learning, the peasantry were consequently ignorant and unreasoning. They indulged their moroseness by speculations in superstition, and conjured together an excellent assortment of incongruous absurdities. The poverty of the country engenders the spirit of selfishness and greed, and "siller" has become the deity of their adoration, and "gear-gathering" the reason of their existence. Nothing else is thought worthy of serious consideration, and, consequently, the finer qualities remain uncultivated. Religion also has played its part, and the peculiarities of the particular faiths of the sectaries have stimulated superstition, with mental narrowness and intoleration. Indeed, in many instances religion has a great resemblance to the carnal feelings of envy, hatred, and malice. But the machinery of their superstition is extensive and operates in a wide and wildering field.

While yet in the untamed condition in his native wilds, the Scot is continually terrorised and tormented by visitants from the unmentionable regions. His footsteps are fettered by the shackles of predestination, and his progress darkened by the evil shadows of a wild and unbounded supernaturalism. Everywhere he is surrounded by phantoms whose influences are malignant, and everything reminds him of unseen dangers that are not always to be avoided. He is continually undergoing a process of supernatural solicitation and supervision, while the fates have never revealed, but suggested, the possibilities of his being spirited away to abodes that are not of the blessed. He is the object of divine solicitude, and his requirements receive special and peculiar consideration. The suggestions of superstition he accepts as facts, and believes the myths of tradition because they are satisfactory to his vanity and congenial to his great and overweening self-importance. He has his attendant familiars. From birth to death, from the cradle to the grave, and beyond it, he is surrounded by sprites and spirits of all and every description. The horizon of his little world is thick with approaching apparitions, jostling to join an already abundant congregation of unreal and bloodless beings, but all animated and active. One portion is engaged in the development of evil and devilish designs, while the other is practising benevolent and good intentions. His orisons and oratory are directed, with greater or less success, in controlling the intentions of these ubiquitous unrealities, and he is continually renewing his efforts to encourage, to appease, and to give deadly defiance. Not infrequently he becomes sorely confused in apportioning the particular proclivities, and thereby misdirecting his invocations and incantations, gives great offence by his contradictory conduct, while at the same time making his spells ineffectual and destroying the power of the compelling exorcism. Yet his powers of fascination must be great and general. He attracts from their lonely haunts the mountain sylph and the goblin-shaped gnome, the water wraith, and the salamander from the fire. The kelpies from the stream and the fairies of the grove pirouette for precedence with the lissome-limbed wood-nymph and the dainty but tantalisingly elusive fay of the forest bower. Poor Anthony's temptation is historical, but the breastworks of the Scot are besieged by the seductive attractions of creatures of such surpassing loveliness that desire is responsive and delight prevails.

But those were only the lighter diversions in his mythological world. He was not dependent upon fairyland alone for his interesting manifestations. His was a fine and varied assortment of entertaining, although phantom, phenomena, whose importance frequently increased with their invisibility. The immaterial was supplemented by the corporeal, the audible, and the visible. There were incomprehensible rappings and tappings, unaccountable gliding ghosts and shuffling spectres, nocturnal interruptions and daylight visitations. Ghost-candles and dead-lights made a respectable illumination which was probably intended to accompany the funeral foregoes and portentous processions. To increase the commotion there were the perturbed spirits and wandering shades of his departed relatives. These restless and roving relics were, once on a time, very plentiful, and the immediate decrease in their perambulatory incursions may be indicative of a settlement amongst the shades, or greater vigilance in the warden of the fort. Be that as it may, and whatever the reason, there is a visible inactivity among those roving midnight raiders, and their excitations are sadly missed. With such a saturnalia of superstition it is supposable that Scottish life was lively, and not a-wanting in stirring incident. And it was so. But there were other agencies of the unseen to raise the riot and boil the broth of demonology.

The aërial nymphs who pressed his pillow and dominated his dreams were of an elvan and unsubstantial character. The fays and fantastic revellers of fairyland were generally altogether invisible, or, when it was their pleasure to expose themselves to mortal vision, they assumed a precariously intangible aspect and indefinable appearance. The return visits of his decaying ancestry were not always entirely satisfactory, as the visitors were generally intangible in substance and incoherent in their utterance. In fact, they had a preference for the sign manual conversation and dumb show, with nodding heads and pointing fingers. But horrors accumulate on horror's head, and the devil is rich in invention. He is always seeking and demanding his dues, and has many of the more power-ful and influential infernal agencies organised as recruiting centres. He conducts his operations with surprising sagacity and great activity, distributing his dainties with a liberal hand in lavish abundance. His servants on earth are more dangerous and to be dreaded than even the elemental emanations. There were the terrible and pernicious orders of witchcraft, with their daylight cantrips and midnight abominations.

Witchcraft was the recognised medium of communication between the enemy of man and his human operators. It was well authenti-cated, and had been long established. It had been exorcised and well banned by bell, book, and candle, but from its vigour it was evident that the anathemas had failed and the applications of holy water were ineffectual. These human agents were more persistent and pernicious than even their master. The Prince of Darkness had occasionally been successfully defied, but the demon mortals were resourceful in their energies. This noble army was composed of warlocks and wizards, witches and wise women; individuals gifted with second sight, and their compatriots in possession of the evil eye. Their gatherings were significant of ill luck, and were con-vened with great circumspection and secrecy. Broomsticks and sieves were their favourite vehicles of locomotion, and the transit was accomplished with surprising swiftness. Their meetings were of an occult nature, and had to be approached with mystic words and meaning knocks, significant signs and supramundane signals, demoniacal incantations and initiatory ceremonials. When the witches were desirous of a horse they secured a bridle, and shaking it over a sleeping member of the male persuasion of the human species, he immediately started up in the form of a swift and sleek steed, which was mounted astraddle and ridden bareback to the secret conclave of some important convocation of the cantankerous clans. That unfortunate mortal who might be selected was never the same after being witch-ridden. The witches, at will, could assume the forms of various animals, and successfully simulate their particular peculiarities—the cunning of the cat or the nimbleness of the mouse, the ferocity of the wolf and the slyness of the fox, the sagacity of the rat with the swiftness of the hare, and the wisdom of the serpent with the fleetness of the wind. These creatures were hard to kill, but their black art was not invariably a secure protection. Cold steel or silver slugs were the only metals that could penetrate their enchanted vitals, and when a suspected hare was sighted there were great endeavours to have a shot at her ribs with a crooked sixpence. When such an animal had been hit and not killed, but only wounded, it was possible to trace her track by the blood drops that led to the hovel of some antiquated crone, when the inhabitant would be found dressing and bandaging a recent and dangerous wound. That was suspicious, and the parish ministers had many such lone women ordered out to be burned. The desire for a similar application of the same drastic treatment still lurks in the minds of some of the older Caledonians, but it has to be remembered that in many localities the old-fashioned and elsewhere obsolete mediæval machinery of hell is yet in good going order. The belief in the pancake form and flatness of the earth has yet its followers, who will assert and asseverate that beneath the surface, somewhere in the bowels of the earth, there is located a good substantial fire, glowing and gleaming, whose sovereign is a real roaring Satan, horned and hoofed, and finding delights in pricking his subjects with a barbed and poison-tipped tail. But a Scotchman is more than a match for the devil in many things.

There is much folk-lore associated with the mystery of nativity. They desire a propitiatory planetary conjunction, and watch for the stars that will control the future and decide the destiny; for well do they know that the heavenly orbs are watchful of the movements of Fate relating to the newly-born child. Every individual at the important occasion has a particular star allotted to his interests, which, rightly understood, foretells his fortune and influences his destiny. A favourable future is indicated by the intensity of its brilliancy, while invarying disaster is plainly foreshadowed by any diminution in its brightness. It will accompany his progress through life, and when it shoots or falls in the sky, that is to be accepted as a friendly warning that the end is drawing near. To minimise the peril and possibly avert the danger, the observer of the shooting star is to vigorously ejaculate "Not mine—not mine!"

The nurse of the newly-born child is surrounded by many dangers and hampered by numerous and mysterious restrictions. The fairies are on the wing and elves on the prowl with a desire to gain possession of the latest addition to the morsels of humanity. It, therefore, has to be guarded against the kidnapping intentions of these troublesome people who are so cunning at snapping away unbaptized Christian children. So greatly do they prefer the human production, that they will sacrifice their own kindred to indulge their tastes, by surreptitiously substituting for the peculated bit of mortality one of their own misbegotten bratlings. That is done to allay suspicion, but the trick is not always successfully performed. If an elfin exchange has been suspected, the test consisted in holding the doubtful infant over the glowing embers of a red-hot fire, and if the substitution has been effected, the impish impostor, with horrible screams, will vanish up the chimney; while the real and original article will, at the same time, come tumbling down. There were other curious methods for the discovery of such undesirable intruders, but the fiery ordeal was the favourite specific and the one most generally practised, as it was considered to be absolutely infallible. It was unlucky to weigh the child, and it was equally so to soothe its cries by swinging it backwards and forwards in the arms. The nails were never to be cut by a scissors or other sharp instrument until the child was at least twelve months old. They might safely be bitten or torn off. Cutting the nails on particular days of the week wrought specific results, and white specks upon them were regarded as of favourable omen and allied to good luck. The cradle was never to be rocked when the lawful occupant was not lying in it, as sickness, perhaps death, was induced by rocking the empty cradle. Washing the infant was another perilous performance that was not lightly undertaken. The operation had to be carefully conducted according to the rules of prescription authorised by the ritual of infantile management and under the personal supervision of the attendant conclave of antiquated crones. It was a miracle that infantile mortality was not universal. No child, under any circumstances, was to be carried up a stair until it had previously been carried down one; and thus we see that the first steps and early progress of the squalling Scot were by compulsion downwards. That fact may account for many after careers. The careful mother slept with the Bible under her pillow, as contact with the holy book was influential in warding off the attack of evil creatures, and a good substantial "family Bible" was no inconsiderable weapon of offence when hurled with unerring aim at the intruding foe. There were many observations prescribed by fancy and tradition for securing happiness and success in life, and dangers were averted by amulets and charms. But man is the plaything of circumstances, and any possible precaution was of no avail if the individual came into existence under an unlucky planet. It was equally disastrous to be born on one of the many unlucky days, and as these were particularly numerous, it was very difficult to arrange for an approximate appearance at the time of a propitious horoscope and on one of the right days. From the number of human failures it is suspiciously evident that a great majority of new arrivals make their descent upon earth under some of these malevolent circumstances. Overlooking was another serious danger to which children were exposed. The influence of the "evil eye" was a real and risky thing to encounter, and "body and beast," when once overlooked by it, would never know health, happiness, or prosperity again, and had only to welcome death with relief to their sufferings. Such a terrible power was regarded with consternation, and the Scot would take a long and roundabout way rather than risk a meeting with the possessor of the evil optic, which was never lightly to be encountered. There were many of them known to be blinking and peering about, and the fervent prayer of the pious Scot was to be preserved from the blithesome blink of a bonnie blue eye—when there was any suspicion of evil about it.

In the life of the rural community the event next in importance to the entry into existence was the connubial confabulation and contract. Marriage had its auguries and omens, and was a serious undertaking never to be concluded without extended consideration and considerable consultation. Hymen had to be propitiated, and there were many attendant complications never to be abandoned or neglected. The observation of a bright light streaming from the windows of a house was regarded as an intimation of an approaching matrimonial venture, the nuptials to be therein celebrated. Youth is unquestionably the season of susceptibility, and the amorous damsel had access to an extensive assortment of preliminary tests and performances in the anxiety to penetrate the mysteries of futurity and decipher her destiny. Spae-wives were resorted to, whose unhallowed accomplishments were believed to have great efficacy in unravelling the thread of life and fortune still hidden in the damsel's future. Love philters were employed, while magical charms were sought and unholy invocations offered in the endeavour to advance their matrimonial machinations. Indeed, there was a period of general demonolatry, when all the resources of superstition were in continual requisition in the vain endeavour to lift the veil and observe the operations of the fateful Spinners. The consideration of their prospective partner in life was of continuous interest, and they always were discovering, testing, and trying new methods for determining which of their acquaintances were to be the highly favoured and lucky individual. These practices were unquestionably of religious origin, and, in fact, the anniversaries of certain old Romish festivals and saints' days were regarded with extra and special veneration, as great occasions when the passion of prying into the mysteries of the future might be indulged with especial and particular success.

There were infallible observances, descended from time immemorial and associated with powerful spells and enchantments, which were performed with sacred solemnity and certain success on those mysterious nights so pregnant with prophecy to the unlettered peasantry and the surreptitiously inclined generally. Festereen, or "Bannock Night," was one of those important occasions that had its mysterious attractions. As a preliminary dip in the divinatory process, a large bowl of "brose" was prepared, and into which was surreptitiously slipped by the matron of the house a gold ring, a silver sixpence, and a bone button. The matrimonially inclined, of both sexes, ranged themselves around the festive board, and, dipping into the brose basin, soon consumed the steaming mass. Whoever got the ring would be first married, the silver betokened wealth, while the unfortunate finder of the button was thereafter to be regarded as a predestinated bachelor or old maid, as the sex might determine. A similar experiment in vaticination was again repeated in the evening, with the variation that the three articles were concealed in a mass of stuff which was made into bannocks on a hot "girdle." Thereafter the bannock banquetters gleefully indulged in games and dancing. Hallowe'en was another anniversary fateful with promise to the unmarried and youthful folk. It had numerous observances, and always and everywhere was regarded as a red-letter night in the calendar of destiny.

But the real oracles and presiding "black and midnight hags" were the extraordinary number of witches, spae-wives, and wise women swarming in every district and infesting all parts of the country. They supplied supernatural information, furnished favours, and dealt out disasters; procured benefits and dispensed destruction; and trafficked in blessings and curses generally, with an impartiality that was seasoned by the remunerative consideration. They had some curious methods for revealing the intentions of Providence in the domains of Mammon, and could sweep the romantic realms of Love with an imagination that might not always be accurate, but was unvaryingly flattering. For ministering to the requirements of the tender passion inspiration was drawn from the dregs of a teacup, and cards were ostentatiously consulted under favour of the amorous deities. And there were many occult and esoteric accomplishments that illumined the darkness of destiny and enabled the weird sisterhood to raise the mystic veil and reveal the advancing crisis to the trembling neophytes. Dreams occupied an honoured position, and the trusted interpreter thereof was highly esteemed by the distracted dreamer. The *Dream Book* is a singularly imaginative and exhaustive compilation that is eagerly consulted by the confiding damsel, and will be found in the possession of many individuals from whose years and position better things might be expected. The floral and vegetable worlds were laid under tribute, and contributed largely to the arts of divination.

The arrangements for propitiating Hymen and the performance of the marriage ceremony were never to be undertaken in any of the admittedly unlucky months. May, in particular, was to be avoided, and certain days of the week were preferable and to be selected for their "lucky" reputation. The state of the weather on the bridal morn was carefully scanned, for it had been established since time immemorial that "Happy was the bride that the sun shone on." If the orb of light rose brilliant in the morning and continued so during the day, the bride smiled; if the sky was overcast and gloomy in the afternoon, the bridegroom frowned. If tempestuous weather prevailed during the entire day, that happy couple were not to be envied, and their married state was likely to be a turbulent existence with a miserable ending. The dismay of the bridal party in any matrimonial procession was complete if they chanced to encounter in the course of their peregrinations a dog or a cat, a priest or a serpent, and familiarity with anything resembling the hare species was not upon any consideration to be encouraged. Happiness, however, was ensured by a meeting with a wolf, a spider, or a toad. On the evening preceding the bridal morn there was an important function to be observed, known as the "feet-washing." It might much more appropriately be designated the whisky-drinking.

The actual marriage ceremony has its peculiar rites and functions, sometimes varied and modified in particular localities. No wedding would be successful without the consumption of a considerable quantity of the national beverage, and consequently the libations to Bacchus are on an extensive and extravagant scale.

During the processional progress noisy discharging of guns is indulged in and much powder wasted, with the hope that evil creatures will be prevented from approaching the interesting pair. Handfuls of rice and old shoes are thrown at the newly-joined couple, and these are not intended as instruments of wrath to do bodily injury, but are regarded as inducements to happiness and good luck. In olden times the "bedding of the bride" was a rather wild and scandalous performance that has beneficially fallen into disfavour and been discontinued. The "kirking" of the young couple was an important event, providing an opportunity to the bride for the spectacular display of her "braws and bravity," and enabling the gossips to decide whether or not she was likely to make a "sonsie eesfu' and working wife," the rural Scot always swearing by a "wirkin' wife." The church-going was also a preventive of any future interference from the fairy folks, as they were never altogether secure until they had presented themselves at church as man and wife. After the birth of a child the mother was always assailable by the little people until she had been "kirked." All those absurdities had been sedulously sown and cultivated by the Romish religion, and they were incorporated into the dogmas of Protestantism. In an ignorant and unenlightened age they were believed by a credulous people, but they are being swept away and forgotten, and morality is probably in consequence considerably advanced.

Regarding the unlucky days and unfortunate months which consumed a considerable portion of the year, it was well known that births and marriages would be unfortunate if occurring upon any such occasions. But journeys were not to be undertaken upon any of them, and they were to be avoided when commencing any great or considerable undertaking. Sickness or accidents occurring on any of these days were always likely to terminate fatally, and no speculation started upon them was ever known to prosper and develop successfully. May was the bad month, and Friday the day of darkness. Of all the days in the week it was considered the unluckiest, and had given terrible evidences of its malignant aspects. In the opinion of the oracular soothsayers it was indeed to be accounted a black day, and numerous were the floating legends devoutly recited for the edification of the ignorant and to prove the contention. Friday has been in disfavour with Christian nations generally, and in tracing the superstition to an unknown origin, far away into the uncertainties of antiquity, the tradition will be found in existence long prior to the Christian era. And its Oriental affinity is secured by the knowledge that in India the penultimate day of the week is in great disfavour with the Brahminic caste. Elsewhere, also, it is regarded with suspicion and terror, and many far-separated races recognise it as an evil day, unlucky, and malodorous with ill omen.

The healing art was another great field always generous with chances and possibilities for the speculations of superstition. For the ailments of the flesh curative concoctions and decoctions were prescribed whose number was only excelled by their nastiness. The peevishness of childhood and the fretfulness of old age provided great and golden opportunities for administering the nauseating specifics of the antiquated conclave; and when we, even dimly, realise the nature of their pharmaceutics, we are astonished that children escaped, even with their lives, the terrible nostrums. Infantile mortality is likely to have been great—it is surprising that it was not universal. But the chirurgical spae-wife and wise woman with her moon-gathered herbs have fallen into popular disfavour.

When we approach the closing of life's fitful drama, the last scene of all, and the impenetrable falling curtain, we are assailed by gigantic phantoms and terrorised by gibbering apparitions. As may be imagined and expected from a people with such susceptibility to superstition, there is a wealth of conflicting controversy and testimony connected with the loosing of the silver cord and the breaking of the golden bowl. Many manifestly false and incongruous notions gather and thickly cling around the mystery that stills the heart and quenches the intelligence. A belief in portents of death is

deeply rooted, and their observance is likely to remain in vigour for
some considerable time yet.   The possession of the second sight was
invaluable in determining the nature of a " call," and the services of
the seers were in great and general requisition.   The narration of a
few of the more common death-dealing warnings may not be
entirely uninteresting.

The rattle of a bridle, without visible agitation, was a warning to
prepare for a messenger of evil tidings ; a champing upon the bit
was indicative of the impatience of fate with impending death.
The fall of a tray betokened the funeral refreshments, and the hollow
rumble of a cart was the preternaturally reverberant echo of the
forego procession to the grave.   Spirits appearing in the forms of
certain animals were always and suddenly accompanied and succeeded
by disasters, afflictions, and death.   The fluttering, flitting corpse-
candles and ghostly gliding dead-lights were widely regarded as
certain intimations that the hour draws near to prepare for the
reception of death, and when these lights gleam and dance in some
swampy ground it is a sure indication that a funeral will in a short
time pass along in that direction.   The howling of a dog at nightfall made the people creep to the ingleneuk, shivering and sad, while
the crowing of a hen was heard with consternation.   Both animals
were presaging death by their vocal efforts, and either was listened
to with enervating terror.   The ticking of the death-watch was a
warning never to be neglected, and the noisy cracking of a chest or
other piece of household furniture was equally significant.   Three
distinct and audible blows, without any visible means, upon a door
were premonitory of the tapping of the coffin-maker or funeral
undertaker.   When corpse-flames were seen hovering over the bed
and then vanishing through the windows, to continue their progress
by slowly moving in the direction of the parish church, that was
known to be the dim light of death, and proverbially was certain to
be followed by an early funeral.   The glowing of the house light
was ominous, and when the falling cinder from the fire was observed
to be of an oblong shape, a coffin on an early date was sure to enter
the house.   The guttering of a candle was a well-recognised summons
from the other world, and the dripping of the melted wax or tallow
was, thereafter, observed to assume the shape of a winding-sheet.
And these superstitions were by no means confined to the ignorant
and the vulgar.   The hallucinations of the peasantry were intensified
in the house of the pompous patrician.

Death omens and family phantoms were favourite delusions with
the aristocratic and wealthy families.   Every old house and ancient
family had the fashionable attendant .weird and wandering spirit
whose appearance always announced a break in the line by death.
The legends about family spectres are innumerable, and the traditions
connected with haunted places have long been familiar.   Many

generations of sentimental damsels have sighed and shivered over the stories of floating swans with bleeding bosoms, white-breasted birds and fluttering doves, croaking ravens and hooting owls. These family possessions were frequently supplemented by the transparent shadow of the sombre nun, the white or green lady with cadaverous complexion and blazing eyes, the fleshless skeletons with waving draperies and eyeless sockets which transfixed with an unknown terror. There may, perhaps, at some far-back period, have been interesting incidents connected with the origin of these picturesque myths, but they long since have been lost and are now forgotten.

When the presence of death was supreme in the house of mourning, the fires were all extinguished and the windows darkened. The tolling of the passing-bell was intended to scare away any spirit of evil that might be hovering around, attracted to the house of desolation by the evidences of mortality. The waking or watching by the dead was the tribute of relatives for the protection of the newly-released soul. It also prevented the removal of the body by unhallowed hands or the powers of evil. That particular violation had sometimes been accomplished, and something substituted to deceive the mourners. At such successes the infernal furies were jubilant and merry. Between death and burial, if the body remained flexible and pliant, that was a sure sign that another dissolution within the family would occur before another year had spent its progress. Sounds and sights were common in the churchyard before the funeral, and the timorous peasantry generally gave the silent city of the dead a respectable distance after nightfall. The proverbial philosophy declared that "Happy was the corpse that the rain rained on," and consequently the drenching of the funeral party was a certain sign that the migratory soul had secured salvation. It also indicated a time of rest and peaceful repose for the spirit of the departed. That was a relief to the relatives at a time when their departed kindred might be doomed to revisit the abodes of their earthly being in ghastly garments. It was customary to watch by the grave till the churchyard received another tenant. That was done with a twofold purpose. It was an antidote and relief to the purgatorial punishment, and it was rendered necessary by the activity of the "resurrectionist." When the body had been removed and buried, the bed straw was burned, but the incineration was suggested rather by superstition than sanitation. On the occasion of a death the community watched for a big illumination of corpse-candles on a grand scale, which showed the activity of Satan and demonstrated beyond all question the malignity of his satellites. At such times his sable majesty and retinue became veritable angels of light, but their unwonted luminosity was intended to deceive and to destroy. Superstition, interpreted by the wily theologians, declared that the heavens were distracted and disturbed when great men died. The passing of rulers was accompanied by a magnificent pyrotechnic display in the sky, of flashing meteors, coruscating comets, shooting stars, and fantastically spinning fireballs. When the darkness was illumined by the dazzling lightning-flash, and the silence disturbed by the reverberations of the rolling thunder, that was a sure omen of the departure of a daring and illustrious spirit. The northern lights shooting athwart the heavens and the fire-flashes were the aërial reflectors of great events, and Scotland has been visited by the phenomena on the eve of many a national disaster, such as the fateful fight on Flodden's fatal field. Such events stirred up the supernatural to unwonted energy, when wonders weird and wild were witnessed on the earth and in the heavens; and even the creatures inhabiting the waters have been observed to assume a distinctly fiery appearance, doubtless for some great and good purpose.

But the romantic realms of tradition can never be thoroughly explored or their treasures exhausted. They defy the antiquarian and dissolve beneath the luminosity of the scientist. They may recede and advance, but never wholly disappear. Driven from their familiar positions, they may depart for a time, to suddenly reappear in some unexpected disguise with renewed vigour and well-defended frontiers. Tradition is tenacious and hard to kill, and the ancient rites and ceremonies are perhaps as common and accredited to-day as they ever were at any time in the history of the race. Only they appear under new forms and fanciful appellations. When the trappings have become tarnished, and they seem to be falling into disfavour, they are refashioned and regilded—and that is all.

JAMES DOWMAN.

# THE DEVELOPMENT OF CRITICISM.[1]

It has often been observed that, although Science has advanced with the advance of time, Art has rather stood a shabby monument of the past. But with one subdivision of literary art it has not been so. The critical work of Ste.-Beuve is hardly less superior to that of Aristotle than is the astronomy of Adams to that of Ptolemy. And in both cases it is not merely that the methods and principles of the earlier master are more accurately applied or more ably developed: the methods themselves and principles are fundamentally different. Very briefly, then, to investigate and discuss the causes and circumstances of this remarkable change—nay, rather but to offer a few hints toward that investigation and discussion—is the aim of this essay. The subject will be found not only curious but also full of instruction and variously suggestive.

"In the days of old, when the world was young," man regarded himself, and that naturally, instinctively, inevitably, as the centre, as the final cause, as the standard and measure of all things. Often in these superior modern times have the capricious showers of careless contempt besprinkled, often has the stern sirocco of solemn scorn enveloped the memory of those gropers in the dusky twilight of philosophy's early dawn, because they endeavoured to erect an imaginary universe, instead of observing and depicting that which lay before them. But this accusation involves a false conception of their aim no less than of their inevitable point of view. To them it never occurred, to them it never could have occurred, that there was aught else to be done than to project their own sensations, their own imaginations, their own feelings outwards upon the screen of actuality : and thus also it happened that they never perceived, that it never even entered their minds that such a thing there might be to perceive, as the broad distinction between this projected, vivified, personified universe and that mysterious, unknowable substratum to all phenomena, that *substance* which forms so familiar a fancy in the philosophy of to-day. Realising these things, may we not readily understand, might we not even confidently have anticipated, that assumptions apparently so unscrupulous should so unhesitatingly

[1] *Sainte-Beuve. Portraits Littéraires.* Paris : Garnier Frères. 1884. *Quintilianus, De Institution Oratorica.* Leipzig : Tauchnitz. 1829. *Horatius, Opera Ononii.* 1885.

have been made, that deities apparently so inconceivable should in truth have appeared almost visible to the expectant eye of faith—in a word, that the science of those days should have been the only science possible or natural to the men of those days.

Turn now to works of art. Suppose a work of genius to have arisen in its splendour before the delighted and astonished soul of such a man, without, however, any knowledge on his part of the fact that it was but the offspring of another human mind: how would he regard it? Must he not, treading of necessity his old accustomed tracks of thought, attribute it to some mind, anthropoid indeed, but great and glorious beyond the measure of humanity—to some god, in fine, the creator and ruler of the realms of art? But now let him learn that the characters have been traced by a merely mortal hand. What then? What, but that the hand, the head, the whole being of the mortal must have been breathed upon and moved by that mysterious divinity: the singer was *inspired*. The hand might be, mayhap, the hand of Æschylus; but the voice assuredly is the voice of Apollo. Accordingly we are not surprised to hear that Socrates, upon examining the poets even of his period, upon discovering their incapacity to expound what they themselves had written, should have been deeply impressed by this so striking testimony to the inferiority of the mere unexalted man, not indeed to his own creations (for by himself nothing had in truth been created), but to that which had been given him to utter of the sovereign Muse. So, again, in Plato's *Ion* we are told that the poet's song is not a work of human skill, but of divine power.

Now to one who approaches a work of art from a standpoint such as this—nor, it may be observed, are we even now wholly unacquainted with readers of the sort, at least as to certain books— what criticism is possible? What shall be his judgment of the poem but a natural birth from that instinctive admiration and reverence which has sprung to life within him under the vivific glow of a celestial fire?

To this there arises an important corollary. As man is the final cause of the universe, as the earth and all that therein is have had their being for his good pleasure, so with the inspiration of the artist. By the impression, pleasurable or otherwise, that it produced upon the hearer's mind, the work was judged: the production, indeed, of a satisfactory impression being the sole satisfactory justification of its existence, or proof of its inspired origin.

It is amusing, by the way, to contrast the new-fangled fad—that is to say, the Modern Ideal—of Art for Art's sake: submission of Poet to Law of his Being (*vice* "for Becoming," resigned), and to the Impulse of his own Imagination, reaching, in good sooth, almost to the theory that the reader was made for the poet, not the poet for the reader.

In close connection with the old view of the poet's function, and yet not inconsiderably modifying it, was the feeling of the subordination of the individual to the State. It did not then appear, as is nowadays conceived to be an axiomatic truth, that the State existed merely to ensure the preservation of the citizens' property, liberty, and life. Far otherwise indeed "in the brave days of old"; "then all were for the State"; then the State claimed, and the claim was unhesitatingly allowed by all that was noble among her sons, that for her sake the citizen should "spare neither land nor gold, nor son nor wife, nor limb nor life."

Accordingly, the labours also of the artist were services to the State. His desire to please, his hope of fame, were directed not, as nowadays, to the vast irresponsible mob of individual readers, but (so great was the social and public element in Greek life) to τους πιλλους at once and in the mass, or rather indeed, at least in many cases, to the State, as representing the collective and considered judgment of the people as a whole.

This naturally leads us to yet another observation of interest. Works of art are, in general, the outward embodiment of the inward emotion or imagination of their creator; and are prone to excite in others also corresponding feelings or ideas. Yet may they be conveniently divided into two classes, according as this or that is their more direct and obvious meaning. Now it is a striking fact, though only what might have been anticipated from the considerations already advanced, that it was the latter class that tended most to flourish in the great art centres of antiquity. Of this sort, for example, are all or nearly all the great monuments of Athenian art, its statues, its temples, its oratory, its drama. But the art of the peculiarly lyric or subjective order found a more fostering *nidus* in the more sequestered spots: though the fact is not to be overlooked that the type of morbid self-revelation or hysterical self-caricature which is exemplified for us in the *Confessions* of Rousseau was in that fresher atmosphere as yet undeveloped and unknown.

A different cause, indeed, has been suggested by a critic distinguished for eloquence, acuteness, and originality, to account for the decisive supremacy enjoyed in Athens by Oratory and the Drama over the rival forms of literary art. It was, he said, because to these alone was offered the stimulus of an adequate *publication*. And true it is that dramas were then published as dramas rarely have been published since. By the ears of a whole city, attentive, earnest, enthusiastic, were the sonorous lines drunk in; the moistened eyes of assembled thousands followed with ardent hope or trembling apprehension the fortunes of the *dramatis personæ*. The same eager and interested audience applauded the glowing periods and soul-stirring sentiments of the orator.

*Agedum pauca accipe contra.* For in truth this cause, though a real cause so far as it *does* reach, is but a secondary cause. Could not such a people, would not such a people, who developed such means of publishing those forms of art which satisfied their instinctive craving for what should address itself to them as a corporate and living whole, surely they had invented some appropriate means also for the publication of other works, had these likewise tended to slake a burning thirst. Nay, what more magnificent publication could be desired by the insatiable vanity of any author than that which the work of Herodotus received, they say, at the hands of Hellas' congregated multitudes? A work, too, we may observe in passing, dedicated to Hellas as a whole, and singing the glories of her united efforts and her common victories. Did not the Greece, again, of an earlier day welcome with a chorus of applause and gratitude the lays of Homer and his fellow-minstrels? To sum up, then, it was not so much that works of other kinds were not produced in Athens because they could not be effectively published, but that they could not be effectively published because they did not jump with the instinct of the times nor answer their demands.

But again we find ourselves loitering along a byway after some stray wanderer or so, but now *revenons à nos moutons* and the main-road. So far as we have hitherto observed, criticism has made no forward step. The great Trilogies of the Drama, the impassioned periods of the orator, were heard, admired, and had obviously produced their effect; or else they failed. Such criticism as was required sprang there complete into existence from the divine intelligence of the mass: it crowned the successful dramatist; it poured its applause upon the weary statesman. *Che dira il mondo—c cio fia sommo onore.*

Yet the more thoughtful observers, struck by these various vicissitudes of success and failure, would be forced to the conclusion that there must have been certain characteristics belonging in common to such works as had achieved success, and lacking in common to such as had achieved but failure. Thus they would be tempted to examine the works, not in the careless impressionable fashion hitherto in use, but by comparison. This problem they might approach from two distinct points of view. First, they might go direct to the very centre and fountain of the matter, and inquire: What are the qualities in the mind of the artist, how developed, how set in motion, which should blossom into such a raceme of loveliness, which should arouse such sympathetic emotions, excite such admiring wonder? But the time for this more radical and profounder method was still in the future; in the far future. Many causes must first operate, both to make men feel any dissatisfaction in the more obvious way, and to hint to them the better one. More obvious, meanwhile, the second method was, and more ready to the hand—to examine, namely, the works themselves, and to endeavour to detect the essential difference of the good. And that this way should be preferred, even had the former suggested itself, was a natural consequence, too, of the self-centring system above mentioned, and of its progeny, the poetic-inspiration theory.

But now a striking observation offers itself to our notice. Wonder is often expressed that a great genius is so apt to be inadequately appreciated in his own day. But the truth is, that when once we have trained our judgment to habits of critical hesitation, deeming ourselves to have attained the dignity of an exquisitely *elegans formurum spectator*, flattering ourselves that "our bravo is decisive," and much to be dreaded "the deep damnation of our bah!"—in such case the wonder would rather be the other way. Doubtless, indeed, when we proceed to the perusal of some mighty masterpiece, whose author's genius has been countersigned by the approbation of all that is most lofty, of all that is most severe among the intellect of our race, we enter upon its contemplation in a spirit of expectancy and reverence, in the assurance that its excellence rather sits in judgment upon our capacity of appreciation than our critical power upon its merit: we are prepared to yield up ourselves to its influence; our attitude, in a word, is that of *faith*. We are comparatively passive, the great magician deals with us as him listeth. But how far otherwise do we treat the artist who is as yet uncrowned, whose power is as yet unacknowledged of the world! Him we approach with the loins of our intellect girt for action, upon his work we consciously and deliberately set in array the forensic and judicial talent of our mind—nay, even though he force us to admire, yet do we insist upon holding an appellate review of the primary decision of our own instinct, and asking, "Do we well to admire?"

Now, no two mental attitudes could be more antagonistic than those of criticism and faith. And whereas in none is the mind so suitably adapted, so happily predisposed for imagination, appreciation, and admiration, as in that of faith; none, on the other hand, is so utterly incompatible with such feelings as that of criticism. And this truth is further illustrated and enforced by the fact that in the general history of the world's intellectual activity the ages of faith have been the ages also of poetry, while the leaven of criticism has, in those periods which it has permeated with its influence and made its own, tended to shunt and wither the productive powers of the imagination. Contrast, as one single instance, the splendid poetical efflorescence of the earnest Elizabethan age with the meagre ill-nourished budding of the eighteenth century. It has been justly and finely observed in regard to Gray that, although possessed of the true poetic faculty, its proper development in him was blighted by the frost of his forbidding, unappreciative times. "He never spoke out."

On the other hand, as ingratitude is a vice only too frequent and

familiar, as generosity, that pleasing flatterer of our self-love, is too
often preferred before tactless and dictatorial justice, so there are
many who long to have their names handed down, exalted with
vicarious glory, to posterity as the discoverers of unknown writers, as
heralds of the excellence of such as are neglected and despised.
They are tempted, too, by the feeling long ago so eloquently expressed by the poet :

> " Juvat integros accidere fontes
> Atque haurire : juvatque novos decerpere flores
> Insignemque meo capiti petere inde coronam."

Thus we find De Quincey proclaiming his pride at having been
perhaps first justly to appreciate and adequately to praise the poetry
of Wordsworth. Nowadays, indeed, so often has the neglect of
struggling merit been adverted to, that this consequence has followed :
many an author is belauded, not so much from real admiration and
a spirit of justice, as because by good luck he *may* turn out to be a
genius, and so confer a subsidiary immortality upon his discoverer.

The plan of criticism naturally adopted by the Greeks was, as we
have already seen, based rather upon the investigation of a poem
conceived as objectively existing than upon any discussion of the
anterior causes and conditions, the various moods and influences,
affecting its conception, development, and birth. But, again, with
a people so exquisitely sensitive to formal perfection and imperfection,
questions of proportion and disposition would be among the first to
attract and firmest to retain their attention. And not only would it,
for this reason, and also because it was in any case the most obvious
point, be the first to shirk them, but they would besides be hardly
likely to go much farther, clogged as they were in their critical
activities by the toils of the inspiration theory ; for it must not be
forgotten that the rigid framework secreted by some old belief,
useful once as a support (like a casing of plaster), though afterwards
a cramping prison-wall, may retain its noxious strength long even
after the belief itself has lost all living power.

The works in which the ancients appear to have approached most
nearly to a discussion of the development and growth of artistic productions are those—and they do indeed bulk very largely in the sum
total of their critical writings—in which advice and information are
offered to intending authors. Yet even here the problem is not
considered *subjectively*. If we regard the immediate cause of a
poem, for example, as the poet's mind ; its remoter cause as, first,
the original constitution of that mind, and, secondly, its subsequent
environment ; we shall at once perceive how far distant from any
such line of investigation was even the nearest of their attempts.
The poem or oration was, as it were, an edifice to be constructed ;
the practised artist taught the apprentice how to set out his founda-

tion, how to choose his bricks, and how to lay them in neat and orderly courses.

Thus we see that this ancient criticism was almost altogether a criticism from the outside. By way of illustration, nothing more is needed than to refer to its three most renowned masterpieces : the *Poetics* of Aristotle, the *Pisones* of Horace, and Longinus on the *Sublime*.

Little difficulty, then, in pointing out why such an art enjoyed but poor popularity and achieved but scant success. First, it was due to this very fact that it did deal chiefly with outward form. But for regularity and beauty of form the Greek, though all untutored, had an innate perception, a delicate and sensitive instinct. Thus, whatever prospects such a system might have had elsewhere, as, for example, among a people such as ours, of feelings dull and untrained in this regard, caring, indeed, for none of these things and ever apt, as one of her most distinguished sons has said, " to think nothing of symmetry and much of convenience " ; whatever force might have been exerted among such a people by the crying need for enlightenment to compel at length some more or less satisfactory development ; among the Greeks the purveyors of this kind of instruction could not boast even the stimulus (so wearily familiar to all those whose consciences permit them not to take their prefaces at the fly) of "meeting an acknowledged want." What need of further words ?

᾿Ατάρ οὐ τέλος ἵκεο μυθος : further considerations there are and weightier. For this criticism had no vitality. Now, although we sometimes hear it stated that such a secondary art, founded as it is itself upon the art of others, must for that very reason be devoid of all innate and vigorous life, still this is not the case with the highest type of criticism. For, like poetry itself, it deals with, it springs from the very life of man, nay, even from its loftiest phase, and from that life imbibes its own animating energy. And every art that offers a true sympathetic ideal of that life offers also the result at once and evidence of its own artistic life. Look at the critical works of Ste.-Beuve.

The criticism, then, of the Greeks neither possessed its own proper life nor perceived that which elsewhere existed. It was an art which painted not the living being, but the dress. It was not a portrait, but a fashion-plate.

Again, there was in those days no true literary history. *Cur hoc ? Dicam, si potero ;* and, indeed, from the same source we may readily draw the explanation. As a true history of a nation consists not merely of the bald annals, however accurate, of events, however interesting, but lays before our eye a picture of the nation's life and growth, so, too, a literary history, to be worthy of the name, must not be an unconnected series of biographies of writers and descriptions of their writings, but ought to expound the generation, birth, and various progress of a corporate artistic life as exhibited in an organically united family of literary works.

One suggestion we may here briefly interject for the benefit of the thoughtful reader who may choose to expand it on his own account. Here, too, as in so many other directions, the Greeks suffered a • grievous want in knowing no other nation, society, literature, whose development they might compare with their own. All the more honour to them, then, for the noble work they did in despite of so many disadvantages and difficulties :

> " Difficile est, fateor ; sed tendit in ardua virtus,
>   Et talis meriti gratia major erit."

As for the extant literature of Rome, it possessed but little originality. It was not, like that of Greece, a great organic whole, the most splendid efflorescence of a national intellect, the natural bloom adorning and displaying the character of the national life from which it sprang, a bloom which, like the chaste authentic flower, as distinguished from the gaudy and artificial hybrid or the painfully painted imitation, bore within itself the seed that should throughout a long futurity perpetuate its living glories. What little originality the Latin literature did possess discovered itself almost entirely in the infusion of a somewhat distinctive and peculiar, a certain Roman colouring, into the borrowed framework of Athenian models, not in striking out for itself a new form or a characteristic art. If we grant Quintillian's claim and allow satire to be an exception, it must be but as the exception that proves the rule. Accordingly this celebrated chapter of his, though so interesting as our almost solitary ancient specimen of general literary history, is after all no history in the true sense of the word. It is but a string of summary appreciations of literary works.

We now take a great leap : we pass to modern times. For the criticism of the Middle Ages was nearly altogether verbal and grammatical, and even when it aimed at something higher—and in this its example was followed during several succeeding centuries, almost down to our own period—it was but an offshoot from the older classical stock.

Nevertheless, with the advance of modern science, gradually winning fort after fort from its antiquated rival, and the concurrent advance of the spirit of sceptical inquiry dashing against belief after belief and rudely shaking such as were but resting loosely upon the hitherto untested and undisturbed detritus of ancient opinion and fossilised tradition, the poetic-inspiration theory fell into conscious disrepute. There arose, consequently, an instinctive desire for some other and natural account of the observed phenomena. The most obvious cause would be the mind of the individual poet.

But on further thought and comparison even of facts that had for ages been well known—for a man confident of his way may pass without perusal an inscription upon a signpost which, when once his suspicions are aroused, he marvels that any could overlook—even from the old familiar facts the long-neglected lesson would at length be gathered.    It would become clear that some more general causes, mysterious in their origin though manifest in their effects, were at work.

Applying the judicious maxim, *Iudicis officium est, ut res, ita tempora rerum, Quærere*, it would be noticed, for example, that not only (as Velleius had long ago pointed out), not only did great poets, together with other great men, make their appearance in clusters, but that each cluster generally presented its own strongly marked characteristics common to its various component individuals.    Thus even through the deepest haze of a distinct antiquity there shines clearly forth the strong, free, vigorous type of early Greece, so well exemplified in Homer and also in Pindar.    The close-clustered group of the Periclean period, again, produced works which, though belonging to such various arts, and so numerous and so diverse in each, did yet unmistakably bewray their characteristic common type, strong still, and full of life, but chastened by a pervading inspiration of ideal beauty and formal finish—the eternal type itself of very art.

Turning now to Rome, we come upon a period full of suggestive interest; the period, namely, of the Ennian and Plautan literature, verging to Terentian, Lucretian, Ciceronian; clearly showing the gradual growth of a taste for Greek formal beauty—a taste which indeed attained in Virgil, Horace, and others of the Augustan age, almost to the penetrative power, the unerring tread of an inborn instinct.    In times still later we discover the veritable Roman genius, strong, earnest, rugged, endeavouring to emancipate and assert itself, and beginning to beget such masculine models as the dark scowl of Juvenalian satire or the throbbing self-coercion of Tacitan energy.    With similar survey we might now pass on through the realms of other literatures, and collect similar conclusions.    Yet, so far as concerns our immediate purpose of indicating a view of the phenomena which could hardly fail to force itself upon the notice of the now alert investigator, that survey has perhaps been already sufficiently extended, even without reminding the reader of those instances, so familiar to us all and so striking in themselves— the English periods of Elizabeth and Anne.

When such facts began to put forth their strength, and such views resolutely to demand the attention of thoughtful inquirers, they could not but compel the recognition of certain queries and deductions that followed in their train.    Thus, for example, how could it happen that so many independent minds should simultaneously be turned out so closely conforming to a single pattern?

And yet a little while, and another set should appear modelled upon a pattern so marvellously changed! Of a surety, then, some other there must be, some cause external to the original constitution of the poet's mind, to produce such striking similarities within these groups of contemporary works. Nay, it was not poetry alone, it was not even the wide extent of literature alone, but all forms together of art appeared to be pervaded by this prevailing influence, this dominant diathesis. And so disproportionate in some cases have its effects appeared, so overmastering its force, that it might even seem as though to it was due the major part of the poet's work, the minor individual characteristics alone being the genuine product of his own personality.

To such a degree indeed (we may observe in passing) has this view impressed some modern critics, that they seem almost to sink the author in the age, to make him merely the facile mouthpiece through which the age pours forth the feelings that ferment within it. So that here again we are afforded yet another noticeable illustration of the truth that extremes are prone to meet, that men will recoil so vehemently and so far to the west from some old belief that suddenly one day to their amaze they find themselves close beside it on the east. For here we discover the old inspiration theory under but a scant disguise: the Muse is replaced by that yet more hazy and intangible personification, the Spirit of the Age. Nay, the poet hardly now attains to the dignity of representing the Pythian priestess, but only to that of the practised clerk who copies down, or, at the most, polishes and edits her utterances.

But this extreme view, though eagerly snatched at and solemnly trumpeted by a few writers more remarkable for cleverness than for judgment, has not, and indeed hardly could have, won any general acceptance. This, however, is not the place to deal with it. Yet let us only compare—and mayhap the mere comparison may be found sufficient—let us only compare as examples of artists closely connected by periodic grouping, although in tone and character essentially dissimilar, Terence and Catullus with Lucretius and Lucilius, Dante with Petrarch, Pope with Swift, Johnson, finally, with Gray.

Meanwhile the facts and considerations briefly suggested above were such as to produce two effects: first, to show that in the generation of the children of an artist's brain some other cause was at work than simply the original complexion of that brain, some modifying cause which, while it varied from age to age, tended, in strikingly similar manner, though in strikingly dissimilar degree, profoundly to stamp its impress on all who come within the range of its mysterious influence; and secondly, to shake to its very basement the old-time careless content with the meagre criticism hitherto in vogue. But, as Newman has observed, though "false ideas may be refuted by argument," " by true ideas alone are they expelled." So also, in order to establish an outlawed art or science in the dominion it would claim by descent from a theory that is true, and therefore by a right that is verily divine, something more is needed than mere dissatisfaction with the reign of the unworthy usurper. Dissatisfaction is but a negation, and emptiness can beget but emptiness. Some clear and vivid conception must form the foundation of any science or art that would deserve the name : any science that consists not simply of a string of dead and isolated facts; any art that is not a mere mechanic skeleton.

*Si quis nunc quaerat,* " *Quo res haec pertinet* ": the conception that was to form the foundation of the new criticism was one to which we have already referred, that of art, namely, as a vital phenomenon. It regarded the individual poem not simply as a series of verses so tagged together as to avoid certain treacherous pitfalls, complying at the same time with certain nice and difficult demands; but as the living utterance of a living soul, as the embodied presentment to other men of some exalted phase of the ideal or emotional power of a sympathetic human spirit. So, too, it regarded the collective poetry of some period of national existence not simply as the sum total of the isolated individual poems, but as the living utterance of a people's mind in its loftiest mood.

To generate this noble conception, the condition of a more profound and searching criticism, divers causes have recently conspired. Such a cause, for example, has been the inward growth and outward expression of national feeling among the peoples of Europe, resulting from the awakening of the several races to a consciousness of their corporeal existence as great united families, who not long since had but been reckoned as the useful or troublesome tillers of a sovereign's domain. Such a cause, again, has been the gradual emancipation of individual thought from the tenacious thraldom of antiquated custom. But perhaps the most effective, and certainly not the least interesting of these causes, was this : the fortunate concurrence of a period of vivid emotional poetry with one that reared up minds trained to careful observation and critical thought.

Among modern nations, even after the Renaissance had aroused their intellect, even after Science had shaken off its leading-strings and started upon voyages of discovery to regions of unfamiliar feature and hitherto unsuspected existence, criticism nevertheless had still continued a willing slave to the unintentional tyranny of earlier models ; nor did that combination soon occur which was to set her free. Thus, during the Elizabethan period in England, when poetry made such a sudden leap into greatness, the observant and critical disposition was rather lacking. On the other hand, although during the age of Anne this void was amply filled, yet the whole fount of the former poetical inspiration (if the metaphor is still permissible) had run dry, and the taste for its sparkling waters faded quite away. In other countries, too, the state of affairs was as unpropitious to the full.

At length, however, the appointed time had come. Towards the beginning of the present century, the mind of Europe being thoroughly prepared by training and education, the angel of romance began to stir the dark and sluggish waters of literature and art. The palsy of the Muses' worshippers was healed, and a period of living, earnest, and strongly subjective poetry set in. Under the fostering combination of many convergent influences the form of the new criticism began faintly to fashion itself before the prophetic eye of genius.

Thus we reach the times and the literature familiar to us all, whose spirit we unconsciously inhale, which to us indeed appears so natural that we find it hard to comprehend how difficult, nay, how impossible it was for our predecessors to perceive what is to us so obvious, I had almost said, so obtrusively self-evident. By far the greatest exponent of these new ideas—*invita fatetitur usque Invidia* —the ablest, in a word, the most sympathetic, the most searching critic the world has ever seen, is one whose name may fitly close this brief review—Ste.-Beuve.

H. T. Johnstone.

# "THE INVALID ABROAD."

## SKETCHES OF INVALID LIFE IN THE HIGH ALPS.

EVERY educated person is familiar with the great strides made of late years in the treatment of consumption, and the keen interest taken by all circles of society, both professional and otherwise, in the struggle of medical science *versus* that dread scourge of humanity, which has arrived at an unprecedented pitch of tenseness. Numberless articles have been written, and are being written daily, on the subject throughout the civilised world; congresses are being convoked, both officially and through private initiative, for the discussion of the all-important question; sanatoria established, &c. &c.

The statement that there is hardly a family in all Great Britain which does not count at least one of its members as affected by lung disease would be by no means exaggerated. For this reason, perhaps, it is not only of interest but of material advantage for those going abroad for the cure of chest troubles—not to mention their relations and friends—to know beforehand what is to be avoided and what striven after while seeking health in one of the deservedly celebrated climatic stations of the High Alps. Hundreds of patients are yearly sent out from the United Kingdom to the highlands of Switzerland, but how few of them know in advance what the "cure" really consists of, and how many have to pay for their apprenticeship by more or less unpleasant experiences! These sketches, therefore, contain a few hints and suggestions which, served in more palatable form than those to be found in the orthodox pamphlet or popular medical tract, may stand the invalid of untried experience in good stead and save him not a few knocks and buffetings, apart from the interest the matter under consideration presents, as the author believes, to the general public.

As met with at home, the consumptive is usually an unfortunate creature, stricken down by a wasting disease, the sight of whom gives rise in our breasts to a sort of conventional pity. He mostly loses himself in the crowd, and his characteristics seemingly differ but little from those of the general mass of humanity, and give the observant onlooker but little chance of special study or observation. But there are certain places upon the surface of the globe which have become colonies for the consumptive. Here his species congregate in large numbers and develop many traits and peculiarities, which have even enabled one to single out from his class certain types not altogether unworthy of the notice of his fellow-men.

As already stated, in later times foremost among these places in Europe are certain health resorts in the High Alps, the manners, customs, and characteristics of whose inhabitants (known in the local phraseology of the lung communities under the name of " Lungers ") will furnish the subject of what is to follow.

In classifying and analysing the numerous varieties of the great Lunger family many subdivisions might be made therein: for instance, that of the Novice, the Reckless One, the Conscientious Patient, the Old Campaigner, &c., *ad infinitum*. But of these we shall single out for closer study only the first three, as the species oftenest to be met with. Thus the Novice, generally furnishing, so to speak, the rough material for the development of those other types, naturally draws our attention to himself at first hand.

The early history of the Novice (of either sex) runs very much on the same lines as that of most Lungers. Congenital tendency, or overwork in a crowded city, a cold, a clumsy local practitioner who perceived the danger only when the disease had taken root, the consultation with an eminent London specialist, his decree——a winter at N—— in the High Alps—these are the usual elements of the story the old resident gets poured into his willing or unwilling ear after *table d'hôte* by the Novice, just come up with the evening train, eager to glean information about the place he intends making his home for the next six months, and to find some one, be he even a stranger, to whom to confide the story of what he innocently imagines to be his unique woes.

He is an optimist, at least in the early beginning. He thinks it necessary to inform you that, although his lungs *are* a bit delicate, " still there is no real phthisis," and he does not intend staying more than one winter. He regards you with but poorly concealed pity if you tell him you are a patient of long standing, and is particularly anxious not to come into close contact with " those people who seem so ill and cough so dreadfully." Contagion is his bugbear, and he is very particular as to whether his room has been properly disinfected before he takes up his abode in it.

Next morning, upon waking and admiring the beautiful Alpine scenery disclosed to his gaze, he makes up his mind he will have as " jolly " a time of it as he can: long walks on the mountains, plenty of sledging, tobogganing, and skating when winter sets in.

At breakfast he is told how well the people amuse themselves in the long winter evenings, what with dancing, theatricals, bazaars, &c. After a bit (especially if the weather be fine) Novice begins to think that it is not half bad to be " touched in the lungs," if one can do so much in the amusement line ; rather a change, in fact, after long hours in a gloomy office, bank, or counting-house.  He imparts his pleasing thoughts to his confidant of last night, but is a bit hurt to find little sympathy in that quarter, and puts his acquaintance down as a surly fellow, soured by his bad luck. . . . (Novice, however, generally has reason to modify his views later on.)

By-and-by, Novice suddenly remembers that he has a letter to the local practitioner from the London specialist, which he had almost forgotten while making his plan for the pleasant passing of his stay at N———.  Armed with this document, and pretty confident of the good report he will hear, Novice walks over to his new doctor's and is admitted to the consulting-room.  And here begins the long and painful process of " disillusionising," which it is the sad lot of so many poor Lungers to go through.

Dr. M———, a serious but kindly Switzer, speaking fairly good English, begins his examination.  This is generally a business that lasts some time.  The chest of the patient is sounded all over, the stethoscope is almost driven into the victim's body, his whole thorax is pencilled with blue lines until it looks like a district map, the doctor scribbling away in his note-book the while.  After this ordeal the patient goes through a long inquisition at the hands of his new medical adviser, the most unnecessary questions—so it appears to Novice—being asked : for instance, as to the number of his great-aunts, what their pet complaints were, &c.  His memory is sorely taxed to furnish a minute record of all the infantile ailments he ever went through, and recall other incidents of his past life.  At last it is over, and Novice awaits what the doctor will say as to his condition.  He does not feel quite as confident as at the beginning of the interview ; the whole proceeding was so very businesslike and impressive.  " Well, well ! " sums up Dr. M———, " although there is considerable damage done to your lung—among other things I detected a small cavity or two—still, with thorough care, there is every chance of a good cure, say, after two years or so in our healing climate ! "

Unfortunate Novice's spirits are further damped after listening to the long list of things in the way of amusement and sport from which he must abstain, and to the still longer catalogue of all he must do to improve his health.  Good-bye tobogganing, skating, &c. !  Even his walks are restricted to half-an-hour's stroll before lunch in the Kurhaus gardens, where the music plays daily.  Instead of mountaineering excursions, young Novice's chief occupation must be the absorbing of an abundance of light nourishing food and unlimited quantities of milk.  In the worst of weathers he is expected to do the " cure "[1] all day long on the verandah of his

---

[1] The "cure" is a local technical term.  To "do the cure" means to lie, well wrapped up, on a deck-chair out of doors in a sheltered position ; such, for instance, as a verandah.

hotel. And all this he must patiently submit to, not to mention, maybe, cold frictionings at an unearthly hour in the morning, and sundry other delightful pastimes of a like nature. For the time his spirits are effectually quenched, and he makes up his mind to lie low and do his best to get well, although he does not see how he will stand the long, weary " cure " for two years at least without going mad in the interval. Also, all his illusions as to *his* not being one of the great invalid herd are brutally dashed to the ground.

But, alas, for the constancy of human nature ! The Novice, at heart an optimist, soon plucks up courage. Even the first few weeks of restful and quiet life at N—— have a beneficial effect on his general health. He has a bad example set him by many of the Reckless type, by the " caretakers," [1] and especially by the healthy sporting fraternity that comes out at Christmas for the skating. The result of all these temptations is a loss of balance and certain hardly noticeable infringements of the doctor's orders.

Novice's backsliding becomes first of all apparent in the lax way he does the " cure." Half the time he should be lying out in the open air he devotes to the stuffy billiard and reading rooms, or else, lounging about the covered terraces, he gossips with his fellow-lungers, particularly of the weaker sex. He even goes the length of making himself useful, and soon develops great skill and dexterity in the tucking-up of the ladies, especially if the latter are young and good-looking. Later on he lengthens his walks of his own accord, and soon you meet him quite a distance from N—— in congenial company trudging through the pine forests or along the pretty roads.

Still, his dissipations, so far, have been quite mild, and he has improved in health, the doctor tells him. But, with the advent of the snow and frost, he begins to petition for a permit to skate. Grudgingly, and perhaps against his better judgment even, mild Dr. M—— allows him half-an-hour a day ; but this time is gradually and imperceptibly lengthened until he spends whole days upon the ice, participating in the " jolly " luncheon parties, practising figure-skating (and paying his way by frequent falls— which do him no good), showing off before the ladies, and generally playing the giddy goat. The " cure " is allowed to look after itself, and Novice goes in for wholly contraband tobogganing, " skiing," and sledging. Slowly but surely the vortex closes over Novice's head, and, one fine day, while he is busy organising some theatricals, he receives a nasty little reminder in the form of a slight hæmorrhage. Of course to bed he goes, and good Dr. M—— shakes his head and remarks : " I am afraid we have been doing too much and neglecting the cure ! We must take better care in future ! "

But, after a few days of quiet, Novice, arisen from his couch of

---

[1] " Caretakers " are friends or relatives who accompany invalids to N——.

sickness, resumes, with even greater zest than before, his old ways of existence, living in the present and not taking the trouble to look ahead and discern the abyss that is opening before his feet.   He refuses warning, and, thanks to the small improvement his health has made in the beginning, and buoyed up by the invigorating mountain climate, he begins to forget altogether that he is ill and abroad for the benefit of his constitution.   He enters himself for the toboggan races, takes a prominent part in the skating tournaments, and has the cheap satisfaction of seeing his name admiringly mentioned in the local *English Gazette* (an honour recorded by that gushing and amiable publication to about two-thirds of the British colony).

If he has a histrionic bent, our Novice finds himself in great request to take the leading parts in all the theatricals, "tableau vivants," waxworks, &c., organised for the benefit of the impecunious lunger.   It never occurs to Novice that "charity begins at home," and that he is neglecting the health of a patient about whose interests he ought to be more solicitous—viz. his own.   Then, of course, towards Christmas, he helps to organise the juvenile amusement department, and parades the streets with others of his tribe, as a sandwich-man, advertising the above-mentioned entertainments. Altogether, his kind obliging ways being well known to the not too scrupulous organisers of all these benevolent undertakings, they take advantage of his ingenuous, unsophisticated nature, and drive him about until he is well-nigh dead-beat.   (It is too well known, alas! what the consciences of bazaar managers and manageresses are worth.)

Of course there can be but one ending to such behaviour on Novice's part (and, to tell the truth, the sooner his eyes are opened the better, although the awakening be rude, and may sometimes end fatally for him): he breaks down.   Some tobogganing party down the Furioso Pass, or else a chill contracted after a dance, help Novice to a grave hæmorrhage, thorough pleurisy, or congestion of the lungs; and his doctor draws a long face and sighs at what he terms the "folly of youth."   But what he now sees is nothing new to him : how often has the same melancholy farce been enacted before his eyes !   All that can be done is done to get Novice out of the predicament his foolishness and inexperience have placed him in; and after months, maybe, of confinement, he weathers the storm. Generally this severe lesson proves beneficial in the long run. Although it may retard Novice's progress for a time, still the steady way he grinds at the "cure" afterwards makes amends for the past. After his allotted term he regains health and returns to his work.

Occasionally his flightiness proves stronger than the lessons of experience, and after he has wasted several seasons uselessly he has to return home, worse than he left, to die.   Or else, if his circumstances permit, he remains in N—— and lapses into an incurable either of the Pessimist or of the Reckless variety, which are such a common feature in the valley of N——.

## THE RECKLESS ONE.

After having disposed of that conglomerate type the Novice, we naturally come to the Reckless variety, as one of the former's outcrops presenting more or less interest.

The Reckless one may be of either sex, and age has not much to say in the matter: all that is necessary is that he or she should still have retained sufficient vital force to play the little game out in a more or less sprightly fashion. This the very nature of the complaint they suffer from permits to a great extent, as a lunger, except when complications ensue, feels little, if any, pain. In many ways their behaviour is much the same as that of the Novice, the difference lying in the fact that the latter goes the pace out of mere ignorance, the former in full knowledge of what they are doing.

The Reckless one generally lives at the gayest hotel in the place. He has some private means, and tries to make the best possible show for his money while there is still oil in the lamp. The Reckless one's inducements to adopt his course of action are either lack of patience and moral strength to attend to the "cure" with the undeviating perseverance it demands, or else the knowledge that in his or her case a more or less complete recovery is out of the question. Hence the decision in favour of a short life and a merry. Of course, this is all very well as long as one is not brought too low. When, however, all capacity for enjoyment is destroyed by the progress the disease has made, it often happens that bitter, but late, repentance sets in. It is pitiful to see the way in which the luckless one, suddenly realising his position and clinging to hope against hope, applies himself to the "cure" with feverish and trembling energy. But the awakening has come too late, and it is one of the saddest sights the world can show to witness the vain, despairing, last efforts to get well of one who has, through his or her thoughtlessness, thrown away that chance of health and life which it is now too late to seek. Some, in the agony of their despair, look for oblivion in death, and nearly all the suicides that occasionally occur in the lung community are perpetrated by those who have thus forfeited the possibility of recovery.

But in the meanwhile the Reckless one manages to burn the candle at both ends pretty briskly. He or she indulges in the boldest flirtations, as there is plenty of opportunity for his or her efforts in that direction; "tailing" or sledging parties to the beautiful surroundings, moonlight toboggan excursions with champagne suppers to wind up with, and so on.

"Tailing" is one of the most favourable pretexts for the carrying on of an active flirtation. The method is as follows: Behind a sledge, with a team of four horses, is attached a long and strong rope. To this the "tailers" tie their toboggans in pairs. The less robust settle themselves in the sledge, well wrapped up, and the rest take their places on their respective sleds. When the horses get well under way, the rope, especially when taking a curve, swings from side to side, the toboggans become very lively on encountering lumps of snow and getting into ruts, and of course the squires have to proffer considerable assistance to their fair partners, if the latter wish to keep their seats. Sometimes the entire dozen or so of couples are precipitated promiscuously into a deep drift, and then a pretty scene of laughter and excitement ensues. For the moment all is confusion. The ladies scream, the men strain to free themselves and extract their charges from the muddle of ropes, toboggans, and human figures half lost to sight in the powdered snow. In a very few minutes, however, things are again put into working order, the driver cracks his whip, and the merry sound of the sledge-bells dies away in the clear distance. These excursions are always made to some place the way to which affords plenty of good long descents. When a convenient declivity presents itself the "tailers" uncouple (to use a technical expression) and enjoy an independent and exhilarating run down the slope, re-attaching themselves to the sledge when it comes to an ascent. This is a very satisfactory arrangement for the tobogganer, and has the great advantage over the ordinary method of coasting, that all uphill work is accomplished by horseflesh. If the road be a winding one and passes through the woods, many a pleasant *tête-à-tête* may be indulged in with great comfort and safety for the parties chiefly interested.

In the evenings the male members of the fast fraternity play poker, faro, baccarat, or hold a private roulette bank by turns. High billiard-playing is also much in favour—quite *à la mode d'Ostende* or Monte Carlo, in fact. Large sums of money are often lost in a single evening, and the excitement the high play generates has, of course, a very salubrious effect upon the robust constitution of the giddy lunger. Sometimes, when a green youngster burns his fingers by, say, losing at a sitting the money that ought to have seen him through the winter, things come to a tragic pass. There are a few very sad stories of this nature on record about which the less said the better.

No racing events at home, or in the local tobogganing or skating world, are allowed to pass unchallenged, and sweepstakes are organised: the names of the favourites, either of the four-legged or biped species, are sold for high prices, and the contests are looked forward to with the keenest interest. If the winner of the toboggan championship is a popular character, he is enthusiastically welcomed and a sumptuous banquet given in his honour. The actors in the grand event, as well as their sympathisers and supporters, are, of course, very careful of their health. For this reason they take the precaution of imbibing a considerable quantity of stimulating fluids, "to keep up the circulation, you know!" early in the day. On the reappearance of their gaily-decorated sledges, after all is over, in the quiet village street, the truth of this can hardly be doubted. If one listens to the uproarious expressions of triumph wafted up from the festive procession on its return, the markedly elevated spirits of all concerned will be patent to the most simple-minded spectator. Thus, the champagne absorbed during the feast adds not a little to the hilarity of most of the partakers, and it is not out of the common to experience some difficulty in gaining their respective habitations later on. Very often comical mistakes are made about doors, and things do not always wind up as peacefully as they began.

Playful little practical jokes are greatly appreciated by the younger members of the Reckless set. It is as likely as not that upon returning to one's rooms after a walk the fact that some of one's fast friends have made a call during one's absence will become apparent by the discovery of the wardrobe and most of the furniture (including the chest of drawers) piled on one's bed, the armchair placed in the middle of the room, and the visiting-cards of these good fellows affixed thereon with your own corkscrew driven through the plush. Or else one may be roused in the morning by a well-aimed snowball alighting in one's face through the open window.[1] Once a young fellow, on returning to his chamber rather late at night after having supped "not wisely but too well," went nearly crazy with fright on discovering that some kind friend had been distributing aperient powders about his room in the most unlikely places. The poor chap, in his dazed condition, thought he had at last got a touch of *d. t.*

Sometimes the Reckless one, by way of a change, takes up the "cure," especially if of late he has not been as fortunate in his flirtations and other amusements as hitherto. Perhaps he is shocked by the unexpected death of a friend or old acquaintance of his "set." And for a time he tries to take things seriously. Reckless knocks off parties, concerts, and sport for a spell. He does the "cure" spasmodically; you may see him taking his temperature in the evening while umpiring a game of billiards. He may have registered 105° Fahr., but, as often as not, he regards that performance more in the light of a good joke than otherwise. Soon he wearies of his voluntary retirement from the noisy little world he has become so used to, and again he relaxes into his habitual ways. So he continues for several months or years. How long he will hold out

---

[1] At N—— all invalids are expected to sleep with their windows open.

depends on what his constitution can stand. Gradually his vitality is sapped, and you see him less and less abroad beyond the precincts of his hotel or villa. He finds himself laid up oftener and oftener. Each time he reappears with less power to resist the vivifying but rude climate of these high altitudes. Then comes a day when he is no longer strong enough to remain in N——, and he goes to warmer climes. This is generally the last scene in the little play, and it is seldom long before one learns of his death from the paper, or receives an intimation to that effect from his relations. Or else, of a sudden, he disappears from the stage without a word of warning, and one is painfully surprised to hear that the poor Reckless one, after a brief sharp illness, has gone over to the great majority to swell the population of the already crowded little graveyard of N——.

### THE CONSCIENTIOUS PATIENT.

What a vast chasm separates the Conscientious Patient from the Novice or Reckless one! In fact, the first is, in nearly every respect, the exact opposite to the latter. In most cases we see him as a person of limited means, who is enabled to stay out abroad one winter at most. In that term he must profit to the utmost by the chances offered him to complete his cure. Under these circumstances he is conscientious perforce, for the prospect of certain and speedy return to unfavourable climatic conditions, and, at all events, to hard work while still in poor health, is hardly an exhilarating one. This ever-present thought takes all the zest out of any stolen or obviously imprudent pleasures he may be induced to participate in.

However, people in the most comfortable circumstances sometimes show from the first great discretion in their mode of living; but there are more exceptions than examples to the rule. If, however, such a case comes under one's notice, it is generally due to a lack of spirit or to a hypochondriacal condition of mind. Mostly the latter is brought on by the patient's ailments. It is a very rare occurrence indeed to come across an invalid who is prudent and does his duty by his health, thanks exclusively to a clear comprehension of his position, and under the sole stimulus of an indomitable resolve to get well at any cost. That such should be the case may seem strange at first, but we shall understand it better when we remember that by far the greater number of these sick people are young folk, mostly of an age varying between twenty and thirty. The juvenile majority gives the tone to the place, and it is no uncommon sight to see solid middle-aged men, who ought to know better, competing with their youthful companions in everything that is foolish and thoughtless.

To combat these injurious outside influences successfully, relying only on the force of one's character and without being driven to adopt a sober course by circumstances, is exceedingly difficult. Still more is it so for a young person of high animal spirits, which the dread disease has had no time to quench so far. If we also take into consideration the mode of life of most lungers previous to their breakdown, we shall comprehend this still better. As before mentioned, the young male lungers generally happen to have quitted a life of steady toil, working hard at business to get well started in life, or else studying for scientific or artistic professions. In other words, they find themselves suddenly plunged into complete idleness, sundered as they are from all regular occupation, with results that we see only too plainly.

Our Conscientious Lunger, of limited or even straitened means, does not have a very lively time of it. For him a stay in N—— signifies serious business. From the beginning he has to steel himself to keep away from all the temptations that encircle him. Having to be very sparing and thrifty, occasionally he will at first even try to get on without a medical adviser, but soon the imprudence of such a course is brought home to him. It is absolutely necessary for him to have in the beginning a Mentor who will tell him exactly where he stands and what he must do; for the conditions of climate and life in the High Alps, at their altitude of five or six thousand feet above sea-level, are very different from those of the low-lying plains. However, he limits the number of his visits to his doctor as far as practicable.

In the hotel or sanatorium or *pension* he is staying at, he is regarded with no great favour by the proprietors. Although, as a rule, an easy person to get on with, and *nolens volens* of modest habits, in most cases he is very exacting in all that concerns the *pension*, for which he pays at a fixed price per diem. At the same time, in his inroads on the cellar he restricts himself either to the cheaper sorts of the "wine of the country," the local beer, or else professes rigid teetotalism. Such an arrangement, although admirably suited to the proportions of his slender purse, does not quite coincide with his host's views on the subject, and his tribe is sooner avoided than sought after in that quarter.

On the other hand, the local druggist makes more profit out of him than the wine merchant. The Conscientious one, however he may economise elsewhere, does not stint himself in the medical department. He purchases large supplies of the best cod-liver oil, meat extracts, peptone, &c. These he takes before and after meals in a little corner of the dining-room, where, on a handy window-sill, he and his brethren keep displayed a little apothecaries' store of tonics, meat juices, emulsions, &c. These potations are known among profane scoffers of a less steady and businesslike kidney under the suggestive name of "appetisers." . . . Our Conscientious one is always absorbing some nourisher or fattener. It is but on rare occasions that we see him without a glass of milk standing by his side, or else a cup of some much-advertised patent preparation.

His favourite reading is that which treats in a popular way of medical subjects; and his symptoms, the progress he makes, his medical or surgical experiences, are almost the sole things he will discuss with any show of interest. When, however, by a more or less skilful manœuvre, he manages to trot out his hobbyhorse, he warms to the subject, and at times becomes almost eloquent. He may have had complications necessitating surgical intervention. In that case, he regards himself somewhat in the light of a curiosity, to interview which is a privilege. He gives most graphic descriptions of his sensations under the anæsthetic, and occasionally quite destroys his neighbours' appetites at *table d'hôte* by his too realistic recitals. If you come to see him in his room, he will insist on showing you relics of his former experiences. Another theme for conversation highly relished by the Conscientious one is that of "mikes"—a caressing abbreviation for *microbes*; on receiving his monthly report from the bacteriologist's he loses very little time in acquainting his various friends with the contents of that interesting document, and is either elated or cast down according to the number of bacilli found in his sputum. It is extraordinary how one-sided many of this class of patient become in the development of morbid tastes. Many take a certain not inconsiderable pride in the fact that their doctor may have told them what an exceptional case theirs is, and that, by rights, they ought long ago to have departed from this vale of tears.

In his recreations and relaxations the hard-up Conscientious one is not a very lively individual. In fact, he hardly indulges in any worth mentioning. He generally tries to profit by his enforced leisure to get up one or two of the modern languages, which may come in useful in his business occupations later on, after leaving N——.

The writer knew a Conscientious one who afforded his companions a good deal of good-natured amusement. He was interested in meteorology, owned a barometer, several thermometers, and other apparatus, which hung out on the verandah. As methodical as one of his instruments, he always visited his scientific pets at given intervals, in the morning, at noon, and in the evening. A favourite joke of his friends was to breathe upon the thermometers on cold nights, and cool their bulbs with salt or snow on mild days, immediately before he went his rounds. These strange and unnatural variations of temperature used to puzzle him sorely; but he never guessed at the truth. Although he did not go in for sport himself, he was always making himself useful by helping to clear the toboggan runs of snow and policing them on race-days—*i.e.*, keeping the street-boys off the track. He skated a little, however, and took part in the cribbage tournaments. Otherwise he was a most harmless and benevolent young man, always ready to oblige, and an example of method and perseverance. Fortune was kind to him, he regained his strength and returned home cured.

Generally the Conscientious one does well in N—— if he has come out in good time. When done with the "cure," he tries to obtain a position in a country with a good climate. His favourite field is South Africa, but he often emigrates to Australasia, America, turning to the mountain States of the West, or choosing the high-lying Southern Republics, for his future home. In British South Africa an "N—— Club" is said to exist, to which all of those hailing from that health resort may apply when in difficulties and meet with ready kindness and assistance. If he is not successful in combating his complaint in the time allowed him, the poor Conscientious one finds himself in a sad plight. He either retraces his steps home, sick as he is, to drag along to the end somehow, or else goes out to one of the above-mentioned countries as a last chance. He may die—in fact he often does—on the journey out. Sometimes, however, he does well, the voyage sets him up, and he prospers in his new home. They say that a great number of the present New Zealanders are descendants of ex-lungers.

Little more can be said on the present subject within the limits of this essay. But before the author brings these little sketches to a close he would like to add a few parting remarks on the Conscientious one who happens to be well endowed with the goods of this world. As a rule, he presents but few striking features. He is the normal type of invalid: for him a year abroad more or less is of no great importance, and his existence is regulated by his doctor and his individual forces. He does not stint himself in what is likely to benefit him, nor does he allow himself anything calculated to impair his progress. He is, so to speak, the ideal type that gets on best. At the same time, as he does not show up boldly against the great background of the commonplace, a detailed description of him would not prove otherwise than insipid and colourless. Let him, therefore, pass from our notice with these closing remarks.

The author now takes leave of his readers, trusting that the foregoing pages out of the life of these afflicted people, a few sides of whose existence he has tried to portray, have not proved too wearisome.

SIMEON LINDEN.

# CONTEMPORARY LITERATURE.

## SOCIOLOGY, POLITICS, AND JURISPRUDENCE.

IT is now nearly four years since Part I. of *The Science of Statistics*, by Professor Mayo-Smith, appeared. Part I. is entitled *Statistics and Sociology*, and Part II.—the volume before us—bears the title *Statistics and Economics.*[1] We cannot help thinking that those sub-titles are somewhat misleading, since both volumes deal with the statistics of sociology. A more accurate title for Part I., which treats of population in its various aspects, would surely be "Vital Statistics"—a term well established for this branch of sociology. The title of the present volume, *per se*, is accurate enough; but it is only one branch of sociology. In fact, the author himself on the first page considers it to be the most important. "The economic," he says, "is the foundation of all social organisation."

The method employed in the classification of economic statistics is the same as that of the statistics of social organisation, as the author terms it, but which we should prefer to call "vital statistics," a method which we described in our notice of Part I. With the author's actual figures we have no fault to find, for, taken as they are from Government or official or trade sources, they are as reliable as are to be obtained; but with his deductions from those figures it is not every one that will agree. We pointed out, for instance, that the official figures for pauperism, from which the author deduces the conclusion that pauperism is diminishing, must be received with modification, since the bare figures do not disclose the actual state of affairs, and leave out of account altogether those relieved by voluntary contribution.

So, too, in the present volume we are not inclined to accept the Professor's optimistic conclusion that the working classes are actually better off than they were fifty years ago because statistics prove that wages are higher and the necessaries of life are lower. Both these may be facts, and probably are so; but no account is taken of rents beyond those showing that, although agricultural rents have fallen generally, the average rent of the labourer's cottage has risen from

1 *Statistics and Economics.* By Richmond Mayo-Smith, Ph.D., Professor of Political Economy and Social Science in Columbia University. Part II. The Science of Statistics. New York: Published for the Columbia University Press by the Macmillan Publishing Company. London: Macmillan & Co., Ltd. 1899.

1s. 5d. in 1850 to 2s. in 1878.   In London and in other great cities
we know as a fact that house rent has increased enormously.
During the last ten years in some parts of the East End house rent
has doubled, and it is said that the average working man pays one-
third and sometimes even one-half of his wages in rent !

In spite of those shortcomings, if they can be so termed, since
the questions we have raised are of a highly controversial character,
there can be no question of the extreme value of this work, which
gives the student or inquirer in social matters in convenient and
scientific form the main figures upon which he may base his
conclusions.   It is a work, however, that must be kept up to date,
and after the next census we shall expect to see Part I. revised.

Sir Richard Temple has doubtless many great qualifications, but
the literary faculty can scarcely be said to be amongst them.   Sir
Richard, in his full and varied life both in India and at home, has
found time to write many works, but the latest production, *The
House of Commons*,[1] will hardly enhance his literary reputation.
After all that has been written on the subject of our chief national
institution, it would be difficult to say anything fresh.

From 1885 to 1895 Sir Richard was an assiduous and hard-
working member, taking part, as he tells us, in nearly three thousand
divisions, and in constant attendance in the Committee-rooms, besides
which he kept a journal, posted up daily, now bound up in ten large
volumes.   Considering all this material, and the fact that those ten
years form one of the most interesting if not the most momentous
decade of our times, one might have expected that the chief incidents,
preeminently suited as they are for dramatic treatment, would have
been described with force and effect.   Instead, we have a mere bald
description of the precincts of the House itself, its constitution and
general characteristics, such as any one who has once visited the
House and has read his daily newspaper is perfectly acquainted
with.

Strong partisan as Sir Richard is, with, perhaps, the exception of
his obvious dislike of the Irish party and everything Irish, there is
no trace of party bias throughout the book.   Sir Richard is absolutely
fair and even generous to political opponents.   The book has evidently been to him a labour of love, but even his strong affection for
the object of his devotion has not been able to effect the impossible
—to endow him with the faculty which nature has denied.

*Advanced Australia*,[2] by Mr. Galloway, M.P., consists of a chatty
account of the author's impressions of a recent tour through the
Australasian colonies.   As an engineer, Mr. Galloway naturally took
much interest in mining, and especially in the gold mines of

[1] *The House of Commons.*   By the Right Hon. Sir Richard Temple, Bart., G.C.S.I.
London: John Long.   1899.
[2] *Advanced Australia.*   By William Johnson Galloway, M.P.   London: Methuen
and Co.   1899.

Western Australia, of which he furnishes comparative statistics showing the enormous development in recent years of this industry.
According to Mr. Galloway, the secular system of free education in
South Australia has been to embitter the relations between the
Orange element and the Roman Catholic. The adherents of the
latter refuse to take advantage of the public schools, which were
intended to weaken and obliterate religious distinctions ; but the
Roman Catholics, true to their traditions, whenever possible provide
schools of their own, thus retaining their hold of their people. The
net result of this secular teaching, highly moral as Mr. Galloway
admits, is a leaning on the part of its pupils to the purely materialistic. This is not a result for which we need feel much anxiety.

Apart from the development of mining in Tasmania, Federation,
opening up the markets of Victoria to Tasmanian fruit and vegetables, would spell increased prosperity for the Garden Island, which
has hitherto been rather regarded as a health resort for Melbourne
citizens.

As in South Australia, so in New Zealand, female suffrage, in the
author's opinion, has caused little difference in politics. This may be
so, so far as the respective strength of parties is concerned, but we
cannot help thinking that its introduction has had much to do with
the development of democratic ideas in colonies where it obtains.

The chapter which will attract most attention is that entitled
" Old Age Pensions in Practice," from which the scheme, both
socially and financially, appears to be a complete success.

The discussion on Federation is perhaps even of wider interest, and
is a good statement of the growth and position of the question.
The figures which abound throughout the book are taken from those
excellent Year-Books and other Governmental publications which
are so little read in this country, in spite of all our tall talk of
Imperialism.

*The Story of the Australian Bushranger,*[1] by Mr. George E. Boxall,
is valuable not merely as a record of crime, but for its delineation of
Australian society in the early days of its growth. Thrilling as the
stories of criminal adventures are, they rather pall on one from their
very number. There are sufficient to form the plots for innumerable
novels. Readers of Rolf Bolderwood's *Robbery under Arms* will
here find the true particulars of " The Terrible Hollow " into which
Will Underwood and his gang were said to retire when hard pressed
or when they required a rest. But, as we have said, the book is not
merely interesting for its sensational stories of crime. In showing
the magnitude of the evil, which had its roots deep down in the
origin and growth of colonial life in the Antipodes, Mr. Boxall has
also shown how the colonists stamped out the plague and built up

---

[1] *The Story of the Australian Bushrangers.* By Geo. E. Bexall. London ; Swan
Sonnenschein & Co., Ltd. 1899.

the fine race which exists to-day. And the task was far harder than is generally realised. The average felon transported to the penal settlements was not in the true sense a criminal, but he soon became one under the grossly oppressive, unjust, and needlessly harsh administration which there prevailed. And even where the convicts were assigned as hands to settlers, they were frequently treated as mere chattels. For trifling misconduct they were tied up and mercilessly flogged. Of course, a magistrate's order for the cat was necessary, but equally as a matter of course this was immediately granted. Under the system in vogue at such penal settlements as Macquarie Harbour, called by the convicts "the Western Hell," one cannot be surprised at any atrocity, however terrible, committed by any fortunate enough to escape. With the cessation of transportation bushranging steadily decreased, and as the population settled down to industrial work crimes against the person or property continued to diminish. It reflects the highest credit upon the Australasians, that from such an ominous beginning they should have emerged into their present flourishing condition, their veins purged of "the bad drop of blood," and their *morale* as sound as that of any other civilised nation.

We have also received the thirty-seventh issue of that hardy annual *Every Man's Own Lawyer*[1] for the year 1900. The present edition is, as usual, well brought up to date, including the recent legislation of the present year, such as the London Government Act, 1899, the Inebriates Act, 1899, &c. Valuable as this book is, it must be used with care by the average man, who, as a rule, is hopelessly ignorant of legal phraseology. The rule that "every man is presumed to know the law" was not in the Middle Ages a mere presumption of law. It was the common case. The average man was well able to follow the intricacies of a fourteenth-century lawsuit, and even to conduct it himself. We wish the publishers would take our advice, and omit the misleading statements on the cover. The work is sufficiently admirable without such adventitious aids.

---

## VOYAGES AND TRAVELS.

WE have seldom more thoroughly enjoyed a book of everyday experiences in a distant land than *A Wide Dominion*,[2] by Mr. Harold Bindloss, who therein narrates in simple and picturesque language

---

[1] *Every Man's Own Lawyer.* A Handy Book of the Principles of Law and Equity. By a Barrister. Thirty-seventh Edition, carefully Revised. Including the Legislation of 1899. To which is added a Concise Dictionary of Legal Terms. London: Crosby Lockwood & Co. 1900.

[2] *A Wide Dominion.* By Harold Bindloss. London: T. Fisher Unwin. 1899.

his varied career in our greatest colony, with his impressions of its inhabitants and many a word-painting of exquisite beauty of its marvellous scenery—not mere "purple patches," but beautiful for their truth to nature. There is not a dull page from first to last. Mr. Bindloss seems to have tried his hand at almost everything, from wheat-grower to dock-hand, in which latter capacity the pecuniary results were much more satisfactory than in the former, although it is only fair to say that want of capital in the former enterprise was the real cause of failure. We hope to have more stories of travels in other lands, to which the author alludes, from the same capable pen.

---

## HISTORY AND BIOGRAPHY.

*In a Corner of Asia*[1] is the captivating title of the latest volume of the "Overseas Library," brought out by Mr. Fisher Unwin. The work is by Mr. Hugh Clifford, the author of *In Court and Campong*. It has the double advantage of being historically accurate, and yet as attractive as the pages of romance. These Malayan tales and sketches will be read with delight even by the indolent reader who cares more for amusement than information. "At the Court of Pelesu" is a most dramatic account of the adventures of an Englishman named Jack Norris, who dared to defy a Malay king. "The Death-March of Kûlop Sûmbing" and "A Daughter of the Muhammadans" are also thrilling narratives. Mr. Clifford has made a special study of the Malays and of their country, and we accept the statement in his preface that "he has striven to convey a picture of realities, not merely to write fiction." This is certainly one of the most interesting of the "Overland Library" Series.

Mr. C. Oman, Fellow of All Souls College, has republished a very curious little book, entitled *The Reign of George VI.*,[2] which was issued anonymously in 1765. The work belongs to what the learned editor calls "prophetical literature," but it is written with all the seriousness of actual history. As a forecast of the early years of the twentieth century it can scarcely be regarded as a successful experiment in the art of prophecy. The anonymous author appears to have been a Tory in domestic politics. Many of his ideas might have been suggested by Bolingbroke's *Patriot King*. George VI. is an English Frederick the Great tinged with some of the homeliness of

[1] *In a Corner of Asia.* Being Tales and Impressions of Men and Things in the Malay Peninsula. By Hugh Clifford. London : T. Fisher Unwin.
[2] *The Reign of George VI.* (1900-1925) : A Forecast written in the Year 1763. Republished with Preface and Notes, by C. Oman Fellow of All Souls College, Oxford. London : Rivingtons.

"Farmer George" and endowed with some of the military genius of Henry V. He engages in a successful war with Russia, and conquers France. He builds a splendid palace at Stanley, where a beautiful city is supposed to spring up. He failed to anticipate the era of railways or steam ; but in one instance he predicted with amazing accuracy a momentous political event. He anticipated a united Italy. Of the great French Revolution he did not even dream. Who wrote this strange book Mr. Oman is unable to tell us. Could it be Dr. Johnson ? Or was it Robert Paltock, the author of *Peter Wilkins* and the *Memoirs of the Life of Parmese, a Spanish Lady?* The modesty of the latter would be a reason for anonymity.

Mr. H. Rider Haggard, who has earned a wide popularity by writing works of fiction full of sanguinary incidents, has reprinted portions of a book written by him so long ago as 1882 on the Boer War of 1881.[1] Of course the present war in South Africa may justify the publication of this work, but Mr. Rider Haggard is not to be relied upon as an historian. He saw many things with his own eyes, but he takes an altogether one-sided view of the position of the Boers. On the question of the annexation he does not attempt to give any reasons for that high-handed proceeding on the part of the British Government. "I believe," says the author, "that the greatest political opponent of the act will bear tribute to the very remarkable ability with which it was carried out." The same remark might be made with regard to most of the late Charles Peace's burglaries. But surely the ability shown in robbing the Boers of their territory is no more a justification for the crime than if it were the act of an individual thief !

As for Mr. Rider Haggard's style, it is unworthy of a schoolboy. In dealing with the effect of the Jameson Raid, he says : "It armed the Boer with a sword of wondrous power" ; and then we have this extraordinary sentence : "Now, indeed, he was able to point to his land violated by the foot of the invader, and to talk of raids as though such a wicked word had never defiled the innocence of his ears ; as though in truth he had never heard of the plains of Stella-land, and of a certain expedition sent by the British Government under the command of Sir Charles Warren to preserve these territories to the peaceful enjoyment of their owners ; nor of that stretch of country which once belonged to the Zulus, but is now called the New Republic ; nor of the trek into Rhodesia that was 'damped'; nor of the extension of authority over Swaziland in defiance of the provisions of the Convention, and of other kindred matters." Surely if a London University examiner wanted to find an example of the misuse of conjunctions in order to test the knowledge of grammar of a matriculating student, he could not find anything more admirably suited for the purpose than this ! Again, speaking of the right to

4 *The Last Boer War.* By H. Rider Haggard. London : Kegan Paul, Trench & Co.

take the black man's land, Mr. Rider Haggard says that, unless we provide him with a just government, the practice is " undefensible." Why not " indefensible " ?   But bad grammar is not the worst fault of his contribution to the literature of the Transvaal question.   In dealing with what he calls " the Transvaal surrender," he declaims against " the farrago of nonsense about blood-guiltiness and national morality."   Is it his view, then, that bloodshed is praiseworthy, and that it is wrong to advocate morality in the dealings of nations and races with each other ?

One service to the cause of " national morality " Mr. Haggard has unwittingly rendered : he has shown the " true inwardness " of the Imperialism of which he wishes to be regarded as one of the propagandists.   It means : " Annex all you can at any cost, and then boast that you have saved the honour of the Empire."   It is a pity that Mr. Rudyard Kipling has not done as much as Mr. Haggard to exhibit in all its naked ugliness the seamy side of Imperialism.

Sir Wemyss Reid[1] has shown his capacity for writing biography effectively in his important volume containing the memoirs and correspondence of Lord Playfair.   The part played by Lord Playfair—better known to many as Lyon Playfair—in the arena of English public life was one of which any man might be proud. His life, which originally promised to be that of a purely scientific man—or, as his biographer, adopting the barbarous expression of the day, says, a " scientist "—developed in many other directions.   Born in India of Scottish parents, he received his early education in " the grey old city of St. Andrews," to which he was sent by his father to avoid the dangers of childhood in India.   He was a quaint, old-fashioned child, as may be seen from a letter written to his father when he was only six years old, in which he puts a number of conundrums or " guesses," as he calls them, to the author of his existence.   He manifested very soon a love of chemistry, which he studied with avidity and enthusiasm.   His intention of joining the medical profession was not carried out, and for a time he occupied the post of chemical manager of print-works in Lancashire. During a visit to Germany he made the acquaintance of the celebrated Liebig, whom he affectionately describes as his " great master."   He was ere long destined to do excellent work as a sanitary reformer, and also as a Special Commissioner of the Great Exhibition of 1851.   It is only right to acknowledge that Playfair was largely helped in his efforts to promote the public welfare by the patronage and friendship of the Prince Consort.   At the period of the Irish Famine he was sent to Ireland, where he investigated the causes of the potato-rot.   We must take leave to differ from the somewhat callous opinion expressed in the autobiographical portion

[1] *Memoirs and Correspondence of Lyon Playfair, First Lord Playfair of St. Andrews.* By Wemyss Reid.   London : Cassell & Co.

of this work that " the famine was not an unmixed evil to Ireland."
A calamity which swept away about two millions of the population
of that island cannot be minimised by the fact that the famine
destroyed the reliance of the Irish on the potato as " a staple food,"
and, " by compelling them to live on more nutritious diet," raised the
rate of wages. This is carrying political economy too far, and
divorcing it from considerations of humanity.

When Dr. Playfair was returned to Parliament as a representative
of Edinburgh and St. Andrews Universities he was in the curious
position of remaining a Liberal, though elected by a Tory constituency. He, however, for some time abstained from mixing
himself up in party politics. His first speech in the House of
Commons was on the abolition of the religious tests in the English
Universities, and it appears to have been " well received by both
sides of the House." Throughout his political career he consistently
supported Mr. Gladstone, and his attitude with regard to Home Rule
will command the approval of all true Liberals.

One of the most unenviable functions ever performed was that of
Chairman of Committees during the period of Irish obstruction, and
this fell to the lot of Playfair. It is a curious fact that the Irish
members whom he suspended privately regarded him with respect.

When he became " Baron Playfair of St. Andrews " he practically
ceased to be a personality in politics, though he did some service in
connection with the question of Old Age Pensions and the Venezuela
dispute. He was three times married, and the fact that his third
wife was an American lady made him take a special interest in the
United States. His kindness of heart is shown by his advice to the
Government in 1885 to allow the late Mr. John Boyle O'Reilly to
return to his native country, and by his gift of a finger-ring to a
deaf, dumb, and blind child at Boston. In spite, however, of his many
amiable qualities and his mental activity—we quote Sir Wemyss
Reid—he " never rose to that dazzling eminence which justifies the
world in describing a human being as supremely ' great.' "

The curious student of eighteenth-century manners will find much
that is interesting in the *Letters from Lady Jane Coke to her Friend
Mrs. Eyre*,[1] which have been carefully edited by Mrs. Ambrose
Rathborne. Lady Jane Coke was the last surviving representative
of the Wharton family. She was the eldest daughter of Thomas,
fifth Baron and first Marquis of Wharton, who was Lord-Lieutenant
of Ireland in the days of Swift, and a sister of Philip, Duke of
Wharton, an eccentric individual referred to in Pope's *Moral Essays* as

> " The scorn and wonder of our days,
>   Whose ruling passion was the lust of praise."

[1] *Letters from Lady Jane Coke to her Friend Mrs. Eyre at Derby, 1747-1758.*
Edited with Notes by Mrs. Ambrose Rathborne.  London : Swan Sonnenschein
and Co.

The reader will find in these letters much gossip, a great deal of simplicity, and, at the same time, no small share of scandal. Ladies of rank in 1749-50 did not invariably wear " the white flower of a blameless life," and yet licentiousness did not always exclude even the fair sex from good society. For instance, Lady Vane—familiarly known as " Lady Frail "—of whom the witty Lady Mary Wortley Montagu said that, " though she did not pique herself on fidelity to any man," she boasted that " she had always reserved her charms for the use of her own countrymen," was one of the fashionable visitors to Tunbridge mentioned in Lady Jane Coke's letters as having been " there with her lord," and having begun " several balls." A century and a half has elapsed since those days; but perhaps we are not much advanced in point of virtue. Truly English morality is a peculiar commodity, which needs some poet like Byron to unveil its seamy side, or hold up to loathing its preference of decorum to honesty, as the author of *Don Juan* certainly did when he wrote :

> " Oh ! for a forty-parson power
> To chaunt thy praise, Hypocrisy."

*The Jonah Legend*[1] is the title of a very erudite work by Mr. William Simpson. It is well to bear in mind that "Old Testament history has been treated unfairly alike by friend and foe." The Bible is, as Mr. Simpson points out, " an Oriental book full of Eastern thought." Certainly a literal interpretation of the story of Jonah seems an absurdity, and yet in such a work as Smith's *Dictionary of the Bible* we are asked to accept the reality of the transactions recorded as unquestionable. The writer of this book explains the story on the principle that " ceremonies had at an early period become legends, and that these legends had been afterwards woven into history as events that had taken place." Numerous examples are given from Babylonian, Greek, and Indian lore. Regarded from this point of view, the Book of Jonah has an historical and ethnological value.

An excellent *History of Greece* from 404 to 321 B C.,[2] forming one of the University Tutorial Series, has been prepared by Mr. A. H. Allcroft, the author of the *Tutorial History of Rome*. The portion of the book dealing with the supremacy of Sparta is admirably written. The student will find in this little volume a mine of valuable and well-condensed information.

Another portion of the Greek history dealing specially with Sparta and Thebes[3] is dealt with lucidly by the same writer. The chapter

---

[1] *The Jonah Legend : A Suggestion of Interpretation.* By William Simpson. London : Grant Richards.

[2] *History of Greece, 404-301* B.C. By A. H. Allcroft, M.A. Oxon. London : W. B. Clive.

[3] *History of Greece, 404-362.* (*Sparta and Thebes.*) By A. H. Allcroft, M.A. Oxon. London : W. B. Clive.

on the literature of the period will interest even the most advanced readers.

Few of those who pass the sign of the "Marquis of Granby" swinging from an old country-town inn or village alehouse could say offhand whom it represented, and fewer still could tell you that this flaunting portrait was intended to compliment the most popular man of his day.   This was John Manners, Marquis of Granby, eldest son of the third Duke of Rutland, who, as a general, in point of time occupied a position between Marlborough and Wellington.   Hitherto biographical notices have not, in the opinion of Mr. Walter Evelyn Manners, the author of *John Manners, Marquis of Granby*,[1] now before us, done sufficient justice to his memory, based as they are upon the writings of "Junius" and Horace Walpole.   The former, he says, practically withdrew all his libels; but the latter, from some hidden motives—possibly, as Mr. Manners suggests, jealous affection for his nephew, General Conway, in whose light Granby stood—persisted in his attacks, although he was not always consistent, admitting in one place that Granby "sat at the top of the world." One of Mr. Manners' chief objects has been to rescue the Marquis from Walpole's misrepresentation and to place him once more in his real position, and we are bound to say he completely vindicates his kinsman from Horry's sneers and depreciations.   "Granby was," he says, "esteemed and respected by the sovereign as a brave and brilliant soldier, a most loyal and chivalrous subject, and disinterested public man."   In an age of corruption, when at the head of the commissariat in the Seven Years' War, instead of growing fat as his predecessors had, and as his contemporaries certainly would have done, he met the deficiencies which existed out of his private purse to the extent of £60,000.   And at a period when the Government was in the hands of one group or the other of the great families, Granby resolutely eschewed all the political intrigues of the time. As a member of Parliament he never hesitated to act according to his principles, although he knew he was endangering his own interests, until the name of Granby, says Mr. Manners, became a synonym for all that was loyal and respectful to his King, and for all that was noble, just, generous, straightforward, brave, and unselfish as regarded his fellow-subjects.   As a general it is difficult to assign a high figure to Granby.   In the Seven Years' War our army formed part of the command of Prince Ferdinand, and, with the exception of the Battle of Vellingshausen, Granby never had a chance of showing what he could do.   In this engagement, however, although Ferdinand was in command, the conduct of the battle at the critical moment

[1] *Some Account of the Military, Political, and Social Life of the Right Hon. John Manners, Marquis of Granby, P.C., M.P., D.C.L., &c.*   By Walter Evelyn Manners. London : Macmillan & Co., Ltd.   New York : The Macmillan Company.   1899.

fell to Granby, who at once showed that he possessed strategic qualities of the highest order, full credit for which was accorded him by Ferdinand himself and other high military critics. Moreover, in smaller engagements, either when alone, or in larger as a subordinate, Granby never failed, as his superior officer, Lord Sackville, so egregiously did at Minden. Mahon, in his work, states that the Battle of Warburg was decided mainly by a charge of Lord Granby and the British horse.

The author modestly states that "the part enacted by him pretends to nothing beyond that of a humble *chiffonnier* wistfully searching for scraps of fact carried upon fitful gusts of disquisition into archival nooks and corners and there left derelict and forgotten." Although, perhaps, as a piece of pure literary work the book does not rank in the first flight, still it enables us to see the man as he was and the times in which he moved, and although, now and then, one feels overweighted with detail, yet, on the whole, one would not have them omitted. We heartily congratulate the author upon a most creditable piece of work. The illustrations could not be bettered.

### RELIGIOUS HISTORY AND BIOGRAPHY.

The study of the lives of England's greatest sons is not only instructive but invigorating, and calculated to stimulate that pride of race the revival of which is one of the characteristics of the latter part of the present century. Time was, and that not so long ago, when we were in the habit of looking abroad—to France, Italy, Germany—for the men who may be considered the makers of modern Europe; but the historical studies which have now become so popular have revealed to us that the sources are often to be found in England, and that we can produce earlier examples equal to, if not surpassing, those of other countries. Such an example is to be found in Robert Grosseteste (the famous Bishop of Lincoln), the story of whose life is told by Mr. Francis Seymour Stevenson in the valuable biography before us,[1] which is a most important contribution to the religious history of the period. Mr. Stevenson describes his book as a contribution to the religious, political, and intellectual history of the thirteenth century, and this comprehensive claim is justified by the important part played by Grosseteste as an ecclesiastic, a religious reformer, a statesman, a student, and patron of learning. Indeed, the perusal of this book has made us marvel, not only at the varied ability of the man, but at the mass of work he was able to accomplish in a few years. His *Compendium Scientiarum* reveals him as the first, and in some respects the greatest, of the encyclopædic thinkers of the century in which he lived. His encouragement of learning, his

---

[1] *Robert Grosseteste, Bishop of Lincoln.* A Contribution to the Religious, Political, and Intellectual History of the Thirteenth Century. By Francis Seymour Stevenson, M.P. London and New York: Macmillan & Co. 1899.

organisation of the University of Oxford, his establishment of a university chest for the benefit of poor scholars raised the university to the first place in the estimation of European scholars. The coming of the friars was due, if not to his invitation, to the support and encouragement they received from Grosseteste. One of his first actions as bishop was to address a letter to the archdeacons, in which he called upon them to rectify various abuses amongst the clergy and to use their efforts to reform the conduct of the laity; to put down vicious customs tending to intemperance, immorality, and irreligion. He defended the Church against the encroachments and exactions of the King as well as against the tyranny and rapacity of the Pope and Cardinals. And yet he could find time to give good advice on the management of estates and the improvement of agriculture. How much we owe to "the Lord Robert" it is impossible to say, but Mr. Stevenson, in some measure, helps us to realise it.

The person who amongst the heroes of the Reformation has the greatest attraction for literary men, of whom Charles Reade and J. A. Froude may be mentioned as noteworthy examples, is Erasmus. The pen was always in his hand, inspired sometimes by a desire to reform religion, sometimes to spread the new learning. His greatness is unquestionable, his defects not to be overlooked. He is not easily understood, and therefore a critical account of his extraordinary career is desirable, and such an account is given us by Professor Emerton, of Harvard.[1] With all his gifts, he lacked moral, perhaps physical, strength, and our author makes it only too painfully apparent that the author of the *Praise of Folly* regarded self-preservation as the first law of nature, and that he lacked many of the necessary qualifications of a hero. Our impression is that Professor Emerton rather overdoes it, and yet it is the only sufficient explanation of the conduct of Erasmus on many occasions. But we must be content to take the man for what he was and to be grateful to him for what he actually accomplished, and what his pen failed to do was done by others with more militant weapons.

The first part of the life of Erasmus is full of an interest that is almost romantic; his struggles, his acquirements, and his success are almost, if not quite, without parallel. This story is well told in this volume. The opposition of Erasmus to the Lutheran Reformation is treated at some length, and we can very well understand how to a man of his temperament it appeared to be a dangerous movement from which he instinctively shrunk; and yet to have gone as far as he had done and then be unwilling to go farther, of necessity provokes a suspicion of inconsistency which Professor Emerton takes no pains to conceal. Erasmus was a great man, but he had his limitations, and perhaps that is all we can say. The interest of

---

[1] *Desiderius Erasmus of Rotterdam.* By Ephraim Emerton, Ph.D. London and New York: G. P. Putnam's Sons. 1899.

this volume is increased by citations from his correspondence and principal works; it also contains a good reproduction of the portrait by Holbein and nearly forty other portraits and plates.

Henry Scougal was Professor of Divinity in King's College, Aberdeen; he died in the year 1678, in the twenty-eighth year of his age; a year or two before his death he had written *The Life of God in the Soul of Man*, the book for which he is remembered. This book was published in 1677, with a preface by Bishop Burnett, and is ranked by Mr. Butler[1] with the *Theologia Germanica*, though in our opinion it is less mystical and far preferable; and this without depreciating much that is beautiful and of enduring worth in the *Theologia*. Mr. Butler also tells us that the young and gifted Henry Scougal was from 1665–68, that is, from his fifteenth to his eighteenth year, president of a religious society at King's College, Aberdeen. The point of this book is to demonstrate the indebtedness of the Oxford Methodists to Scougal, and the author's contention is, first, that the Oxford Society which was called "Methodist" was suggested to Charles Wesley, the real founder, by the example of Scougal at Aberdeen, though there is no ground for supposing that the idea was not spontaneous and the resemblance accidental. The other contention, which is better founded, is that the Wesleys were largely influenced in their religious development by Scougal's book. The *Life of God in the Soul of Man* was read in their home at Epworth and was a favourite book with the Oxford Club; and Charles Wesley gave a copy of it to George Whitefield, who afterwards wrote that he never knew what true religion was until he read it.

In a work on ecclesiastical matters written entirely by laymen, and edited by a Fellow of the Royal College of Physicians and of the Society of Antiquaries, we expect to find much that is interesting and suggestive, and in *Some Principles and Services of the Prayer-Book*[2] we are not disappointed. The essays are but four in number: "The Ceremonial Use of Lights in the Second Year of the Reign of King Edward VI.," by Cuthbert Atchley; the "English Altar and its Surroundings," by J. N. Comper; "The Act of 1872 and its Shortened, Hurried, and Extra-Liturgical Services," and the "Regalism of the Prayer-Book," by the Editor. The essays are full of curious information of an antiquarian character and not without interest in the present state of the Church. Mr. Legg contends that the Act of Uniformity Amendment Act of 1872 is the main cause of the liturgical anarchy in the Church, as the Public Worship Regulation Act is the cause of the anarchy of discipline. The confusion is patent and Mr. Legg may have hit upon the cause.

---

[1] *Henry Scougal and the Oxford Methodists; or, The Influence of a Religious Teacher of the Scottish Church.* By the Rev. D. Butler, M.A. Edinburgh and London: Blackwood. 1899.

[2] *Some Principles and Services of the Prayer-Book Historically Considered.* Edited by J. Wickham Legg, F.R.C.P., F.S.A. London: Rivingtons. 1899.

Another glaring fault he denounces is the extraordinary fashion of hurrying through the service. " People complain especially of the rate at which the Confession, the Lord's Prayer, and the Belief are taken, so as to make it impossible, without the wind of Achilles, to keep up with the reader." These readers, we suppose, imagine it is " Catholic " to be unintelligible. It must not be supposed that these criticisms of some modern vagaries, on the part of the editor, detract anything from the real historical and antiquarian value of this work.

Mrs. Humphry Ward has lately spoken of the English Unitarians as the left wing of the old Presbyterians. This is a common opinion, but the grounds on which it rests appear to be sentimental rather than historical. If " left wing " is the correct expression, the left wings of the old Independency and of the early Baptist bodies would seem to have contributed as much, or more, to the ancestry of the existing Unitarian body, while that which gave it cohesion was the action of Mr. Lindsey, a seceding Anglican. Mr. Walter Lloyd, the author of the *Story of Protestant Dissent and English Unitarianism,*[1] as the minister of a Unitarian congregation originally Independent and founded by one of the ejected Independents of 1662, is naturally free from the trammels of what he calls the English Presbyterian " Legend." Quite apart from this particular point, the very careful and very readable account which he presents of the origin of Liberal tendencies in Protestant Nonconformity, and of the process of their development, is valuable and instructive, bringing to light many new factors in an interesting story. Mr. Lloyd also makes clear the ecclesiastical position of Richard Baxter and the reasons which led him and others to refuse to conform in 1662. We have also a description of the Protestant Dissenters after the passing of the Act of Toleration, the building of the meeting-houses, and the characteristics of Liberal Dissent during the eighteenth century. One thing which strikes us very forcibly is the curious instability of Calvinism, which exhibits itself from time to time in great and even in recurring strength, but seems incapable of maintaining itself anywhere for any lengthened period. John Wesley's Arminianism has already held its ground for a longer space of time than can be claimed continuously for Calvinism in any community in England. Mr. Lloyd's remarks upon the future of the Evangelical Free Churches are both wise and sympathetic.

[1] *The Story of Protestant Dissent and English Unitarianism.* By Walter Lloyd, Minister of Barton Street Chapel, Gloucester. London : Philip Green. 1899.

## BELLES LETTRES.

IT is rare to find a novel nowadays free from the vice of affectation and sham sentimentalism. *Over the Edge,*[1] by Mr. George Wemyss, is a novel of this kind. It draws a picture of the evils of mercenary marriages, without the introduction of any high-strung platitudes. The character of Bertie Fergus, the genial but somewhat apathetic critic of social follies, is admirably drawn. Rhona Lendy is also a splendid study. The author is no superficial observer, and the only fault we can find with his latest work is that it is too short. He should have painted on a broader canvas. If he had done so, *Over the Edge* might almost be worthy of comparison with *The Newcomes.*

*Terence,*[2] though a very readable novel, is an utterly exaggerated picture of Irish life. The hero, the gentleman-coachman, is one of those things which may exist out of latter-day Ireland, but which certainly cannot be found in it. Mrs. Croker has only a very limited knowledge of the ways of the Irish peasantry. Her book will pass a few hours pleasantly, but it will not add to any reader's knowledge of the Irish people.

*The Bread of Tears*[3] is an extraordinary story. It throws a curious light on the Armenian question, and in his treatment of the subject Mr. Burgin shows great cleverness. The character of Kara Oglou is a most complex one, and seems to show that an Oxford education is not good for Armenians. That blandly murderous "patriot" is scarcely preferable to the average Turk. The heroine, Fenella, is a most interesting personality.

In *Ready-made Romance,*[4] Mr. Ascott B. Hope has given us a number of excellent stories of adventure for young readers. A great deal of the matter in the volume is drawn from rare and curious sources, and has an historical interest which entitles the stories to some attention from even more mature readers.

The ninth volume of the Eversley edition of Shakespeare's Works[5] contains *King Lear, Macbeth, Antony and Cleopatra.* The introduction to *King Lear* does justice to the sublime quality of that great play, and gives, at the same time, a lucid account of the various editions. In the introduction to *Macbeth* Dr. Herford deals learnedly with the supernatural element. He points out that, where no supernatural cunning is concerned, the style shows an unusual inclination to the Sophoclean irony of innocent phrases covering sinister depths of meaning.

[1] *Over the Edge.* By George Wemyss. London : T. Fisher Unwin.
[2] *Terence.* By B. M. Croker. London : Chatto & Windus.
[3] *The Bread of Tears.* By G. B. Burgin. London : John Long.
[4] *Ready-made Romance : Reminiscences of Youthful Adventure.* By Ascott B. Hope. London : A. & C. Black.
[5] *The Works of Shakespeare.* Vol. IX. (Eversley Series.) London : Macmillan and Co.

*The Conscience of the King*[1] is the title of a work which might, if it were written in a scientific fashion, perhaps come under the head of Jurisprudence. The author, Mr. James Carmichael Spence, has, however, dealt with the philosophy of the statute-book, if we may use the phrase, in a speculative and rather fanciful style. His book is really rather a readable collection of essays on the ethics of law than a scientific inquiry. As such it merits appreciation. The sweeping remark that "more genuine crime and more barbarous cruelty has been committed by the law than by all other criminals put together" must be taken *cum grano salis.* Of course there is some truth in the remark; but it is one of those dangerous half-truths that should be avoided. The chapter on "Political Dementia" is one of the most interesting in the book.

*Richard Carvel*[2] is a very fine novel. It reminds us of *Esmond,* and it would seem as if Mr. Winston Churchill had made Thackeray his model. The story is told with wonderful vividness in the style of the last century. The period is that of the war with the American colony, and the hero takes the side of the colony against the King. The book is far above average fiction in point of literary merit.

The *Blenheim Roll,*[3] 1704, is a volume in which explorers of the past will take delight. It gives information as to the names and pay of the officers who served under Marlborough in Germany. It also gives the names of the officers killed at the battle of Blenheim. Mr. Dalton has done his work well.

*Zur Modernen Dramaturgie*[4] is the title of a series of interesting studies of the German drama, by Herr Eugen Zavel. The author gives us a critical analysis of the works of Auerbach, and the later plays of Sudermann are critically dealt with. The last essay in the volume is on "Jenny Lind."

Those interested in the history of German journalism will read with deep interest Herr Ludwig Salomon's work, *Geschichte des Deutscher Zeitungswesens.*[5] The subject is treated historically, and the book is a monument of research.

*La Macédoine,*[6] by Dr. Cléanthès Nicolaïdès, is a very elaborate work on the history and political development of Macedonia. The author shows that in the various phases of the Eastern Question Macedonia occupies a foremost place. The sketch of Macedonian history is very lucid and as far as possible complete.

[1] *The Conscience of the King.* By James Carmichael Spence. London: Swan Sonnenschein & Co.

[2] *Richard Carvel.* By Winston Churchill. New York: The Macmillan Co.

[3] *The Blenheim Roll, 1704.* By Charles Dalton, F.R.G.S. London: Eyre and Spottiswoode.

[4] *Zur Modernen Dramaturgie.* Von Eugen Zavel. Oldenburg und Leipzig: A. Schwartz.

[5] *Geschichte des Deutscher Zeitungswesens.* Von Ludwig Salomon. Oldenburg und Leipzig: A. Schwartz.

[6] *La Macédoine.* Par Dr. Cléanthès Nicolaïdès. Berlin: Johannes Raede, éditeur.

We have received a copy of the *London University Guide and University Correspondence Calendar*, 1899–1900,[1] which contains an immense quantity of information as to subjects of examination, courses for degrees, &c.

Few living writers possess more descriptive power than Maurus Jokai. Perhaps the most popular of his works is *The Poor Plutocrats.*[2] It has been translated in German, Danish, Swedish, Dutch, and Polish. The English translation of the work, by R. Nisbet Bain, reads smoothly, though it would have been better for the translator to have given the English equivalents of a number of Hungarian words in the text rather than in footnotes. The descriptions of mountain scenery in the novel are splendid. The characters, too, are all limned with a masterly hand. The various members of the Lapussa family seem to live and move as if everything were actually happening before our eyes.

Mr. Lipos, the lawyer, and his nephew, Lyilard, are two very life-like personalities. The mysterious robber, Fatia Negra, is one of the most interesting characters in the book. Some of the incidents will strike the English reader as almost impossible; but then England is not Hungary. The volume is one of the most attractive of the series of translations of this gifted writer published by Messrs. Jarrold and Sons.

*A Passing Fancy* [3] is a very readable novel, but the plot is quite unreal. Mrs. Lovett Cameron writes well, but she draws too much on her imagination, and this is, perhaps, the least " convincing " of her books.

*The Young Master of Hyson Hall* [4] is a capital boys' story. The scene is laid in America, and Mr. Frank R. Stockton shows considerable humour in relating the adventures of Phil as temporary master of Hyson Hall in the absence of his uncle. The book is breezy, natural, and wholesome, and, though the plot recalls that clever story, *Vice-Versâ*, Mr. Stockton has treated the entire subject in an interesting fashion of his own.

Miss May Crommelin has written nothing more picturesque than her charming book, *Kinsah : A Daughter of Tangier.*[5] The revelations of life in the harem are painful and, at the same time, evidently true to life. The gaudiness, formality, and cruelty of Moorish life are admirably depicted. The readers' sympathies will be at once aroused on behalf of the young girl Kinsah, mated at fourteen to a licentious old man. After a series of sad experiences she is finally

[1] *London University Guide and University Corr. Calendar (1899–1900).* London : University Corr. College Press.
[2] *The Poor Plutocrats.* A Romance. By Maurus Jokai. Translated by R. Nisbet Bain. London : Jarrold & Sons.
[3] *A Passing Fancy.* By Mrs. Lovett Cameron. London : John Long.
[4] *The Young Master of Hyson Hall.* By Frank R. Stockton. London : Chatto & Windus.
[5] *Kinsah : A Daughter of Tangier.* By May Crommelin. London : John Long.

united to her true lover, Ahmed, and thus the story has a happy ending. Miss Crommelin is evidently a very keen observer, and her book is valuable as a study of life in Morocco, quite apart from its merits as a novel.

*Charming Miss Kyrle*[1] is scarcely equal to Miss Mina Sandemann's previous efforts. It reads well, but its unreality is too much for many readers.

*Boffin's Find : A Tale of the Fifties,*[2] is a most exciting narrative of Australian adventure. Mr. Robert Thynne explains that his work was written before De Rougemont's book saw the light. The story has all the ring of a true record of fact. It never flags from beginning to end. We are not surprised to find that the character of " The Parson " is really a portrait of a person whom the author knew well.

There is much to interest thoughtful readers in *Rural Life : Its Humour and Pathos,*[3] by Catherine Geary. Some of the remarks on the effect of the spread of education are somewhat narrow-minded ; but it is undeniable that new ideas are calculated to rob country life of much of its primitive character. One story told in the book is open to the observation, *Si non vero, è ben trovato.* It appears to have been told to the authoress by a gentleman living in Devonshire. An old couple who were rather above the rank of the labouring class were left a small sum of money and some furniture, together with some oil-paintings, by a relative. " The largest of these canvases represented Saint Joseph with the Virgin Mary before the birth of the Saviour, when Saint Elizabeth comes to greet her cousin. On the frame of the picture beneath was inscribed the legend, *Ave Maria.*

" ' Have you any idea what this picture means ? ' asked the gentleman tentatively.

" ' Yes, sir, yes,' answered the old man cheerfully. ' I think we've pretty well a-made it out by this time. There's no doubt that he,' pointing to Saint Joseph, ' is wishing to marry she,' indicating the Virgin ; ' but she don't want to take him, so she's a-pointing to the other one, and sayin', " Ave Maria." ' "

If this anecdote is founded on fact, rural England must have very misty notions as to the New Testament.

*The Love Affairs of a Curate*[4] is a book that will furnish much amusement. Of course, the author may be accused of trifling, for his curate is a little too silly. However, all curates are not philosophers, even though they may pass for theologians.

*The Progress of Pauline Kessler*[5] is a very painful study of a type of woman such as, one would hope, is not very common in real life.

[1] *Charming Miss Kyrle.* By Mina Sandeman. London : John Long.
[2] *Boffin's Find : A Tale of the Fifties.* By Robert Thynne. London : John Long.
[3] *Rural Life : Its Humour and Pathos.* By Catherine Geary. London : John Long.
[4] *The Love Affairs of a Curate.* By Marcus Reay. London : John Long.
[5] *The Progress of Pauline Kessler.* By Frederic Carrell. London : John Long.

The author knows how to sustain the interest up to the *dénouement ;* but the ending is much too abrupt and blood-curdling.

The translation of the *Theætetus* of Plato,[1] published by the firm of Messrs. Maclehose & Sons, merits the utmost praise that can be bestowed on it. The dialogue is one of the most interesting of all Plato's writings. Professor Dyde has, if possible, improved on Jowett's fine translation of the dialogue. The introduction is luminous and scholarly.

---

## POETRY.

LADY LINDSAY has by this time established her claim to be regarded as a true poet. Her new poem in blank verse, *The Apostle of the Ardennes,*[2] is a charming version of the story of St. Hubert. It recalls in some passages Gustave Flaubert's beautiful story, *La Légende de S. Julien l'Hospitalier.* The tone of Lady Lindsay's poem is thoroughly mediæval, and some of the quaint lyrics introduced here and there have an exquisite simplicity and a sort of old-world fascination. The stately verse of the poem itself makes it not unworthy of comparison with some of Tennyson's *Idylls of the King.*

*Dursch Frost und Gluthen*[3] is a charming collection of German lyrics appealing to the patriotism of different nationalities. The lines on Luther and Beethoven are exceptionally fine.

---

[1] *The Theætetus of Plato : A Translation with an Introduction.* By S. W. Dyde, D.Sc. Glasgow : James Maclehose & Sons.

[2] *The Apostle of the Ardennes.* By Lady Lindsay. London : Kegan, Trench, Trübner & Co.

[3] *Dursch Frost und Gluthen.* Gedichte von Heinrich Bulthaupt. Oldenburg und Leipzig : Schulzesche Hof-Buchhandlung und Hof-Buchdruckere : A. Schartz.

## ART.

THE successive volumes of Messrs. George Bell & Sons' five-shilling illustrated handbook of " Great Masters in Painting and Sculpture " are faithful to the promise of the first number.    An excellent general plan has been adopted by the editor.    This secures clearness of text, without too much technical wandering under plea of criticism, historical interest, the information useful to the visitor of art collections, and the apparatus (index, catalogue, bibliography, chronology, &c.) needed by the student from the beginning.    The illustrations are also sufficient from the point of view of modern photographic methods, which alone make such handbooks possible.    They give a fairly exact idea of the master's design and of the present condition of his pictures.

*Andrea del Sarto* [1] has been entrusted to the hands of Mr. H. Guinness.    The English general reader, in most cases, derives his interest in this particular old master from Robert Browning's poem. He will find a basis of intelligent appreciation of the master's art, as well as of his history, from the chapters of Mr. Guinness, who has evidently written his book from very personal and sympathetic researches.    His notes on the works found in easily accessible collections are such as are desired in a competent handbook.

In her *Luca Signorelli* [1] Miss Cruttwell has armed herself with quite the newest criticism, which is also very good, and not spoiled in the telling.    She has made an interesting figure of an old master, whose work has always been much less *simpatico* than the exuberant Renaissance spirit he embodied ought to warrant.    This side of the painter's work is brought out in agreeable relief, and the work he left is made clear and intelligible.

[1] *Andrea del Sarto.* By H. Guinness. *Luca Signorelli.* By Maud Cruttwell. (Third and Fourth Volumes of "Great Masters in Painting and Sculpture.") London : George Bell & Sons.  1899.

# THE

# WESTMINSTER REVIEW.

### VOL. CLIII. No. 2.—FEBRUARY 1900.

## THE WAR AND AFTER.

### EMPIRE WRECKERS—PARASITES, NOT PATRIOTS.

"Another thing, which the British reader often reads and hears at this time, is worth his meditating for a moment: That Society 'exists for the protection of property.' To which it is added that the poor man also has property, namely, his 'labour,' and the fifteen-pence or three-and-six-pence a day he can get for that. True enough, O friends, 'for protecting *property*;' most true: and, indeed, if you will once sufficiently enforce that Eighth Commandment, the whole 'rights of man' are well cared for ; I know no better definition of the rights of man. *Thou shalt not steal, thou shalt not be stolen from:* what a Society were that : Plato's Republic, More's Utopia mere emblems of it."—CARLYLE.

"Foolish men imagine that because judgment for an evil thing is delayed, there is no justice but an accidental one here below. Judgment for an evil thing is many times delayed some day or two, some century or two, but it is sure as life, it is sure as death ! In the centre of the world-whirlwind, verily now as in the oldest days, dwells and speaks a God. The great soul of the world is *just.*"—CARLYLE.

" He's true to God who's true to man, where'er wrong is done
To the humblest and the weakest, 'neath the all-beholding sun.
That wrong is also done to us ; and they are slaves most base
Whose love of right is for themselves and not for all their race.

" Then to side with Truth is noble, when we share her wretched crust,
Ere her cause bring fame and profit, and 'tis prosperous to be just;
Then it is the brave man chooses, while the coward stands aside,
Doubting in his abject spirit till his Lord be crucified,
And the multitude make virtue of the faith they had denied."—LOWELL.

SHOULD the serious checks that the British arms have received in South Africa result in the discomfiture and ultimate extinction of "the vulgar and bastard Imperialism of irritation, and provocation, and aggression, of clever tricks and manœuvres against neighbours, and of grabbing everything, even if we have no use for it ourselves,"[1] then the lives of the brave men—Britons and Boers—lost in this shameful war will not have been altogether wasted.

[1] Sir Henry Campbell-Bannerman.

This insane policy of expansion for mere expansion's sake, regardless of all right or justice, decency, truth, or honour—this policy of meanness, dishonesty, and cowardice—must be abandoned once and for all if the British Empire is to be saved from utter ruin. It was this policy of expanding, ever expanding, the empire, regardless of the fact that the empire was not sound at heart, that resulted in the downfall of Imperial Rome ; that has resulted in the downfall of many empires in ages dead and gone ; and it must, if blindly and hypocritically persisted in, result in the downfall of Imperial England.

Fortunate indeed shall we be if we learn this lesson at the hands of the plucky and indomitable Boers, instead of at the hands of an outraged Europe.

Disguise it how we may, this Transvaal War is naught but sheer buccaneering—the Jameson Raid on an Imperial scale ; and, whatever the result, this country cannot come out of it with honour. A magnificent spectacle, is it not? An Empire of upwards of 300,000,000 straining its resources to crush two small Republics, numbering all told—men, women, and children—not more than 160,000 souls! It is all of a piece, moreover, with our treatment of the Boers from the first. Misrepresentation and misunderstanding and an arrogant over-reaching policy have marked the whole course of our dealings with the Boers. Time and again have they trekked far beyond our borders with the cry on their lips, " We complain of the unjustifiable odium which has been cast upon us by interested and dishonest persons, under the name of religion, whose testimony is believed in England to the exclusion of all testimony in our favour."

The present raid has many features in common with the stealing of the Kimberley diamond fields. The very men, indeed, who benefited most by that steal are the men who have promoted and engineered this war. The theft of the diamond fields is thus referred to by Mr. J. A. Froude in his *Oceana* :

" Perhaps there would not have been " any further breach " had no new temptation come in our way. But . . . diamonds were discovered in large quantities in a district which we had ourselves treated as part of the Orange Territory before our first withdrawal, and which had ever since been administered by Orange Free State magistrates. There was a rush of diggers from all parts of the country. There was a genuine fear that the Boers would be unable to control the flock of vultures which was gathering over so rich a prey. There was a notion also that the finest diamond mines in the world ought not to be lost to the British Empire. It was discovered that the country in which it lay was not part of the Free State at all, and that it belonged to a Griqua chief named Waterboer. This chief in past times had been an ally of the English. The Boers were accused of having robbed him. He appealed for help, and, in an ill hour, we lent ourselves to an aggression for which there was no excuse. Lord Kimberley gave his name to the new settlement. The Dutch were expelled. They did not resist, but they yielded under protest to superior force, and from that day no Boer in South Africa has been able to trust to English promises. The manner in which we acted, or allowed our representatives to act, was insolent in its cynicism. We had gone in as champions of the oppressed Waterboer. We gave Waterboer and his Griquas a tenth of the territory. We kept the rest and all that was valuable for ourselves. . . . We have accused " the Dutch " of breaking their engagements with us, and it was we who taught them the lesson. . . . Our conduct would have been less entirely intolerable if we had rested simply on superior force—if we had told the Boers simply that we must have the diamond fields, and intended to take them; but we poisoned the wound, and justified our action by posing before the world as the protectors of the rights of native tribes whom we accused them of having wronged, and we maintained this attitude through the controversy which afterwards arose. I had myself," continues Froude, "to make inquiries subsequently into the details of this transaction, perhaps the most discreditable in the annals of English colonial history."

Must not the verdict of history be that this Imperial Raid is a transaction even more discreditable?

It is not many months since that the English Press—and who more loud-voiced then than the Yellow Press of to-day?—was premising the decadence and predicting the downfall of France because of the Dreyfus scandal. But have not we ourselves condemned, on manufactured evidence and without fair trial, a whole race? By how much more, then, is the decadence of England apparent? By how much more is the downfall of England imminent?

Well might Mr. Leonard Courtney, M.P., write:

" Against this " (the desire to subjugate the South African Republics) " I urge invincible hostility, feeling persuaded that this engrossing arrogance, which men call Imperialism, will be the ruin of our country."

Well might Mr. Bryce, M.P., speaking at Aberdeen, say:

" We may find that in our impatience to assert British supremacy everywhere we have set in motion forces that will ultimately destroy it. For the experience of the American revolutionary war has shown that self-governing colonies can be retained by friendship only, and not by arms."

Well might Mr. F. C. Selous, whose intimate knowledge both of the country and of the people entitles his opinion to great weight, warn us that " if all arbitration and discussion of the points in dispute should be arbitrarily refused by the Colonial Secretary," and war should follow,

" in that case we shall have entered upon a course which, though it may give us the goldfields of the Transvaal for the present and the immediate future, will infallibly lose us the whole of South Africa as a British possession within the lifetime of many men who are now living. Through arrogance and ignorance Great Britain lost her American colonies, and if arrogance and ignorance prevail in the present conduct of affairs in South Africa history will repeat itself in that country."

Have those who are responsible for the present war—has Lord

Rosebery, who recently emerged from his semi-retirement to protest against any repetition of Mr. Gladstone's great and courageous act of magnanimity and justice after Majuba Hill—the most magnificent, as the present raid is the most dishonourable, action of Britain in South Africa—have these gentlemen forgotten the weighty words of Lord Randolph Churchill on that very point ?

"Better and more precise information, combined with cool reflection, leads me to the conclusion that, had the British Government of that day taken advantage of its strong military position and annihilated, as it could easily have done, the Boer forces, it would, indeed, have regained the Transvaal, but it might have lost Cape Colony. The Dutch sentiment in the colony had been so exasperated by what it considered to be the unjust, faithless, and arbitrary policy pursued towards the free Dutchmen of the Transvaal, that the final triumph of the British arms, mainly by brute force, would have permanently and hopelessly alienated it from Great Britain."

A buccaneering policy is in the nature of things foredoomed to failure ; and though judgment be delayed, it comes at long and at last, the heavier perchance for the delay. Right down through the ages history enforces the great truth that, to use the words of Goldwin Smith,

"the Power which rules the universe is just, and no nation ever tramples upon the liberties of others without in the end forfeiting its own."

As Carlyle more picturesquely, though not less forcefully, puts it : [1]

"Mights . . . do in the long-run, and forever will in this Universe in the long-run, mean Rights. . . . Howel Davies dyes the West Indian seas with blood, piles his decks with plunder; approves himself the expertest Seaman, the daringest Sea-fighter : but he gains no lasting victory, lasting victory is not possible to him. Not, had he fleets larger than the combined British Navy all united with him in buccaneering. He, once for all, cannot prosper in his duel. He strikes down his man ; yes ; but his man, or his man's representative, has no notion to lie struck down ; neither, though slain ten times, will he keep so lying ; nor has the Universe any notion to keep him so lying ! On the contrary, the Universe and he have, at all moments, all manner of motives to start up again and desperately fight again. Your Napoleon is flung out at last to St. Helena ; the latter end of him sternly compensating the beginning. The Buccaneer strikes down a man, a hundred, or a million men : but what profits it ? He has one enemy never to be struck down ; nay, two enemies : Mankind and the Maker of men."

England must put far from her her present buccaneering, if she would not, with suicidal folly, range herself against mankind.

Has it never struck those who aver that private business and national and international affairs can never be safely conducted on the lines of right and justice—those Bishops of Peterborough who declare that were this nation to conduct her affairs in accordance with the Sermon on the Mount she would inevitably go to the wall—

---

[1] *Past and Present,* chap. x.

has it never struck these gentlemen that it is only the few, the very few, that can benefit by a policy of plunder, rapine, and murder; that the many must always "pay the piper," both in blood and in goods; that, therefore, it is to the interest—the best and highest interest as well as the most sordid interest—of the great majority of mankind to put an end to buccaneering in every shape and form? that, therefore, it is only a question of education and enlightenment —that sooner or later, and sooner rather than later, the majority, whether of the nations of the earth or of individuals, will inevitably rise in their might — Heaven grant that it may be peacefully done!—and put an end to buccaneering, if not to the buccaneers?

Shall we, then, call the promoters of the present raid " Empire Builders "? Shall we not rather call them Empire Wreckers?

Who in this war are we fighting for, and who against?

"For the Outlanders," say you? Even so, would it not be in very truth a spectacle for gods and men? "Tommy Atkins"—so cheap, poor fellow, that even as "food for powder" he can only command 1s. a day above and beyond his kit and rations—Tommy Atkins—recruited, doubtless, by Hunger and Want, best recruiting sergeants of the British Army—fighting for the franchise for, fighting to redress the grievances of, Outlander miners earning their £1 a day!

Nay, it is not for these that we are fighting. They have nothing to gain, but everything to lose, by the present war. Let the yellowest of the Yellow Press instruct us on this point. What says the Capetown war correspondent of the *Daily Mail?* What to the miners is the result of this war?

" Along Adderley Street, before the steamship companies' offices, loafed a thick string of sun-reddened, unshaven, flannel-shirted, corduroy-trousered British working men. Inside the offices they thronged the counters six deep. Down to the docks they filed steadily with bundles to be penned in the black hulls of homeward liners. Their words were few and sullen. These were the miners of the Rand—who floated no companies, held no shares, made no fortunes, who only wanted to make a hundred pounds to furnish a cottage and marry a girl. They had been turned out of work, packed in cattle-trucks, and come down in sun by day and icy wind by night, empty-bellied, to pack off home again. Faster than the shiploads could steam out the trainloads steamed in. They choked the lodging-houses, the bars, the streets. Cape Town was one huge demonstration of the unemployed."

For whom, then, are we fighting? Again we turn to the Yellow Press for information:

" It is disgusting to leave these men (English officers), and turn into one of the Cape Town hotels to find yourself surrounded by the rich refugees from Johannesburg, and to hear them cry like children as they tell you what they will lose if the British do not hurry up and take the Transvaal before the Boers destroy Johannesburg. They actually cry in their plates at dinner, and half strangle themselves by sobbing as they drink their whisky at bedtime. The Mount Nelson, the Queen's, and the Grand Hotels are full of these merchants and millionaires, faring on the fat of the land, idle, loafing, all of every day, and discussing what per cent. of their losses the British Government will pay when they put in their claims at the end of the war. . . . The war has jeopardised their property, and they have a keener interest in it than any Tommy or any officer now at the front. How can they see the cream and flower of English manhood rushing down here to spill its precious blood for them and never feel a blush of shame or a pang of any emotion except grief over losses which will still leave many of them rich?"—Mr. Julian Ralph, of the *Daily Mail*, on the War.

And *against* whom are we fighting? Says Froude in his *Oceana*:

"The Boers of South Africa, of all human beings now on this planet, correspond nearest to Horace's description of the Roman peasant soldiers who defeated Pyrrhus and Hannibal. There alone you will find obedience to parents as strict as amongst the ancient Sabines; the *severa mater* whose sons fetch and carry at her bidding, who, when those sons go to fight for their country, will hand their rifles to them and bid them return with their arms in their hands—or else not return at all."

Is it not only too evident that Great Britain has espoused the cause of the Mammon of Unrighteousness—the cause of the exploiter—the cause of the land thief?

What the "rapacious vultures" of the Rand stand to gain by the war they themselves have told us. The recent report of the Consolidated Gold Fields Company of South Africa points out that when the Government of the Transvaal is "reformed," the company, which already pays cent. for cent., will "earn" an additional dividend of £4,000,000 to £5,000,000 a year! "Good government" in the eyes of these gentlemen, means the abolition of the Transvaal mining laws, the most liberal in the world, perhaps[1]—mining laws specially directed against monopoly of the mines—mining laws which the miners of Alaska petitioned to have enacted there. Then, as the De Beers Consolidated Mines swallowed up and absorbed all interests in Kimberley, so the Consolidated Gold Fields Company would swallow up and absorb all interests in the Rand. The Witwatersrand Mines would be worked on the same "compound" (slavery) system as the Kimberley mines, wages would be at once cut down by 50 per cent.

[1] "RHODESIA WORSE THAN THE TRANSVAAL.—At the meeting of the United Rhodesian Gold Fields, Limited, this afternoon, some strong remarks were made by the chairman, Mr. Clarendon Hyde, in reference to the Chartered Company and its relations with Rhodesian mining enterprises.

"He said the mining ordinance of the Chartered Company threatened to weigh with crushing severity upon the mining industry. *Under the ordinance* the Chartered Company was entitled to *one-half interest in every claim and reef;* that was to say, either one-half of the gold won or one-half of the vendor's scrip received by the owner on the sale of any claims to a mining company. . . . At the present moment he said unhesitatingly that the position of a Rhodesian mining company under the mining ordinance was worse than anything in the Transvaal, and that the uncertainty of the conditions under which they were at work in developing the mines must render investors doubtful of placing money in the mining industries of the country until the position was made plain."—*Westminster Gazette,* November 28, 1899.

—to swell the "earnings" of the company!—and the Outlanders would be reduced to the position of mere serfs.

Small wonder that, as the special correspondent of the *Daily Telegraph* told us ere the war began :

"Whatever may be said to the contrary, there are large numbers of Outlanders, English and other nations, who have enrolled themselves and taken up arms in defence of their adopted country."

Or that Mr. Julian Ralph should say :

"He (Padre Robertson) tells me that there are Englishmen, Irishmen, and Scotchmen among them (the Boers), as well as the mercenary Germans and Scandinavians, who are serving for a gold Kruger a day—which is to say, a pound sterling Dutch."

How astonishing is it, on the other hand, that so many workers here at home have been misled by Yellow Press lies into cheering for this war! That our colonies—even Canada, whose history, one would think, should have led her to sympathise with, and aid to the utmost of her power, those who sought for a peaceful solution of the racial difficulties of South Africa—should unite to send their sons to fight and die in such a cause !

The colonies, however, were by no means so unanimous as has been represented in "rallying for their Homeland and their Queen."

On the platform, in the pulpit, in the Press, and in the Senate men were found to speak for right and justice. Witness the *Sydney Bulletin* :

"Let British speculators gorge themselves with plunder if they will. Let British politicians bring town after town, and State after State, and country after country, within the Imperial clutch. . . . What affair is it of ours? save to express contempt for the methods, detestation of the means. If we sympathise, let us at least sympathise with the patriot, not with the bully; let us assist the men who fight for their fatherland, not the men hired to realise a bloodstained dream of worldwide empire. . . .

"Who believes that the Australian troops are going for love of Britain ? They are going for excitement, for change, for vainglory and the tawdry lustre of military honour; and because the man who professes to be a soldier, who is trained to the soldiering business, naturally wishes to test his courage and his weapons. Without war, he conceives that he has wasted the time spent in preparing for war. It is to the undying disgrace of Australia that the Governments should have yielded to the military clamour—in such a shameful cause.

"History, proud to chronicle the defence of the little Swiss Republic against the Empire of Austria, will not fail to mark the dishonour to the British Empire of the similar war of aggression against the brave little Republic of the Transvaal. And though Britain may extend her empire farther than Rome dreamed of, may depopulate States and destroy communities in her campaigns for greed and 'glory,' upon her also each fresh aggression will recoil with ruinous force and each new conquest will carry with it the seeds of deserved disaster. The measure which Britain metes to weaker peoples will some day be meted to her. Her Goth will come."

Ay, her Goth will come—unless her people, using the God-given light of intelligence, set themselves to purge the land of the spirit of the buccaneers. The dangerous classes are the very rich and the very poor; and material progress, striking like an immense wedge between the upper and the lower strata of society, tends ever to widen the gulf between the two. The danger that the very rich are running the country into is all too obvious to-day; the danger that is to be feared from the lower classes—is it not written in letters of blood and fire in the pages of the history of the French Revolution?

It but adds to the danger to be for ever extending the boundaries of the Empire, while there is rottenness at the core.

Dealing with the housing problem at Manchester the other day, Sir Henry Campbell-Bannerman said:

"Surely we cannot acquiesce in a state of things which is cruel, scandalous, and a danger to society. Here is a grievance, compared to which the complaints of the Outlanders are a mere empty cry . . . for not until it (the housing problem) is solved, whatever be our political or military success at the other end of the world, can we say that the heart of our Empire is sound."

The language is not a whit too strong. In our October number, in the article " On which Side art Thou ? " was reviewed at considerable length the *Daily News* Extra[1]—" No Room to Live "—in which it is shown that in London to-day there are nearly 400,000 people living in " the soul-destroying conditions of the one-roomed house ; " and that 900,000 people—more than the total population of any other city in the United Kingdom—live more than two in a room, with less than the 400 cubic feet of space to each person prescribed by the Public Health Acts; while it was also shown that "there are in Glasgow 31,000 one-room houses containing 100,000 people, or $3\frac{1}{4}$ persons to each room ; and 53,000 two-room houses containing 263,000 persons, or $2\frac{1}{4}$ each room." Since then the commissioner of the *Daily News* has extended his researches to the country districts, and the result of his investigations is to show that the housing problem is, if possible, even more terrible in the country than in the towns.

Here, for instance, is a short extract from his report as to the condition of affairs in Wiltshire. We have not space for more:

"I came across some positively horrible cases of crowding. The people have emigrated in crowds from round about here. But the old houses have fallen into decay more rapidly than the people have made their exodus. The result is that practically all the habitable cottages are occupied—and more than occupied. What is more, if the Rural District Councils exercised their authority to close all the houses that are not safely habitable, all the labourers' cottages in the villages about here would at once become impossibly unhealthy by the evicted tenants crowding in to share their accommodation. Therefore, more cottages must be built. But to get back

---

[1] Sad, indeed, is it to find the *Daily News* on the side of the spoilers.

to the cases of overcrowding. I have come across fifteen instances where more than five people are occupying one small bed-room, ten cases where more than six, eight more than seven, six more than eight, three more than nine, two more than ten, and one where eleven people— mother, father, and nine children, eldest a girl of fifteen—are sleeping in a single bed-room.

## "Overcrowding and Insanity.

"And this is what the medical superintendent of the Wilts County Asylum says in the cold official language of his report :

" ' We may conclude that . . . bodily ailments such as anæmia, general debility, and emaciation caused by insufficient and improper food are an excessive cause of insanity in Wiltshire; that much immorality exists, including incest, of which several cases have been met with. These probably have their origin to some extent in overcrowding.' "—*Daily News*, November 28, 1899.

Who, in the face of such facts and figures, shall say that " the blacks " in the Transvaal are not infinitely better off than poor Hodge ?

What sharp social contrasts our country affords! Cause and effect, surely, are to be discerned by those who read between the lines in the following cases :

### The Duke.

"We regret to announce that the Duke of Westminster died at ten minutes past ten last night. . . . The late Duke can scarcely be described as distinguished in the ordinary sense. But two distinctions he did undoubtedly possess which marked him off from every other man in England. Though one of the smallest of the great landowners in point of acreage, he was not only the wealthiest of them all, but the landlord of all the rest. Throughout Belgravia there is probably not a single social magnate who does not, directly or indirectly, pay ground tribute to the Grosvenors. . . . When the Westminster property came into their hands by marriage in the seventeenth century, it was a farm of about 500 acres, letting for £21 a year. Now the rental is nearly a quarter of a million and the capital value is—how many millions ?

"The late Duke once complained that the Harcourt succession and death duties would mulct his successor in a million and a half. On another occasion, he resented the imputation of being worth £800,000

### The Sempstress.

" 'Natural causes' is perhaps the proper verdict for a coroner's jury to return upon the death of an old woman of sixty-nine, who had earned a precarious six shillings a week by shirt-making, and who had slowly starved to death. Six shillings a week, as Dr. Westcott said " (at an inquest) "at Shoreditch on Saturday, is 'just enough to starve on.' So it proved in the case of Caroline Oswald, who, earning this sum as a maximum, grew steadily thinner and weaker, was carried to the infirmary in an emaciated condition, and there died of starvation. Can nothing be done for the sweated multitudes of London, who, at this very moment, are pining to death like Caroline Oswald ? Can nothing be done to the sweaters ? Parliament has made some more or less futile efforts. It must be urged to try again, for the bitter lot of the starving sempstress is a scandal to the whole nation."— *Daily Chronicle*,[1] January 8, 1900.

[1] Now, alas ! one of the Yellow Press.

a year, on the ground that the real figures were a mere trifle of something over £400,000.

"But the £800,000 are well within the horizon. A great number of 99-year leases fall in during the next twenty years, and men talk with bated breath of values increased by twentyfold.

"Viscount Belgrave is heir to the dukedom. He is the son of the Duke's eldest son, Earl Grosvenor, who died in 1884. The Viscount is now twenty years of age, and acts as secretary to Sir Alfred Milner, in Cape Town.

"Amongst other prospects may be reckoned the probability of his becoming the richest man in the world."—*Morning Leader*, Dec. 23, 1899.

*Man must live on the land.* It is his only foothold in space, his only storehouse for food and raw materials.

*Man must live on the products of labour*—his own labour or another's. If we have, therefore, an idle few "rich beyond the dreams of avarice," we must as a necessary corollary have the toiling masses receiving bare starvation wages.

Do not these two truths, italicised above, at once explain, when taken in conjunction, the dire poverty of the toiler and the vast wealth of the land " owner " ?

But the many not only pay in rent a heavy tax to the few. They pay a still heavier tax of disease and death. Says Dr. C. R. Drysdale in his *Report of Industrial Remuneration Conference*, p. 130 :

" At present the average age at death among the nobility, gentry, and professional classes in England and Wales was 55 years; but among the artisan classes of Lambeth it only amounted to 29 years ; and whilst the infantile death-rate among the well-to-do classes was such that only eight children died in the first year of life out of some 100 born, as many as 30 per cent. succumbed at that age among the children of the poor in some districts of our large cities. The only real causes of this enormous difference in the position of the rich and poor with respect to their chances of existence lay in the fact that at the bottom of society wages were so low that food and other requisites of health were obtained with too great difficulty."

Ay ; but was not " the only real cause of this enormous difference " the enormous rentals paid by the workers to the few ? Given private property in land, where rents are high wages *must* be low.

While such things be, " can we say that the heart of our Empire is sound " ?

" Latifundia perdidere Italiam "—Great estates ruined Italy—was Pliny's epitaph for the Roman Empire. It may yet serve also as epitaph for the British Empire. According to Mulhall's *Dictionary of Statistics*, p. 266, the landlords of this country (all, that is to say, owning more than a field or a cottage each) number only 180,524, and they between them own *ten-elevenths* of the total area. Less than two hundred thousand men have, therefore, legal power to expel the whole of the population from ten-elevenths of the British Isles, and the vast majority of the British people have no right whatever to their native land, save to walk the streets or trudge the roads. To them may be fittingly applied the words of a tribune of the Roman people :

"Men of Rome," said Tiberius Gracchus, " you are called the lords of the world, yet have no right to a square foot of its soil ! The wild beasts have their dens, but the soldiers of Italy have only water and air ! "

Said Mr. Dillon in the House of Commons last session :

" No one could say that the Irish soldiers had ever turned their backs to the foe. And yet all the reward they had given for the services of men whose bodies were scattered over the hills in South Africa, and whose reckless bravery had probably saved the troops from terrible disaster, was the tearing down of the rooftrees of their fathers and leaving their mothers on the roadside. Those were the sort of men that during the whole of this century the Government had endeavoured to exterminate and eradicate. Yes, the Government had done that until they had succeeded in reducing the population of Ireland."

While " An Old Soldier," writing to the *New Age*, points the same moral :

" I do not know," says he, " of any more harmful fallacy than the blind feeling of patriotism which is supposed to inspire all those persons who are now shrieking for the continuance to the bitter end of the present most unjust and disastrous war. Our soldiers are said to be fighting for ' Queen and Country.' What arrant nonsense ! The Queen is in no danger of personal attack, and even if she were the soldiers might well ask what she does for them that should induce them to risk life and limb in her defence. And as for 'our country,' about which these patriots rave so loudly, will some of them please explain what he means by a country in this sense ? Is it the houses, or the land, or the people? And why should the average soldier, who does not possess enough land to fill a flower-pot, fight to the death in defence of such a chimera ? As far as he is concerned it matters nothing whether he is ruled and robbed by Mr. Kruger or by Mr. Chamberlain. When a man picks my pocket, his nationality is a matter of indifference to me."

Cannot the people of this country see that the present robbery and buccaneering abroad are of a piece with the robbery and buccaneering at home ; that it is in the nature of things that our "Landlord Government" should aid the buccaneers, the landgrabbers of the Rand, in their fell designs ? Your Landlord is your Prince of Buccaneers. And these men—Rhodes, Beit, Eckstein,

Werhner, Newmann, Joel, and many another patriot whose name betrays his extraction—what are they? "Financiers, capitalists all," says the Socialist. My friend, is Rhodesia land or capital? Are diamond fields and goldfields land or capital? "They are land most certainly," says the economist. "Capital is wealth used to assist labour in the production of further wealth. All capital is wealth—though all wealth is not capital—and all wealth is, in the last analysis, produced by labour from the land. 'The term land embraces . . . all natural materials, forces, and opportunities, and, therefore, nothing that is freely supplied by nature can be properly classed as capital.'"

"The rapacious vultures" of the Rand and "our old nobility" are, it will be seen, "birds of a feather."

But this Landlord Government claims also to be the Patriotic Government. True, they love their country. They love it so well that they will not part with one foot of it unless they are compelled! They must know that the titles to "their" land are based on force and fraud; they must know that land monopoly is the canker-worm at the heart of the Empire; they must know that so long as they live in idle luxury the workers must of necessity consequence toil and moil day in and day out for bare starvation pay; they must know all this, yet these "patriots" hold fast with avaricious clutch their ill-gotten estates. Nay, more, in conjunction with the "Empire builders," they peril the very existence of the Empire itself, in the endeavour to steal the gold-bearing lands of the Transvaal and enslave, in South Africa, blacks and whites alike.

Empire Builders! Patriots! Nay, rather, Empire Wreckers! Parasites!

> "The Feudal Aristocracy, I say, was no imaginary one. To a respectable degree, its *Jarls*, what we now call Earls, were *Strong Ones* in fact as well as etymology; its Dukes *Leaders*; its Lords *Law-words*. They did all the Soldiering and Police of the country, all the Judging, Law-making, even the Church Extension; whatsoever in the way of Governing, of Guiding, and Protecting could be done. It was a Land Aristocracy; it managed the Governing of this English People, and had the reaping of the Soil of England in return. . . . Soldiering, Police, and Judging, Church Extension, nay, real Government and Guidance, all this was actually *done* by Holders of Land in return for their Lands. How much of it is now done by them; done by anybody? . . . We raise Fifty-two millions from the general mass of us, to get our Governing done—or, alas, to get ourselves persuaded that it is done: and the peculiar burden of the Land is to pay, not all this, but to pay, as I learn, one Twenty-fourth part of all this. Our first Chartist Parliament, or Oliver *Redivivus*, you would say, will know where to lay the new taxes of England! Or alas, taxes? If we made the Holders of Land pay every shilling still of the expense of Governing the Land, what were all that?"
> —CARLYLE.

It is surely, then, the bounden duty of the Liberal party, in view of the present crisis—

(1) To cry HALT! To insist upon an armistice—in order that, before our armies fall upon the devoted Republics in overwhelming numbers, a last effort, and a genuine effort, may be made to settle our difficulties peacefully—by arbitration or otherwise.

"But," say you, "the Boers were the aggressors. They must, at least, be first driven from British soil. By their insolent ultimatum they left us no option but to go to war."

Is that ultimatum so insolent, reading it now in the light of what had preceded it—is it so insolent as it, perchance, appeared on the first perusal? Is it not rather a dignified and a spirited protest withal against the aggressive, the hostile action of this country in ostentatiously massing troops in South Africa while the negotiations were pending? Would not Britishers, had they been placed in that position, have acted as the Boers did? Would they not have protested, and have struck home if their protest proved of no avail, much sooner than the Boers did? Of course we should.

The "insolent ultimatum" of the Boers contains four demands, of which the first is:

"That all points of mutual difference shall be regulated by the friendly course of arbitration or by whatever amicable way may be agreed upon by this Government with her Majesty's Government."

Mr. Kruger has all along favoured arbitration. But—was it with a view to forcing the present crisis?—the Government objected to the presence of Transvaal delegates at the Hague; and the claim of "Suzerainty," buried in oblivion for fifteen years, was resurrected by the Colonial Secretary, with the necessary, if not the all-along-intended consequence of exasperating the Boers and rousing the Jingo spirit in this country to such a height that the very idea of going to arbitration with a "vassal State" was scornfully rejected.

"But," urges the Jingo, "what about the widespread conspiracy amongst the Dutch in South Africa, and the continuous arming of the Transvaal, ever since Majuba Hill, to drive the hated Britishers into the sea?"

My dear sir, you cannot produce one jot or tittle of evidence in support of such a contention. On December 7 last Mr. Hugh Price Hughes, editor of the *Methodist Times*, wrote:

"It is now in evidence that for many years before the Raid President Kruger had been doing his utmost to anticipate the day of battle, and that immense sums—in fact, all that the so-called Republic could afford—had been spent in preparing for an attack upon the British Empire."

Will it be believed that, though pilloried for more than a week in the editorial and correspondence columns of the *Morning Leader*, and doubtless of other papers also, this "champion of Nonconformity" has not produced a scrap of solid evidence in substantiation of this statement ?

"Dagonet" stated recently, moreover, in the *Referee*, that Mr. Fitzpatrick had "effectively disposed" in the *Contemporary* (*sic*) of the contention "that it was the Jameson Raid that caused the Boers to increase their armaments." But this was promptly and effectively disposed of by the *Star* of December 2, which, adopting "the deadly parallel" argument, showed that Mr. Fitzpatrick's ingenious, but scarce ingenuous, method was to omit the date of the manifesto published just before the Raid, and to change the tense from the future to the past, thus :

| *Fortnightly Review*, Dec. 1899. | *The Transvaal from Within.* By J. P. Fitzpatrick. |
|---|---|
| "In 1894 we had seen the commencement of preparations on a large scale which are to-day demanding toll in British blood. In the manifesto published before the Raid, the Uitlanders complained of the £250,000 spent on Pretoria forts, £100,000 on Johannesburg fort, the importation of cannon, Maxims, and small arms, and the hiring of German mercenaries." | "£250,000 is *to be* spent upon the completing of a fort at Pretoria, £100,000 is *to be* spent upon a fort to terrorise the inhabitants of Johannesburg, large *orders are sent to* Krupps for big guns, Maxims have been ordered, and we are even told that German officers *are coming out* to drill the burghers." |

The Liberal party, therefore, on the platform, in the pulpit, in the Press, and in Parliament, should insist upon an armistice—upon the immediate cessation of our present career of wholesale murder for gain.

(2) It is the duty of the Liberal party to insist upon a just, a liberal, nay, a generous, settlement of our differences with the Boers—a settlement in the best interests of both countries—not in the interests of the speculators.

In his Guildhall speech Lord Salisbury said :

"We seek no goldfields. We seek no territory. What we desire is equal rights for all men of all races, and security for our fellow-subjects and for the Empire. I will not ask by what means these results are to be obtained. The hour for asking that has not yet come. But those are the objects, those are the only objects that we seek ; and we do not allow any other considerations to cross our path."

Were proposals on such lines definitely submitted to the Transvaal, together with an undertaking that all further differences between Boers and British should be settled by arbitration, both the Transvaal and England could with honour accept such terms.

(3) It is the duty of the Liberal party to insist upon a full, free, and impartial inquiry into the hidden causes, the secret intrigues, and the dishonourable wire-pulling that led up to this war.

In their own interest—if they be guiltless—and in the public interest, Cecil John Rhodes, Joseph Chamberlain, and Alfred Milner should be put upon their trial; and the Hawkesley *dossier*, part of which has already been published, with damning effect, in the *Independance Belge*, must be published in full in order that this unspeakable crime may be sheeted home to the guilty.

(4) The War Office scandals must also be thoroughly investigated, and steps must be taken to put the army upon a proper footing.

(5) *It is the bounden duty of the Liberal party to be upright and downright, honest and businesslike in regard to domestic reforms.* The Empire, if it is to be a worthy and a lasting one, must be founded on the impregnable rock of right and justice—not on the shifting quicksands of opportunism, force, and fraud. The heart of the Empire must be sound—and to that end the canker-worm of land monopoly, and of injustice in every shape and form, must, as soon as may be, be stamped out. The "Liberal Forwards," for example, must no longer be backward on such matters. They must be as straight and as strenuous in home politics as they are in foreign politics. And "the Nonconformist Conscience"—"the backbone of the Liberal party"—one had almost been tempted to think that the party is absolutely invertebrate—must do its duty honestly and effectively.

Sir Henry Campbell-Bannerman has recently been speaking out in a style that would be distinctly encouraging were his utterances more encouragingly distinct. Speaking at Birmingham on November 24, Sir Henry was more explicit than he had been at Manchester, but even then there was much to be desired. After dealing in a businesslike fashion with the temperance question, he said:

"Then there is the housing question calling aloud for action, and that housing question what is it but one phase and part of the land question; and who among us can fail to see that the forces which demand the opening of the land question are strengthening among us day by day? Our people—the British people—have no desire to be unfair to any man, but they have equally no desire that any man should be unfair to them; and it appears to them to be an unfairness that an additional value created by their industry and energy should all go to an individual without even a contribution to ease the burden which they bear. Ladies and gentlemen, these are called social questions. A social question often appears to me to be interpreted as being some proposal to be beneficent at the public expense. These are more than social questions. These are political questions. They go down deep to the very roots of political liberty, and if you are to carry the reforms you desire in these matters it will require all your hardihood, all your earnestness, all your tenacity as active reformers."

At Aberdeen, too, on December 20, Sir Henry, alluding to religious equality, electoral reform, the House of Lords, the land laws, and old age pensions, said:

"Well, gentlemen, there need be no doubt as to the manner in which we should deal with any of these questions if we had the opportunity.

We should simply apply to them our immortal Liberal principles. We would put an end to monopoly and privilege where it was found to be injurious to the public interest, and we would endeavour to secure to every man the best conditions of living, and, so far as can be done by laws and customs, to secure him also an equal chance with the others of a useful and happy life."

Brave words, doubtless; but no definite line of action is mapped out. No distinct pledge is given. Yet the democracy have a right to demand—and the more intelligent among them do demand—both.

Sir Henry, moreover, endorsed at Birmingham the idea that has given more force to the Imperialistic reaction, perhaps, than anything else. "Ladies and gentlemen," said he, "we have in this country an overflowing population, and we are bound to find for their industrial energy ever fresh fields and outlets."

What about the 26,000,000 acres in this country—26,000,000 out of 72,000,000!—lying absolutely idle, and the millions more only half used? Twelve million, at least, of these idle acres would readily support a family to every ten to twenty acres—from 600,000 to 1,200,000 families, or from 2,400,000 to 4,800,000 souls.

Before domestic reforms can be considered, moreover, we must, according to the Liberal leader, first settle our foreign difficulties. At Birmingham he said:

"But we must first—before we come to any such subjects as these—we must first dispose of our difficulties and perplexities beyond our own shores. We are all anxious, and must all desire when the present calamities are over, to see the people of South Africa united and harmonious on a footing of absolute equality between race and race. It is only by such happy results, not only in South Africa, but elsewhere in the dominions of the Queen, that we can be free to apply a cure to evils which, as they stand, are a hindrance and almost a barrier to the prosperity and happiness of our people."

And so it is with all the Liberal leaders.

In view of the "financial poltroonery" displayed by the late Liberal Government; in view of Sir William Harcourt's repeated failures in 1893, 1894, and 1895 to redeem the Budget pledges upon which the Liberal party got into power; in view, moreover, of the manner in which, under the leadership of Mr. Shaw-Lefevre, an ex-Liberal Cabinet Minister, the Progressives on the London County Council have not only failed to carry out their pledges, but have adopted as their own the programme of the Moderates with regard to the taxation of land values; the people of this country must have very clear and very definite pledges from the Liberal leaders if they are again to place any confidence in them.

The Liberal Press, too, must look to its laurels. Some of the old champions of Liberalism, like the *Daily News* and the *Daily Chronicle*, have espoused the cause of the buccaneers abroad. On the other hand, papers like the *Westminster Gazette*, the *Morning Leader*, the *Star*, the *Manchester Guardian*, the *New Age*, and *Reynolds's* have spoken out straight and true against the buccaneers in South Africa. With regard to buccaneering at home, however, even the best of them is little, if any, more explicit than are·Liberal leaders themselves.

Said *Reynolds's Newspaper* the other day :

"This war will cost £100,000,000 in direct cash, it will enormously increase our taxes, dislocate trade, increase the unemployed difficulty, postpone indefinitely old-age pensions and other reforms. . . ."

That depends upon the Radical party and in large part upon the leading given by the Radical Press.

How is it that neither Liberal leaders nor Radical editors can be brought to face fairly and squarely the fact that the House of Lords is debarred, by the resolution of the House of Commons in 1687, from interfering with the Budget? Why is it that Liberal leaders and Radical editors alike fail to realise the splendid opening that this gives the democracy?

Let the Liberal party place on present values the land tax of 4s. in the £, now fraudulently levied on the values of 1692, and bringing in £1,000,000 only, and they would then net £40,000,000 a year. With this they could—

I. Give Old Age Pensions (£25,000,000);

II. Abolish the Breakfast Table Duties (£5,000,000) ;

III. Give Payment of Members and of Election Expenses (£1,000,000) ;

IV. Pay Interest and Sinking Fund Charges on £100,000,000, the probable cost of the present war (£5,000,000 a year, say) ; and yet

V. Have some £4,000,000 to spare to knock a penny off the Income-tax, and reduce the taxes on tobacco, or what you will.

Moreover, one cannot find a better remedy for the dislocation of trade and the unemployed difficulty than this same taxation of land values.

At Aberdeen in December last, the Scotch Liberal Associations, while declaring for the taxation of land values, temperance reform, &c., bluntly laid down the abolition of the House of Lords as the main issue before the country at the next General Election.

Where is the common sense, or the common honesty, in so doing, when it is practically impossible to take the position by a frontal attack? There must be a Budget each year, and the Budget outlined above could be carried in the teeth of the Lords. Why not, then, take them on the flank by taxing land values—a form of attack which they cannot face if pressed resolutely home ; secure the other

Budget reforms above mentioned at the same time; and use the taxation of land values, the power of the purse, to force through other much-needed reforms, and, if necessary, to bring the Lords to their knees and compel them to resign their legislative privileges?

This the Liberal party can do if they are honest—if they are in earnest. Let us have plain speaking and honest dealing. They are the *sine quâ non* of national stability. Let the Liberal leaders, the Liberal Press, the Liberal party, and the Nonconformist Conscience array themselves on the side of right and justice—on the side of "Mankind and the Maker of Men"—and against buccaneering, whether abroad or at home.

# DO THE CONTAGIOUS DISEASES ACTS SUCCEED?

It is evident from the foregoing that there never was any necessity for exceptional action on the part of her Majesty's Government with regard to venereal disease. That it is *absolutely impossible* to make prostitution safe. That a sanitary law applicable to one sex only can never succeed. That only a small fraction of prostitutes can ever be brought under control. *That the danger from mediate contagion is insuperable.* That the examinations are worse than useless. That they spread disease, while the whole system by giving men inducements and a false sense of security is a fruitful source of injury to the innocent wives and children we are so earnestly called upon to protect.

Since the Acts are so manifestly useless, injurious, and iniquitous, how do you account for the kind of public feeling which has been manufactured in favour of them? Well, the Committees and Commissions which have sat to consider this question have been mainly composed of avowed supporters of the system—men who fancy that if they can lock up even one woman in a licensed brothel or imprison her in a hospital they have done wonders, and no evidence would change their opinions. Again, the persons examined have been generally the police and officials employed in carrying out the system. Benjamin Constant has said, "Si vous voulez savoir si un Institution est bon, n'ecoutez pas les raisons de ceux qui en vivient," and everybody knows that any Act of Parliament which involves the expenditure of vast sums of public money is certain to find plenty of thick-and-thin supporters. Besides the people, especially innocent ladies, have been frightened out of their senses by the grossest fabrications and exaggerations as to the extent and virulence of venereal diseases ; for instance, the Association for extending these Acts have stated officially "That the venereal disease is a disease of the grossest character constantly transmitted from parent to offspring." What do they mean? Every one knows that the vast majority of cases of venereal disease are as trivial as trivial can be, and there is no disease whatever of venereal origin that is constantly transmitted from parent to offspring. Again, they tell us that from one-fifth to one-third of the sick poor of

London are suffering from this serious malady—the truth being that only about 1 in 25 is affected and that the vast majority of these are readily cured; that it is a rare event for disease to be transmitted to children and that its influence is never felt beyond the immediate offspring.

"Even if the statistics herein afforded were unquestionable, we should be no nearer the solution of the question we want answered. Apart from the fault of grouping all venereal diseases together, as proper matter for State intervention, *grave doubt has been thrown upon the statistics*, such as they are, which the Association parades. The medical officer of the Privy Council has taken some pains to test their accuracy. At the Children's Hospital, in Great Ormond Street, he finds, on inquiry, that of 118,590 children of the poor treated there during *the last ten years for all sorts* of diseases, the proportion recorded to have been syphilitic has *only been* 1½ *per cent.* From a very careful investigation conducted by Mr. W. W. Wagstaffe, who visited for this purpose several of the largest general hospitals and dispensaries in London, it appears that, of 9363 out-patients in all departments of these charitable institutions, only 8·71 per cent. were affected with venereal diseases of any kind, and only 4·21 with syphilis, the remainder · being mostly cases of gonorrhœa. Mr. Wagstaffe extended his inquiry to the in-patients treated in hospitals, workhouse infirmaries, and by the parochial out-of-door surgeons, with the result 'that 6·92 will probably represent the percentage of the sick poor population affected with some form of venereal disease,' of which about half, or 3½ per cent., would be infecting syphilis. *Surely 456 persons suffering from true syphilis in one form or another, in a poor population of a million and a half, such as that which seeks gratuitous medical aid in our London population, cannot be held to be a proportion so large as to call for exceptional action on the part of any government.* And Sir John Simon adds, ' it must be remembered that London, probably, illustrates *the utmost dimensions which the evil can attain* in this country.' "—*British and Foreign Medico-Chirurgical Review*, Jan. 1870.

Again, we are assured that there was much less disease at stations under the Acts than at stations not under them, but this is owing to the fact that soldiers, where the Acts are in force, predominantly conceal their diseases : they hate the fuss that is made about what they consider a trivial matter, and, as Lord Roberts remarked before the · Departmental Committee, decline to point out the woman who has infected them; if pressed, they point out perfect strangers or respectable women—thus, in Hong Kong during six months, out of 139 women denounced by British soldiers and sailors as having communicated contagion, 102 were on examination found to be free from disease ; again, on another occasion, out of 103 women denounced, 101 were found to be free from disease ; hence, although venereal diseases may apparently fall, the druggists' shops are crowded by applicants for anti-venereal remedies. Take the evidence of Inspector Smith given before the House of Commons Committee.

The Chairman asks the inspector whether he had ground for believing that there were many diseased soldiers going about who had not given themselves up and were not in hospital. He replies: "Yes, I have for a considerable time been impressed with the belief that many men are at large who are diseased." Inspector Smith induced one of the chemists to take the number of men whom he served with medicine for venereal disease, and handed in the report, which is as follows, to the Committee: "On Monday, June 14, there were 16 soldiers applied for this purpose ; on Tuesday the 15th there were 13 ; on Wednesday the 16th there were 17 ; on Thursday the 17th there were 18 ; on Friday the 18th there were 11 ; on Saturday the 19th there were 23 ; the total being 98 in one week." There were four chemists at Aldershot, one other shop did an equal trade, and two others not quite so much ; this would give an average of about 320 men in one week at Aldershot alone under treatment for venereal diseases contracted under the so-called protecting provisions of the Contagious Diseases Acts, and excluded from the returns which are paraded as proofs of the success of the system.

Again, stations were compared one with another which do not admit of any legitimate comparison ; for instance, the Board of Admiralty had been accustomed to publish in the *Navy Report* a yearly return exhibiting the alleged sanitary benefits of the Contagious Diseases Acts, comparing the results in certain ports under the Acts with certain ports not subjected to the Acts. This comparison was first made in the *Navy Report* for 1876, and published by the House of Commons in 1877. Immediately after its issue, it was pointed out to the Admiralty that the comparison was fallacious, because the "protected" ports embraced large training ships containing many thousand boys, whilst there were no such ships or boys in the "unprotected" ports, and these thousands of boys were all ranked as men in the comparison ; and the absence of venereal disease among these boys, who had no chance of contracting it, was put down to the credit of the Acts, the comparison nowhere stating that "per 1000 of force" embraced thousands of boys in the one set of ports, and no boys at all in the other set. No attention was paid to this criticism, for the comparison was republished without change in the following *Navy Report ;* and this was repeated year after year for twelve years, notwithstanding that the criticism was again and again brought before the notice of the Admiralty, and was officially acknowledged, admitted to be correct, and yet disregarded.

It must be noticed that women evade the examinations *when they are on the register,* especially if they have the least reason to suppose

that they are suffering from venereal disease.   In an official report
M. le Dr. le Pileur, Médicin de Saint Lazare, says: I must acknowledge—

> "Qu'aucune prime n'est capable de faire franchir a une femme les portes
> de Saint Lazare et qu'il est patent que celles qui ont des doutes sur leur
> santé fuient la visite avex une énergie qui couronne presque toujours le
> succès."

Commenting upon these facts M. le Docteur Lutaud says:

"Women evade these examinations for two reasons.   First,
because it is the prison and not the hospital that may be the consequence of this visit.   Second, because the examination is forced
upon them, and is resisted because it is an attack upon their liberty.
Everybody knows that Saint Lazare is a prison rather than an
hospital, and no one is likely to enter who can keep out.   Is it
necessary, therefore, to abandon all attempts to treat prostitutes
who are diseased?  the Doctor asks.   By no means, he says.   There
is at Paris a hospital for the treatment of women suffering from
venereal disease.   It is called the Loureine, and it is always full
because women go in when they please and come out when they
please, while Saint Lazare is never full, although the most shameful
raids are practised in order to force women to enter.   I am
convinced, says M. Lutaud, that the day that coercion ceases,
the day when disease ceases to be a pretext for imprisonment,
women will hasten to the doctor instead of flying from him;
instead of having 1500 treated by force, you will have 150,000
who will gladly accept treatment whenever there is any necessity
for it.   You will have in this way and at small cost and by
honourable, praiseworthy means organised a simple, acceptable, and a
thousand times more efficacious means of treatment than anything
you get by violence to-day."

What are the means, quite unobjectionable, and in full accord
with the free spirit of all English institutions, which, in your
opinion, would suffice, so far as is possible, to mitigate venereal
diseases?

The establishment of voluntary hospitals and dispensaries and
drug stores freely accessible to all classes and both sexes at little
expense or no expense at all.

Is it not a fact that this end has been attained by the building of
Lock Hospitals under the Contagious Diseases Acts?

No; it is not.   These institutions are prisons; they are in fact
penal institutions; and the authorities have done their best to defeat
the object of the Legislature by making it difficult, indeed impossible,
for a vast number of persons suffering from venereal disease to enter
them.

How so?

They pretend that these institutions provide gratuitous medical relief for females suffering from venereal diseases, but they require, before admission, that the woman shall be registered as a common prostitute; that is the *sine quâ non*, and they expect women to be stamped with lifelong infamy before they will accord them medical treatment, which is quite enough to prevent any woman in her senses from accepting it.

What is the objection to registration?

The objection to registration is this:—It means what Dante wrote over the gates of Hell—" Abandon hope who enter here."

Dr. Mireur, of Marseilles, an eminent authority, in his great work on Prostitution (p. 549 remarks): " The system of registration which regulates and legalises the sorrowful industry of the prostitute is, in fact, the sinister stroke by which women are cut off from society, and after which they no longer belong to themselves, but become merely the thing of the administration. They are cut off, not from society only, but from heaven, from hope, and from the power to repent."

What woman who could help it would ever submit to this for the sake of medical treatment? Certainly only the lowest, most abandoned, or terribly diseased: so that you at once shut out nine-tenths of the women who are prostitutes and sources of disease, compel them to become clandestines, conceal their maladies, and thus become sources of infection infinitely more dangerous than before. And this is not all. It is proved by the returns of the London Lock Hospital that 30 per cent. of the women treated in that institution are not prostitutes at all, so that, irrespective of the clandestines actually manufactured by the Acts, you shut out from suitable treatment nearly half the sufferers who ought to be treated; and, in addition, have altogether neglected those very active sources of contagion—men; and make no provision whatever for the innocent children, about whom we have heard so much.

Do you think women who were diseased would attend voluntarily?

Certainly; if they were free to come and go. If there is one fact established beyond dispute by the evidence taken before the Lords' and Commons' Committees and the Royal Commission, it is this—to use the words of the Chairman of the Lords' Committee—" The evidence before us shows that women are most willing to enter the Lock Hospitals."

Is it not a fact that they decline to remain till cured?

Not if they are really diseased. This difficulty occurs only with women who have nothing the matter with them; and there can be no question that a vast number are sent in because the surgeon does not know whether they are diseased or not. It is, in fact, a matter of doubtful medical opinion. In proof of this I refer to the 609 women sent to the Royal Albert Hospital by the examining surgeon, and the following quotation from the *Bombay Gazette Budget* of December 25, 1880:

"THE WORKING OF THE CONTAGIOUS DISEASES ACT IN BOMBAY.

"At the time the Government so arbitrarily declared its intention to help itself to Rs. 15,000 from the municipal funds to extend the working of the Contagious Diseases Act, with which the Municipality had declared that it would have nothing to do, the excuse which was put forward was that there was great need of the money. The hospital, it was stated, was full to overflowing. Over two hundred cases of the worst type of disease filled the wards, and it was found impossible to provide for other cases quite as bad, which were being constantly sent up by the staff of medical examiners. The necessity of providing further hospital accommodation was declared to be undeniable and urgent. Negotiations were actually entered into for the leasing of a large building in Parel Road, for the accommodation of the patients for whom the existing hospital had no room. The state of affairs was very bad. The need of the Act had been fully demonstrated by the ascertained prevalence and intensity of disease of the worst form. The one need was money to enable the Act to be worked on a scale commensurate with the magnitude of the evil to be combated. A second and a larger hospital, an enlarged staff of medical examiners, a few more thousands of rupees expended monthly, and all would be well. It is true that the Act had failed egregiously when it was tried before. But now it was working admirably, and no hitch or abuse of any kind could be detected in its operation. Those who had prophesied that it would break down a second time as ignominiously as it had at first were covered with confusion. The Government, which had introduced it by a fiat of power in the teeth of all remonstrance, was proud of its work. Nothing was wanting but funds, and to secure them Rs. 15,000 were requisitioned from the Municipality. The big building on the Parel Road was all but taken; everything promised well; and nothing remained but to give a vigorous impulse to the working of this beneficent Act.

"Now at this satisfactory stage it occurred to the Surgeon-General, Dr. Beatty, to test by personal inspection the reports sent up by Dr. Anderson and the medical examiners. He visited the hospital and was considerably astonished at what he saw. He visited the offices of the medical examiners, and his astonishment was, if possible, augmented. There seemed to him to be no reason why the better half of the population of Bombay should not come upon the books, according to the system which was acted upon. He communicated with the Government. The result was the appointment of a medical committee, composed of Dr. Blanc and Dr. Knapp, to investigate the matter. These doctors examined the hospital and—it will scarcely be credited—they found that of the two hundred women detained in the building for treatment for a specific disease, nearly one-half of them—ninety in exact numbers—were not suffering from that disease at all! They had been taken to the hospital and detained there in accordance with the provisions of the Contagious Diseases Act, and they were actually treated for contagious diseases with which they were not affected! The fact is indisputable. It is placed beyond all doubt by the independent investigations of the Surgeon-General himself, and of Drs. Blanc and Knapp. Dr. Anderson, who was in charge of the hospital, confessed that he had been mistaken in his diagnoses, but he pleaded that he was not responsible for the error by which these ninety women were sent into the hospital. That was due to the blunder of the medical examiners. It was their business to detect disease in the women sent up for examination by the police, and when they found them diseased to send them for treatment to the hospital, where they must remain, of course, still under police surveillance. Dr. Anderson's excuse is, of course, not valid. It was his business to see whether his patients were really sick people or not, and if they were not suffering from disease to send them home. The only excuse that can be really urged on his behalf is that he is no longer young, and he was not, therefore, quite capable of detecting the multitudinous blunders committed by the staff of medical examiners. He has practically admitted the correctness of this view of the matter by sending in his resignation, on the ground that his age renders the burden of his present office too great for him. With regard to the medical examiners, it appears they all, with one exception, signalised themselves by the zeal with which they devoted themselves to the detection of disease—even where it did not exist—and they seemed to have vied with one another as to who should send up the greatest number of cases for hospital treatment. The one exception is that of Mr. De Souza, who sent up so few that he was for some time under a suspicion of lukewarmness in the good cause, and his competence for the post of examiner came to be doubted at headquarters. But when it was found by the Committee of Inquiry that the cases which he had sent up were really cases of disease, it began to be surmised that, perhaps, he alone of the medical examiners possessed the requisite qualifications for his office, and knew how to combine a certain proportion of care and circumspection with zeal for the public health. It is needless to say that Mr. De Souza is now rehabilitated in the opinion of his superiors, and that some of his colleagues are, in their turn, under a cloud. Some changes in this department are regarded as certain. The hospital, being freed from the presence of one-half of its inmates, is found to be sufficient for the wants of those whom the operation of the Act is likely to bring to its doors. The proposal to open the second hospital has been abandoned.

"Is it too much to ask that Government should now reconsider its precipitate action in regard to the re-introduction of the clumsy and most objectionable Act into this city? The failure which was experienced when it was first introduced, before this second *fiasco*, was signal, and the experiment had to be abandoned as entirely mischievous. It is a great mistake to suppose that a measure which may prove efficacious for a particular purpose in a cantonment, or amongst a population of limited numbers, will necessarily prove equally efficacious when brought into operation in a vast city numbering a million of inhabitants. It is a mere delusion to suppose that any system which brands those who come within its influence with an indelible stigma can succeed in bringing any considerable number of persons to submit to that stigma where such ample means of evading it exist as are found in cities such as Bombay. And the attempt to work the Contagious Diseases laws, if it be not successful, is always mischievous, not only in its moral but in its physical results. For to avoid falling into the clutches of the police, persons who would otherwise when smitten with disease seek medical relief in hospitals or dispensaries, are deterred from doing so lest, the secret of their calling being disclosed, their names should be brought upon the police books. The successful evasion of the law is found to be possible even in cities where the police are so well-organised and so ubiquitous as in Paris, Berlin, and Hamburg. The Act has now been in force since the 1st of September, and how many of the 9000 women supposed to be living a profligate life have been brought under police and medical supervision? *Not one in eighteen.* In Paris the proportion is about one in fourteen. Every expert knows that the real foci of disease are to be found amongst those who are not on the police books, and are scared away from the hospitals and the doctors by fear of a discovery which would bring them into the hands of the police. The great scandal which has already attended the attempt to work the Act in Bombay ought to cause the Government to seriously reflect upon the wisdom of continuing in the course to which the hasty resolution of Sir Richard Temple committed them."

Dr. Beatty's observations as to the better half of the population of Bombay coming upon the books is exactly paralleled by the remark of Mr. Lister before the Hong Kong Commission.

Do you suppose that when women are diseased they would remain until cured?

Certainly. Mr. Wolferstan, for four years Surgeon to the Royal Albert Hospital, Devonport, says that he never had any difficulty in keeping women who were really diseased.

Would they know when they were diseased?

They would certainly know better than any doctor could tell them; and they have a very crucial test in the fact that their paramours accuse them. A woman so accused would, under a free system, apply at once to have the doubt cleared up; and if satisfied that she was diseased, would be most thankful to be cured. She need not become an inmate of a hospital or prison for this purpose; she need not even, in many cases, be examined; the vast majority of cases are better treated as out-patients. If she had sores, their infectious character could be at once destroyed by appropriate caustics; and if she were suffering from the constitutional disease, the infectious nature of the secretions would be neutralised by injections, and the constitutional affections cured by the administration of remedies which would be far better given at home. Women badly diseased would be only too thankful for admission to hospital, and glad to avail themselves of treatment until cured. As to soldiers and sailors, simple precautions and cleanliness on their own part would suffice to protect far more certainly than any Contagious Diseases Acts. If I wanted to inoculate an unabraded surface, and the patient washed the matter off after it was applied, I should say there is no possibility of inoculating under such circumstances; and if a soldier with an abraded surface had intercourse with a woman, he would be as likely to disease her as she him.

Marriage is also a certain cure; and I don't see why a soldier should not marry as well as a policeman. Boys brought up in barracks, and accustomed to military routine from babyhood, would make the best of soldiers; and we should have an army ready to our hands without the very expensive process of manufacture. Keeping troops stationed as long as possible at one place is also an excellent means of diminishing venereal disease. Dr. Balfour says he never knew troops move without an increase of disease; in fact, if they stay long in a place they form permanent attachments, and are practically married, and so escape disease. This is the secret of the small amount of disease among the Belgian troops, owing to their having been years in one place, and so forming engagements which had the same effect as marriage.

Women are undoubtedly far better treated as out-patients. When it was suggested to Mr. J. R. Lane, an ardent supporter of the Acts, that men should be sent to hospital, he indignantly repudiated the notion, remarking (Q. 14,646, Royal Commission): " I think that would be a great evil to take all diseased men into hospital. The greater number of diseased men can be treated perfectly well as out-patients ; you would be stopping their industrial occupations if you took them in."

Now the same remark applies to women. But a very small portion of those who require treatment need be sent into hospital; a vast number could be treated at a very slight expense, and without going into hospital at all. Cases of syphilis are better treated out of doors, with plenty of fresh air and exercise.

Dr. Jago, in his evidence before the Royal Commission, says : "The moment you instil into the minds of these women that there is a penalty, remote or contingent, then you lose more than you would gain by keeping them in hospital." He adds : " By a voluntary principle you would get men and clandestines far more than any force could obtain. Twenty, thirty, or fifty women, abandoned, heartless, wretched creatures, mixed with young girls of different ages—one limit, one law—will those less degraded become more degraded, or *vice versa ?* Will the mass go up or down in moral feeling ? It will certainly go down. These women may have every virtue under heaven except chastity. Ah ! we are all sinners, and that is the way they sin. *You are going contrary to common sense, common reason, and common humanity."*

Duchatelet says that " Middle-aged or old prostitutes are far more dangerous to their own sex when past middle life than ever they were in their youth to the other ; " so that it is evident that the worst thing you can do to a woman is to make her a prostitute (by registration), and the next is to forcibly associate young girls with veterans in the profession. Now this is exactly what the Contagious Diseases Acts do, as is evidenced by the following extract from the Report of the Rescue Society :

The Society for the Rescue of Young Women and Children, 85 Cheapside, London, has been established for many years, was presided over by the late Lord Shaftesbury, and has eleven homes for the reception and reclamation of fallen women. The testimony of the officers of this society is therefore invaluable, and is entirely corroborated by the evidence of the managers of all other female reformatories in London ; indeed, these gentlemen are the authors of a pamphlet entitled "An Exposure of the False Statistics of the Contagious Diseases Acts," published by Tweedie, Strand, statistics which have been presented by the special police to Parliament in the hope of bolstering up the Acts. If the reader will turn to the Twentieth Annual Report of the Rescue Society (p. 14) he will find the following :

" 1. It is alleged that the Acts have been successful in reclaiming unfortunate women. The Committee have elsewhere dealt with the monstrous mis-statements and exaggerations put forth upon this point. It is, moreover, proved to demonstration that the success of such efforts on the part of official persons is of the smallest character. There is no need to go further in proof of this than the records of the Royal Albert Hospital at Devonport, an institution which is the citadel of the system. From 50 per cent. of the admissions of women to hospitals, under a voluntary system recommended to homes, the rate of such recommendations under the compulsory system of these Acts has dwindled down year by year to 13 per cent. The last issued Parliamentary Paper on this subject shows that, of 3748 cases of women admitted into hospital from all the districts during the year 1872 (including 264 left from the preceding year), 3020, or 80 per cent., returned at once to prostitution, while of the balance of 728, only 10 per cent. of the whole number, or 395, returned to their friends or entered homes, and 330 remained in hospital, 3 others being incurable. These recommended cases consist almost exclusively of the younger girls most recently brought under the system. Even the officials themselves seem to have awakened to the fact, so long perceived by this Society and by other observers, that the moral reformation of women who have been long subjected to the hardening influence of the examinations is almost hopeless."

There is a terrible table in the last issued Parliamentary Paper on this subject, which shows the character of permanency given to the pursuit of prostitution, and the longer persistence of women in an evil career under this system. As against 44 per cent. over twenty-one years of age of the whole number of women brought under the Acts in 1866, 75 per cent. (or nearly double) over twenty-one years of age of the whole number were found so soon after as 1872. To get hold of the younger girls the most desperate efforts, as this Committee well know, are made. *They are hunted down if there is the slightest pretext for supposing them to be unchaste, are registered, examined, and hurried into hospital, as has been over and over again proved, without adequate medical cause.* Whatever may be the justification to some minds of this course of procedure, the Committee express their solemn conviction, founded on a very close observation and much experience of the system, that in numberless cases it ensures the final moral ruin of the hapless young creatures. To thrust over the brink with rash, rude grasp a young female, whose moral fate is trembling in the balance, whose feet have perhaps from the pressure solely of penury, or from trust and affection betrayed, approached the verge of the vortex, and who may just be wishing and seeking a way of retreat from the horror seen to be impending, is an act involving a terrible responsibility. Deprived of the last remnants of self-respect, galled to madness by a forced subjection to an instrumental violation of her person, committed by officials at a shameful rendezvous, and under circumstances dreadfully humiliating to her feelings, insulted by immediate registration as a common prostitute by being placed at once on a level with the lowest, by being compelled to attend for inspection again and again at brief intervals, by being treated as one of themselves by the vilest outcasts, the girl sinks into savage recklessness and despair, and accepts the life of the streets as her doom.

Mr. Parsons, in his evidence before the Commons' Committee (Q. 252), informs us that many women were brought up to him by the police who willingly offered to take their oaths that they were modest women. Do modest women then submit rather than go before a magistrate? Yes, he replies, unquestionably. One woman he happened to know personally himself who was a respectable married woman. He also tells us (Q. 377) that the number of registered prostitutes has been doubled, owing to the police having discovered—*i.e.*, made into common prostitutes—a number of young girls who were *attempting clandestine prostitution*. There is abundant evidence to show that women are very willing to go into hospital to be treated, and the statement that they will not remain until cured is sufficiently met by Mr. Wolferstan, House Surgeon to the Royal Albert Hospital under the Acts for four years, who says (Q. 3508, Royal Commission): "My experience is that if you can convince a woman that she has contagious disease there is no difficulty whatever in *keeping her* in hospital."

Mr. Sloggett, to Percy Windham (Q. 98, Commons' Committee): "They all express their great willingness to go into hospital,"—*i.e.*, on a purely voluntary system.

(Q. 388.) To the Chairman: "The imperfections of the Acts never became apparent until after January, because a sufficient number of diseased persons were so easily found to fill the beds; there was no difficulty about it; even those who came voluntarily and asked for admission were sufficient to fill the beds."

(Q. 428.) The women come up quite willingly to be treated.

(Q. 757.) A number of soldiers being diseased, and closely following each other, having connection with them, different affections are dispersed among *them by mediate contagion*, a danger that cannot be overcome.

(Q. 3816.) He never had in his experience *bad cases of syphilis* at Devonport *before the Acts*.

(Q. 3357.) Under voluntary system, of 162 cases of syphilis, only 33 went out uncured; so that the effect must have been to have cured 114 cases of syphilis.

Under the voluntary system 41 per cent. were sent home or into reformatories; since the Acts have been in force the percentage has gone down to 19 per cent.

(Q. 3618.) Mr. Wolferstan : "You cannot always tell when a woman has constitutional syphilis—*that is a large class*, and of course cannot say whether she would be safe or not."

(Q. 3638.) The system prevents women going to be cured, for fear of being found out.

(Q. 3641.) A vaginal or uterine discharge will usually be accompanied by visible secondary symptoms, will it not ?—No, not always.

(Q. 3642.) But usually ?—*No, not usually.*

(Q. 3657.) The cases that escape detection are those of constitutional syphilis.

(Q. 3788.) Not advisable to detain the women, because the uterine discharge is incurable—may detain her any length of time and not cure it.

(Q. 6868.) Square : Women have syphilis and know nothing about it.

(Q. 6976.) The visiting surgeon found cases of secondary disease, who consulted Dr. Jago : he said, you see secondary disease has nothing to do with the visiting surgeon, they have bad eyes, &c.

Dr. Jago says : "Have no inquisition or tribunal ; let each individual come as to an ordinary hospital. Under this law you set up a barrier or policeman to frighten the woman, to tell her her liberty is endangered, and the surgeon has to deal with a patient who is an opponent."

The effect of gonorrhœa is not of the slightest importance to any government.

Dr. Jago : The proportion of cases treated in hospital under the Acts is ludicrously below the actual bulk.

Only a small proportion of women and men really ought to go into hospital. You could treat a large number of cases for very little money while they reside at their own homes.

(Q. 8584.) Mr. Littleton : I have heard the women say that they would only be too glad to go to hospital, provided they would be treated as diseased patients, and not *subjected to periodical examinations.*

(Q. 10,731.) The number who come voluntarily to hospital and admit they are diseased is a class very much on the increase.

Captain Harris (Q. 13,548), by Mr. Buxton : "Are you aware that there was, *before these Acts came into operation*, a very remarkable and rapid decrease in the amount of disease of this character ?" "No ; I am not at all aware of it, nor can I credit it."

(Q. 13,548.) "Will you allow me to ask if you have observed Dr. Balfour's returns, which show in 1862, in the six protected districts which then existed, taking Devonport, Portsmouth, Chatham with Sheerness, Shorncliffe, Woolwich, and Aldershot, 2040 men per 6000 soldiers were affected with this disease, whereas before the Acts were brought into operation in 1865, when the thing was still voluntary, the number of soldiers so afflicted, taking 6000 together, was only 1600, showing a far more rapid diminution of these diseases among the soldiers before the Acts were brought into operation than there has been subsequently?"

(Q. 14,267.) The women were only too glad to have the advantage of the Lock Hospital. And that is all that is necessary. Periodical examinations are a farce.

(Q. 14,676.) Seventy-five per cent. of the patients voluntarily stayed until cured.

(Q. 14,777.) Each of these returns shows that there are numerous prostitutes who are not registered.

(Q. 16,174.) Canon Gregory to Dr. Balfour : I am taking your own figures as to primary venereal sores; the reduction was greater in 1866 over 1865 than between any other years—namely, 29 per 1000.

| | | | | | | |
|---|---|---|---|---|---|---|
| Reduction | 1866 | . | . | . | . | . 29 per 1000 |
| „ | 1867 | . | . | . | . | . 4 per 1000 |
| „ | 1868 | . | . | . | . | . 14 per 1000 |
| „ | 1869 | . | . | . | . | · 11 per 1000 |
| „ | 1870 | . | . | . | . | . 6 per 1000 |

You see that the 29 per 1000 from 1865 to 1866 is nearly equal to all the rest put together. (Q. 16,218.) *There were no examinations when the great reduction 29 per 1000 took place.*

(Q. 16,749.) No systematic periodical examinations. No Contagious Diseases Acts really until 1869, 1870. Dr. Balfour : *I was not aware of that until you informed me.*

(Q. 16,266.) Dr. Balfour : No diminution of gonorrhœa, but a slight increase per 1000.

(Q. 16,289.) Showing steady and important diminution before the Acts were brought into play. 1860 to 1866, diminution of 706 without the Acts.

(Q. 16,606.) In slight cases of gonorrhœa a man may do his duty with perfect safety.—Armstrong, Navy.

Men on leave necessarily bring back disease. In Malta disease imported by English sailors. *A French man-of-war always causes an accession of disease.*

(Q. 17,652.) A woman affected with secondary symptoms might disease a person, and a woman may have secondary disease and yet by a *careful examination you shall not make it out upon her at all.*

(Q. 17,687.) Fortnightly examinations inefficacious.

(Q. 20,158.) Almost impossible to detect gonorrhœa in the great majority of cases. Contagion in the woman for years.

(Q. 20,227.) Impossible to say when a woman is cured of syphilis; would not be certain after two years. After disappearance of eruption she may give disease, although she seems perfectly healthy·

(Q. 20,223.) Men object to registered women.

(Q. 20,303.) As to staying in hospital, of 350 patients admitted to venereal wards, 58 only discharged themselves.

(Q. 20,332.) At Plymouth, Southampton, Woolwich, Chatham, Dover, has met considerable number of clandestines.

(Qs. 1500–1519.) Sixty women requested to go into hospital on purely voluntary system; only two refused.

(Q. 386.) Dr. Wilks: One might have constitutional syphilis which would pass unnoticed unless carefully looked for, and yet give the disease. Disease almost unknown in the coastguard ships, owing to the men being allowed to marry.

(Q. 1873, Venereal Commission.) Women go on infecting men long after the period of primary affection ceases, and after all trace of constitutional disease has passed away.

(Q. 1876.) By far the greatest proportion of men are infected by women in secondary stage, which so often cannot be detected.

(Q. 2427.) Dr. Barclay: The old soldiers kept women, and, of course, escaped disease.

(Q. 897.) Dr. Dodson attributes the immunity of the natives to the fact that they are allowed to marry.

Mr. Whitbread's Committee of 1862 ascertained from the police and local authorities that, if voluntary hospitals were set up, the badly diseased women would gladly go into them. Whitbread's Speech in Discussion in the House of Commons, 1876. *Medical Enquirer*, p. 109, vol. ii.

Mr. Whitbread says: " The voluntary system was tried, but it had a most unfair trial—one small ward only at each of three stations, and it was tried for a short time only. The fact was, that it was starved in point of accommodation, and it was voted a failure upon the very smallest evidence that could be brought against it, without an attempt to find a remedy for the weak points discovered in it. It was tried at Devonport with twenty-five beds, and the contribution to the ward containing them was only paid on the quarterly certificate of the Commander-in-Chief, who was the Admiralty visitor, that the beds had been fully occupied during the quarter; but the moment coercion was put in force they had four times the accommodation. Was that a fair trial ? No one could deny that the wards opened on the voluntary system were filled, but it was charged against them that the patients went out before they were cured, and that they did not go in soon enough; and now the great stamping-out theory came in. The voluntary system had been voted a failure, but the solid fact remained that the voluntary wards were popular and full. Women were induced to enter the voluntary wards who could not have been forced by a coercive system."

" Under the voluntary system women came in ; no questions were asked ; they were cured and went out ; and no one was able to point at them in their future life. Now they cannot come in without having *their names placed upon the register ;* the result was that many women were kept out who, under the voluntary system, would have been brought in. (If they had wanted to keep them out they could not have adopted a better scheme.) As to the women leaving before being cured, that could have been met."

The relation between the police and brothels is one of co-operation. Alluding to this point Mr. Kingsford Bannister, in his able analysis of the evidence taken before the Royal Commission, remarks: "There is no reason to doubt that the public would afford adequate support by voluntary contributions, if a proper appeal were made for that purpose. If Government aid were necessary, it would be more justifiable to give it for the general relief of venereal disease than to give it, as is done under the Acts, for the exclusive relief of registered prostitutes. A horror of going into the workhouse does not mean an objection to go into hospital."

Mr. Lane, speaking of the London Lock Hospital, says: " There are about thirty beds for females on the voluntary side. They have been always filled, and double the number or more could be filled readily ; a great many applicants are dismissed for want of room every week. The worst cases are selected for admission."

The fact that women at voluntary hospitals are badly diseased proves only the eager competition for admission and the insufficiency of accommodation provided. Mr. Acton in his work (p. 247) shows that it is successful severity that obtains admission, and that, in order to secure this, the women render themselves as bad as possible on purpose.

In the subjected districts many prostitutes do all they can to avoid being sent to hospital, although they know they are diseased ; but that is only because they are not bad enough to require confinement, or because the hospital is a prison—a penal institution.

Before the Venereal Commission there is evidence that, under the voluntary system at Devonport, tried from December 3, 1863, till March 31, 1865, all the beds provided were kept full. Voluntary hospitals in London, Bristol, and Liverpool have proved an entire success—(Qs. 11,747-9, 12,934, 18,163, Royal Commission)—and generally, that prostitutes, when diseased, are most anxious to obtain medical treatment. Perverse and reckless women, who will not go into hospitals, are just as difficult to manage under a compulsory system as a voluntary one. If any disadvantage could be proved against the voluntary system, as not bringing women under prompt treatment, it is more than counterbalanced by the fact that voluntary hospitals would secure the clandestines as well as the men, and thus do more to diminish disease.

Mr. Kingsford continues : Dr. Deas, in his evidence before the Venereal Committee, stated that voluntary patients would leave hospitals on occurrence of any fresh excitement, &c.; but Dr. Deas is there speaking, not of voluntary hospitals, but of twelve beds at Portsmouth, provided under the Act of 1864, and filled by the compulsory process of that Act, detention being left to the discretion of the hospital authorities. Apart from the general statement of opinion on this point, we have two facts in support of the necessity for compulsory detention—viz., that under the voluntary system at Devonport, from December 3, 1863, to March 31, 1865, "forty-eight syphilitic patients and twenty cases of gonorrhœa were discharged uncured at their own request;" and that from the voluntary side of the London Lock Hospital, between 23 and 25 per cent. of the patients are self-discharged. But against the 68 who were discharged uncured are to be set 214 patients who remained in the Devonport Hospital till their cure was complete, 114 of whom were syphilitic patients. There is no proof whatever, in either instances, that the women discharged uncured were prostitutes, or, if prostitutes, that they practised prostitution while in a state of disease. Thirty per cent. of the women treated in voluntary hospitals are not prostitutes, but married and other women who probably have children, or are engaged in employments making it necessary for them to leave hospital after a certain stay there. And of the prostitutes who left uncured, some may have done so with the intention of reforming, returning to their friends, going to refuges, continuing medical treatment at their own home, &c., or, at any rate, without any purpose of continuing prostitution while diseased. No doubt it is a fact that a certain percentage (say, making deductions above suggested, 8 to 10 per cent.) did return to prostitution; but this, in the face of the facts that a chief proportion of the patients were cured, and that all were treated for some time, by no means proves that the voluntary system was useless or a failure, unless the only purpose of that system be taken to be, not the cure of disease and the relief of suffering, but the provision of clean prostitutes.

There seems no reason to doubt that, by proper management, the number of patients leaving uncured might be reduced to a minimum. It is not surely impossible, where the hospital is in a proper position and subject to proper regulations, to prevent the inmates from knowing of the arrival of regiments and ships, and of those other attractions which are said to affect them so much. A little tact in relieving the monotony of hospital, kindly influences and persuasion, and voluntary promises on admission to remain till cured, would all have their effect. At St. Bartholomew's Hospital, in London, there were, in the years 1868 and 1869 respectively, 350 and 373 women admitted to the venereal ward. The number self-discharged was 55 and 61, and of these a considerable proportion were married women, who returned to their families, while others went away to employment or returned to their friends. A small voluntary hospital was established by two benevolent ladies at Bristol some years ago: of 60 patients treated, *only two left uncured*, and one of these two had some good reason for leaving.   In a similar hospital at Liverpool, a promise, given on admission, to remain till cured, has been found effectual.

One may add, as an argument from analogy, that, in homes and refuges, compulsion, other than that induced by kindness on one side and gratitude on the other, is not needed to detain these women, though the period of detention is considerable, the regulations often strict, and temptations to leave strong.

Further, the alleged necessity of coercion in getting prostitutes into hospital and detaining them there rests very much on the *assumption, altogether fallacious*, that there is a general tendency among prostitutes to continue to practise prostitution while diseased. Now every motive of self-interest, operating on the brothel-keeper and the prostitute, is opposed to such a tendency.   The truth seems to be that the tendency exists only in the poorest and lowest class of prostitutes, because compelled by want to continue their course of life ; and that the tendency in this class, except in merely exceptional instances, is altogether removed when the provision of free and adequate hospital accommodation takes away the cause of that tendency.   It is just the poor and wretched class, whose life has few attractions, which is most ready to go into and remain in hospital.

The certified hospital only treats registered prostitutes ; no other person affected with venereal disease can obtain admission.   There is no authority in the Acts to justify the admission to hospital of any woman except such as are found diseased on examination by the visiting surgeon ; no other person could have the expense of her treatment charged on the Contagious Diseases Act Fund ; and no authority to detain her unless on the certificate of the visiting surgeon.   Thirty per cent., one-third of the women who obtain treatment for venereal disease in the London Lock Hospitals, are not prostitutes ; so that the certified hospitals shut the door to one-third of the patients who require treatment.

The Albert Hospital, Devonport, cost for building £15,000,—that does not include the land ; and for hospital charges alone £4000 is required every year.   Mr. Kingsford says : "What must be the lesson to the individual and the public, of a system which refuses aid to an honest woman suffering from no fault of her own, but accords help readily to a diseased prostitute, simply because she is a prostitute ?   If a prostitute infects a man, the man is always a consenting party to the risk ; but it is only a man who can communicate disease to an innocent person—his wife or child.   Voluntary hospitals would treat venereal disease among all classes without distinction of character or sex, and would thus reach a far larger area of disease than any compulsory system can possibly do."

With regard to innocent sufferers, married women infected by their husbands, and children through their parents, it is only voluntary hospitals that could afford treatment to the married women or the children, or afford prompt relief to the husband or father himself.

It is not justifiable to keep a woman in hospital on the ground that she is suffering from disease, because no one knows whether she is or is not; it is a matter of mere doubtful medical opinion; certain forms of disease, such as uterine leucorrhœa, mistaken for venereal disease, are incurable; so that it is utterly useless to detain them, and yet they may infect their paramours.

On this point M. Mauriac, a celebrated Parisian physician and specialist in syphilis, says:

> "Si vous pensez que la santé publique est une loi supreme et qu'il faut employer touts les moyens pour le sauvegarder frapper l'homme et la femme vous exigez des garanties pour la santé des hommes, et quelles sont celles que vous donnez aux femmes. Aucune, les mesures de police sont un legs de la barbarie du moyen age—vous infectez et vous ne voulez pas etre infectés.
>
> "Qu'on organise contre la prostitution touts les systèmes, de defense, d'assanissement et de securité que suggeresent l'hygiène et la medicine, Rien de mieux mais qu'en renonce aux mesures contre la femme seule. Inscrivez aussi les hommes, c'est impossible, alors n'inscrivez personne voilà la justice."

Here are a few instances of what is constantly going on wherever such Acts are in force; they will be found with full details in M. Yves Guyot's (ex-Ministre d'Etat) well-known work on Prostitution. A young girl who had been on the register was desirous of abandoning that mode of life; she procured lodgings, got work, and was doing very well; one day she saw two of these ignoble *agents de mœurs* prowling about her dwelling; they had discovered that she was attempting to lead a respectable life, and meant to stop it. One commenced to ascend the stairs, when, mad with despair, she threw herself from the window, fell on to a glass roof, broke both legs and was literally cut to pieces. "Send for a cab," said some one. "Oh, it is not worth while," said the man below, "she is going to burst up; *elle va crever.*" She died next day, raving about the *police de mœurs.*

A poor workwoman in lodgings was watching her sick child. Suddenly it struck her that it might die. It was late at night, but she must, at all risks, procure a doctor. She was no sooner in the street than she was seized by an *agent de mœurs.* "Let me go," she cried, "my child is dying." "Oh, we know all about that!" and he dragged her off to St. Lazare. Here she was shut up with a number of women supposed to be attempting clandestine prostitution. She screamed, begged, implored, entreated; and as she would not be quiet, was shut up in a padded room reserved for such cases. Here she went mad, and became so violent that she was sent to the Salpetrière (the Paris hospital for the insane), where she died three weeks later. The child succumbed a few hours after her mother had left her.

Towards the close of September a young girl of twenty was seen talking to a young man of her own age, and both were seated upon a bench in the public promenade of Paris; they were talking, nothing more, when a *sous-brigadier* of police and a morals agent who were passing took them both into custody. The commissioner of police, seeing nothing to justify their arrest, set them free. The sequel is given in the words of the editor of an influential Parisian journal: "What do you think the modest *sous-brigadier* did? his sole apology was to gravely take down the name and address of the young girl, and on dismissing her to say, 'If the inquiries we are about to make respecting you are not satisfactory I shall have you registered and taken to the examination house.' Knowing how utterly without protection women are where such a system prevails, terrified by the threat, timid by nature, and half frantic at the idea of possible dishonour to herself and friends, this young girl left her workshop at an early hour next day and drowned herself in the canal." The editor of the *Evenement* continues: "Nevertheless, examples of such mistakes are by no means rare; *indeed, they abound*."

Madame de Grandpré, the well-known philanthropist, tells us that these police agents force their way into poor workgirls' apartments. "How much are you earning?" The poor child shows a few francs. "That's not enough: you must be a prostitute; show your hands." No needle-marks! "But I am a florist, a burnisher, or work in a printing-office." "No matter. I must have you on the register and examined."

The shocking condition to which society is reduced by this detestable system is also well illustrated by the occurrences at Lille which led to a celebrated trial for murder. Here a number of ruffians, by only pretending to be policemen employed under these Acts, outraged girls and respectable females with impunity. One of the band confessed that 500 women had thus passed through his hands in the course of five years. "Where wrong is legalised all must suffer." Madame Daubié, in her well-known work "La Femme Pauvre au Dix Neuvième Siècle, says that no young woman of the middle class dare venture a single step without a protector in Paris, a system which permits any dissolute ruffian to frighten a girl out of her senses by the common threat, "Je te ferai mettre en carte." In Berlin women belonging to the industrial classes notoriously dare not walk out unprotected, as the Berlin special correspondent of the *Daily Telegraph* remarks.

"*Hosts of women* walking quietly along the streets of this city are apprehended every day and night by policemen in plain clothes, even if they be as chaste as Diana herself. This," he adds, "is particularly hard upon tradesmen's wives and young women in employment, who may wish to visit churches, theatres, or concerts on foot in order to avoid the expense of cab hire."

Marie L——, who was left a few minutes on the boulevard in Paris by her *fiancé*, was dragged off, subjected to the surgical outrage, and imprisoned for days by two *agents de mœurs*. She was a virgin, and the shock ultimately killed her. Remarking on this case, the *Marseillaise,* a Paris journal, says, "Who killed her? The agents of morals! We will no longer endure this police inquisition which slaughters women. If this is your civilisation it is the civilisation of assassins." Here are a few newspaper extracts:

At Lyons a girl of about twenty named Melanie M—— was accosted at the railway station of Perrache by an agent of the police dressed in plain clothes, when she had just joined company with a traveller. At a sign from the agent two guardians of the peace came up, laid hold of the girl M——, and, in spite of her vehement resistance, dragged her towards the police station. A terrible scene ensued. The unhappy girl, struggling desperately, threw herself on the ground and tried to kill herself by dashing her forehead upon the pavement. The agents pulled at her in all directions with extraordinary violence. An hotel omnibus was coming along; the driver could not stop his horses in time, and the wheels rolled over and crushed the girl's feet. A crowd formed: many persons honourably known in the quarter, moved by a feeling of charity and pity, wished to interpose. They requested the agents to leave the injured girl at the Hôtel de l'Univers, where they might come for her next day. As to the expenses, they offered to pay them. The agents refused, and succeeded in dragging the poor girl to the poste of the tobacco manufactory; the girl, notwithstanding her cruel sufferings, struggling more than ever. A surgeon demanded her removal to the Hôtel Dieu. A cab passing by, she was thrown into it; one of the agents placed himself by her side, the other got up in front. Coming to the Quai de la Charité, the girl suddenly opened the door and threw herself into the Rhône, where she was drowned. Her dead body was found two days afterwards. This occurrence took place on Friday, September 1. The Monday following, towards seven o'clock in the morning, an agent of the *service des mœurs* presented himself at the Hôtel Duguesclin and proceeded to arrest another girl named Marie Dans. Seized with terror, the girl Dans opened her window on the second floor and threw herself into the courtyard. She was taken up in a most deplorable condition. At the end of the same week—Saturday, September 9—a girl named R——, who was one of those subjected to the Acts, tried to commit

suicide at the Hôtel de Police of the Rue Luizerne.   Not succeeding
in strangling herself with her apron-string, she stuck herself several
times with a knife.   Happily the weapon which she had seized had a
round blade, and the wounds inflicted were not deep.   In this
condition she was taken to the Prison de Saint Joseph.   "Evidently,"
says M. Yves Guyot, "the treatment which girls undergo at the
hands of the police, which incarcerates them and then enrols them
in the number of registered prostitutes, is such that these poor
creatures prefer death to the existence which the police prepares for
them."

Oh ! but it is different here ; such things could not happen with
respectable English policemen, or anywhere under the protection of
the British flag.—Why not ?  Like causes will produce the same
effects all the world over ; nor need we feel surprised that Englishwomen in their wretchedness and despair should seek relief even in
death from the cruel persistence of their police tormentors.   A girl
of twenty, named Brown, drowned herself from this cause at Plymouth in July 1874, after a previous attempt to cut her throat.
Another girl named House committed suicide by throwing herself
from the window of the Royal Albert Hospital, Devonport ; and
another named Mulcarty drowned herself at Millbay in April 1873 ;
and in 1876 Mrs. Percy, an actress of repute, rather than submit to
the surgical outrage with which she was threatened, drowned herself in the canal at Aldershot.   Her daughter, who was similarly
threatened, was rescued and taken away by a benevolent lady ; and
it is well known (the case was brought before the House of Commons)
that two of these men chased a poor girl till she threw herself into
the Granville Dock, when they left her to drown.   It is also well
known that a superintendent of police, an Englishman, specially
selected by the British Government to carry out the Contagious
Diseases Acts at Hong Kong, broke into a private house in the dead
of the night in the hope of discovering something, and drove two
girls who were sleeping together almost frantic with fright, so that
they escaped from the window on to the housetops.   One girl fell
and was killed ; but no matter, Mr. Inspector continued his chase till
the other fell and was also killed.   At the inquest it transpired that
three weeks previously the same man had broken another woman's
leg in a similar way.   Surgeon-Major Curran tells us that it was
necessary to put gratings over the cesspools in India in order to
prevent the girls from throwing themselves into them ; and I have
already quoted evidence to show that thousands of girls were driven
from their homes in the Indian towns where the Acts were in force,
preferring starvation and even death to submission to the outrages
which the police were determined to force upon them.

And now, in spite of repeal and admitted failure from a sanitary
point of view of the Acts, especially in India, we are to have the Acts

again in India under some so-called cantonment regulation, and the pro-Act party are endeavouring even now to create a panic with a view to a similar infliction upon the people of England. I wonder if it will ever occur to these gentlemen that they are altogether wrong; that they cannot possibly have any right to hunt women about, drive them to despair, and periodically to violate them by the score or hundred with a speculum, for no reason on earth except to see if they are fit for fornication. The idea is monstrous! the blunder complete! and the whole business as illegal as murder, rape, or any other crime! I am told that the woman has been guilty of prostitution. Perhaps!—perhaps not! It is well known that some of the women examined in Paris and elsewhere are virgins. Moreover, the only evidence, if any evidence is adduced, is that of a spy paid to accuse, and he only has to say that he thinks something —such testimony as has never been accepted before by any tribunal except the Spanish Inquisition. Besides, if the woman has committed an act of prostitution, as it is called, what of it? Prostitution is not a crime! When Mr. Ayston, M.P., proposed in the House of Commons to make it a crime he could not find a seconder, and before you can lay a finger on any woman on the ground that she is a prostitute you must make prostitution a crime. You must prove, and to *the satisfaction of a jury* (for no more serious charge could be brought against any woman), that she has committed that crime, and as the offence can only be carried out by twos, you must treat both sexes alike. Even then, to examine a woman with the speculum against her will is, as the late Professor Francis Newman has remarked, " an indefensible atrocity, an intrinsic wickedness, an outrage that nothing human ought to submit to."

As to the re-introduction of the Acts in India, it was not possible for the Government to make a greater mistake; there could not be any more formidable bar to successful colonisation anywhere. Nothing makes an invading army so hated, so detested, so execrated by the natives as this seizing upon and violating of their women. Anybody can understand that if the British flag is to carry freedom with it, if the natives under that ensign are to become their own masters, as we boast, and get justice for the asking, then we must decide at once and for ever never again to carry this equally foul and silly despotism in our train. As I have already pointed out, the Acts have failed in India as they have failed in England, and for precisely the same reasons that they have failed in every known clime and age, to attain the end in view. They have more than failed. They have degraded the whole nation by enslaving women. They have imperilled the public health by offering men inducements to go astray and a guarantee which is false. They have subjected women who have committed no crime, who are not even suspected of any legal offence, and who are absolutely free from disease,[1] repeatedly to the most indecent and humiliating outrage that it is possible for a man to perpetrate upon a woman, and as a net result they have aggravated every evil, both physical and moral. Let us thank God, therefore, that from a sanitary point of view these Acts have failed and must inevitably fail, for a more cruel and cowardly attack upon the constitution, upon liberty, justice, and the sacred rights of the individual, has never been perpetrated in the name of law since the world began.

## APPENDIX.

M. LE DR. ALFRED FOURNIER, Professor à la Faculté de Médicine de Paris, Ricord's successor and Physician to l'Hôpital St. Louis, has recently (November 1899, shortly after the Brussels Congress, which he attended) formulated his views as to the prophylaxis of syphilis in a paper which he has presented to the Academie of Medicine of Paris.[2] He says, the best of all methods of preventing syphilis is by the inculcation of moral and religious principles, in other words, as M. Ricord has remarked, "the only way" to escape syphilis is to avoid the risk of catching it; syphilis does not fall down from heaven, and no man need inoculate himself unless he deliberately chooses.

As to the actual system of the *Police de Mœurs* in Paris—a system which we are asked to copy in England—M. Fournier, and no higher authority can be quoted, declares that it is "insuffisante, impuissante et caduque"—insufficient, powerless, and rotten to the core. This is, he says, owing to the fact, on which I have laid stress, that the police can only bring under control a few women (two or three thousand), while six, eight, and ten times as many escape control and spread syphilis among the population of Paris; the police, he says, do the little they can, and we must thank them, but it is impossible for them to check the spread of venereal disease. "Elle est impuissante à endiguer le flot debordant des contaminations vénériennes."

M. Fournier adds, little as the police have done, they will do still less in the future, and for the following reasons:

(1) Because the licensed brothels are steadily and inevitably diminishing in number; women cannot, much as the police try, be driven into them and kept there prisoners.

(2) Because of the immense increase of clandestine prostitution, which is constantly increasing.

(3) Because of the strong public feeling which is opposed to the

[1] Five hundred thousand of these examinations were perpetrated during the régime of the Contagious Diseases Acts in England upon women pronounced perfectly healthy.

[2] *Bulletin de l'Academie de Médicine*, No. 39 ; Séance du Nov. 14, 1899, p. 475.

arbitrary action of the police (upwards of 20,000 women are arrested every year in Paris, outside of all legal forms, and may be detained from a few weeks to a year) ; and

(4) Because of the demonstrated *impuissance* of the system to prevent syphilis or diminish venereal diseases, in proof of which M. Fournier says we have syphilis with us now as we have always had it :

"A-t-elle par exemple jamais diminué de frequence depuis une quarantaine d'années que j'en en fait l'objet de mes etudes speciales ? Impossible a moi de le croire d'apres ce que j'ai vu de mes yeux vu ! A-t-elle au contraire augmenté de frequence ? Je le crois fermement "—

an impression which is shared by M. Fournier's colleagues, who have unanimously declared : "Des syphilis on en voit aujour-d'hui partout *et plus que jamais.*"

M. Fournier adds, syphilis is flourishing in Paris to-day, it abounds and surabounds, the special hospitals are not large enough for the numerous cases which overflow into the general hospitals ; all this, he adds, shows how impotent are the *Police de Mœurs* so far as the repression of syphilis (the only venereal disease of any consequence) is concerned ; he adds : "Telle est en effet la stricte verité des choses." All this is evidently *the direct result* of the system we are asked to introduce into England. With what object ? To stamp out syphilis.

Is it not too ridiculous ?

If the inhabitants of Paris are so badly off with their system, would they not be worse off without it ? They could not be worse off, no doubt, if a voluntary system of hospital treatment was substituted ; they would be better. Anyway, as I have already pointed out, syphilis has been falling off in England without any regulation with each succeeding decade, till we can hardly recognise the disease described by our forefathers. Was not M. Fournier formerly a great supporter of the French system ? He was ! hence his testimony is the more valuable !

# EXILES IN ENGLAND AND THE WAR IN SOUTH AFRICA.

In this country, as well as abroad, Professor Vambéry enjoys a well-merited reputation as one who has largely contributed to our knowledge of Central Asia by his travels and adventures in regions little known until he went there in the disguise of a dervish. By his learned works on Eastern languages he ranks high as an Orientalist scholar. Through his lectures in England and his letters to the Press he has often given timely warning as to Russian designs in regard to India and Constantinople. Having personally met him years ago, I need not say how highly I esteem him and his widely ranging activity.

In the *Humanitarian* of December he had an essay: "The Origin and Cause of my English Sympathies," which certainly contains a great deal that is worth pondering upon. At the same time its conclusion might easily give rise to the opinion that it was the duty of all friends of progress, as well as of those who dwell as exiles on English soil, to take the side of England—in other words, of any Government which may temporarily be in power here—in whatever wars of conquest she may embark upon; nay, strictly speaking, in any dealings of hers with a foreign Power.

Lest I should unwittingly do wrong to the distinguished author, I will quote in full his concluding sentences. He says:

"Perfection is very rare in human doings, and the English, too, are labouring under many mistakes in their administrative policy in Asia, but in spite of that, no nation in the world is equal to them with regard to the salutary results produced hitherto in the different parts of the globe. The ground conquered by the British flag is indiscriminately an open field for the trade, industry, and cultural aspirations of the French, Russians, and Germans. Only intentional blindness fails to see and to acknowledge this state of things. Is it not sad and afflicting to find that most of the foreign countries, instead of hailing with joy the propagation of our culture in savage and barbarian regions, produced by the daring spirit of British manliness and courage, are not only constantly cavilling and condemning its enterprise, but they rejoice in the reverse and mishap of the English pioneer of civilisation? Lurid jealousy and naked envy is continually blinding the eyes of England's rivals, and the nations of Europe utterly forget the great loss and detriment which might accrue to themselves, through any eventual weakening of the country whose Liberal constitution has always served as a shining pattern to their own Liberal aspirations, and whose shores were greeted as the safest harbours of refuge to those who had to fly before the tyranny of their own government. Where will the future Kossuths, Louis Blancs, Karl Blinds, Stepniaks, Midhat Pashas, and many other martyrs of liberty find a shelter, if the power and might of Great Britain will be weakened."

I do not know whether I rightly appreciate the drift of these remarks. But as all this is said without any restriction whatever, I cannot but think that the mass of the readers will understand it as meaning that, lest the power and might of England should be weakened, we are always bound to go with her—even when her Government is manifestly in the wrong, and when, in our view, England's own best interests are injured by the mistaken or reprehensible action of men who happen to be at the helm. A moment's reflection will show that this would be an impossible attitude for real freemen and true friends of this country.

For the sake of that liberty of the Press and of public speech, which has hitherto been the pride of the English people, a different bearing undoubtedly recommends itself. Unfortunately, recent occurrences have shown but too plainly how much damage that liberty has already suffered. I have been present on Trafalgar Square when sheer violence, manifestly organised by a party which has provoked the present deplorable war, crushed any utterance of warning voices. Since then, one editor after the other, who simply adhered to the lines once laid down by the Colonial Secretary himself, has been removed from his position, or compelled to write against his own conviction lest he should lose his means of livelihood. We know the capitalist agencies that brought about this terrorism. These are truly most evil fruits of alleged " civilising," or humanitarian, tendencies on English soil itself.

Perhaps I may here quote what a well-known French lady writer —whose name frequently figures in a Paris paper which is the organ of the Humanitarian movement there—said to me in regard to this terroristic treatment of the Press. " Yes," she remarked, in reference to some recent vulgar outbreaks in French papers, " it is quite true that we have a great deal of license in our Press; but we have, at any rate, also freedom of the Press. English journals, as a rule, do not indulge in such license. But where is the freedom of the English Press now, when men who wish to serve the cause of truth and justice can thus be ousted one after the other?"

There is a better England and there is a worse one. It was not the better England which tried to promote the dismemberment of the great American Republic by helping the Slaveholders' Rebellion; for which criminal act this country had afterwards to pay a heavy sum of indemnification to the United States. How much quicker might that frightful war, which cost so many human lives and made hundreds of thousands of widows and orphans, have been ended, had the then governing classes of England not acted contrary to the laws of civilisation and of neutrality!

Shall I mention that when the German people of Schleswig-Holstein, having natural right and even ancient Treaty law on their side, wanted to be freed from foreign dominion, Palmerston, Russell, and Gladstone sought to form an alliance defensive and offensive with Napoleon III. for the purpose of making war upon Germany? The offer was spurned because the Man of December had, just before, experienced a rebuff from, and felt a grudge against, England in the matter of the Polish insurrection. Had he accepted the English proposal, what a world-conflagration would have been lighted up—with the armies of all Germany, to which Austria then still belonged, being in the field! How would the small English army have fared in such an unrighteous war? Yet, fifteen years afterwards, Mr. Gladstone still boasted of having been one of those in the Cabinet who had proposed such a war against the whole German nation which had set its heart on the deliverance of its brethren in the North.

What a spectacle for humanity would it have been if Palmerston, Russell, and Gladstone had had their way! Queen Victoria, to her honour be it said, is supposed to have in this Schleswig-Holstein case, as in the case of the American Union war, expressed her disapproval of the fatal policy of the then leading English statesmen.

Again, was the Government of Mr. Gladstone right when suddenly bombarding Alexandria, even without a declaration of war, whilst Arabi Pasha and those who acted with him nobly sought to reform Egypt? John Bright denounced that bombardment as a gross "violation of international and moral law." He thereupon left the Cabinet, in which an "inner ring" had, unknown to him, resolved upon this lawless attack.

Arabi Pashi had not only the Mohammedan population of Egypt on his side, but also the full support of the Christian, Coptic, and Jewish communities, whose recognised heads and notabilities stood forth for him in manifestoes under their signatures. Yet "England," or rather Mr. Gladstone—whose hatred of the adherents of Islam was such that he could not brook the idea of a Mohammedan people reforming itself from within—suddenly and arbitrarily smashed the germ of better popular government in Egypt by shot and shell. That was an act which Professor Vambéry, I believe, cannot but reprove.

Having been a member of the London Egyptian Committee, I recollect but too well how near the danger even was of Arabi Pasha

being disposed of, I would say murdered, by court-martial bullets.
Our Committee exerted itself for saving his life.    But to this day
that Egyptian Reformer is living as a deported captive exile in
Ceylon, after a lapse of eighteen years !   Is this in accordance with
true English notions of liberty, humanity, and civilisation ?

As a member of the London Transvaal Committee of 1881, I have
felt it a duty to join in the protest against the lawless annexation of
the South African Republic.    It was by Mr. Disraeli that unjust
deed was done when the Boers were harassed by war with the savage
natives.    I hold that the best interests of England suffered from
that high-handed act; the Dutch population at the Cape being
deeply offended by the wrong inflicted upon their kinsmen.

Again the same injustice has been committed of late.    I believe
the harm thus done to England herself to be truly incalculable,
whatever issue the present war may have.    Mr. Chamberlain himself
has foretold it; and there is only too much ground to fear that his
prediction will come true in every sense.

Morally, politically, and from the military point of view, England
has already gone down sadly in the estimation of the world.    The
consequences will, I fear, show themselves in course of time.
People in this country, though they have grown anxious indeed, do
not, perhaps, fully realise yet the enormous damage wrought, seeing
that the war takes place in a distant land, and that it is apparently
so easy to shout defiance from behind a sea-wall at home.    But the
watchful and friendly observer whose power of judgment is not
restricted by insular notions, experiences an uncomfortable presenti-
ment as to the ultimate result and the coming mischief.    Albeit it
may travel with a seemingly limping foot, it is sure to arrive.

I have referred to Mr. Chamberlain's own prophecy as to this
immoral and unwise war.    Now, is it to be expected that men who
conscientiously held, and still hold, the same principles and opinions
as Mr. Chamberlain expressed in 1895, should turn their backs upon
themselves because a man in power, from motives that I will not
enter upon here, suddenly threw his own views to the winds?

Have not even prominent Tories, like Sir Edward Clarke, as well
as Liberal leaders, like Sir William Harcourt, acknowledged the utter
baselessness of that claim of "suzerainty" which was formally
abolished in 1884, but which yet has been continually held as a
threat over the South African Republic during the negociations
which preceded this war ?    Can any one doubt that this claim was
put forward for the very purpose of making a peaceful settlement
impossible and so provoking war ?

The party which, with a light heart, worked for this war, thinking
that there would be an easy "promenade to Pretoria," is the same
which, in trade matters, aims at a protectionist policy of the English

World-Empire—in other words, at a lock-out of foreign competition in an immense territory which already comprises a sixth part of the inhabitable globe. The idea that the ground conquered by the British flag should be "indiscriminately an open field for the trade and industry" of the whole world, is not one which that annexationist party relishes. Now, here, again, a danger arises lest the continued increase of an already enormous extent of territory should lead to conflicts with foreign Powers, which could only be met—and even then met with but doubtful results—by utterly changing English institutions in the sense of the most complete Militarism. Yet that is a change which the mass of Englishmen look upon with the greatest aversion !

The best foreign friends of England, men who have often supported her cause under great difficulties, saw with regret, of late, the rapid growth of a domineering spirit, which found signal expression in the famous "Abracadabra" speech of Mr. Chamberlain. They who had frequently enough pointed to England as a land of free, representative government, were unpleasantly struck by this aggressive note of disregard of all treaty-faith and of common respect for other people's rights. Knowing how little prepared England was in a military sense, some of them had a strong misgiving of that which is happening now. I may claim to have done so, as shown by numerous writings both on this and on the other side of the Atlantic.

Need I say that I have always wished for the friendliest relations between England, the United States, and Germany ? For that very reason I regard it as necessary to protest against a haughty spirit which is apt to throw this country into conflicts and perils that may some day culminate in a fearful catastrophe.

There are cases when the most sensible friends of England, those who wish to see her Indian Empire strongly protected against Russian designs, feel bound to warn against penetrating into "savage and barbarian regions," such as the Chitral territory. Not from jealousy and envy, but from a belief that India would be more secure if the tribes of that region were left for the present undisturbed, have even some foreign writers declared that the unfortunate campaign made in that direction was a grave mistake. They thought the independence of those tribes would form a belt and bulwark of India, whilst an attack upon them might serve the aims and objects of the military and bureaucratic caste of St. Petersburg. Or was that campaign not an ill-advised one ?

English statesmen cannot, certainly, be said to have always correctly judged in such matters, and real well-wishers of this country, even if they are foreigners, must be allowed to have their say on the subject. Professor Vambéry will, no doubt, agree to that. I remember a long conversation I once had with **Mr. Disraeli** at the House of Commons. It was before the last Russo-Turkish war. Having said that Russia incessantly pursued her twofold aim of breaking down Turkey and coming nearer and nearer to India, the Tory statesman exclaimed:

"The Russians have now enough on their hands in Central Asia. And, after all, I do not think there is any cause for complaint or alarm in that direction."

From Mr. Disraeli's well-known views on Central Asian affairs, I was quite prepared for that remark, and I answered:

"You will pardon me when I say that I have never been able to understand how quietly England, upon the whole, nay, with what surprising assent, not a few men here have regarded this pushing forward of Russia through Independent Tatary. After all, her final aim is India. . . . . I believe Russian autocracy will never rest, as long as it has great power, until England has been brought down from the pinnacle of her greatness. Russia knows of what value India is for the commercial prosperity of this country; a prosperity in which the working classes of the English towns are deeply interested. Hence the Russian Government will always aim at coming nearer and nearer to India, by first pushing in the outer bulwarks such as Turkestan, Turkey, and Persia. When that work is done, she will try to bring about the final catastrophe and convulsion."

Soon after this conversation there came the Russian war against Turkey. Since then the Czar's frontier has been pushed up to, nay, into, Afghanistan. And now we are ironically informed that, by way of simple experiment, on account of certain false rumours, Russian troops have been transported from Tiflis to Kushk, when it was found that, "in case of an emergency," an army could be transported there in eight days!

Considering all this, is there not good ground to say that the truest foreign friends of England have sometimes ample reason for not following, through thick and thin, the policy, or the astounding occasional tergiversations, of some statesman who turns his back upon himself, and leads his country into a Slough of Despond?

The fact of an exile having found safety on English soil does not destroy his right, or even his duty, to act in accordance with the principles for which once he fought, and for which he was proscribed. Rather than give up this right, an exile, true to his convictions, would have gone to the Scandinavian high North as a place of refuge, or to the southernmost islands of the globe. England, be it not forgotten, is an asylum for the vanquished of all political parties abroad. When in 1848 Louis Bonaparte, the Imperial Pretender, still dwelt here, there came, in rapid succession, Louis Philippe, the Prince of Prussia (the later King-Emperor), Louis Blanc, and many others as refugees to London. Later on, there arrived Italian, German, Hungarian, and French democratic exiles after the December state-stroke of 1851 and the Paris Commune rising of 1871.

So also Polish refugees after 1864, and, in more recent times,
Russian ones.   Despots, Constitutionalists, Republicans, and
Socialists stepped on the English shore as political shipwrecked.
Who knows from what camp the next batch may come?  It is not
for the champions of freedom alone that the shores of England are
open.

But those who struggled in the cause of popular rights abroad
are the very men who, from love of the liberty and of the welfare of
England, are bound to raise their voices when they see injustice done,
and harm wrought to her renown and her welfare.   It is in this
spirit of true friendship that I have written these lines, fully feeling,
as I do, the grave perils ahead for this country—perils frivolously
brought about by men who have shown little foresight in regard to a
struggle the inevitable consequences and the future increased cost in
blood and treasure of which may yet send a shudder through all
mankind.

KARL BLIND.

*Postscript.*—Since the above was written, a letter of Professor
Vambéry has appeared in the *Times*, in which he asserts that the
Continental opponents of the present war are actuated "either by
gross ignorance or by envy," and pleads for the energetic and
unswerving continuance of the struggle.   He indiscriminately
declares that " the mainspring of Continental enmity is and remains
the wealth, power, and liberty of Great Britain."

To speak of Germany only, does he thus account for the opinions
expressed by the mass of Liberals and Democrats of that country, many
of whom had hitherto pointed to England as to a preferable example
in regard to freedom?   Is he not aware that men in Germany and
France, honorary members of the Cobden Club, who, until lately, were
noted for their philo-English views, have since the attack upon
Transvaal independence turned wholly round in sorrow and indignation?   Is he not aware that the International Address of 1881
(drawn up by the author of the present article) in favour of the full
restoration of the South African Republic was signed by a galaxy of
men of science, of philosophers, poets, legists, university professors,
politicians, and parliamentary leaders in the Netherlands, in Germany,
Austria-Hungary, France, and Italy—containing the most illustrious
names of world-wide renown?   Not a few of them were personal
friends of mine.   Does he think that they have changed their views?
If so, the proof to the contrary could easily be given.   Truly, it is a
pity that the public opinion of England should thus be misled by
an untenable wholesale charge.   As to " ignorance of geography
and ethnography," and so forth, by which it is alleged Continental
ideas are influenced, I regret to say that since 1881 I have found

the grossest ignorance among a great many politicians, writers, even members of Parliament, and educated men in general in this country. To how many had I even to explain, privately or in the Press, until quite recently, that there were two Treaties with the Transvaal, one of 1881 and one of 1884? In Germany, certainly, no such ignorance exists among the leaders of public opinion. Even the fact of the speech of the Boers being the same as that of the Dutch, and far removed from English, I had to fight out against a friendly antagonist, only a few years ago, in the columns of the *Times*.

K. B.

# TO THE ELECTORS OF THE UNITED KINGDOM.

THE railways of the United Kingdom are the most expensive in the world, and stand to-day destroying internal industries in all its branches.

The revenue of railways is enormous. Passenger and parcel traffic for fifteen companies for the half-year was £17,300,000 for 1897 and £18,000,000 for 1898. Merchandise grew from £10,000,000 in 1897 to £11,000,000 in 1898, and each year a corresponding advance takes place.

Gross receipts for the half-year show £38,000,000 and an increase of £1,400,000 over the previous year. Working expenses are about £22,000,000, leaving a sum of £16,000,000.

Railways are capable of producing splendid profits, only they are closely watched by a hungry, extravagant, and grabbing Government. The cost of railways is necessarily enormous. The rates and taxes are exorbitant, and when is added to this enormous charge legal expenses and parliamentary charges, what benefit can the shareholders get?

Thirty years ago the railways of England and Wales were assessed at £4,800,000 for local taxation; five years ago this rose to £13,000,000, and neither the increase in railway capital, or the increase in mileage or in traffic receipts, is relatively equivalent to such a tremendous charge. In the half-year ending December 31, 1896, the London and North-Western paid £208,000 in rates and taxes; for the same period thirty years earlier the sum was £53,000, but the revenue had only increased from £3,000,000 to £6,000,000 sterling, or say, for six months ending 1897, equal to a dividend of 3s. 6d. per cent. on the then consolidated stock of £31,000,000; those paid in the second half-year of 1897 would have sufficed to pay 10s. per cent. dividend on the present consolidated stock of £41,000,000.

The construction of the South-Western cost £4000 per mile; London and Birmingham, £6300 per mile; London and Brighton, £8000 per mile; London, Chatham and Dover, £150,000 per mile.

The nature of the cost of construction depends on many conditions —viz., the nature of the district traversed, labour, &c.; for the

United Kingdom it averaged £44,000 per mile. The "Inner Circle," the most expensive in the world, cost £600,000 to £1,000,000 per mile; the South Eastern, between Charing Cross and Cannon Street, including two large stations and two bridges over the Thames, with hotels—two miles in length—cost over £1,000,000 per mile.

Heavy cost for land: £120,000 has been paid for what was worth £5000—land in most cases consisting of narrow slips before it is disturbed for laying sleepers.

Then we have parliamentary charges, lawyers' and counsels' charges, many of whom are members of the House of Commons, also hard sweating experts, and other privileged expenses.

One company was so extravagantly over-capitalised that when Lord Salisbury and Lord Cairns sat as members of an arbitration board to consider what was to be done, they applied a remedy by wiping off £12,000,000 of liabilities. Who paid the piper? The public.

### RAILWAY RATES.

Sugar, from Paris to London, a distance of 340 miles, pays 30s. per ton. Home-made sugar from London to Sherbourne, a distance of 118 miles, pays 37s. 6d. per ton. English sugar from Hull to Manchester, 15s. 10d. per ton; from Hamburg, *via* Hull, to Manchester, 15s. 3d.

*Glass.*—British glass, from London to Bristol, costs 35s. per ton; foreign glass, 20s.

*Timber.*—Rates of carriage of home timber are 100 per cent. more than those of foreign timber.

Foreign pianos are carried from Liverpool to London for 25s. per ton; English pianos, 70s.

Belgium can send its iron 100 miles by rail to Antwerp and thence by sea to London for considerably less than is charged from Staffordshire to London.

Finished iron and steel are transferred on the Belgian railways at an average of ·51 per ton per mile; in England the rates vary from 1d. to 1½d. per ton per mile.

Instances can be multiplied indefinitely through every class of goods.

The charges for home-grown vegetable produce are far above what is charged for foreign produce, favoured by special import rates by the railway companies, *and the difference paid by the British farmer is equal to £2 per acre on the cost of British land.*

Forty-eight years ago, when Mr. Gladstone introduced his Railway Bill and the companies' capital was, I think, £23,000,000, he warned the public that railway monopoly would become unbearable as soon as their capital reached £30,000,000. Have we not arrived at

£1,000,000,000 to-day? and has not the prediction of the late Right Hon. gentleman been amply fulfilled?

No use fighting the companies through the House of Commons, for are not the bulk of its members shareholders?

No use making the attempt through the House of Lords, for there we find members chairmen and directors. So the remedy must lie with the voice of the elector, when the elector has been educated to the fact.

Agriculture is a most important question, next to that of an efficient navy.

London to-day stands on honeycombed ground, undermined with locomotive traffic, where people fly morning and night to their daily labour. The mysterious ruler of man's destiny gave him the surface of the earth on which to perform his daily labour. But the modern Babylon has adopted the bowels.

Our country lands are neglected, deserted, and uncultivated, for have not the people flocked to the great towns and cities? In consequence, the great mass have to "exist" under circumstances below the brute level, to satisfy the selfish greed of a combination of City vultures who can smoke guinea cigars, while people in sight of its walls have to exist on what its ash would produce.

No nation can be prosperous whose limited sources of agriculture are neglected.

At the close of the Crimean War home-grown wheat produced 17,500,000 quarters, and we bought 2,900,000 quarters from abroad.

In 1874–5 our produce fell to 12,900,000 quarters, and we purchased 11,700,000 quarters. In 1895 we produced 4,800,000 quarters, and bought 23,300,000 quarters.

In 1888 we expended £46,000,000 sterling on wheat, £80,000,000 on meat, £31,000,000 on tea and sugar, making a total of £157,000,000, or £4 5s. 0d. per inhabitant. In 1897 we expended £189,000,000 on food out of a total of £481,000,000, showing an increase over 1888 (ten years earlier) of £30,000,000, *which sum is far in excess of the requirements of the increased population during that period.* Value of food imports, common necessaries of life, such as wheat, sugar, meat, butter, cheese, tea, coffee, rice, eggs, and potatoes, fresh fruit, spirits and wine, was in 1860 £69,000,000; 1870, £91,000,000; 1880, £160,000,000; 1889, £153,000,000; 1897, £189,000,000. In tons, total amount of food for year from 1860 was 3,500,000 tons, rising to 10,910,000 tons in 1889, or 640 lbs. of food per inhabitant; and allowing for a corresponding rise from 1889 to 1899, we should have something like 12,000,000 tons of food for which we are depending on the foreigner!

Our farmers declared last harvest that they would grow 3,000,000 quarters more of wheat (English wheat 30 bushels to acre) were it not for the fact that they could not get the price. How can they when railway companies favour the foreigner with favoured import rates? Our farmers are called upon to pay prohibitive rates—from 12s. to 18s. 6d., against 5s. from America, 7s. 6d. Russia, 4s. from France—while 60,000 acres of land are uncultivated outside London.

We feed 1,000,000 paupers on foreign grain at a cost of £12,000,000 annually to the ratepayer.

We pay £52,500,000 annually for breadstuff. We have 100,000 able-bodied men among those who are relieved by the rates, and the consolation for that from some people is that we are getting cheap food—a much-used and favourite handful of sand for the eyes of the British public, while Lombard Street thrives on the "fat bulls" representing foreign transactions at the expense of the industrial class, the—what ought to be—honey-bees of the Empire.

The beet-sugar could be cultivated in England: there is nothing to prevent it. London is the centre of the sugar market of the whole world, and the United Kingdom does not produce one pound. There is no difficulty against the cultivation, for several experiments have proved it a success in Reading. *The only obstacle* against such an undertaking is financial influence. The cultivation of the beet would cause £20,000,000 of capital to be invested at home. It would employ 400,000 men, 300,000 families. It would pay £10,000,000 per annum in wages.

In many parts of this country rents are lower than in beetroot districts of the Continent, so most suitable to crop. In 1897 Austrian agriculturists obtained 78,000,000 florins more by 40,000,000 florins than would have been got if planted with wheat, wages being paid to 250,000 workmen, 30,000,000 florins (£2,500,000), and this when they were unable to obtain any other employment. They pay 190,000,000 florins annually in wages. Official statistics show that 58,695 men and 15,841 women are employed in sugar factories puffed up with bounties *which protect the foreigner in our market.*

In 1898 a deputation waited on the Right Hon. A. J. Balfour, and pointed out the loss sustained by the decline of sugar refining, and that the people of Greenock had suffered greatly from the decay of sugar industry, the falling off of refining amounting to 300,000 tons per annum, which meant a loss of £500,000 annually, and of that loss Greenock had sustained half.

Six towns with their great disused industry was one of the most melancholy sights.

Sir E. Hall spoke for Bristol, which for centuries had been the home of sugar refining, now defunct.

In India the grievance was the same, but her Majesty's Government preferred that the tribes of the Khyber Pass should slice our troops in place of slicing " beet."

The beet-sugar and twin-brother the mangold is cultivated as field crops in Behar successfully, for turnips grow to perfection in Afghanistan, and there is no reason why the beet-sugar should not prove a valuable crop in the north-west frontier of India.

In 1896–97 India imported 2,682,463 cwt. of refined sugar.

Believing H.M. Government to be in earnest, a deputation waited on the Chancellor of the Exchequer to remind him of his promise, which had been given on his taking office. The deputation, introduced by Mr. Tomlinson, M.P., represented 400 trade and labour associations as well as from manufacturing and agricultural districts. The labour memorial was one of the most important ever presented to Government. The Government, however, refused, and have not troubled to put forward any counter-proposals, thus not "doing all in their power," and thereby breaking their word, their solemn pledges to the country, and rudely snubbing the deputation representing about 1,000,000 votes. The cause is not difficult to see. The bankers of London, whom no doubt the Prime Minister soft-soaped at dinner, petitioned against it. The Government abjectly obeyed the demands of this " class," which all experience proves is the most selfish and tyrannical in the world, for whom " solely " the British Empire Syndicate is run.

*Any attempt to mature and encourage home industries is opposed by this class with their " hog policy," and any revolution to change the channels of clearing bankers' profits will meet with powerful opposition from the Shylocks of modern Babylon.*

In 1897 the transactions of the London Clearing House stood at £7,491,281,000 0s. 0d. In 1898 it rose to £8,097,091,000 0s. 0d., showing an increase of 606,010,000 0s. 0d., or 8·1 per cent., equal to our import and export trade combined. Is it any wonder that Raphaels and Rothschilds can die and leave a million and a half each behind them?

*What are Governments doing, Conservative or Liberal?* Are they benefiting the country? Certainly not. The present Government have not a brilliant record. Hear the sound and the blast on the trumpet of the noble Marquis at the head of the Government:

" The Empire is advancing and must advance. The great strength you have must be used unfailingly, unsparingly, but still prudently, for the advancement of the interests of the Empire, for the benefit of mankind, and happy will be the Minister in future days [God help him!] who will be able to render you as good an account as, I think, we can render you to-day."— Lord Salisbury at the Constitutional Club.

What has been the record? A grant of £780,000 from the British taxpayer to Egypt, to put the Egyptian Government in a borrowing position for the benefit of the bondholders—*Bondholders' and Stock-jobbers' Session.* Cattle Diseases Bill—protection for our meat producers—("*no good ; railway rates too high.*") The Agricultural Rating Bill gave £2,000,000 a year to landed interest—*Landlords' Session ;* £600,000 a year to Voluntary Schools—*the Parsons' Session.* Then we have Mr. Chamberlain's scheme : "Old Age Pensions," "Working Men's Dwellings Bill," "Poor Law Reform," "Compensation to Injured Workmen," Increase of power of local authorities for the better housing of the poor, Prevention of pauper immigration—*Hope Session and bait for future election, with further useless promises.* A Tory scheme to square the workman's vote, for whom the Tory Government have done nothing. These propositions will reap advantage to the present generation at the expense of the taxpayer in the future generation. Well may the noble Marquis say : " Happy will be the Minister," &c.

The Empire stewing in its own juice.

Imports annually rising, which means more for the people to pay.

Exports annually decreasing, which means less purchasing power for the mass.

Local debts growing.

|  |  |  |  | £ |
|---|---|---|---|---|
| In 1875 it was | . | . | . | 92,000,000 |
| In 1881 ,, | . | . | . | 144,000,000 |
| In 1892 ,, | . | . | . | 207,000,000 |
| Lady Day 1895 | . | . | . | 235,000,000 |

The sum of £27,000,000 being added in three years.

How is money spent ?

|  |  | £ |
|---|---|---|
| Highways and Street Improvements | . | 7,000,000 |
| Elementary Education | . | 6,000,000 |
| Public Lighting | . | 1,000,000 |
| Fire, Libraries, Prosecutions | . | 800,000 |
| Police | . | 4,600,000 |
| Paupers | . | 10,000,000 |
| Annually | . | £29,400,000 |

In London gross expenditure on relief comes to 14s. 0¾d. per head, against 6s. 1¾d. for other towns.

Local taxation is annually growing, and Governments, Liberal and Conservative, are spending money "like water." People are taxed for *what does not concern them,* and fattens the bondholders and stock exchange speculator. Taxed for the food they eat ; for it is the heaviest tax to pay what it is difficult to meet ! Taxed for the produce of the foreigner, the most rotten foundation for any government. Taxed heavily in endless ways. Taxed when going abroad by extortion of railway tariffs.

The great secret of all evils is this. A powerful railway monopoly with one thousand millions at their back. The " Goliath " that stands in the valley, the "brag," the "bully," the "coward;" can there no David be found to go against this foe?

The electors must do it and rally round the Ministry, whether Liberal or Conservative, and support them on the Railway Reform question which, like the "Old Man of the Sea," is choking and throttling the autumn life of the Empire for the sole benefit of a class.

No Englishman, except those endowed with the "hog policy," can read our newspapers without feelings of shame and disgust at what appeared in the *Times* of April 29, under the heading of "Thousands of Little White Slaves," and yet £5,000,000 was voted for elementary education, and sends 53,000 children to school with empty stomachs. The British elector to-day seems to be totally indifferent to his responsibilities, and plays into the hands of political adventurers with "fads" like Local Veto, temperance, women's suffrage, prompted by pulpit advice, which has done so much of recent years to cause complications and divisions among governments of both creeds. Misguided public opinion prompted the formation of the opium commission, chiefly originating from Exeter Hall and local pulpits, and very near plunged India into another revolt, ending in costing the taxpayer of this country £40,000, and a dispute as to who should pay it.

Hurled Turkey at the throats of the Greeks with an "after-lunch" telegram from one hundred members of the House of Commons.

As long as the Liberal party go in for such folly they will *never* be of service to the country, neglecting questions of sound, useful policy such as I have indicated here, and with such they will be called upon to deal with sooner or later.

Let the electors consider these questions. Let them put on their considering cap, and perform their duties, the first and most prominent, of doing their duty towards their neighbour, and meet this bold demon of financial influence which, if longer tolerated, must soon complete the already downward progress of a once great and influential Empire. The time has arrived for giving the matter serious consideration; let the new century record a start for a change and reform in the right direction for the good and progress of the mass of our fellow-men.

*Proposition.* For Railway Reform. Nationalisation of Railways.

*Advantages.* Markets nearer home best known to traders. Our farmers could cultivate more wheat. No waste of energy, time, capital, or damage on way by sending to markets farther off. Ease, to some extent, surplus of congested population. Give employ to people at home. Make many happy and contented. Reduce gambling, crime, and evil consequences of drink. Would reduce taxation £8,000,000 annually.

The Empire would not be at the mercy of the foreigners for food supply in the event of our becoming involved in war with any European Powers. This would entail a small sacrifice on behalf of those representing a thousand millions of capital which is at the back of the great railway monopoly. Agricultural development would then be encouraged, and the mass of congested capital in Threadneedle and Lombard Streets would gradually circulate through the country districts and eventually have the same effect on an Empire tied to the foreigner as the blood of life to a human being. Monetary reform would eventually follow, but not until such change as I have indicated had commenced to work.

The opposing forces are powerful and represent £5,000,000,000 of wealth, so that a change cannot be hoped for at an early date until the masses have been educated as to its necessity.

A writer in one of the Reviews, in an article where England is supposed to be engaged in war with the "Dual Alliance," France and Russia, remarked as a consequence "that the people behaved well under the symptoms of starvation." What right has Government to put people in that position? Any Government so acting would be unworthy of the confidence of the country.

To-day 40,000,000 people of the British Isles are solely depending on the foreigner for our ordinary necessaries of food, and when we consider that from 150 to 200 vessels, each carrying 1 to 2000 tons of food, floating towards our shores, with a week's supply, representing 1,000,000 tons, manned chiefly by foreigners, our prospect would be a bright one.

The present Conservative Government opened their career with a costly war on the Indian frontier.

At Tel-el-Kebir, in September 1882, 3000 dervishes were killed; at El Obeid, in October, 11,000 were killed, and Hicks Pasha's army destroyed; at El Teb, in February 1894, 1500 were killed, at Tamai 2000, at Abu Klea 1000, Toski 1200, Firket 900, Atabara 3500, and on the closing drama of the drop scene 26,000 killed, wounded, and uncared for on the brinks of the Nile.

And now, at their close of office, one of the most dreadful and appalling wars known in the history of the Empire in South Africa, for which we have already paid dearly for in loss of life, to be eventually followed by expense and complications, all for the stock-jobber and the bondholders, no matter what construction her Majesty's Ministers—many interested directors—may put upon it.

England to-day, the Governor of 300,000,000 people, with an Army whose home establishment is 100,000 men—for which the public pay dear enough—is called upon to send a force against a band of undisciplined shoemakers, farmers, and traders; and for this to put 80,000 men in the field she has to call up 20,000 reserve, organise her Militia, and draw 5000 men from the Indian establishment. What better proof could there be of the utter rottenness of our military system, thanks to the ill advice of the present Commander-in-Chief? I trust the country will have an explanation and be fully informed as to the origin of such deplorable mismanagement. I have already pointed out in the pages of this REVIEW the extravagant and inefficient way the British establishment of the Indian Army is run, the brutal way our countrymen and countrywomen are shipped to the East. The Indian Army to-day, on paper 70,000 strong, could not put 10,000 fighting men on the frontier. We have had bitter experience in South Africa; are we to wait and buy our Indian experience at an equally bitter cost?—for pipeclay and bullet-headed Secretaries of State and Officialdom are immovable.

Debts are growing, and the grip of financial influence, like "the old man of the sea," is year by year tightning its grip. No better illustration of results could present itself than reviewing the past. What have Governments done for home with all their talk and promises? Encouraged extravagance by the London County Council to pull down London and build it up again.

That will benefit the sub-contractors for a time—a most important influence—trade for a time, labour for a time; yet later on things must change, and the piper will have to be paid.

Food prices must rise as land grows old. Shipyards must get slack as money gets scarce. The London County Council must draw a line somewhere, and reaction must follow.

Where are our resources? No attempt having been made even to consider them.

Surely rising imports, decreasing exports, growing local debts, increasing population, extravagant frontier wars cannot be symptoms of good honest government. One grows sick of the bully policy where the foe is weak, and doing Europe's dirty work for her bondholders at the expense of the British taxpayer. The Powers which would treat us to-morrow as the bullies—Russia, France and Germany—treated Japan, while Great Britain looked on without even a protest when Russia occupied Port Arthur, in the bully's presence the metal may be seen, for anything honestly carried out carries strength, which no human power can master. Her Majesty's Government is not so constituted, the Liberals less so. The tiny cloud is gathering, and unless checked will burst over the head of our Empire as it burst over Rome, where similar symptoms to those amongst us to-day foreshadowed its doom.

The Liberal party, under the leadership of the Right Hon. gentleman the Leader of the Opposition, are going to the poll with the "Temperance banner," endorsed by the Very Rev. the Dean of Canterbury. The Temperance party are going to unfurl their banner and reform the people. Let the Right Hon. gentleman reform himself and leaders, and he may eventually reform his party with honest, useful legislation, not leading his party to the House of Commons, whose existence in the past has depended on the Home Rule vote and the Irish Convention, by whom the Liberal party has existed in the past under the auspices of the late Right Hon. Leader.

Unless the Liberal leaders put forward an " honest policy " they will never be of service to the Empire. The time has come for them to consider seriously.

Let the elector support a candidate for railway reform, and send a railway candidate to the House of Commons at the next election. It must be a great fight.

Force the railway candidate at all costs and bring Governments to their senses, for appeals to them is useless waste of time. You are only appealing to chairmen, directors, and shareholders, which constitute Cabinet Ministers and Right Hon. gentlemen, members of the House of Lords and Commons, for whom solely the thousand millions of railway capital is run.

Let the British workman drop his pipe and beer for an hour and go to the poll. Let people cease to vote for those good, generous members who give cheques and coal tickets and buy rags at church bazaars. Let every honest-minded man look to the national needs—crying needs—of his country, the overcrowdings, children dragged up in the filthy slums of London, overcrowded like brute beasts, a vanishing agriculture, a desolate and neglected and deserted country, ruined and crippled by railway monopoly. The railway question is the thin edge of reform, the remedy for meeting a gloomy outlook, and a first step towards putting the Empire once more on the foundation of prosperity for the good of the honey-bees of the Empire. Support a railway candidate.

Frederic W. Tugman.

# THE PERPLEXING PREDICAMENT
## AND THE WAY OUT OF IT.

IN our first article in November number on "England and the Transvaal," by Mr. W. J. Corbet, the two sides of the case between the present Government of Great Britain and the Transvaal were stated as clearly and fairly as appeared to be possible, with the view of giving the public the principal facts, to enable people to see where the blame lay for going into this most unwelcome, destructive, and cruel war—such a war as was not expected to befall the world ere the nineteenth century closed, and far less was it expected that the twentieth century would be ushered in amidst the clash of arms from the most destructive instruments of warfare that ever have been invented; and that, too, by the greatest national Power of Europe. What is most astonishing is that this war has broke out immediately on the back of the great and propitious Peace Congress at the Hague, which was pretty generally considered to be the harbinger of national amity of the widest range. But, alas! the new century is coming in with a very unfriendly and disappointing countenance, portending no good-will to men in general, but the reverse.

Even for the short time the war has been going on civilisation has been very terribly arrested, and the old barbarous and murderous customs of fighting introduced again with tenfold ferocity: dumdum bullets and quick-firing guns, which give men no chance for their lives in the battle-fields. Living men are thereby mowed down like fields of corn. The old romance of war is gone, and the so-called patriotism of men being led to death up hillsides against hidden foes is in the meantime encouraged by the Jingoes who stay at home. But the soldiers and their families are to be deeply pitied. People are "whistling to keep up their courage." Perhaps that will not continue long if there is no good to show for all the military ardour which is presently shown to soldiers as they are marched and carried off to where—ay, where to, and what to do? In a country cottage lately in my neighbourhood there was a family in great grief. The mother was crying and three of her children; the father was there, and waiting to see and say farewell to his son, who was just returning from school; he came in, and the father took an affec-

tionate embrace of his wife and all his children, and then hurried off
to the train to go to the port of shipment. A letter has since arrived,
saying he has come through two battles safely, but his name has now
appeared in the list of the lost. There are many sad cases like
that.

The outbreak of the war has come upon the country when it was
enjoying the benefits of good trade and plenty of employment for
working men, and there was the prospect of a continuance of
prosperous times, but a great financial set-back has already taken
place, following upon the bad news from South Africa. There has
been a great shrinkage in the value of all high-class securities on
the Stock Exchange. At the commencement of the campaign the
public were led to believe that the British army would carry all
before it, and that the war would soon be over, and Pretoria taken;
but just when the stock markets were most buoyant three reverses
took place to the British army. The Bank rate was then advanced
to 6 per cent.—that is, 1 per cent. above the ordinary rate even at
tight times—the Bank rate never rose above 5 per cent. before the
Bank Act was passed in 1844, but after that the Bank got so great
a command of the money market that it can almost charge what the
directors like, without respect to the requirements of the mercantile
community, as has been exemplified at different times of *panic.*

At the present time there was no need for raising the rate of
discount, as the Bank has a most abundant *reserve* of funds on
hand under various heads to employ in banking to any extent likely
to be required. There was on November 30 in the banking department £64,691,130, and only £32,014,391 in " other securities "—
that is, discounts, &c., and advances in business—and £13,340,990
in Government securities, which can be used for other business if
required. There was £17,571,610 notes unemployed. That reserve
of notes alone may show that the pretence of the Bank being short
of reserve is all a false alarm and an excuse for raising the rate of
discount, for there is no shortness of reserve for the home trade or
circulation. The stock of bullion is superabundant. Gold is not
really wanted for the home circulation ; indeed, the Bank could issue
a great many more notes if it would do so, but the Bank Act, 1844,
operates against its issuing as many notes as it might do on
national security. The Governments of the United States, France,
Germany, and other States now issue national notes to large amounts
amply sufficient to support the home circulation and encourage trade
by that means. But these Governments and large national banks
are not so " *hidebound* " as our Bank of England is, for since the Bank
Act of 1844 was passed our Bank is bound to restrict its issue of
notes according to the amount of gold in its coffers : that restriction
has brought Britain into very serious monetary predicaments on
these occasions, when the Bank Act had to be suspended. After

that was done trade got on quite well again; the pity is that the Act was not suspended altogether. With free trade in banking all good banks would have got fair play, and with wholesome competition there would have been no monetary crisis, as the Bank of England and other banks would adjust themselves to the circumstances in which they were placed. At the present time the country is threatened with another great monetary crisis, unless the Government steps in and suspends the Bank Act at once, ere ever the crisis comes on. It could easily and very properly say to the Bank that it must no longer be restrained from issuing a sufficient amount of notes to sustain the currency of the country to its requirements, and if necessary the Government should authorise it to issue notes on Consols, which will be as secure as gold. The same privilege could also be given to other good banks, so that the difficulty about the supply and the exportation of gold would be easily got over, and the country saved from any monetary crisis.

The rush into war with the Transvaal has brought this country into a far worse conflict than the military one, as it has upset the whole financial and business conditions of every trade. The present crisis makes it very clear that some change must now be made in the British monetary and banking system in order to cope with and meet without difficulty any alteration in the value of gold, which was, by the Act of 1816, made the basis of money in Great Britain, whereas before that time Bank of England notes were *legal tenders,* and in Scotland bank-notes for £1 and upwards were the regular and still are the *circulating medium,* and are considered to be far better for that purpose than *gold coin,* which, to the amount of £7,000,000, lies locked up uselessly in the Scotch banks by the stupid Act of 1845.

Now, the occasion has come at last for reconsidering the legislation which made gold bullion, or a gold sovereign, to be the legal *standard of value.* But it has so happened that gold has recently been found in such abundance that it is wonderful that it has not dropped in value, as silver did, to only one-half of its former price. The Government of the United States passed laws to buy up all the silver by the Treasury, at the full old price, for some time, in order to maintain the value of the silver coin; but that Act was a failure, and bi-metallism too, so that silver now fluctuates in price in the market like other metals, and it is a marvel that *gold* has not as yet followed the same course, seeing the total production of gold in the world now is no less than double what the outcome of the mines was only five years ago. The mines at Johannesburg have been and still are the most productive of all the world; until the war broke out they turned out and sent to England £600,000 monthly, which, by Act of Parliament, the Bank of England was bound to buy at the fixed price of £3 17s. 9d. per oz. and to sell it out again to any buyer at a profit of only 1½*d*. per oz.—no great profit—although the author of that Act said that " England should always buy in the cheapest market and sell in the dearest." However, it cannot do so in this case. It stands to reason that now, when gold has become superabundant, the Bank should be allowed to buy in its *gold* when wanted as *cheap* as possible—just as *Cape wool* is bought and sold by public sale in London—by public competition. If this system of free sale of gold was adopted there would probably be a change in the price of gold. There is no saying what the price would fall to, but the probability is it might fall as much as silver did. This would be *a great boon to Britain*, because it would give us *free trade in gold*, which would complete the scheme of Free Trade which Mr. Cobden and others designed, but which has not yet been accomplished because of the fixed price for gold and the Bank monopoly preventing *perfect* freedom.

This subject is of the utmost importance at the present time, as it has an immense bearing upon the proper settlement of the Transvaal differences. I have been led to believe from my long experience in trade and observation of the consequences of the Bank of England being bound to buy and sell gold at the fixed prices stated, and its being restricted from issuing bank-notes as wanted for the home circulation, I feel certain that *free trade in gold and in banking* would, in the first place, make the Johannesburgers and the Transvaal Government more *dependent* on the British Government by that means than by any other means, even by this horrid war. It could be done simply by the Bank of England giving over the buying of their gold at the price of £3 17s. 9d. per oz. when in an open market it could probably be bought at a much lower figure. That would make a great change in the Boer's policy, as then they would not have the money or means to buy so many munitions of war or equip so many fighting men as now. In short, this probable reduction in the value of gold would most likely turn the Boers back to be farmers, as they were before the mines were discovered and their heads turned thereby.

The next party to be benefited by *free trade in gold* would be the Bank of England, as it would then be able to buy its stock-in-trade at such a price as it could make a profit by, just as wool merchants do when they buy Cape wool! Then, having bought gold cheap enough, the Bank could sell it at a profitable price; moreover, if it could not obtain a good price for it, the Bank could keep it in stock until wanted. Then the Bank, with its stock of bullion, could sell it or export it to any country it pleased at any price. It could then at all times get any amount of stock of gold it wished at market-price, and would not be obliged to sell, except at a fair price. The trade of the country would then get into a fair way of dealing; gold would then rise and fall in price according to demand and supply, and the *price* of gold would fluctuate according to the rate of exchange between different countries. For instance, if the balance of exchange happened to be against Britain, then the price for gold would rise here, and this would throw the demand for exportation to be on British *goods*. In this way free trade in gold would inevitably stimulate and establish free trade *internationally*. Thus free trade would enforce itself on every nation; foreigners could not then sell their own produce without taking as much value in exchange from other countries as to balance accounts, and when they could no longer get *gold cheaper* than other produce or goods they would just have to deal by fair exchange, which will undoubtedly be best for all parties.

The next most important consideration in connection with this question is to show how it would benefit our home trade; it goes without saying that whatever benefits the foreign trade will at the same time increase our home trade. But by improving our banking and currency system the trade in general will be so much improved and extended that it will be like getting out of slavery into freedom, for, if we will think of it, the laws of our country since 1816 have been made more with the false idea that it was the duty of the Legislature to do all that could be done to *hinder* giving banking and currency facilities, rather than to give every possible *facility* for the spread of trade.

This anti-free-banking and currency idea must now be entirely overcome, and as many new banks set up in Great Britain as required, on a properly organised system, such as there is in Canada, the United States, France, Germany, &c. In the two last-named countries great facilities have lately been made for giving banking facilities to all, even to the very smallest customers, and this is found to give great encouragement to all classes and trades.

One of the worst prejudices which has to be contended with in England is the idea that gold coin only is sound money. Hence the Bank of England and other banks keep on hoarding up gold uselessly; whereas the real strength of banks is the responsibility of the shareholders and their stocks of money held in reserve.

The Government should establish a National Bank, or Treasury, for the issue of national notes, which will be the very best and most handy kind of money, as it is found to be preferable to coin where people have both coin and paper notes. Above all, there is the recommendation that a good Government currency would be a great gain, and at present might provide money to meet the extra expenses incurred and save taxes.

The way out of the present predicament for Great Britain is to give the gold-diggers the "go-bye" and to adopt *free trade in banking*, and to open up good banks throughout England, Scotland, and Ireland, which would be as good as opening mines, or better, as they would discover and distribute wealth, and give employment at home, and encourage trade at home and abroad by the circulation of good ready-money in the form of national or secured bank-notes, which would be preferable to gold coin, as described in this article and in the one in our number for November.

ROBERT EWEN.

# THE DEVIL AND HIS ALIASES.

## "SATAN, AHRIMAN, SIVA, LOKI, THE EUMENIDES AND TLACATECOLOTL."

THE conception of a personal "Power of Evil" has prevailed in all ages of the world, and, as a cardinal doctrine, exists in most of the great creeds of the present day. To any theological or metaphysical discussion of the case, however, from either the "advanced" or the "orthodox" point of view, it is not my purpose to devote space. My desire is merely to trace the diverse modifications of the same idea in distinct parts of the world—to show, in fact, that the Hebrew "Satan," the Persian "Ahriman," the Hindu "Siva," the Scandinavian "Loki," the Greek "Eumenides," and the Mexican "Tlacatecolotl" are all modifications of the one basic principle.

The Origin of Evil has, as is well known, been the battleground of the creeds, but it is the incarnate "element" more than the moral attribute to which our comparative analysis shall be applied. In his admirable work on the *Christian Doctrine of Sin*, the late Principal Tulloch threw out the suggestion that "Evil" in all the earliest religions was invariably "physical" and "objective" in its character. More recent investigations have proved the substantial proof of the assertion. Nay, as Dr. Pfleiderer has pointed out, all the remains as well as the myths that have reached us from prehistoric times, indicate that "Evil" was originally esteemed to be personal in its nature, and that an incarnate "Devil," as the direct author and agent of "Evil" to mankind, held a co-ordinate place with a "Power of Good" in the theogonies current in the grey dawn of religion—as, for instance, in that dim epoch prior to the Vedic hymns. The dragon "Tiamat," for example, with which the older gods of Babylon and Assyria were said to be perpetually at war, and whose representation can be traced so frequently in the recently discovered remains at "Nippur," appears to be the lingering memory of that mighty incarnate "Force of Evil" which, alternately with the "Good," dominated the dualism of the earliest ages after men had emancipated themselves from the degradations of Fetichism. The reason is not far to seek.

The destructive natural phenomena peculiar to the "Far East"—

where the consensus of opinion has placed the cradle of the human race—would at once explain the predominance of the "Power of Evil" in the early dualism.   To witness, as has been the lot of the writer, a tropical tornado passing over a belt of country not exceeding a few hundred yards in width, and sweeping houses, trees, cattle, human beings, and all else before it, while by any person standing at a short distance from the direct track of the hurricane scarce a breath of air can be felt, fully explained to me the origin of the Melanesian's saying that "the tornado was the battle between 'Good' and 'Evil.'"   From lengthy residence in the East, and a careful study of the varying phases of religious belief in the countries where I lived, I have been led to the conclusion that, in every case, "Evil" was originally a physical experience, and that the moral signification which the term afterwards assumed was of a purely subordinate and secondary character.

Principal Fairbairn, in his excellent work on the *Philosophy of Religion and History*, Dr. Tiele, in his *Outlines of the History of Religion*, the late Professor Rawenhoff, in his *Religions Philosophie*, and M. Albert Reville, in his monumental works on the *History of Religion*, amid numerous differences, have this one feature in common that, in their conception of the earliest form of the "Power of Evil," they all prefer an incarnation of "destructive physical phenomena" to any other explanation of that "Principle of Maleficence" which looms darkly against the background of the first Aryan creed.   I am of opinion that the "God of Storms" was the earliest form under which the power we term the "Devil" appeared in religion. Professor Menzies and Mr. Andrew Lang rather incline to a more subjective explanation.   But from a study of the question among Central Australian tribes, whose association with "whites" has been of the smallest extent, also from the facts gleaned from an investigation on the spot, of the superstitions current among the inhabitants of New Guinea, the New Hebrides, and the Marquesas Islands, the conviction is driven home to my mind that both "Evil" and the power producing it were originally "physical" and "objective" in their character.

My intention in emphasising this point so strongly is thereby to explain that prominently personal and realistic presentation of Satan, Siva, Loki, and the Eumenides which appears in the earliest references to them in the respective religions to which they belong. The Hebrew "Satan" is, in the first notice of him in the Book of Job, one of the "Beni Elohim," *Sons of God*, though there is an obvious differentiation drawn between him and the others of the same category.   Satan, whose name, as is well known, means "the adversary," was, in this scene, represented as an incarnate being who came into the presence of God "from going to and fro in the earth, and from walking up and down in it," but who also was definitely entrusted by the Deity, with the function of working evil upon one who was admittedly without peer in the earth—" a perfect and an upright man, one that feared God and eschewed evil."

In the Azazel of Leviticus, which was simply a synonym for Satan, as Hengstenberg has shown, the same personal character is maintained, and in the vision of Zechariah the same feature is even more strongly affirmed, " he showed me Joshua the high priest standing before the Angel of the Lord, and Satan standing on his right hand to *resist* him," or, as the Revised Version reads, " to be his adversary." The first conception of " Satan," therefore, was an incarnate principle, personified in a being that possessed many human attributes, but whose office was to inflict evil upon men ; probably, in the very earliest forms of the belief, as the minister of God ; but in the later epochs of pre-Exilian history upon his own account.

But the Hebrew " Satan," during the exile in Babylon, underwent a notable metamorphosis. Here the distinctively Jewish conception came into contrast with that of the Persian Ahriman, the impersonal " Power of Evil " in the great system of Zoroastrian dualism. On this subject a recent but anonymous writer remarks : " The Jewish Satan grew greatly in power and in definiteness, under the shadow of Ahriman, and henceforth it is from him directly that moral and physical harm towards men proceeds. Yet it must not be supposed that this was due to direct borrowing, and that the Jewish Satan was not substantially an original evolution of the native Jewish mind." And from this point, the Jewish Satan assumes the character more and more of an agent whose function is the promoting of moral as well as physical evil, of leading men on to sin against themselves and their better light, as well as against their fellow-men. From the Captivity to the time of Christ, Satan's character loomed up ever larger against the background of Divine Goodness, until, in the form in which he is presented in the system of our Lord, he appears as the relentless enemy of all good, as the rival, though the unequal one, of the Deity, as, in fine, the tempter of the Son of God. Of Christianity, it is a cardinal doctrine that the great warfare between Good and Evil was brought to a conclusion in the overthrow of the latter, when Christ proved victor over death and the grave.

Ahriman is the " Devil " of the Perso-Iranian Zoroastrianism, now chiefly professed by the Parsees. According to the system of the great religious reformer Zerdusht, there existed from the beginning of things, two supreme Spirits or Powers, Ahuro Mazdao or Ormuzd, and Angro Mainyush or Ahriman, the former representing the agency producing the " Good " that is in the world, the other that to which is due the " Evil." The problem of the Origin of Evil is thus overcome in the ancient religion of Persia by ascribing an eternity of Existence to it as well as to the Good. As Professor Geldner, of the University of Halle, remarks : " Ormuzd is light, and life, and all that is pure and good; in the ethical world law, order, and truth; his antithesis is darkness, filth, death, all that is evil in the world, lawlessness, and lies. When the two are spoken of as "a pair," this is not to be interpreted as meaning they are "twins"; it simply means a "duality," an opposed couple. The two spirits had, until the creation of things, exactly counterbalanced one another. Though at present the "Evil" strives with "Good," a cardinal principle of Zoroastrianism is the ultimate triumph of Ormuzd over Ahriman. In the *Zend-Avesta*, the great battle-field of the two Supreme Powers is the world, with man as its centre, and in the soul of mankind the hottest of the conflicts take place. Ahriman is represented in earlier Zoroastrianism as a spiritual essence, possessing the faculty, however, of incarnating itself at will.

In later Persian theology, however, and at the present day in the system of belief professed by the Parsees, Ahriman appears solely as a moral essence, a subtle indefinable influence for evil that exercises over mankind a fascination somewhat akin to that power possessed by the snake. The only hope, says the pious Parsee, is to resist Ahriman from the very first. He gains strength as the resolution of man becomes weaker, while if resisted he is put to flight. What is this but the familiar Christian doctrine: "Resist the devil and he will flee from you"?

The hope cherished by every godly Parsee is that the end of the present world is at hand. The present is the time of Ahriman's triumph. When "the end of things" arrives, Ormuzd will summon together all his powers for a final decisive attempt to break the sway of Ahriman forever. By the help of Ormuzd, the "faithful" will achieve the victory over Ahriman and his allies in the great Zoroastrian Armageddon. Then Ormuzd, supreme now over all, will hold a "Vîdaite" or last judgment upon all mankind and judge strictly accordingly to the deeds done in the body, punishing the wicked and assigning to the good the hoped-for reward. Ahriman will then be cast (according to the *Zend-Avesta*) into the abyss, along with all those who have been delivered over to him, to suffer the pains of hell, where he will thenceforward remain, powerless. Then begins the one undivided kingdom of the "Good" or God in heaven and on earth.

There are two clearly marked stages in the development of the conception of Ahriman, the first wherein he is represented as merely a man possessing superhuman powers for evil, but still a man with all a man's vices and particular sins. During this stage Ahriman achieves his conquests by direct temptation, appealing to the natural senses. Every misfortune, every disease, every accident, every incitement to sin are all ascribed to the personal presence and agency of Ahriman. But with the lapse of centuries the conception gradually modified its characteristics. It became more impersonal, more subjective in its influence, though its powers were regarded as more mysterious and awful because less clearly defined. From an incarnation of physical disorder, Ahriman has now become a mere moral quality or essence, terribly real and powerful, yet no longer appealing to the natural senses. To the educated Parsee of to-day Ahriman is simply a moral quality embracing within itself everything that affects mankind of an unfavourable, harmful, or pernicious character.

Siva, the "Devil" of the Hindus, presents to us features of an altogether different nature. Only by laying emphasis on one phase of his character can he be held to exhibit any family affinity at all with the Hebrew Satan or the Persian Ahriman. Siva is typical both of destruction and of reproduction. But the latter attribute was doubtless a later addition to the sum of his qualities. The original conception of this deity was that of a power delighting in destruction, in the achievement of physical evil and wrong, and in hurling death and devastation upon the people and their land. He is represented in the Sacred Books of the Hindus as "the terrible destroyer"— "the one who delights in the destruction of men." But in all this there is no whisper as yet of any moral qualities of evil. The conception is entirely one of physical power, used with the utmost malevolence and injustice against men. Along with his principal wife, who is variously called Devi, Durga, Uma, and Kali, he is portrayed as the incarnation of physical evil, wrong, injustice, or misfortune. In the *Puranas* Siva is described as wandering about surrounded by ghosts and goblins, inebriated, naked, and with dishevelled hair, covered with the ashes of a funeral pile, ornamented with human skulls and bones, sometimes laughing and sometimes crying. Devi, his consort, is represented with a hideous and a terrible countenance streaming with blood, encircled with snakes, hung round with skulls and human heads, and in all respects resembling a "Fury" rather than a goddess. The only pleasure which Siva and Devi feel is when their altars are drenched with blood, which, of course, could not be shed without the destruction of some form of life.

Only comparatively recently has an element of moral evil made itself visible in the current Hindu conception of Siva. Into the nature of this mighty "third" in the great Hindu "Trimurti" or Trinity, there has slowly crept an attribute of affinity with the "Not-good," directly emanating from his function as the physical "destroyer." Siva loves evil simply because it brings men within his "power"; but I can discover no trace of him ever assuming the *rôle* of the Tempter so as to induce men to evil. Siva differs from Satan in having no complex intermingling of objective and subjective attributes, of moral with physical evil. He was, until very recently at least, purely human in all his qualities, and was rather an infinitely magnified type of man than an incarnation of moral qualities. Hence the "sins" of the Hindus were, and are, largely those of ceremonial, offences against personal or caste purity, and without a trace of subjective moral quality attaching to them. Siva's animosity towards man proceeds rather from his innate love of "destroying" than from any desire to achieve the moral ruin of the race. Of course, as has already been pointed out, Siva is also "The Reproducer," and some writers have argued that his love of "destroying" proceeded from the wish to reproduce in a better form. But this is a forced explanation of the attribute, and, besides, the fact must be borne in remembrance that Siva's attribute of "The Generating One" is of comparatively late growth, subsequently, in fact, to the time when the worship of Brahma "the creative principle" had fallen into decay. The analogous qualities which he exhibits to Satan and Ahriman are his thirst for blood in the material sense, his hatred towards light, truth, beauty, and purity, his desire to annihilate —not merely to ruin—the human race, and, finally, his absolute antagonism towards the "good"; in Hindu mythology represented by Vishnu, "The Preserver."

Loki, in the Scandinavian pantheon, is more distinctively akin to Satan and Ahriman than to Siva. He belonged to the older theogony of North Saxon deities, and not to the Odinic race of the Aesir. The Edda styles him "the calumniator of the gods, the grand contriver of deceit and frauds, the reproach of gods and men. He is beautiful in his figure, but his mind is altogether evil and his inclinations towards wrong continually. He surpasses both gods and men in perfidy and craft, and delighteth in evil as the other gods in good." From this statement one would gather that the dualistic doctrines of Eastern Zoroastrianism had here a curious analogue in the far Western mythology. Probably there has existed here, in long bygone ages, a variety of Dualism, whereof Loki, the "Principle of Evil," is the sole remaining trace. He is like none of the other Scandinavian deities. His qualities savour rather of that pre-Odinic worship wherein the physical powers of nature played so large a part. Loki, in his earliest character, was, I have every reason to think, the personification of that destructive principle in the forces of nature which is present in devastating storms, in floods that sweep away the cattle and crops of a whole district, in the winds and rains, and so forth. In fact, wheresoever the physical forces of nature inflicted suffering, loss, disaster, and death, there was Loki esteemed to have been at work.

But after the institution of the Odinic pantheon, Loki was taken over from the older mythology. He had, however, undergone somewhat of a change in the process. He exhibited now an element of moral evil which he never possessed before. Nay as time went on the tendency became more marked to ascribe physical disaster to the inferior divinities, and to regard Loki's work as lying more in the temptation of mankind to wrong-doing, and the inflicting upon them such subjective "evils" as impure desires, evil thoughts leading up to evil deeds, and more especially murder and slaughter. Loki must not be confounded with Thor, a sufficiently bloodthirsty personage, who was God of Thunder and of the "Noise of Battle"—not "God of Battles," for that was Odin's title. Thor and his father Odin did not consider it at all derogatory to slay their enemies whenever and howsoever they might come across them; but Loki was of so essentially evil a nature that he turned his weapons against his own friends, especially against the gentle and beautiful Balder—the Scandinavian Christ. Loki, therefore, may be esteemed the incarnation of the "Essence" or Power of Evil. The very fact that he does not belong to the Odinic theogony is testimony how ancient is the problem among the Scandinavian race of the Origin of Evil. Loki is not so definitely individualised as the Hebrew "Satan," but he is much more clearly defined as a moral principle than any of the other types of the "Devil," with the exception, perhaps, of the "Eumenides" of the Greeks. Abriman possesses a larger moral element, but he is not definitely and clearly personified as Loki.

Regarding the Greek "Eumenides" or *Erinnys* but little need be said. Every schoolboy is acquainted with their characteristics. They were originally "the avengers of wrong-doing," but in the course of time they assumed the additional attribute of "ministers of evil" and agents of that grim providence which led the doomed ones into the path of calamity and destruction. These three goddesses, Alecto, Megaera, and Tisiphone, had distinctive duties assigned to them, but they were all in the line of punishing mankind for crimes, and even tempting them into fresh deeds of wrong-doing in order to achieve their destruction. The "Furies" as they were called, amid many characteristics utterly dissimilar to those peculiar to Satan, Ahriman, Siva, or Loki, yet resembled them in this particular that they wrought evil from the love of it. Their nature inclined them to the terrible task laid upon them and they discharged it *con amore*. Aeschylus in his tragedy "The Eumenides," and Sophocles in "Œdipus Coloneus," represent with overwhelming majesty and power the dread mission of these "Ministers of Fate." Within the scope of the associations investing their triune personality must be included all that solemn ethical atmosphere, which in Hellenic literature surrounds the mysterious problems of Sin and its atonement. By the sheer relentlessness of their pursuit and punishment of wrong-doing, they inscribe, as it were, in letters of fire against the deep moral background of Greek tragedy, the awful doctrine that the area of expiation is practically unlimited, and that the innocent descendants of the original criminals, even unto the third and fourth generations, may become the vicarious sufferers of a long by-gone offence.

Finally, the last *alias* of the "Devil" which presents any features of interest to us is that of the Mexican god "Tlacotecolotl"—or "He who revels in Sin." This power is representative of both physical and moral evil. In the Aztec Pantheon the conception of a divinity whose energies were wholly directed towards inflicting disease, misfortune, sorrow, and death upon humanity, was one which at any early date took shape, and succeeding generations increased the attributes of maleficence associated with the name. Many of the qualities afterwards ascribed to the Mexican Mars,—the frightful Huitzilopochtli, God of War, whose altars reeked with the blood of 10,000 human sacrifices every year,—were originally identified with Tlacotecolotl. A subtle form of dualism was also present in the Aztec mythology, being found in the perpetual antagonism existing between the latter and the Supreme Power, the beneficent "Tloque-nahuaque," whose name implies "he who is all in himself," or "he in whom all things live." The struggle between the two deities has existed from "the beginning of days" and will continue, says Mexican tradition, until Quetzalcoatl, the Mexican Christ, reappears and crushes Tlacotecolotl under his feet. While, in the earlier ages of Aztec history, Tlacotecolotl exhibited only attributes associated with physical suffering, disease, disaster, and death, in the later epochs of Mexican civilisation he gradually assumed certain moral qualities that rendered him closely akin to Satan and Ahriman. He was the "Power that induced men to commit the deeds that brought destruction upon them." He also exhibited other characteristics that remind one of "Satan the Tempter," in being the agent that instilled evil thoughts, evil suggestions, and evil impulses into the minds of men—impulses, moreover, which he fostered until they took shape in action. Tlacotecolotl dwelt in darkness, whence his title of the "Man-owl of Evil," and his abode, to which the wicked would be sent after death, was beneath the world. From this inferno he only issued to execute purposes of evil. His name occurs again and again in the "picture-writing" of the Aztecs, being always represented as an owl with a grotesque human head.

Such, then, are some of the *aliases* that the "Power of Evil" which we call "the Devil" has assumed in various parts of the world. Others might be named, such as the "Taipo" of the Maories, the "Looern," or "Wiwonderrer," of the Australian aborigines, the "Gauna" of the Hottentots, the "Erlik" of Altaian Shamanism, the "Eblis," or "Azazil," of Mohammedanism; but these are decidedly of inferior importance to the principal designations mentioned above. Look where we will we find evidences of the conflict of Good and Evil, which has formed so insoluble a problem to the theologians of

" Christendom " from the time of Christ to the present day.    Alas!
the problem is not confined to Christianity.    It has been the mighty
stumbling-block to faith in every religion that has been formulated
under heaven, and in all probability will continue to be until " time
shall be no more."    The fact that in our own age such minds
as John Stuart Mill, Rathbone Greg, Hartmann, Helmholtz, and
Ritschl have sorrowfully renounced the attempt to reconcile the conflicting issues save by the mechanical doctrine of Dualism, is significant of its difficulty.    Let Professor Maudsley's confession voice the
testimony of the others when he remarks in *Body and Will*—" The
facts of organic and human nature, when observed frankly and
judged without bias, do not warrant the argument of a Supreme and
beneficent artificer working after methods of human intelligence, but
perfect in all his works ; rather would they warrant, if viewed from
the human standpoint, the conception of an almighty malignant
power that was working out some far-off end of its own, with the
serenest disregard of the suffering, expenditure, and waste which
were entailed in the process."    Unquestioning faith is the sole torch
that can light humanity through this labyrinth of perplexity !

OLEPHANT SMEATON.

# ISRAEL BEFORE THE PROPHETIC REFORMATION.

FOR the moment there is a pause in the perennial conflict between High Church and Low, and no apology should be needed for a short excursion into the field of biblical criticism.

The Higher Criticism of the Old Testament is effecting a revolution in the way in which we conceive of the history of the Hebrew people, and the recent appearance of the third volume (in point of time) of the *International Critical Commentary* affords us an opportunity of acquiring some idea of the nature of the work which is being accomplished in this field.

The volume in question deals with the Books of Samuel, and has for its author Dr. Henry Preserved Smith, Professor of Biblical History and Interpretation in Amherst College, Massachusetts. The Introduction comprises an analysis of the composition and sources of Samuel, and a short account of the. Hebrew text and versions, a dissertation on the religious ideas of the books, and a reference to the various commentaries. The bulk of Dr. Smith's work is his own commentary on the text. An appendix deals more fully with the criticism of the text, and with certain theories on the literary process which has given rise to the Books of Samuel as we now know them. This is not the place, even if the present writer felt himself competent, to undertake a critical estimate of Dr. Smith's work. The most uncritical reader cannot, however, fail to appreciate the care, thoroughness, and breadth of erudition to which every page bears witness. The emendations of a very corrupt text seem altogether admirable, and, if the account of the literary process which explains its present form as the work of two main narrators and a redactor appears hardly to account for all the facts of the case, this arises from the extreme difficulty of the problem, and we feel that the theory proceeds on true lines of criticism, and is likely rather to be supplemented and modified than to be displaced by a totally inconsistent hypothesis. A duplicate narrative we clearly have in many cases, and the present unity of the books proves the existence of a redactor. Dr. Smith errs, therefore, if at all, on the side of conservatism and caution, that is to say, on the right side. To the general reader, however (if, indeed, theological works ever come the way of that reader), the main interest of the book will probably consist in the light thereby thrown on the social and political state of Israel in early times.  The state of Israel before the prophetic ethical movement made itself felt is indeed one of the most interesting topics to the student of Jewish history and will form the subject of the present article.  We shall, however, take the liberty of not confining ourselves to the Books of Samuel for its elucidation, but will take our information from whatever sources are open to us.

To the discussion of such questions the work of the Higher Criticism has been an essential preliminary.  It is not too much to say that what may be called the traditional view constituted an absolute bar to any attempt whatever to investigate Hebrew antiquities by the same historical methods which have been applied to inquiries into the origins of other races and systems.  Adopt the traditional standpoint and you cannot, by the exercise of any ingenuity whatever, form a conception of the history of Israel which does not stand in startling conflict with every canon of historical probability.  A race of herdsmen, escaped from Egyptian serfdom, emerge from the desert after forty years of wandering equipped with a mass of ecclesiastical and sacrificial ordinances, combined with some moral and social precepts.  These laws are clearly framed for a nation in a state of considerable wealth and civilisation and settled political institutions.  They are intended for a people cultivating the soil and inhabiting cities.  For the transition to this settled state, however, there are no regulations whatever, nor are there any provisions for civil government, or machinery for the carrying into effect of the elaborate code.  Canaan is taken and divided among the tribes—for the most part by lot.  Then the code drops utterly out of sight and is ignored, as if non-existent, even by the most virtuous and pious men, who act, apparently in entire good faith, in flagrant neglect of the clearest precepts.  The history of the people in general becomes a monotonous course of wrong-doing, punishment, penitence, forgiveness, renewed prosperity.  The series repeats itself again and again, but the Law is always out of sight. Prophets rise up and denounce in no measured terms the low state of morality which prevails and the gross and superstitious character of the popular religious observances and the ideas which underlie them ; but the prophets, too, ignore the code and make statements inconsistent with its existence.  Hundreds of years pass, and the nation is carried away captive to a foreign land.  A remnant eventually returns, and then, for the first time, the Law comes into sight and takes the position which its existence demands for it.  Systematic steps are taken to enforce its precepts ; a mass of tradition grows up around it ; it henceforth becomes the prevailing study and interest of the Jewish life.

To state this view of the case now seems of itself enough to refute it, and the difficulty is to understand how it can ever have been accepted. Unhappily, the older commentators were *capables de tout.* We now know the true account of the matter. History did not take this bewildering course. If Israel was unconscious for so long of the Pentateuchal law, it was because that law had not yet come into existence. Our minds once freed from the shadow of the law, Israelitish history appears in a new light. The straits in which the nation finds itself from time to time are seen to be, not punishments for sin, but the natural conflicts of the race with its warlike neighbours as it slowly consolidated its position, while the captivity appears the inevitable result of the coming into contact of Palestine with the great world-empires. The ethical teaching of the prophets is now seen to lead up to the legislation of the book of Deuteronomy in the reign of Josiah, while the priestly code introduced by Ezra is recognised as the result of the purifying influence of the prophetic teaching on the ancient customary ritual, which, in the process of revision and codification, undergoes a complete metamorphosis and loses its original spontaneous character. If political and governmental institutions find no place in the sacred law, the explanation is a simple one. They are presupposed, being, of course, supplied by the secular Persian Government. The history of Israel, indeed, presents its own strikingly peculiar phenomena (chief of which is the rise and activity of the prophets), and it would be hard to exaggerate the interest and importance of these phenomena; but the traditional view obscures them by placing them in a non-historical environment, and it is not until we are able to bring them into their due position in the growth and evolution of the religion of Israel that we can properly appreciate them, or consider the history of that religion in its proper place among the religious systems of mankind.

To form an idea, then, of the state of Israel at the outset of the history of that nation, we must not turn to the priestly, or even the Deuteronomic law, or the associated narratives of the Hexateuch, though from the oldest sections of that compilation much may be learned. Our information on the subject is mainly derived from the earlier historical books—Judges, Samuel, and Kings. Hence the importance of a careful study of those books, and the value of a commentary such as that of Dr. Smith. These books, indeed, have undergone revision from the point of view of Deuteronomy, and the framework of them is Deuteronomistic. It is to this editing that we owe the crudely pragmatic theory of history in which misfortune always springs from sin and repentance is followed by renewed prosperity. Apart, moreover, from this final revision, examination of the various narratives discloses several sources more or less removed from the most primitive tradition. Sufficient, however, of the latter remains to allow us a considerable insight into the early history, ideas, and institutions of the people of Israel.

Who was Israel ?  Israel stands for a number of tribes of Semitic origin recognising their blood kinship with other peoples, such as Moab and Edom, but claiming a closer relationship with each other. When the history of Israel begins with the exodus from Egypt the tribes were probably united in some sort of league which still subsisted—perhaps in a looser form—during and after the conquest of Canaan.  Israel was hardly a political unit until the time of the monarchy.  Before that the unit was the tribe.  Various tribal or clan leaders from time to time lead the Israelites on to victory as they obtained and made good their footing in the land of Canaan. They fought on foot, having · until Solomon's time no horses, and bows and arrows were at first unknown to them.  Swords, spears, and darts are mentioned, and slings were no doubt usual weapons. Shields were carried, and men of rank at an early date seem to have had armour of some description.  The "Ark of Yahweh" went out to battle, and no expedition was taken in hand unless divine approval had been first signified by the sacred lot.  The campaign was preceded by sacrifices.  A military expedition had a quasi-sacred character, and those engaged in it were subject to certain taboos.

Before the monarchy the rulers of the people were the Sheiks or Elders.  The Sheiks decided on questions of peace and war, and of alliances, and exercised the functions of judges.  Law and morality were wholly customary.  "It is never so done in Israel," "That is folly in Israel," are the phrases applied to deviations from the recognised standards of conduct.  In judicial proceedings, ordeals played a part.  The usual death punishment was stoning, an act of the community, in which "all the people" take part.  Blood feuds were common, and in certain cases the sacred altars were places of sanctuary from private revenge.  Marriage was by purchase, polygamy being freely practised by the rich.  The husband had an unfettered power of divorce.  Concubinage was a recognised institution, and slavery existed.  The practice of circumcision prevailed, but this rite was not a distinguishing mark of the Hebrew people, as is shown by the reservation, for the Philistines in particular, of the epithet " uncircumcised."  Witchcraft was believed in and practised, though early condemned and proscribed, and the story of the witch of Endor and the apparition of the ghost of Samuel seems to indicate a belief in some shadowy spirit existence of the individual after death, though there is, of course, no trace of the conception of a future world as the sphere of punishment or reward.  Men known as " seers " existed, who were believed to possess a power akin to that of second-sight, and were prepared, for a small fee, to use their powers for— *e g.*, the tracing of lost property.  Of the idea of taboo we find numerous vestiges.  It lies at the root of the distinction between clean and unclean, and the law of ceremonial purification.  Firstlings were taboo, as were the first fruits of young trees.  Mourning was shown by howling, fasting, the tearing of clothes, the wearing of sackcloth and ashes, the gashing of the flesh with knives, and the polling of the hair and the beard. The invaders of Canaan were shepherds; but the settlers seem to have soon adopted the practice of agriculture and the growth of the grape, and begun to reside in cities.

Pressure from without, and in particular from the Philistines, led to the foundation of the monarchy. The first king was the man who came to the front at the critical moment. The view of the monarchy as a lapse from the path of devotion to the divine ruler is not a contemporary one. The king is Yahweh's anointed, and he fights the battles of Yahweh. The earlier narrative in the Book of Samuel gives the true account of the matter. The seer announces to Saul the mission of the latter, and is proved to be right by the subsequent event. Saul was a man of war simply, and his life was spent in war. It was left to David to found a stable dynasty and consolidate the royal power.

One permanent bond of union between the tribes was their religion. Yahewh was the God of Israel, and Israel was the people of Yahweh. His relation to Israel was that of protector. Israel may incur his wrath for a time, but lasting estrangement is inconceivable. Yahweh *must* be on Israel's side. The enemies of Israel are his enemies, and their extermination is pleasing to him. The early conception of Yahweh was purely anthropomorphic. He is a local god. His original seat is at Sinai. Thence he visited his people at Kadesh. Afterwards Palestine became his home. Go into a foreign land, and you leave his presence and must serve other gods whose existence is as real as his. He acts in haste and repents his action. He instigates to sin and hardens men's hearts in order that he may afterwards punish them. It is the spirit of Yahweh which clouds and darkens the mind of Saul. It is Yahweh who instigates David to take the census, the taking of which is punished by a pestilence falling upon Israel. When Ahab is to be lured to his doom, it is Yahweh himself who makes the spirit of prophecy become a lying spirit in the mouths of his prophets, that the king may be deceived. The ways of Yahweh are, indeed, past finding out. To see him is death, and to approach him rashly is dangerous. He seeks to slay Moses in the night. The ark of Yahweh becomes the cause of a deadly plague in the land of the Philistines. Uzzah, laying his hand upon it as it journeys towards Jerusalem, is smitten with sudden death; yet it becomes a source of prosperity to the Philistine Obed-Edom, in whose house it is lodged. Yahweh is, however, conceived of as a moral being. Offences against customary morality are displeasing to him, and he punishes the violation of oaths and vows, visiting the sins of the fathers upon the children. Swift and sudden as is his anger, he may be appeased by sacrifice, and to those who find favour in his eyes he is very gracious. His power is not unlimited. Even with his assistance the men of Judah could not drive out the inhabitants of the plains " because they had chariots of iron."

Yahweh was worshipped under various forms, frequently that of a calf or bull. We have no doubt a reference to the fact in the story of the worship of the golden calf in the wilderness. We know that the altars of Dan and Bethel, at which there were golden calves, were both sanctuaries of Yahweh, and figures of oxen appear in the description of Solomon's temple. There was, in fact, in præ-prophetic times no objection to the use of images. Teraphim and ephods were both, down to comparatively late times, used in connection with the worship of Yahweh. Both were images, teraphim being of human shape and usually to be found in every house. Rachel steals her father's teraphim, and David's wife puts the household image in his bed to deceive the messengers of Saul. Down to the time of Hezekiah a brazen serpent was worshipped in the temple at Jerusalem. Older still, no doubt, than the use of " graven images " was the worship of sacred stones or pillars, which were smeared with blood and anointed with oil. Springs or running water had a sacred character—" Spring up, O well ; sing ye unto it "—and there are numerous traces of tree worship. The ark of Yahweh itself was probably a stone image or pillar. (Note that the Philistines place it in the temple of Dagon, treating it like the image of their god.) The historical mention of it in Samuel is entirely at variance with the notion of the ark given by the narratives of the Pentateuch, where the names " Ark of the Covenant " or " Ark of the Testimony " are used to denote a box for the tables of the law. As with the ark so with the ephod. In the earlier references in the historical books the ephod is an image. In the law it becomes the name for a priestly garment.

A place of worship is not arbitrarily selected by man. It is chosen because the deity shows himself there. Yahweh reveals his presence in various places which become his sanctuaries because they are known to be places of his abode. The Yahweh of one place is, to popular apprehension at least, a distinct personality from the Yahweh of another. Absalom must go to serve Yahweh at Hebron although the ark is at Jerusalem. Nearly every sanctuary had the legend of its theophany, some of which legends appear in the patriarchal narratives in the Book of Genesis. When these stories grew up the places they referred to were still sacred places, and hence the interest of the legends, the meaning of which is, of course, lost under the influence of the later law when the cultus at these shrines became proscribed and regarded as irregular and idolatrous. Jacob's ladder is not the unsubstantial fabric of the patriarch's vision. The ladder which he sees is always at Bethel, which is thus shown to be the house of God. Among other holy places were Shiloh Hebron (the ancient capital of Judah), Beersheba, Mispah, Mahanaim, Shechem, Dan, Gilgal, Gibeon, Mount Carmel, Zoheleth, Gihon. No doubt they were very numerous. Under the kings, Bethel became a royal sanctuary for the kings of Israel. Solomon's temple was nothing more than the royal chapel of the kings of Judah. It was part of the palace building to the scandal of Ezekiel at a later period.

If the older sanctuaries had their legends to explain their existence, it must not be thought that the legends contain the true explanations. The narratives are in such cases invented when the real origin of the shrines has been long forgotten. The Israelites, in fact, took over the holy places of the Canaanites, and hence arose a syncretism, distressing to the prophets, between Yahweh and the gods of the older worshippers—the Baalim—divinities of fertility and growth, givers of corn, wine, oil, wool, and flax. Probably the older sanctuaries were beside wells or springs of water like Beersheba, but the later altars, the bamoth or high places, were on the hilltops amidst groves of trees. We must imagine the city on the hillside, below it the well, above it the bamah. The oldest altar was the great stone or pillar (itself originally both idol and altar), the habitation and symbol of the deity (it is the *pillar* at Bethel which is God's house), and the oldest form of sacrifice was the pouring out against it of the blood of the sacrificial victim or the anointing of it with oil. Later, altars were of earth or unhewn stone (a reminiscence of the ancient pillar) and on these burnt offerings were offered. The blood and the fat of the intestines were peculiarly sacred and must not be eaten, but, for the rest, except in the case of the holocaust, a sacrifice was a meal in which the deity shared. The flesh placed on the altar was previously boiled in the same way as that eaten by the worshippers, boiling or seething being probably the older method of cooking flesh among the Israelites; a method which was later to some extent superseded by that of roasting. Although cereal offerings were made, animal sacrifice holds a far more important place than these. There was no killing without a sacrifice. A feast implies a sacrifice and a sacrifice usually a feast. The later and more refined conception of the sharing of the deity in the meal was the inhaling of the smoke, the smelling a sweet savour. Hence the origin of the use of incense, which was unknown in early times. Wine was not placed on the altar, but poured out at its base. It is the blood of the grape and appears to be used as a surrogate for blood.

Human sacrifices are frequently mentioned by the prophets, and seem to have come into prominence in the period before the Assyrian captivity. In early times they were probably rare, and it would be a mistake to regard them as primitive. There are, however, several early references to such sacrifices. The story of Jephthah and his daughter is an example. Other instances are the hewing in pieces of Agag before Yahweh, and the sacrifice to Yahweh by the Gibeonites of the seven sons of Saul as an expiation for their father's breach of the national treaty with that people. This is an interesting case, because we are told that Yahweh was propitiated by the sacrifice, and that the famine with which he had afflicted the land came in consequence to an end. The story of Abraham and Isaac seems to indicate a tendency to a moral feeling against the practice. By the divine command an animal was in this narrative substituted for the human victim.

Certain sanctuaries naturally came to acquire pre-eminence in size and importance, and with the growth of these great sanctuaries professional priests make their appearance. In early times laymen sacrificed without the intervention of a priest, but some one is naturally needed to take charge of the temple and the image (which might well have been stolen) which such a building contains. The priesthood was not until late in the history of Judah confined to a particular tribe or family, but often at a particular sanctuary tended to become so. As time went on the priests, or some of them, claimed Levitical descent. The first stage in this process was probably the tendency to regard Moses or Aaron (both Levites) as founder of the priesthood. Possibly many of the priests were Levites in fact. In earlier times, however, the proprietor of a place of worship appointed his son or any one he pleased as priest. Sometimes the actual guardian of the temple would be, not the priest, but a subordinate official. We know that Samuel, acting in that capacity, slept in the temple of Shiloh. In Israel and Judah alike the kings (who themselves offered sacrifices on occasions) absolutely controlled the royal chapels and the regius-priesthood. They did not hesitate, in fact, to deal freely with the ritual practice. The subordinate offices of Solomon's temple were filled by foreign slaves—"slaves of the house of Yahweh." The sacred oracle was in the hands of the priests, and they naturally became the depositaries of the ritual tradition and of the learning with regard to the ancient rules as to ceremonial cleanness. The priest depended for his livelihood on the bounty of the worshippers at the shrine, it being customary for him to receive a share in the sacrificial offerings. At a later time he became entitled to fixed dues. The royal sanctuaries were no doubt maintained at the king's expense. Tithe was at first a royal tax, and only in the latest legislation became a priestly due.

Yahweh's will was made known in various ways to his people. Omens might be sought in the most casual occurrences, such as the unpremeditated remarks of men, or the sound of wind among the tree-tops. The usual method of inquiring of Yahweh was, however, by Urim and Thummim, the sacred lot. For this the intervention of the priest with the ephod was necessary. The inquirer put his question to the priest, who drew forth the lot giving the answer. Questions were put in the alternative form, one answer being shown by Urim, the other by Thummim. The Urim and Thummim were material objects, and the priest seems to have drawn one or the other with his hand from the receptacle, which may have been a cavity in the image. The divine will was also revealed through the prophets, or *nebiin*, a kind of dervishes who consorted in troops. They used musical instruments and uttered inarticulate sounds and ravings, acting, in fact, like men deprived of reason (who also possess a sacred character). In public estimation they do not seem to have stood high. Under the monarchy they were very numerous. The prophets of whom Ahab inquired before undertaking the siege of Ramoth-Gilead are stated to have numbered 400. These men appear to have exercised their prophetic office as a means of livelihood. Not all those, however, to whom Yahweh's word came belonged to the prophetic guild. Amos, for instance, expressly disclaims all connection with this professional class.

An ethical movement, however, seems early to have originated among the prophets. How far it influenced the bulk of them may, indeed, be doubted, but that it was felt to an extraordinary degree by a minority is certain. How this movement arose is a question of great difficulty and cannot be completely answered. The phenomenon is connected with the rise of ethical monotheism, in which the prophets had so large a part. The prophet always regarded himself as the mouthpiece of Yahweh. Once, then, you have a man possessed of ethical instincts in advance of his age (and such individuals will in any society from time to time arise), and the utterances of such a man possessed with this belief in his divine mission must, if he be a man of strong character, acquire transcendent power. In such a man's mind the conception of Yahweh would become purged and heightened, would tend to lose its *naïf* primitive attributes, and to acquire a more definite moral character. On the negative side, the strong national and conservative bent of the prophets helped to keep Israel apart from his kindred races and to resist, as displeasing to Yahweh, foreign innovations in religion. In the foregoing sketch of Israel there seems little of a "sacred" character (using that word in a popular sense), little, if anything, so far as we know, to distinguish the Israelites from their neighbours—the people of Yahweh from, say, the people of Chemosh. Why in Israel's case only the prophets and prophecy became the mighty force which gave to the religion of Israel the character which subsequent religious formalism could not destroy we cannot say, but it was the prophets of Yahweh who, by their lofty ethical conception of his character, laid the foundations of a religious universalism of which not even the greatest of them dreamed.

C. G. B.

# AN EVERY-DAY CRIME.

OF course this is absurd on the face of it. Crime, with most of us at any rate—say with the readers of this magazine—is a long way off. It may be among some people's near concerns; with us it is the very opposite of an every-day matter. To give such a name to anything done by ordinary persons is to make mountains out of molehills.

I shall have something to say presently of proverbial lore, but here I will content myself with remarking a detail in the nature of mountains and molehills not infrequently overlooked. If you get enough molehills and put them together they will make a mountain; and some respectable people are, as time goes on, accumulating offences of the molehill order in their record at a pretty fair rate. Take the case of the most every-day, reasonable, orderly, and English among my readers. He has probably two or three connections who are obliged by force of circumstances to spend a good deal of their time in his company; who live with him, in fact, more or less; and who have to get on with him, and with whom he has to get on (for there are always two sides to a question) as well as temperament and circumstances allow. When two people are thus chained together for the whole or a part of their lives it is open to either of them to make the time which they spend together either a pleasure or a burden to the other, and that without doing anything which would excite much remark. If anybody, let him be as every-day as he will, makes a large portion of another person's life, or two or three people's lives, a burden to them, it may fairly be maintained that he has come about as near to the limits of a crime as he need aspire to do. The difference between habitual rudeness and habitual politeness in his own behaviour will probably be as great a difference as he will ever be able to make to the general sum of happiness. Let it be fully understood, by-the-bye, that the masculine pronoun, wherever the context allows it, should include the feminine for good and evil. We terribly need the common gender.

Almost everybody has had some acquaintance—quite an ordinary person—without criminal tendencies, respected, very likely, or even beloved at a sufficient distance, but never desired as a close companion; dreaded, in fact, in that capacity as one dreads the mosquito. A gasometer, it has been observed, is not so very ugly at a distance, and when quite out of sight is even rather nice. So is it with people of this nature. "She's very good-hearted, you know!" He has a great many virtues." How well we know those anxious exculpating phrases which form the preface or the conclusion when the bottled-up aggravation of relatives and friends can be bottled up no more! The bottling is much to the credit of the said friends; but the outburst, though an ineffable relief, is attended with a haunting sense of guilt; and that little justifying phrase is dictated by a twinge of really unnecessary remorse. Did the "good-hearted" and "virtuous" people who have been the subjects of conversation ever feel any remorse, one wonders, for making themselves so disagreeable that their intimates could suppress their feelings no longer? It is a curious but undeniable fact that those who are blamed in such cases by outsiders and by themselves are usually not the aggressors but the sufferers. The aggressor is always "so good-hearted, you know." "It is a shame to say anything against such people;" they "mean so well;" and so on to the end of the chapter. But only ask whether anybody not already in bondage would like to live with those excellent people, or even to have much to do with them. "Not for worlds!" "See them further first!" "So beastly disagreeable." "So very difficult to get on with." In some such terms, according to age, sex, and temperament, the proposed victims begin to make excuse. The people in question are like the gasometer—so nice when quite out of sight! None of their friends want their company, even for a week; and think of the unfortunates who have to be their companions always!

"But," somebody will say, "it is a pity to brood over trifles, and it is not fair to condemn anybody for little things." "Don't brood over trifles" is a delightfully easy dictum, has given the speaker no trouble in inventing it, is as simple as recommending you not to cry over spilt milk or not to answer a fool according to his folly, or moralising about mountains and molehills as suggested above. The copyright of these remarks is out—anybody can use them; and they are always effective, because they sound, and are in themselves, so sensible. But it should never be forgotten that there are two things to be considered in a remark: firstly, whether it is in itself good; and secondly, whether it is applicable to the present situation; and though Solomon may have invented the remark for us, in which case it is probably good, we have to depend on ourselves for the application, which therefore frequently could not be worse.

In the present case the injunction not to brood over trifles is excellent; the only thing to be settled is whether the matters in question are trifles or not; and in the case of every-day behaviour there is a good deal of misapprehension on this point. You are staying with the Browns, and, with the best intentions in the world, probably meaning to fill up an awkward gap in the conversation, you make some not very deeply-considered remark about, let us say, the course of study for a medical degree. The eldest Miss Brown instantly sets you right, and, not satisfied with your meek acceptance of her information, brings works of reference to impress upon you what a ridiculous mistake you have made. Not wishing to be discouraged by the first unpleasantness, you try Miss Brown with the last book, play, or piece of news in which you have taken an interest, and are given to understand that she never wastes her time over such matters, having, it is plainly implied, a better use for it. These, in themselves, are trifles, and you would certainly be foolish to brood over them. The probable explanation is that when Miss Brown is tired she is apt to be a little snappish, and very likely she has good reason enough to be tired. But that you should always feel that when Miss Brown is in company an innocent remark, meant to show your goodwill, will be snapped up in the same way if she happens to be tired, and should therefore be driven to take refuge in silence; that all the Browns' friends, and, still more deplorable, the Browns themselves, should be made to feel the same—this creates an atmosphere which is not a trifle. The Brown family can tell you so, if they will speak the truth; but probably they will prefer, from motives which command respect and sympathy, to suppress it. Nobody, least of all Miss Brown herself, will appreciate the deadliness of the blight thrown over all conversation, or be aware of its true cause. Visitors will only think the Browns a very silent family. They expect to be snubbed whenever they attempt to speak, and consequently do not attempt it on any subject that they care about. Conversation becomes nearly impossible, and confidence entirely so. "I want to talk to you, Rose," is the tentative introduction thrown out by a friend, who perhaps thinks a good deal of Miss Brown, relies on her judgment, is fond of her, and would like, at the present moment, the advice and sympathy of some one she can trust on a delicate subject. "Talk, then," says Rose, who has a headache, or perhaps has made that homely mistake of getting out of bed on the wrong side; and obviously the friend's only course is to say, "Not if you're busy," and to make an excuse for getting out of the way. Who can unfold a cherished scheme, make an interesting confidence, even enter on an argument, in the face of that "Talk, then"? Pleasant intercourse of any kind flourishes in proportion to the expenditure, on somebody's part, of sympathetic interest and polite self-restraint; and to cast a blight over pleasant intercourse is no trifling offence. Rose does not realise that if there is to be conversation, somebody must "make it go;" but she would soon recognise a difference if the people who habitually perform that good office in her family were to abandon it suddenly, and frame their manners on her model. She has never seen herself as others see her, for the very simple reason that none of

those about her behave as she does. People have remonstrated with
her; but she has always been able to answer that all the things to
which they take exception are " mere trifles." So they are; and
that is one reason why rudeness—in the abstract—is so readily
excused. It has to be attacked, if at all, on the ground of some one
petty offence the mention of which seems puerile when much .stress
is laid upon it. It is impossible to make the offender realise the
difference between one petty rudeness and the habit of being rude.
Politeness, it may be observed here as well as elsewhere, is a virtue
which is apt to get little credit ; like many other unobtrusive sources
of happiness, it is often not perceived till it is gone, and even then
the want which is vaguely felt is not traced to its right source.
Rose is quite aware that she enjoys being with her friend Miss Jones
—at any rate, when Miss Jones has gone away, she knows that no
one else suits her so well. But she does not connect this with the
fact that Miss Jones suppresses the unfavourable criticisms which
occur to her until they are asked for ; waits to tell her story or make
her point till she can do it without interrupting somebody else; is
often crowded out of the conversation in consequence, but is never
unwilling on that account to listen sympathetically to other people ;
and, when she has to say something unpleasant, does it, not in the
manner which Rose would call " truthful," but in the manner which
will convey the truth with as little pain as possible. These and a
hundred other little restraints make up her charm to a great extent,
but it will be observed that many of them are in their nature negative. They do not strike Rose's imagination, and probably will never
impress themselves much upon her conscious thoughts.

Rose has, however, according to the formula mentioned above,
many virtues, and goodness of heart is among the number. If only
her goodness of heart would lead her to exercise that virtue which
would make more difference to her fellow-creatures than she will ever
be able to make in any other way—what a different life it would be
for her friends and family! She has worked her way well; she was
persevering and industrious at school and college; she is a conscientious and successful teacher, honest, morally courageous, very much
in earnest, generous with her money and her time. But if only she
would have done less for her friends in the way of unasked and
unexpected kindnesses, even given less excellent lessons on the Tudor
period and the fourth book of Euclid, and respected the feelings of
friends and pupils in her daily transactions with them, the total of
wasted energy would have been less. As it is, friends and pupils
count the minutes till her departure enables them to converse and
carry on life generally with some freedom and satisfaction. That the
whole of one's intercourse with a friend or relative should be a perpetual self-defence against aggressive rudeness leads not infrequently
to the decision that peace is better than friendship—a serious

decision, which may be disastrous to two lives. Moreover, even in trifles there is such a thing as classification. Even trifling grievances are either just or unjust. There is a story—disinterred, I believe, from a tract—of a little boy who asked for the loan of his brother's ball. The brother refused, which, as far as the outside public can penetrate the case, he had a perfect right to do. The first little boy being in an unreasonable frame of mind, the two came to blows; and the parents, for the sin of quarrelling, shut them both up in a dark cupboard for the rest of the day, quite oblivious of the fact that one boy was in the right and the other in the wrong. I have forgotten now what moral was supposed to be pointed by the tale, but it will serve to illustrate a very common mental confusion. No doubt it saved the parents a great deal of trouble—for getting at the rights of a case is an endless business. Probably the Sunday pie was burning, and the mother was in a hurry to get at the oven, and under these circumstances two clamorous children are much handier in a dark cupboard than squirming about the kitchen floor. One feels for the mother, but one feels also for the little boy who was in the right. In the same way, it is a great deal of trouble to inquire whether the grievances of the Brown family are just or not. It is much easier to say to Rose's brothers and sisters, "Don't brood over trifles." They will probably offer less resistance to a little undeserved blame than Rose would to any kind of criticism, though it were no more than the truth demanded.

"But again," it is said, "you are hard upon Rose. She does her best really, and she is so good-hearted with it all, you must not mind her temper." If Rose does her best, criticism is certainly disarmed, though she may have to be forgiven until seventy times seven. Rudeness is often not deliberate, and Rose's friends and victims plead on her behalf that if she has less tact than other people that is not her fault. It is sometimes maintained that tact is an intellectual quality not to be acquired. It may be so; though for my own part I believe that a real conviction of the importance of courtesy, combined with a sincere desire to practise it, will in time work wonders—perhaps all that can be desired. But it is very certain that a great deal of ungraciousness is due either to a notion that there is no duty in trifles, and that those who attach importance to them are foolish, or to the fact that politeness often involves the trouble of thinking, or the suppression of something which people have taken it into their heads to say. " Really, I don't want to be rude, but—— " is the formula constantly prefixed to some astounding impertinence; and the natural reply is, "If you don't want to be rude, why *are* you rude?" The formula intended to palliate the rudeness is as honest as some others in frequent use; but it is hardly sufficient not to want to be rude. People should want not to be rude, which is a different thing.

As for the second plea, Rose may be as good-hearted as she likes. Some people would say that they set little value on the goodness of heart reserved by its possessor for great occasions only. They are not altogether right there ; for humanity is strangely inconsistent, and gentle actions and mean cruelty may be found in the same nature. Dr. Johnson was guilty of many a brutal, unprovoked, and unpardonable insult; but we need not on that account deny him his goodness of heart when he carried the destitute girl to his home, loyally maintained blind and unamiable Miss Williams out of his own means, and—perhaps a more lovable trait than either— went out on an undignified errand himself to spare the feelings of his servant. To some extent, frequent lapses add a pathetic charm to contrasting excellence, and it is often the nature which can be brutal whose gentleness is so exquisite. But when a man of Dr. Johnson's type, in the habit of launching insults at his daily companions, ends, say, by risking his life to save them from drowning, I think the universal expectation that the habit of insult shall be forgotten and cancelled is rather a large demand to make. Some people—and those not the worst—would excuse him from the final rescue if he would keep his insults to himself through life. There are prices too high to pay for any one's friendship, and among them is the demand that a man should put up with rudeness unworthy to be committed or suffered by a gentleman, at the caprice of his associate.

Besides—and now for one of those non-copyright dicta which save so much trouble—life is made up of trifles, and good conduct in trifles is often said to be rarer and more difficult than good conduct in great matters, which is perhaps the reason why it is found convenient to ignore trifles, and lock them up in dark cupboards. We all feel pretty certain that we shall not more than once or twice be called upon to act in great matters ; we are quite sure that we must act in trifles every day ; and therefore it is much pleasanter and easier to say that trifles do not signify, and to be very much in earnest about those great questions which we shall never have to decide. But, after all, a great decision—even a great sacrifice—resolves itself into a procession of every-day matters when it comes to be worked out. It is not the moment of renunciation which is the test of a character ; it is the living up to that renunciation through the days and weeks which follow, when the exaltation is gone and the sacrifice is felt.

Let it be clearly understood, by-the-bye, that politeness—or courtesy, to use the better word—does not necessarily mean smooth insincerity. There is a mischievous habit of confounding *brusquerie* with honesty and fearlessness, and imputing a desire to flatter and deceive to any one who treats his friends as one gentleman treats another. "The assumption is," I was once told, "that if people are very

polite they must have something to gain by it." The view of human
nature implied in such a doctrine speaks for itself. But it is a
mistake to suppose that every omission to cram unwelcome facts
down people's throats constitutes untruthfulness, and it is also a mistake
to think that *brusquerie* is bound up with sincerity. There is a
tendency to imagine that he who tells an unpleasant truth can have
nothing to gain by it; but the notion will not bear examination.
To some people, the telling is in itself something to aim at. They
think it adds to their own consequence to pull down somebody else
in his own and other people's estimation; and conversely they think
themselves lowered by admitting that anything belonging to another
person can be admired. That unsolicited and unfavourable opinion
of your bicycle or your hat or that paper which you have just succeeded
in getting into *The Unique Review,* and of which, being human, you
think a good deal—that unsolicited opinion, I say, which they think
themselves both clever and honest for throwing in your teeth, is it
not, on the whole, best described as a childish impertinence? Not
that you would do much good by telling them so. "Oh, well, if
you want to be flattered," is their usual answer, "don't come to me.
If you want my opinion, you'll have to hear the truth." But the
legitimate reply is, "I don't want your opinion." "I *am* ugly," said
Priscilla Lammeter to the Miss Gunns. "But law! I don't mind—
do you? The pretty 'uns do for flycatchers—they keep the men off
us." I have always felt that the Miss Gunns deserved sympathy.
Priscilla afterwards remarked that she was "a bad 'un to live with
for folks when they didn't like the truth." That was her way of
putting it.

Of course there is no doubt that circumstances alter cases.
Any one who has asked a candid opinion from a friend should take
blame along with praise, and be grateful to the person who has
undertaken, at his instance, a delicate and often difficult task. It is
to the last degree unreasonable to complain under such circumstances
of an adverse criticism. But you do not ask everybody's opinion;
and even if it does not suit you always to have your bicycle in perfect
condition, or the paint on your front door absolutely up to date, you
may not see the force of being called to account by all and sundry
for these lapses. The Miss Gunns had not asked for Priscilla's
opinion on their personal attractions.

Moreover, "unpleasant truth" is rather a wide term, and is often
made to cover what might be more appropriately called unpleasant
assertion, if nothing harsher. The person who enjoys making a
disagreeable remark does not always stop to inquire whether his
remark is founded on fact. Such a process might deprive him of
the pleasure of making it; and to go through life telling people
only what they do not like to hear brings him no nearer to sincerity
than to say only what is agreeable. The plain rule is—to say

nothing untrue, and nothing that it is not your place to say; and it must be admitted that this maxim, if carried out, would deprive some conversationalists of much of their capital.

There is a good deal of the bullying element about rudeness—the element of hitting those who are down. Some people, it is true, are rude impartially, and one respects the impartiality; but even then one does not respect the rudeness, and it is pitiable to confound a morose habit of mind with fearless honesty. But most rude people—one regrets to say—are rude when they dare; and the bully is generally a coward. The rude person is the last to tolerate rudeness against himself. He is the first to commend people who " don't brood over trifles," and " can take a joke;" and he probably intends to be credited, and sincerely credits himself, with this Spartan habit of mind. But if you put him to the test you find that it is rudeness to other people of which he is so remarkably tolerant. Turn the tables on him, even in just self-defence, and it is an outrage. It is never he who has been the aggressor—it is you who are " so easily offended."

The denunciation of a fault is an ungrateful task, and perhaps can hardly be undertaken without suggesting a low view of human nature. The remedy is to present to contemplation the corresponding virtue. " It is better to fight for the good than to rail at the ill." And courtesy is not a negative quality. It is not simply the absence of discourtesy. It is that active desire to confer benefits, which in great things is called devotion, carried into the trifles of daily life. It is the extension to all sentient creatures of that chivalry which, absurd in its exaggerations and its limitations, had yet in it a splendid disregard of self. It is that large and honourable respect for the human rights of a human being which in all its delicate ramifications makes the character of the lady and the gentleman; that fine and cogent sense of justice from which the highest generosity springs.

FRANCES HEATH FRESHFIELD.

# HEALTH'S IMPROVEMENT.[1]

As the title-page sets forth, it " Discovers the Nature, Method, and Manner of Preparing all sorts of Food used in this Nation," Written by that ever Famous Thomas Muffett, Doctor in Physic.

The original work seems to have fallen into oblivion from which it was rescued. " Corrected and Enlarged " by Christopher Bennet, Fellow of the College of Physicians in London 1655, not for his " own glory and honour," but, as he explains in the Preface, " to restore the fame of the one time most famous doctor," or, to give his own words :

" It is not an itch to be in print, but my Profession to keep men alive, and when gone to recover and revive them, that hath induced me to this undertaking. Blame me not therefore for useing means to raise our Author out of the dust, and long oblivion, wherein he was buried. 'Tis true, his own relations and their interests much sollicited my help; but the merits of the man were my greatest motives, and his old Fame most quickend me to restore him, upon perusal, I found so much life and Pulse in his dead Works, that it had not been Charity in me to let him dye outright, specially when it is for the worlds good and your (Health's Improvement). This is all, only if it may be any advantage to have my Judgement, tis a Piece for my palate, not likely to dis-relish any, where so much pleasure is interlarded with our profit. I may safely say, upon this subject I know none that hath done better ; and were Platina, Apicius, or Alexandrinus, with all the rest of the Dietetick writer's now alive, they would certainly own, and highly value this Discourse."

And so ends Christopher Bennet's preface to his friend's book, what he himself terms " An Epistle to the Reader ;" but the book itself is full of interest, not only as showing how we have changed in the last 200 years in our foods, but in the way in which we regard them. Dietests, as they called themselves in those days, looked upon certain foods as causing all ills that flesh is heir to, and others as not only having a physical but mental and moral effect upon the body; and though, no doubt, there was a grain of truth in their theory, they were carried far beyond the bounds of possibility in their enthusiasm for their science. As when they assumed that food properly chosen would enable men to live to the age of the patriarchs, or by eating the flesh of long-lived animals or birds one could increase their length of years. To quote my author :

[1] Written by that ever Famous Thomas Muffet, Doctor in Physics in Queen Elizabeth's reign.

"Divine Hippocraté, compareth diet most fitly to a Potters wheele, going neither forward nor backward, but (as the world it self moveth) equally round; moistening that which is too dry, drying up that which is too moist, restoring true flesh if it be decaid, abating proud flesh (by abstinence) if it be too much, neither drawing too much upward nor downward (as peevish Sawyers do), neither clapping on too much sail (like unskillful Mariners), but giving (like a wise Steward) every part his allowance by geometrical proportion, that the whole household and family may be kept in health. Such a Steward was Asclepiades, who cured by only Diet infinite diseases.

"Such a one was Galen, that famous Physitian, who being three or four times sick befor he was twenty eight years old, looked more strictly afterwards to his diet; in such sort that a hundred years following he was never sick but once, and died only through want of radical moisture.

"Such an one finally was Hippocrates, who lived till he was a hundred and nine years old without any memorable sickness, and yet he had by Nature but a weak head, insomuch that he ever wore a night cap. Wherefore let us neither with the impudent, call diet a frivolous knowledge, or a curious science, but embrace it as the leader to perfet health, (which as the wise man saith) is above gold, and a sound body above all riches.

"The Romans once banished Physitians out of Rome, under pretence that physick druggs weakened the peoples stomacks; and cooks, for corrupting and enforcing appetites with strange sawces and seasonings; and Perfumers, and Anointers, and bathe-masters, because they did rather mollifie and effeminate the Roman Mindes, than any whit profit or help their bodies. Yet they retained Cato, the chief dietist of that time, and all them that were able (without physick) to prevent or cure diseases."

Foods themselves seem to have changed somewhat in England during the 300 years that have passed nearly since our old friend Dr. Muffett first penned his notes. According to him, wild boar, red deer, and hedgehogs were as commonly eaten as beef, and goats and kids as mutton and lamb. His chapter on the flesh of wild beasts is so amusing that I must quote it fully. He says:

"Of all Venison, Hippocrates most commendeth the flesh of a Wild Sow, because it is not only an excellent nourishing and strengthening meat, but also medicinable to keep us from costiffness, Reason teaching us that it is far above tame Pork or Swines flesh: First because it feeds more purely; Secondly, because it hath not meat brought to hand, but it gets it by travail, and hath choice of diet to feed whereon it listeth. Thirdly, it is not penn'd up (as commonly our Swine be) in a little close and stinking Stie, but enjoyeth the benefit of a clear aire, which clarifieth bloud, as much as any meat can augment it. It is a rare meat now in England, and found only (as I have been enformed) in my Lord Latimer's Woods, who took pleasure in hunting them, and made also wild Buls of tame ones, as our fore-Fathers (more wisely) made tame of wild.

"If they be young, fat, fully grown, and taken in chase, in the winter time (presently after mast is fallen) they are unfit for few mens stomacks, being thus prepared as I have seen them done in High-Germany. First, after the flesh is thoroughly cold, parboil it in Rhenish Wine, wherein ripe Juniper berries were sodden; then having taken it out and sliced it, season every slice or cut with Pepper, Salt, Cloves, Mace, Ginger, and Nutmegs, of each a sufficient quantity, last of all make it in paste, with good store of sweet butter and it will prove a most excellent meat to be eaten cold.

"Wild Calves are common in Wales upon the mountains; whence one was brought this last Christmas to Ludlow Castle, where I did eat of it rosted and bak'd ; and by taste I find it more firm and dry, and by the effects of digestion, more wholsom and passable then our ordinary Veal.

"Now concerning Deers Flesh, some imagine it to be the worst meat of all others, and some conceive it to be the best, Galen numbereth amongst hard, melancholique, and gross Meats, comparing, yea almost preferring Asses flesh before it; ascribing also unto it ill concoction, ill nourishment, stoppings, and Quartane Feavers. Roger Bacon thinks it one of the best meats, if it be so young that we can digest it; For, saith he, That which long liveth by its own nature, maketh also others to live long. But by his leave, we may then feed better upon Ravens than Capons, for these never live above seven yeares, and a Raven liveth to nine hundred yeares, if Virgil be not deceived. Plutarch thinketh Deer an unwholsom meat, because it is of a cold and melancholick constitution. And how proveth he that ? forsooth, first; because he is fearful ; secondly because if he were of a hot complexion (as the wild Bore is) his teares would be sweet, as his be ; but the tears of a Deere are salt. Furthermore they are thought to be unwholsom, because Bucks and Staggs feed much upon Snakes ; yea as an Ass is to a Lions mouth, or hony to Bears, or Bees to Martlets, so are Serpents to them a desired meat; whereupon the Grecians call them, Serpent Catchers.

"Might I be a sufficient Arbrirator between two Learned Men, I would determine the truth to be on either side : For indeed young Venison, whilst it is sucking, is very restorative ; Nay young Bucks and Does, Hinds and Staggs (whilst they are in season) are a wholesom and delicate meat, breeding no bad juice of themselves, yet bearing often the faults of bad Cooks (which know not how to dress nor use them aright). The Italians also have this opinion of Venison, that eaten in the morning it prolongeth life, but eaten towards night it hasteneth death.

"Contrariwise old Venison indeed is dry, and perhaps too cold likewise ; full of gross, clammy, and incorrigible humors : So that the same meat may be wholsom at some age, in some times, and for some certain complexions, which otherwise in contrary circumstances is unwholsom ; yet is it never so pretious as that a man should venture his life to get it by stealth, as many doe, and have done in Noble mens Parks, yea perhaps in their Princes Forrests and chief Chases. Cardau affirmeth that Bucks and Does have no Galls in their bodies, which is rather a signe of good temperature and lightness, then of any dull, dry, or heavy meat.

"This one thing only I will add, That Keepers of Parks, or at least their servants and young children, have, upon my knowledge fed all the year long of little meat else, and yet remained as strong, healthful, and active as any persons could be. Finally, admit Deer to be dry ; doth not butter amend them ? Suppose they be cold ; doth not pepper and salt, and baking, give them sufficient heat ? Thus howsoever it falleth out, they are either by preparation (which none can deny) or by nature (as I verily believe) a good nourishment, so that they be chosen in their due season, just age, and moderately fed upon :

"Neither have we any reason from their unwholsomness to dispark our Parks, or to cut down Forrests provided for their succour ; nay rather we ought to cherish them for maintenance of Hunting, whereunto if young Gentlemen were addicted, as their Fathers were heretofore, they would be more ready (whereof Hunting is a resemblance) to warlike purposes and exploits."

Our author imputes so many virtues to the flesh of the hedgehog, that one is inclined to think it must have been one of his favourite dishes. He says :

"When I consider how cleanly the Hedghogg feedeth, namely upon Cows milk (if he can come by it) or upon fruit and mast; I saw no reason to discontinue this meat any longer upon some fantastical dislike, sith books, nature, and experience hath commended it unto us. For as Martial made Hares flesh the daintiest dish of the Romans, so in Hippocrates time the Hedghogg was not of least account among the Grecians; which he commendeth for an excellent nourishment, were it not something too moist and diuretical. Nay (as some affirm) it nourisheth plentifully, procureth appetite and sleep, strengthneth Travailers, preserveth women with child from miscarrying, dissolveth knots and kernelly tumours, helps the Lepry, Consumption, Palsy, Dropsie, Stone, and Convulsion."

He not only tells us what are the best means, but also how to cook them, and the book is filled with quaint receipts. I do not know what the Society for the Prevention of Cruelty to Animals, however, would say to some of them. Take, for instance, his general receipt of cooking fish, or, as he says himself :

"A VERY GOOD WAY HOW TO DRESS MOST PART OF SCALED FISHES.

"Prepare it after this sort. Set a good quantity of white strong vinegar, and stale ale, with a cursey of salt, a little mints, origanum, parsly, and rosemary; and when your liquor boileth fast upon the fire, stop the mouth of your fish with a nutmeg thrust down into his throat, and cast him skipping into the liquor keeping him down till he be thorow dead and perfectly sodden; dress Pikes, Roches, Carps, Grailings, Mullets, and all great fish of the River in the like sort; for it will make them to eat pleasant, crisp, brittle, and firm, not watrish and flaggy, as most fish do, because we know not how to use and order them.

"OF FISH GENERALLY.

"As amongst Poets there is some called Coryphæus, or Captain-poet, so fareth it likewise amongst meats. Some prefering fruit as being most ancient, cleanly, naturall, and needing either none or very little preparation. Others extoll flesh; as most sutable to fleshy creatures, and giving most and best nourishment. But the finest feeders and dainty bellies did not delight in flesh with Hercules, or in fruit with Plato and Arcesilaus, but with Numa and Philocrates in variety of fish; which Numa made a law, that no fish without scales nor without finns should be eaten of the people, whereupon I may further collect and gather, that he was not ignorant of Moses law. Also (according to the vain dream of Gregory the Great Bishop of Rome, and author of the Carthusian Order) he put more holines in fish than in flesh, falsly imagining flesh to be a greater motive to lust then the use of fish; which frivolous conceit is befor sufficiently confuted in the seventh Chapter, and needeth not to be shaken again in this place. Now I will not deny, that fish is a wholesome meat, if such fish could be alwaies gotten as may sufficiently nourish the body; but now a daies it so falleth out through iniquity of times, or want of providence, or that our Sea-coast and Rivers are more barren of fish than heretofore, that in the Spring time, when we ought to feed on the purest and most wholesome nourishment, our blood is not cleansed but corrupted with filthy fish, I mean salt-herrings, red-herrings, Sprats, Harerdin and greenfish which are not amiss for Sailers and Ploughmen, but yet most hurtful and dangerous for other persons. Gatis Queen of Syria made a Law, that no meal should pass through the year, without fish: which if it were as firmly made and executed in England, no doubt much flesh would be spared, and

Navigation and fisher men maintained through the land : neither should we need to imitate Gregory the Lent-maker, perswading men to eat only fish at that time, when it is most out of season, most hardly gotten, and most hurtfull to the bodies of most men. Also in high Germany there is both fish and flesh continually set upon the table, that every mans appetite, humour, and complexion, may have that which is fittest for it : in which country though no Lent be observed (except of a few Catholicks) yet is there abundance of flesh, all the year long, restraint being onely made in Spring time of killing that which is young."

Though our ancient physician devotes quite half of his book to flesh and fish, he yet is half a vegetarian, judging by his own showing, for in the chapters given over to fruit and vegetables, he says :

"Now we come to the last course, which in ancient and more healthful ages was the first and onely, whilst mens hands were neither polluted with blood of Beastes nor smelt of the unwholesome sent of fish.

"This kind of meat is commended (like the Hebrew tongue) for three principal reasons : antiquity, purity, and sufficiency ; for it is more ancient than either flesh or fish by two thousand years ; it is so pure of itself that it never defiles the hand nor needeth any great dressing ; and that it is sufficient to maintain us long in life, not only the history of the first twelve Patriarches, but also whole nations living at this day in India, Africa, Asia, and some parts of Europe, of sufficiently declare, feeding wholly or principally of fruit ; whereof I find three chief or especial kinds, namely, Orchard-fruit growing upon trees ; Garden-fruit growing upon shrubs herbs and roots, and Field-fruit concluded under the name of Graine.

## " OF ALL ORCHARD FRUITS.

"Abricocks are plums dissembled under a peaches coat good only and commendable for their last and fragrant smell, their flesh quickly corrupting and degenerating into choler and wheyish excrements, engendring pestilent agues, stopping the liver and spleen, breeding ill juice, and giving either none or very weak nourishment ; yet they are medicinable and wholesome for some persons, for they quench thirst ; and sirup made of the infusion of dried Abricocks, qualifies the burning heat and rage of fevers : They are least hurtful to the stomach, and most comfortable to the brain and heart, which be sweet kerneld, big and fragrant, growing behind a kitchen-chimny (as they do at Barnelms) and so thoroughly ripened by the sun, that they will easily part from their stone. They are best befor meat, and fittest for hot stomacks ; but let not women eat many of them and let them also remember to drown them well in Sack or Canary wine.

"Apples be so divers of form and substance, that it were infinite to describe them all ; some consist more of aire then water, as sour Puffs called Mala pulmonea ; others more of water then wind, as sour Castaras and Pome-waters. To be short, all apples may be sorted into three kinds, Sweet, Soure, and Usavory. Sweet apples ease the cough, quench thirst, cure melancholly, comfort the heart and head (especially if they be fragrant and odoriferous) and also give a laudable nourishment. Soure apples, hinder spitting, straiten the brest, gripe and hurt the stomach, encrease phlegm, and weaken memory. Sweet Apples are to be eaten at the beginning of meat, but soure and tart Apples at the latter end. All Apples are worst raw, and best baked or preserved. . . . Philip of Macedonia and Alexander his son (from whome perhaps a curious and skilful Herald may derive our Lancashire men) were called Philomeli Apple-lovers, because they were never without Apples in their pockets, yea all Macedonians his Countrymen did so love them, that having neer Babylon surprised a Fruiterer's boy, they strived for it that many were drowned.

"Honey and bread was a great Meat with Pythagoras and his Scholars, and counted a sufficient food for a temperate life. For bread strengthens the body, and honey both nourishes much, and also cleanseth away superfluities. Pollio Romulus being asked by Augustus the Emperor, how he lived so long! By nourishing (saith he) my inwards with Honey, and my outward parts with Ayle. The like answer likewise made Democritus, being demanded the like question. Furthermore, it is so general a Meat thorough Russia, that the Children eat it on their bread every morning as ours do Butter to their breakfast: with whom, and with Old Men it agreeth exceeding well, clensing their breasts, opening their pipes, warming their stomachs, resisting putrefaction, and engendering sweet and commendable blood; Raw honey is never good, therefore clarifie it throughly at the fire; also let it be honey that ran and was never puffed out of the combs, and of young bees rather than old, feeding upon thime, rosemary, flowers, and such sweet and wholesome herbs. Then may you boldly give it as meat to young children, to cold and moist complexions, and to rheumatick old men, especially in Northern Countries, and cold climates, and in the winter season.

But enough of extracts: these will prove to you how quaint and old-world a book we have before us, and that our learned author, if a good "dietest," as he calls himself, was but a poor physician, as we count physicians now; and, for the sake of our bodily wellbeing, it is better to be living in our Victorian Age than in the days of Good Queen Bess and Scotch Jamie, when our friend Muffett lived and wrote "The Nature, Method, and Manner of Preparing all Sorts of Food used in his Nation." One wonders on turning over the book, if the Englishman of those days managed to keep well and strong on the strange and highly-spiced and most indigestible food of his time; what he would have been, fed on the more simple and plain foods of nowadays—a very giant in strength, I have no doubt, and rivalling the Patriarchs in their length of days.

# CONTEMPORARY LITERATURE.

## SCIENCE.

ECLIPSES of the sun have been so frequently observed, and the facilities for transporting observers to all parts of the globe are so great, that it might be imagined that most of the features of these phenomena have already been observed and explained. For several reasons, however, the interest of astronomers in eclipses of the sun has of late years increased rather than diminished, and every civilised country now fits out expeditions to enable qualified men of science to make the fullest observations. Many features which had escaped the notice of former observers still await explanation, while improved scientific apparatus and methods open up entirely new fields of research. The Shadow Bands and Baily's Beads are still unexplained, and spectroscopic observations on the sun's atmosphere will probably never be complete. The forthcoming total eclipse of the sun on May 28, 1900, is an event which is being looked forward to with great interest, the more so as the line of totality will pass through Portugal and Spain, and will therefore be easily accessible. Much valuable information concerning this and previous eclipses is contained in a little book by Mr. G. F. Chambers,[1] which appears at an opportune moment, and will be found most useful by all who take an interest in the subject. Although the author explains fully the technical terms used in connection with eclipses of the sun and moon, yet this is done in popular language which can be understood by any educated reader. A large portion of the book is devoted to historical eclipses of the sun, which are not only of interest to the astronomer, but also to the historian, because they fix clearly many dates, especially in classical history, which might otherwise be open to dispute. All who take interest in the phenomena of nature will derive pleasure as well as instruction from the perusal of Mr. Chambers' book. Those who intend observing the eclipse of May 28 should not fail to study the Appendix, which contains much useful information with reference to the journey to Spain or Portugal.

The solar eclipse of January 22, 1898, forms the subject of a special volume issued by the Meteorological Department of India,[2]

---

[1] *The Story of Eclipses.* By G. F. Chambers. London: G. Newnes, Ltd. 1899.
[2] *Indian Meteorological Memoirs.* By J. Eliot. Vol. XI. Part 1. Calcutta: Government Printing Office. 1899.

A large number of observations are recorded, which were made at 154 stations in India. Most of the observers were natives, and it speaks well for the organisation of the Indian Government, and for this department in particular, that it should have been possible to obtain such accurate results at so small a cost. We may remark that it is through the Meteorological Department that the Indian Government obtains the first warning of the approach of those famines which periodically cause such loss of life. Without this warning the mortality would be enormous, and the difficulty of obtaining food and transport would be greatly increased.

*The Advance of Knowledge* is the somewhat ambitious title of a work by Lieutenant-Colonel W. Sedgwick[1] which has just reached us. A very small portion of the book is devoted to general knowledge, but considerable space is occupied by the special views of the author, especially on atoms, molecules, periodicity, and similar subjects. Some of the views expressed are, at any rate, original; but we would have preferred if they had been accompanied by a few facts in confirmation. The forms of atoms, for instance, are supposed to vary according to the valency of the substance. The form of the metalloid atom " is that of a chipped sphere with flat pieces on its surface, which provide seats on which hydrogen atoms can sit safely." Other atoms are shaped like ninepins; in fact, the gallant author does not hesitate to chip off or add pieces wherever they may appear necessary.

There are many original ideas in this work, but we cannot look upon it as an accurate record of even those branches of knowledge which are referred to in it.

---

## PHILOSOPHY AND THEOLOGY.

THE theology of Christianity, as influenced by the spirit of the times, might very well be given as the title of the Gifford Lectures by the late Dr. John Caird.[2] Theology, to the learned lecturer, was not a matter of doctrines or history, but of ideas; and in these lectures he tries to show how, at least from his point of view, the Christian idea fits in with our other ideas of God, nature, and man. Principal Caird was, through all his fruitful life, desirous of getting rid of the divisions between the religious and the secular, faith and reason, God and man, which have characterised nearly all forms of Christ-

[1] *The Advance of Knowledge.* By Lieut.-Colonel W. Sedgwick. London: G. Allen. 1899.

[2] *The Fundamental Ideas of Christianity.* By John Caird, D.D., LL.D., late Principal and Vice-Chancellor of the University of Glasgow; with a Memoir by Edward Caird, D.C.L., LL.D. Two vols. Glasgow: James Maclehose & Sons. 1899.

ianity.  So in these lectures Christianity is regarded rather as a philosophy of life than a scheme which interrupts the natural order. This was his justification for treating it under the scientific aspect required by the terms of the Gifford trust.  The mode of treatment may not, certainly will not, satisfy all Christians, but it must be confessed that the theme is treated in a lofty and reverential spirit, even if at times the lecturer's idealism seems to border upon mysticism.

However that may be, his brother tells us, in the interesting memoir prefixed to these lectures, that in his preaching—and as a preacher he was deservedly famous—it was upon the practical and ethical side of Christianity that he delighted to dwell.  The life of a preacher, a Professor of Divinity, and the Principal of a University, all spent within a limited area, is not likely to be very eventful; and, indeed, the three or four appointments thus indicated are the only events of importance related in the essay devoted by Dr. Edward Caird to the memory of his brother.  This memoir is therefore necessarily and principally concerned with the mental and religious development of John Caird, whose portrait is painted for us by a hand guided with the deepest admiration and affection for its subject. There is ample testimony that Principal Caird has largely moulded the religious thought of the Scotland of our generation, and the host of readers whom he may count as his disciples will heartily welcome these volumes.  A striking portrait of the great preacher and teacher is included in the first volume.

The origin of Christianity is, curiously enough, still an open question, and Mr. Nesbit holds the view very strongly that Jesus was an Essene.  We are glad to see that his very interesting book has reached a second edition.[1]  This is no mere reprint, but contains a large amount of new matter and is a great improvement on the first edition.  Mr. Nesbit learns as he goes along and gives the reader the full benefit of his acquisitions.  Apart from his especial point, the book contains a good deal of just criticism on Judaism and orthodox Christianity.  It is written from the Theistic or Unitarian point of view.

*Jerome and the Vulgate*[2] is the title of an address delivered by the Rev. J. E. Manning, M.A., at the opening of the last session of the Unitarian College, Manchester.  The address gives a vivid sketch of the great scholar, and an accurate account of the history of the *Vulgate* and its influence upon theology.

*Can I believe in God the Father?*[3] by William Newton Clarke, D.D., is a wholesome contribution to present-day religion.  Dr. Clarke

[1] *Christ, Christians, and Christianity, or Jesus an Essene.*  Second Edition.  By E. Planta Nesbit.  Manchester and London : John Heywood.
[2] Manchester : H. Rawson & Co.
[3] Edinburgh : T. & T. Clark.

approaches the subject of Theism from its ethical, rather than its intellectual, side, and is much more persuasive than dogmatical.

A scholarly and useful book, very appropriately published at the present time, is Mr. Kidd's history and explanation of *The Thirty-Nine Articles.*[1] It appears almost to be forgotten by many people, clergy not excepted, that the Church of England has any doctrinal standards, but as long as the Thirty-nine Articles stand the Church of England cannot evade them. It seems a pity that articles which are to be taken " in the literal and grammatical sense " should stand in need of so much explanation. Some of them, no doubt, refer to controversies long since forgotten, and are in a manner obsolete; but this can hardly be said of the main doctrinal and ritualistic, or anti-ritualistic, articles. Those who wish for a thoroughly trustworthy exposition of them should read Mr. Kidd's book. In an appendix the author gives the text of the Articles of 1553 and 1563. The text taken for explanation is that of 1571.

The glory and wisdom of Solomon[2] are known of all over Europe and the East, and here comes Mr. Conway to tell us that they are mythical; though the myths associated with this name are not without their lessons. According to Mr. Conway, the subject is deeper and wider than is commonly supposed, and it is only by a comparative study that it can be understood. Mr. Conway, as might be expected of him, has produced an entertaining and enlightening book which no theologian or folk-lorist should miss.

Everybody has heard of the Sibylline Oracles, but few people have read them, or, perhaps, even know what is meant by them. Professor Milton S. Terry has generously come to their assistance and produced an easily read translation of such as are extant.[3] The author gives Lactantius's and Justin Martyr's accounts of the Sibyls, and in the preface gives an account of the text, which is also elucidated by scholarly notes. The English blank verse is not up to our standard, but this may be forgiven, as the translation and notes will be found useful.

We are in full agreement with Mr. Thomas Parker, the author of *The Coming Bible,*[4] that the essence of Christianity is to be found in the Gospels, but we are not prepared to go his length and entirely put the rest of the Bible on one side. The Gospels themselves would be unintelligible without some knowledge of the Old Testament, and the author seems to forget that some of the post-Christian (apostolic) writings, as he calls them, were probably written before the Gospels. The Gospels have to be taken with the whole of their

[1] *The Thirty-Nine Articles: their History and Explanation.* By Rev. B. J. Kidd, B.D. Two volumes in one. London : Rivingtons. 1899.
[2] *Solomon and Solomonic Literature.* By Moncure Daniel Conway. London : Kegan Paul, Trench, Trübner & Co. 1899.
[3] *The Sibylline Oracles.* Translated from the Greek into English blank verse. By Milton S. Terry. New York : Eaton & Mains.
[4] London : Swan Sonnenschein & Co.

environment: what is wanted amongst the masses is a more rational understanding of the Bible as a whole; even the Gospels must be subject to criticism.

A diagram upon the cover of a religious pamphlet leads the reader to expect further eccentricities on the part of the author, but he will not find any others in the case of Mr. Viner, the writer of a booklet, *Unity and Variety in Religion : A Twentieth Century Forecast.*[1] The diagram is the key to this essay; it gives a bird's-eye view of the comparative proportions of the different religions in the world. His thesis is that there is only one religion, but it is divided into classes, families, genera, and species. The best cure for intolerance is to know something about the opinions of other people, and to this end this tract may contribute.

The English translation of Professor Th. Ribot's work, *The Evolution of General Ideas,*[2] will enable those who have not read the book in French to appreciate the author's masterly analysis of abstraction and generalisation. The chief aim of the work is to show that these two operations advance by an evolutionary progress from the lowest form to the most elevated species of symbolism. The account given of the lower forms of abstraction, which is characterised by the absence of words, and of which we find illustrations in the case of animals, children, and deaf-mutes, will be read with considerable interest. It may startle the orthodox to learn that animals can count, and that they have the power of recognising such qualities in objects as hardness, sharpness, and weight. With regard to children, Professor Ribot points out that the problem is not to be stated in the terms that intelligence progresses from the general to the particular, but from the indefinite to the definite—which is a distinct proposition. Few more lucid treatises on an important branch of psychology have ever appeared.

---

## SOCIOLOGY, POLITICS, AND JURISPRUDENCE.

WE have scarcely the patience to treat seriously *The Case for Protection,*[3] by Mr. Ernest Edwin Williams, Fellow of the Royal Statistical Society and author of *Made in Germany*, a pamphlet which was effectively disposed of by the late George Webb Medley. Mr. Williams bases his argument for Protection upon what he calls General Principles.

[1] London : Williams & Norgate.
[2] *The Evolution of General Ideas.* By Th. Ribot, Professor in the Collège de France. Authorised Translation from the French by E. Welby. London : Kegan Paul, Trench, Trübner & Co.
[3] *The Case for Protection.* By Ernest Edwin Williams, Fellow of the Royal Statistical Society. London : Grant Richards. 1899.

British exports increased from £35,000,000 in 1798 to £57,000,000 in 1847, a period representing the last half-century of absolute Protection.

This increase, he assumes, was due to Protection, and, he asserts, "helps to explain why the growth did not altogether cease during the first generation of Free Trade."

That this increase during the first half of the century was due to Protection is obviously the merest assumption. It would, indeed, be curious if, under the circumstances of our trade, when we were the workship of the world, and with a rapidly increasing population, this increase had not taken place. A Free Trader would assert that this result was obtained in spite of Protection. Mr. Williams once more trots out the hard case of the English farmer. We are all now fairly well acquainted with the actual causes of his present position, and we know that, as far as he is concerned, protection of food stuffs would not benefit him a halfpenny. The landowner would pocket the difference in increased rent, as he did in the good old days of Protection, and the consumer would supply the wherewithal. Mr. Williams frankly admits that Protection would not prove a panacea for all the ills of the agriculturist, and very properly points out the grave defects of the agricultural mind, which neglects proper organisation and modern methods of culture. Preferential railway rates also very properly excites his indignation, and he is perfectly correct in stating that the whole of our wheat supply might be produced at home, as was pointed out long ago by such eminent agriculturists as Mr. Lawes, Mr. Caird, and the late Lord Derby.

After the hard case of the farmer comes that of the manufacturer, who is asked to believe that Protection would prove his salvation. Mr. Medley has disposed of this belief in his *German Bogey*, and Mr. E. J. Smith has shown in his *New Trades Combination Movement*, which we noticed last month, that under the new system what little foreign competition there is becomes a negligible quantity.

Mr. Williams then runs a-tilt at such exponents of Free Trade principles as Fawcett and Professor Bastable, and fares little better in the encounter that his more famous prototype in his Quixotic enterprise, and finally winds up with an ardent advocacy of Mr. Chamberlain's Zollverein, which we thought had scarcely breathed ere it was consigned to an early grave by its heartless parent. One looks for something more than this from a Fellow of the Royal Statistical Society.

We expected better things from Professor Smart, the author of *Studies in Economics*, than we find in his latest work, *The Distribution of Income*.[1] Not but what it contains much with which we are in

[1] *The Distribution of Income.* [By William Smart, M.A., D.Phil., LL.D., Adam Smith Professor of Political Economy in the University of Glasgow. London : Macmillan & Co., Ltd. New York : The Macmillan Company. 1899.

agreement and much that is fresh and of considerable value. It is with his main conclusions that we quarrel. It is perfectly obvious, as the Professor says, that "the national dividend is at once the aggregate net product of, and the sole source of payment for, all the instruments of production within the country." And Professor Smart is equally correct in stating that this aggregate wealth is not sufficient for the 40,000,000 in this little island which provided for 15,000,000 in greater comfort. In his chapter entitled "The Socialising of Consumption" in the former work, we think Professor Smart was on the right road. All honour to the Professor if, with greater experience and riper knowledge, he has found himself obliged to modify his views and recant his opinions. In writing the present work he says it became clear to him that "of the vast national income which this country enjoys a great deal is distributed while and as it is made. That, in short, the production process as we know it is also a distribution process. Following this clue I began with the personage who, in the present state of things, is primarily the paymaster of organised industry, the employer, and tried to find how his payments are conditioned and overruled. Working along this line, I was forced to see that whatever hard names may be applied to the results of this distribution, the distribution is not arbitrary, much less chaotic." The Professor admits that one may perhaps imagine a better distribution, and that there is something wrong with the student who begins his economic studies in admiration of the *status quo*! Great heavens! what a falling off from the writer of *Studies in Economics*, who advocated a more equitable distribution of the national wealth by means of municipalisation of some of the great necessaries and pleasures of life. From an advocate of dynamic sociology Professor Smart has retrograded to a more one-sided individualistic phase; and in his acknowledgments to the assistance rendered by Mr. Edwin Cannan we think we can readily guess what influence has been at work. His general conclusion may be gathered from the following passage: "But when the question is whether a regulated State control, according to any social or socialistic ideal, would bring us conditions of life wherein all would have the possibility of realising their moral being, or of being what is called 'happy,' I am disposed to think that the 'invisible hand'—however one interprets Adam Smith's reformer—is bringing about those conditions more quickly than any deliberate arrangement of industry would." We presume that the Professor understands evolution as the "invisible hand." But evolution does not always spell progress. We know how the evolution of the land system ruined Rome, just as it is responsible for many of our economic troubles to-day. So the evolution of the industrial system must not be left to chance, to *laissez faire*, to "invisible hands." It must, as far as possible, be directed along the right road. What the right road is, is the economist's business to find out and inform the public. That a fairer distribution of the present national wealth is imaginable is obvious. That it is possible is almost equally obvious. One could point to many systems of taxation by which the present inequality might be sensibly modified. Under-consumption means under-production. With a fairer distribution greater consumption would follow, accompanied with greater production; and with increased municipalisation, the enjoyment of wealth would be extended so as to result in greater happiness to the greatest number. In making these remarks we must not be taken to disparage a work of great merit and value quite apart from its conclusions, which every reader can form for himself after a perusal of what, after all, is the real object of the book—viz., the ascertainment of the methods of the present distribution of wealth.

## VOYAGES AND TRAVELS.

*Portuguese Nyassaland,*[1] by Mr. Basil Worsfold, is scarcely a book of travels, although, as a resident for many years in South Africa, it is probable that the author speaks to some extent from personal experience. The information here collected is, we are told, derived from three main sources—viz. (1) The records of travellers contained in their works and in the Transactions of the Royal Geographical Society, (2) the British Consular Reports, and (3) the reports furnished to the administration of the Nyassa Company by its officials, and by the experts placed in charge of the various expeditions which have already been sent out. The work commences with a brief sketch—which might well have been extended—of the discovery of the east coast, followed by an historical account of the Portuguese in Africa.

The present condition and prospects of Portuguese East Africa are then described, together with an account of the Nyassa Company, to whom was entrusted in 1891 the administration of the northern district of the Province of Mozambique. If there is any truth in the current rumour of the partition of the Portuguese possessions between Great Britain and Germany, that portion of the book which deals with the resources of this vast region—agricultural and mineral—becomes of even greater importance. From this we learn of the

---

[1] *Portuguese Nyassaland.* An Account of the Discovery, Native Population, Agricultural and Mineral Resources, and Present Administration of the Territory of the Nyassa Company. With a Review of the Portuguese Rule on the East Coast of Africa. By W. Basil Worsfold. Illustrated. London: Sampson Low, Marston and Co., Ltd. 1899.

immense value of these possessions to a strong colonising Power.
In the littoral zone, sugar, indigo, tobacco, cotton, cocoa, and tea may
all be grown most profitably with native labour under European
supervision, whilst the highlands are especially suitable for the
cultivation of a coffee which is the finest in the world.   In addition,
these upland regions are particularly adapted for European settlement.   Timber is plentiful and of high class, and a large trade,
which only requires development, is already in existence in ivory,
beeswax, gum copal, india-rubber, oil-nuts, rice, &c., whilst wheat
can be grown in abundance and there is ample fine pasture for sheep
and cattle.   Throughout these uplands, too, there are indications of
considerable deposits of coal, iron, gold, silver, and other valuable
minerals, which only await development ; and lastly there remains
the ordinary trade and commerce with a large native population.
Much of the book is taken up with statistics relating to the above
subjects, and thus are rather dry for the general reader, but it is
none the less valuable for that.   The chapter on the Nyassa Company is contributed by Sir Robert Edgcumbe, to whom we are also
indebted for a series of interesting photographs of the east coast.
Two large maps are conveniently placed in a pocket, a new feature
which is much to be commended.   Mr. Worsfold is an acknowledged
authority upon South Africa, and this work will considerably add to
his well-deserved reputation.

*L'Empire du Milieu*,[1] by M. Marcel Monnier, forms the second
volume of that writer's *Le Tour d'Asie*, the first of which dealt with
Cochin-China, Annam, and Tonkin.   At the present moment the
attention of Europe—with the exception of England, who has no
thought but for South Africa—is fixed to a large extent upon the
affairs of the Celestial Empire.   The real struggle is one for para-
mountcy in the Far East.   Is this to be secured by Russia, France,
or Great Britain ?   Thus France is naturally much concerned in
extending her political influence and developing her commerce.
The moment is therefore well chosen for presenting to the general
public of France a popular, lively, and striking account, supported
by reliable evidence, of the present position of affairs in China, the
condition of the Great Powers, and relations with each other and with
the Chinese Empire.

The work before us fully realises all these requirements.   The
illustrations are numerous and much more original than most of
those which have appeared in recent English works upon the same
subject.

[1] *Le Tour d'Asie—L'Empire du Milieu.*   Par Marcel Monnier.   Paris : E. Plon,
Nourrit et Cie.   1899.

## HISTORY AND BIOGRAPHY.

THE biography of the late Mr. John Mills, the author of *Vox Humana*,[1] will be read with deep interest. To Mrs. Mills this work must have been a genuine " labour of love." It is impossible not to admire her devotion to her husband and her thorough appreciation of his great virtues as a man. The autobiographical reminiscences contributed by herself are in themselves exceedingly interesting. She presents us with the picture of an English home so long ago as 1830. We see a group of children watching the unfolding of a newspaper printed in golden letters, the contents being a minute account of the coronation of William IV. There is something singularly picturesque in the scene. As Mrs. Mills quaintly remarks : " To have a whole newspaper about one's self printed in letters of pure gold was royalty indeed ! " We have also a remarkable description of the lighting of a dip-candle by means of a flint and a tinder-box. Such old-world recollections are delightful, and give us a glimpse of a state of society which, considering how civilisation has advanced, seems two centuries rather than barely seventy years ago. Mrs. Mills makes some striking observations on the effects of improved methods of lighting, which appear to show that there has been loss as well as gain by some of our modern inventions. The following passage is worth quoting from this point of view :

" It is doubtful whether the much be-lighted young folk of this day could find their way in the dark about a house, putting their hands on any given article, in the ready, unhesitating fashion that we had to do it. We were not permitted to carry lamps or candles about the house ; if on a winter's evening a book or any forgotten article were wanted, we had to fetch it in the dark. Not to keep our clothes in certain parts of the drawers, or books on a shelf, so that we could lay our hands on them in the dark, was to be dubbed untidy and shiftless. At the top of the stairs was an opening to a long passage that led to dim and mysterious attics. Past this opening some of us would fly breathlessly, with a vague dread of some unseen presence. What a relief it was when our ever-busy brother Joseph one day put up in the lobbies and on the stairs small brackets, on each of which stood a glass tumbler filled three-parts with water, and a fourth with oil, on the surface of which floated small round bits of cork, with a tiny wick in the centre. When these were lighted after dark the house was illuminated, and we kept on running up and down stairs to enjoy the brilliance. Not so very long after this gas-lights were introduced ; but they made no such impresssion as did those welcome little oil-floats."

[1] *Life of John Mills. With some Early Century Recollections.* By his Wife. Manchester : Sherratt & Hughes.

After all, perhaps, we make too much of the material advantages of electric lighting. Mrs. Mills gives an account of the Bright family, which enables us to see that every member of it was an enthusiastic worker for the great cause of progress. When seizures of property were made in Rochdale for church rates, a stormy meeting of ratepayers was held in the churchyard, at which Mrs. Mill's father, with Jacob Bright, senior, John Bright, and others attended. John Bright moved, " That the rate was illegal," and after successive polls on the question, there was found to be a small majority in favour of the rate. Thereupon it was determined to raise subscriptions to defend any one who was prosecuted for non-payment. This certainly is a practical illustration of having the courage of one's convictions. Mrs. Mills tells some good stories about her father. He was of Irish descent, and was born in Belfast in 1791. He married a Yorkshire yeoman's daughter, and, starting in business at Rochdale, rapidly prospered. He was short of stature, but well-knit, with a high forehead and laughing grey-blue eyes. We learn that up to the age of ninety his walk was so jaunty and quick that " any stranger following him expected to see him break into a run." We can bring up before our mind's eye this portrait of a fine old man, healthy both in body and mind. John Petrie, Mrs. Mills's father, became a Methodist early in life, and in politics he was a Progressive Liberal. He was chairman of the Rochdale branch of the Anti-Corn-Law League, of which he was one of the earliest members. In 1846, when he was only fifty-five, he had the only serious illness of his life. He was losing flesh, and, though he went to Harrogate for treatment, only grew worse. One day he said, " I will go home and put my house in order ; my days are numbered." On the journey home he was persuaded by his wife to turn aside and try Ben Rhydding and hydropathy. He returned home six weeks after, with " a new lease of life." Is not this like a chapter of romance ? Mr. Petrie died in 1883, in his ninety-second year, leaving about one hundred and forty living descendants.

Of John Mills, the main subject of the biography, it would be hard to speak too highly. He was born at Ashton-under-Lyne in 1821. Though devoted to commercial pursuits, he was a man of fine literary taste, and some of his poetry is full of beauty and shows a deep love of nature. Like Pope, he seemed to have " lisped in numbers," for at the age of ten he wrote a humorous elegy on the death a favourite cat, and a comic ode on Saturday beginning :

" Saturday, Saturday, terrible day !
When cross-tempered housewives will have their own way."

When he was twenty-one he wrote a splendid poem entitled " Who are the Living of the Earth ? " which he read at a literary meeting in Manchester in 1842. Here are the concluding lines :

"Are the flowers fair in their dewy dreaming?
Are the streams pure on their moss-beds gleaming?
Are bird-voices sweet in pleasant green places?
Is their soul in the smile of our human graces?
Why bare the great Mother this lavish birth?
'Twas for you—ye living of the earth!"

Mr. Mills was an example of self-culture carried to a high pitch in the midst of the cares of a commercial career. He admired the great brain-workers of the century, and was an earnest student of Goethe, Jean Paul, Ruskin, Strauss, and Mill. In 1848 he met Emerson, who gave him his autograph accompanied by the words:

"As sings the pine-tree in the wind,
So sings in the wind a sprig of the pine."

The letters in the volume unfold to us the life and the mind of this gifted and noble-hearted man. In his literary tendencies he was a Wordsworthian. In politics he was a thorough-going Radical, and agreed with Jacob Bright in advocating Home Rule for Ireland. He met Kossuth in 1850 when the Hungarian patriot visited Manchester. Mrs. Mills has admirably brought together the facts of her husband's life, and in this charming volume has depicted a most attractive personality.

*The Psychology of Woman* [1] is a work of a very remarkable character. It is such a book as could only have been written in an age of transition and of new ideas. The writer, Laura Marholm, is a woman of rare perception and philosophic insight. She discusses the subject from nearly every possible point of view. She does not shrink from unveiling the hidden cancers of modern society. Her analysis of different types of the modern woman—the *detraquée*, or morbidly disordered woman, the *grande amoureuse*, or intensely ardent woman, and the *cérébrale*, or the woman who tries to think with her brain—is masterly and almost scientifically accurate. The chapter entitled "The Demand for Happiness" is calculated to make the reader think. Let us quote the opening portion of it:

"'We wish to be happy!' It is the cry of the age. This demand, so far as our knowledge of past civilisation extends, has never come forward so nakedly before. It has always been clothed in some garb, oftenest in that of religion. Christianity, which has impressed its forms and ideals upon our life and morals, transfers all harmonious happiness to the other world, and at the same time converts that happiness into something impersonal, non-individual; by the mystics happiness is regarded as reunion with the Infinite Soul. Amongst our old fathers of culture, the Greeks and Romans, there was but one idea of personal happiness—enjoyment, sensation. . . . We, as they, seek enjoyment and sensation. Mankind has never

---

[1] *The Psychology of Woman.* By Laura Marholm. Translated by Georgia A. Etchison. London : Grant Richards.

done otherwise; we have never had in our unconscious consciousness any other cause for existence. But in this century something new has been added, something which was never before so openly avowed, never set itself up so insolently and self-assertingly; this is the declaration—We will be happy."

The "modernity" of this passage is perhaps its most striking note. There is a certainly unhealthiness is this craving for "happiness." A neurotic age adds to its miseries by the pains of oversensitiveness and unrest. This fact is not overlooked by the ingenious writer of this interesting work. She recognises a physical and moral deterioriation of the species in the midst of intellectual progress. For the women who can never become wives she proposes a scheme of productive work and co-operation. In such a scheme there are inherent difficulties, and we fear too much reliance is placed in the enthusiasm of women and their willingness to renounce life for themselves to live into the lives of others. The work of philanthropy is rarely congenial to the female temperament. However, the book gives us such a wide outlook in woman's future and its possibilities that we are inclined to accept all its suggestions with reverence rather than criticism. The volume has been· admirably translated by Georgia A. Etchison.

One of the most original, daring, and, at the same time, thoroughly philosophic books recently published on the woman question is *Woman and Economics* by Charlotte Perkins Stetson.[1] It puts aside all cant about motherhood, and shows that the existing human method of maternity is injurious to the race. The sexuo-economic relation is revealed to us in a new and somewhat startling light. Woman being merely a consumer must wait till she can "afford to marry." The economic dependence of the human female on the human male has tended to produce an abnormal condition of society. As the writer of this book puts it : "In no other animal species is the sex-relation for sale." One of the results is that we have in prostitution "the flower of the sexuo-economic relation." The remedies for the present state of things are partly suggested. The decline of the family and the emancipation of the individual by the economic independence of women is one of the obvious tendencies of true sexual evolution. This book is one of the best ever written on a most difficult and perplexing question, and we hope it will be widely read.

Is it true that the world is still "lamentably ignorant" of Cromwell's "real character"? This, at least, is the opinion of his latest biographer, Mr. Arthur Paterson. Perhaps we should qualify this description of Mr. Paterson, having regard to Mr. John Morley's Life

---

[1] *Women and Economics.* A Study of the Economic Relation between Men and Women as a Factor in Social Evolution. By Charlotte Perkins Stetson. London : Putnam's Sons.

of the Protector. The character of Cromwell is regarded by some students of history as exceedingly complex. This is not Mr. Paterson's view.[1] According to him, Cromwell was a simple and a sincere man with a "genius for taking pains." This estimate of the Protector is, to some extent, borne out by the correspondence of which Mr. Paterson makes such copious use ; but in assuming that Cromwell's conduct was wholly free from ambitious motives he seems to us to have been guilty of sophistical reasoning. Moreover, the apology made for the horrible cruelties attending Cromwell's campaign in Ireland is entirely unsatisfactory. At the same time it is evident that, though a fanatic, Cromwell was a genuine English patriot. This much Mr. Paterson establishes by very convincing evidence. It is a pity that in the seventeenth century "religion" meant hatred of your opponents. Cromwell can only be called a champion of religious liberty in a very limited sense; and Mr. Paterson in holding him up as the friend of freedom of conscience seems to view the case from the standpoint of 250 years ago rather than from that of nineteenth-century ideas. In doing so he is possibly right, for a man should be judged by the state of public opinion in his own time. We cannot, however, ignore the fact that Cromwell's notion of toleration would nowadays be rightly looked upon as downright intolerance. The book has been brought out in a very attractive form by the publishers, Messrs. Nisbet and Co.

Most people who read at all must have heard of Sir Thomas Urquhart as the translator of Rabelais. But the facts of his life are not known to the majority of readers. For instance, it has been stated by Motteux, the Frenchman who supplemented Sir Thomas's version of Rabelais, that he was "a learned physician." This, of course, is erroneous. Mr. John Willcock[2] has given us in his charming volume a vivid portrait of Urquhart, a gallant Sc who was always in debt, but who took a careless view pecuniary troubles, fighting when occasion arose in those turbulent politics, and then writing books containing a w new-fangled words. In addition to his services to liter presenting us with the best English version of Rabel Thomas Urquhart also gave the world an interesting account "Admirable Crichton," which, however, like most of his stat as to matters of fact, must be taken *cum grano salis.*

The admirers of the great musician, Johannes Brahms, will be much interested in the *Recollections*[3] of him, contributed by Professor Albert Dietrich and Dr. J. V. Widmann, and translated

[1] *Oliver Cromwell : His Life and Character.* By Arthur Paterson. London Nisbet & Co., Ltd.

[2] *Sir Thomas Urquhart of Cromartie.* By John Willcock, M.A., D.D. and London : Oliphant, Anderson & Ferrier.

[3] *Recollections of Johannes Brahms.* By Albert Dietrich and J. V. Wid lated by Dora E. Hecht. London : Seeley & Co.

by Dora E. Hecht. The impression gained by a perusal of the letters in the volume is that Brahms was a delightfully simple, affectionate, and unconventional being, in whose soul love of music was the dominant passion.

*How Tolstoy Lives and Works* [1] is the title of a very readable volume translated from the Russian of P. A. Sergyeenko by Isabel F. Hapgood. Of course, deep interest is taken in Tolstoy as one of the most original and extraordinary men of his time. In some respects, he seems to have gone back fifteen centuries; in others, he is much in advance of the age. The volume, of which an English version is now presented to us, gives only a partial glimpse of the man Tolstoy. One strange but beautiful characteristic of Tolstoy is his absence of vanity. For instance, we find him depreciating his own work, *Childhood and Boyhood*, as " a frivolous little book." This is probably due to his power of taking an impersonal view of his own life and writings—a very rare faculty. Another great characteristic of Tolstoy is his deep, passionate love of the common people. He has taught one great lesson to the nineteenth century with its money-worshipping tendencies—the nobility of the agricultural labourer's simple toil, and the comparative worthlessness of luxuries. Any work on so remarkable a man as Tolstoy must be welcomed. But the life of the great author of *War and Peace* has yet to be written. It will be a most curious and, perhaps, astonishing book.

Mr. Kegan Paul has not, in his *Memories*,[2] given us a glimpse into his inner life. He says himself: " These pages will not pretend to tell everything. The morbid self-analysis of Rousseau needs all, and more than all, his genius to make it tolerable, and if it be pleasant reading under any circumstances, it is unprofitable." This may be Mr. Kegan Paul's opinion; but we fear he does not appreciate the true value of Rousseau's self-analysis. The *Memories* must be described as " pleasant reading "; but they belong to the region of the commonplace. The recollections of Eton may interest a few Etonians, but how many others? Mr. Kegan Paul was originally a Protestant clergyman, and it would seem as if that career suited him admirably. However, he was destined afterwards to take part in the practical work of publishing. His chapter on that portion of his life is interesting. One of the most interesting passages in the book is the account of Shelley's descendants, Sir Percy and Lady Shelley. As for Mr. Paul's reasons for becoming a Catholic, they do not strike an unprejudiced reader as convincing. Pascal and Newman influenced him a great deal; but he seems to have ignored the physical cause of Pascal's superstitious weakness, and the scepticism

---

[1] *How Tolstoy Lives and Works.* By P. A. Sergyeenko. Translated from the Russian by Isabel F. Hapgood. London: J. Nisbet & Co.
[2] *Memories.* By C. Kegan Paul. London: Kegan Paul, Trench, Trübner & Co., Ltd.

which underlay Newman's Catholicism. As for the readiness of Mr. Paul to believe the Lourdes "miracles," it can only be compared with his funny theory that the imposture known as spiritualism is partly due to "satanic agency." Mr. Paul refers to M. Huysmans's novel *La Bas* in support of this somewhat mediæval notion; but can we really take M. Huysmans seriously? He is a gifted artist who has suddenly plunged into mysticism after a sad experience of "the fleshpots of Egypt."

With some hesitation we have decided to deal with the book entitled *Pages Catholiques*,[1] which is made up of extracts from *En Route* and *La Cathédrale*, as a portion of this section. The Abbé Mugnier in his preface maintains that M. Huysmans is, while narrating the history of Durtal's confession, really telling the story of his own change of opinion from Free Thought to Catholicism. The account of Durtal's morbid struggles with sensuality and sentimentality until at length church music and sculpture and religious pictures become to his unhealthy soul a sort of substitute for the luxuries of an indolent literary existence is interesting as a study in decadence. The "conversion" of a man who had formerly despised religious forms simply by the appeal of a cathedral and its artistic surroundings to his imagination is not an admirable spectacle. The beauty of M. Huysmans's style must be acknowledged; but it is evident that his reason has become debilitated, and that he is the victim of an illusion. He may interest psychologists as a reactionary and a sentimental dreamer, but the absurd reasons given by him for abandoning Free Thought, and spending his time in prowling through churches like a phantom, will only excite in every robust mind a sense of pity for the artist and man who could sacrifice his intellectual freedom for a sickly mediæval mysticism.

Lieutenant Paul Kollmann's interesting book, *The Victoria Nyanza*,[2] has been well translated by Mr. H. A. Nesbit, M.A. The great lake now called the Victoria Nyanza must have been known in remote antiquity, but, partly owing to the exaggerated accounts of travellers, its history was obscured in a cloud of myth. The work of Lieutenant Kollmann throws a vivid and picturesque light on the subject. One noteworthy fact mentioned is that the river Kagera is a source of the Nile, so that all the sources of that great river are to be sought in German territory. The account of Uganda is full of curious details. The inhabitants of this negro kingdom may probably be regarded as a blend of settlers and natives. The Wagandas must get the credit of having a comparatively high degree of culture, and they have advanced much further in civilisation than the neighbouring countries. Msukuma, another district near the Victoria

---

[1] *Pages Catholiques.* Par J. K. Huysmans. Avec Préface de M. l'Abbé Mugnier. Paris: P. V. Stock.

[2] *The Victoria Nyanza: the Land, the Races, and their Customs, with Specimens of some of the Dialect.* By Paul Kollmann. London: Swan Sonnenschein & Co., Ltd.

Nyanza, is described with great minuteness of detail in the book. The Sultan of the country has the advantage of an additional hedge round his dwelling, and we learn that it comprises living-rooms for the monarch himself as well as for his retinue and womankind. There is a primitive simplicity about his Court which would scarcely excite the envy of European potentates. However, as the number of wives a Msukuma may possess varies according to his wealth, the Sultan has the privilege of keeping a hundred beauties, while a common man must confine himself to five. The fact is emphasised that a strong Msukuma woman " needs no assistance in childbirth " —and the circumstances may recall to the lovers of Tennyson the words of the hero of " Locksley Hall " :

" I will take some hardy woman : she shall rear my dusky sons."

The illustrations in the volume are excellent, and it has been beautifully brought out by Messrs. Swan Sonnenschein & Co.

We have received the *Proceedings of the Royal Society of Canada* for 1898, and must pronounce it to be a most important and luminous publication.[1] The proceedings of the Society range over a great variety of subjects. We notice with satisfaction that the Society has paid that talented author, Mr. Gilbert Parker, the compliment of making him a Corresponding Fellow in the Department of Literature. In doing so the Society showed its appreciation of literary genius, for Canada has just reason to be proud of the man who wrote *The Seats of the Mighty.* Incorporated with the volume is a most absorbing sketch of the death of La Salle, by M. Benjamin Sutte, in the *Memoires of the Société Royale du Canada.* This contribution to Canadian history reads like a chapter of romance.

In *Imperialism and Liberty* [2] Mr. Morrison J. Swift denounces the policy of the American Government with regard to the Philippines. He holds that the United States cannot justly annex the Philippine Islands, and he sees in what has happened only political corruption and commercial greed. Incidentally, he points out that British Imperialism has made use of the United States as a tool, and he concludes by expressing the view that if the American people are not dead, the present Administration will be " cast into the depths of the sea."

*The New Zealand Year Book* [3] for 1899 contains an immense quantity of useful information. It has been prepared under instructions from the Premier, the Right Hon. R. J. Sedden, P.C., and E. J. Von Dadelszen, Registrar-General. It appears that the Year

[1] *Proceedings and Transactions of the Royal Society of Canada.* Second Series Vol. IX. Ottawa: James Hesse & Son. 1898.
[2] *Imperialism and Liberty.* By Morrison J. Swift. Los Angeles, California : The Pembroke Press.
[3] *The New Zealand Official Year Book, 1899.* (Eighth Year of Issue.) Wellington N.Z. By Authority. John Mackay, Government Printer. London : Eyre & Spottiswoode.

Book was completed at an earlier date than usual, and owing to this cause some of the departmental reports presented to Parliament were not available for statistical purposes.   However, the facts embodied in the volume fully enable any reader to realise the progress of the colony during the year 1898.   The population showed an increase of about 14,000 as compared with 1897, and it may be assumed that in the years to come there will be a much larger increase.   The gold-mining industries of the colony are holding their own.   The wheat harvest cannot be regarded as quite satisfactory, for the total amount of wheat exported during the year 1898 was only 10,090 bushels, while the imports were as high as 60,860 bushels, showing that New Zealand had not grown as much as was required for consumption by her own people.   The harvest of 1899, however, shows a big increase. The political and social development of New Zealand is shown in the improvement in the marriage and divorce laws by which women are placed on an equality with men, and the admission of women to the Parliamentary franchise.

## MEDICINE.

To the second edition of his *Crime and Criminals* [1] Dr. Sanderson Christison has added an appendix dealing with the cases of Merry, Windrath, and Luetgert.   The two former were executed for murder, but Dr. Christison's review makes one hesitate as to whether the penalty should have been enforced.   For Merry he put in the plea of degeneracy, and says that he was "an indigenous product" of the worst crime-breeding section of Chicago.   His description of it recalls the "Rectangle" of Mr. Sheldon's popular tale.   He adopts as true in the main the confession of Merry as to the manner in which his wife came to her death and his flight under the fear of being suspected.   The article respecting him was written for the *New York Herald* during the trial, and dwells upon his "abnormal inheritance" and his "moral obtusity" as pointing to a "degree of insanity as yet comparatively unrecognised because so common."

The review of the Windrath case was written for the *Journal of the American Medical Association.*   The author and two other physicians were for the defence on the ground of insanity, while six others testified that the accused was sane and shamming.   The arguments of the State experts are examined in the article, and the author, who witnessed the execution, holds that the criminal was insane at the time.

The Luetgert case is a much more difficult one.   Its medical and psychological aspects were discussed by the author for the *Chicago*

[1] *Crime and Criminals.*   By J. Sanderson Christison, M.D.   Second Edition. Chicago. 1899.

*Law Journal*, and the article is here reprinted. He holds that the crime charged—so atrocious that its announcement shocked the civilised world—without any rational motive, could not have been committed except by a lunatic, but that, under the most trying ordeals of court-room and jail, extending through ten months, the accused's conduct betrayed absolutely nothing of guilt, and not the slightest indication of mental abnormality. This case is the most fully considered by the author, who is convinced of Luetgert's innocence, although he was sentenced to imprisonment for life. Of course this review partakes of the nature of a counsel's plea for the defence, but so many facts are marshalled against even the possibility of guilt that the reader cannot resist the conclusion, in the absence of rebutting evidence, that a sad injustice seems to have been done. Photos of the accused are given, and also some alleged portraits, which look like caricatures, and which were published in the newspapers at the time. This and some other proceedings are distinctly Transatlantic, and we hope will never be imitated by the most enterprising papers on this side.

Another brochure by Dr. Christison has also just come to hand, entitled *Brain in Relation to Mind*.[1] This is "addressed to physicians and laymen." This necessitates the statement of certain anatomical facts already familiar to one set of readers. But the work is brief enough to render this of minor importance to those who know, and may, indeed, serve as a useful reminder. There is a general outline of the development and functions of the brain and a consideration of the notion that some part of the brain is most subservient to thought. Some deductions the author postpones to a future psychological work. Meantime he agrees with Dr. Hughlings Jackson that states of consciousness are utterly different from nervous states of the highest centres, and psychical states cannot be said to be functions of the brain. If mind were a secretion of brain-cells as bile is of liver-cells, we should expect a parallelism in the development of events and in the results. But this is not the case. Cell-products are all cast out of the system and destroyed, adding nothing to the power of acquiring more. But the acquisitions of the mind are permanent, each adding to the power of acquiring more. Thus the tests of time and space—ever-present conditions of matter and energy—do not apply to mind. "If mind were a mere cell-product, memory," says our author, "could not exist," and he holds in derision the "phosphorescent" deposits and "memory images," like dents upon a phonographic cylinder, that some writers have propounded.

That some persons cannot conceive of mind apart from brain is simply due, in Dr. Christison's opinion, to their habit of thought. We distinguish a lovable personality in a repulsive form in some

[1] *Brain in Relation to Mind.* By J. Sanderson Christison, M.D. Chicago, 1889.

people as easily as attractive features in a criminal character. Though physical defects are often associated with mental or even moral irregularities, the one is not necessarily dependent on the other. Virchow and others have proved that persons who had ape-like brains were destitute of the mental characteristics of the ape and differed in no degree from their fellows, and when we see that a large part of the brain may be absent, and no peculiarity noticed in the life of the person, the fact, well known to physicians, may give pause to many a hasty theorist. Again, brain-form is supposed by some to exercise extreme control. The facts do not support the notion. So, too, brain-size is a very unreliable indication of mental power, as will be seen from the tables of weights collected in the book under notice, in which also other interesting facts will be found. His concluding chapter passes in review the mental faculties, considers the state of decadence, and arrives at the conclusion that, "for the same reason that matter is indestructible, mind is immortal, and because similar results can only follow similar conditions, character cannot change *post mortem* in any way possible *ante mortem,* so that the exit from this life must fit an entrance of the next."

---

## BELLES LETTRES.

THOSE who can derive satisfaction from the perusal of a poor imitation of *She* or *Treasure Island* will find their requirements fulfilled by *An African Treasure: A Tale of the Great Sahara,*[1] by Mr. J. Maclaren Cobban; a story with a threadbare plot and impossible situations, and characters who egregiously fail to sustain their parts.

*An Obscure Apostle*[2] is the work of a Polish novelist, Madame Eliza Ozeszko, who is unfortunately little known to English readers. She is a talented and prolific writer, and this book appears to be one of her finest efforts. It is a very beautiful story. It deals with the history of the Jewish community of a town called Szybow. The hero, Meir Ezofowich, is a young emancipated Jew who wishes to lead his brethren out of the slough of ignorance and superstition. His life is, indeed, a species of martyrdom. The account of the feud between the Ezofowich and Todros families is deeply interesting. The strange fanatical character of the Rabbi, Izaak Todros, is drawn with much dramatic power. The translation reads very smoothly, and is apparently very ably done by C. S. De Soissons.

*Wise in his Generation*[3] is a cleverly-written novel. Mr. Dave-

[1] *An African Treasure.* A Tale of the Great Sahara. By J. Maclaren Cobban. London : John Long. 1899.
[2] *An Obscure Apostle.* By Mme E. Ozeszko. Translated from the Polish by C. S. De Soissons. London : Greening & Co., Ltd.
[3] *Wise in his Generation.* By Philip Davenant. London : John Long.

nant had already shown his power of character-painting in *Cicely Vaughan*, and this book is an advance on its predecessor. The character of the girl Sylvia is a unique study.

A good book of amusing Irish stories ought to be welcomed by those who sympathise with Celtic ideals. *In Chimney Corners*[1] is a collection of charming Irish folk-tales by Seumas MacManus. The author professes to unveil the secrets of "the Country Beyond." He does it delightfully. "The Apprentice Thief" is a most absorbing story. The illustrations are very attractive.

*Ashes Tell no Tales*[2] is described on the title-page as "a dramatic story." It certainly is a very startling narrative, and the plot does credit to Mrs. Bradshaw's ingenuity. The character of Julie Van Zant is an extraordinary one, and might have been borrowed from the annals of criminal jurisprudence. Some of the incidents in this lady's career seem improbable, but we know that "truth is stranger than fiction."

Mrs. C. W. Earle's book entitled *More Pot Pourri from a Surrey Garden*[3] is very readable. Like her previous work, it is a medley of literature, horticulture, and cookery. Her quotations from well-known poets are numerous but sometimes not quite felicitous. As for her ethics, they are more than conventional. In one passage (p. 400) Mrs. Earle declares that, in her opinion, some forms of hypocrisy are necessary. We prefer on this question to side with Mohammed, who quite properly consigns hypocrites to the lowest pit of hell. The volume, in spite of its shortcomings, shows a wide range of knowledge. Mrs. Earle frankly avows that she knows nothing about any class but the well-off class. She takes a rather optimistic view of life, and necessarily a superficial one. Both her style and her ideas are amateurish; but a great many persons will find her book very enjoyable.

---

## POETRY.

It is not easy to do justice to a poem like *Without a God*.[4] It might be described as a novel in verse. The author's name is not given, and we fear that, if even his identity were revealed, he would not have a just title to the name of poet. Still, the work is a remarkable specimen of a rare species of literature. It is a singular combination of the narrative poem, of which Scott and Byron were

---

[1] *In Chimney Corners.* Merry Tales of Irish Folk Lore. By Seumas MacManus. Illustrated by Pamela C. Smith. London and New York: Harper & Brothers.
[2] *Ashes Tell No Tales.* A Dramatic Story. By Mrs. Albert S. Bradshaw. London: Greening & Co.
[3] *More Pot Pourri from a Surrey Garden.* By Mrs. C. W. Earle. London: Smith Elder & Co.
[4] *Without a God.* By a Singer from the South. London: Kegan Paul, Trench, Trübner & Co.

the greatest masters, and of the philosophical treatise in verse. It is, perhaps, to be regretted that the work was not written in prose. The story is deeply interesting. It shows how a man may even sincerely love and pity a fallen woman, and how even his sufferings on account of her frailty may shatter his early faith. There is an appendix attached to the poem containing some very impressive lines dealing with the Fall of Man and the history of the Christian Church. The writer evidently has seen life with the eyes of sad experience. He speaks of himself as a Freethinker, but he vents his wrath and indignation on what he calls the "shams" of the age. His creed is purely negative and nihilistic, and is, therefore, opposed to all true conceptions of progress. Some readers will feel a little curiosity as to the real basis for this curious volume of verse extending to nearly 600 pages, and will probably ask themselves how far it may be regarded as an autobiography. It is a volume entirely out of the common, though we cannot speak very highly as to its purely literary merits.

The volume by Mrs. Aylmer Gowing, containing *Boadicea*,[1] a play in four acts, and other poems, will sustain that talented lady's reputation. The career of the "British Warrior Queen" is admirably adapted to dramatic treatment, and, though we cannot place this effort on a level with the highest tragedies, it contains many striking passages, and the *dénouement* is effective. Of the shorter poems, perhaps the most spirited is "Martin Sprague: a Fireman's Story," which will be probably very popular with those who recite on public platforms. Of the sonnets in the volume, we think the finest is that on "Speranza"—Lady Wilde—of which we quote a portion:

> " Proud Hecuba of sorrows, in thy arms
> Could woman's anguish weep its bitter fill,
> Touched by this kiss with sweet companion's balm.
> Oh, rich in mother-love unquenchable
> Our human spark of everlasting flame,
> Caught from the heart of God."

The verses are not unworthy of the gifted woman to whom they are a well-merited tribute. Many of Lady Wilde's lyrics have a Hugoesque grandeur, and we rejoice to find that Mrs. Aylmer Gowing has thrown a charming wreath of verse, so to speak, on the tomb of "Speranza."

---

[1] *Boadicea.* A Play in Four Acts. Poems for Recitation, &c. By Mrs. Alfred Gowing (Emilia Aylmer Blake). London: Kegan Paul, Trench, Trübner & Co.

## THE
# WESTMINSTER REVIEW.

## VOL. CLIII. No. 3.—MARCH 1900.

## THE PROBLEM IN SOUTH AFRICA.[1]

### BOER *V.* BRITON.

ONE naturally shrinks from adding to the already enormous mass of printed matter dealing with the tangled skein of South African politics, but when one seeks almost in vain, in leading text-books, books of the day, magazines, and leading newspaper articles for any impartial and coherent account of the subject as a whole, it becomes the duty of the mere critic to sift and weigh the evidence with as

[1] *The History of the Great Boer Trek.* By the late Hon. Henry Cloete. Edited by W. Broderick-Cloete. London : John Murray. 1899.

*The Last Boer War.* By Rider Haggard. London : Kegan Paul, Trench, Trübner and Co., Limited. 1900.

*Boers or English? Who are in the Right?* Translated from the French of Edmond Demolins. London : The Leadenhall Press Limited. 1900.

*The Problem of South African Unity.* By W. Basil Worsfold. London : George Allen. 1900.

*A Century of Wrong.* Issued by F. W. Reitz, State Secretary of the South African Republic. With a Preface by W. T. Stead. London : *Review of Reviews* Office. 1900.

*The Transvaal Trouble. How it Arose.* Being an extract from the Biography of the late Sir Bartle Frere. By John Martineau London : John Murray. 1899.

*Britain and the Boers. Who is responsible for the War in South Africa?* By Lewis Appleton, F.R.H.S. London : Simpkin, Marshall, Hamilton, Kent & Co , Limited 1899.

*The Transvaal from Within.* By J. P. Fitzpatrick. London : William Heinemann. 1899.

*The Scandal of the South African Committee.* By W. T. Stead. London : *Review of Reviews* Office. 1899.

*Some South African Recollections.* By Mrs. Lionel Phillips. With 36 Illustrations. Fifth Impression. London, New York and Bombay : Longmans, Green & Co. 1900.

*Impressions of South Africa.* By James Bryce. Third Edition. London : Macmillan and Co. Limited. 1899.

*Arbitration or War?* Edited by Francis Parker. London : Harrison and Sons. 1899.

*Blacks and Whites in South Africa.* By H. R. Fox Bourne. London : P. S. King and Son.

*Le Transvaal et l'Angleterre en Afrique du Sud.* Par Georges Aubert. Paris : Ernest Flammarion. 1900.

*Natives under the Transvaal Flag.* By the Rev. John Bovill. With Illustrations. London : Simpkin, Marshall, Hamilton, Kent & Co. 1900.

much judicial impartiality and freedom from all national, party, or class sympathies or prejudices as he can muster. Upon one point, at any rate, we are all agreed. Whatever the original cause of quarrel between the contending parties, the nation with practically absolute unanimity has determined to prosecute at all costs the struggle to a successful termination. Until the British flag flies from the Zambesi to Simon's Bay, nothing must be allowed to interfere with our operations.

At the same time, however, assuming ultimate success for our military operations—and no other assumption can be entertained—it will never do to wait till the settlement is upon us before making up our minds upon what principles affairs are to be arranged. It is, therefore, the bounden duty of every citizen to acquaint himself with the leading facts of the case and to form upon them some clear conclusions to guide his action when the time comes. My object, then, is to assist the average man, who is unable to wade through and sift the mass of evidence, by indicating the main questions involved, freed, as far as is humanly possible, from all tinge of party spirit, passions, and prejudices.

In order to understand the present position of affairs some acquaintance with the history of the past is invariably necessary in all cases; but it is particularly essential here, since the Boers, like all pastoral races, have long memories, and these have been deliberately kept alive by the irreconcilables.

The first period, then, with which we have to deal is that from 1814 to 1852, a period known as the Great Boer Trek, which resulted in the creation of the Orange Free State and the Transvaal Republic.

During this period the Boer case is almost irrefutable. The transference of the Boers by their own nation to foreigners was the first grievance; but with good government this would have died away, as, in fact, it did in Cape Colony and Natal, and as it has done in Canada and elsewhere; but this is just what the Dutch did not obtain for the moment. The trek into the unknown was no new thing; it had been going on for years, partly owing to want of land for the growing population, and partly to the tyrannical *régime* of the Dutch East India Company, against whose rule the Boers had twice risen in rebellion. The English Government was admittedly better than this, but it only formed part and parcel of an ill-informed, prejudiced, self-interested, and muddle-headed system, aggravated by ignorant and high-handed Governors, who treated Boers and British alike with arrogant and senseless harshness.

In the early portion of this period the three main grievances all fall under the Native Question, one aspect of which, I feel convinced, has lasted till now as the primary cause of all the trouble. These three may be classed as (1) the Hottentot Question, (2) the Slave Question, and (3) the Kafir Question.

The first owes its origin to the officious and ill-conceived zeal of the missionaries, prompted by well-intentioned but ill-informed and over-zealous philanthropists at home. These missionaries proclaimed themselves the champions of the black population against the white, and they stand convicted of formulating absolutely false and baseless charges of ill-treatment of the natives at the hands of the colonists. In 1811 some seventy to eighty of such charges were preferred before the High Court.

"There was hardly," writes Mr. Theal, "a family on the frontier of which some relative was not brought as a criminal before the judges to answer to a charge of murder or violent assault. Several months were occupied in the trials, and more than a thousand witnesses were examined, but in every instance the most serious charges were proved to be without foundation. Only a few convictions, and those of no very outrageous crimes, resulted from those prosecutions, which kept the whole colony in a ferment until long after the circuit was closed."

Of those summoned to appear before a similar Commission in 1815 to answer a charge of ill-treatment of a Hottentot was a farmer, named Fred. J. Bezuidenhout, who was killed in resisting the warrant issued for his arrest. This led to the rebellion of that year, which resulted in the notorious execution of five of the ringleaders at Slachter's Nek, which, said Henry Cloete, speaking in the year 1853, had left a far more indelible impression in the minds of the Boers than even their losses in the Kafir Wars or the abolition of slavery, and which Mr. Reitz to-day describes as "the first blood-stained beacon which marks the boundary between Boer and Briton in South Africa." A distorted view, no doubt, but still a sentiment with which we have to reckon. The rebels were rightly convicted and executed, but the original cause of their disloyalty lay with the authorities in allowing the missionaries to exercise their powers for evil. Miss Kingsley has recently told us that all our troubles on the West Coast of Africa are traceable to the missionaries, and we know that in India these gentry have been strictly confined in their operations.

In Cape Colony, in addition to setting the law in motion as described, those emissaries of the Aborigines Protection Society, many of whom had married native women, entered every homestead and made life unbearable for the colonists. In the north and north-eastern districts, where hired native labour was customary, the natives were seduced into missionary schools in which they passed an idle life, and encouraged the rest, who were too destitute or ill-behaved for admission, to hang round the towns, to which they became a nuisance, and even a terror.

In the south-western districts, on the other hand, slavery prevailed, though not to the exclusion of hired field-labour. Nine-tenths of the slave population consisted of domestic slaves, who were, as there is ample evidence to show, treated on the whole with great humanity.    After the peace of 1815 the British people, and through them the Government, became imbued with the philanthropic spirit of anti-slavery, one of the greatest moral movements of the century, but spoilt by the crude and precipitous action of its advocates. A local ordinance was passed in 1826 instituting the office of guardian or protector of slaves, who, by himself or his deputies, could interfere on behalf of the slave, but the Home Government, not satisfied with this, by an order in Council in 1830, increased the number of guardians and rendered the regulations still more stringent.    These laws tended to entirely destroy the good relationship hitherto subsisting between the slaves and their owners.

The colonists themselves were perfectly willing to abandon the system, provided their interests were duly considered.    In fact, two or three hundred female slaves were freed by voluntary effort, and Parliament was asked to contribute some £8000 annually, by which, in the course of ten years, at a cost to Great Britain of £80,000, slavery would have ceased to exist.    This moderate request met with a flat refusal.

By the Act of 1833 slavery was abolished throughout the British colonies at a cost of £20,000,000, out of which it was estimated that £3,000,000 would be available for Cape Colony.    Upon the figures being worked out, it was found that £1,200,000 only could be awarded, and that the compensation would only be payable at the Bank of England.    This necessitated the employment of agents at ruinous commissions, and so disgusted were some owners that, according to Cloete, they indignantly refused to accept the paltry sums tendered by the Government.    The result was in many cases absolute ruin, and in all very considerable loss, and a feeling of bitterness only accentuated by time.

It is a mistake, however, to suppose this to be a special grievance of Boers of the Great Trek, since these were principally drawn from the north and north-eastern district where slavery was almost unknown.    However, even by them it has ever since been regarded as one more instance of British breach of good faith.

It was the Kafir question, however, which was the proximate cause of the Great Trek.    It is impossible to describe here the details of the numerous Kafir wars, and it must suffice to say that from 1815 to 1834 the whole frontier was in a chronic state of fermentation.    Even when there was no actual war, not a week passed but some looting or murder took place, and when the sufferer complained he was generally accused of exaggeration or downright falsehood.    If a collision occurred the blame was always thrown upon the colonist.    The borderland was now taken from the Kafirs, now declared neutral ground, only to be again reconquered and in turn restored, until the invasion of 15,000 Kafirs on

Christmas Day, 1834, brought matters to a crisis. This attack was successfully repulsed under the Governor, Sir Benjamin D'Urban, and the whole of Kaffraria up to the Kye cleared of the Kafirs. The neutral territory was to be given to those farmers who had specially suffered from the war, the total amount of damage being assessed at £300,000, but D'Urban's proposals were overruled by Lord Glenelg, then Secretary of the Colonies, who, in a despatch which might have emanated from Exeter Hall, made the following extraordinary declaration :

"Through a long series of years the Kafirs had an ample justification for war ; they had to resent, and endeavoured justly though impotently to avenge a series of encroachments : they had a perfect right to hazard the experiment, however hopelessly, of extorting by force that redress which they could not otherwise obtain ; and that original justice is on the side of the conquered (the Kafirs) not of the victorious party."

Other grievances are mentioned by Henry Cloete—the alteration of the land system in 1813, the redemption in 1825 of the paper currency at only thirty-six hundreds of its nominal value, the abolition of the courts of Landdrost and Heemraden, and the substitution of the English for the Dutch language in the courts. Yet these measures, however distasteful at the time, are now recognised by the Dutch in Cape Colony as having been necessary and beneficial.

And the three great grievances, too, might have been forgotten but for the idiotic policy of Lord Glenelg. From the moment of his fatuous despatch a general exodus was determined upon, and in two or three years some 10,000 bade farewell for ever to the land of their fathers and trekked out into the great unknown, which was to be to them a land of war and famine, of cruel hardships and terrible tragedies, relieved by victories oftentimes dearly bought. Their history forms the romance of South Africa unequalled by any fiction.

"And so," writes Mr. FitzPatrick, "they fought and worked and starved and died for their land of promise, where they might hope to be alone, like the simple people of their one Book, where they might never know the hated British rule, where they might never experience the forms and trammels, the restlessness and changes and worries, the necessities or benefits of progressing civilisation."

The first emigrants, after the loss of some small parties which were practically wiped out, finally rolled the Matabele across the Limpopo, and their numbers increasing they spread themselves over the district south of this river, and gradually formed themselves into small and scattered communities, from which were evolved the two Dutch republics of our time.

A party of those under Retief having crossed the Draakensberg, found the country unoccupied save for a small settlement of English at Port Natal, was quickly followed by nearly 1000 waggons. Those English settlers who had been there since 1824 had repeatedly petitioned for recognition as a colony, but Lord Glenelg had expressly "disclaimed in the most distinct terms any intention on the part of his Majesty's Government to assert any authority over any part of this territory."

Here, after terrible struggles with the Zulus, the Dutch emigrants established the Republic of Natalia, the cession of the country by the notorious Dingaan being afterwards found in a leathern pouch still attached to the skeleton of the ill-fated leader, Retief.

Meanwhile Sir George Napier had despatched Captain Jarvis with a detachment to hold Port Natal, but a few days before the great Boer victory over Dingaan, finding the Secretary of State for the Colonies unwilling to support his policy of occupying this district, he sent orders to Captain Jarvis to withdraw.

Thus the Boers were left in undisputed possession of Natal, and regarded themselves both *de facto* and *de jure* masters of the country.

In spite of the establishment in 1840 of a settled form of government, by 1843 the country was in a state of anarchy. A raiding expedition having been made against the Kafirs bordering on Cape Colony, Captain Smith was sent with a small force in 1842 to restore order and demand satisfaction. He arrived without opposition at D'Urban, and at once conceived the plan of a night attack on the Boer position at Congella. His every movement, however, even before leaving camp, had been carefully noted by the Boer scouts, and instead of surprising the Boers he was himself caught in a skilfully prepared trap, losing 103 out of 140 men. When will the British officer learn by experience? We might be reading here an account from to-day's newspapers.

Shut up in his camp for a month, Smith was at length relieved by a force from the Cape under Colonel Cloete, who speedily reduced the Boers to submission to the English Crown. Under the able guidance of Henry Cloete satisfactory terms were arrived at, and the district was incorporated within the Queen's dominions.

So satisfactory were those terms that a memorial was presented by the farmers of the Orange River praying for a similar constitution under the Crown. But another Governor had replaced Sir George Napier, who replied "that the application could not be entertained." The settlement in Natal, however, had not been effected without opposition, and the irreconcilables in considerable numbers abandoned their farms and retired at first into the Free State, where a few remained, whilst the majority wandered northwards over the Vaal River. This fact alone explains the keener spirit of hatred against the British felt to this day by the Transvaal Boers. But for the vacillating policy of the Home Government of at one time recognising and at another of repudiating their independence, this particular grievance would have had no foundation.

It was an axiom during the earlier portion of this period that British subjects could not divest themselves of their allegiance by leaving the country and forming independent States.[1]   When the Boers seemed likely to establish a State in Natal with a maritime border this principle was put into force, the ostensible reason for interference being the conflicts between the emigrants and the natives, as already described.   This principle was again enforced in 1848, when a British Resident was appointed to the Free State.   Pretorius gave him forty-eight hours' notice to quit.   Thereupon followed the British victory at Bloomplaats, with the subsequent annexation by Sir Harry Smith of the "Orange River Sovereignty."   Troubles speedily arose with Moshesh, the chief of the Basutos, and upon request for assistance the Free Staters responded but coldly.   In 1851 a despatch from Earl Grey to Sir Harry Smith declared all this to be a mistake:

"The ultimate abandonment of the Orange River territory," it stated, "must be a settled point of our policy.   You will distinctly understand that any wars, however sanguinary, which may afterwards occur between different tribes and communities which will be left in a state of independence beyond the colonial boundary, are to be considered as affording no ground for your interference."

And so Sir Harry Smith was recalled in disgrace, and his policy reversed.

In 1852 Sir George Cathcart signed the Sand River Convention, by which the Transvaal became an independent State, and two years later the Orange Free State became equally free.

The native trouble, however, soon became too much for the Free Staters, and in 1858 the Raad by resolution proposed reunion by federation or otherwise with Cape Colony.   Notwithstanding Sir George Grey's support, the Colonial Secretary, Sir E. Bulwer Lytton, decided against it, and so a golden opportunity was lost.

This fact is not noticed by Mr. Reitz in his special pleading of the Boer case.

In 1868, in spite of our declared policy of non-intervention, it was thought fitting to rescue the Basutos from annihilation by the Free Staters.   Mr. Reitz prefers to call this "well-merited chastisement on the Basutos."   In the examination of the Boer treatment of the natives it will be seen whether we were not fully justified in our intervention.

The discovery of the diamond mines at Kimberley in 1870 gave rise to another dispute.   Froude asserts that we ourselves had treated this as part of the Orange River territory.   It was necessary to establish some sort of order in a large mixed mining population, and Kimberley was thereupon occupied by our forces upon the plea that

[1] Legalised by 6 & 7 Will. IV. c. 57.

it was within the boundary of Waterboer, a native chief who had ceded the district to us. According to Froude, "there was a notion that the finest diamond mine in the world ought not to be lost to the British Empire." I am inclined to think that this was the real motive. However, order had to be maintained and the Free Staters made no real attempts to effect it. The boundary dispute was settled by the payment to the Free State of £90,000. According to Reitz, the British Government acknowledged its guilt and paid this sum for the richest diamond fields in the world, and, in the words of Froude, "from that day to this no Boer in South Africa has been able to trust to English promises."

Froude can hardly be accepted as a reliable authority upon boundary questions in South Africa, and if there were anything in black and white describing the boundaries of the Orange River territory Mr. Reitz would surely have produced it. By English promises, Froude meant those contained in the Aliwal Convention of 1869, by which we bound ourselves not to intervene in the internal affairs of the Free State.

Wilmot, who cannot be described as a pro-Boer, roundly asserts that "there is no doubt that the great dry diggings at Kimberley were all really within the Free State boundary," and that "the Republic in due course sent its officers to exercise jurisdiction," and that then Waterboer made his claim, which was defeated in the courts.[1] It is also asserted by the Boers that when we were in occupation of the Orange River territory our magistrates exercised jurisdiction there.

Mr. George Lacy, a well-known hunter and pioneer, tells a very different tale. At the time he was there,

"The country round," he says, "was in dispute as to ownership, being claimed both by the Orange Free State authorities and by the Griqua chief Waterboer. Arbitration by the then Governor of Natal resulted in its being awarded to Waterboer, and by him it was made over to the British Government."[2]

Mr. Lacy is very sceptical upon Froude's reminiscences. He fell a victim to that reprehensible colonial practice elegantly termed "filling up the jimmies."[3] But Froude has had his revenge. He has "filled up" Mr. Reitz! The truth seems to be that there had been no real delimitation of the frontier, and this particular grievance appears to me "not proven."

Speaking of a more recent visit to Kimberley, Mr. Lacy says that the De Beers Company is probably the most gigantic and iniquitous monopoly the world has ever seen. No competition is allowed.

"At its instigation the Cape Parliament passed the most iniquitous Act ever enacted by a civilised legislature—the notorious I.D.B. (illicit

---

[1] Wilmot, *Expansion of Southern Africa*, 173.
[2] George Lacy, *Pictures of Travel, Sport, and Adventure*, p. 159.　　[3] *Ibid.* p. 189.

diamond buying) Act.  Under this Act the police have the right to search at any time and without warrant the persons and houses of any one they choose ; and if a diamond is found the person or occupier has to prove that he had a permit to purchase that particular stone, in default of which he is liable to a long term of penal servitude." [1]

The second period in the history of the Transvaal Boers, from the Sand River Convention to the annexation in 1877, is not so creditable to the trekkers.  Whether the Boers ill-treated the natives in the earlier period is a moot point.  There does not appear to be any evidence upon which they can be convicted generally of ill-treatment, although isolated instances have been proved.  The Boer standpoint is frankly stated by an Afrikander writer :

"The Boers, while treating the blacks kindly and humanely, do not believe that blacks and whites were intended to be on an equal footing in this world.  They contend that even the Bible teaches that the children of Ham shall be servants to the children of his brethren." [2]

The English, on the other hand, desired to place the natives on an equal political footing with the whites.  In carrying out this, no doubt they acted too hastily, as they did in the emancipation.  The old social order was too rudely shaken.

It is clear, as Mr. Rider Haggard says, that the Boer looked upon the "black creature" as an inferior being delivered into his hand by the "Lord" to be shot or enslaved.  This view was naturally strengthened during the Great Trek by the bloody struggle that ensued in the Free State, Natal, and across the Vaal.  Just as in Cape Colony in the early period, so in the Free State and the Transvaal, only on a far larger scale, the Boers dispossessed the natives of their land and cattle by fraud and chicane.  It was a common practice to obtain licences to graze from some petty chief, and after a few seasons of occupation to claim not only the ownership but damages against the owner for trespass !  If the dispute became serious, a small force was collected under a field cornet, which, proceeding with a small present of cattle for the head chief, obtained his signature to a document alienating large portions of his territory.  Such documents do not appear ever to have been explained to the chief.

"In Secocoeni's case they allege that his father Sequati cedes to them the whole of his territory (hundreds of square miles) for a hundred head of cattle." [3]

Cattle were obtained in much the same way.  The process is thus described by an eye-witness :

"A few well-armed colonists assemble together ; then falling suddenly on an isolated body of natives, they compel its members to bring up all

[1] George Lacy, *Pictures of Travel, Sport, and Adventure*, p. 205.
[2] "Clos," *Life in Afrikanderland*, 1897.
[3] Rider Haggard, *The Last Boer War*, p. 7.

their cattle; then they select therefrom the animals which best suit them and give for them whatsoever price they please. This is what used to be called 'making a purchase with a loaded rifle.'"[1]

But the Transvaal Boers did not stop at fraud and chicane. Their occupation was, says Elisée Reclus, "sometimes accompanied by wholesale exterminations; each advance of the whites in a northerly direction had to be purchased at the price of blood." One of the most notorious examples took place in the Zoutpansberg War of 1865, when the blacks after a defeat took refuge with their wives and children in some caves, where the Boers smoked them to death. The place is thus described by Dr. Wangeman:

"The roof of the first cave was black with smoke; the remains of the logs which were burnt lay at the entrance. The floor was strewn with hundreds of skulls and skeletons. In confused heaps lay karosses, kerries, assegais, pots, spoons, snuff-boxes, and the bones of men, giving one the impresssion that this was the grave of a whole people. Some estimate the number of those who perished here from twenty to thirty thousand. This is, I believe, too high. In the one chamber there were from two hundred to three hundred skeletons. The other chambers I did not visit."[2]

For a long time, says Demolins, the Boers asserted that this was a resort of cannibals and that here a native tribe held fearful orgies, but the real facts are now established. Other instances might be given of similar atrocities on a smaller scale.

The existence of slavery in the Transvaal has been strenuously denied. There is ample evidence, however, that it existed as late as 1881. The Boers called the system "apprenticeship," but in addition to this, by which destitute children whose parents had been killed were apprenticed to farmers till they came of age (an event which seldom happened till they were decrepit with age), a regular slave trade was carried on. Mr. Rider Haggard, who, it must be remembered, was secretary to Sir Theophilus Shepstone, asserts that President Burgers himself was one of the greatest slave-dealers.

No sooner had the Boers to some extent settled down than the leading families engaged in a series of feuds for the headship. One Republic was established at Lydenburg and another at Pretoria, which were incorporated in 1852, but no President was elected till 1872, when Mr. Burgers was returned for that office. Circumstances, however, were too strong for Burgers, who was one of the few honest politicians in the country. But the majority of the Boers cared nothing for progress. They only wanted to be let alone and to do as they liked. In other words, they had a rooted aversion to paying taxes and were determined not to abandon their custom of "forced labour." Then they split up into factions. Paul Kruger became the leader of the Dopper party and intrigued against the President.

[1] Levaillant, *Deuxième Voyage.* Vol. I. 19-20. Cited by Edmond Demolins.
[2] Cited by Rider Haggard.

By 1877 the Transvaal was bankrupt; 12*s.* 6*d.* was in the Treasury and the liabilities amounted to £300,000. On March 3 Burgers resigned, saying, in his address to the Raad:

"I would rather be a policeman under strong government than the president of such a State. It is you—you the members of the Raad and the Boers—who have lost the country, who have sold your independence for a drink. You have ill-treated the natives, you have shot them down, you have sold them into slavery, and now you have to pay the penalty."

One of the terms of the Sand River Convention was that slavery should not be permitted by the Republic. It was also mutually agreed that the sale of firearms and ammunition to the natives should be prohibited by both parties to the treaty. Mr. Reitz makes a great grievance of the breach of the latter term by the British, but maintains a discreet silence upon the breach of the former by the Boers.

Thus it would appear that the old spirit of individual liberty and national independence had degenerated into mere licence. By their cruel aggressions the Boers had brought the natives down upon their heads, and, in the state of anarchy which prevailed, were in no condition to resist their hereditary enemies.

So far three points are clearly evolved. First, upon the Native Question the ideas of Briton and Boer are diametrically opposed; secondly, the Boer detests law and order when coupled with taxation; and lastly, there was an utter lack on the part of the English Government of any continuity in their South African policy.

HUGH H. L. BELLOT.

(*To be continued.*)

# WHO OUGHT TO PAY FOR THE WAR?

REBUKING some time ago some indiscreet person who had used the word "almsgiving" in the course of an appeal on behalf of the funds being raised for the wounded and disabled soldiers and the widows and children of those killed in the present most shameful war, the *Daily Chronicle* indignantly said:

"'Almsgiving,' at any rate, is not the word that has been generally associated with this outburst of national sympathy, in which all sorts and conditions of men have hastened to join. 'We do not ask you to join in any act of charity,' said the Duke of Devonshire the other day, 'but to do your duty, to bear your share of the war, the full burden of which is falling on our soldiers.'"

True, the word "almsgiving" is not one that has generally been used in this connection. "Almsgiving," most certainly, is not the word that one would apply to any provision made for the brave soldiers who may be wounded and disabled, or for those near and dear to them who may be made widows and fatherless as a consequence of the blundering and plundering policy of our Government of landlords and "patriots." To make such provision is a national duty, and is in no sense charity.

But, if we look more closely into the matter, if we probe it to the core, there is a sense, and a very real sense, in which "the notable, the unexampled movement on behalf of those who are fighting our battles," "this outburst of national sympathy, in which all sorts and conditions of men have hastened to join," may be stigmatised as almsgiving pure and simple.

Surely, it must have been with tongue in cheek that the Duke of Devonshire uttered the words quoted above.

Had his Grace spoken with a greater regard for the truth he would have said: "We, the landholders of England, in inviting contributions to these funds, crave your alms. We ask you to join in an act of charity towards us—not that to bear a share of the cost of the war, the full burden of which should fall on our shoulders, is any part of your duty."

That the full burden of this and of all other wars should fall on the landholders—that, in fact, they should bear the whole of the burdens of State, both local and general, cannot be denied by those who have studied to any purpose the history of land tenures in this country, and have any regard for truth and honesty.

That the large sums raised during the past few months on behalf of our soldiers at the front and those they have left behind them really operate in the long run as alms to the land-"owners" is obvious enough to those who have any real grasp of economic principles.

> " Pass the hat for your credit's sake, and pay—pay—pay ! "

said that Jingo jingler, Rudyard Kipling.

Had he said

> " Pass the hat for the landlord's sake, and pay—pay—pay ! "

he would have been far nearer the mark.

There can be little doubt that while land-grabbing abroad —the " collaring " of the gold-bearing lands of the Transvaal— was the main object of the Rhodes-cum-Chamberlain Raid, a secondary object—perhaps a primary one with Lord Salisbury and some other members of the Cabinet—was the postponing for an indefinite period of land reform at home.

The reduction of the Government majority from 142 to 34 on February 10, 1899, on Mr. E. J. C. Morton's amendment with regard to the taxation of land-values for local purposes, was a portent that did not escape Lord Salisbury's attention ; and a vision of a preconcerted Radical attack on " property, and especially private property in land," evidently presented itself, for in the following May, addressing at the Hotel Cecil the Knights Imperial of the Primrose League, the noble Marquis said :

> " If it is possible within a reasonable time to cause again a bitter controversy, by which parties in England shall be divided into two well-marked lines, undoubtedly the question of property must be brought in. Property is marked out as the next object of Radical attack when the Radical party resumes its activity and unity. Their efforts can only be met by a corresponding effort on the part of those who wish the ancient principles of property, and the system on which this country has reached so vast a height of civilisation and prosperity, to be maintained and upheld. It will depend upon the efforts of those who hold that such attacks should be repelled. But do not imagine that we can stand aside, one of us in a country house, another of us in a city office, a third in any other field of activity, following his own vocation, thinking of his own immediate interests, and abstaining from combining together for the co-operation in which salvation alone is to be found. Unless we co-operate together we are lost."

What motive, except that he could see that a war would probably shelve for a long time the social reforms he so much dreads, could have been strong enough to induce Lord Salisbury to allow Mr. Chamberlain to carry on the negotiations with the

Transvaal with his pushful, Brummagem bluff? Lord Salisbury had somewhat of a reputation as a Foreign Minister to lose, Mr. Chamberlain had no reputation to lose. What more probable than that Lord Salisbury, on the principle—

> "Let laws and learning, art and commerce die,
> But save, oh save, our old nobility "—

that is to say, "our noble selves"—should permit Mr. Chamberlain to make a diversion in the interests of "property, and especially property in land," by pushing matters to extremity with the Transvaal.

The idea may to some seem far-fetched, but Mr. G. W. E. Russell, who, on July 10 last, took the chair at a public meeting held in St. Martin's Town Hall, "to protest against reckless threats of war with the Transvaal," prefaced his introductory remarks by the following significant utterance:

"I remember very well that when the present Government was being formed, one of the most experienced politicians then in the House of Commons, who was leaving it and looking back over a long Parliamentary life, made to me this prediction: ' I expect that this Government will go on pretty quietly for three or four years, and then at the end of that time, when they find their popularity waning, they will stir up a war in one part of the world or another.' "

Mr. John Morley voiced the same suspicion when, in addressing his constituents at Arbroath early in September last, he said:

"But it is idle, when you hear the sound of approaching war in your ears, to talk about ground values or old-age pensions, or any of those things; and, without being uncharitable, I wonder whether some of those who send this hurricane of rumours of war into the air are not quite alive to the fact."

The _Chronicle_, dealing with the meeting of the Tory Caucus at Dewsbury, and that of the Liberal Unionists at Leicester, put the same point very forcibly:

"We have awaited the Liberal Unionist gathering at Leicester in the faint hope that we should find a sign of more progressive policy in their resolutions than in those passed at Dewsbury by the Conservatives. We cannot say that the results have justified the ingenuous hopes which we entertained. Things are not, indeed, quite so bad as with the Tories. With them social reform is dead, and has been given a pauper's funeral. The Liberal Unionists still cling to a shred of the tattered garment, and there is a beautiful gradation in the degrees of detachment. Sir Fortescue Flannery, who sits for an 'Old Age Pensions' seat, moved an omnibus resolution covering pensions, employers' liability, and—strange partnership!—Irish over-representation. On the suggestion of a puzzled delegate, the resolution was divided into three parts. On cutting down the Irish seats, the Liberal Unionists, like the Tories at Dewsbury, are unanimous. But on the mild proposal to extend employers' liability there was a division of opinion while on Old Age Pensions there was a considerable minority

against.  In other words, these things are virtually shelved.  Truly the
Unionists must regard the war as a blessed event, especially created to
postpone social reform."

While Mr. Chaplin at the United Club dinner, December 9, 1899,
very naïvely gave the whole case away:

"I have often been under obligations to my hon. friend," said he, "but
I do not know that I ever felt more indebted to him than when he told
you just now he had abandoned all intention of asking me to-night to
express my view, and the opinions and intentions of Her Majesty's Government, with regard to the very vexed question of Old Age Pensions.  I
accept with gratitude the invitation of your chairman to confine my
observations to that question which occupies the mind of everybody at the
present moment—namely, the progress of the war in South Africa which
has been forced upon us."

The Tory party, more especially Mr. Chamberlain, were utterly
discredited by their failure to carry out their programme of social
reforms.  They could not, or rather would not, rehabilitate themselves by redeeming their pledges as regards Old Age Pensions, for
the very simple reason that in order to secure the necessary funds
the Chancellor of the Exchequer would have had to tap the only
source of revenue large enough for such a purpose—the source
whence the landlords derive their unearned, their perpetual and
perpetually-increasing pensions—land values; and to tax land
values is to the Tories *anathema maranatha*.  Their only alternative, therefore, was a war, because a war would enable them to
"call upon all patriots, regardless of party distinctions, to stand
shoulder to shoulder with them in defence of Queen and country."

The war was to have been "a military promenade picnic" from
Cape Town to Pretoria, but it has proved a much tougher and a
much more costly job than was anticipated by its promoters, and it
may yet prove that in more ways than one they have far over-reached
themselves.

Sir Michael Hicks-Beach proposed to make the gold mines of the
Rand bear at least a large part of the cost of the war, and, said
Mr. Bryce, M.P., at Aberdeen:

"It is an excellent idea, which ought to receive a great access of support
from the figures recently published regarding the increased yield to be
expected from the mines under a better administration.  More than two
millions sterling a year are given by an experienced authority, while others
look for a still greater increase, and, as far as I can judge, with good
ground.  It is quite equitable to appropriate this increased revenue, or
nearly the whole of it, towards paying the cost of the operations which
will have brought the increase about.  Do not let us repeat the mistake
made in Egypt, when the action of Britain in 1882 came near to doubling
the value of the bonds, and the profit which ought to have been secured
for Egyptian purposes went to benefit the bondholders only."

An excellent idea, indeed.  Let a substantial tax be placed on the land values of the Rand ; but a large part of such revenues should surely be earmarked to indemnify the Boers for the losses caused by their being "jockeyed" into this infamous war. A similar tax might well be levied on the land values of Kimberley, and the revenue so obtained might be applied to compensate Cape Colony and Natal for their losses by the war. Again, Mr. Chamberlain is a man of wealth, and Mr. Rhodes is said to be worth £10,000,000. Let these two men be impeached together with Sir Alfred Milner, and let those of "the millionaires of the Rand" who are also implicated in the engineering of this act of piracy, this wholesale murder for gain, be put upon their trial. If found guilty, they might well congratulate themselves if they escaped with their lives, even though sentenced to long terms of imprisonment and allowed to retain a tithe only of their wealth.

It were only just and fair that these men should be made to suffer for the incalculable loss and suffering that their "vaulting ambition" has caused ; but to meet the greater part of the cost of this war and to make generous and adequate provision for the wounded and disabled, the widows and fatherless, we ought to tap, and we shall have to tap sooner or later, those land values which are, in the eyes of the present "Landlord Government," so sacred. The revenues derived from other sources have reached the limit of the taxpayer's endurance, and while Lord Mayor's Funds, &c., may to a certain extent relieve the tension, and so tend to put off the evil day (for the landlords), the "relief" to the landowners can only be of a "temporary" character. In the words of the villain of melodrama, "A time will come!" And that that time may come quickly is the wish of every lover of fair play and justice : ·

Said Cobden fifty years ago :

"If you were to bring forward the history of taxation in this country for the last 150 years you will find as black a record against the landowners as even in the corn laws. If they want another league on the back of this one then let them force the middle and industrial classes of England to understand how they have been cheated, robbed, and bamboozled upon the subject of taxation."

The historical and legal aspect of the question is admirably stated by Mr. Dominick Daly (barrister-at-law) in his pamphlet, *The Feudal Theory of Landlordism: a Plea for its Revival,* [1] from which we need make no apology, considering the vital importance of the question, for making somewhat lengthy extracts :

"Thus," says he, "something resembling feudal tenure—or the holding of lands on condition of service to the State—existed among the Anglo-Saxons, though, as Hallam says, the prevalence of actual feudality is not clear. It is, however, very certain that the Normans introduced, in an unmistakable form, the feudal principle of land tenure. . . . The stringent

[1] Midland Educational Company, 91–92 New Street, Birmingham, September 1882.

rule was then at least laid down and stringently enforced throughout the country that *every holder of land was a mere tenant and that the ultimate freehold in fee simple was vested in the sovereign as chief landlord and lord paramount.* This principle was indeed the very root and essence of the feudal system, which would have ceased to be a system at all without it. . . . As Mr. Froude puts it, ' the owner of the soil was an officer of the commonwealth. If he was false to his trust the sovereign power resumed its rights, which it had never parted with, and either sold or gave his interest and his authority along with it to others who would better discharge the duties expected of them.' Those original conditions of English land tenures have been considerably broken in upon, but down to the present day the feudal theory as to tenure survives. In contemplation of English Law no man is the absolute owner of land, but can at most hold only estates or interest therein of longer or shorter duration.[1]

" With few exceptions . . . the all-prevailing principle of land-occupancy was that the occupier, however he became so, should render a substantial and not a mere nominal return to the State for the privilege he enjoyed.

" This substantial return constituted originally almost the entire resource available for the purposes of carrying on the government of the country. The holders of the soil had to bear the national expenditure, either directly as tenants-in-chief of the Crown, or indirectly through intermediate lords. Military service was a mode of paying for the privilege of occupying the land convenient to all parties, agreeable to the spirit of the age and indeed necessary at a period when the idea of a standing army and of a permanent navy had no existence. Accordingly, such service—Knights' service, as it was designated—was a usual condition of land tenure, and was, at the same time, regarded as being the most honourable ; this service was regulated by the extent or value of the land held by the tenant. The unit of measurement, as it may be called, was a 'knights' fee' or the possession of twelve ploughlands—680 acres according to some, and 800 acres according to others. . . . It is known from Doomsday Book that in the time of William the Conqueror the entire kingdom was in this way divided into some 62,000 knights' fees, from each of which the service of a knight could be demanded, once a year if necessary. . . .

" The occupants of the soil were further liable for the maintenance of the naval forces of the country whenever it was deemed necessary to organise such forces. . . . In short, the cost of maintaining the military and naval forces of the country fell directly upon the occupants of the land, and they likewise contributed largely to the civil expenses of the Crown and Government. . . . It was a practical recognition of the principle that the individual upon whom was conferred the privilege of monopolising a portion of the ' original inheritance of all,' to the necessary exclusion of others, ought to contribute more than those others to the national expenditure."

Mr. Daly shows how *escuage*, scutage, or " shield money " was afterwards substituted for actual service in the field, and how by various evasions, culminating in the reign of Charles II., the landlords by means of landlord-made law gradually shuffled off the feudal dues and services, and, though retaining the land, imposed all the burdens of State on the people.

He says (page 22) :

" It was on November 21, 1660, that the Act was passed uncondition-

[1] Williams' *Real Property.*

ally abolishing the seignorial rights of the Crown over the great landholders, but it is a noteworthy fact that those who wrought this vast change refused to entertain a proposal for granting a corresponding relief to the sub-tenants, and insisted upon the maintenance of *their* obligations to the superior landlords. The passing of this Act accomplished a revolution which materially changed the character of our Constitution, and conferred upon the country the institution of landlordism as we now know it.

"The Act is divisible into two great parts, one the necessary consequence of the other. The one destroys sources of revenue, the other opens up new sources. The landowners were relieved of their ancient burdens, and these were cast upon the shoulders of the people in the form of excise and other taxes. . . . The lands which had previously been regarded as the property of the State passed absolutely into the hands of private individuals, free from all the conditions and obligations which had originally attached to their occupancy, and the position of the Sovereign, as the only real landlord of the country, became a mere legal fiction. . . .

"English landlordism is clearly a departure from our original Constitution. It is a departure which was begun and continued by evasions of the law, and was completed in the throes of a national revolution and through the instrumentality of an irregularly assembled Parliament. That completed departure has had the effect, on the one hand, of making those who were formerly mere rent-paying tenants of the State private and absolute owners of the nation's lands; and, on the other hand, of casting upon the general body of the public the whole of the national expenditure. . . . Circumstances may make it desirable that the land should be partitioned out amongst individuals—as in the feudal system—for purposes of national discipline, but it is a flagrant violation of the theory of a common property in land when portions of it are completely taken out of the national ownership and set aside for the aggrandisement of private persons or families. This is not only a wrong to the nation at large in the persons of its existing members, but also an injustice to the unborn generations of the nation, who, on coming into being find themselves wholly, or in part, disinherited. Their share in the national birthright is monopolised by others, and they find in effect that they have been born trespassers in their native land, having no business there, and no right to cumber it without the permission of the lords of the soil."

Mr. Daly, further, deals with the land tax of 4s. in the £, originally imposed in 1692, and with regard to the difficulty that a portion of the land tax has been redeemed, he makes the important statement that

"it was never a condition attaching to the redemption of the tax that it should not be re-assessed, or that a further tax of the same kind should not be imposed. On the contrary, when the measure of 1798 was before Parliament, Mr. Pitt, in reply to certain inquiries, distinctly said that the redemption of the land tax '*would not preclude that or any other Parliament from imposing another land tax, or from re-assessing the existing one.*'

"Here, then," he continues, "is a resource for restoring to the nation in a perfectly justifiable way the advantages of which it was unfairly, if legally deprived in 1660; and the landowners who, since the passing of Mr. Pitt's Act (to go no further back), have been enjoying the advantage of making mere nominal payments on a fictitious tax of four shillings in the pound cannot decently object to the tax being made real at that figure. Pending the settlement of the great question of restoring the lands of the country to the nation, it will be something to secure the payment of a large part . . . of the annual national expenditure out of the vast rent-roll of the landlords. The whole of that rent-roll, whatever its precise total may be, belongs of right to the nation and should represent imperial revenue."

The land tax of 1692, when first levied, brought in a revenue of £2,000,000, about one-fifth of the total revenue of the country. Small wonder that Carlyle, in his *Past and Present*, should indignantly exclaim :

"We raise £52,000,000 from the general mass of us to get our governing done—or, alas ! to get ourselves persuaded that it is done ; and the ' peculiar burden of the land ' is to pay, not all this, but to pay, as I learn, one twenty-fourth part of all this. Our first Chartist Parliament or Oliver *Redivivus*, you would say, will know where to lay the new taxes of England ! . . . If we made the holders of the land pay every shilling still of the expense of governing the land, what were all that ?"

To-day "the peculiar burden of the land" is—how much think you ?

In the article on the land tax, in the *Financial Reform Almanack* for 1899, it is shown that while " the people of this country pay the landowners some couple of hundred millions of pounds a year for permission to live upon the land of their birth," out of this large sum the landowners "contribute to the people, in the shape of land tax or state rent, about £1,000,000 a year ! " That is to say, about one one-hundred-and-fortieth part of our total revenues, local and general.

If, however, against the £1,000,000 that the landlords pay by way of land tax, we set the £2,000,000 per annum that they receive through the Agricultural Rating, or " Landlord Relief," Act, and the £13,000,000 to £14,000,000 that they receive through grants in aid of local taxation—Mr. Chaplin even has admitted that these grants ultimately filter into the pockets of the landlords—we find that the " peculiar burden of the land " to-day is *minus* £15,000,000— that is to say, that through the Rating Act and the grants in aid the landlords receive from the State some £15,000,000 *more than they pay in land tax or state rent !* .

As for local rates, income-tax, and death duties, since not one of these has any tendency to force idle land into the market, the landlord simply passes them on to the tenant, as the veriest tyro in economics must know.

"But," objects the now oft-quoted "man . in the street," "the Army and Navy protect you ; why shouldn't you help to pay for them ?"

To which we reply—My dear sir, we do now pay for them. We pay for them twice over—once in taxes, and again in rent. Whatever advantages such protection confers all materialise in ground-rent, and the landlord who does nothing and is therefore entitled to nothing sends in his little bill. It is the same with police protection and all public services and public improvements, local and national. As Thorold Rogers has well put it :

" Every permanent improvement of the soil, every railway and road, every bettering of the general condition of society, every facility given for production, every stimulus applied to consumption *raises rent.* The landowner sleeps, but thrives."

It is the landlords, and the landlords alone, who benefit by our lavish expenditure upon " expansion," and it is they, therefore, who ought to pay for it.

Said Mr. Purvis during the last Budget debate :

" If ever the time came that we should stand still in regard to expenditure on our Army and Navy, we should have to stand aside and allow a stronger nation to reap the fruits of empire. . . . *Then the grass would grow in the streets of our great cities.* . . . But until that time came we must make up our minds to bear the burdens as well as to reap the fruits of empire."

By Mr. Purvis's own showing it is the landlords that " reap the fruits of empire," and they " must ere long make up their minds to bear the burdens as well."

We pay the State and the Municipality £140,000,000 a year " to get our governing done " for us ; and over and above this, we pay the landlords, who do nothing of all this, who do nothing useful of any sort, who, in fact, monopolise one branch of the legislature on the strength of their " stake in the country," and use the power so obtained to obstruct all useful legislation—we pay the landlords £200,000,000 a year ! That is to say, £5 for every man, woman and child in the United Kingdom, or £25 per family !

Well may Henry George say :

" So far from there being anything unjust in taking the full value of land-ownership for the use of the community, the real injustice is in leaving it in private hands—an injustice that amounts to robbery. . . . We propose that for the future such robbery shall cease—that for the future, not for the past, land-holders shall pay to the community the rent that to the community is justly due."

As a beginning the Democracy of this country should demand that the land tax of 4s. in the £ be levied on the land values of to-day, instead of on those of 200 years ago. The sum thus realised would not only suffice to meet the charges of this war, and to make ample provision for the wounded and disabled, and the widows and the fatherless, but there would be a large surplus remaining to secure Old Age Pension and other important home reforms now unfortunately eclipsed in public interest by the present foreign complications.

# THE WARRIOR BARD:

## ANCIENT AND MODERN.

NOT till comparatively modern times did poet dare to invoke the god of battle while he himself remained in the peaceful but inglorious security of his own home.

In the palmy days of Athens such a counsel would have been regarded with unutterable contempt, and if by any chance it should have been offered and accepted, with defeat as the result, an ignominious death would most surely have awaited the giver of it at the hands of his fellow-citizens when the war ended.

But it would be extremely difficult to find a single instance in Greek history where either poet or orator counselled a resort to arms without being himself prepared to stand shoulder to shoulder with his fellow-countrymen. Themistocles, Alcibiades, Pericles, were all prepared to act upon the counsel they offered in times of State crises.

Themistocles it was who counselled the Athenians to embark in their ships and face the Persian host at Salamis; for this he was elected general, and the unhappy wight who counselled submission was stoned to death, and his wife was stoned by the Athenian women. More than one of the immortal triumvirate of Athenian dramatists threw down the pen in favour of the sword when the independence of their gallant little State was threatened by the Persian invader.

Most memorable of all, perhaps, was the action of the great Demosthenes when he counselled the little citizen army of Athens to oppose the victorious march of Philip of Macedon on the fatal field of Chaeroneia.

The Athenians were defeated, and soon made to feel that they were strangers in their own city. The half-drilled citizen army proved no match for Philip's disciplined and well-trained veterans. Years after, when Aeschines, the political rival of Demosthenes, accused the latter of bringing defeat and disaster upon the city, Demosthenes put his opponent to shame and confusion in one of the noblest orations which he ever delivered. But the argument that told most on the Athenians was the fact that, when Demosthenes had pointed the direction in which the only hope of courage lay, he marched in the ranks of his countrymen to play a man's part in the field of battle.

The following lines breathe something more than mere sentiment :

> " The minstrel boy to the war is gone,
>     In the ranks of death you'll find him ;
> His father's sword he has girded on,
>     And his wild harp slung behind him—
> ' Land of song !' cries the warrior-bard,
> ' Though all the world betrays thee,
> *One* sword, at least, thy rights shall guard,
> *One* faithful harp shall praise thee !'
>
> The minstrel fell !" &c.

For, skipping the centuries, we find that bards were cunning with the sword as well as with the harp-string.

On the morning of Hastings, Taillefer asked and obtained permission from William to lead the onset. He sang in a loud voice the *Song of Roland* in the front of the Norman army, then, striking spurs into his horse, he rode forward still singing, and dashed his life out in an ecstasy on the Saxon spears.

Students of the Elizabethan dramatists cannot fail to be impressed by the realistic touches of battle scenes which are scattered through their pages ; and the secret of this martial strain is that most of them bore arms in some capacity or other in the service of their country. Evidence exists, internal and external, that Shakespeare himself was in this respect not behind his contemporaries.

The poets who inspired the Cavaliers with their songs sustained at the same time the cause of the King in many a well-contested battle.

Coming to still more recent times, we find that Lord Byron not only inspired, in undying verse, the Greeks to strike for independence ; he staked his fortune—ay, and his very life—on the issue.

But it is in the Border ballads that we see the Warrior Bard at his very best, for nowhere breathes the martial spirit so intensely.

Sir Philip Sidney said long ago that the ballad of *Chevy Chase*, although " sung by some blinde crowder," stirred his blood " more than a trumpet." And the reason that this ancient ballad fires the blood and tingles to the brain is, that its author, whoever he was, like the moss-trooper minstrels, played a part in the scenes which he describes.

The drawing-room war-whoop invariably gives out a hollow sound, be the martial strain ever so well affected. It lacks of fire ; the simulation is apparent in every line. This species of poetry cannot be imitated in cold blood, and the greatest of modern poets have wisely eschewed it.

Far otherwise is it with the moss-trooper minstrel. Ever in the thick of the fray, he encounters perils with as gay a heart as he treads a measure with a rustic beauty or enshrines the charms of his lady-love in immortal verse.

The Scotch moss-troopers have been across the Border with the dawn, and are now pushing rapidly homeward with flocks of sheep and a hundred head of cattle. The alarm has spread for miles, and Cumberland is mounting in hot haste with spear and lance. Across barren waste and up steep ravine a bloodhound is already baying on the robbers' track. Men are posted on every ford on the Liddel; and afar on the Souter moor, Will, stalwart Wat, and long Aicky are sitting with a sleuthhound on the watch. "We have fairly trapped the Scots to-day, and before nightfall there will be wild work, and many an empty saddle in their troop."

The Minstrel is in the thick of the turmoil, and in his graphic and spirited description of it you hear the clatter of the horses' hoofs and the clash of the steel. You look through the iron corslet of the marauder and see the fierce heart heave beneath.

The finest of the Border ballads is *Kinmont Willie*, remarkable alike for the daring deed it celebrates and the light and laughing scorn of danger which it exhibits. Lord Scroope, the English Warden of the March, has, thanks to the traitorous Sheriff Salkelde, succeeded in capturing Kinmont Willie, the most dashing and notorious robber on the Marches, and he promptly claps him into Carlisle Castle. The word goes forth that Kinmont must be rescued. "To horse, lads, to horse!" The moss-troopers rally round their chieftain, the "bauld Buccleuch," in Branksome Hall. Mark how he receives the news of Kinmont's capture:

> " He has ta'en the table wi' his hand,
>      He garr'd the red wine spring on hie;
>  ' Now Christ's curse on my head,' he said,
>      ' But avenged of Lord Scroope I'll be.'
>
> O is my basnet a widow's curtch?
>      Or my lance a wand o' the willow tree?
> Or my arm a ladye's lilye hand,
>      That an English lord should lightly me?
>
> And have they ta'en him, Kinmont Willie,
>      Against the truce of Border tide?
> And forgotten that the bauld Buccleuch
>      Is keeper here on the Scottish side?
>
> And have they ta'en him, Kinmont Willie,
>      Withouten either dread or fear?
> And forgotten that the bauld Buccleuch
>      Can back a steed and shake a spear?"

They march to the rescue.

" He has called him forty marchmen bauld,
    Were kinsmen to the bauld Buccleuch ;
With spur on heel, and splent on spauld,
    And gleuves of green and feathers blue.

There were five and five before them a',
    Wi' hunting-horns and bugles bright ;
And five and five came wi' Buccleuch,
    Like warden's men arrayed for fight."

The movement of the verses descriptive of the march it would be difficult to surpass.

But the ballad must be read in its entirety to be thoroughly appreciated. Kinmont Willie is rescued, for the moss-troopers batter down the castle gates.

"Wi' coulters and wi' forehammers,
    We garred the bars gang merrilie."

It is significant that the poet says *we*, not *they*.

In this simple fact lies all the difference between the old Warrior Bard and the new.

AUSTIN M. STEVENS.

# HOW TO LOWER THE RATES.

THERE are two difficulties to be overcome in bringing about any substantial reduction of the rates, the first being, strange to say, the apathy of the average ratepayer, the man who will chiefly benefit by the change. The reason why the householder or tradesman takes so little active interest in the movement for securing a more scientific method of rating is, however, not far to seek. The daily struggle for a livelihood absorbs all his attention, and he is almost hopeless of any relief being possible. Yet it must be plain that the rates add greatly to the keenness of that struggle, and it should, therefore, be considered an important, an essential part of the day's work to see that the rates are fairly levied and used to the best advantage.

The second difficulty arises from the opposition which will be made by those who profit by the existing system. This is, however, hardly worth our consideration, because, once the spirit of reform is roused among the majority of the people, no opposition on the part of a privileged few can succeed in blocking progress.

That there is something fundamentally wrong in the present system can hardly be denied, but it requires some little study of economics to trace the injustice to its source. Once discovered, however, it can never again be lost sight of.

This fundamental injustice of the present system cannot be better illustrated than by taking the case of an outsider who has recently come into one of our large towns. Noting the great population, he would consider that there should be no difficulty in exchanging his services for the livelihood he needs, providing only he can secure a suitable site for a house, or shop, or workshops. He approaches the owner of a vacant plot and inquires the terms for use. The reply is £20 a year ground-rent. "Is not that far too much?" says the visitor; "I can secure the use of a plot of land of this size at my home for half-a-crown a year!" "That may be quite true," says the landlord, "but the use of such a plot as you name does not carry with it the advantages of such streets, pavements, lighting, police and fire protection, schools, libraries, parks, &c., and such an enormous population close at hand for trading, as this plot does."

"Certainly," says the stranger, "I can quite see the advantages that this site possesses over the other, and these advantages I must pay for in increased rent." The agreement is concluded, the house, shop, or factory built, and then what happens? The rate-collector calls with his demand-note. "What's this?" says the tenant. "Well," says the collector sarcastically, "I suppose you don't expect all these roads, pavements, schools, police protection, lighting, and the rest of the public benefits you enjoy, for nothing, do you?" "Certainly- not," says the tenant; "but you've made a mistake— you've come to the wrong man. *I* am already paying for these advantages. I am paying £20 a year ground-rent for the use of this bit of land that isn't worth half-a-crown without these other things. You must go to the ground landlord. If he is not going to provide for the keeping up of roads, &c. &c., what am I getting for my £20 every year? He can't pretend that he is providing the land! That has been here for thousands of years; as well say that he provides the air, or the sun, or the rain. If he is not going to pay for the lighting, police, roads, &c., I am getting nothing for my £20. He is charging the price of these public benefits, and yet he pays nothing whatever towards providing them!"

Here, I think, we see clearly the injustice that inheres in the present system. The ground landlord is receiving ever-increasing public values without paying for them, yet with no protest whatever on the part of the ratepayers, to whom in equity these land-values belong. Enormous wealth is thrust upon those who provide nothing whatever in return, while, on the other hand, on the thrifty industrious tradesman, who puts in a new shop-front (thus employing labour and adding to the appearance of the town) is levied a fine (it is termed a rate) of £2 a year. A drunken man is let off with his 5s. fine, but this sober and industrious citizen is fined regularly £2 each year so long as his property continues in existence.

Need we be surprised that trade is crippled and that we have a cut-throat and deadly competition under such an absurd system of rating, a system that rewards the idler and penalises the worker!

We have seen how unfair is the present system; what, then, should be the law in regard to rating so as to provide a scientific and just method of obtaining funds for local needs?

The essential basis of a scientific method of rating is that the ratepayer shall pay in exact proportion to the public benefits he receives; that he should receive an exact equivalent for the amount he expends in rates. Who would object to paying rates levied under such conditions that the ratepayers would receive a pound's worth of benefits for every twenty shillings expended?

Land, and land alone, increases in value through the expenditure of the rates, and that without any exertion on the part of the owner. Land alone owes its value to the presence and activity of the community, to the constant expenditure of rates for the keeping up of roads, drainage, lighting, police protection, &c. Land-values, therefore, form the true basis of local taxation, and should be rated in order to provide for the cost of those improvements by reason of which alone the land has value.

Such a system of rating would be in harmony with the ethics of property, and could be gradually introduced without injustice to any man ; for, in proportion as the rate on land-values was increased the rates on labour-values (capital) would be lowered, until eventually the whole of the worker's earnings—using the term "worker" in its widest sense—would be left to him, undiminished by any rate, to be expended on his house, food, clothing, &c. On the other hand, those land-values which the community creates, and which may properly be termed " social earnings," would be more and more used for social needs. Thus there would be a rendering unto society of the earnings of society, while the security given to individual earnings would act as a great incentive to the people to add to the comfort and value of their homes.

There is no difficulty whatever in estimating land-values. Such estimates are made daily, and it is very interesting to note the enormous increase which has taken place in the value of the sites of large towns, especially during the last half century. Let us suppose that the total value of any particular property is put down at £3500. The worth of the improvements, the bricks and mortar, the machinery or fittings is then estimated, and we will assume that in this case it is £2300. Then it is evident that the value of the bare site, or plot of land, will be just the difference between the total value, £3500, and the worth of the improvements; that is, the land-value will be £1200. This would, of course, be the " capital value " of the land. The annual value at 4 per cent. would be £48, and on this annual value the land would be rated—*whether it were put to use or not.* In all cases the land-value can be ascertained with far more ease and certainty for rating purposes than the value of improvements. In fact, an expert, without even seeing the land, with only a map and a knowledge of the town to guide him, can form a very accurate estimate of the value of any particular site.

Any district which shows an increase of population will furnish an instance of increasing land-values. This follows from the fact that land-values are due to population, and vary directly as the population and the public improvements that population brings in its train. If the three hundred and fifty thousand inhabitants of Sheffield were to migrate to Salisbury Plain, the Duke of Norfolk would wait in vain for his ground-rents. These would now appear in the new settlement, and the owner of Salisbury Plain would quickly see to their collection for private use, and, no doubt, in time, be created a duke for his pains. Just as we expect to find honey where bees have made a home, so we know that land-values will spring up in any civilised community of human beings, forming thus a natural fund for communal needs, had men but the sense to see it.

The following instances of increase in value are instructive :

The Corporation of Glasgow over a hundred years ago sold the site upon which the municipal buildings now stand for about £800 ; but when, about twelve years ago, they bought back the same site, they had to pay for it £175,000. Curiously enough, this sum was paid to the daughter of the man to whom the site was previously sold ; and thus, in one generation, it may be said, the plot increased in value more than two hundredfold !

In 1830 the outside price of any acre of the heath and pine-woods on which Bournemouth is built was £100 ; but of recent years portions in the heart of the town have been sold at upwards of £100,000 per acre ; and one strip, in 1897, was sold at £5 6s. 8d. per square foot, or at the rate of £232,320 per acre !

In the heart of London £37,000 has been paid for 1285 square feet—that is to say, nearly £29 per square foot, or £1,260,000 per acre !

In Chicago, in 1830, when the population was only 50, a quarter-acre lot was sold for 20 dollars. To-day that quarter of an acre is worth 1,250,000 dollars. The fact that there is now a population of a million and a half centred in Chicago at once explains this enormous increase in value.

The increase of rent that the present system renders possible is, moreover, not a fair one. It is a monopoly price that is paid to ground landlords to-day. Owing to the present system of rating, landowners are under no compulsion to use the land (in fact, in many cases, it pays them to prevent men using it), and there is what the Americans term a " corner " in land. There is thus placed in the hands of unscrupulous landowners a most powerful weapon. At the end of the lease the earnings of the tenant are practically confiscated. As the late Mr. William Saunders, M.P., said :

" Would it be wrong to say that as each house falls to the ground land-lord, a legal robbery is perpetrated ; and that the many who are ruined by this system, and die broken-hearted, are legally murdered ? "

There is not a family but has felt the ill effects of this monopoly. To quote from Henry George :

" Every blow of the hammer, every stroke of the pick, every thrust of the shuttle, every throb of the steam-engine pay it (landlordism) tribute. It claims the just reward of the capitalist and the fruits of the inventors' patient effort ; it takes little children from play and from school, and compels them to work before their bones are hard or their muscles are firm ; it robs the shivering of warmth ; the hungry of food ; the sick of medicine ; the anxious of peace. It debases and embrutes and embitters."

Towards the breaking up of land monopoly, through the rating or taxation of land-values, progress is being steadily made. At every by-election this question comes more prominently to the front. When this reform was discussed in the Commons on February 10, 1899, Mr. E. J. C. Morton, who moved the amendment, concluded:

" But whether the Government take up the question or not, it is one to which the people are turning their attention, and one for which they are determined to find a solution."

Sir John Brunner, Mr. Asquith, Mr. Haldane, Mr. Provand, Mr. Billson, and Mr. Fletcher Moulton, with others, supported the amendment, Mr. Moulton opening his able speech by saying

" that the taxation of ground-values was the next step to be taken if taxation was to be put on a just and firm foundation."

Moreover, the majority against the amendment—" And we humbly express our regret that there is no indication in your Majesty's gracious speech that measures will be submitted to this House dealing with the ownership, tenure, or taxation of land in towns "—was only 34, though the normal Government majority was 142.

Another sign of the times is to be seen in the following quotation from the *Daily News* of March 29, 1898:

" It should by no means escape notice that the movement for the taxation of land-values has received the powerful support of the Association of Municipal Corporations. At the annual meeting, apparently without opposition, the representatives of 266 towns in the United Kingdom, including all the county boroughs, and all the non-county boroughs of over 15,000 inhabitants, except one, declared that the growing burdens upon ratepayers made it urgent that 'some means should be provided by which owners of land (whether occupied or vacant) should contribute to the local revenue.' The meeting, it should be noticed, was presided over by a well-known supporter of Lord Salisbury, Sir Albert Rollit, and can certainly be considered eminently respectable. The Municipal Corporations in the United Kingdom represent a very strong, and, perhaps the best Conservative element in the country, and now they are found supporting a measure which, when put forward by the Progressives on the London County Council, was characterised as revolutionary, and at least impracticable.

" The demand that the owners of land shall be taxed for local improvements from which they largely benefit is now made by the whole of the large urban communities in Great Britain and Ireland, and it cannot be much longer resisted."

During the past year, moreover, largely attended and representative conferences at Bradford, London, Glasgow, and Huddersfield, held under the auspices of the English Land Restoration League, the Scottish Land Restoration League, the Financial Reform Association, the Land Nationalisation Society, and the Land Law Reform Association, have declared most emphatically in favour of the rating of land-values, while the Trades Congress once more affirmed the principle.

The London County Council has twice obtained the passage of a Bill through the House of Commons authorising the separate taxation of ground-rents to pay for the public improvements which have increased land-values, but each time the House of Lords has defeated the Bill.

Glasgow controls its tramways and gas and water works, but finds that the pecuniary advantages are secured by the landowners, and, by a majority of its City Council, has now petitioned for power to tax land-values, and has drafted and submitted to Parliament a Bill for that purpose.

The Legislature of New Zealand, in 1891, imposed a graduated tax on land-values varying from 1s. 8d. to 6s. 8d. in the £ (annual value). For twenty years prior to this date the Government has owned and operated the railways, telegraphs, and telephones; but, in spite of this public control of certain monopolies, the country passed through a period of fearful commercial depression. It was overwhelmingly in debt and the population was decreasing at the rate of 20,000 a year. After the passing of the Land Value Tax Act real prosperity came to New Zealand; population began to increase, and the annual increase now exceeds the annual decrease before the passage of the Act. United States Consul Connolly says of New Zealand that it is the most progressive community on earth. In ten years the private wealth of the people has increased over 40 per cent., which is double the rate of the increase of population in the same period, and shows that the government is based on sound economic principles.

The result of the first instalment of natural taxation in New Zealand was so satisfactory that in September 1896 a Home Rule Local Taxation Act was passed, permitting municipalities to levy all their taxes on the improved or site value of land. This has been adopted in a number of municipalities, and the beneficial effects are so soon realised that neighbouring towns are following the example of those which have already adopted it. Queensland also has local taxation of land-values. As a result of the rates being removed from improvements and levied on the site value, the relief to workers and capitalists has been very considerable. The only sufferers are land-grabbers and speculators, but even these will eventually enjoy earning an honest living in preference to exacting tribute from their neighbours.

" Can the landlord shift the tax ? " is the question often asked.

It is proposed to tax, or rate, land-values—the premium which the " owner " can command for permission to use " his " land.

If tea, or tobacco, or anything produced by labour be taxed, the producer lessens the supply by lowering the rate of production until the scarcity has sent up the price sufficiently to recoup him for the tax. Should consumers refuse to pay the increased price, then production is entirely discontinued, and when the tax-collector calls he finds nothing to tax. But this plan cannot be adopted by landowners. They cannot stop producing land, because it is not a thing of human production; nor can they hide it, or carry it away, or destroy it. The tax-collector is bound to find it, and the fact has to be faced that the tax must be paid or the land given up to the State. There are two sources from which the tax may be paid : (1) Out of the rent received, in the case of used land; or (2) from the owner's pocket in the case of unused land.

If the tax be paid out of the rent, the owner's income from land-values is reduced, as all income-tax payers know, by the exact amount of the tax levied. Thus, if an income (land-value) be £10 and the tax-collector take £2, there will be but £8 left for the land "owner."

But it is suggested that, since the tenant will be freed from a certain portion of tax and be able to pay more rent, the landlord will therefore raise the rent and thus obtain the same net return. Now he can and will do so unless all land, unused as well as used, is taxed on the full value. Here is the crux of the whole argument, because as soon as unused land, which now escapes, is taxed as if it were bringing in rent an entirely new factor is introduced; for we have the landowners paying out a tax though no rent is received. Now land is kept unused only so long as it is profitable to do so, and while there might be a few landowners who would for a time be willing to suffer this constant outgoing (and even these would be forced to let go as the tax was, step by step, increased to 20s. in the £), there would be a tendency on the part of the majority to at once secure tenants, so that out of the rent obtained the tax would be paid and the loss stopped. But to secure tenants the land must be put on the market; hence, as a result of the tax, we have not, indeed, a supply of newly created land, but, what is quite as advantageous to the tenants, more land in the market. This increased supply would lower prices, so that in place of rents being raised they would be lowered. The "corner," or monopoly values, which now exist would, as a result, approach fair competitive prices, and, in place of a deadly struggle among the landless to secure land, there would arise a competition among landowners to secure tenants, with the inevitable results of lower rents, better terms, and greater security for improvements.

It is thought that a tax on land-values would be unfair towards the small owner. Now, exactly the opposite would be the case, as he would be the one who would benefit not only directly by the reduction of taxation on improvements, but still more indirectly from the enormous impulse given to trade by the abolition of land monopoly. The land would remain his as much as ever, and although the speculative price would be reduced it would matter nothing to him, since he would be unable to live without land of some sort, and the only reason he would want to part with it would be to exchange for another plot at the same reduced price. His rates and taxes on improvements would be gradually abolished, and, since his land is but small in value, the new tax would be so light as hardly to be noticed. His children, in place of having in their turn to struggle half a lifetime for a home, would find on all sides landowners anxious to have them as tenants on almost any terms, so long as the land-tax was paid. Hence in a generation or so there would hardly be a family but had a home of its own; and, unless a man expected his neighbours to pay all his rates and taxes, he could wish for nothing fairer than to pay a land-value tax—a tax which would be in exact proportion to the public benefits he received.

Should there arise any apparent hardship, as in the case of a widow whose income is derived from land-values, there would be no difficulty about arranging for a continuance of the income, and a portion of the revenue obtained from a tax or rate on land-values would be set aside for this purpose. In a generation or so education on this question would be so spread abroad, and there would arise such a feeling against using funds which were the property of others, that the need for any special provision of this nature would die out. Just as in the days of negro slavery it seemed uncharitable to a widow to assist any of her slaves to escape and be free men or women, yet it was finally seen that the slave belonged to himself, not to the widow; so the widows who to-day live on other people's earnings run the risk of that diminution and ultimate loss of income which is bound to come when the said "other people" awaken to a knowledge of the situation.

As we have seen, a tax or rate on land-values would undoubtedly break down the monopoly of land which now exists. It would tend also to prevent the monopolising or "cornering" of the fruits of labour, and would, moreover, go a long way towards the solution of, if it did not completely solve, the housing problem.

Any attempt to monopolise food, clothing, houses, &c., anything produced by labour is harmless, provided that land, which is the storehouse of all, is open to labour; but so long as land can be monopolised at the will of a few, we may regret it, but we need not be in the slightest degree surprised that the many have to go short of proper food and decent housing or clothing. It is this fundamental monopoly—land monopoly—that must be first attacked, and this can only be done by the rating or taxing of land-values.

The housing question so plainly depends on the land available that little study is needed as to the remedy. It is often, however, proposed to buy up land and provide municipal homes. Now if it be desired to send up land-values, there can be no better way than for the various municipalities to enter the market to buy land out of the public purse. Just as fast as they purchase so will land-values rise, and the worker will find it increasingly harder to secure a plot. In place of making homes easier for the masses to obtain, such a plan would at once harden the market.

The taxation of land-values, however, would have exactly the opposite effect. As soon as the land was assessed and rated on its full value apart from improvements, it would be found that the owners of slums would replace them with good houses, for it would not pay the owners to have unsanitary dwellings on land that would cost them no more in taxes if good dwellings were erected on it.

The present system offers a premium to slum-producers, provided their property is sufficiently decayed, for the better the house the higher the rates, but the poorer and more insanitary the house the lower the rates. Just as the rewards offered in America for wolves' and snakes' heads led to the breeding of these noxious creatures in order to obtain the reward, so the buying up of slum property must lead to the production of slum properties. If it is desired to abolish slums their owners must be penalised by the taxation of land-values instead of being rewarded, as they now are, by our absurd and iniquitous rating system.

It is evident that a considerable increase in local revenues will be available as soon as the building land, now held idle and at present unrated, is assessed for rates at its full value. The increase thus obtained will vary in different localities, but when the various plots are assessed at something like what the owners contend they are worth, the increase in revenue will probably be not far short of 25 per cent.

This additional revenue would not be required for present needs, but would allow of a substantial reduction in the rate levied—say from 7s. to 5s. 6d. in the £, or from 5s. to 4s. in the £. The present ratepayers would be directly benefited by the reduction in rates, due to the ground landlords contributing their quota; and indirectly benefited by the reduction of rent, and by the better trade and less keen competition that would result from the breaking down of land monopoly.

No sympathy need be wasted on the ground landlords. They are few, but wealthy indeed compared to their millions of victims.

We suggest, however, no retrospective demand for the arrears of rates which they have shirked for years past. Let bygones be bygones. They have profited enormously by the ignorance and apathy of the public; but sooner or later this confiscation of the people's property must be stopped, and if to some it should appear that the proportion of their income from land-values demanded for rates and taxes is too large, it must be remembered that the whole of that income is unearned by ground landlords, while it is earned by and due to society.

The value of land is created by the community, without any effort whatever, either original or continuing, on the part of the owner. He makes no return and renders no equivalent. What possible return can he make? He does not provide the cost of drainage, lighting, police, schools, libraries, &c. None of these requirements of civilisation are paid for by him. That is, indeed, the cause of our complaint. He cannot pretend for a moment that he created the land. That is absurd on the face of it. It is this system, by which the tenants are first charged ground-rent for the use of public benefits, and are then made to pay a second time, through the rates, for the very same advantages—it is this system that must be ended. *One* payment is enough, and if the ground landlord receives the money, it should be paid on condition that he provides for the cost of those improvements which add to and maintain the value of his property and enable him to obtain rent.

The working of the present system, as far as landlord and tenant are concerned, has been well summed up in the following clever lines. To complete the case, however, the rate-collector should be represented as keeping *his* " eagle-eye " on Mary's proceedings, and fining her so much in the pound for every improvement she makes :

### MARY AND HER LANDLORD.

Mary opened a little shop
　To help her on life's way ;
And honest toil found its reward
　And it began to pay.

" How's biz ? " the landlord often asked,
　And Mary was imprudent ;
Of course she never guessed he was
　An economic student.

But Mary's landlord's eagle eye
　Was watching how things went,
And when the 1st of May came round
　He doubled Mary's rent.

The imposition staggered her,
　But what could Mary do ?
Subsistence bare is the tenant's share,
　All above is the landlord's due.

So Mary kept on as before,
　Improving as time went,
But step by step with increased trade
　The landlord raised the rent.

And thus the merry game went on,
　Till Mary's life was spent.
As fast as God could prosper her,
　The landlord raised the rent.

W. CHAPMAN WRIGHT.

# THE REVIVAL OF BUDDHISM
# IN INDIA.

THAT more than a mere local interest has been aroused by the recent itinerary in India of the Anagārika H. Dharmapala, the founder of the Mahabodhi Society, is evidenced by the references to it which have appeared of late in the European Press. When this society was first formed at Colombo in 1891, its objects then declared were to make known to all nations the teaching of the Buddha, to conserve and maintain the holy shrines in India and to re-establish a monastery at Buddha-Gaya. Since, however, the transfer of the society's headquarters to Calcutta, its efforts have been more distinctly concentrated on the colossal design of restoring to the people of India that ancient faith which, under the rule of King Asoka, became the State religion of the whole continent of Hindostan some 250 years before Christ.

This movement to revive Buddhism in its native land is somewhat similar in conception to the scheme for the restoration of the Jews to Palestine. India is the holy land of the Buddhists. There the great *Sakya Muni* was born, lived and died; and many of the spots rendered sacred by his memory still retain the names they bore 2400 years ago. Some authorities maintain that no means would more effectually prepare the soil for the subsequent reception of the highest ideal of essential Christianity than a prior conversion of the people of India to their pristine faith in Gotama Buddha, and that under the regenerating influences of his gospel of tolerance and love the evils of caste, superstition and bigotry would disappear and leave the field open for the propaganda of a universal brotherhood—the religion to be—when our little systems have had their day and denominationalism will be a thing of the past. Sir William Hunter in his "Indian Empire" when referring to the objects of the Mahabodhi Society wrote: "A revival of Buddhism is, I repeat, one of the present possibilities of India. The life and teaching of Buddha are also beginning to exercise a new influence on religious thought in Europe and America."

In order, however, to predict such an eventuality with any degree of confidence, as well as to estimate the value of Buddhism in this connection, it is expedient as a preliminary step to endeavour to look at the position from a Buddhist point of view by approximating in thought to a tolerably clear apprehension of the nature of the Buddhist cult. It will not, I think, be disputed that only a microscopic minority of non-Buddhists has yet arrived at a just and correct conception of what true Buddhism really consists in, and that some of its ablest investigators have failed in their attempts to expound it. At the same time I by no means wish to contend that the subject requires any special ability to grasp, but it most certainly demands the power of getting outside existing notions and a continued effort to retain oneself in that position. When we come to consider that even Christianity has been misconceived by Western theologians for want of an Asiatic and mystical training, it is scarcely to be wondered at that so little progress has been effected in the comprehension of Buddhism by Occidentals of the present day. Notwithstanding this absence of a clear insight into Buddhism, the main features, as presented to us in the Pali Scriptures and various works on the subject, have succeeded in riveting the attention and continue to claim the admiration of a constantly increasing number of cultivated people in Europe and America. The reasons for this are not far to seek. First, there came the element of surprise. People were staggered by the discovery that there could be embodied in a "heathen" system, a product of idolatrous and benighted India, so much that was so ethically sound and incontestably religious in the highest sense; which was, moreover, based on a philosophy strikingly in accord with the latest developments of scientific thought and research. Then, as was quite natural, there arose in every truly Christian heart a great respect and affection, that could not be logically withheld, for the character and precepts of Gotama, which show so close an affinity with those of Jesus and his Gospel. Further, the quaint, archaic and beautiful setting in which the stories of the Great Renunciation and the Great Decease are enshrined did not fail to make a profound impression upon all those in possession of poetic fervour and insight; and it must be added that the sympathetic treatment which the Sacred Books received at the hands of Western translators greatly helped towards this end. The psychologist, too, was not slow to recognise that the philosophy of Buddhism contained speculative matter of considerable value, which lent itself to assimilation in the task of formulating theories of a positive science in his own field of special research.

Never before in the whole known history of mankind has the influence of a single personality been so largely diffused, numerically speaking, as that of the young Indian nobleman who, some twenty-four centuries ago, separated himself from his kindred, and unaided and alone evolved from the depths of his own struggling soul the wondrous thing which we now call Buddhism.

From one point of view this extensive circulation of the doctrine cannot be accounted strange or opposed to the natural order of things. The much oppressed proletariat of India who were brought into immediate contact with Gotama, and subsequently with his disciples and missionaries, were ripe to receive a gospel which upheld the equality of all men and breathed forth in ever-recurring beauty those solemn truths touching the existence of sorrow, the cause of sorrow, and the cessation of sorrow which formed the refrain of Gotama's pathetic utterances. Yet it was by no means only the poor and oppressed whose minds were directed to a realisation of the pain inseparable from a clinging to life, and who pushed into the background for a season mystic speculations. The movement extended also to princes, plutocrats, and notorious courtesans, many of whom abandoned luxury and pleasure to unburden their consciences by a life of holiness. It was precisely those ideas most liable to darken the conscience that became, through Gotama, the means of illuminating it. It was not so much the grandeur and sublimity as the simplicity and sweet reasonableness of his doctrine that appealed with such strength to all classes. In place of dependence on intermediaries, each man was raised to the position of individual responsibility. Henceforward he was to stand alone. No God, no priest, no mediator could save him. Herein lies the superb optimism of the Buddhist, who believes that man can be his own saviour. The readiness, too, with which this doctrine was received implies a certain robustness of spirit with which the reliant nature of the Indian is not usually credited. Sin could not be condoned by making soft supplications to others, however high in authority these might be in heaven or on earth. Each individual has to work out his own salvation with diligence. Yet the good influences shed by him and his fellow-creatures all work in to the fulfilment of. life's highest aim—emancipation from the thraldom of the senses—and finally to the extinction of being or becoming. The Christian aims at salvation from hell ; the Buddhist looks forward to the ultimate freedom of man from the impermanency of a conditioned existence. There were many in the early days of Buddhism who were dissatisfied with the claims of an exclusive ecclesiasticism ; who thirsted for a comfort and support which would alleviate the burdens of life made intolerable by sacerdotalism. There was at least freedom in the thought that there was to be an end to the devices invented by a hereditary priesthood for the escape from sin or the acquisition of spiritual benefits.

In order to prove his point that the Buddhist movement was not directed towards the redemption of the lower classes, Dr. Oldenberg lays great stress upon the fact that nearly all the named converts belonged to the higher ranks of society. By denominating Gotama's simple formula of the causes leading up to sorrow as " the dialectic of the law of the painful concatenation of causes and effects," he seeks to show that Buddhism could hardly have been intended for the uneducated; that it was only suitable for the cultured classes, and not for the ordinary working-man. Misleading his readers in this connection, he quotes, "To the wise belongeth this law, not to the foolish." Would he have us forget, we may well ask, "the woman at the well," "the young mother and her dead child," "the leper Suppabuddho," and many others in the same category whose hearts were touched and comforted by the doctrine of the Blessed One, and who received the "clear, undimmed light of truth"? Buddhism was non-democratic in the sense that it did not encourage the lower orders to overturn existing authority. Any change that had to take place in the attitude of the postulant to his surroundings was an internal one, not external. The internal change would have been no longer Buddhistic if it had resulted in the exhibition of outward dissatisfaction with the accepted order of things. The acceptance of Buddhism involved simply a μετανοια: the process was entirely a mental one. Buddhism cannot by its very nature concern itself with politics, the strife of parties, the, tumult of disputants. There are two alternatives for the holy man—either righteous discourse, or, in the absence of that, the noble observance of silence.

Great and far-reaching as was the fame of Gotama—though kings and princes, travelling with their gorgeous retinues, and wise men versed in all the subtleties of Indian dialectic, came from distant parts of the land to do homage to the Perfect One—yet, at those times when not engaged in preaching to these splendid audiences, he, the Exalted One, the enlightened, the world-famous reformer, was to be seen standing, with downcast eyes, in the slums of the city or in the outskirts of the village to receive the free offerings of food needful for his daily sustenance.

Such is the picture that has been drawn of this man, untainted by adulation, unmoved by the overwhelming enthusiasm of his admirers. As he wended his way from place to place among the people, the majesty of seclusion and the happiness of repose suggested by his appearance led captive to his feet the proudest in the land, and the convincing beauty of his apothegms appears to have overcome on every occasion his most obstinate opponents. How supremely he soared above the level of his age is evident when we recognise how at every turn, in every dubious position, all obstacles gave way before his saintly persuasiveness. That which must strike every one acquainted with the general outlines of the inception of Buddhism as unaccountably strange is the reception which was given to the subversive teaching enunciated by Gotama in respect of the nature of the soul. A complete *volte-face* had to be made by the people of India in order to assimilate this doctrine; yet the opposition met with was so insignificant that the readjustment of thought it

entailed was scarcely perceptible at the time, and resembled more an
unconscious development than a violent upheaval of pre-existing
ideas. The egocentric theory of the nature of man was boldly
proclaimed to be a delusion—a delusion as clearly established and
demonstrable by empirical reasoning as that of the geocentric theory
of the universe. Rarely has so momentous and far-reaching a
change in the views of mankind been accomplished with so little
friction and with such brilliant success. In this connection it forms
an interesting study to note how, from the days of Democritus
upwards, theories of Buddhistic origin, such as the non-egocentric
theory, have sprung up and withered under the blighting influences
of alien and inhospitable conditions, until finally they culminated in
the full blossom of the philosophy which Schopenhauer gave to a
scornful and incredulous world. Positive psychology has now abandoned
the egocentric theory, and Buddhistic monism is incorporated in all
modern and standard works on the subject. Within the prescribed
limits of Gotama's revelations to mankind I would venture to apply
the term agnostic to the impression conveyed by some of his
deliverances if this word were not so debased and misconceived in its
common application. On the other hand, there is no denying that
the general tenor of the philosophy pervading Buddhist scripture
leads one to the conviction that Gotama's view of things was
monistic. He set free for the moment the abstract ·from the
concrete, but only to bring them together again into one indivisible
whole. Heraclitus advanced as far as Gotama in perceiving that all
was "becoming," but the latter limited (which the Greek philosopher
failed to do) this state of things to the conditions of the sensational.
Mr. Lafcadio Hearn says : " The Buddhist denial of the apparitional
world is not a denial of the reality of phenomena as phenomena, nor
a denial of the forces producing phenomena objectively and subjectively. The true declaration is that what we perceive is never reality
in itself, and that even the ego that perceives is an unstable plexus
of feelings which are themselves unstable and in the nature of
illusions." In the apparitional world there are plurality and variety,
but there is unity throughout. When consciousness ceases then
there is that utter nothingness which is "nothing to us now, but
will be everything to us hereafter." Reality, when sensation ceases,
is not "known." It is knowledge itself; for "known" implies a
differentiation of object and subject. In the language of the
Upanishads, "God knows, but knows nothing." No attempt was
made by Gotama to throw light upon an ultimate cause. The
origin of matter, for instance, was frankly admitted to belong to the
category of the "Unthinkables." Gotama was practical if he was
anything, and he chiefly confined his teaching to facts of experience
as they are or seem to be. Omniscience is ascribed to him as a
Buddha, and this implies a knowledge the nature of which is not

always communicable to conditioned beings and cannot be transferred
to phenomenal language without danger of misinterpretation. Holding this view it would be impossible to agree with even so eminent
an authority as Dr. Oldenberg when he more than hints that Gotama
shirked giving a definite answer to some of his interrogators because
he did not possess the necessary knowledge, and for the reason that
a direct statement one way or the other might have gone far to shatter
the fabric of his system and discredit his philosophy in the estimation
of astute Brahmins. With considerable acumen Gotama met his
interlocutors on some occasions by telling them that their questions
were wrongly formulated. When asked by Vaccha if the saint who
has attained to Nirvana in this life is reborn after death, he replies:
"To say that he is reborn or not reborn, to say that he is both
reborn and not reborn, that he is neither reborn nor not reborn
would not fit the case." Then he puts this question to Vaccha:
"If some one were to ask you, 'In which direction does the fire
(which has become extinct) go—east or west or north or south?'
what would you say?" Vaccha replies: "The question would not
fit the case. For the fire which depended on fuel of grass and
wood, when that fuel has all gone and it can get no other, being
thus without nutriment, is said to be extinct."

"In exactly the same way, Vaccha, all form and consciousness by
which one could predicate the existence of the saint, all that form
and consciousness have been abandoned, uprooted, become non-
existent and not liable to spring up in the future. The saint
who has been released from what is styled form and consciousness
is deep, immeasurable, unfathomable, like the mighty ocean. To say
that he is reborn or not reborn, that he is both reborn and not
reborn, or that he is neither reborn nor not reborn would not fit the
case."

Gotama in his discourses utilised the phraseology and figures of
speech then prevalent with the Brahmin community; he also
adapted the current folklore to the illustration of the particular
doctrines he endeavoured to implant in the minds of the people.
Consequently in reading the *Pitakas* it is necessary to be on our
guard to avoid falling into those misapprehensions to which the
terminology employed naturally gives rise. It is scarcely possible
to exaggerate the importance of premonition in this respect, when
we consider that quite a large number of the utterances attributed
to Gotama seem at first sight to be in direct antagonism with those
very tenets which formed the groundwork of his system.

A brief reference to certain Buddhistic expressions and doctrines
which are very commonly misapprehended may not be out of place
here.

The terms Nothingness and Emptiness present ideas to the
Buddhist very different from those with which we usually associate

these words. Such expressions as "vacuum," "emptiness," &c., are pregnant with meaning to the Buddhist. They must not be interpreted solely in a negative sense; there is a positive sense also to be taken into account. The positive aspect of such terms has been very clearly set forth by the great Chinese philosopher, Lautoze, in the following manner: "The thirty spokes [of a wheel] unite in the one nave; but it is on the empty space [for the axle] that the use of the wheel depends. Clay is fashioned into vessels; but it is on their empty hollowness that their use depends. Therefore, what has a [positive] existence serves for profitable adaptation, and what has not that for actual usefulness."

Of *Sunnata* (emptiness), Professor Rhys Davis writes: "The misunderstanding of the term has led to the use of the term ' Buddhist Nihilism,' which connotes a great deal more than is warranted by the primitive use of the phrase it is supposed to represent." As applied to Nirvana, "nothingness" means "that which is nothing to us now, but will be everything to us hereafter."

Due to its originality and isolation, considerable interest attaches to the Buddhistic conception of the soul, self, or individuality. According to the definition of Brahmin philosophers in the time of Gotama, the soul or self, *Atman*, was taken to mean an immutable unit. The use of this word *Atman* is frequently employed in Buddhistic writings, and has been rendered by various translators self, the ego or soul. But to read Buddhism aright we have to discard the ordinary significance of those terms which carry with them the implication of an indestructible individuality. Gotama contended that if the soul was conditioned, it was liable to the fate of all compounds—that is, to dissolution. He says: "Even unto a grain of sesamum fruit there is no such thing as a compound which is permanent. All are transient, all have the inherent quality of dissolution. Having come into existence, having reached a *state*, they are surely dissolved. For all these things come into existence, taking an individual form; and are dissolved, being broken up. To them as soon as there is birth there is what is called a *state;* as soon as there is a *state* there is what is called disintegration. For the unborn there is no such thing as *state*, and there is no such thing as state without disintegration. All these component things, therefore, without exception, are impermanent, momentary, unstable, disintegrating—as temporary as a phantom, as the mirage, or as foam."

While thus the eternity of the self or soul in its usual sense is shown to be a doctrine opposed to empirical reasoning, the word "self" is nevertheless used to denote what may be styled the sensational self. As the body is only apparitionally separated from the material universe, so the self is only sensationally individualised.

Speculations, as to the existence or non-existence of the ego after death, starting from predicates of material form, were considered vain and unprofitable, because "they do not conduce to progress in holiness; because they do not contribute to peace and enlightenment. What contributes to peace and enlightenment, Buddha has taught his own: the truth of suffering, the truth of the origin of suffering, the truth of the cessation of suffering, the truth of the path that leads to the cessation of suffering."

Under the general terms mysticism and asceticism may be included all the practices of Yoga which prevailed in India at the time of Gotama's appearance on the scene. Professor Rhys Davis has pointed out in his Yogavacara Manual how in the annals of most ancient times and of a great variety of races we find a belief existed that when an individual was rapt from all sense of the outside world he could acquire a state of sanctity and knowledge of the secrets of the universe which were unattainable under ordinary conditions; and this belief has persisted in many lands to the present day. The Platonists and the neo-Platonists, the Gnostics, the Yogis of India, and later on the Dervishes, the Sufis of Persia, and the Christian mystics all worked on the same lines. To these many others might be added, so it is not overstepping the mark to say that this belief and the practices involved have been almost universal. But to Gotama belongs the signal honour of having, with unwonted freshness and perspicuity, assigned to mysticism and asceticism their proper position in the scheme of things and of having shown that as things in themselves they do not necessarily conduce to holiness; that they are not the end, and the end can be reached without them. In the domain of Buddhism the current practices were sanctioned and formed part of the training of a member of the order of monks. These were considered useful as means to an end, but "to seek for Nirvana by the mere practice of the four Jhanas was held to be a deadly heresy." Professor Rhys Davis has emphatically stated that Yoga, as practised by the Brahmins, was "physical and hypnotic, whereas the Buddhist method (though it has its physical side) was predominantly intellectual and ethical."

If a man desires to arrive at perfection, he places no reliance on mystical conditions; he articulates no prayer to an unknown power; he asks not for the mediation of a Buddha, a priest or departed saint; he subscribes to no formula; no sprinkling of water or any sacred mysteries will regenerate him; caste or sect are powerless to help. If a man should desire to arrive at perfection, what then is needful? The Perfect One has said: "Let him fulfil all righteousness, let him be devoted to that quietude of heart which springs from within, let him not drive back the ecstasy of contemplation, let him look through things, let him be much alone."

That Gotama's teaching was unpractical and not adapted to the needs of every-day life and the conditions of a complex civilisation has often been urged in condemnation of Buddhism. It is natural, perhaps, that this should have been the case. The rules laid down for the guidance of the order of monks and the general tendency of the Buddhist Scriptures to give prominence to the advantages of a life of seclusion and to emphasise on the other hand the manifold hindrances to holiness to be encountered in a mere worldly career, are liable to convey this impression. The object, however, which Gotama had in view in this direction was to secure a class of people such as the monkhood to serve as exemplars to the laity of the highest self-sacrifice, tolerance and humility; and not to impose a rigid asceticism upon the householder whose duties would render such a life impracticable. This is very clearly set forth in the record of an interview between Gotama and Anātha-pindika.

Anātha-pindika says: "My soul yearns to do what is right and to be a blessing unto my fellow-beings. Let me, then, ask you, 'Must I give up my wealth, my home, and my business enterprises, and, like you, go into homelessness in order to attain the bliss of a religious life?'"

And Buddha replied: "The bliss of a religious life is attainable by every one who walks in the noble eight-fold path. He that cleaves to wealth had better cast it away than allow his heart to be poisoned by it; but he who does not cleave to wealth, and, possessing riches, uses them rightly, will be a blessing unto his fellow-beings.

"I say unto thee, remain in thy station of life and apply thyself with diligence to thy enterprises. It is not life and wealth and power that enslave men, but the cleaving to life and wealth and power.

"The Bikshu who retires from the world in order to lead a life of leisure will have no gain. For a life of indolence is an abomination, and lack of energy is to be despised.

"The dharma of the Tathagata does not require a man to go into homelessness or to resign the world unless he feels called upon to do so; but the dharma of Tathagata requires every man to free himself from the illusion of self, to cleanse his heart, to give up his thirst for pleasure and lead a life of righteousness.

"And whatever men do, whether they remain as artisans, merchants, and officers of the king, or retire from the world and devote themselves to a life of religious meditation, let them put their whole heart into the task; let them be diligent and energetic, and, if they are like the lotus, which, although it grows in the water, yet remains untouched by the water, if they struggle in life without cherishing envy or hatred, if they live in the world not a life of self but a life of truth, then surely joy, peace and bliss will dwell in their minds." [1]

[1] *The Gospel of Buddha according to Old Records.* Paul Carus.

The important question of matrimony was not left untouched by Gotama. An invitation he accepted to attend a marriage feast at Jambunada afforded a suitable opportunity for the deliverance of a brief homily on the married state. An excerpt from the above-quoted source will make clear his views on this subject: "The greatest happiness which a mortal man can imagine is the bond of marriage that ties together two loving hearts. But there is a greater happiness still: it is the embrace of truth. Death will separate husband and wife, but death will never separate him who has espoused the truth.

"Therefore be married unto the truth, and live with the truth in holy wedlock. The husband who loves his wife and desires for a union that shall be everlasting must be faithful to her so as to be like truth itself, and she will rely upon him and revere him and minister unto him. And the wife who loves her husband and desires for a union that shall be everlasting must be faithful to him so as to be like truth itself: and he will place his trust in her, he will honour her, he will provide for her. Verily I say unto you, their wedlock will be holiness and bliss, and their children will become like unto their parents, and will bear witness to their happiness."

The ideas connected with the mention of Brahma, angels and spirits in Buddhist literature are nearly everywhere presented to us in the garb of Brahmanic metempsychosis, and unless we are forearmed with a knowledge of this fact, it must inevitably follow that an entirely false view of the subject will be acquired. For instance, when Gotama is asked by his disciple as to the ultimate fate of some good man,[1] after death, there occurs some such reply as the following: "He is re-born in the Tāvatimsa heavens where he outshines all other deities or angels." In order to arrive at the meaning of this answer, which appears on the surface so anti-Buddhistic in form and thought, we must first possess a clear comprehension, in its broad outlines, of *Karma*, a doctrine which was substituted by Gotama for the heresy of metempsychosis. This doctrine, briefly summarised, is that "effects" are abiding and continuous as long as and wherever sentiency, organic or inorganic, exists to receive their impressions. A man walks on a road: the effects upon the inorganic are interminable within the limits of causality. In like manner the acts of an individual in his social relations, whatever they may be, are followed by effects which are eternal. It is precisely these effects that are the only continuing and permanent " I." Being thus equipped with a general idea of Karma, we are at once delivered from any difficulty presented by the opening phrase of the above-quoted reply. The " He " that is re-born is

---

[1] Not to be confounded with the saint who attains to Nirvana in his lifetime.

only the effect of that man's actions as received by other sentient beings.

The names given to the various heavens and hells may be taken to denote conditions or grades of happiness and suffering. The word "*Niraya*," constantly translated "hell," means literally "the exit, the downward path, the evil path."

Connected with the belief in demons and spirits, there is a strange creature, the Yakkho, worthy of passing mention, who alights upon the stage with great theatrical effect in some of the stories related of Gotama's life on earth.

The Yakkho is described as an inhuman being, though of human shape, and generally hostile to mankind. Some of them were converted to Buddhism. The females, Yakkhini, famous for their beauty, acted the part of sirens, and, moreover, devoured human flesh ; a curious effect of this being that their bodies after such an orgie were cold to the touch—an unexplained phenomenon to which the myth-reader and latter-day physiologist might direct their attention. One of the many stories in which a Yakkho appears runs as follows : "When the Blessed One sat meditating in a monastery garden, in the deathlike stillness and profound darkness of a tropical night, while from an overhanging cloud there fell one by one huge drops of rain, a Yakkho, conceiving a desire to test the imperturbability of the Blessed One, crept up close behind him and uttered three piercing shrieks. Seeing that this made no impression upon the Blessed One, the Yakkho stood before him humbled in spirit. Then the Blessed One breathed forth this solemn utterance :

"When the holy man, in knowledge, has passed beyond the
  conditions of existence,
Him neither goblin nor fiend can terrify."

To sum up, Buddhism is the great exorcist of delusions. As a religious system it makes no demand upon the credulity of its adherents : it does not attempt to account for the origin of evil beyond the established fact, based on empiricism, that ignorance or the absence of enlightenment is the cause of suffering. Its synthesis is this, "Be good ; not for your own sake, but for the advantage, the welfare, the happiness of mankind, and out of compassion for all living things. Experience is the material of its philosophy and the foundation of its metaphysic. The absence of all that is sectarian and exclusive, the appeal it makes to common sense, its adaptability to the progressive march of science, the welcome it gives to all that is true and pure in other religions, the honour it accords to all great religious reformers and the allowances made for the errors to which man is naturally subject ; these qualities seem to point to the possibility that in the distant future every sectarian difference in the domain of religion will be laid to rest in the everlasting arms of this all-embracing system.

It is, in fact, no more nor less than the larger Christianity, the religion of Christ, as differentiated from the splendid but misunderstood symbolism which is now called by that name.

It is to be devoutly hoped that if in the future there is destined to be any rivalry between these two great religions in connection with the Revival of Buddhism in India, that this rivalry may be of a friendly nature and manifest itself in an emulous endeavour to follow as closely as possible those noble precepts and examples inherited by them from their founders, rather than in any undignified controversies with regard to doctrinal differences.

In one of the Jataka stories it is related how a peacock, of golden plumage, stands, at the hour of dawn, upon the purple ridge of a mountain and sings this hymn of praise :

> " Arises, now, the all-seeing, only king,
> The golden one—all earth illumining!
> Praise be to him, the golden one, the king!
> May he this day our mighty guardian be."

The peacock, of golden plumage, then descends from the summit and feeds upon the mountain slopes.

Once more at the hour of sunset he stands upon the purple ridge and sings this hymn of praise :

> "Departs, at length, the all-seeing, only king,
> The golden one, all earth illumining !
> Praise be to him, the golden one, the king !
> May he this night our mighty guardian be."

Such, poetically expressed, was the attitude of reverence towards the Buddha when he arose in the East and diffused his light over the vast plains of India.　Such, too, did it continue to be when he departed from the world, and was no more seen of men.　Surely we can little wonder that the pure radiance of so resplendent a sunrise should still illumine more than one third of the inhabitants of this globe.

D. M. Strong.

# BISMARCK AND THE GERMAN EMPIRE.[1]

ACCORDING to a quaint fancy of the mystical poet Novalis every Englishman is an island. Most of us are too closely absorbed in our nearest pursuits and aims to bestow much time and zeal on the careers of foreign statesmen. Hence it is well that we should welcome the first critical survey of Bismarck's life and work written in our own tongue.

Journalists like Whitman and Lowe have given us glimpses and sketches (somewhat lively and vigorous), but no historical treatment in the true sense. The writer of the work before us scarcely yields to them in sympathy and reverence for his hero, without doing injustice to the aims and motives of his foeman or losing sight of the social and spiritual forces of the era. It is possible to quarrel with his verdicts, but not with his thoughtfulness and care.

The question whether Bismarck has been a blessing or a curse to the slow march of the world may be handled in many ways, but hardly allows of an answer on this side of the Styx. More scrupulous statesmen (such as Stein and Cavour), if they achieved less, ran less terrible risks and caused less sadness to the angels over the woes of the earth-born. Gervinus was of opinion that the whole Prussian policy of his day had corrupted the nations of Europe by its ruthless enforcement of the idea that might was right. Even the brilliancy of results cannot of itself make the absorption of Hanover moral, as the writer admits on page 268.

Nearly all English Liberals were against Bismarck and the king throughout the period of conflict with the old Prussian Parliament, five-and-thirty years ago. As Mr. Headlam puts it (page 287), only the cannon of Königgrätz really settled the matter. One of Shakespeare's kings suggested an invasion of France as the best way of stifling the cry of discontent at home, and the ideas of Bismarck's opponents were, perhaps, not less laudable in their way than those of the Lollards and Reformers who vexed Henry V. It is well known that Bismarck had made up his mind to perish on a Bohemian battlefield rather than face the odium of failure and defeat at the hands of the people of Berlin.

[1] Putnam's *Heroes of the Nations.*

Treitschke the historian, in a letter to the man of blood and iron on the outbreak of the war with Austria, frankly stated his opinion that it was needful and just. Later on, in the preface to the fourth of his stirring volumes, he said that the task of blending all Germany in one could not have been brought to pass without liberal help nor yet, on the other hand, through liberal methods. Most Germans believe that the clear advantages of union on so weatherproof a rock outweigh the misery and bloodshed for which Bismarck was answerable, as he avowed to Busch on a snowy evening in Varzin.

The writer's bent for description (as shown in his handling of the old life in Pomerania, or the scenery of the Black Forest, pages 12 and 275) at once suggests a regret that he has not given us more. Perhaps some of the subtle points of international dispute (such as the Ems Telegram or the Schleswig-Holstein question) might have been more compressed in the pages of a popular volume, where space and time pinch. Almost the only mistake in matters of positive fact is that which concerns the real situation of Fredericsruhe (page 439), for no one has ever got there as quickly as the writer asserts, even by a fast train. It is about half an hour from Hamburg, but several hours from the city which has been the arbitress of Europe for the last thirty years.

The comparison of Bismarck to Augustus (page 293) as a builder on foundations which others had laid sounds happy and suggestive. Like Augustus, he somehow lacked the ideal grandeur of soul belonging to the saintly kings and heroes of the far-off springtime who were found fit to dwell in the fresh and happy fields. Both were of the earth earthy (when all has been said), and would not have been congenial comrades for Virgil or Dante on their strange voyage. Bismarck's moral stature, in spite of all his achievements, was as many cubits lower than Stein's as Augustus was behind Assaracus.

That Bismarck was nevertheless a believer (without much taint of Agnosticism) can hardly be doubted by any one who studies the steps of his career. Mr. Headlam rightly refers to the deep and lasting influence of the pietistic set from which his wife came, but makes no mention of the curious fact that Schleiermacher equipped him for the rite of confirmation. At no time of his career did the orthodox Kreuz-Zeitung party regard him as one of themselves, according to his own avowal to one of his newspaper friends. Still less was he a champion of old British bibliolatry in a land where critical ideas have long ago taken hold of the learned and thoughtful classes. Perhaps the mystical influence of Frau von Klettenborg on Goethe (which is known to have been the source of the *Confessions of a Beautiful Soul*) may afford the closest parallel to Bismarck's case. It may be safely said that the simple theism of Psalmist and

Prophet entered more into his being than the ideas of the Fourth Gospel.

Mr. Headlam remarks (page 289) that the cause of representative government never sustained so serious a blow as at Bismarck's hands.   Perhaps Englishmen were at one time too hopeful of planting that which they had themselves evolved by slow degrees, and with the help of sunshine and fresh spiritual rain on a less happy soil.   Bismarck was all along aware that what had been successful in London failed wretchedly in Cracow, and only a strong crown seemed likely to hold a large nation together in the middle of Europe.   Nor should it be forgotten that the Germans, in the days of a *régime* that might almost be called feudal from a Western stand-point, had attained more spiritual freedom than either England or France.   Men like Fichte and Kant would hardly have been able to run riot in Oxford in the last century.   No late German prose writer or heretic of any hue carried his loyalty to Bismarck further than D. F. Strauss.

The gift of Universal Suffrage (page 255) made Socialism and Catholicism stronger, to Bismarck's surprise.   No one who has ever lived and studied in Germany can doubt that the milk-white hind has far more hold on the masses than any evangelical church.   In the villages of the Rhineland and Baden the contrast between the worshippers of the two confessions is striking, although the air of the less crowded buildings is more healthful and pure.   Poles in the Eastern Provinces pass from the brandy-shop to the church and then back to the brandy-shop; but they do not doubt that the priest who stands by their sick-bed in the flesh possesses the key to admit them to the palace of the King of Kings.   The future of Socialism is, so far, a book with seven seals.

Catholics and Radicals and Socialists by a grotesque alliance were able to wreck Bismarck's last measure in the Reichstag.   His speech during the Cultur-Kampf, which went back to Agamemnon in Aulis and made mention of possible "gesta Dei per Francos," had been one of the bitterest attacks ever made against priestcraft in politics (page 401).   Windthorst is charged with religious unbelief by Bismarck in his memoirs, but led the Catholic party with unmistakable skill.   Richter (a Radical of the type of J. S. Mill or Cobden) and Bebel, who looks forward to a day when goods and wives shall be in common, scarcely agreed on anything except dislike of the Chancellor.   Some of them were charged with seeming to think it would have been better for the Fatherland if they had guided its destinies.

Few men look back on events with entirely the same eyes.   A good deal of water (to borrow a German adage) will probably flow down the Rhine before the last historical portrait of Bismarck can be drawn. His friends can point to the unique glory of his great success, his foes to the fact that his life was not, after all, more congruous than that of commonplace men. In the meantime, such as may desire to refresh their knowledge of the outline and meaning of his whole work (both at home and abroad) cannot do better than turn to this sober and useful volume.

# COURTESY IN MODERN LIFE.

THE motto[1] which has been handed down with the traditions of the Great Wyckamite College has shared the fate of many a well-intentioned proverb in affording laughter to the many and reflection to the few. But never perhaps until of late has any serious question arisen as to the real meaning of the proposition that "Manners makyth man." It has seemed to many who have been closely connected with university life and training as it probably seemed to the founders of the "Novum Collegium" in its early days, that there was a certain deep appropriateness in a motto which emphasised in a place so largely devoted to intellectual interests, the corresponding influence of external charm. For that the words were then as now interpreted according to their most obvious signification, there can hardly be the shadow of a doubt. They served, as they still serve, to impress alike upon young or aged, peasant or prince, the essential value of courtesy.

But, consistently with the modern spirit of readjustment, a new interpretation has lately been brought to bear upon the venerable words. It has been suggested that for "manners" we should now read "character," and so fashion the corpse of an imperfect truism into a more accurate semblance of truth. To the philosopher who is ill-disposed towards the fitting of the many-angled facts of life into the round hole of a generalisation, both the motto and its amendment must leave something to be desired. Both are necessarily imperfect, limited in view; while yet both are expressions of a truth which cannot be disregarded. For the fact is that the correlation between manners and character is closer than is perhaps generally recognised; and in so far as the new interpretation has recalled our attention to the fact, it may have some claim upon our gratitude. Nevertheless, one cannot avoid the reflection that the criticism is strongly and not too happily characteristic of the present age. It is certain that the trend of modern life and discipline is moving farther and farther from the former ideals of courtesy which, without undue insistence upon formality and rule, are yet essential to the beauty and harmony of social intercourse. For there is nothing so charming as courtesy, and beautiful manners embellish life. Without them

---

[1] "Manners makyth Man." Motto of New College, Oxford.

the laurels of scholarship are but imperfectly borne, and the highest
gifts of fortune may fail of their influence. They "make" a man,
inasmuch as they do undoubtedly increase his popularity, enlarge his
opportunities, and indirectly—a point which recalls one to the
influence of manners upon character—augment his very pleasure
and enjoyment in daily life.

It is a curious fact, however, that while theoretically the value of
good manners is seldom openly denied, yet practically we are allowing—and even, as it seems, encouraging—their neglect. It may
be that in a more hurrying and keenly competitive age we have less
time and less inclination to be polite; it may be that the loosening
of certain old aristocratic and political barriers has reacted upon the
manners of those to whom their independence has become a snare;
and it may be also that a certain spirit of egoism—not reasoned,
but unconfessed and often unsuspected—has crept in among the
many wholesome developments of our emancipated youth to the
destruction of its charm. But, from whatever cause or combination
of causes, the fact remains; and it is evident that courtesy is no
longer the natural and graceful accompaniments of the educated
world. And the pity of it is that nothing else that exists can in
any way replace it. The bonds of formal etiquette are but meaningless and servile imitations if, severed from the animating spirit of
courtesy, they only are retained. All social restraints, moreover,
and the interdependence of the classes will become more and more
strained and artificial in proportion as manners are allowed to decline.
But side by side with the growing laxity in private and in public,
in the university and in all grades of social life, a curious misapprehension seems to have arisen, more especially among the younger
men of the day. Brusqueness, it would seem, has come to be
confused with manliness, and gentleness with effeminacy.

The men of the previous generation, "gentlemen of the old
school," a few of whom yet linger among us, are of a type now
rapidly passing away. We may have improved upon their acquirements: our educational curriculum is wider, our advantages greater
than were theirs; but we shall never improve upon that dignified
and beautiful conception of human relationship which expresses
itself alike in every form of intercourse, and which gives to every
kindly act and every trifling service a peculiar charm. And there
is no reason why in the most active life, amid the most varied
interests, this delicate balance between outward and inward should
not duly be maintained. The secret of it lies in that tactful consideration for others which is the essence of good breeding and the
surest qualification of social success. But it is just this quality in
which our modern life appears to be so curiously lacking, and,
indeed upon many, more especially public occasions, it shows a
tendency to vanish out of sight. The stronger, the younger, are

not now impelled by custom or by courtesy to give place in crowded assemblies to the aged or the weak. The primæval doctrine that might makes right need no longer be delicately veiled in deference to the prevailing ethical standard : all may fight on an equal footing, and the battle is to the strong. Or, as we may add, to the selfish.

And this deplorable blunder has consequences worse than the mere ugliness of the effect. The mischief of it not only disfigures society, and destroys the best ideal possibilities of human life, but it reacts—and seriously—upon the individual. The want of *savoir faire* which betrays itself in carelessness of word or action ; the brusqueness which to the finer nature often causes pain ; the neglect of the little courtesies upon which in all classes and relationships so much depends ; the more flagrant breaches of good taste and politeness which are unhappily not uncommon ; all these things are to be regretted as much on behalf of the individual who offends, as for the sake of the many who suffer. And this is a point which is apt to be overlooked by those who would replace " manners " by " character." For that the success and happiness of men and women depend only upon character does not hold good in the manifold relationships of life. It might be true for a Thoreau in his remoteness, or for any one who held intercourse only with the planets " in the milky way " ; it is emphatically not true for us who are members of a complex civilisation. For our environment demands from each and all of us a practical recognition of human brotherhood, and a gracious and swift response to the obligations which that bond implies. Such a response is the saving grace of our civilised existence. It issues in the finer developments of sympathy, of all gracious and kindly deeds. It is the forerunner of good taste and delicate perception : without it lives are closed to their widest possibilities ; they are hampered and incomplete.

And here the correspondence between outward and inward before alluded to is again brought to our view : here we may resolve the two conflicting propositions into their fundamental unity. It may be said—and this, no doubt, is the contention of the modern critics —that the *savoir faire* of polite society, often existing merely as an outward gloss upon inward deficiencies, can therefore exercise no worthy influence upon that character which " makyth man." But we would urge against this view the laws of reflex action. A beautiful manner is either the simulation or the actual reflection of an unselfish and considerate mind. The cultivated and reasoned attitude which we call courtesy habitually gives another the preference over self. It is not restricted to the mere utterance of pleasant words and cheap civilities : a readiness to sacrifice one's own pleasure or convenience, and to express such a willingness in the most graceful way, is the essential characteristic of good manners. It is always

possible that the external charm may be more beautiful than the
intention. Good breeding is not *necessarily* unselfish, though it
must certainly appear so in the ordinary intercourse of life; but, on
the other hand, a character that is habitually trained to habits of
gentle consideration can hardly fail to become in some degree that
which it seems. Thus, then, does education aid and supplement the
gifts of Nature. That all-determining quality which we call "charm"
is largely the outcome of a natural gift and faculty. But it would
be untrue to say that cultivation cannot nourish and sustain its
growth. From the earliest years of infancy formative influences
may so surround the character as to impress upon it a habit of
courtesy that will endure through life; and the neglect of this so
essential training is greatly responsible for the ill-success of many
otherwise liberally endowed.

It were idle to seek from history and biography illustrations
which our own observation can as readily supply. But from many
a page such examples could be gathered; lives of men and women
who have received liberally of life, and who have contributed, it may
be, by virtue of their gifts and their position to the history and the
thought of their time, and yet whose career has failed of its ideal
possibilities through lack of personal charm. And if even great
acquirements and striking qualities are not of themselves sufficient to
make the personality harmonious and complete, how is it with the
average individual? The answer, alas! is only too obvious in the
present day. It is conceivable that to genius at times discourtesy
should be forgiven (though it can never be excused); but the lesser
lights have no such power or privilege. The average man and—
more especially—the average woman, who follow the prevailing habit
of the day in brusque self-assertion and neglect of the common
courtesies, are entirely without cloke for their deficiency. However
estimable they may be in character and purpose, their virtues do not
commend themselves to the impartial gaze; they must be left to the
imagination, and will therefore inevitably, if unjustly, be overlooked.

A great deal is put down to aristocratic prejudice, which is simply
the natural bias of a refined and cultivated mind. It is impossible
for such an one to take pleasure in the society of those who offend
his more fastidious sense by want of taste and manners. The barrier
is not one of prejudice, but simply of difference—and the difference
is one which "no geometrical ratio can express." It is an old
truism that a crime is more readily forgiven than a blunder—that is,
than an error in taste; for such an error strikes at the root of all
civilised human intercourse, and there is no separation so complete
and inevitable as that which it tends to generate.

It may, indeed, be said that deficiency of taste and manner is one
of the most fertile sources of disunion and disagreement. Many
things in friendship can be forgiven; many moral and intellectual

differences condoned, while even the personal injury may leave but a scar which the kindly years obliterate. But the discourteous action—the rude or unseasonable speech—leaves an influence never to be outgrown or forgotten ; an influence which, as a disintegrating factor, is sorely antagonistic to the harmony of social life.

" Manners makyth man." It would surely be well if the ancient motto were more universally respected for the truth which it still conveys. For the life that is lived in the " sweetness and light " of habitual courtesy falls not far short of the highest ideal attainable by man. Keeping in touch with all kindness and love, swift in response, liberal in sympathy, it radiates happiness and receives it ; it blesses, and in turn is blest. And in the " largior æther " of its serene and cultivated being, no petty discords, offences and quarrels can take root. Courtesy is the perfected flower of discipline : only the character that is trained to self-control can easily and habitually practise it, so intimate is the true relation between the " manner " and the " man."

But if this be so—if courtesy has the deep and potent influence which we have claimed for it, and if in a measure it is susceptible of cultivation, do we not greatly err in its neglect ? The present age is one of vast activity, widespread interests, ever widening knowledge and ever changing views. It is not for us to regret the narrow interests and comparative stagnation of a more leisured time ; nor would we welcome a return to old and stereotyped formalities. Only, among all the changes, truths which are grafted upon the very nature and necessities of human life still hold their own. We cannot afford to neglect them, and we cannot isolate ourselves from the laws and conditions of a gregarious existence wherein personal relations largely determine our success.

" Beauty in the inward soul " was the prayer of Socrates, and that " outward and inward might be at one." And with that wise insight into the heart of things which characterised so much of the ancient world's philosophy, the words still find an echo among the changed conditions of our modern life. For still does that " beauty in the inward soul " appeal to our highest instincts ; and still does it hold sway over our hearts and minds when, finding its due expression through the medium of external charm, it creates for us the gracious ideal of harmonious personality.

E. G. WHEELWRIGHT.

# ORIGIN OF MUSIC.

## THE PASSAGE BETWEEN BRUTE AND MAN.

### I.

IN the WESTMINSTER REVIEW, February 1899, I made an attempt to show that the deadlock created by the problem of the origin of human language might be broken, by way of a new interpretation of certain well-known and incontrovertible facts about the earliest musical habits of our race. Avoiding the use of the word "music" for sounds which might have been, in the words of Sir J. Hawkins, "hideous and astonishing" rather than musical, I indicated that there were abundant evidences of a "want" of artificially produced impressions of sound having been felt in the remote past history of man; I tried, further, to point out how the vocal organs of our remote ancestors must have been forced into the service of supplying this peculiar "want" without any ulterior object whatever, and thus the raw material of language was produced; finally, it was suggested how this raw material was made into language by way of dramatic play. But the crux of the matter, the question of the nature of this "felt want," the mysterious, insatiable want of music, how and why this found a beginning before man acquired language remained to be considered.

Now, in scanning the best records extant of man's remote past, there is nothing about which it would be easier for the scientific multitude to feel honest doubts than of the remote antiquity of the Art of Music. For instance, what is there in the geological records of our race to encourage a belief in even the merest rudimentary existence of the Art among races considered in geological speculations on prehistoric man? Who thinks of the Art of Music in pondering on the Stone Age? No sign of music is found in the Danish Kitchen-Middens, nor among the remains of the Swiss lake-dwellers; I believe that the word "music" does not occur in any of the great works on prehistoric man; and it appears quite natural to ignore the existence of the art, even in the more imaginative speculations on the beginning of human life. Moreover, those who take most interest in geological remains would be inclined to say that it matters very little to Science whether the stone-chippers were musical or not. They will say that it is work, and not play, which was the main lever in human progress during prehistoric times as well as to-day; and there are lots of axes, arrow-heads, pottery, fishing-gear, &c., to support the assertion, while music has nothing except the supposed whistles made from the phalanges of the reindeer found in the caves of Périgord and elsewhere, the flute-like tubes found in the caves of the Pyrenees by M. Piette, those found at Langerie Basse by the Abbé Landesque, and at Rochebertier in Charente by M. Fermond.

But, if we ignore the probability of the existence of music at any place or time except where we have direct records of it, the truth about the matter will inevitably suffer, because, even in historical ages, this art is the least assertive of all human habits. Is it not true that, as high as music stands in the affections of the people of our own time, it is, nevertheless, too close to their lives from childhood upwards for them to dwell spontaneously upon the wonders of it? We are led naturally from childhood to take the immense mystery of the pleasures of music for granted, just as we are led to take the mystery of life itself for granted. Music has been with us as long as we remember, and when it came to us individually it required no exponent, not even so much as the very simplest truth of Nature. Not one of us could recollect the period when the pleasure of music first dawned in our minds; it grew with us. Look at a group of slum-children banging some sounding thing or other, and tramping noisily to the rhythms they send echoing about the slum-walls. Look at the child in the nursery beating drum or rattle, and la-la-ing, often with a decided sense of correct interval and time.

" This natural inclination of man toward music shows itself from the first. The infant's eye, we have seen, is aimless for a season; but its ear is alert from the beginning; it enters upon life with a cry, and its first sorrow expressed in a sound is soothed by the first sound of its mother's voice. One half of a nurse's time, I suppose, is spent in singing; and baby, when not sleeping or drinking, is either making or hearing music." [1]

How could we pause to wonder at the possession of a pleasure like that of music? It could never occur to us to think of existence without it. We take the wonders of it quite easy, and need not, therefore, be surprised that people of past ages did likewise. With all their treatises on the structure of scales, and with all their philosophic niceties of comparison with planetary systems, the Greeks never troubled to leave a record of the character or depth of the pleasure of music as they experienced it. The symmetrical skeleton of the art appealed to the enlightened curiosity of philosophers, but the pleasure from living, pulsating music must have been too closely bound up with the various actions of life for it to be thought of by itself. The few gleams of reflected light that mythology and history

[1] Dr. George Wilson, *Five Gateways of Knowledge.*

throw upon the art among any of the ancient cultured nations only
embarrass the historian of music; he would not dare to claim for his
art such power as is suggested, for instance, by the fact that the
Hindus represented their divinities as performers on musical instruments, the supreme Seraswati herself as a drummer, nor by the fact
that the ancient Greeks regarded all their deities as being susceptible
to the pleasure of dancing—Venus, Hebe, the Houris, the fair-haired
Graces holding each other's hands, while Phœbus Apollo struck the
harp, taking grand and lofty steps. And when the historian comes
to actual historical record he dared not claim that his art has existed
so long as suggested by the fact that music is performed in parts of
the East to-day in the same way, apparently, and with the same
kind of instruments as are represented on Egyptian sculptures three
thousand years old. But who can help wondering how old was music
when these musicians were sculptured on the tombs? Was it three
thousand years old then? Who can say it was not? In the fossils
of the Aurignac and other caves have been found unquestionable
traces of funeral gifts to the dead. Were these things done without
music? Were they done without at least such rhythmic utterances
and dances as make up the funeral ritual of native races which have
been found in our own days at a stage of development corresponding
to that of the Stone Age? Music that consisted of rhythmic cries
and pantomimic dances could leave no record buried in the earth;
if, like the ancient Egyptians, the stone-chippers performed pantomimic dances representing the actions of the dead man we should
know no more about it than we do now.

In ancient Egypt evidence of the position occupied by music must
be gathered almost exclusively from drawings and sculptures on the
tombs of kings; but there is one characteristic which must immediately strike the most casual reader—namely, the dramatic roots
that the art rested on in public life. A dancer immediately preceded the hearse in the funeral procession and acted the deeds of
the deceased to the accompaniment of musical sounds.[1] Now, even
if it was only kings' lives that obtained musical representation of
this kind, the spectacular and public character of the performance
indicates that pantomimic music was not itself a mere fad of greatness, but a thing that appealed to the emotions and understanding
of those who looked on.

In the pursuit of my own studies on this subject I have often
thought that the modern thinking world would much more easily
appreciate the position occupied by music among the ancient cultured
nations if the art had become entirely extinct in modern life. An
art which is to us a recreation, an evening amusement, a superfluous
accomplishment, cannot very well be regarded as a fundamental

---

[1] For a picture of such a procession, see Wilkinson's *Manners and Customs of the
Ancient Egyptians*, plate 69.

concern of life in times gone by, although some of our best modern critics assure us that it must be so regarded.

"Their education," says Mr. Walter Pater, speaking of the Greeks, "which, indeed, makes no sharp distinction between mental and bodily exercise, results as it had begun in 'music'—ends with the body, mind, memory above all, at their finest—on great show-days in the dances."

If we could for the moment forget entirely what music is to ourselves, and keep our present-day notions of the art from darkening our vision, when we think of the music and pantomimic dances of the ancients, then we might see in this mysterious union of bodily and mental exercise a good reason for putting the question, whether the thoughts and words of the ancients were not, historically and psychologically speaking, abbreviated, atrophied pantomimic dances? Right through the web of ancient history there runs a thread of apparent buffoonery in the form of pantomimic play. For instance, when we learn that Sophocles was anointed, and danced in public to the music of the lyre after the victory of Salamis, we are apt to be quite in sympathy with the commentator who suggests that the great dramatist was drunk; and if we are told that all the Greek dramatists were dancers, we will probably think that a modern dramatist may be quite an enthusiastic dancer, without the fact furnishing any evidence whatever on the process of the origin of man; but some at least of the ancient dramatists, as we are told by Athenæus, certainly danced their plays; and, so far, pantomimic dances to some extent constituted and expressed their thoughts. Beyond a doubt the language of the Greek dramatists possessed a firm and assured mental and intellectual independence; if it had passed through stages wherein bodily movements were necessary to give it adequate significance, that period must have been long passed in the time of Sophocles; but yet the impulse of utterance was likely to revert to its original forms when fired by the excitement of national triumph.

And in this regard how can we help calling to mind some of the prominent and well-known instances of religious dancing in the ancient world? Is there any more reason why great poets and priests among the ancients should have expressed national and religious fervour by buffoonery than there is for modern poets and priests to do so? We must suppose that such men in ancient times no less than to-day resorted to the grandest and truest forms of utterance on occasions of religious and national fervour, such forms of utterance as would appeal most powerfully to their people. Was the dancing of the ancient poets and priests one of their grandest and truest forms of utterance, and the most powerful in appealing to the emotions and understanding of the people?

Was it a reversion to forms of utterance through which the human race had passed, and to which the greatest speakers were driven, even in historical ages, when they were fired by deep emotion? If not, then, no matter what is said about leaping and dancing being a natural expression of joy in all living creatures, the conduct of the ancient speakers stands out in history as a psychological mystery.

A luminous sentence occurs in Quintilian's *Institutes of Oratory*:

" I do not wish," he says, " the gesture of an orator to resemble that of a dancer, but I would have some influence from such juvenile exercises left, so that the gracefulness communicated to us while we were learning may secretly attend us when we are not thinking of our movements."

In directing the young speaker toward the truest lines of oratorical education, may we not trace in Quintilian at least an intuitive grasp of the process through which the race passed in its education towards speech?

The Romans, at all events, were imbued with the instincts of pantomimic dancing; the Salii, some of them selected from citizens of the highest rank, went through the streets holding javelins and shields, singing hymns and dancing; and in the theatres entire dramatic representations were given in dances. We are told that at a time when all strangers, even including philosophers and public teachers, were excluded from the city through scarcity of food, the dancers were retained because of the extreme popularity of their play.[1]

It need hardly be said that no claim is made here of extracting out of historical records of the musical habits of ancient times any proof that speech is a direct product of these habits in the pre-historic past; all that is definitely claimed is, that the position occupied by music shows that the art lies at the very root of all human culture in the earliest ages, and among contemporary native races; and, moreover, musical habits were never regarded as things to wonder at as a recent acquisition would be. And now, to come at once to our point, unless we accept one of the thousand myths of music being a gift of the gods, we must recognise that the pleasure of it made a beginning like other things, starting with little and growing strong by degrees, until it established itself among those pleasures and concerns of life already strong with the prerogatives of their age and foundations in all animal life. At what point of man's history did the beginning take place?

If, as I have tried to show in considering the origin of language, sounds uttered under a musical impulse supplied the vocal material out of which words were made, and bodily movements made under a musical impulse supplied the words with significance, then the origin of music is referred back to pre-human days. But, it may be asked, what is the use of referring to pre-human days? Are we not now

---

[1] Gibbon's *Decline and Fall*, chap. xxi.

removed from all possibility of either proving or disproving by
experiment what happened in the passage from brute to man ?
Perhaps we are ; but I venture to invite my reader's attention to
some considerations showing that the way of rhythmic movement and
sound was the only path by which brutes could ever get educated
into human ways through a strictly natural process, and entirely
without miracle.

The choice of methods of bringing forward these considerations
lies between using Simians of prehistoric days and contemporary
brutes as a starting-point : and in choosing the latter I beg my
reader to put from his mind every thought of the petted and tutored
monkey of the show-cage. It is merely for the sake of finding an
objective point for our thoughts that we will suppose a zoologist was
found bold enough to undertake the experiment of educating a horde
of brutes, which are our own contemporaries, into human ways.
Suppose this zoologist felt that he could, as it were, get behind the
scene of brute life and play the hidden prompter, could he obtain any
guidance toward the initial stages of the plot that was once so effectively developed to its grand *dénouement ?* Let us picture these
subjects of his as we may, giving them sufficient space of forest,
plain, or mountain for the free exercise of their brute activities
of life. There is no call for drawing a strict line about the grade
of brute intelligence they must have attained before we think of the
experimenter approaching them. Give them what craft or prowess
we will, there is one thing which will form an almost insuperable
barrier against the educator—namely, the enchainment of the brute
ATTENTION within the circle of his appetites and instincts.

The first thought of every educator, whether of brutes or man,
has always been, and always must be, how to attract and hold
ATTENTION. Now what could attract and hold the attention of the
subjects of our inquiry ? It would be a waste of time to ask my
reader to look out upon nature and the surroundings of our horde
of brutes for an attention-drawing influence.

Certainly there were always the great changes of nature, the
rising and setting sun, thunder, lightning, &c. ; but, after all, the
great impressions of nature are but a part of the charmed circle in
which the brute's attention lies imprisoned. It would be presump-
tious for me to attempt any ground-clearing of theories formed by
zoologists about grades of brute intelligence ; I will, without further
preface, point out my reason for believing that there existed only
one kind of experience in brute life which could form stepping-
stones to entice the brute attention from the thraldom of brute
passion and instinct. Ages before the advent of man on earth, a
mine of rhythmic experience was already formed in the brute nature ;
a certain set of favourable conditions and circumstances was required

to open this mine; then music originated. What were these conditions and circumstances?

First of all, regarding the fact of this mine of rhythmic experience in brutes, it is open to everybody to observe that, during the moments of a brute's greatest bodily elation, when absorbed in action and passion, something of the nature of rhythmic experience had to be lain by in the body from beats of the heart, movement of respiratory organs, from muscular sensations of moving limbs in rushing upon objects of desire. There is at least a prepared ground for any stimuli capable of acting on the brute body in a rhythmic way; and I think it could be maintained that, within the compass of the entire possibilities of nature, nothing possesses the natural prerogatives of rhythmic stimuli for creeping upon the brute attention; if brutes only had a motive to let them thus creep on attention, to meet them, as it were, to ATTEND to them.

But where is the motive, the spur, the inducement to ATTEND to rhythmic stimuli? Our subjects are still brutes; whether we think of them in the remote past, when the psychological moment of the beginning of man's education came in reality, or whether we think of them as contemporary brutes, with the psychological moment brought about by artificially made conditions, they are simply brutes, without a vestige of human understanding, without speech, without concepts. We may take the guidance furnished us by the position of rhythmic play in the early life of our race; we may infer that, if play had a part in the first steps of man's education, then the playing brutes must have had a fair chance of security, a security acquired by their prowess and cuteness, no matter how. If we take this guidance, we must then ask what there is in play to furnish a motive for bringing in rhythmic stimulation, and making a special thing of it, such as is made in the rudest forms of rhythmic play? It will, of course, be said that the brute's springs of action are simply promptings of brute instinct and appetite. This is true, but in play brute instinct might well prompt to a vague attempt to sustain and promote the pleasure of the putting forth of superfluous nerve-energy. Did brute play require any sustaining and promoting?

This question deserves, I think, the most careful attention; for if a horde of brutes dominated an entire continent, and had long periods of plenty, with unlimited time for the outlet of play energy, their habitual and instinctive alertness to environment must still dominate the brutish attention, and render their play a matter of fitful outbursts, subject to constant interruption. In these circumstances an impulse to sustain the pleasure of play, however slowly it came to life, must lead to the opening of the mine of rhythmic experience in the brute.

## ·II.

As the writer traces his own interest in the problem of the Origin of Music to Herbert Spencer's well-known essay on the subject, it must be with diffidence that he points out how the great philosopher's failure to make a single decisive step beyond the crude physiological aspect of the putting forth of nerve-energy in play kept him from opening an entirely new source of knowledge of man's origin.

After following Mr. Spencer's collation of facts of early human music, and seeing their connection from a physiological point of view with the "play" of animals generally, let us take a step farther and assert a principle which has all the appearance of a mere truism—the principle that anything which checked the output of play energy checked the pleasure of play, and anything which promoted the output in like degree promoted the pleasure. Having laid down this principle, let us bring in face of it the question, How a motive to attend to rhythmic stimuli was ever created in brutes?

The commonest observation of brute life establishes the inference that the alertness to environment which is characteristic of the brute would be a check upon the free outlet of play energy; and we may ask ourselves whether anything which enticed the brute's attending faculties, and robbed them of this alertness, would tend to remove a great and permanent obstacle to the free outlet of play energy? Now, would the tendency to remove this great obstacle furnish a motive to attend to the rhythmic stimuli which are thrown, so to speak, gratuitously into all brutes' play? Of course it may be, at first, a vague, far-off, slow-working motive; it may have taken long periods to become effective in creating during play a demand for rhythmic stimuli—a demand which would impel the playing brutes to bring their movements into rhythmic form. But, no matter how far below the plane of conscious effort the motive worked at first, if a playing brute once moved a muscle, let us say, stamped a foot, and ATTENDED to the muscular sensation of it, or the sound of it; if a brute once ATTENDED, and stamped again, and ATTENDED again to the succession of stamps, at that moment the great obstacle to the free output of nerve-energy in play would be in some degree removed, and the motive to ATTEND again would be established. Thus would begin that growth of rhythmic movement and sound which we call the Art of Music, thus would begin that unique sort of pleasure which is brought into existence while we ATTEND to rhythmic movement and sound; thus our race must have learnt to attend to constructed rhythms until this act of attention became as natural to man as the breath of life; so natural, that the infant is capable of it long before it is capable of any other act of attention; so natural that it is no easy task for a sanguine theorist to separate the act of attending to musical constructions from the pleasure of music in order to show that this pleasure may be simply the animal delight of play; only in music it has become specialised in its great reservoir of constructed rhythms.

This theory may be left to the judgment of the more critical reader, who will see how small is the speculative element it contains; and to the reader who, for one reason or another, may magnify the speculative element, and demand experimental fact pure and simple on all points, there remains the possibility of a zoologist some day being able to produce the necessary conditions for experiment on brutes now existing. If such a one is ever found he might work confidently to prove, under the guidance of the law which impels all animals to grope after means of sustaining pleasurable states of feeling, that his subjects would feel out a way of continuing and making still more effective the sort of play movement which made rhythmic stimuli absorb attention during play. Zoologists, however, may not encourage a hope that such favourable conditions can be produced; and an element of speculation will have to remain for the present at least in this account of the prehistoric event of the origin of music. But if our particle of speculation is false, it will surely collapse before the great fact of music as we know it. I will try to anticipate this test in the briefest form possible.

Passing over the prehistoric beginning, we may depend that the first inkling of an increase of pleasure in the sensations of play activity must have given the feeding of attention the position of a new appetite, a new spur of ingenuity, an inducement to feel out for further means of enticing attention. Yet, the "musical" results at first might be the veriest wildness; not improbably it turned the brutes into yelling, leaping monsters; and the heightened play excitement might well have kindled brute passion by the sheer violence of outlet. The rhythmic excitement of savages encourages such a supposition. But this could matter nothing; once felt, the strange new pleasure must take care of itself, once connected with the making of rhythmic stimuli, play might end in orgies of brute madness; but when the next playing mood came the movements of play would again become rhythmic; the spur for seeking absorption of attention being always the psychological motive. Thus, slowly but inevitably would be established the first condition of education from brute to man, thus would be built the first schoolhouse wherein the brute attention could be broken from the slavery of brute instinct and appetite.

What happened in this schoolhouse when the education of man was actually accomplished we know to some extent in the ultimate results; the exact way in which these results were reached science may have means of learning. Language,[1] concepts, and the other characteristics of human understanding arose within its sheltering walls. Yet in all its great work, and through the vicissitudes of long ages the central kernel of this psychological motive has not been destroyed, nor even warped from its first character. In the structure of music it possesses a living witness. From the rudest rhythmic noises of aborigines to the highest development of music this psychological motive can be traced as the sole developing force.

It requires the following of no particular theory of music to demonstrate this fact; from the first time the art is mentioned in human history, and through the din of the various theories of origin and significance up to our own time, there may be traced an impulse of the "musical sense" to demand sounds in such grades of difference as will best and most smoothly absorb attention.

Leaving the merely rhythmic stages of musical development, and taking any bit of tune, let us for the moment consider its subjection to the principle of what is called "tonality," namely, the subjection of every note in its composition to a tonic- or key-note.

Now, what is the relation between a key-note and all the tones forming a melody? Helmholtz, in chapter iv. of his *Study of Sensations of Tone as a Physiological Basis for the Theory of Music*, tells us that every musical note possesses what he calls "upper partials," and that these upper partials are audible and are perceived vaguely by the ear. In chapter xiii. we are told further that the entire melodic relationship of tones depends upon their upper partials, and in chapter xix. it is made perfectly clear that the Octave, Fifth, and Fourth became the most commonly used intervals and laid the foundation of the musical scale, because they are the most prominent upper partials in a musical note. Now, taking the work of the early makers of music as we find it, without for a moment thinking of how the appetite for rhythmic stimulation felt a way towards sounding things which could produce musical tones; taking bits of tune as we find them in the light of history when rhythmic beats had become grouped into the rudiments of bars, and bars into the rudiments of phrases—let us ask why the early musician, when he succeeded in producing musical notes of varying pitch, preferred notes to follow each other in intervals of Octaves, Fifths, and Fourths? In other words, why did he prefer that the fundamental of the second note should be a certain upper partial tone of the first?

If my reader puts entirely from his mind the considerations previously put forth in this paper, could he not gather from this last-mentioned fact alone that there is some strong reason why the

[1] See "A New Approach to the Problem of the Origin of Language," WEST MINSTER REVIEW, February 1899.

enjoyment of the early musicians should have been deeper when the second note of an interval consisted of the loud fulfilment of a whisper contained in the first ? Does not this fact alone oblige us to recognise that something in the pleasure of music impelled the early musician to seek and find in tones a continuous fulfilment of a continually excited expectation—the smooth and easy absorption of attention by tonal relations ? May not the same question be asked regarding every step in the development of music ? In harmony, from the first days of simple concord to the gradual development of dissonant combination and the discovery of the chord of the dominant seventh, we may observe the musician striving to keep sight of the pole-star of musical pleasure, the point of relationship by which the listener is drawn into the absorption of his keenest perceptions, namely, the Tonic. "Although," says Helmholtz, "the chord of the dominant seventh is dissonant, its dissonant tone so nearly corresponds to the corresponding partial tone in the compound tone of the dominant, that the whole chord may be very well regarded as a representative of that compound tone" (chapter xvii.). From the point of view of the origin and development of music is it difficult to understand why this chord "plays the second most important part in modern music, standing next to the tonic"? Is it not because of the smoothness and ease of its relationship for the mind, because of its power of making the attention wait, expect, look for, the fulfilment of the promise of the tonic chord?

It is not possible to bring into review here all the great and salient points in the development of music, or it would be easy to trace the "musical sense" spurring ingenuity onward to feel out for a means of further enticing attention, and yet at the same time staying the intrepid hand of the innovator when he dared to wander too far from the track mapped out by the very physic need which originated music, the need of absorbing the perceptive faculties. Among all the varieties of musical tastes this need is never stifled. There have been periods when it seemed to have been swept aside ; for instance, when musicians were in the early surprises of the effects of harmonic combination. Among the Polyphonic Schools the organic unity of melody was drawn out and distributed among voices until the grasp of its unity must have been beyond the perceptive powers of hearers. But the physic need was there still, and in time overcame the mistaken technology and succeeded in drawing melody back to the source from whence it sprang.

Rhythm is touched upon here only in vague generalities, but every step in the development of rhythmic symmetry is an obvious result of the demand of this exacting "musical sense," the grouping of rhythms, the periodical occurrence of heavier beats, the phrase, and every variety of measure, including even bizarre deviations from metrical rule.

It is little wonder to find thinkers tempted by the symmetry of the rhythm of music, more than by any other character of the art, to place musical pleasure under the wing of the delight man takes in order and symmetry generally. The mystery of the Art of Music in both origin and development has attracted so many interpretations that the great critics of music have been obliged to apply their best power of analysis and reasoning in showing not what music is, but what music is not. Against the supposition that the pleasure given by order and symmetry as such was sufficient to account for musical delight, Hanslick says that "the musical sense demands ever new symmetrical formations" (*Vom Musikalische Schoenen*, p. 93).[1]

Nothing is more natural than the attempt to account for this or that form of music by referring to the preferences which the human mind shows in other arts—in poetry, sculpture, architecture. If music is the actual mould·through which the human mind had to pass in the process of becoming human, then the forms of this art must be the paragon, the model, the ideal of all human art whatever.

What remains to be said of the content of these forms; in other words, the thoughts and emotions that are brought into life within these most ancient storehouses of human thought? Should the emotions awakened by music bear the stamp of origin? Should they, even to-day, appear like vague memoranda of the time when the nascent pleasure of music drew forth the brute voice and compelled it to utterance, compelled it to sing, when the uttered sounds had no meaning beyond the rhythmic play movements that accompanied them, and in time curdled them into thought? Should emotions awakened by music still bear traces of the music dramas that fixed meaning upon articulate and rhythmic sounds? The question might be asked, Do they not? Can it be denied that, although the emotions awakened by music may touch any point of the whole compass of human thought and feelings, they are in their general trend, before and above all else, essentially dramatic?

J. Donovan.

---

[1] Against the adequacy of the pleasure in orderliness to account for musical pleasure Edmund Gurney advances the same objection: "The forms, when they occur, and as far as they are impressive, are each new and unique things, not like new expressions or postures, or alterations and reminiscences of known things ; each melodic presentation which is profoundly felt, is felt as till then wholly unknown." (*Tertium Quid.* ii. 260). For a searching examination of orderly structure as accounting for the beauty of music, see Gurney's *Power of Sound*, chap. ix. It is interesting to note that Hanslick and Gurney might be echoing a *critique* of music in Plato's Republic. "There are certain novelties ever taking place in dancing, and all the rest of Music . . . and in the same manner as you have said occur in Egypt" (Bk. II. chap. v.).

# MILITARY LIFE IN INDIA.

IN May 1845 I took my passage by steamer to Allahabad. We were four days going through the Sunderbunds, a strange labyrinth formed of the mouths of rivers flowing into the sea, with dense jungle on either side, the abode of the Bengal tiger, and one day one of these denizens of the forest stood fearlessly at the water side gazing at the passing steamer, and was fired at repeatedly before it sprang away. I did not, however, reach Allahabad by the steamer; because, having been seized with an alarming attack of typhoid fever, and the doctors on board having declared it as their opinion that I should not survive the twenty-four hours, I was taken ashore at Dinapore in a miserable condition, with the May hot winds blowing like a furnace; and they returned to the steamer having placed me in an empty bungalow to die as they thought. And I should have died had it not been that Captain Buller (the brother of Judge Buller) acted the part of the good Samaritan and took me to his own house, got a soldier servant to wait on me, and took the greatest care of me, and so, by the mercy of God, my life was saved. After a most marvellous recovery I proceeded to join my regiment, the 19th N.I., stationed at Bareilly.

Glad was I to get to the end of my hot weather journey. Indian life was now regularly commenced. Servants had to be engaged; a Hindoo bearer to awake me early in the morning for parade, darn my socks, put on buttons, help to dress me, announce callers, and carry letters out to friends, who were made most expeditiously. A fellow I have hardly exchanged half a dozen words with, belonging to a different regiment, writes to me familiarly as " My dear White," in a chit containing half a dozen lines, saying for instance, " Come, old fellow, to my bungalow quick, and see a snake charmer or a conjuror." Or it might have been a note to come and smoke a cigar over a glass of brandy paunee; but never an invitation to take tea, as afternoon teas were unknown meals in those days, and if any one had ventured to introduce such an innovation he would metaphorically have been flayed alive. I had, moreover, to get a khidmeitgar to get my breakfast, and to stand behind my chair at mess, at the two principal meals of the day—tiffin and dinner—and wait on me there.

Now with regard to the officers, I must say that they were a

harum scarum set of fellows, making no profession of religion or
virtue. "Man is man's devil"[1] was true in my case, and under such
evil influences the strong religious feelings I had before joining the
19th N.I. evaporated. I liked Colonel Syers, our commanding
officer, a hospitable and good-natured man, and his wife Mrs. Syers,
a genial, kind-hearted motherly woman, and one of the nicest ladies
I ever met; Lieutenant Shute, the adjutant; but the two officers I
most remember from their subsequent sad fate were two ensigns:
Norman Leslie, afterwards Sir Norman Leslie, who was murdered by
the Sepoys in the Indian Mutiny, and Penson, who was afterwards
imprisoned in gaol for a year for manslaughter.

I did not, however, stay long at Bareilly, as I was anxious to be
near the frontier, where a war with the Sikhs was imminent. I
therefore exchanged into the 59th Regiment N.I., stationed at Meerut.
But before leaving the station some of the officers who lived there
invited me to a nautch, which I attended; but I think I need
not repeat the oft given description of the dancing of native women
of very doubtful reputation.

As in duty bound I at once called upon my commanding officer,
Lieutenant Colonel T——. I soon made the acquaintance of my
brother officers, Dunsford,[2] the adjutant, a very handsome fellow, a
decidedly smart officer, and a pleasant companion; Harry Lumsden,[3]
the interpreter and quartermaster, a capital fellow and very popular
in the regiment.

Ladies at this time, it must be admitted, were exposed to great
temptations from idleness and the great abundance of unmarried
officers, who loved to bask in their sunshine, and there were some
who had no compunction of wounding their married brother officers
by the crime of adultery. I have heard an officer of my regiment
openly boasting of his success in a shameful intrigue of this sort.

Some other officers must here also be mentioned, viz., Lieutenants
Blackwood, Dwyer,[4] and Gibney, the latter fond of playing jocose
and irritating tricks upon my poor long suffering steed, and Ensign
Scot, a very pleasant fellow, Phillips and Presgrave, called by the
natives Parsgreen Sahib. With these rollicking companions I was
destined to pass my time for many a long day to come. At this
period I was what was termed a griff, or greenhorn, who, during his
one year's probation, must contentedly submit to be the butt to
provide amusement for the other officers. This contemptuous treatment naturally irritated me, since no one who possesses any spirit
likes to be made an object of ridicule and laughter. Practical joking
in India at this time was carried on to a frightful extent. Indeed

---

[1] *Vide* Hindustanie Baghbahar.
[2] Afterwards General H. F. Dunsford, C.B., who died in 1887.
[3] Afterwards Lieut.-General Sir H. B. Lumsden, K.C.S.I., C.B.
[4] Afterwards Major-General H. A. Dwyer.

once at Bareilly I nearly lost my life through a practical joke; a brother officer having for the sake of a little fun induced me to mount a most vicious brute, which nearly occasioned my going over to the great majority.

After taking part in the Sutlej campaign, my regiment, the 59th N.I., was cantoned in the Punjaub. We had not been long at this delightfully cool station—Hoshiarpore—when we were ordered off to form part of a column, under the command of Brigadier Wheeler, to put down the insurrection of Shaick Imamoodeen in Cashmere, lately made over to Raja Golab Singh.

I was in high favour with my brother officers one day, because during the night part of the march I witnessed a most amusing *contretemps*, which sent the gossiping quidnuncs into fits of laughter. Our commanding officer had given orders that no camels or elephants, &c., should be allowed to go in advance of the troops. But very early on that particular morning I observed an elephant gliding along in the darkness; whereupon Lieutenant-Colonel T——, enraged at such a glaring defiance of his orders, made a rush at the mahout and ordered him to turn back. The driver pleaded something about the Brigadier Sahib, which our gallant colonel evidently did not understand. So once more in great wrath he ordered him back. But it was no go. The mahout was an immovable fixture to deal with, as was the elephant itself, and since our commanding officer could neither pull nor push the big beast back by its tail or otherwise, and as he dare not venture on such an extreme course as to fire at an animal that was Government property, it was puzzling to know how this exciting embroglio would end. Happily I had not long to wait for the *dénouement;* for a startling apparition suddenly became visible. Ah! What was that queer thing emerging from the top of the howdah? There was first a nightcap, and then a man's head, and an angry one to boot. Verily, it was that of the Commander of the Army! I then listened with schoolboy delight to a most amusing dialogue. Our commanding officer was dreadfully crestfallen when he found how he had got into a mess by disturbing the old boy's slumbers. Fury indeed changed sides when the Brigadier, in high displeasure at the disturbance, demanded to know who it was that had dared to stop his elephant and thus disturb his repose. Poor Colonel T—— was in a regular fix, and could only apologise for his inopportune temerity and explain his mistake away as best he could, and in doing so he furnished a splendid illustration of what is meant by "drawing in one's horns." This exquisitely amusing incident happened a little before daylight, but it was not dark enough to prevent me seeing what I have here narrated.

We advanced to the borders of Cashmere, but were disappointed about having any fighting, as Shaick Imamoodeen made his submission.

Now for a brief description of military life, beginning with the regimental coffee-shop, which might, with some propriety, be called the station slander-shop. The morning parade being over the officers adjourn to this familiar spot, where visitors are cordially received and bidden to partake of the invariable chota hazree (preliminary break-fast) at a camp table in the shade of the mess-house, where the station *on-dits* with a choice assortment of scandal were in due time ventilated and commented upon by a lot of jolly fellows and a few regular bricks. Then a light having been called for and brought by Pitumber, the bearer, in a small pair of tongs, cigars are lit, and a brisk confidential chat is commenced, perhaps to be interrupted by the welcome arrival of an itinerant peddler, who forthwith spreads out with alacrity the contents of a large box of miscellaneous stores upon the floor, and respectfully invites your attention thereto. Sometimes a snake-charmer, a conjurer, an acrobat, or an Indian horsedealer turns up to vary the scene. In the case of a valuable horse buyer and seller meet with their hands under a cloth, and settle the price by pulling each others' fingers.

Formal calls are made between 11 A.M. and 2 P.M. Much time is generally spent at the mess, playing billiards, &c. Then the officers sit down to tiffin about 1 P.M., and in the evening, when it is suffi-ciently cool, all the panting residents of the station order their horses, buggies, and carriages to go out to eat the air, as it is expressed in the vernacular, proceeding for that purpose either to the bandstand or other places of diversion. Thence they generally betake themselves to dine in uniform at mess, or at home in mufti. Shooting, races, theatricals, balls, and such-like gaieties occupy much of the attention of the officers and other station residents.

At this period Anglo-Indian Society was exceedingly irreligious. A pious officer, as I well know, was indeed a rarity, at least in the Bengal Presidency. Military officers, generally speaking, lived as though there were no God, and no such thing as a judgment to come. The most they did to show themselves Christians was this, that a certain number of the more staid ones, having sobered down to matrimony, thought it decent and the proper thing to do to attend the cold formal service at the Station Church. The state of morals then amongst Anglo-Indians was simply awful. I have an excellent memory, and I speak of Indian Society on the whole from the stand-point of Bareilly, which may be considered as a representative can-tonment for the illustration of the moral condition of military officers. Of course Bareilly was not nearly so large as some other stations like Meerut and Umballa, but I see no reason for supposing things in this respect were better in the big cantonments. Doubtless at some places the condition of morals was a trifle better than at Bareilly, and at others they may just as probably have been worse. I shall merely observe with regard to certain immoral entanglements with

native women, which decency forbids me to enter into particulars
about, that the Mahomedan and Hindoo Sepoys, judging of Christianity only by the dissolute and profane lives of their officers, might
well be excused if they thought they should not better themselves by
becoming Christians, who, in addition to their other faults, ate the
flesh of the sacred cow and that of the unclean pig.

Talking about balls reminds one of the doleful dearth of spinsters
that prevailed in the North-Western Provinces at this period.  The
demand in fact far exceeded the supply from the home matrimonial
store (if I may be pardoned for using such an unpolished expression).
Anyhow, it seemed rather hard when my regiment gave a ball to the
station, that I should have to pay the same quota towards the
expenses (namely forty rupees, or four pounds) as that contributed by
those at the top of the tree, as well as by those who enjoyed all the
benefits of the entertainment ; since there was but little likelihood of
my getting a single dance owing to the great scarcity of ladies, and
the cautious tactics of Belgravian mothers, unfavourable to the
presumptuous advances of a poor ensign to any spinster daughter
of theirs, when there were better fish to fry in the shape of
dashing adjutants and captains, and, above all, members of the Civil
Service, regarded as the best prizes of all in the matrimonial
market.

At Nynee Tall I formed the acquaintance of General Richards,
who had served with the Duke of Wellington at the capture of
Seringapatam in 1799, and who preferred the Himalayas to England.
I also made friends with Captain H. Ramsay,[1] the Magistrate
of Nynee Tall, at whose house I dined nearly once a week.
There was a dreadful duel fought here by Lieutenant M—— and
Lieutenant C——, on which occasion Lieutenant C—— was very
severely and, as it then appeared, mortally wounded.  This sanguinary
transaction originated at a ball, where one of the combatants felt
terribly jealous of the dancing favours bestowed by a certain lady
upon his rival.  No official notice was taken of this wretched
business, as duelling in India was then regarded as the proper thing
for the settlement of affairs of honour between gentlemen, and I was
imbued with the same sentiments so long as my principles of action
were formed on the code of worldly opinion.  Duelling was generally
connived at by the Indian military authorities, till Sir Charles Napier
exerted himself by the most stringent measures to suppress these
affairs of honour, which were considered to be a necessity to avoid
the imputation of cowardice.  Yet, after all, I cannot help thinking
that the un-Christian practice of duelling can be defended on just as
good grounds as those whereon many of our national wars are
excused !

---

[1] Afterwards General the Hon. Sir H. Ramsay, C.B., K.C.S.I.  General Ramsay
died in 1893.

The plea of the one is that it is necessary for the vindication of the honour of an individual. The excuse of the other is that it is necessary for the defence of the nation's honour. In one case two hot-headed duellists may get wounded in a personal quarrel, or, perhaps, lose their lives, which would be no great loss to the community. But in the other case, thousands who have no personal quarrel with their opponents are ushered into eternity, making many widows and orphans, and a great many millions of the public money are misspent in an invasive war that might have been used for the substantial benefit of the nation.

But I must now mention that after returning to Bareilly in October my regiment, under the command of Colonel Syers, marched to Berhampore in the cold season of 1849_50.

I soon applied for an exchange into the 42nd Regiment, N.I., commanded by Lieutenant-Colodel T. Polwhele (afterwards General Polwhele), one of whose favourite sayings was : " Fools give dinners and wise men eat them." When a certain King of Scotland heard this old saw at one of his feasts, he pulverised it with another : " Wise men make proverbs, and fools repeat them."

I now got married. This was rather a bold stroke, considering that I was not merely only an ensign, but at the very bottom of the list of ensigns in my regiment, and that officers, who are mostly unmarried, don't like their young brother officers to leave them in the lurch by wiving. Anyhow, our adjutant made a remark to me on the occasion that I did not much relish. If I remember aright it was : " If I were the Governor-General I would pass an order forbidding ensigns to marry."

My new regiment was cantoned in the large military station of Barrackpore, distant about fourteen miles from Calcutta, and a very agreeable and desirable cantonment on account of its pleasant park and Zoological Gardens, and its proximity to the city of palaces, the metropolis of British India, and the general port of embarkation for all Anglo-Indian birds of passage residing in the Bengal Presidency, as there was then no railway to take one any part of the way to Bombay.

When an officer died, a captain and two subalterns were appointed to make a catalogue of all his effects, which were soon afterwards put up to an auction sale, and as a frequenter of these mournful sales I can say that to a reflecting mind there was often much seen and heard there calculated to call up very sad and sombre thoughts; because all who had a rupee to spend were at perfect liberty to discuss freely the merits or demerits of any and everything submitted for sale, regardless of the fact of the garment having recently adorned the person of one who had been the life of the regiment, whose well-known horse, dog, and gun were eagerly and excitedly bidden for. Prized presents of a mother, sister, or the deceased

officer's *fiancée* could not be excepted if needed for the payment
of his debts.

Then, as I well know, how soon after the march back from the
cemetery was their dear old chum almost, if not quite (apparently),
forgotten by his boon companions, those jolly carousers, capital
fellows, gallant officers, and regular bricks, who, after the depressing
funeral was over, were only too glad to dismiss their old comrade
from their thoughts and drown all melancholy misgivings in copious
draughts of brandy and soda and other stimulants, singing " Begone
dull care," and doing their utmost to avoid thinking of one they had
been eating and drinking with every day of their lives for a good
many years.

In November 1853 I was promoted to lieutenant in the newly
raised 3rd European Regiment at Chinsurah. As soon as my name
appeared in orders I lost no time in hiring a small sailing-vessel,
known as a budgerow, in which primitive craft I and my dear wife
sailed down the Ganges and the Hooghly Rivers, and arrived in due
course of time at Chinsurah, a cantonment about twenty-six miles
from Calcutta. I soon became acquainted with the officers of my
regiment, commanded by Colonel J. C. C. Gray, who, having entered
the service in 1814, became a general afterwards, and died, I believe,
six years ago (1893) at a very advanced age. Without mentioning
the names of all the officers I shall only notice briefly those with
whom I had most to do, some of whom are still alive, though most
have joined the ranks of the great majority. W. Carnell was our
smart adjutant; Thomas, the interpreter and quartermaster, was a
nice, quiet, pleasant fellow; so was Strover; Cooper Fellows was a
particularly gentlemanly fellow; Alexander Pond was a very able
and intelligent officer; Ross and Thompson agreeable and possessing
fair abilities, the latter, despite his plebeian name, boasting a
pedigree as old as the Druids; and Roberts, a good-natured fellow,
not overburdened with brains. Moreover, we had with us some
decided topers afflicted with morning dry throats and want of
appetite for breakfast; such as Captain S—— and Lieutenant
H——. The latter on account of his potations was compelled a
few years afterwards to leave the service. We had some rollicking,
jolly fellows with us, like Stephenson and Barclay, including others
weighed down with heavy debts, such as L——, who had an odd
way of expressing his assent to everything he agreed to by the
unvaried stereotyped formula of " I believe you, my pigeon "; and
F——, a man over head and ears in debt, who possessed a wonderful
command of words and power of speech for gaining conversational
victories and cozening tradesmen to supply his wants, despite his
known impecuniosity. He eventually retired from the service to
practise his undoubted natural gift of oratory in Indian courts of
law. The third officer awfully in debt of my regiment was poor

B——, a charming fellow with lots of pluck, besides being a very promising officer. But, alas! his pecuniary difficulties ruined him in the crisis of his career. Oh, the insane cravings of some young officers to purchase things on credit that they could well do without, and which they must know, if they give the matter a thought, that they cannot pay for when the time for payment comes! B—— at Gwalior became seriously impressed by the earnest sermons of the chaplain. But it is a melancholy fact that money troubles made poor B—— desperate, and he was forced to leave the Army.

With my new regiment parades were the order of the day; but all I need to relate on this head is a very droll incident that occurred at one of them, when an enormously stout gentleman posted himself right in front of the regiment, expecting to see a few quiet manœvures, when, to his horror and surprise, the commanding officer mischievously gave the word of command: "Charge," and as the men went at the double it was most laughable to watch the frantic efforts of the corpulent old boy to get out of the way. And though the officers managed to suppress their risibility, it was too much for one of the soldiers, who was so much tickled that he committed a military offence by bursting out laughing in the ranks, for which I believe he was brought up afterwards before the commanding officer at the orderly room. I cannot remember exactly what was the result, but I suppose he got off as he ought to have done. Here I obtained the prize of a thousand rupees for high proficiency in two languages, but, having no local interest, it did not enable me to get a staff appointment.

After the final suppression of the Mutiny my regiment came back to Agra.

I returned with Captain Nixon, an officer on political employ, with whom I dined in the mud fort of Bhurtpore, so celebrated for its successful resistance to the victorious General Lake, and its subsequent capture by Lord Combermere in 1826, when it was regarded as the strongest fortress in India. We were soon on the march again. But before proceeding with my narrative I think it will be well just to give a brief description of the state of morals and religion among the Anglo-Indian community at this period. *Imprimis*, there was certainly an improvement in the tainted moral atmosphere. Old Indians will understand my meaning in remarking that the unblushing profligacy, so characteristic of Anglo-Indian society under the *régime* of old John Company, soon became, under the direct government of our Empress-Queen, a thing of the past, and a better order of things was introduced. But I must make one reservation in noticing this betterment, inasmuch as the legalisation of vice was still continued for the benefit of the health of the European soldiers, in whose behalf depravity was safeguarded in opposition to the claims of morality and religion. I could not help hearing a good deal of this whilst I was in India, where things were done which decency forbids me to particularise. I never came personally in contact with these abominations. I was interpreter to two European regiments, but was never called upon to do what another interpreter told me he had been required to perform. If I had received such an order I should certainly have refused to obey it, which I would not have done for all the money in the Bank of England!

The auction sales were a source of amusement, which were made more attractive by the handing round very bountifully of champagne and sandwiches for lunch, in the hope of promoting the sale of things. Whether it proved a good business speculation I should doubt; but the sparkling Moselle was most acceptable. There was an old general's lady who spent her time in frequenting these sales, and I can't think what she did with all her purchases, unless she re-sold them for fun or profit.

S. DEWE WHITE,
Colonel late Bengal Staff Corps.

# A PIONEER OF UNIVERSITY
# REFORM.

WE hear a great deal in these days of the inevitable defects attaching
to our older Universities, in common with most ancient institutions,
and in many people's minds there seems to exist an undefined notion
that Cambridge and Oxford are very much where they were two or
three centuries back.   Such worthy persons are far from realising
the immense changes which have already taken place, let us hope
for the better.   We can only rightly appreciate them by imagining
ourselves, in true journalistic fashion, back in one of our ancient-
Universities about the middle of the last century.   We take Cambridge for the purpose, as being the home of that pioneer who forms-
the subject of our sketch.

First, then, we should find all undergraduates divided into three
classes : (1) noblemen and fellow-commoners, or greater pensioners ;
(2) lesser pensioners ; (3) sizars.

Noblemen and fellow-commoners had the privilege (granted them
by an incomprehensible statute of Elizabeth) of obtaining a degree
without passing any examination whatever.   In other words, they
had practically no motive for doing any work during their time at
college unless they chose.   Human nature being what it is, we can
scarcely suppose that they frequently did choose.   They had also a
separate table, and various other privileges.   The lesser pensioners
answer very much to the ordinary undergraduates of our own day.
The sizars were the "poor scholars" on the foundation—lads with
brains and industry, but no money.   On their miserable condition
and the shameful humiliations to which they were subjected there
is no need to dwell here.   They have been often and eloquently
described by various distinguished authors, as likewise the licensed
insolence of the noblemen and fellow-commoners.   These last were
not always well-born, but they were generally the sons of rich men,
to which fact alone they owed their immunities.

Both sizars and lesser pensioners had to pass one examination,
and one only—the final, as we should now express it.   There was
no "Little Go," no "Additionals," and (for passmen) no "General."
Those terrible institutions known as "Mays" (because always held in
March, June or December) had scarcely yet been dreamt of.   Dr.

Powell, the Master of St. John's, was the first to inaugurate them. Somewhere about the year 1770 he introduced an examination of all undergraduates in his own college twice yearly, from which even the sacred persons of noblemen and fellow-commoners were not exempt. The practice spread by degrees to other colleges, and at last became universal.

The subjects for the degree examination were practically restricted to mathematics and natural science, though moral science and metaphysics were nominally included. Classics received no recognition whatever, save for some scholarships and prizes. The Classical Tripos was not established till 1822, and down to 1850 it could only be taken by men who had already gained honours in mathematics. The Moral Science and Natural Science Triposes date only from 1848.

The degree examination lasted three days. It was *vivâ voce*, varied by problems, solved, we are quaintly told, in remote corners of the Senate House. Candidates had also to maintain in Latin (of the genuine canine description pretty often) " a public disputation on some scientific or metaphysical question." The class lists were divided, as in the Mathematical Tripos now, into wranglers, senior and junior optimes. Then came the οἱ πολλοά or pollmen whose only ambition had been to scramble through. Failures were rare among this class, as the standard required of them was a very low one.

Such was the condition of things which Dr. John Jebb, the " pioneer" of our title, worked zealously, though unavailingly, to improve. His name is little remembered in our time, but by his own generation he was highly esteemed both as a reformer and a man of letters. He came of a family which has long had traditional associations with Cambridge University, associations never more brilliantly maintained than at the present day. His father, the Dean of Cashel, is mentioned by Swift as one of the few congenial companions who solaced his long exile in Ireland. It is rather a shock to find that young John was sent successively to no less than seven schools in England and Ireland, among which we may mention Shrewsbury and Drogheda. Perhaps that spirit of rebellion against the established order of things, which afterwards distinguished him, manifested itself thus early. Yet this supposition is scarcely consistent with the excellent progress which he made in his school work.

He began his college career at Dublin University, but soon migrated to Peterhouse, Cambridge, where he took his degree as second wrangler in 1757, at the age of twenty-one. Four years later he was made a Fellow of his college, took orders as a natural consequence, and was inducted into several college livings of no great value. We are bound to admit that he was an unblushing pluralist, and, moreover, lived nearly always away from all his parishes, at Cambridge, where he was in great request both as a lecturer and a private coach. The university system of which he disapproved so strongly had certainly not had a cramping effect upon him. He was as strong in classics as in mathematics, an excellent Hebrew scholar, and barely missed the Arabic Professorship.

It was in 1773 that he brought forward his great scheme for reforming Cambridge University by means of an annual examination. It seems, perhaps, rather an inadequate remedy, but we must remember that the educationalist visionary of those days sighed always for more examinations, just as he sighs now, for fewer, or none at all. Jebb proposed that all undergraduates, including noblemen and fellow-commoners, should be subjected to an annual Senate House examination during their first two years of residence. The subjects were to include classics, history, and English composition. By this means he hoped to encourage a wider range of reading, to check the idleness to which even Honour men were prone during their first two years, and, above all, to force some measure of industry and information upon the privileged idlers of the aristocratic class. He considered a public examination much more likely to produce good effects than the college examinations newly instituted by Dr. Powell, owing to the greater scope given to emulation.

His proposals were debated with the utmost excitement for over two years. Cambridge was divided into two camps. A brisk warfare of pamphlets was carried on, in which Mrs. Jebb, under the pseudonym of " Priscilla," took her husband's part with great vigour. Her literary efforts gained the applause of so competent a critic as Archdeacon Paley, who observed of her opponent that "the Lord had sold Sisera into the hand of a woman." But Jebb finally lost his cause, owing mainly (such was the logic of those times) to his theological opinions.

So early as 1770 the undergraduates had been prohibited, much to their dissatisfaction, from attending his divinity lectures. We cannot greatly wonder at this as, by his own avowal, he had, for at least two years previously, taught Unitarian doctrines. He honestly held the extraordinary view that such teaching ought to be permitted in the Church of England, and took an active part in organising a petition praying that clergymen should no longer be bound to subscribe the Thirty-Nine Articles. This remarkable venture failed, as was to be expected, and Jebb, realising at last the falseness of his position, resigned his benefices, and renouncing for ever the University career in which he had been so distinguished, betook himself to the study of medicine.

A part of his seemingly inexhaustible energies was now thrown into organising a Unitarian congregation in London. The chapel, now Essex Hall, was built in Essex Street, and his friend, Mr. Lindsay, like himself a former clergyman of the Established Church, became the first minister. Mr. Lindsay was most anxious that Jebb should be his coadjutor in this office, but he preferred his medical work. He passed through his course with credit, supporting himself the while by private teaching, and became a successful and popular physician. But his attitude in politics was quite as uncompromising and revolutionary as in theology, and this made him obnoxious to the party then in power, and twice lost him the appointment of house-physician in one of the London hospitals.

He carried the reforming spirit into his new profession, and one of his unattained ambitions was to institute courses of ambulance and first-aid lectures, intended especially for country clergymen.

He had worked too hard to be a long liver, and in 1786 he died at the age of fifty. His wife, a Miss Ann Torkington, with whom he had lived most happily, survived him. He had no children, none at least who lived to grow up. As a Unitarian, he was buried in unconsecrated ground, but even bishops adopted the peculiar compromise of sending their carriages to his funeral.

The reforms which, since his time, have taken place at Cambridge have been, of course, on different lines from those which he laid down. But he deserves all honour for helping to spread the conviction that reform of some kind was urgently needed.

CAMILLA JEBB.

# DRAMA ON THE DOWNWARD GRADE.

## 1868–1898.

"THE old parrot-cry," I hear the reader say as he scans the title of this article, "about the decline of the drama—bosh!" But wait; that is not my meaning. Art, like everything else, is subject to that law of necessity which induces change.

My meaning is that one form of drama is degenerating only to give place to a form of a higher kind.

In all things the process of degeneration runs parallel with the process of development.

The truth is that during the last thirty years stage art has been going through a refining process, a kind of disintegration which old actors, old-school critics, old playgoers, and essentially stage drama-tists cannot grasp.

The art of acting and the art of writing for the stage was, until about thirty years ago, constituted upon the same principles as apply to scene-painting, without any discrimination of the fact that the sense of hearing and the intellectual perception are much finer than the nerves of sight. The eye, though in some respects the most marvellous of the animal organs, is yet limited in its power and singularly liable to delusions, and rendered in some degree abortive under extent of distance, of point of view, or degrees of power, or conditions of light.

Stage scenery, under old conditions of stage lighting, had to be painted in very broad, exaggerated lines and perspectives and colours. These, under improved conditions of stage lighting, have been modified.

A comparison of the methods of the best provincial acting with the best London acting will show the difference between two distinct methods of art production in effect.

Thirty years ago exaggeration was the essence of both play-writing and play-acting.

But during the last three decades the best artists and the best public have learned that in theatric art, as in all other art, effect is lost when the contemplative vision of the spectator is disturbed by too violent an appeal to the emotions of the will.

Neither the dramas nor the actors of thirty years ago would be

acceptable by the public now.   The best public in those days were
attracted to the theatre only by the Opera, or by Shakespeare (when
adequately performed), or by the light comedies and burlesques
performed at the Strand, the Prince of Wales's, and the newly
opened Gaiety Theatre.

In the lighter forms of dramatic entertainment one may see how
the change from burlesque which was exaggeration to burlesque that
is entirely *jeu d'esprit* has developed, by comparing W. S. Gilbert's
burlesque, *Robert the Devil; or the Nun, the Dun, and the Son of a
Gun*, with *The Circus Girl.*

After the death of Charles Kean and Samuel Phelps, Barry
Sullivan tried to infuse interest with Shakespeare ; but his method
was too broad for a public who wished to see Shakespeare interpreted
and not accentuated, underlined, and stagefied by the artifice of the
actor's emphasis.   This was how it came about that in 1875 Irving
made such an impression as *Hamlet.*   Drama of the morbid
type had been slipping down the grade for seven years and
was now fairly rushing down to that Avernus which it has nearly
reached.

The philosophical drama, which Mr. Edward Maitland hoped for in
*Higher Law*, was in the throes of birth.   I mean the drama for
the Age, because, of course, Shakespeare's dramas are all a mixture
of philosophy with poetry, but require essentially, first, an artistic
setting ; second, an intellectual interpretation.

That form of drama which aims only at the delineation of the
passions, and which Schopenhauer rightly assigns the origin of to
French dramatists and actors, is clearly on the decline and acceptable
now mainly to provincial audiences, and the chief cause is the rise
and development of Music-drama.

Such fine dramas as *The Two Orphans* and *Peril* (*Nos Intimes*)
will hardly please audiences who sit out *A Doll's House* or *Ghosts*,
who enjoy *A Happy Life, Rosemary*, or *The Liars*, and positively
revel in *Lohengrin* and *The Meistersingers.*   Yet amidst all this
Shakespeare holds his own, and, after Irving's *Hamlet*, we get Tree's
and then Forbes Robertson's, and people flock to Alexander's revivals
of *As You Like It* and *Much Ado About Nothing* and the revival of
*Julius Cæsar* at Her Majesty's Theatre.

It is that particular form of drama which moralists and theologians
have taken under their protection which is distinctly passing into
contempt and oblivion, notwithstanding the success attained by a
play called *The Sign of the Cross*, which was absurdly puffed by a famous
statesman, who ought to have known better than to lend himself
to such nonsense, and which was one of the most remarkable per-
versions of human nature, history, and the laws of true dramatic
effect that ever was placed upon the stage.

This play, however, did not appeal to unbiased minds, nor did it attract the real body of theatre-goers—I mean people who accept the theatre for what it is, a place for rational amusement.

Dramatic art is the representation of ideas in action—pathetic scenes.

The fallacy that all art is exaggeration has been derived from the contemplation of French art, which is, as a rule, the depiction of the passions at white heat. This makes French dramas marvellously effective at one hearing; but they pall upon repetition, because they out-Herod nature. Shakespeare never exaggerates. *Romeo and Juliet* is his only play of intense high-wrought passion, and it is natural to two young, fiery Italian hearts. His women are all sublimated; but not impossibilities nor distortions.

Moreover, none of his women are depicted as embodiments of false purity or senseless ignorance.

The drama that depicts passions only and delineates them in characters moved by *one* passion alone is, let us hope, dead for ever, for such drama is false. It is the moral drama which seeks to shape human nature according to the theories of moralists and professors of theology, who are the most absurd people that the sun shines upon.

I am afraid that truth compels us to say that the purely oral or intellectual drama is passing away as a lost and needless art. The mechanism of the theatre has killed it. If a second Shakespeare were to arise now he would probably write great books, grand poems, or noble novels, but not dramas. In Shakespeare's day imagination filled the theatre. Now, the stage-manager, the musician, the scene-painter, and the *costumiere* have turned imagination out into the street through the stage-door. People talk not of *Julius Cæsar*, but of the marvellous crowd that is mimicked in it.

In fact, while the art of the theatre has grown more refined, it has narrowed its limits, focused itself upon such scenes as can be realistically imitated. The text of a play now has to be so concentrated, so attenuated, to make room for increased details of actor's business and scene-painter's craft, that there is no room either for poetry of language or natural development of plot, hardly even for the clear depiction of character.

Moreover, music has proved itself more effective than poetry in theatres.

Great novels like *Guy Mannering, Hard Cash, The Mill on the Floss, Our Mutual Friend, The New Magdalen, A Mummer's Wife, Far from the Madding Crowd,* or *Tess of the D'Urbervilles,* are the satisfying forms of literary art for a complex civilisation. But what are these dramatised, however skilfully done? Nothing but coarse shadows or faint *simulacra* of the great originals. Great and faulty as Ouida is as artist, who can tolerate her stories dramatised? Fancy *Ariadne* reduced to actor's text!

The fascination which the stage has for many writers (notably as it had for Charles Reade) takes its rise from the mad desire to see their creations realised. In meaner mortals this insanity is the belief in their individual immortality.

But it is the contemplation of a thought that makes men great. If the contemplation of objects were as ennobling the very surface beauty of the world would make men gods. But it is only through the crucible of thought that great minds learn to know true greatness. That is how art " reveals to men the true nature of the world."

In the modern theatre it is not the idea that is seen, but the formal objectivation of it.

In the music drama only do ideas take forms that are immaterial.

For the contemplation of really great art work, solitude is requisite, or the companionship only of those we love.

Primarily the theatre is a temple of pleasure : pleasure ennobling to good natures, harmful to bad ones.

Before a mixed audience a great play must be *caviare*. I am inclined to think one of the finest plays of the modern theatre is Mr. H. A. Jones's *Saints and Sinners*. But such a play reveals, I fear, the limits to which dramatic art of the oral theatre can go. *The Crusaders* did not attract audiences.

The introduction of musical plays like *The Gondoliers* and *The Geisha* really indicate the new path which theatric art will ascend in the future. Opera in all its forms is now at least ten times as popular as it was thirty years ago.

In these plays there is more refinement, amusement, and exhilarating enjoyment than in the dramas of the *Lost in London* type, with their artificial griefs, lurid situations, and strained sentiment.

In an opera like *Shamus O'Brien*, or even *The Lily of Killarney*, one gets beautiful ideas without the over-colouring of actualities which were found in the old Irish dramas of Boucicault, though, of course, the last-named is only *The Colleen Bawn* extra-idealised.

The reception given to Ibsen in this country has led many to think that the oral drama will develop in the future on the lines he has laid down. Much as I admire him as an artist, he has one glaring defect which forbids any such possibility. I mean his unrelieved gloom. If this were a truth in art, or a reality, which it is not, it would nevertheless prove fatal in the theatre. Only the morbid mind can find pleasure in gloom : it is unnatural.

Shakespeare, who probably read few books, but observed human life keenly, knew this absolutely, that in life the terrible and the absurd are grossly intermingled. One may be watching the death throes of those we love, and a piano outside may be playing " Oh, what a difference in the morning."

So in *Macbeth*, close on the horrid murder comes the coarse knocking on the gateway and the gross humour of the drunken gatekeeper.

Ibsen is too steeped in one vein. *Ghosts* is all horrible. *A Doll's House* very human, but too confined to one set of people. His finest piece of dramatic work, *Lady Inger of Ostrat*, has never been acted in this country. Are the Norwegians a people wholly devoid of humour? Happily for the British they are not. If there is to be a modern British philosophic drama humour must appear in it.

The music-drama, however, conquers the field, for in music there is not only mirth and pathos and true tragedy (the expression of the will's denial), but there is the removed atmosphere, the mystic veil which stands between the ideal and the real and prevents the vulgarisation of the former. At least as long as there is music and not mere cacophony.

Another proof of the gradual extinction of oral drama (as a popular pastime) is the limited success of comedy—*i.e.*, comedy that does not merge into farcical extravagance. Comedy appeals almost solely to the intellect, and is, moreover, untrue to life; for in life pain and sorrow are the positive elements. The comedies of Shakespeare are not as popular as his tragedies. The three most frequently acted—*As You Like It, Much Ado About Nothing*, and *The Merchant of Venice*—are successful because of the strong humanity and passion in them. The best comedy in the English language, *The School for Scandal*, has a drama of passion and malice underlying it. But comedies, as a rule, do not appeal to the emotions and do not satisfy the cravings of the will. The end, usually marriage, is not a true finality. In comic opera it is the exhilaration produced by the music that satisfies the will, so much so that music lovers will go and see a comic opera twenty times in the course of its career. Farce is often successful because of its boisterousness, which temporarily cheers by the violence of the laughter it excites, though often a reaction of depression is produced. This is not felt in music, because in all well-composed music there is an underlying sadness that we are not always conscious of; for music appeals directly to the will-to-live, which is the important thing upon which all depends, as Schopenhauer justly tells us. But whether music-drama will develop quite on the plan set forth by Richard Wagner time alone can reveal.

The play which consists solely of action and speech will probably proceed upon an intellectual plane after the type of drama appealing to the savage instincts of man has become defunct.

In the four masterpieces of Oscar Wilde and the best work of H. A. Jones and Louis N. Parker, we now see the beginnings of a drama dealing with humanity in its complex state under high pressure. Romance can never vanish from life as long as human beings are gifted with imagination, and the power of imagination is likely to increase with the broader evolution of intellect. It is the moralists who fetter art. Those who call Shakespeare gross and seek to banish such gems from poetry as Suckling's ballad on *A Wedding*, and Burns' *The Lass that Made the Bed to Me*, or Aphra Behn's *The Juniper Tree*. Art can never reach its fullest perfection while thought is fettered or the expression of ideas veiled. Neither drama nor novel can become true revelations of humanity until human character is depicted in its complex individuality without regard to mere tabulated tenets of morality set according to either theological or philosophical systems of thought. Nor do I believe that any writer can produce a great play, either for speech or music, if he be writing always with the stage and set-scene before his eyes and the requirements of actors or the limits of particular actors' powers of expression in his mind.

Mr. A. W. Pinero is a specimen of the clever, day-labourer sort of manufacturing dramatist, successful because he fits in with an unimaginative period and a class of audiences and actors who seek for conciseness rather than amplitude of expression. In *Trelawney of the " Wells,"* however, this author has composed a work the effect of which is absolutely life-like, while at the same time it is pure art.

The over-elaboration of acting makes the theatre more effective, but it dwarfs the play. A very poor play seems a wonderful work if it be splendidly acted; and only indifferent acting or a private reading of it will reveal the wretched stuff of which it is composed. Such plays as *Mrs. Tanqueray* and *Mrs. Ebbsmith* do not advance dramatic art one step. The first was a heartless attempt to fasten another rivet in the chain of abominable injustice which women have suffered at the hands of priests and men for ages. The second was one of the poorest pieces of mere playwright's puppet-show workmanship that I have seen in twenty-five years' experience.

Such plays as *Lady Windermere's Fan, A Woman of no Importance, An Ideal Husband, Rosemary, Love in Idleness, Gudgeons, Saints and Sinners*, and *The Middleman* leave a decided impression behind them. But the one thing that can save even the intellectual drama from descending the grade that the sordid drama, founded on the Seven Cardinal Sins, has already gone down, let us hope for ever, is this: that every dramatist shall write a drama for the sake of the dramatic form, because it is the best for action as opposed to that of the novel which is for narration; but not for the theatre, as " cabined, cribbed, confined " by the scene-painter and stage-manager.

We shall then get again plays that make actors: at the present epoch nearly all the plays are made by the actors, and, indeed, are nothing without them, which is as abortive as if the music of an opera could never be heard or sung except by an opera-singer in an opera-house. Mr. H. A. Jones is right: if a play be not worth reading, or being heard read, it is most decidedly little worth the trouble or expense of being acted.

There is a fallacy abroad that drama exists only for actors, but this is a huge error. In all true art drama must be. Nature herself is dramatic. In sculpture, painting, music, great poetry, the novel, even in architecture dramatic form must be. When all is said the drama of the theatre is but a puppet-show and poor shadowgraph of the great drama created by the will in Nature.

And as mankind are mere players on the world's stage, ruled and worked by the fateful cords bound on them by the great law of necessity, so the actors in a theatre are but the recorder-pipes stopped by the hands of the great creative artists.

As man, when he seeks to transcend the laws of nature, is smitten with degeneration and extinguished in insanity, so the actors who seek to mould the art of drama to their own aggrandisement are destroying the very roots of their existence; for in the *facilis decensus averni* of the drama all actors must be swept together into the abyss, from which there is no recovery nor re-ascent.

ALLAN LAIDLAW.

# EDUCATION AND THE ENGLISH PARENT.

THERE is, perhaps, no subject which receives more of the public attention in these latter days than education; there is certainly none on which more nonsense is talked. You go to a lecture and hear a cultivated and literary person discourse on the facility with which the young idea may be taught to shoot in the proper direction, if only you will adopt his simple and natural method. You prick up your ears—if you are a teacher—when he begins to apply it to the teaching of languages. Without any unnecessary preliminaries as to the size of the class, the resources of the teachers, or the general mental condition of the victims, he naïvely propounds the uncontested fact that a universal language is needed, and what so obvious as that Latin should be that language? Nothing is easier: children are known to be able to pick up a language without any effort if they only hear it; plainly, then, all that is necessary is to talk Latin to them. Every one is at once convinced of the greatness, and at the same time the simplicity, of the discovery; the turning to account of children's known facility for picking up a language is a master-stroke; the audience regard the matter as settled, and applaud with emotion. All, that is, except an insignificant sprinkling of teachers, one of whom may be overheard to say to his, or her, neighbour on the way home: "Does the lecturer know that there are commonly not less than thirty children in a class, and that the time allowed for teaching languages *may* amount to some four or five hours a week? Does he really think that a dead lion is better than a living dog? Can he believe that a language which is full of grammatical inflexions such as no modern tongue possesses can be picked up without a definite study of its grammar?" But of all this the lecturer hears nothing, and he goes his rounds propounding his airy theory, making teachers melancholy, and inspiring parents with dreams from which they will sooner or later experience a rude awakening.

This is, however, a digression; it is intended merely as an illustration of the statement that nonsense is sometimes talked in connection with the subject of education.

We are accustomed to being told wonderful things of the progress

of education abroad ; there is hardly a single country of Europe—
with the possible exception of Turkey—which has not been held up
as a rebuke to us by one enthusiast or another ; and with the
patience mingled with complacency which distinguishes us from
other nations we sit quietly and listen to the rating, apparently
rather enjoying it than otherwise. Our attitude is perhaps explained
by the existence of a strong under-current of conviction that, though
all this may be true, yet one Englishman will lick three foreigners
any day in the week.

As to the causes which lie at the root of this admitted inferiority
we have also heard much. It is the Board School system ; it is the
Voluntary School system ; it is the Pupil-teacher system ; it is the
Payment-by-result system ; it is the system of half-time ; it is the
want of training of teachers ; it is the over-training of teachers ; it
is, in short, anything which the faddist of the moment happens to
object to. But there is still one cause which has never been properly emphasised, and that is what we may call the Parent system.
So far the parent has come off very much better than he deserves at
the hands of educationists, and if we subject him to some rather
severe strictures in this survey, it must be attributed to a rankling
sense of justice delayed.

Roughly speaking, we may say, adapting Tennyson's words,.
" Parents in the loomp is bad," and the man who remarked in his
haste that the life of a schoolmaster would be bearable if it were
not for the parents, would probably have said the same at his leisure..
It is not too much to say that the English parent has less sense of
his responsibility towards his children than any known species. We
are not speaking of the depraved section of society ; we are speaking
of the respectable Englishman of all ranks who sends his children
to school, or otherwise provides for what the universal looseness of
our language allows him to call their " education."

To begin at the beginning, he has too many children. He has
been told this in various ways by various people, but the only effect
produced on him is a pious shudder at the reckless atheism of the
propounders of such doctrine. Indeed, as Matthew Arnold says,
" One has heard people, fresh from reading certain articles in the
*Times* on the Registrar-General's returns of marriages and births in
this country, who would talk of our large English families in quite
a solemn strain, as if they had something in itself beautiful, elevating
and meritorious in them ; as if the British Philistine would only
have to present himself before the Great Judge with his twelve
children in order to be received among the sheep as a matter of
right !" There exists a pious formula to the effect that if the Lord
sends another mouth He will send something to put into it, and it is
held to be both profane and indelicate to argue against the premises
assumed here. The origin of the doctrine and of the formula is a

little obscure, but it is vaguely believed to be founded on certain
texts in the Bible.  When we assert, however, that the English
parent has too many children, we do not necessarily mean that he
has more than he can afford to feed, but rather that he has more
than he can bring up and provide for properly.  Every one must
have noticed that in large families, especially in the middle-class, it
is commonly the case that the elder children are carefully trained
and brought up according to some kind of system or theory, but
that the mother is often too busy or too much of an invalid to give
the same attention to the ninth or tenth child, while the father's
growing cares and responsibilities make it impossible for him to
spare any time for what is, after all, his most sacred duty, and the
children are neglected physically and morally.  Large families have
a reputation of bringing themselves up well, and one can see that
there are possible advantages in the influence of the children on each
other ; but most people's experience is against this sanguine view of
the case, and anyhow it would seem to be in spite of their circumstances rather than because of them.

The same beautiful trust in Providence is illustrated in that
entire absence of any provision for the children's future, which is so
common in England.  The English parent is content that his
daughters should be as the polished corners of the Temple, but he
sees no necessity to provide them with dowries, with husbands, or
with annuities.  It may be said that to find husbands is no part of
his duty ; but here we would respectfully join issue with the romantic
but unpractical objector, and say that it is his duty to provide, if not
husbands, at all events the alternative, namely, the means of living.
The case is better where sons are concerned, but even with them
there is too much of a kind of drifting policy, and too little care
expended on the choice of an occupation which is suited to the needs
and capacities of the boys : they are often put into the first post
that affords an opportunity of earning money, and who can calculate
the loss which the nation suffers from the prevalence of square men
in round holes ?

But it is when we come to the subject of education that the
English parent is seen at his worst.  England is, we believe, the only
civilised country where we find a rooted sentiment of opposition to
the systematic education of children.  It may be thought that this
is too strong a statement, but we appeal to teachers of children in
every class of society for confirmation.  Take the Board schools :
the children are sent to school late, unnecessary absence is frequent,
the parents abuse the school and the teachers in presence of their
children, and the poorer ones use every means in their power to evade
the laws for compulsory attendance, and to send them to work before
they have reached the necessary standard, not to mention the fact
that many parents hamper their children's progress by making them

work at unhealthy trades during the hours which ought to be given
up to play and real recreation.    Or take the secondary schools.
The difficulties here are fewer, because the parents of these children
have not the same pecuniary temptations, and the middle-class
Englishman, as a rule, prefers to secure the full value of his money.
But is it not a fact that the work of the teacher is hampered in all
kinds of ways by want of co-operation on the part of the parents?
They allow their children to be late; they keep them at home on
the most trifling pretext; they make no effort to ensure the home-
work being properly prepared; they criticise the teaching with an
omniscience only possible to ignorance; they do everything, in short,
to minimise the lasting effects of the school-training.    We recently
heard an educated lady complaining, before the assembled family, of
the unreasonableness of the mistress who had objected to let her
daughters leave their classes before the end of the morning in order
to attend some festivity, and of the insolence of the headmaster of a
public school who had insisted on the carrying out of certain regulations in the case of her sons.    It is, at bottom, a want of the true
spirit of education.    In Germany or in Switzerland, for instance,
education is the great matter: everything is regulated to fit with
school arrangements; the ordinary parent sees that it is to his
interest to support the school system; and the effect may be seen by
the most casual visitor in the manners and discipline of the children.
Or, again, take the case of children educated at home by private
governesses.    In many families it is rarely that a week of regular
adherence to the specified school-hours is to be counted on: everything is made an excuse for a holiday, and systematic training is
simply an impossibility.

What is the *fons et origo* of all this open or concealed opposition
to education?    We believe its sources are complex, and reach far
back into those remote ages when learning was regarded as " only
fit for clowns," when to be a scholar was also, in many cases, to be
a beggar; when profound learning was associated with the Evil One,
and was both disliked and distrusted by gentle and simple; when
the noble looked with contempt on the clerk who transacted his
business for him, and the churl feared the effect of his spells.
Shakespeare has crystallised this sentiment for us in the words,
" Hast thou a mark to thyself, like an honest plain-dealing man?"
A man might be trusted if he could not write.    In England respect
has always been paid to the solid things of this life, to the possession
of physical strength, of wealth, and above all, of land, the very
symbol of all that is solid, immovable, imperishable.    From time
immemorial brains have been associated with villainy, stupidity with
virtue.    To this day we find ladies of culture and refinement sighing
for the good old times when servants could neither read nor write.
Some such traditions as these we have inherited: a gentleman must

do things, but he need not know anything—what does a gentleman want with learning? This survives in the view taken by the upper classes. In the middle classes, the objection to learning was its inevitable association with poverty. In the lines which Mr. Glegg quotes to Tom Tulliver:

> " When the land is gone and money spent,
>    Then learning is most excellent,"

we hear an echo of this conviction, and even now it is at the bottom of the tone in which the middle-class parent clamours for concrete rather than abstract learning for his children. In the poorer classes there was in addition the lingering suspicion of unhallowed arts. The English mind, in short, has never taken kindly to the idea of education; it has had to be driven to it by State regulations, and submits with a very ill grace indeed.

We do not find this peculiar antagonism to learning outside England: even the most ignorant and uncivilised peoples entertain respect and admiration for it, and in civilised countries education has now almost invariably taken its true place in the national life. In Scotland, to get education is the universal ambition: parents are willing to undergo all kinds of privations in order to secure it for their children: the children themselves pursue it with a courage and endurance that are often heroic; and the existence of this spirit is abundantly illustrated in the life of almost every famous Scot.

Where is the remedy to be found? How are parents to be taught to take a right view of their duties? To the civilised man it might be supposed to seem that no duties could be so binding as those of a parent to a child, for he assumes them deliberately, while the child has no say in the matter. We are apt to lay more stress on filial piety, but this is surely only because it is of the nature of the voluntary, whereas parental " piety " is obligatory. That is to say that, as the child did not undertake to have parents, their claim on him is less strong than his own on them, since they have deliberately chosen to be responsible for him. It is one of the problems of the age: and the appalling part of it is that civilisation seems to go hardly any way towards solving it. People must be made to see that they are to undertake only as many children as they have reasonable expectation of being able to give a fair chance to. In an ideal state of society we might say that every one should marry for love, not without prudence, however; that all should face the children question soberly and squarely, leaving out of sight the old pious platitudes, and remembering that, if the Bible says comparatively little about the duty of parents to children, it is doubtless because it is so natural and obvious a duty as to need no insistence; and that the tendency of all training and legislation should be to heighten, not to minimise, the conception of the parents' responsibility for their children. Alas, how far have we strayed from this path! People object to the statement that we are not civilised; but, if we look at the question from this point of view alone, is there not ample confirmation of it to be found in the course of our ordinary newspaper reading? People marry for money; divorce is common; child-murder is frequent; and neglect, which is virtually murder; there exists a Society for the Prevention of Cruelty to Children, which is constantly having to interfere between parent and child; there are numerous institutions and societies for the care of forsaken children. Surely to a person with this question burning in his heart, it may well seem that civilisation, in this matter at least, has not even begun. There are societies for housing the poor, for spreading a knowledge of sanitary laws, and for a hundred other social objects; but the greatest work of all is reserved for a society which shall adopt some means of beginning at the very beginning, which shall point out to men and women the most elementary, the most obvious, the most essential of all human duties—the duty of parents to their children.

EDITH SLATER.

# FRIENDSHIP BETWEEN THE SEXES.

" FRIENDSHIP, mysterious cement of the soul, sweetener of life, and solace of society ! "

In a recent number of the WESTMINSTER REVIEW there appeared a brief but very interesting article upon this subject, and, being written by a lady, it is, perhaps, just as well if " mere man " should answer it. " Why is it that women cannot be allowed by the world at large to have male friends ? " she asks. The reason is, I think, because so many of the fair sex are too silly. The average girl is not one of whom it may be said, " Grace was in all her steps, heaven in her eye, in every gesture dignity and love." She spends more time in dressing and undressing, and admiring herself in the looking-glass, than the small minority of her sex does in improving their minds. In writing upon this subject I wish to treat it impartially from a man's point of view. I happen to be the fortunate possessor of a platonic friendship, and my friend has had the candour to tell me that she has never made a girl friend. She also gives me as her reason that she never learns anything from the frivolous maiden bent on fashion-study and the dissection of female character, and says it is impossible to confide in women as a rule, that they invariably betray her secrets—in short, that they are not sincere. I have spent many a pleasant and profitable hour in the company of this friend, but then our conversation has not been upon dress and mere amusements, but upon a thousand and one topics of literary, artistic and general interest. Charlotte Brontë very truly remarks : " If we would build upon a sure foundation in friendship, we must love our friends for their sakes rather than for our own." I thank heaven that I am unconventional myself, and always admire— when I do happen to meet with one — an unconventional maiden.

The fault I find with most of the sex is that they will not dare to be themselves, but slavishly copy other people. 'Tis truly refreshing to meet with a girl who thinks and gives you the benefit of those thoughts. Who that has read Homer does not remember that fine passage

> " Shall I with brave Laodamas contend ?
> A friend is sacred, and I style him friend."

If we are to enjoy the interchange of thought and mental experience, it must be as friends and not mere acquaintances.

How much longer will the gentler sex live in mortal fear of what Mrs. Grundy will say? Banish the old lady to limbo, I say, rather than be in perpetual thraldom. We have much to gain, if only we will encourage our lady friends to give us more of their inner thoughts. Seneca gives us a delightful picture of what friendship ought to be. He says: "True friends are the whole world to one another; and he that is a friend to himself is also a friend to mankind. Even in my studies the greatest delight I take is of imparting it to others; for there is no relish to me in the possessing of anything without a partner."

When man is necessarily so much engaged during the day in pursuits of a sordid nature it is imperative that he should look for some refining influence when his day's work is done. One of the problems of my life, however, is the fact that so very few women realise the potentiality they possess of influencing for good the other sex. The average girl I meet with gives me no inspiration and little stimulus to higher thoughts. And why is this? The answer, I fear, is plain—too often, alas! it is not in her. What Miss Moulder says about the conceit of some men is quite true. But who is it that "makes a man a lover directly he pays the slightest attention to a woman?"—who but a number of silly women? I do not blame Ruskin a little bit for all he says about the failure of women to influence men for good. If Ruskin "does not make enough allowance for the conventionalities of life with which women have to contend," I fear I do not make any more allowance. Once let girls show that without losing any of their modesty and self-respect they can still have independent minds of their own—worthy thoughts and aspirations—men will be only too eager to pay homage to them as platonic friends. There can be nothing more ennobling than the friendship of a good woman, and friendship, says Cicero, is infinitely better than kindness. Let all good women be careful, then, upon whom they bestow their friendship. I have always had such a high ideal of women that my friends at times consider me unduly severe in my criticism of them; but this is only because so few come up to my high standard. Girls must become less sensitive upon the point of being talked about; if their own conscience does not condemn them, why need they trouble about what people will say? Study to be both *sans peur et sans reproche.*

Depend upon it, any reform in this direction must come from the ladies themselves, and the sooner they unite together with this object in view the better it will be for all concerned. I would say, let them commence with the male friends they have, and show them by their conversation and manner that they desire platonic friendship. Personally I have a great objection to those silly musical evenings that are given to thirty or forty people, who, in turn, "favour us with a song," .&c. Some empty compliments are passed, and, when the evening is over, you come away without having had any real conversation with any one, but merely an hour or two of chatter. Better far if ladies would only invite, say, half a dozen gentlemen at a time, and know something more of these same six friends on parting.

There are some men, immaculately dressed, whom I would not dream of introducing to my sisters, nor allow them to dance together at a ball. If ladies, with their greater intuition, would only invite men in smaller numbers, they would sooner know those who are worthy of being invited at all. And let the ladies be as a friend of mine is, frigidly cold and distantly polite to all unworthy ones. Men would value their lady friends more highly, and there would be more true friendship between the sexes, if ladies would only be more particular about whom they asked to accept of their hospitality.

WILLIAM GARLAND.

# THE SOCIAL NE'ER-DO-WEEL.

THERE is one section of humanity which is generally ignored, but which, nevertheless, deserves much sympathy and considerable study : that class is represented by the social ne'er-do-weel. The species is by no means rare ; it is well known in every drawing-room, in every community, in almost every circle of relatives. Nature seems to have given certain social types a genius for spoiling sport ; a kind of paupers who take all the advantages that society has to offer and pay it back in boredom and *ennui*.

There are many varieties of the social sinner. Often he is not, properly speaking, a sinner at all ; he has the best intentions in the world, and is perfectly irresponsible for his bungling. This is quite the worst kind to deal with. The person who deliberately treads on his neighbours' toes may be brought to a sense of his guilt. Society has only to express its righteous wrath and he will generally find it the best policy to desist. But the good-natured blunderer, who never dreams that he is an infliction, who says and does the wrong thing by an unerring instinct without the faintest notion that he is driving his friends to the verge of madness—this is the true monster of social life. No patience, no cunning, is proof against him, and you have not even the satisfaction of feeling that some one is to blame.

The most formidable shape under which such persons appear is the meddling type. It is generally feminine, but male specimens exist and are much to be dreaded. To these people not a little of the tragedy of life is to be traced. They appear to be so constructed as to have no clear apprehension of the meaning of " mine and thine " ; it is impossible for them to keep their fingers out of other people's concerns ; interfere they must or die.

In general their first aim is to get at a clear understanding of their neighbours' affairs prior to controlling them. The instrument of torture they employ for this purpose is a system of interrogation in public and private, in season and out of season. Now for a truth-loving Protestant this kind of procedure is sometimes highly embarrassing ; the sharpest of us are not prepared to concoct at a moment's notice and for any personal question that may be asked us, an answer which shall be at once truthful and discreet ; perhaps a more difficult mental exercise could hardly be imagined than the attempt to parry

a volley of questions, without being uncivil, without committing
yourself, and without perjuring your soul. As a rule the task is
a perfectly hopeless one. You might as well expect, with Mrs.
Poyser's friends, to carry water in a sieve, as hope to keep your own
counsel under such painful and harassing circumstances. One is
disposed to agree with Bacon that dissimulation is "the skirts or
train of secrecy," and that a laudable taste for privacy excuses some
measure of deceit. However that may be, our meddling friend is
rarely satisfied until she—or he—has unriddled the mystery of how
you spend your evenings, your salary, your Sunday, with countless
other hows, whys, and wherefores which might reasonably be considered as private matters. Your dress, your hobbies, your conscience,
—nothing is too momentous or too trifling to be publicly inquired
into, and the result is a good deal of domestic and social heart-
breaking. Certainly, in dealing with such persons "an habit of secrecy
is both politic and moral." As we all admit, knowledge is power. We
are in many respects the slaves of those who know our histories and
foibles; by a little judicious interference, well-timed and persistent,
they can often rule us completely. Freedom of action is not always
worth having when it means continual self-defence. For the sake
of peace we soon find it wisest to give way. A servile acquiescence is
easier than constant opposition, and sooner or later most of us
submit to these self-appointed tyrants and censors, who often aim at
nothing but our good and woefully defeat their own ends.

Secondly, there is the irrepressible talker. Most people know
what it is to have cherished leisure interrupted by a ceaseless and
soulless flow of small talk, which nothing short of brutal insistence
will put an end to. It is wonderful how much pain may be
inflicted by this seemingly innocent habit of telling stale jokes,
dragging out yarns to an immoderate length, dosing the patient
listener with family history and other frowsy topics of no interest to
any one concerned. The blissful unconsciousness with which many
persons unintentionally make martyrs of their audience is quite
touching to behold; one cannot but regret that Nature has given us
no patent method of discovering our own social frailties, and thus
abstaining from trampling on our kind. How is it that books, mere
dead things comparatively speaking and a poor substitute for vital
human contact, have yet one inestimable virtue: they give us
society without its *ennui?* Books are sincere with us, and in
return we treat them honestly. In their presence we never cloak
boredom under smiles and conventional flourishes. Throughout the
volume we are deep in, our author is talking his best, exerting his
conversational powers to the utmost, often turning his soul inside out
for our perusal; yet no sooner do the faintest signs of drowsiness
begin to assail us than we stop his mouth with an effectual slam-to
of the pages, without apology, sometimes without even waiting for

the end of his sentence. It is refreshing, this audacious way we have of gagging genius itself when it begins to tire us; its power over us is greatly enhanced by the liberty to measure our own quantities. Would that the same freedom could be used where it is far more urgently needed, towards people who are not geniuses at all and who unwittingly consume our precious hours with vacant and vapid commonplaces.

Again, not the least of social offenders is the person who never knows when his presence could be dispensed with, when he is in fact *de trop*. What dark and vengeful feelings this guileless individual sometimes arouses in those who have the misfortune to be acquainted with him! What lost opportunities and "defeated joys," he is responsible for; how many of the "best-laid schemes o' mice and men" have gone "a'gley" through the dulness of such good-natured simpletons, many of whom are far from suspecting the anguish they inflict, and would sometimes betake themselves to any quarter of the globe rather than be a burden to their associates.

There are numerous other varieties of the adult *enfant terrible*, and, socially considered, they are—like wives and children in Bacon's opinion—"a kind of discipline of humanity." Their vagaries are the thorn in social life, without which it would perhaps be unmixed pleasure and solace; and probably the friction they give rise to, and the patience they demand of us, are not without a modifying effect on the general egoism.

It is interesting to notice that the species in question does not by any means always consist of insipid mortals and nonentities. Perhaps dullards are even less to be found in it than men and women of intellect and marked personality, and the reason is, I think, not far to seek. Natures which have a fixed bias in any direction find it difficult to bend to the moods and whims of others. Yielding comes easiest to the thoughtless majority, to characters without much innate stability, who have no scruples about doing as Rome does, and can therefore make themselves fairly at home anywhere. An enthusiast generally lacks the elasticity of mind of the social genius. He is too independent to be good at making concessions. That subtle sensitiveness which responds to every change in the surrounding mental atmosphere and sways with every varying wind of thought and feeling is seldom one of his gifts. It looks to him too much like ignoble yielding. He wants society to conform to his standard, and will not come half-way to meet it. Hence many great men are disliked or ignored in private life, until fame has procured them the sufferance, perhaps the homage, of the world. After this they are sufficiently hunted and lionised, but we do not often hear of them as drawing-room favourites unless they have been, so to speak, forced down people's throats by their public notoriety. "The great man," says J. S. Mill, "should not enter general society unless he can do so as its prophet. He should confine himself to the few picked souls by whom he is known and understood." Yes, and there is more than one reason for this. He should not hold aloof only because his acquaintances fail to satisfy him, for all social life is an education, even when composed of the most empty-headed triflers. But the point is that if society does not look on him as its prophet, it will almost certainly receive him as its pensioner. In nine cases out of ten he will find himself largely at a discount among the many, may possibly be rather tolerated than welcomed, and it is a question whether submission is altogether consistent with his dignity. Perhaps, like Brutus, he should "bear too great a mind" for public and unmerited ignominy. But, be that as it will, it can hardly be denied that the great man is not often made a popular hero on the ground of social talent. If society opens its arms to him, it is generally in spite of his oddities, gaucheries, and whimsicalities, not because of them.

Those who are best able to make themselves socially acceptable are in general well-balanced, supple natures, who combine excellent common sense with a tendency to take life much as they find it, who neither dictate to society nor grovel at its feet, but have enough imagination to understand it and enough wit to amuse it.

A genius for taking life casually is almost the one thing needful, and its possessors can generally hold their own under the least favourable conditions. Thus we notice in the French nation an inherent lightness and *abandon*, on which their charm of manner is largely dependent. The English character is too rigid for such piquancy; it clings too sternly to principle and received tradition, is too politic and cautious; hence the proverbial scarcity of social talent amongst us. For the same reason women have—as a writer in a recent magazine has pointed out—"a livelier and more penetrating social genius in all respects than men." The feminine nature is more elastic and mobile than its counterpart, and has often immense adaptive power. The tact of woman is generally acknowledged, and her old Saxon appellation of the peace-maker has not been entirely undeserved. In society gatherings she appears as the reconciler of mind with mind. Her smiling ease, her ready fund of conversational trifles, filling crude pauses and hiding masculine blunders, are the very salt of social intercourse. Undoubtedly there has been another side to this question, one which is fast disappearing in favoured modern days. The starving of woman's intellect has made her less able to look beneath the surface in questions of character. Her penetration, if subtle, has been largely superficial, often confined to details. Deep knowledge of life and how to deal with it has not been her *forte;* she can smooth and adorn society, but has failed to understand its under-currents of motive and thought; hence, her beauty once vanished, that grand excuse for every kind of failing, she has not seldom rendered herself a very tiresome appendage to the social world.

It is extraordinary and perhaps rather pleasing to note to what a degree society allows itself to be victimised by its bores and super-fluities. Centuries of Christianity have not been without their effect, even in our drawing-rooms; there is yet some life, some charity, in our most crystallised conventions. It is ingrained in us from child-hood that we must give quarter to the unwelcome guest; he must be borne with and indulged, within limits, of course, and on the surface, but this partial toleration means no inconsiderable measure of self-control and witnesses to a wide recognition of society's duties towards its members. Not that the world is without its weapons of defence against the class; its honours, its lordings, and lionisings, are seldom granted to the socially unworthy; unless he has some strong reason other than personal for claiming them, the ne'er-do-weel is ousted from many of its choicest privileges. But for all that, it is surprising how widely he is received, if he chooses to be, even amongst those least favourably disposed towards him. On the ground of family connections, standing, influence, or some such pretext, he can generally elbow himself into a very fair share of social advantages and make it the custom for a large number of persons to invite him and support his visits with a good grace. Thackeray has somewhere pointed out the feasibility of making your way in society by taking advantage of its easy temper. Tread on your neighbour's toe, he tells us, and ninety-nine cases out of a hundred he will move it away. And even without violent measures or any malevolent intentions, a great deal may be accomplished. No one, be he never so lacking in the power to please, need be without sincere friends and partisans, and through these he can link himself on to general society, and is often received where he is least welcome without a murmur.

It is a question, however, whether the habitual politeness and suavity of humankind towards such persons is altogether worthy of admiration. It often savours not a little of deceit, and robs the poor ne'er-do-weel of many a salutary lesson. Sometimes it would be a great relief to feel that the world could be trusted to express its opinion of us in something plainer than hieroglyphics; it is so unwilling to utter hard truths in anything but a covert and round-about manner, that not a few persons find it wholly unfathomable, and are at a loss to discover how they stand in its estimation. And since no one of average Christianity wishes to make himself socially obnoxious, it is a pity that more of us are not allowed to know our crimes. The question of how, when, and why they are burdening their acquaintance might indeed be puzzling to the shrewdest philosophers. Possibly a good many social faults would soon be eradicated were the general disapproval more plainly manifested, but in practice this doctrine might prove a dangerous one. If every one took to passing open judgment on his neighbour without restraint or ceremony the results would certainly be preposterous; any amount of well-bred lying would be preferable to such a state of things.

As it is, however, the difficulties of the class in question are much to be felt for. In general they command little sympathy, though they are not amongst the least of human ills. A vague sense that he is socially superfluous often haunts the well-intentioned bore. He is conscious of being in some mysterious way out of harmony with the men and women about him. Like Jerome's shy man, "he moves about the world, but does not mix with it. Between him and his fellow-men there runs ever an impassable barrier—a strong invisible wall, that, trying in vain to scale, he but bruises himself against." People patronise him and have missions to him, good-humoured and self-sacrificing persons lay themselves out for his benefit, feel it kind to invite him and pretend to a great deal of liking for him which they do not really feel. Under these circumstances the species acquit themselves variously according to temperament; the better sort "pass on with pride over men's pity," live superior to society's verdict on them, and in so doing often greatly modify or even conquer their unpopularity. Some take an injured, some a grovelling attitude; some are really too thick-skinned and callous by nature to feel any cold-shouldering short of positive affront and hence thrive excellently on their reputation as bores. Many go through life in blissful ignorance, looking on themselves as amongst the benefactors of society. But for the sensitive nature even a moderate degree of social odium is difficult to support, more difficult than is at first sight apparent. Hasty judgment is often passed on these unfortunate persons, who, for one reason or another, have not the key to the hearts of their generation. For such the effort to be at once dignified and inoffensive, to sustain a virtual outlawry without taking a mean revenge on the world, makes life none the easier, and those who succeed in it are neither fools nor egoists. Old maids have formerly had a hard task in this respect. When youth and wifehood were regarded in women as a kind of passport to society, those who had neither qualification were not welcomed with much enthusiasm and had in general but a sorry time of it. "Pray observe," says Swift, "how insignificant things are the common race of ladies when they have passed their youth and beauty, how contemptible they appear to the men, and yet more contemptible to the younger part of their own sex, and have no relief but in passing their afternoons in visits, where they are never acceptable, and their evenings at cards among each other, while the former part of the day is spent in spleen and envy, or in vain endeavours to repair by art and dress the ruins of time." Nowadays it is hardly an assumption to claim that this state of affairs, if it ever really existed, is altogether a thing of the past. Even the good Dean, in his benighted age, makes an exception of intellectual women, who, he tells us, are sometimes sought after by " all the polite part of the town and court " merely for the benefit of their conversation. Certainly the nineteenth-century woman who drops out of society for such reasons as the above has only herself to thank for it.

To conclude, it is much to be regretted that social arts are so little cultivated in " Merrie England." By careful training in youth, by a more studious attention to the graces of life, to the subtle and intricate laws that connect mind with mind in common intercourse, we might render existence an altogether more tolerable thing. That we should thus exterminate the unpopular class is too much to claim, but certainly it might be greatly diminished. Matters might be so far improved that there would be less unsociability amongst us ; fewer interesting and original persons would find the world irresponsive or complain of it as dull ; there might chance to be more *bons camarades* and fewer examples of the social ne'er-do-weel.

H. G. WORTLEY.

# CONTEMPORARY LITERATURE.

## SCIENCE.

THERE was a time, and it is not far distant, when most people allowed their standard of morality to be laid down for them by unscientific sectarians, and in many minds there is still a confused idea that religion and morality are almost synonymous. To those who still hold such opinions we can confidently recommend the perusal of Mr. G. Gore's work on the *Scientific Basis of Morality*.[1] In it the author takes the view that the great laws of science are the chief guides of life, and that human beings must accept these laws and regulate their conduct by them whether they like it or not. Although Mr. Gore has much to say about theological theories and superstitions, yet his criticism is not of an unfriendly kind, and mental phenomena are treated in the same impartial manner as other scientific observations. The quotations from other writers are extremely numerous, perhaps rather too numerous in the case of some poets, and show much patient research on the part of the author. The chief rules of moral conduct are summarised under nine headings or moral rules which would, no doubt, be safe guides from a social point of view. Mr. Gore's work is replete with original ideas, and can be recommended to all students of social and religious problems.

A work treating of somewhat similar subjects is Dr. P. Topinard's *Science and Faith*;[2] but here the author frankly takes the view that science and faith mutually exclude each other; "science is knowledge, faith is belief." A considerable portion of the work is devoted to tracing the origin of human society and social evolution generally, and the high position of Dr. Topinard as an anthropologist gives great weight to his views on these subjects. The chapters on Psychical Needs and on Education are well worth the attention of all who are interested in the mental evolution of the human race.

We have received the latest volume of the "Contemporary

[1] *The Scientific Basis of Morality.* By G. Gore. London: Swan Sonnenschein and Co., Ltd. 1899.

[2] *Science and Faith.* By Dr. P. Topinard. Translated by T. J. McCormack. London: Kegan Paul & Co., Ltd. 1899.

Science Series," [1] which maintains fully the high standard of these summaries of various branches of science. Mr. Deniker's account of the various races of man leaves nothing to be desired either on the score of clearness or compactness, and the facts stated have been well selected and arranged. In such a work one of the chief difficulties is to find a system of classification which shall be applicable to the numerous varieties of the human race. The first division adopted by the author is the geographical one, the five geographical groups being further subdivided into linguistic regions. A copious bibliography adds considerably to the value of the book, and the anthropometric tables in the appendices and in the body of the book will be welcomed by those who know the difficulty of getting such information in an accessible form even in much more pretentious volumes. The illustrations are in most cases good ; but some of the photographic reproductions show the indistinctness so frequently found in these useful aids to science.

In his *Ethical Sunday School* [2] Mr. W. L. Sheldon gives a record of the system adopted in a Sunday School with which he is connected. As compared with the ordinary Sunday School course of instruction it is claimed that the ethical course of tuition develops tendencies of thought or a certain attitude of mind; it does not merely impart knowledge. We are glad to see that the miracle side is kept in the background, teachers being advised to say that "the subject is not in the lesson " if asked for an explanation of water being turned into wine, for instance. We think the author of a really satisfactory ethical work will have to grapple with these matters instead of shirking them.

Another volume of the " University Tutorial Series " has appeared, the subject being *The Elements of Co-ordinate Geometry*.[3] The problems appear to be clearly stated and the exercises well chosen.

We have received a report of the opening ceremony of a new wing of the Parsee Lying-in Hospital, Bombay, and of the unveiling of a marble bust of the chief physician of that charity, Dr. Temulgi B. Nariman.

The meeting, which seems to have been attended by most of the philanthropic leaders of the Parsee community, was presided over by Sir Jamsetjee Jejeebhoy, Bart., who pointed out the increasing favour with which the hospital is regarded year by year. From statistics given at the meeting it appears that a third of the poorer Parsees have come to avail themselves of the hospital, notwithstanding the obstacles of prejudice and social customs. The enormous benefit conferred by the hospital is proved by the mortality returns of the

[1] *The Races of Man.* By J. Deniker. London: Walter Scott, Ltd. 1900.
[2] *An Ethical Sunday School.* By W. L. Sheldon. London: Swan Sonnenschein and Co., Ltd. 1900.
[3] *The Elements of Co-ordinate Geometry.* Part II. By J. H. Grace and F. Rosenberg. London : W. B. Clive.

inmates, as compared with that among the women confined in their own homes. The statistics of the last three years show the death-rate outside to have been from three to four times higher than in the hospital. The result is such as the medical staff may well be proud of.

The new wing opened on December 9 last was erected by the widow of the late treasurer and generous benefactor, Mr. N. J. Wadia, to perpetuate the memory of her husband, who had devoted years of labour and much money to the institution. In the new N. J. Wadia wing accommodation for fifteen additional beds is provided, with quarters for the matron and nurses.

After the formal opening of the wing Sir Jamsetjee Jejeebhoy proceeded to the further ceremony of unveiling the bust of Dr. Temulgi B. Nariman, who has been physician to the hospital from its inception, and has visited the chief lying-in institutions of Europe with a view to securing that the equipment of his own shall be worthy to rank with the best.

It is a rare event for a statue to be erected to a doctor—much more in his lifetime—so the recipient of this honour is to be congratulated. The oil portrait of his wife also adorns the institution. Both portrait and statue have been paid for by funds collected for the purpose by the late N. J. Wadia, who unhappily did not live to see the completion of the statue.

---

## SOCIOLOGY, POLITICS, AND JURISPRUDENCE.

*The New Democracy*,[1] by Mr. Jethro Brown, Professor of Law and Modern History in the University of Tasmania, comes as a useful reminder of what valuable nursery grounds for political experiments we possess in our colonies, which vie with each other in the introduction of democratic reforms. "The original student of modern politics," says Professor Brown, " may be disposed to remark that democracy is an excellent form of government but for two difficulties: no means exist for securing the adequate expression of public opinion, and the opinion would be of little value even if such means could be found." Although, as the author says, most impartial men would dissent from such a view, it possesses a large measure of truth. "The attempts that have been made to adapt the representative machinery to new social and political conditions have

[1] *The New Democracy.* A Political Study. By W. Jethro Brown, M.A., LL.D. ; Barrister-at-Law ; Professor of Law and Modern History in the University of Tasmania. London: Macmillan & Co., Ltd. New York: The Macmillan Company. 1899.

proved lamentably inadequate. As a result, democracy has been compelled to face a new and almost overwhelming complexity of problems, under conditions which encourage a spirit of corruption and chicanery." As solutions of the problem of representation, Professor Brown offers the Hare system and the referendum. The solution of the problem of character has always been the same— popular education. This education ought to consist in a study of history which possesses, as he thinks, " in a most unusual degree, the power of informing and directing the political judgment, of arousing interest and of stimulating enthusiasm."

We doubt very much whether history, as usually taught in our schools and universities, possesses very much political value. The intelligent artisan who has studied economic problems first-hand has in our experience sounder political views than the average student of history. But Professor Brown means something very different. The history of economics and of other social problems, their origin and evolution, are the phases which make the study of history of political value.

For the details of the Hare system in actual operation in Tasmania we must refer the reader to the book itself. There he will find this most complicated voting machine most lucidly explained.

The referendum is regarded by Professor Brown as a temporary specific until proportional representation is established. And even then he would limit it to certain defined purposes. In this we think he is right, since, if the latter worked out as it should, there would be little occasion for the former. The Hare system appears to have been thoroughly successful in Tasmania and in some cities in the United States ; but whether it would be practicable with a large population like our own seems somewhat doubtful.

Of course our present system is deplorable, but then the ignorance of the average voter is also deplorable. We take it, however, that under such a system large classes of intelligent voters would not be excluded, as they are at present, owing to absurd registration regulations, otherwise our last state would be worse than the first.

We have always understood that in practice the referendum had been found to be retrogressive. The precedents from Switzerland and the United States are examined, and Professor Brown comes to the conclusion that the scheme is unsuited to English and Australian politics. Just as industrial progress is only possible where full scope is given to the utilisation of special ability and special information, so political progress is subject to the same law. The will of the majority must ultimately decide ; " but the majority can only lose by having its momentary inclinations gratified with invariable promptitude."

If proportional representation brought with it social and economic reforms, it would, of course, be well worth the trouble and risk of change; but until the average political knowledge is raised a little higher, we much doubt whether any changes in our political machinery would be of any great practical importance. However, whatever conclusions may be drawn, there can be no question that we have here the work of a thoughtful man of the world, of more than ordinary breadth of view and impartiality.

Professor Brown is no mere doctrinaire. He does not make his facts fit his theories, but establishes his theories upon his facts, an obviously proper mode of procedure, which is not, unfortunately, invariably followed. We cannot speak too highly of the practical value of this work.

At no time could such a work as *Droit Politique Contemporain,*[1] by M. le Vte. Combes de Lestrade, have been more welcomed than at present, when the majority of political organisations are eagerly called in question, and even social organisation itself disputed. M. de Lestrade's work is, of course, based principally upon the political organisation of the more important States of the world, but it is well to notice that the smaller ones are not forgotten. For instance, on page 46 will be found a note on the position of the Uitlanders in the Transvaal; on examining their situation M. de Lestrade is of opinion that the problem of their position is " absolutely identical " with that of the Arabs in France and the Jews in Russia, whose position he has just been discussing. We get a very fair idea of the plan of this voluminous work from a narration of the chief matters dealt with : the State, its social composition—Constitutions and Governments (and we may notice in passing that the English Constitution is placed by M. de Lestrade as a " class apart "— unique)—the sovereign power—the legislative power—the executive power—popular suffrage—constitutional " guarantees." The work is so modern, so very much up to date, that one might almost suppose the author to have been able to foretell in commencing his work the political difficulties that were to exist at its close.

---

## VOYAGES AND TRAVELS.

MR. GEORGE LACY is better known in this country for his *Liberty and Law*, published in 1888, in which he successfully disposes of the extreme doctrines of Individualism taught by Mr. Herbert Spencer and his school. Whether one agrees or not with his conclusions this book displays a depth of knowledge and of thought which one

---

[1] *Droit Politique Contemporain.* By Vte. Combes de Lestrade. Paris : Guillaumin, 14 Rue Richelieu.

does not usually look for in a sportsman.   And yet in South Africa
to this day Mr. Lacy is remembered as a daring hunter of big game,
a keen sportsman, and an experienced pioneer.   In *Pictures of Travel,
Sport and Adventure* [1] we have Mr. Lacy's experiences graphically
described not only in South Africa, but also in New Zealand and
Australia, where he appears to have been chiefly engaged in
journalism.   In the former country his remittance went astray, and for
a month, unable to obtain employment, he literally starved, living on
little but hawthorn-berries, watercress and spring-water.   Whilst
here he was employed to compile a guide-book to the entire Hot
Lake Districts, and although the famous pink and white terraces
have frequently been described, Mr. Lacy's account, especially since
their destruction, will be read with interest.   He also visited the
Victoria Falls in 1868.   Mr. Lacy is particularly strong in descriptions of scenery.   It is not often that a hunter or a traveller,
however keen an observer he may be, is also able to put his
observations to writing in suitable form.   Mr. Lacy is a keen
student of nature, and his journalistic training has enabled him to
convey to others exactly what he has seen.   In describing this
eighth wonder of the world Mr. Lacy has given us a really splendid
piece of descriptive writing.   Of good hunting stories and exciting
tales of adventure, the book is full from beginning to end.   Some
of these must be taken with a grain of salt, but all the same they
are good reading.   Much of this hunting took place in a district to
which all eyes are now directed—the country lying between the
Drakensberg and Maritzburg.   As far back as 1866 Mr. Lacy
rode down the Drakensberg one pitch-dark night to Utrecht,
crossed the Tugela at dusk next evening, reaching Grey Town in the
early morning, a ride of 215 miles in fifty hours, with scarcely a
mile of level road anywhere.

It is men like these whom our military officers at the present
moment ought to consult.   They are still to be had, men who know
every inch of the country.   We know several instances where the
services of such men have been offered and contemptuously rejected
by the War Office five or six months ago, and only at the end of
January one was suddenly ordered to the front.   In the chapter
entitled " Sport and Adventure in Natal " will be found a good
description of the present theatre of the war.   The illustrations are
good, but one photo of a native in his war-paint is wrongly described
as a " Swazi masher."   He is really dressed as a Zulu.

[1] *Pictures of Travel, Sport and Adventure.*   By George Lacy (The Old Pioneer).
London : C. Arthur Pearson, Ltd.   1899.

## HISTORY AND BIOGRAPHY.

THE recollections of an experienced journalist are sure to be interesting. Sir Edward Russell, the editor of the *Liverpool Daily Post*, has written a delightful book entitled *That Reminds Me*——/[1] It is perhaps too discursive a volume to be regarded as a perfect work of art. Its author is, however, too modest to claim for it anything more than the record of a working newspaper editor's experience. The claim of such a book can perhaps be best illustrated by a few extracts. The subjects dealt with range over a wide area — politics, literature, the drama, and that curious field for speculation, the private and public characters of celebrated persons. In the entire volume there is not a particle of malice. The tone of the book is manly, candid, and sincere. A great portion of Sir Edward Russell's recollections are associated with Mr. Gladstone. As a staunch Liberal, the author could not fail to take a special interest in the man whom he looked up to as the leader, if not the prophet, of the party. One anecdote told about Mr. Gladstone shows that he scarcely appreciated the greatness of Cromwell. We give it in Sir Edward Russell's words: " Coming from ' our friend the enemy,' the following story ought to be received with caution ; but it was told with all positiveness. It was said that Mr. Gladstone had mentioned in conversation with the author of the story, a new book on Oliver Cromwell. ' Now,' quoth Mr. Gladstone, ' do you think Cromwell was a very great man ? ' ' Yes, I think he was a very great man,' replied the biographer. ' Ah ! ' said Mr. Gladstone, ' now I should not have said myself that he was a very great man, not greater, for instance, than the late Lord Althorp.' " It is no wonder that an admirer of Mr. Gladstone, who happened to be present, should have exclaimed : " For Heaven's sake, don't tell anybody he said this ; at least, not till after he is gone."

There is a reference to " the Parnell scandal," as Sir Edward Russell is pleased to call it. Credit must be given to the *Liverpool Daily Post* for the advice given by it to " let Mr. Parnell down gently," and to do all that could be done to prevent the Liberal-Irish cause from being ruined, as it ultimately was. Mr. Parnell committed the unpardonable sin (in certain eyes) of being " found out." Those who see beneath the surface of politics are inclined to think that if the Irish party had unanimously stuck to Mr. Parnell after the divorce case, Mr. Gladstone would have reconsidered his decision, and Home Rule might by this time have been won.

Sir Edward Russell does more than justice to Lord Beaconsfield, whose great virtue, according to him, was perseverance. There is a

[1] *That Reminds Me* ——/ By Sir Edward Russell, Editor of *The Liverpool Daily Post*. London : T. Fisher Unwin.

somewhat mysterious story told about a quarrel between the author of *Vivian Grey* and Sir Robert Peel, which is scarcely creditable to the delicacy of the former.

The references to the late Lord Randolph Churchill presents that gifted politician in a most aimable light. Lord Randolph possessed a charming simplicity of character. Here is an example of it : " Many years ago, when Sir (then Mr.) Henry Irving was playing Hamlet in Dublin, a message was brought into the dressing-room one night that Lord Randolph Churchill would be much obliged if he would see him. Mr. Irving asked who he was, and was informed that he was a son of the Lord Lieutenant. Lord Randolph came in, asked leave to light a cigarette, and, after a few compliments, went into general conversation. This was between the third and fourth acts. Presently Irving told him that he must now say good-bye, as he was nearly due on the stage for the next act— the play, remember, being 'Hamlet.' Lord Randolph said, ' What occurs in the next act ? ' Irving explained to him that the young lady he had seen in the former part of the piece got into more trouble, and at this and other explanatory expressions Lord Randolph said, ' Dear me, this is very sad.' Presently, when he was nearly going, he said, ' Will you tell me how it all ends ? ' Irving told him, entering into the spirit of the thing, that in the fifth act most of the characters would be found lying on the stage, struck with swords or disposed of by poison, and Lord Randolph seemed to think this a very interesting condition of things. He said, as he was going, 'I am not much of a playgoer, and in point of fact I have never seen a play of Shakespeare's before, nor have I ever read one.' " Subsequently Irving was invited to dine with Lord and Lady Randolph Churchill, and on this occasion Lord Randolph informed the great actor that since the night when they had talked of " Hamlet " he had read that and four other plays of Shakespeare, adding, " I feel that you have really introduced me into a new world." The naïvete of Lord Randolph Churchill is most refreshing in an age of priggery and self-sufficiency.

There is a deep pathos attached to the circumstances under which the late Mr. John Richard Green's *Conquest of England* [1] was written. His widow explains in the preface how the two works, the *Making of England* and the *Conquest of England*, were produced. Mr. Green was suffering from severe illness before the fourth volume of his *History of the English People* was finished. Then came an interval of renewed health, and he hoped that some years of life might be before him. With the ardour of new hope he threw himself into schemes of work hitherto denied him. He had, however, only just begun to shape his plans when they were thwarted by a fresh

---

[1] *The Conquest of England.* By John Richard Green, M.A., LL.D. Two Vols. London : Macmillan & Co., Ltd.

attack of illness. The *Making of England* was thus commenced
under the shadow of death. The courage, the enthusiasm of the
man who could carry out a task involving great intellectual effort
under such circumstances cannot be too highly praised. In the
scheme which was drawn up at the time the book to which the title
of the *Conquest of England* was given was to have ended with the
period when the Danes became masters of the country. The work,
as it stands, is a monument of patient toil, research, and accumulated knowledge. The opening chapter, dealing with the social and
political changes which followed the settlement of the English in
Britain and the introduction of Christianity, is a luminous picture of
the conditions under which the English nation was built up. The
account of the Danish invasion is very minute and, on the whole,
accurate, though it is a singular fact that the share taken by Ireland
in crushing the Danes is ignored by the author. In the second
volume the narrative is brought forward to the Battle of Hastings,
and it seems to us that less than justice is done to the heroic
character of Harold. This portion of the work is somewhat fragmentary, being supplemented by an article written by Mr. Green in
the *Saturday Review,* in which Harold is referred to as narrow in his
views and incapable of great things. On the other hand, a glamour
surrounds the barbaric character of William the Conqueror in the
eyes of Mr. Green. It is to be regretted that a man of such deep
learning and philosophic insight should take a superficial view of the
true lessons of history. The marauding spirit of the Conqueror had
much to do with the creation of that abominable aggressiveness
which still survives in England under the name of Imperialism. It
must never be forgotten that conquest for the sake of conquest brings
with it eventually an inevitable reaction towards barbarism. We see
this to-day in the horrible war waged between British and Dutch in
South Africa.

*The Mind of the Nation* [1] is an attempt to "analyse the machinery
of National Government, and the motive forces which have actuated
it during the present century." The author also endeavours to
indicate the direction and balance of power at the present day, and
the tendencies of modern constitutional development. The book is a
very useful guide to the student of modern politics, and it is to be
regretted that, having regard to the great variety of its contents, it
has no index. Mr. Dormer's account of the political history of
George III., George IV. and William IV. is an admirable example
of systematic and comprehensive marshalling of facts. The Queen's
reign is sketched in a somewhat fragmentary style. The view of
the Home Rule movement taken by Mr. Dormer is rather super-

[1] *The Mind of the Nation.* A Study of Political Thought in the Nineteenth
Century. By Marcus R. P. Dormer, M.A., M.B. Cantab. London: Kegan Paul,
Trübner & Co., Ltd.

ficial. He, moreover, fails to appreciate the true measure of the influence of the Press in the nineteenth century.

Mr. John Hogben's monograph of the late Mr. Richard Holt Hutton,[1] of *The Spectator*, is a sympathetic and appreciative study of one of the greatest English journalists of the century. As a critic and a thinker Mr. Hutton was the foremost—or, at least, one of the foremost—amongst the Englishmen of his day. Mr. Hogben displays extensive knowledge of Mr. Hutton's work in journalism and literature. This delightful little volume is, indeed, an ideal monograph.

The *Letters of Ricardo to Trower*[2] (1811–1823) will be read with keen interest by all who are concerned with economical problems. Ricardo was a man of liberal views, and, considering the narrow intellectual atmosphere in which he lived, he was in advance of his age. It is unnecessary to dwell on the controversies between Ricardo and Malthus on the question of capital and interest. Of far more importance, from a social and political point of view, is Ricardo's opinion on the evils of the English Poor Law system. He regarded an increase of wages as the proper remedy for the grievances of the poor, and not an undiscriminating charity. With regard to Ireland, Ricardo must get the credit of having in 1821 strenuously supported the Catholic claims, and he went so far as to suggest a Catholic Established Church for that country just as Scotland has a Presbyterian one. This, of course, would be a doubtful experiment. He says in a letter to Trower, dated January 25, 1822 : "The evils of Ireland I, in my conscience believe, arise from misrule." If he were living to-day it is probable that he would regard Home Rule as the right remedy for this "misrule," of which, judging from the recent attempts to stifle liberty of speech in Ireland, we have not yet seen the end.

*The Life of Madame de Longueville*,[3] by Mrs. Alfred Cock, is the biography of a woman who played a very remarkable part in French history. The sister of the great Condé and the cousin of Louis XIV. possessed rare intellectual qualities, and, in spite of her faults, she must rank with the women who have done good by stepping "out of the beaten track." The chapter dealing with Madame de Longueville's penance gives a curious insight into the blend of daring and abject superstition of which we find so many examples amongst the old nobility of France. How much nobler was Hawthorne's Hester Prynne than Madame de Longueville!

---

[1] *Richard Holt Hutton of the "Spectator"*: A Monograph. By John Hogben. Edinburgh : Oliver & Boyd.
[2] *Letters of David Ricardo to Hutches Trower and Others (1811–1823)*. Edited by James Bonar, M.A., LL.D., and J. H. Hollander, Ph.D. Oxford : Clarendon Press.
[3] *The Life of Madame de Longueville (Anne Genevieve de Bourbon)*. By Mrs. Alfred Cock. London : Smith Elder & Co.

### RELIGIOUS HISTORY.

IN a codicil of his will, Ernest Renan, amongst other posthumous publications the care of which he left to his family and his publishers, indicated *un volume d'Etudes sur la politique du régne de Philippe le Bel.* This original and notable contribution to the history of the Papacy and the political action of Philip in relation to it is now happily given to the public by M. Calman Lévy.[1] It was one of Renan's contributions to *l'Histoire littéraire de la France*, undertaken at the request of a committee of *l'Académie des Inscriptions et Belles-Lettres*, of which he was elected a member in 1856. The volume is not only written in Renan's masterly manner, but is a monument of research, and abounds in new and important information relating not only to the policy of Philip, but to the Papacy under Boniface VIII., Benedict XI., and Clement V. The aim of Philip, in which, indeed, he ultimately succeeded, was to reduce the Pope to the position of a vassal to France. The conduct of Boniface afforded Philip a good excuse for his interference, and neither Benedict nor Clement were strong enough to resist the pressure brought to bear upon them. The most important contribution to this history of the times is the discovery of the leading part taken in carrying out the policy of Philip by his agents Guillaume de Nogaret (Nogaretius) and Pierre du Bois. It is remarkable that until recently so little has been known of Nogaret, who appears to have been the most active enemy of Boniface VIII., and to whom are due many of the libels against that Pope. Boniface was bad enough, but Renan shows that he was not the scoundrel he has been painted. The volume is in three books entitled respectively "Guillaume de Nogaret," "Pierre du Bois," and "Bertrand de Got" (Clement V.). The 450 pages which compose this volume are so full of intense interest that it is impossible to do justice to them in a brief notice, but no student of the history of France and of the Church can afford to leave them unread.

The comprehensive *History of the Christian Church*,[2] left unfinished by the late Dr. Moeller, was wisely entrusted for completion by the publisher to the author's colleague, Dr. G. Kawerau. The result is the present volume dealing with the period of the Reformation and Counter-Reformation, 1517–1648. Dr. Kawerau has proved himself worthy of the task entrusted to him, and though he is modestly described as editor, a very considerable portion of this volume is direct from his own pen. Dr. Kawerau confesses himself a Lutheran, but there is no evidence of undue bias in his work, and we can

[1] *Etudes sur la Politique Religieuse Régne de Philippe le Bel.* Par Ernest Renan. Paris : Calman Lévy. 1899.
[2] *History of the Christian Church, A.D. 1517–1648.* Third Volume. Reformation and Counter-Reformation. By the late Dr. Wilhelm Moeller. Edited by Dr. G. Kawerau. Translated from the German by J. H. Freece, M.A. London : Swan Sonnenschein & Co. 1900.

believe him when he says he has endeavoured to write intrepidly only what is true.   Testing the author's fairness and accuracy by his account of the Reformation in England and the struggles between the Puritan and Anglican parties in the seventeenth century, we can affirm without hesitation that he is to be fully trusted, not only for his accurate statement of facts, but for his intelligent understanding of principles.

Though this history of the Church may be regarded primarily as a book of reference, it is sufficiently full to prove interesting to the general reader whose taste lies that way, as well as to the student of ecclesiastical history.

Mr. Hunt's history of *The English Church* [1] is full of details and is, therefore, highly interesting reading.   None the less so because he does not exclude everything that many will regard as only legendary ; thus as miracles occupy a prominent place in the history of the early years of the Church, he has noticed them wherever he deemed it necessary—but he goes further than notice them, he defends them ; and, we suppose, therefore, he believes them.   Miracles present no difficulty to the writer.   " To those who deny miracles altogether," he says, " as contrary to the ' law of nature,' it is easy to reply by asking when that law was declared.   Was it settled before the discovery of the Röntgen rays, or only the day before yesterday ? Have men of science as yet brought psychological phenomena under this law ? "

Perhaps the state of mind evidenced by such sentences ought not to prejudice us against an historian, but it is calculated to do so. Nor, perhaps, ought we to say that this history is written with a purpose ; but when we are taught that the Church of England began with the Roman Mission, and that the State may be said to owe its existence to the instrumentality and example of the Church, we are driven to the conclusion that the writer has his eye upon the present crisis, and that in some measure the history is affected by a tendency or motive.   Apart from this it is only just to say that the volume is crammed with information and written in a bright and readable style.

The Rev. Henry Cobbe, who died in November 1898, just after his eighty-first birthday, was the brother of Miss Frances Power Cobbe, rector of Maulden and a well-known scholar and antiquary.   For many years he had been engaged on a history of *Luton Church*,[2] but he had only corrected the proofs of Part I. at the time of his death. The work is now completed, and is presented to the public by Messrs. George Bell and Sons in a massive volume.

1 *The English Church from its Foundation to the Norman Conquest (597–1066).*   By William Hunt, M.A.   London and New York : Macmillan.   1899.
2 *Luton Church, Historical and Descriptive.*   By the late Henry Cobbe, M.A., Rector of Maulden, Bedfordshire.   With Portrait, Illustrations, and Plan.   London : George Bell & Sons.   Bedford : F. Hockliffe.   1899.

This is probably the most exhaustive work on a parish and parish church which has ever, and, perhaps, ever can be produced, for Luton is exceptionally rich in its records. The volume is, therefore, of much more than local importance, as it throws a good deal of light upon the development of the English Church, for what went on in Luton for several centuries was doubtless going on in other parishes where the records have been lost or have perished.

It is difficult to say what this volume contains, for it contains everything the learned writer could find which relates to Luton and its fine old church, of which latter there is a full architectural account with numerous illustrations; as also of the inscriptions and monuments. The historical description extends from the seventh century to the present day. To all this is added a short biography, as far as ascertainable, of each of the persons who have been most intimately connected with the Church. The volume is also enriched by the reproduction of numerous valuable and interesting documents. One of the most interesting biographies is that of Thomas Pomfrett, who became vicar at the Restoration; he was father of John Pomfrett, the author of the once popular but now almost forgotten poem, "The Choice." There is also a good account of the "intruded ministers," 1645–1660. No praise can be too high for such a work as this; it is not only a monument of industry, but almost a unique example of what may be done by a man who is sufficiently well informed, and who is really in love with his subject.

A striking contrast to the above, but no less admirable in its way, is Mr. Perkins' account of *Wimborne Minster and Christchurch Priory*.[1] This is only a small and inexpensive work, uniform with Bell's Cathedral Series, which is so deservedly popular. The historical description is very scanty, probably owing to the lack of data. Wimborne Minster was founded early in the eighth century—the dates vary from 705 to 723 A.D. It is known to have been the burial-place of King Æthelred, the brother and predecessor of Alfred. Reginald (Cardinal) Pole was Dean of Wimborne 1517–1537. A few notes of this kind exhaust the historical description. The main feature of the book is in its architectural descriptions, which are full and exact. Much the same has to be said of the account of Christchurch Priory, the origin of which is even still more obscure. The author states that the Priory is one of the finest churches in England below cathedral rank; and, judging by the description and illustrations, we have no difficulty in believing him. The illustrations are almost as numerous as they are excellent.

---

[1] *Wimborne Minster and Christchurch Priory.* A Short History of their Foundation and Description of their Buildings. By the Rev. Thomas Perkins, M.A., F.R.A.S. With Illustrations from Photographs by the Author. London: George Bell & Sons.

## BELLES LETTRES.

*Notes of an Outlook on Life*[1] is the title of a little volume consisting of selections from the private MSS. of Dr. Alexander Gardiner Mercer, a distinguished American theologian and philosopher. It is worthy of note that Dr. Mercer's private benevolence was in harmony with his humane and enlightened views. Though his mind was overshadowed by theological bias, he was anything but a conventional churchman. Let us extract a few of his finest aphorisms: "Many a heart not yet noble perhaps, but kindred with all nobleness, will when meeting nobleness turn to it with loyalty deeper than design or duty." "The greatest fool is not much of a fool until he thinks himself wise." "If a man believe himself great, let him know that he is to do something unexpected, yet regular— a miracle in look, and yet the most orderly and natural." "Despair is to the weak what resolution is to the strong: both carry us through until time works its gradual change." "There is at present no real doctrine as to morals. It is held not as a philosophy or a religion, but as a superstition."

The fault, perhaps, of these "Notes" is that they embody a certain amount of unconscious prejudice. The clerical attitude of mind rarely shows an emancipation from blind belief in the miraculous. Dr. Mercer, too, is afraid of pushing thought to its logical conclusion. He is terrified by the bogies of anarchy and revolution, which could not frighten a bold thinker like Nietzsche.

*Appearances : How to Keep Them Up on a Limited Income*[2] is one of those books which will either be accepted as an oracle or as a waste of time. Mrs. Praga knows the art of housekeeping, but she should remember that in housekeeping, as in everything else, "one man's meat is another man's poison." The advice given with regard to servants is not quite as original as that of Swift ; but to those intent on "keeping up appearances" it may be more useful.

The tenth volume of *The Works of Shakespeare*[3] in the "Eversley Series" contains "Coriolanus," "Timon of Athens," "Venus and Adonis," "The Rape of Lucrece," the "Sonnets," and "The Passionate Pilgrim." The Introduction to "Coriolanus" shows that the play is only partly the work of Shakespeare. Dr. Herford, the editor, makes this manifest by referring to the peculiarities of style by which certain passages are distinguishable from others. The theory as to the Sonnets is unsatisfactory. In fact, it leaves us "where we were." The printing of this excellent edition of

[1] *Notes of an Outlook on Life.* By Alexander Gardiner Mercer, S.T.D. (1817–1882). London : George Bell & Sons.
[2] *Appearances : How to Keep Them Up on a Limited Income.* By Mrs. Alfred Praga. London : John Long.
[3] *The Works of Shakespeare.* Vol. X. (Eversley Series.) London : Macmillan and Co., Ltd.

Shakespeare leaves nothing to be desired in point of clearness and accuracy.

*Aradia, or The Gospel of the Witches,*[1] belongs to that class of books which may be best described by Poe's words, "quaint and curious volumes of forgotten lore." Mr. Leland has studied Italian folk-lore with enthusiasm, and this work is one of the results of his labour. The book really deals with Pagan witch-lore. Diana largely figures in it. Some of the original Italian verse given by the author, with one exception, where he has scarcely elucidated a doubtful passage, is most fascinating. Diana is invoked by votaries who threaten her, in case of non-compliance with their wishes. The whole subject is, at the same time, uncanny and grotesque.

*Billy*[2] is one of the most charming books for children ever written. The hero of it, a little boy, is a philosopher in embryo. His questions about life, the lower animals, men and women and God, are astounding. The book, in its way, has flashes of genius. It is far more natural, more human, and more dramatic than Dickens's carol. We congratulate the author of *Chronicles of Westerley* on having given the world a masterpiece in child-litera-ture. The illustrations are excellent.

*Things I have Seen in War,*[3] by Irving Montagu, late War Corre-spondent of the *Illustrated London News,* presents us with some startling adventures, including *The Torture of Karl Hoffmann,* a story of the Commune, *A Woman in a Thousand,* a sketch of a heroic Frenchwoman, and others. The book is defective in style. Each sketch opens in the most conventional manner, but Mr. Irving Montagu writes about his actual experiences, and the matter of his book is certainly very interesting.

The volume, by Herr Heinrich Bulthaupt, entitled *Dramaturgie des Schauspiels*[4] deals with a number of well-known dramatists, including Shakespeare, Schiller, Goethe, Ibsen, and Sudermann. The author had studied the drama from what might be called an international point of view. His criticism is luminous and convincing, and he throws much fresh light on this most interesting subject.

[1] *Aradia or the Gospel of the Witches.* By Charles Leland. London : David Nutt.
[2] *Billy : A Sketch for "The New Boys."* By an Old Boy, author of *Culmshire Folk,* John Orlebas, Chronicles of *Westerley,* &c. London : The Leadenhall Press, Ltd.
[3] *Things I have Seen in War.* By Irving Montagu. With Sixteen Illustrations. London : Chatto & Windus.
[4] *Dramaturgie des Schauspiels.* Von Heinrich Bulthaupt. Oldenburg und Leipzig : chulzesche Hof-Buchhandlung und Hof-Buchdruckerei : A. Schwartz.

## POETRY.

Dr. Charles Stuart Welles has written a charming little volume of poems with the title of *The Lute and Lays*.[1] Some of the verses have a rich colouring, which reminds us of De Musset. For example:

> " Lo, the touch of velvet fingers,
> And the music of her breast,
> Beating full, majestic measures,
> Soothe my weary soul to rest."

The lines entitled " Bohemia " are also worthy of praise. Altogether, it is a book of verses which will delight lovers of purely lyrical poetry.

The fact that a book of American lyrics has been translated into German shows how literature binds nations together. *Lieder aus der Freinde*[2] is the title of a charming little volume containing German versions by Herr Karl Knortz of short poems by John J. Piatt, Thomas B. Aldrich, Minot J. Savage, Bret Harte, Ella Wheeler, and others. The selections display taste, sympathy, and appreciation, and show that Transatlantic genius finds genuine admirers in the " Faterlandt."

*Neue Lieder*,[3] by Marie Itzerott, is a volume of beautiful poetry, the product of a muse inspired by true natural emotion and sympathy with all high and noble ideas. " Sappho " is an exquisite fragment, " Nein, nein! " and " Juni " have a splendid lyrical ring. The writer of these verses is certainly enslaved by " the vision and the faculty divine."

---

## ART.

A very entertaining " Chapter in the History of the Music of the Past in Edinburgh " has been written by the Lecturer on Physiology in the University of St. Andrews, under the title of the hall where the music was produced—*Saint Cecilia's Hall in the Niddry Wynd*.[4] " The very walls still stand that vibrated to the strains of the *Messiah* as a *new* oratorio, that echoed to the tenor of Tenducci and the falsetto of Corri; in this very hall an old gentleman was overheard to say, on hearing for the first time a sonata of Haydn's, ' Poor new-fangled stuff! I hope we shall never hear it again ';

[1] *The Lute and Lays.* By Charles S. Welles. London : George Bell & Sons.
[2] *Lieder aus der Freinde : Frieie.* Uebersetsunken. Von Karl Knortz. Oldenburg und Leipzic, Hof-Buchandlung und Hof-Buchdruckerei : A. Schwartz.
[3] *Neue Lieder.* Von Marie Itzerott. Oldenburg und Leipzig, Schulzesche Hof-Buchhandlung und Hof-Buchdruckerei : A. Schwartz.
[4] *Saint Cecilia's Hall in the Niddry Wynd.* By David Fraser Harris. Edinburgh and London : Oliphant, Anderson & Ferrier. 1899.

that very cupola looked down upon the flirtations of the beautiful Eglantine Maxwell, saw behind the facile fan of Jane, Duchess of Gordon, and watched the rhythm of the melody flush the damask cheek of the heavenly Miss Burnet with a matchlessly delicate hue."

This is a brave beginning, which is justified in the sequel. The book is one of those careful descriptions of places and local events, with their contemporary colour and life of personages of local renown, which have their great use now that the memory of the past is fading in mere tradition. It helps to form an enlightened consciousness—*conscientia informata*—in the citizens of Edinburgh that they are denizens of no mean city ; and it further enlightens the general reader as to the realities of a century ago in a typical and not unimportant fragment of civilised society. Bibliography, maps and plans, anecdotes of players and singers and audience, are all satisfactory from one who loves so " fervently Edinburgh—queen of cities—and her romantic story."

The new volume in Messrs. Bell and Sons' series of " Great Masters in Painting and Sculpture " is by Mr. Henry Strachey, and deals with *Raphael*.[1] It has all the excellent qualities of a popular kind noted in the previous volumes of the series—plates and text, indexes and, particularly, the catalogue of the Master's works, classified by the museums or collections in which they are to be found. We have only to regret that the drawings of Raphael in the principal museums could not have been indexed for the fuller satisfaction of the many who will use this little book as a guide in their art studies. But the work done is good—very good, indeed— all the more so that the author loves and defends his subject.

He is evidently right in saying that Raphael ended the Middle Ages as far as art was concerned, and he notes the curious fact that this Roman Catholic of the Rome of Luther's abhorrence fixed the Puritan imagination of Biblical scenes. Surely this lasting deed done in art history amply balances whatever still remains of the criticisms of Ruskin, whose mind was sealed up against even Puritan humanism, and of the admirers of a Velazquez whom the great Spanish painter never recognised in himself. The book is, however, not all controversial or even critical, but simply wellinformed, sensible, and sympathetic. Rio, who is a little forgotten as an art-writer, would have confirmed usefully many of our author's ideas. Perhaps the severe Morelli's higher criticism might have been noted in regard to the Louvre *Young Man's* portrait. But this is the best and completest handy-book of its subject yet published.

[1] *Raphael*. By Henry Strachey. ("Great Masters in Painting and Sculpture ' ' Series.) London : George Bell & Sons. 1900.

# THE

# WESTMINSTER REVIEW.

Vol. CLIII. No. 4.—April 1900.

## THE PROBLEM IN SOUTH AFRICA.

### BOER *V.* BRITON.

### II.

In 1874 Lord Carnarvon became Colonial Minister, and encouraged by the success of the Canadian Confederation of 1867, in which he had taken a leading part, he forwarded a similar scheme to the Governor at the Cape. As an exponent of his policy he sent out Mr. Froude, but before his arrival the Cape Assembly had passed a resolution (June 1875) to the effect that such a movement should originate in South Africa. The prevailing opinion was clearly in favour of some form of Federation, and a man of some diplomatic experience and tact might have revived and led the movement, but Froude, possessing neither, by his ill-considered public utterances speedily found himself in antagonism with the Governor, his Ministers, and public opinion throughout the colony.

At the special request of Lord Carnarvon, Sir Bartle Frere went out to carry through, if possible, a South African Confederation under the British flag. He had scarcely landed when the annexation of the Transvaal by Sir Theophilus Shepstone, on April 12, 1877, was announced.

The Republic, as we have seen, was in a parlous state. Its treasury was empty, its civil and military organisation had collapsed, its President had resigned, its forces had been repulsed by the Matabele under Secocoeni, who was carrying fire and sword through the northern districts. On the east three large bodies of Zulus, between 30,000 and 40,000 in number, were gathered on the border, only waiting the word from Cetewayo to carry destruction up to the very walls of Pretoria. If Shepstone had delayed the annexation a few months longer—Mr. Rider Haggard says a few weeks [1]—it is probable that the Boers would have been wiped out, together with such English settlers as there then were.[2] He would appear, however, to have been somewhat premature. It was, of course, a delicate situation. A larger pressure from without might have resulted in the transference taking place in a more voluntary fashion. Voluntary union was preferable to annexation. Out of 8000 voters only 3000 had recorded their votes for annexation. The remainder sullenly acquiesced.

Shepstone's grave mistake, however, as Mr. FitzPatrick rightly points out, was his secret arrangement with the Boer leaders, who, whilst privately encouraging him to take over the government, prevailed upon him to allow them, for the sake of appearances as they said—" to save their face " with the Irreconcilables—to make formal protests through the Executive and the Volksraad against the annexation. It is clear that Shepstone was hoodwinked. These leaders, at any rate Kruger and his party, wished to be in a position, when the British Government had pulled the chestnuts out of the fire, to agitate for the restitution of their dearly loved independence. In fact, the delegates, Kruger and Jorissen, immediately started for England to agitate against the annexation, although it does not appear that either of them had much faith in their mission.[3] As Mr. FitzPatrick rightly says, the compromise was a most improper one.[4] With this view Mr. Martineau also agrees.

Both Secocoeni and Cetewayo acquiesced in the situation, and on the return of Kruger and Jorissen the latter resumed his office of Attorney-General, a post for which he was totally unfitted, and the former became a member of the Executive Council. It had been one of the terms of the compromise that these men and some other leaders, notably Joubert, should enjoy salaried positions in the new Government. It was soon found necessary to dismiss Mr. Jorissen on the ground of incompetence, and when Mr. Kruger's appointment expired, in November 1877, he was not reappointed. He had made repeated applications for an increase of salary, and there was a serious charge of misrepresentation in money matters preferred against him. At any rate, from this moment he joined the agitation against the British rule.

This had been commenced in the western province of Cape Colony by a party consisting chiefly of Hollanders, whose organs were the *Volkstem* and the *Natal Witness*, edited by the notorious Aylward, a professional agitator, said to have been one of the murderers of

---

[1] *The Last Boer Trek*, p. 61.
[2] Mr. Haggard effectually disposes of the charge that Shepstone had called up the Zulus to constrain the Boers into accepting the annexation.—*The Last Boer Trek*, pp. 59–64.
[3] *The Transvaal Trouble*, p. 20.  [4] *The Transvaal from Within*, p. 15.

the Manchester policeman, and who was in receipt of the moneys subscribed by the Irish rebel societies for the purpose of inciting the Boers to rise.

It had been the intention of Sir Bartle Frere, as High Commissioner, to go up to Pretoria to settle the provisions of the new Constitution, but, unfortunately, unforeseen circumstances prevented him from carrying this out for two years. Shepstone was occupied for some months in settling the Zulu boundary dispute, receiving the submission of Secocoeni, and discharging the liabilities of the late Republic. Meanwhile Sir Bartle Frere was occupied with the Galeka rising, which had scarcely been repressed when the Gaikas rose. The latter war led to differences as to its conduct between the Governor and the Molteno-Merriman Ministry, which resulted in the latter's dismissal and the succession to office of Mr. Gordon Sprigg, under whom the war was brought to a successful conclusion.

In March 1878 Secocoeni, at the instigation, it is alleged, of a Boer named Abel Erasmus, rose, and although kept in check by a small force under Major Clarke, was only finally defeated after the Zulu War by Sir Garnet Wolseley.

Just at this moment came the news of Lord Carnarvon's resignation, which Mr. Martineau describes as

"the first blow to the prospect of Federation and to a consistent policy in South Africa."

And such Frere evidently regarded it. It was particularly unfortunate, as the new Sprigg Ministry had promised a hearty support to the policy of Confederation.

In December the Zulu storm burst forth, and on the 11th Frere delivered his ultimatum. In answer to his and Lord Chelmsford's repeated applications for reinforcements Sir M. Hicks-Beach, who had succeeded Lord Carnarvon, declared that the Government were not prepared to comply, stating that

"all the information that has hitherto reached them with respect to the position of affairs in Zululand appears to them to justify a confident hope that by the exercise of prudence, and by meeting the Zulus in a spirit of forbearance and reasonable compromise, it will be possible to avert the very serious evil of a war with Cetewayo."

A second despatch, which arrived two days after the ultimatum, was to the same effect, but it was impossible then for Frere to withdraw.

The war commenced disastrously with the fatal field of Isandhlwana, a result entirely due to the lack of precautions urged by Kruger, Joubert, and other colonials experienced in Zulu warfare. The news was received in England with the utmost consternation, and Frere fell a victim to the cry for a scapegoat. The wisdom of his action was then, and is now, a matter of controversy, but in the opinion of those on the spot best capable of judging, Frere was right in carrying the war into the enemy's country. Had he not done so, Cetewayo would have overrun Natal and forced the colonial Zulus, who as it was remained neutral, to join his impis.

The arrangements for the war having now passed into military hands, Frere was at liberty to pay his long-promised visit to the Transvaal.

Meanwhile, matters had been going from bad to worse in the Transvaal. A second deputation to England had met with no better success than the first. In July 1878 a petition had been forwarded to Frere complaining that the Volksraad had not been summoned and no constitution of any kind created; an unfamiliar system of justice introduced; the contract for the Delagoa Bay Railway repudiated, and public meetings suppressed. It also alleged that Shepstone was not a *persona grata*, and, above all, that the promised protection against Secocoeni and the Zulus had not been afforded. Early in January 1879 Shepstone ceased to be administrator of the Transvaal, and Colonel Lanyon was appointed in his place. According to Frere, Shepstone was not the man for the post. He was too reticent, procrastinating, and fond of diplomatic subtlety, and had no sort of sympathy with the Boers; but the appointment of his successor was an even graver mistake. His administration was necessarily autocratic in form, and became autocratic in spirit also. He was described to Mr. James Bryce

"as stiff in mind and arrogant in temper, incapable of making allowances for the homely manners of the Boers, and of adapting himself to the social equality which prevailed among them. A trifling cause aggravated their dislike. His complexion was swarthy, and they suspected that this might be due to some tinge of negro blood. He refused to listen to their complaints, levied taxes strictly, causing even the beloved ox-waggon to be seized when money was not forthcoming, and soon turned their smouldering discontent into active disaffection." [1]

Halfway between Heidelburg and Pretoria Frere came upon the Boer camp which had been formed shortly after Isandhlwana, and had soon become the centre of disaffection whence emissaries had been sent to native chiefs inciting them to follow Cetewayo's example. Beyond stopping the mail carts, however, little overt action had been taken. Joubert is described by Mr. FitzPatrick "as the only honest Protestant" amongst the malcontents. But the following incident somewhat belies this flattering estimate. On the return of Kruger and Joubert from England, a meeting was held at Potchefstrom, which resolved upon regaining the independence of the Transvaal, and Joubert was deputed to go and see Frere, which he did at Maritzburg, when the latter told him it was impossible, but gave him written and verbal promises of local self-government.

[1] *Impressions of South Africa*, p. 157.

When Frere was discussing the position with the Committee at the camp, it appeared that Joubert had never delivered his messages. Joubert admitted the breach of faith and was angrily dismissed by Frere, who declared he would have nothing more to do with him.

In this instance Joubert would appear to have lived up to his reputation of "slimness." The last thing he desired was a settlement, and so he deliberately held back anything which might bring it about.

Then followed the historic Conference at Erasmus Farm and the arrangement of terms for the future settlement of the country. On April 18 the camp broke up and the Boers dispersed, fortunately before Reuter's telegram announcing that the Government had, in a despatch to Frere laid on the table of the House of Commons, censured his action, became known in the Transvaal. Thus Frere was thrown to the wolves by his own party, scarcely a man in either House venturing to defend him. Frere's Zulu policy, as I have said, is open to question, but it had been supported by the Conservative Government up to a point when it was impossible to change it. If any one man is to be picked out as responsible for the muddle, it is Sir M. Hicks-Beach. The despatch containing the censure was accompanied by a general expression of continued confidence!

But the Government had a curious way of showing such confidence. Sir Garnet Wolseley was sent out to supersede Frere as High Commissioner of the Transvaal, Natal, and all the adjoining eastern portion of South Africa. He was also appointed to supersede Lord Chelmsford, but before his arrival the latter had settled the Zulu War by the battle of Ulundi. Having settled the Zulu question in a very perfunctory fashion, Sir Garnet proceeded to the Transvaal, and by one blow broke the power of Secocoeni and took him prisoner.

Returning to Pretoria, Wolseley announced the new Constitution, which was to consist of a nominated council, thus falsifying Frere's pledges of an autonomous government. Meanwhile, the malcontents were openly preaching rebellion, parts of the country were disturbed and ammunition plundered. A mass meeting was held, December 10, on the High Veldt advocating these views and threatening the absentees.

On December 25, 26, and 27, Mr. Gladstone delivered the famous Midlothian speeches, which are declared by Tory writers to have been direct incitements to the Boers to rebel. Upon an examination of these speeches it will be found that they contain nothing but a general objection to premature expansion of the Empire and to the assumption of burdensome obligations. The Transvaal is given as an instance. Egypt, Cyprus, Armenia, and Afghanistan are given as others. In some Mr. Gladstone was mistaken in underrating the strength of the country, in others he was right. The pledges then

made by the Tory Ministry to Armenia have been broken by the
present Government.   In a speech delivered to a small Liverpool deputation on December 29, Mr. Gladstone was more specific.   He asked :

> " Is it not wonderful that those who are free men, and whose fathers have
> been free men, and who consider that freedom is an essential condition of
> civic life, and that without it you can have nothing great and nothing
> noble in political society—is it not marvellous . . . that we are to march
> upon another body of free men, and against their will subject them to
> despotic government ? " [1]

Here Gladstone was blaming, and rightly blaming, the Government
for the measures they were taking.   He was not objecting to the
annexation, but to the manner in which it was being carried out.
Frere himself some months previously had written :

> " It was clear to me that it was not the annexation so much as the
> neglect to fulfil the promises and the expectations held out by Shepstone
> when he took over the Government that has stirred up the great mass of
> the Boers and given a handle to agitators."

As Mr. FitzPatrick rightly says, the disaffection was caused by
" the failure to fulfil the conditions of annexation." [2]   Upon this
subject Mr. Haggard writes as a mere political partisan.

There is no doubt that the malcontents took advantage of
Gladstone's language, and a Boer meeting held on March 18, 1880,
sent a letter to him, expressing thanks for his sympathy.   In April
Gladstone was returned to power, and on June 8 he wrote in answer
to their letter :

> "Our judgment is that the Queen cannot be advised to relinquish her
> sovereignty over the Transvaal ; but consistently with the maintenance of
> sovereignty, we desire that the white inhabitants of the Transvaal should,
> without prejudice to the rest of the population, enjoy the fullest liberty to
> manage their local affairs.   We believe that this liberty may be most
> easily and promptly conceded to the Transvaal as a member of a South
> African Confederation."

Such a Confederation, however, had been rendered impossible by
Frere's recall in August.   Under Frere the colonists were quite
prepared to enter upon this policy, but were naturally reluctant to
commit themselves to the hands of a new and unknown High
Commissioner.   Frere's authority, too, might have been sufficient
with the Boers themselves.   But he was strongly attacked by some
of the leading Liberals, such as Mr. Courtney, Sir Wilfrid Lawson,
and Mr. John Morley, and Gladstone had not forgotten his Afghan
policy and the Zulu War.   Moreover, his Conservative friends gave
him practically no support.   Meanwhile, Kruger and Jorissen had
in May arrived in Cape Town to intrigue with members of the
Legislative Assembly, and to make preparations for an armed
rebellion.   They were so far successful in their first object that a

---

[1] *Times*, December 30, 1879.          [2] *The Transvaal from Within*, p. 29.

division was not taken in the Assembly upon the Conference proposals, which were thus indefinitely postponed. This refusal of the Cape Parliament "to take even the preliminary step of a conference" was the ostensible reason for Frere's recall.

A mutual friend of Frere and Kruger went to see the latter and reminded him of Frere's promise of local self-government, and ultimately of a constitution as liberal as that of Cape Colony. Kruger and Jorissen declared

"their willingness to accept such a constitution provided the annexation were rescinded and the English flag hauled down for a single day as a confession of national error and apology for national wrong-doing."

They declined, however, to allow this proposal to be officially laid before Frere

"because the Governor's power was gone, and he was, they were assured, to be recalled."

Frere asked them

"to postpone their departure from Cape Town till Sir George Colley, then daily expected, arrived." [1]

This they did, but Colley, underestimating the disaffection and the military resources of the Boers, declined to see them. With the return of Kruger and Jorissen the agitation was renewed with increased vigour. A mass meeting was convened for January 8, 1881, but in consequence of the Bezeidenhout incident the meeting was summoned for December 8, 1880. In November of the latter year Bezeidenhout had refused to pay his taxes. His waggon was thereupon seized in execution and put up for sale, when a party of armed Boers prevented the sale. The force sent by Lanyon to arrest the rioters was too weak, and on his appeal for more troops Colley was unable to respond owing to the outbreak of the Basuto war, to which Lanyon had himself allowed a body of 300 trained volunteers to depart. The Transvaal was practically undefended. The mass meeting was held at Paarde Kraal, at which the independence was declared, and the famous triumvirate—Kruger, Joubert, and Pretorius—was appointed. On Dingaan's Day, December 16, the Republic was formally proclaimed.

The Boers had chosen the most favourable opportunity for their revolt. The country was denuded of English troops, the Government was fully occupied with the Basuto rising, and, above all, the Zulus and the Secocoeni had been crushed.

Mr. James Bryce considers the destruction of the Zulu power to have been the third blunder of the Government; the other two being the failure to grant local autonomy and the appointment of Lanyon.

[1] *The Transvaal Trouble*, p. 239.

" It was," he says, " probably necessary to deal with Sikukuni, though the British Government seems to have forgotten its former doubts as to the right of the Boers to the territory of that chief, but in extinguishing the Zulu Kingdom the High Commissioner overlooked the fact that he was also extinguishing the strongest motive which the Republicans had for remaining British subjects."[1]

Whether the Zulu war would have broken out but for Frere's ultimatum is a moot point. As we have already stated, the better opinion is that it would. Mr. Bryce himself seems to forget that the protection of the Boers from the Zulus was a term of the annexation, and, in fact, the principal motive for its acceptance.

Mr. Bryce, no doubt, followed Gladstone in denouncing the war, but the latter certainly did not denounce it on the ground that the destruction of Zulu power would extinguish the strongest motive for the Boer acquiescence in British rule. This allegation appears to me a mere afterthought.

To the many virtues claimed for the Boers common gratitude can scarcely be added. Just as the voortrekkers in Natal gladly availed themselves of British assistance against the Zulus, and when the danger was past rejected British control, so in the Transvaal their descendants accepted annexation to save their skins, and when they no longer required protection, and the British Government was occupied with native troubles, they seized the opportunity to sever the British connection. On the other hand, political gratitude is never expected by politicians, and is always regarded as a broken reed. In the non-fulfilment of the British promises of autonomy they had ample excuse for remonstrance. Technically they had a perfectly sound *casus belli.* If some earnest had been shown of carrying into effect Frere's pledges, the rebellion might have been averted. In their neglect of this both Beaconsfield's and Gladstone's Ministry stand convicted, and both were equally to blame in allowing a noisy minority of malcontents to gain the upper hand. Upon this point Frere wrote, July 25, 1881 :

" No doubt the non-fulfilment of our promises of some sort of self-government was the cause which kept in the ranks of the malcontents many Boers who would otherwise have reluctantly acquiesced in the annexation of the Transvaal. For this breach of faith Liberals and Conservatives are equally to be blamed, perhaps the Conservatives most, for it was they who divided the authority Lord Carnarvon had united in my hands, and prevented the consideration of my proposals for a constitution such as Mr. Sprigg and Mr. Brand concurred in suggesting. But the Liberals cannot escape blame, for it was they who allowed six months to elapse without any sign of willingness to repair the omission of their predecessors, which I specially brought to Lord Kimberley's notice in the only interview I had with him after my return home."[2]

Culpable as this neglect undoubtedly was, the Boer leaders must have known perfectly well that the delay had been caused by circumstances over which the Government had little control, and from

---

[1] *Impressions of South Africa,* p. 185.　　[2] *The Transvaal Trouble,* pp. 251-2.

Gladstone's speeches they might have gathered that eventually the fullest form of local self-government would have been granted. From their actions, however, it is clear that they would be content with nothing less than independence. In their proclamation, it is true, they declared their willingness to enter into confederation and to guide their native policy by general rules adopted in concurrence with the Colonies and States of South Africa.

A letter covering this proclamation to Lanyon contained the following paragraph :

" We declare in the most solemn manner that we have no desire to spill blood, and that from our side we do not wish war. It lies in your hands to force us to appeal to arms in self-defence."

A reply within forty-eight hours was demanded. On the very same day that this was despatched a Boer force opened fire on the English garrison at Potchefstroom, and Lanyon's reply could barely have reached the Triumvirate at Heidelberg when a detachment of the 94th was ambushed at Bronkers Spruit, some eighty miles from the rebel camp.

It is impossible to resist the conclusion that the Boers committed a deliberately designed piece of cold-blooded treachery. They advanced under a flag of truce, which they violated directly they had surrounded and marked our troops. In a few minutes 157 men fell out of 250.

The next incident is even more outrageous. Captains Elliott and Lambert, the two surviving officers of Bronkers Spruit, upon reaching the rebel camp as prisoners, accepted the offer of release on parole. An escort was provided to put them over the border, but before this was reached the escort disappeared. Left to themselves, they followed the Vaal for some days looking for the ferry, when they were stopped and accused of breaking their parole. The Boers then forced them to ford the river in their cart, which had scarcely entered the river before it overturned, and the Boers, on the pretence that the prisoners were seeking to return, opened fire. Elliott was struck and swept away by the current, and Lambert, on reaching the opposite bank, was still under heavy fire for some 200 yards.[1]

A more infamous murder was never more deliberately planned.

These instances of cowardice and treachery do not stand alone. Several other similar murders occurred, and at Ingogo the white flag was treacherously abused and the red cross disregarded.

These incidents are sadly inconsistent with the alleged character for Boer simplicity and piety.

We may well pause here to inquire whether the Boer character had deteriorated or whether it had merely retained its seventeenth-century standard. Mr. Martineau remarks that

[1] *Transvaal from Within*, p. 33.

"the Boers have lost, it is said, in the course of generations, under changed conditions of life, and by contact with savage races, much of the truthfulness which marked their Puritan ancestors of the seventeenth century."

But, he continues, the old ideal, if not so well acted up to, is still held in reverence. And Frere showed that a successful appeal to it could be made.

Upon the evidence as to character before and after the Great Trek, it would appear that, cut off from all contact with civilisation and engaged in constant savage warfare, the Transvaalers cannot be placed in the same class with the old Dutch colonists. They certainly imbibed in warfare the spirit and methods of their hereditary native opponents. Whether they deteriorated in civil affairs is not so clear. In 1879 Mr. George Lacy, who, amongst other things, was an itinerant trader, roundly asserts that they were a parcel of thieves,[1] and his description is corroborated by Mrs. Lionel Phillips, who states that to this day special attendants are appointed in the stores to watch Boer customers. When a Boer is caught pilfering nothing is said, but the price of the article annexed is silently added to the bill, which is paid without dispute.[2]

Of their piety, of course, there is no question, but it may be doubted whether religious professions have any more effect upon conduct in the Transvaal than elsewhere. Men must be judged not by their religious or political professions, but by their conduct. The morality of the Boers seems to me to be greater in the breach than in the observance. It is quite clear that Boer character will not bear comparison with that of the Cape and Natal Dutch, which has developed with the advancing tide of progress and civilisation.

It must not be supposed, however, that the graphic pictures of Boer life, with all its pastoral simplicity, drawn by such writers as Olive Schreiner, Du Plessis, "Cios," and other Transvaalers are untrue. They represent, perhaps, more truly the homely, hard-working, simple-minded but ignorant, God-fearing farmer of the past than of to-day; but the Boer of to-day may display all these virtues and many others in the bosom of his family, and yet in his relations with the hated Englishman be guilty of untruthfulness, treachery, duplicity, and deceit.

Much of this, as I have said, he has learned from his black antagonists, but much more is due to his study of the Old Testament, in whose demoralising precepts he is steeped to the full. From the Old Testament he draws his belief in the system of slavery and in the wholesale extermination of the conquered foe—man, woman, and child. His code of honour in his dealings with strangers is no higher than that of the semi-civilised tribes of Israel. In short, the

[1] *Pictures of Travel, Sport and Adventure*, p. 237. [2] *South African Recollections*, p. 13.

Boer is a fanatic, a sincere fanatic no doubt, but still a fanatic. Criminal offences amongst themselves appear to be practically non-existent. But a Boer who would never dream of robbing a fellow Boer seems to have no scruple in pilfering the stores of a Hollander or Englishman. They would appear to have one code of honour in their dealings with one another and quite a different one in their transactions with strangers. Their contact with wandering traders, prospectors, adventurers, and ne'er-do-wells, who flooded the country in the early seventies and who preyed on the unsophisticated Boer community in the most unscrupulous manner, had also, no doubt, a demoralising effect, and filled them, at any rate, with that suspicion which they still entertain for all foreigners.[1]

Another peculiar and discreditable trait in the Boer character is within my personal experience. Of recent years numerous educated Transvaalers and Free Staters have entered our Inns of Court in order to be called to the Bar. Whilst here they are hospitably received and entertained by Englishmen. Their object in becoming members of the English Bar is to increase their professional standing and consequently their emoluments. And yet they all expressed their hatred of England, and one before leaving for the war last year said he should die happy if he could shoot six redcoats! I hear that he has himself been shot. One would have supposed that men with such feelings as these would have had too much pride to solicit and receive favours from a nation they profess to hate and despise.

To return to the events of the war. On January 28 Colley was severely repulsed at Laing's Nek; on February 8 he fought a drawn battle on the Ingogo Heights; and on February 27 he met with the crushing defeat and his own death on the Majuba.

Few events have been the subject of more bitter controversy than the reversal of the annexation of 1877 which now followed. Public men did not hesitate to describe it as a cowardly surrender, and no statesman was ever more savagely attacked than Gladstone. And writers of to-day like Mr. Haggard and Mr. FitzPatrick still continue to denounce him and to compare his tactics to those of a pettifogging attorney. The Boers admit that Sir Evelyn Wood held them in the hollow of his hand. To prosecute the war then would have been a mere blood feud of revenge. To stay his hand was an action which was likely in the highest degree to appeal to a man of Mr. Gladstone's nobility of character; but he was too good a politician to suppose that such an act of magnanimity, thoroughly unpopular as it was, would redound to his political credit, or would be appreciated by the enemy. It may be that this formed one of the motives for his action, but the principal reason, and probably the only one, lay deeper. We have seen how even the Cape Assembly, under the thoroughly patriotic Ministry of Sprigg, had sympathised with the Boers, and this feeling had been increased by the continued neglect to grant them autonomous government and by the suspicion that there was no intention to grant it.   The successes of the Boers, writes Mr. Martineau,

" had the additional bad effect of obtaining for them sympathy and adhesion among the Dutch population elsewhere, and there was danger lest out of the war should arise a bitter hostility between the Dutch and English throughout South Africa." [1]

"The British Government," says Mr. Bryce, "were advised from the Cape that the invasion of the Transvaal might probably light up a civil war through the two colonies."

"Whether such a race conflict," he adds, "would, in fact, have broken out all over South Africa is a question on which opinion is still divided, and about which men may dispute for ever.   The British Government, however, deemed the risk of it a real one, and by that view their action was mainly governed.   After careful inquiries from those best qualified to judge, I am inclined to think they were right." [2]

Additional evidence tending to confirm this view is given by Dr. Jorissen's *Transvaalsche Herinneringen*, published in 1897 in Dutch.   It has long been known that as early as February 12—four days after the drawn battle of Ingogo—negotiations were in progress between Colley and Kruger, and on the 21st of that month Colley offered to suspend hostilities, in order that a Royal Commission of Inquiry might be appointed, and a liberal constitution for the Transvaal framed.   Unfortunately Kruger had been called away by a Kaffir rising, and Colley receiving no reply recommenced hostilities. Sir Evelyn Wood, who succeeded Colley, was not only General in Command, but also High Commissioner for South Africa and Governor of Natal.   At this moment Brand, President of the Orange Free State, offered his services as mediator, and an armistice was arranged from March 6 to 14, afterwards prolonged to the 23rd.   Jorissen's evidence must be taken for what it is worth, but it is to the effect that on March 19 an arrangement was made at Laing's Nek between the Boers and De Villiers, Commandant of Harrismith in the Orange Free State, and Rath, a member of the Volksraad, by which, if acceptable terms were not granted to the Transvaal, a commando of Free State Boers, equal to two British regiments, should descend into Natal and intercept the movements of fresh troops landing at Durban.   And on the same day a proclamation was prepared, appealing to all Dutch Afrikanders as kinsmen, and demanding their assistance in prosecuting the war.   Early on the 21st, before the hour fixed for the Conference, Brand sought a private interview with Sir Evelyn Wood :

" The recognition of Transvaal independence was conceded on that very day, and in two days was approved by telegraph from London." [3]

---

[1] *The Transvaal Trouble*, pp. 245-246.       [2] *Impressions of South Africa*, pp. 162-3.
[3] Du Plessis, *The Transvaal Boer*, p. 119.

In a recent speech Lord Kimberley has assigned the same motive for this sudden reversal of policy.

Mr. Chamberlain, speaking at Birmingham, subsequently declared that Lord Kimberley must be mistaken, as such a reason was in itself improbable. The reason was, he asserted, at any rate speaking for himself,

"that the Transvaal had been annexed under an evident misapprehension. It had been taken by Lord Beaconsfield on information conveyed to his Government that the majority of the Boers were themselves desirous of annexation. It was proved afterwards that that was not the case. We thought, rightly or wrongly, that under these circumstances the annexation should be cancelled, provided we could get conditions which would secure our rights and secure the rights of British subjects. And accordingly, when the Boers expressed their willingness to assent to these conditions, we did not think it was the duty of a Christian country to prosecute a war for which they had no longer a policy of justification, but a policy of revenge. We thought at that time that the Boers, partly from gratitude, partly from self-interest, would observe the conditions to which they assented. We were egregiously mistaken." [1]

It seems to me that Lord Kimberley's version of the motive which influenced the Cabinet is more likely to be correct, since he was Colonial Secretary at the time. The motive assigned by Mr. Chamberlain for his share in the transaction may have influenced him and others in the Administration, but it would not by itself be a sufficient reason for abandoning the loyalists and the natives in the Transvaal. As Mr. Bryce truly says, the loss of the Transvaal seemed a slight evil in comparison with a civil war, which would have destroyed the prospects of peace and welfare of the two colonies for many years to come.

As events have turned out, it must now be recognised that it would have been wiser to have run this risk and have established the supremacy of Britain as the paramount Power in fact as well as in name.

The annual celebration of Majuba Day as a national holiday by the Boers has no doubt been gall and wormwood to the British in South Africa, but its importance has been much exaggerated. Mr. Balfour struck the right note when he recently described it as

"a very small military action—in which I think less than half a regiment was engaged—and which, in my judgment, may be absolutely ignored, both in the present controversy and in any future consideration connected with South Africa."

Whatever the disgrace, however, it is now wiped out by Paardeburg.

Gladstone did not stand alone in committing mistakes, if mistakes were made. The original cause of the trouble beyond all dispute was the neglect of the Conservative Government to establish a liberal constitution in the Transvaal. In this neglect Gladstone must take his share, although in his case the delay was more due to the action of the Colonial Office in putting off the matter until the Confederation scheme could be carried through.

I fail to see that Gladstone's policy was widely different from that of the Conservative Government, which through Frere had promised a constitution as liberal as that of Cape Colony. What Gladstone denounced was not the annexation, which he accepted as an existing fact, but the failure to grant any local self-government whatsoever. In his own words we had

"put ourselves in the strange predicament of the free subjects of a monarch going to coerce the free subjects of a Republic and compel them to accept a citizenship which they decline and refuse."[1]

He also declared that Cyprus and the Transvaal had been acquired by "means dishonourable to the character of our country." With this view must be associated Mr. Chamberlain, the Duke of Devonshire, and Mr. Goschen. Whether this is the correct view is still a matter of controversy. Mr. Chamberlain, at any rate in the passage from his recent speech quoted above, assents to it.

The main charge against Gladstone must be his abandonment of the loyal settlers who had invested their capital and made their homes in the country upon the assurances of the British Government that the Queen's authority would never be withdrawn.

The compensation of £1,400,000 allotted to them, according to Mr. FitzPatrick, was reduced to £400,000, but he does not state how this larger sum was arrived at, nor does he explain the reduction. Mr. Haggard, who goes more fully into this point, says nothing about the odd million. In any case this abandonment of the loyalists is a deplorable feature of the settlement. The native chiefs also bitterly resented the retrocession, declaring that they had been perfectly contented under the Queen's Government, and that the country originally belonged to them and not to the Boers, who had always ill-treated them. But if in view of graver eventualities these two bodies had to be sacrificed, due provision ought to have been made for their protection in the Convention. By the Convention of Pretoria, 1881, Great Britain was declared to be the suzerain power, with the right (1) to appoint a Resident; (2) to move troops through the State; and (3) to control the external relations of the Transvaal. By Article 5

"all sentences passed upon persons who may be convicted of offences contrary to the rules of civilised warfare during recent hostilities"

were to be carried out. By Article 12 all loyalists were to have

"full liberty to reside in the country with enjoyment of all civil rights and protection for their persons and property."

[1] Speech at Dalkeith; *Times*, November 27, 1879.

And by Article 16

"no slavery or apprenticeship partaking of slavery"

was to be tolerated.

This last provision is specific enough, and we shall see later how far it was observed by the Transvaal State.   Article 5 proved a dead letter owing to the composition of the Commission and the fact that no Boer jury could be found to convict the murderers of Elliott, Barber and Malcolm.   No other perpetrator was even put on trial. For their own honour the Boers should have brought these criminals to justice, but apparently these crimes had the approval of, at any rate, the governing classes in the Transvaal.

Article 12 must be left for future examination, and also Article 26 which deals with the rights of future aliens.

But the Boer Government chafed under the restrictions imposed upon their foreign relations, and finally, in 1884, induced Lord Derby, then Colonial Secretary, to agree to a new Convention. The introduction to the Convention of London, 1884, contains the recital that the articles of the new Convention shall be substituted for the articles of the old Convention.   There has been much controversy as to whether the preamble of the 1881 Convention, which contains the words

" complete self-government subject to the suzerainty of her Majesty,"

is still in force or not.   The Boers contend that it is not.   If so, then it is said that the independence goes with it, but the answer to this is found in the Introduction of the new Convention, which recites that the Transvaal State shall be known as the South African Republic.   But whether it remains or not is, to my mind, immaterial.   In law a preamble to a statute has no force *per se*.   It only explains, and it cannot extend, the scope of the statute.   In the case of the old Convention the word suzerainty was confined to the Powers described in Article 2.   Assuming it to be still in force it is now defined by Article 4 of the new Convention.

Both parties to the treaty, however, would appear to have acted upon the assumption that the preamble had gone.   Lord Derby, in explaining the treaty in the House of Lords, said :

" We have abstained from using the word suzerainty because it was not capable of a legal definition, and because it seemed a word which was likely to lead to misconception and misunderstanding."

And on another occasion, when asked by the Earl of Cadogan whether by the Convention the suzerainty was abolished, he replied that the substance if not the name remained as defined by Article 4.

Mr. Appleton's contention,[1] then, that the Convention of 1884

---

[1] Lewis Appleton, *Britain and the Boers*, p. 6.

did not supervene or cancel that of 1881, would appear to be ill-founded.  However this may be, Earl Spencer is correct when he says that from 1884 until the recent negotiations the word suzerainty was never used.[1]

The fact that Lord Derby in preparing the new treaty deleted the preamble and the passages relating to suzerainty in a copy of the old Convention, is only some evidence of his intention to abandon it, but is by no means conclusive as some writers contend, as it is equally compatible with the view that he only used the old Convention as a draft.

Mr. Reitz contends that under the London Convention the South African Republic became a Sovereign Independent State, and compares it with Belgium.  "Sovereignty," he asserts, "need not of necessity be absolute."[2]  This proposition is obviously self-contradictory.  Belgium is in a peculiar position, whose independence, like that of Switzerland, is guaranteed by the Great Powers in return for perpetual neutrality.  The Transvaal may be more correctly compared with Egypt, which, under the suzerainty of Turkey, is forbidden to conclude any treaties containing political arrangements with foreign Powers.  All these States, although in diplomatic documents the name is not applied, are classed by writers on International Law as "Part-Sovereign States."[3]

"The Boer Republic cannot," says Professor Lawrence, "in strictness be said to possess the full rights of independence, though it is called an independent State in treaties and despatches."

Upon a consideration of all the circumstances it appears more reasonable to conclude that the new Convention was a substitution *in toto* for the old one, and since the substance of the preamble still remained under the new Convention, Mr. Chamberlain was most unwise to renew a useless controversy by reviving the Convention of 1881.

HUGH H. L. BELLOT.

[1] Speech of Earl Spencer at Chator Moor, October 30, 1899, p. 7.
[2] *A Century of Wrong*, p. 36.
[3] T. J. Lawrence, *Principles of International Law*, c. iv.

(*To be continued.*)

# HOW TO CONSOLIDATE THE EMPIRE.

How may we best consolidate, strengthen, and safeguard the British Empire?

Such is the grave, the vital problem that confronts our people and our statesmen to-day.

"Consolidate the British Empire!" cries the Jingo. "This war has consolidated the Empire."

Dr. Conan Doyle, replying to the toast of his health at a dinner given by the Authors' Club prior to his departure for South Africa, is reported to have said :

> "He was very optimistic about this war and the effect of it. It marked a turning-point in the life of Great Britain. . . . Why should they punish Kruger? That man had solved a question which every statesman had found insoluble. He would build a monument to Kruger the size of St. Paul's—putting him under it!—and he would write across it : 'To the memory of the man who federated the British Empire.'
>
> "Kruger was the man in all the world who had made the British Columbian feel that he was blood-brother with the Queenslander."

"Strengthen and safeguard the British Empire!" exclaims the Jingo, slapping his breeches pocket. "The Empire is strong enough and safe enough. We've got the ships, we've got the men, and, by Jove, we've got the money too!" In his opinion, blood and iron and gold will suffice to firmly weld together the Empire. In common with the Jingoes of all the dead and gone empires of the past he believes that blood and gold and iron are omnipotent. He has yet to learn that

"Righteousness alone exalteth a nation."

That lesson Great Britain must learn, or, like Greece and Rome, Egypt and Babylonia, perish miserably.

Opportunism, force, and fraud must be put on one side by those who wo̶u̶ld build up the British Empire upon a firm and lasting found̶a̶t̶i̶on. They must dare because right is right, to follow right in ̶t̶h̶e̶ ̶consequence.[1]

̶Herbert Spencer say, in his *Social Statics*—would that ̶the Spencer̶ of to-day were the Spencer of fifty years ago:

---

[1] "And, because right is right, to follow right
  Were wisdom, in the scorn of consequence."
  —TENNYSON.

"Our social edifice may be constructed with all possible labour and ingenuity, and be cramped together with cunningly devised enactments, but if there be no *rectitude* in its component parts—if it is not built on *upright* principles, it will assuredly tumble to pieces. As well might we seek to light a fire with ice . . . or otherwise disregard the physical laws of the world as go contrary to its equally imperative ethical laws.

"Not as adventitious, therefore, will the wise man regard the faith that is in him—not as something which may be slighted and made subordinate to calculations of policy; but as the supreme authority to which all his actions should bend. . . . We are not to pay lip homage to principles which our conduct wilfully transgresses. . . . But, on the contrary, we are to search out with a genuine humility the rules ordained for us—are to do unfalteringly, without speculating as to consequences, whatsoever these require; and we are to do this in the belief that then, when there is perfect sincerity—when each man is true to himself—when every one strives to realise what he thinks the highest rectitude—then must all things prosper."

This is as true of nations as it is of individuals. For nations, as for individuals, honesty, though an old-fashioned virtue, is the best policy. For nations, as for individuals, the right course is in the long run ever the best course, the most expedient course. And with nations, as with individuals, when each nation is true to itself—when each nation strives to realise what it thinks the highest rectitude—then must all things prosper.

Small wonder, therefore, that Herbert Spencer condemns the present war.

Writing to the *Morning Leader* on the day when, to use the words of Mr. W. T. Stead, it "blossomed forth into the foremost morning Liberal daily newspaper in London,"[1] Herbert Spencer said:

"The crowds who shouted to the departing troops 'Remember Majuba!' displayed the same passion as the lowest savages who make blood-revenge a primary duty. And the pride of mastery which prompts the Indian to wear as a trophy the scalp of his fallen foe is the same in nature as that which will hear of nothing less than taking the chief city of a conquered nation. Is the sentiment of the prize ring—'I am stronger than you are'—so very noble?"

Mr. Stead is himself one of the most outspoken advocates of the application of the principles of right and justice in our dealings with other nations, and he condemns the present war in good set terms. Just to read the "programme" which he "keeps standing"

---

[1] Mr. Stead's words are worth quoting in full, for the *Morning Leader* deserves every credit for the noble, the courageous stand it has dared to make against the blatant Jingoism of the hour. Says Mr. Stead, in *War against War*, Feb. 9, "the *Morning Leader* on Monday blossomed forth into the foremost morning Liberal daily newspaper in London. The foremost did I say?—the only morning Liberal daily newspaper left in London. For organs that are tuned to the keynote of Brummagem Jingoism may be daily and morning newspapers, but they can hardly pretend to be regarded as in any sense the organs of the Opposition. The *Morning Leader* has served a long apprenticeship. It has now served its time and takes its proper place as a skilled and trusted veteran in the ranks of British journalism. It started on the new shape and increased size with a chorus of benedictions from eminent men and women of letters."

on the front page of *War against War* is a splendid moral tonic. Here it is:

"PROGRAMME.

"1. What do you want to do?—Stop this war!
"2. When?—Immediately!
"3. Why?—Because we are in the wrong.
"4. How?—By confessing our sins and doing right.
"5. What sins?—Lying to cover conspiracy. Fraud in making false claims. Bad faith in going back on our word. Wholesale slaughter.
"6. And to do right?—Expose and punish the criminals. Compensate their victims. And make peace!"

A "Stop-the-War Committee" has also recently been formed, with the Rev. John Clifford, D.D., as Chairman of the General Committee, the Rev. Silas K. Hocking as Chairman of the Executive Committee, and as Hon. Sec. Mr. W. M. Crook, who, to his lasting honour, resigned his position as Editor of the *Echo*, just as Mr. H. W. Massingham resigned his as Editor of the *Daily Chronicle*, rather than be false to his principles. The Committee is doing yeoman service in the cause of peace and justice.

On February 14, moreover, there was a grand Liberal rally at the Westminster Palace Hotel, and a National Liberal League was formed to combat the prevalent spirit of Jingo-Imperialism. Mr. Lehmann, the convener of the meeting, presided, and some 300 delegates attended from all parts of the country, among those present being Sir John Brunner, M.P.; Sir William B. Gurdon, M.P.; Mr. Lloyd-George, M.P.; Mr. F. A. Channing, M.P.; Mr. Thomas Burt, M.P.; Sir Wilfrid Lawson, M.P.; Mr. Bryn Roberts, M.P.; Mr. C. P. Scott, M.P.; Mr. Maddison, M.P.; Mr. Frederic Harrison, Mr. G. W. E. Russell, and Mr. Cronwright Schreiner.

The *Morning Leader*, in summarising the proceedings, said:

"The resolutions, it is true, dealt mainly with the present war, but the scope of the speeches was much wider. Mr. Burt and Mr. Maddison emphasised the unanimity of the Labour members of Parliament in opposing this war, and both of them ventured to prophesy that an uprising was imminent against a war engineered by capitalists and a policy that must destroy all hope of social reform at home. Mr. Burt informed the meeting that the Northumbrian miners who had returned from the Rand are unanimous in agreeing that there were no Uitlander grievances that justified war. They had no ill-treatment to complain of, and they did not want the franchise. Mr. Herbert Paul, speaking with an intimate knowledge of the facts, dealt wittily with the conspiracy myth, the legend of armaments, and the Boer atrocities propagated by the Rhodesian Press. Mr. Channing and Mr. Russell recalled the meeting, in speeches of genuine eloquence, to the old Gladstonian tradition, and one speaker reminded it that the Liberal rallying cry in 1878 had been, ' Down with Imperialism.' In this connection it was significant that most of the speeches were in favour of severing all connection, if necessary, with that section of the Liberal party which supports a policy of aggressive Imperialism. As to practical measures, the feeling of the meeting was that the right of Free

Speech must be vindicated at all costs, and that the constituencies must be educated regarding the real facts of the present crisis by open meetings. The greatest enthusiasm was manifested by the meeting, and the resolutions were unanimously carried."

These resolutions, six in number, are of such importance that they may well be given in full. They are :

"(1) That this Conference denounces the present war in South Africa as a crime and a blunder, committed at the instigation of irresponsible capitalists; condemns the official excuses for it as insufficient and insincere; and demands from the Government a declaration of the objects for which they are sacrificing blood and treasure.

"(2) That this Conference, considering the belief in a Dutch conspiracy against British power in South Africa void of foundation and regarding the Transvaal armaments as defensive preparations due to the Johannesburg conspiracy, the Jameson Raid, and the suspected complicity of Imperial officials, demands the full publication of the suppressed correspondence and of other unconsidered evidence relating to the Raid.

"(3) That this Conference protests against a constantly increasing expenditure on armaments, which makes political reform and social improvement impossible; and would regard with alarm and indignation a proposal to introduce conscription in any form.

"(4) That this Conference, recognising the supreme importance of a policy of peace, as affirmed by Richard Cobden and John Bright, and further asserting its adherence to the uniform Liberal tradition, maintained by Fox, Canning, Lord John Russell, and Mr. Gladstone, of supporting and stimulating the independence of small nationalities, records hereby an emphatic protest against the use of bluster and vulgar insult as aids to diplomacy, and declares its unwavering faith in Mr. Gladstone's principle that courtesy and a conciliatory spirit should be displayed in our conduct towards all foreign Powers, and not the least towards those who are weaker than ourselves. This Conference, therefore, desires to place on record its deep sense of gratitude towards Sir Henry Campbell-Bannerman, Sir William Harcourt, Mr. Morley, Mr. Bryce, Mr. Courtney, and all others who have, during this crisis, courageously maintained the true principles of Liberalism, and affirms its entire confidence in the leader of the Liberal party in the House of Commons.

"(5) That this Conference desires to express its appreciation of the sincere efforts for peace made by the Ministers of Cape Colony and Natal, and especially to express its sympathy with the Dutch, on whom a terrible strain is imposed by a war with which they are entirely out of sympathy.

"(6) That it is desirable to raise a substantial fund for the purpose of forming a permanent organisation to enforce by means of vigorous political propaganda the principles enunciated in the foregoing resolutions, and that this Conference requests the convening Committee, with such additions as may be desirable, to take the necessary steps for carrying out this object."

So far as they go, we have no fault to find with Mr. Herbert Spencer, Mr. Stead, the *Morning Leader*, the Stop the War Committee, or the National Liberal League. In our opinion their condemnation of this war is not a whit too strong.

With Mr. Stead we want "to stop this war immediately because we are in the wrong," and "to expose and punish the criminals, compensate their victims, and make peace."

We do find fault with Mr. Herbert Spencer, Mr. Stead, the

*Morning Leader*, the Stop the War Committee, and the National Liberal League, however, because, in our opinion, *they have not gone half far enough.*

They have failed to consider the question—and it is a fundamental question—"Who ought to pay for the war?" And they have utterly failed to get at the root cause of this war—the root cause of the power of Jingo Imperialism.

But for the economic driving forces behind it Jingo Imperialism would cut no figure at all in politics. Go to the root of the matter, remove the cause, and in a generation or so the only representatives of the cult would be a few fossilised militarist survivals of a bygone age.

In the *Fortnightly Review* for December last Professor Holland (Chichele Professor of International Law) summed up as follows his judgment upon the Peace Conference at the Hague:

> "Not to contracts, the drafting of which can hardly be secured from ambiguity, and the performance of which can never be absolutely relied upon, but to a gradual elimination of the causes of war, must we look for a reduction of the armaments by which the world is now over-burdened."

And it is to "the elimination of the causes" of Jingo Imperialism rather than to their present line of action, that the Anti-Imperialists must look for a diminution of the blustering, bluffing, buccaneering Jingo spirit now so rampant.

Now, what are the economic driving forces behind Jingo Imperialism—the forces that give it all its weight and all its power for evil?

Broadly speaking, there are two such forces.

The first is indicated by Thorold Rogers, when, speaking of the law of entail, "under which the possession of land may be a danger, and is the means of fraud," he says:[1]

> "It [the law of entail] perpetuated the poverty of the younger son and the system of quartering him on the public purse. It was the origin of the principle of vested interests, perhaps the most anti-social and dangerous doctrine which has pretended to justify the robbery of all labour, and will justify the antagonism of all labour to privilege. The development of the younger son as a social pauper and a social leech is at the bottom of most of the financial extravagances and all the financial meanness of the English administrations to our own day. It is difficult to be thrifty in the public expenditure where one should be, and impossible to be generous where one ought to be."

To this he attributes "the retention of sham offices in the public service," and the quartering of young scions of the nobility on the church, the Post Office, the civil list, the War Office, &c. To this also, as he points out (p. 293), are to be attributed many of our wars—

> "The great resource of the younger son without land or means, and

[1] *Six Centuries of Work and Wages*, p. 295.

therefore sure to be quartered on the English people, was the army. The great war with France was maintained in the interest of the younger son."

The second is embodied in the oft-used phrase, "We must peg out claims for posterity," and was voiced by Sir Henry Campbell-Bannerman at Birmingham, when he said:

"Ladies and Gentlemen,—We have in this country an overflowing population, and we are bound to find for their industrial energy ever fresh fields and outlets."

This, in spite of the fact that out of the 72,000,000 acres in the United Kingdom, 26,000,000 acres—half, at least, of which is good, cultivable land—are held absolutely idle, and millions more are only half used—labour starved! This, in spite of the fact that this country could, according to Prince Krapotkin, Alderman Mechi, and other authorities, readily support twice its present population on home-grown food, and at the same time afford ample provision for all their other wants! This, in spite of the fact that, as Lord Rosebery told his audience at Edinburgh three years ago:

"You have acquired so enormous a mass of territory that it will be years before you can settle it, or control it, or make it capable of defence, or make it amenable to the arts of your administration. . . . In the (last) twelve years you have added to the Empire, whether in the shape of actual annexation, or of dominion, or what·is called a sphere of influence, 2,600,000 square miles of territory! . . . to the 120,000 square miles of the United Kingdom, which is a part of your Empire, you have added . . . . twenty-two areas as large as the United Kingdom itself!"

Why, in the face of such facts, this constant cry for "ever fresh fields and outlets"?

Says the *Financial Reform Almanack* for 1900:

"We own already about one-fourth of the inhabitable surface of the globe. Surely we need not be afraid of others obtaining slices out of what we have left."

Well might Lord Rosebery say, "the foreign policy of Great Britain until its territory is consolidated, filled up, settled, civilised, must inevitably be a policy of peace"; but it is hard to reconcile with that statement of opinion his action during the Fashoda crisis; and all that he has done and left undone at the present juncture, his disclaimer of "the Majuba policy," and his demand—for such his recent speeches in the House of Lords amounted to—for the mobilisation of the Fleet and the introduction of the Militia Ballot. Practically speaking, "the sole causes of disagreement between the Great Powers are to be found in their industrial and commercial rivalries, and their frantic efforts in the direction of colonial expansion; "[1] but statistics show that, as a matter of fact, the assumption upon which colonial expansion is advocated, the assumption that

---

[1] "Towards Universal Peace," WESTMINSTER REVIEW, April 1899.

" trade follows the flag," is false.   In the article " Our Expenditure on Armaments " (*Financial Reform Almanack*, p. 28), it is shown that whereas our naval and military expenditure in the period 1894_95 to 1898_99 was £56,792,000, or £11,358,000 a year, in excess of that for the period 1880_81 to 1884_85, there was a *decrease* in the exports of British goods to British colonies, possessions, and protectorates in 1894_98, as compared with 1880_84, of no less than £12,574,000, or £2,515,000 a year!

That explodes one of the fallacies that form the stock-in-trade of the Jingo-Imperialist.   A thorough and enlightened advocacy of free-trade principles—absolute free trade, not our present hybrid system—would dispose of all the rest.

The Protectionist idea that the industrial and commercial interests of one country are necessarily opposed to the industrial and commercial interests of the rest, must be nailed to the counter as a " damnable heresy ; " and free traders must not hesitate to push their principles to their logical conclusion.   They must show that before trade can be truly free, not exchange only, but production also, must be free; that it is impossible for production to be free while the land, the only raw material of labour, is the subject of a close monopoly; and that, therefore, to carry out the principles of Cobden and Bright in their entirety, land monopoly must be abolished.

Were the Herbert Spencer of to-day the Herbert Spencer of fifty years ago, we should find him striking straight at the root of the matter and expounding with all the vigour displayed in *Social Statics* the text, " Equity, therefore, does not permit property in land."

Were Mr. Stead an economist—which, unfortunately for himself and for the rest of us, he is not—he would realise with Mr. Henry George that [1]

" He who would insure peace—aye, he who would bring peace in its full, true meaning—must look deeper than to arbitration between nations; he must endeavour to build the very foundations of the State upon the firm rock of justice.   War comes from injustice ; peace comes from justice ; from the securing to each man of his right; from the giving to each of that which is his due."

If to each man in this country were secured—by Henry George's " sovereign remedy," the taxation of land-values—his " right to the use of the earth," if our social adjustments gave to each his due, peace and plenty would abound ; in the supply of home needs we should find ample market for all our goods and ample employment for all idle hands, and there would no longer be any need to seek for the " industrial energy " of our people " ever fresh fields and outlets." The topsy-turvy idea, moreover, that it is more honourable to be " quartered upon the English people " than to work for one's living,

[1] *Financial Reformer*, Oct. 1898, p. 187.

more honourable to live by slaughter than by labour, would soon die a natural death. And, further, as shown in the article "Towards Universal Peace," quoted above, the taxation of land-values would vastly strengthen England's position in regard to other nations. In case of need, land-values could be taxed up to the full £200,000,000 of ground-rent without increasing the burdens of labour and capital —and by absolute free trade such tendencies would be set in motion as must in the long run federate and consolidate, not only the British Empire and the English-speaking races, but all mankind.

Mr. Stead has lent additional emphasis to his programme by putting it in the form of question and answer. May we venture to extend that programme as follows :

(7) Who ought to pay for the war ?

The landholders. Under the old Feudal System they had, in return for the land they held, to support the army and navy, police the country, act as an unpaid magistracy, maintain the roads and bridges, and, in short, render practically all those public services for which we now pay rates and taxes. They shuffled out of those dues and services by a long series of landlord-made laws ; and it is only fair that we should, as quickly as may be, reverse that process.

(8) How ?

By means of the Budget. Gradually substitute a tax on land-values for all present rates and taxes.

(9) But doesn't "the House of Lords block the way " ?

No ; by virtue of the resolution of the House of Commons in 1687, and as Lord Salisbury himself admitted in the House of Lords the other day, "the House of Commons holds in regard to Supply the power of the purse." The Lords cannot interfere with the Budget.

(10) We agree with your views upon foreign politics, what about domestic politics ?

I promise thorough-going administrative reform. With the exception of the Budget, the House of Lords can block all legislative reforms ; but I promise you a thoroughly Radical Budget. As a first step, I propose to levy the existing tax of 4s. in the £ on present values, instead of on the values of 200 years ago. That will bring in some £40,000,000, which I would apportion as follows :

(a) Payment of Members and of Election Expenses (£1,000,000) ;

(b) Abolition of the Breakfast-table Duties (£5,000,000) ;

(c) Old-Age Pensions (£25,000,000) ;

(d) To meet the interest and sinking-fund charges on the debt caused by the present war, say £5,000,000 ;

(e) To reduce the tobacco duty, the income-tax, or what not, £4,000,000.

On such a programme Mr. Stead, we venture to say, might well successfully contest West Birmingham against the Right Hon. Joseph Chamberlain himself.   "Joe," with all his cleverness, could not over-trump that 4s. in the £ Budget.

Moreover, Mr. Stead might show how, by using the taxation of land-values as a lever, the Liberals could force through the House of Lords such measures as Home Rule all Round (thus removing one of the greatest obstacles to Imperial Federation), Registration Reform, Adult Suffrage, Second Ballot, Temperance Reform, &c.

We would commend this programme to Sir Henry Campbell-Bannerman and to the "backward Liberal Forwards."

Were Sir Henry to strike out clearly and courageously on such lines, he would soon get rid of all cross-currents in the Liberal party, the democracy would rally to his support, and his success at the next General Election would be assured.   He has been fairly outspoken on the land question and kindred problems of late, but before he can hope to rally the party to any purpose he must crystallise into a clear and definite programme the policy he has as yet only vaguely outlined.

Surely the Liberal Forwards, for they are the backbone of the National Liberal League, can see that it rests very largely with them whether or no the war policy of the present Government shall "destroy all hope of social reform at home."   Surely they can see that while "Down with Imperialism" is an excellent rallying-cry, "Down with Imperialism and Down with Landlordism" is at once more radical and more logical, and in view of the great urgency of the housing problem—"the housing question is the land question," says Sir Henry Campbell-Bannerman—is likely to be a much more popular and effective battle-cry.   Surely they can see that while it is necessary "that the right of Free Speech must be vindicated at all costs," it is at least equally necessary that "the equal and inalienable rights" of Englishmen "to life, liberty, and the pursuit of happiness"—that is to say, their equal rights to live and move and have their being in their native land—should also be vindicated at all costs.

Why, then, do they hesitate to champion these rights as well as the right of Free Speech?   Why, then, do they hesitate to be as straight and strenuous in regard to domestic politics as they are in regard to foreign politics?   Why, with so tender a regard for the lives and liberties of Boers and "blacks" 6000 miles away, have they seemingly so little regard for the lives and liberties of the white slaves of England?

# WAS WAR NECESSARY? [1]

## THE STORY OF THE NEGOTIATIONS.

THE Boer ultimatum, couched in impossible terms, tantamount to a declaration of war, and followed up by the invasion of Natal, furnishes an obvious answer to that question. From that point of view war was necessary; and the country has loyally stood by the Government and voted the necessary supplies, and now follows with keen and sympathetic interest every movement in South Africa.

But the question is, what led up to this last step? For it is not the person who strikes the first blow who is necessarily to blame for the breach of the peace. This question is a political one, and the answer is to be got from a study of the diplomatic correspondence and negotiations between the Government and the Boers during the last couple of years, and particularly the summer and autumn months of 1899. No apology is now needed for this discussion, for during the progress of the negotiations the Opposition was necessarily and properly silent, and it was only in the course of the debate in the House of Commons in October 1899 that Mr. Chamberlain announced that discussion now would not embarrass the Government; indeed, he welcomed it as a relief.

This paper is not written in support of the Boers, but with a desire to look at the attitude of both parties to the negotiations impartially, criticising, condemning, approving, as the case may require, but throughout having regard to the tremendous issue of war which these negotiations involved; and remembering that war is a coarse remedy, a pitiless and illogical remedy, for it strikes the innocent instruments and brings suffering and sorrow to unoffending homes.

In regard to the earlier history of the two South African republics it is not necessary to do more than remind the reader that in 1852, by the Sand River Convention, and in 1854, by the Bloemfontein Convention, the Transvaal and Orange Free States respectively acquired their independence—the right of self-

[1] The Blue Books cited are titled "South African Republic" and bear the following official numbers and dates—but for brevity's sake are quoted by the Roman number here appropriated to them and the page: C 8721 February 1898, I.; C 9507 August 1899, II.; C 9415 July 1899, III.; C 9518 August 1899, IV.; C 9521 September 1899, V.; C 9530 October 1899, VI.

government without any interference from the British Government, no slavery being, however, permitted in either case. The Orange Free State has continued to enjoy this right till the present time. But in 1877 the Transvaal was annexed by the British Crown. This was done, as explained by Mr. Bryce, at a time when the Transvaal was weakened by native troubles and internal disorders, and practically bankrupt. A British Commissioner, Sir Theophilus Shepstone, was sent to investigate, but with secret instructions to annex if he should deem it necessary and be satisfied that the majority would approve. After three months' inquiry he exercised the power, without the inhabitants being consulted in any way, and the annexation was approved by the High Commissioner at the Cape, Sir Bartle Frere, and by the Government at home. The President protested and retired to the Cape. The Vice-President, Kruger, and the Executive Council also protested and sent delegates to London to remonstrate. A large majority of the Boer population signed a memorial praying for a reversal of the Act of Annexation, although, no doubt, the few English approved of the change. The unauthorised annexation was not followed by the promised grant of local autonomy, and the administration became autocratic. Accordingly, when the native powers that had proved dangerous were broken by the British in the Zulu war of 1879 and 1880, the Transvaal again demanded a restoration of their independence, but the new Liberal Government were advised that the annexation could not be undone, and refused it. Then followed a Boer call to arms and the successes over the small British forces that could be got together at Laings Nek, Ingogo, and Majuba, and the peace which was conceded, about which so much interest has recently been revived. We are content to take the explanation recently offered by Mr. Chamberlain of the motives and action of the Cabinet of which he was a member, given in view of the recent utterance of Lord Kimberley :

" Our reason was that the Transvaal had been annexed under an evident misapprehension. It had been taken by Lord Beaconsfield on information conveyed to his Government that the majority of the Boers were themselves desirous of annexation. It was proved afterwards that that was not the case. We thought, rightly or wrongly, that under these circumstances the annexation should be cancelled, provided we could get conditions which would secure our rights and secure the rights of British subjects ; and accordingly when the Boers expressed their willingness to assent to these conditions we did not think it was the duty of the Government of a Christian country to prosecute a war for which they had no longer any justification but a policy of revenge. That, at all events, was the view of the case which influenced me, and which, as I believe, influenced the Duke of Devonshire and many other distinguished members of that Administration." [1]

Mr. Chamberlain here, no doubt, includes Mr. Gladstone. In short, the essential and paramount consideration in the policy was

[1] Speech at Leicester, November 29, 1899.

justice to the Transvaal Boers. It is as erroneous to represent it as dictated by fear of the Boers as to base it upon a sentimental though splendid magnanimity.

For the present purpose the leading points of the Pretoria Convention of August 3, 1881,[1] may be summarised :

1. By what is called the "preamble" the Commissioners, on behalf of her Majesty, guarantee that complete self-government, subject to the suzerainty of her Majesty, will be accorded to the inhabitants of the Transvaal territory, upon the following terms and conditions and subject to the following reservations and limitations.

2. Her Majesty reserves right to appoint a British resident whose duties and functions shall be :

To act as Chargé d'Affaires and Consul-General.

To report upon the treatment of natives both in and outside the Transvaal.

To be the means of communication with native chiefs outside the Transvaal, and control the conclusion of treaties with them.

To be the medium of communication between the Transvaal Government and foreign powers.

3. Her Majesty reserves right to move troops through the Transvaal in time of war or threatened war between Britain and any foreign state or native tribe.

4. Her Majesty reserves the control of the external relations of the Transvaal, including the conclusion of treaties, and the conduct of diplomatic intercourse with foreign powers.

By the docquet at the end the Transvaal representatives

"agree to all the above conditions, reservations, and limitations under which self-government has been restored to the inhabitants of the Transvaal territory, subject to the suzerainty of her Majesty,"

and undertake to get the Convention ratified by the Volksraad, which was done.

It is worth while quoting a sentence or two from a despatch dated March 31, 1881, of Lord Kimberley, then Colonial Secretary, which is an almost contemporaneous exposition of the Convention, and which has been frequently appealed to as such both by Mr. Chamberlain and the Transvaal representatives.

Lord Kimberley says :

"Entire freedom of action will be accorded to the Transvaal Government so far as not inconsistent with the rights expressly reserved to the suzerain power. The term suzerainty has been chosen as most conveniently describing superiority over a state possessing independent rights of government subject to reservations with reference to certain specified matters. The most material of these reserved rights is the control of the external relations of the future Transvaal State, which will be vested in

[1] Blue Book, South Africa, 1881. C 2998.

the British Government, including, of course, the conclusion of treaties and the conduct of diplomatic intercourse with foreign Powers."[1]

Ere long the Transvaal State, through its representatives, expressed themselves greatly dissatisfied both with the Convention itself and with its working, and sent a deputation to London " to negotiate with her Majesty's Government concerning a revision of the Convention of 1881."[2]   Their objections were fundamental, and in 1898 they refer to their object as having been "to obtain the abolition of the suzerainty."[3]   Mr. Chamberlain has recently challenged this and declared that they did not then claim the abolition, "but some restriction of the extent of the suzerainty. That is the exact word."[4]   But the letter of the deputation to Lord Derby, dated November 14, 1883,[5] does not bear this out.  They say :

" We feel ourselves bound at the outset to state that our people and their representatives in the Volksraad object not only to certain stipulations of the Convention of 1881, but to the said Convention in its entirety as being a document which neither in origin, nor in tendency, nor in practical working meets the requirements of the country."

Further on they add that

"a satisfactory settlement of mutual relations will not result from the modification of certain articles of the present Convention, but can only be expected from a new arrangement."[6]

It is true that " the extent " of the suzerainty is referred to, but in quite a different connection.  They say :

" The impracticability of the Convention has appeared chiefly in the following points : . . . (b) The extent of the suzerain rights reserved to her Majesty by Articles 2 and 18."[7]

It is a pity that Mr. Chamberlain should have misrepresented their position.

Of course the important point is not what the Transvaal claimed in 1883, but what they obtained in 1884 ; and while, for practical purposes, it is of little consequence what the relation is called, provided it be clearly defined, it will appear from the sequel that the discussion which has raged round the word " suzerainty " has led to very serious consequences.

The result of these negotiations was the Convention of London of February 27, 1884,[8] containing a new preamble and articles in which the word suzerainty does not occur, and the provisions in regard to a British resident and the movement of British troops are absent ; while the provision affecting the control of external relations is altered so as to permit negotiation with foreign Powers and

[1] II. 8.            [2] II. 19.            [3] II. 8.
[4] Speech in the House of Commons, Oct. 20, 1899.        [5] II. 19.        [6] II. 21.
[7] II. 20.   .        [8] South African Republic 1884.  C 3914.

tribes, but to prohibit the conclusion of treaties without her Majesty's approval. This Article (4) is so important that its exact words may be here given:

"The South African Republic will conclude no treaty or engagement with any State or Nation other than the Orange Free State, nor with any native tribe to the eastward or westward of the Republic, until the same has been approved by her Majesty the Queen. Such approval shall be considered to have been granted if her Majesty's Government shall not within six months after receiving a copy of such treaty (which shall be delivered to them immediately upon its completion) have notified that the conclusion of such treaty is in conflict with the interests of Great Britain or of any of her Majesty's possessions in South Africa."

If the substance of the matter be alone regarded, no difficulty need be felt in accepting Mr. Chamberlain's statement in December 1898[1] that what the substance of suzerainty is was described by Lord Kimberley in 1881 in the passage already quoted, viz.:

"Superiority over a State possessing independent rights of government, subject to reservations with reference to certain specified matters";

and that these words accurately describe the relations between Britain and the Transvaal under the Convention of 1884. The reserved matter was of course the conclusion of treaties with foreign Powers and tribes. Not less emphatic was the declaration of the Transvaal representatives in 1898[2] that, not for the first time, but to prevent any misunderstanding, they desired to state clearly that the Transvaal was "prepared in every respect to abide by the stipulations of the Convention of 1884"—a declaration renewed more than once in the course of the subsequent negotiations.[3] Accordingly, Mr. Chamberlain, pointing to the foreign treaty stipulations of the Convention of 1884, declared in 1898[4] that there was

"thus no controversy as to the essential point in the relations between the two Governments, which gives to Great Britain a position of superiority."

If the word "suzerainty" be used, it is not too much to say that the beginning, middle, and end of the suzerainty under the Convention of 1884 was the veto upon foreign treaties in conflict with British interests.

It is unfortunate, however, that both parties adopted, if not more extreme views, at least more extreme language in expressing them, for the Transvaal representatives, while acknowledging the veto on the conclusion of treaties, claimed not only that the British suzerainty was abolished, and that no suzerainty existed, but also that the South African Republic was a Sovereign International State; and, on the

---

[1] II. 28.  [2] II. 7.  [3] VI. 13.  [4] II. 22.

other hand, Mr. Chamberlain claimed that the preamble of the Convention of 1881, with its assertion of a general suzerainty, still remained unchanged, and governed the articles substituted in the Convention of 1884. It is not necessary to pursue the subject further at this point, but the effect of these divergent views will become apparent later on. In the meantime, it may be observed that, by Article 14 of the Convention of 1884, it was provided that all persons, other than natives, conforming themselves to the laws of the South African Republic should have the following rights :

(a) Full liberty with their families to enter, travel, or reside in any part of the Republic.

(b) To hire or possess houses, manufactories, and other premises.

(c) To carry on their commerce either in person or by agents; and

(d) They will not be subject in respect of their persons, property, commerce, or industry to any taxes, whether general or local, other than those which are or may be imposed on citizens of the Republic.

These provisions, together with an Article affecting customs duties, and the assurances of equal protection and treatment given at the Conference of May 1881,[1] in view of the restoration of self-government to the Transvaal, constitute the charter of the Uitlanders' rights. They entitle Britain, both on the ground of international right and the Convention, to interfere for the protection of its own subjects, and to secure fulfilment of their common law and treaty rights.

For the purposes of this paper it is assumed and admitted that the Uitlanders' grievances are real and substantial, and that Britain has a right and duty to insist upon redress, first no doubt by negotiation or arbitration, and in the end even by force. It is admitted that the Uitlanders' grievances are the ultimate cause of the war; but the question to be examined here is whether the remedy by negotiation was exhausted and nothing remained but to apply force by war.

The import of the diplomatic correspondence prior to the Bloemfontein Conference of May and June 1899 may be shortly explained. In 1896, after the Jameson Raid, the Volksraad passed the Aliens Expulsion Act,[2] conceiving that notwithstanding the 14th Article of the Convention of 1884 they were entitled to expel foreigners whom they deemed dangerous to the peace and safety of the country, that being a right inherent in every State on the principle of self-preservation. The Act gave the Executive the power to banish without trial, and was no doubt a breach of the

[1] IV. 8.     [2] I. 69.

Convention, and was objected to as such. Thereafter the Volksraad
resolved to revise the law in the sense of requiring the offender to
be tried, and subsequently repealed the Act altogether.   In reporting
the Volksraad's first resolution, her Majesty's agent at Pretoria
called particular attention[1] to the fair and sensible tone of the
supporters of the motion, and to the temperate nature of the
discussion.

After the repeal Mr. Chamberlain had occasion, on October 16,
1897,[2] to reply to the Transvaal despatch of May 7 on the subject,
and expressed satisfaction at the repeal.  He then went on to
expound the doctrine that the preamble of the Convention of 1881
was still in force, and that under *these Conventions* her Majesty holds
towards the South African Republic the relation of a suzerain who
has accorded to the people of that republic self-government on
certain conditions.  From this he deduced the not very obvious
inference that it would be incompatible with that position to submit
to arbitration the construction of the conditions on which self-
government was so accorded ; and he concluded by refusing to
submit to the arbitration of a foreign State or its nominee questions
as to the " infringement of the Convention."

The reply of Dr. Leyds of April 16, 1898,[3] discusses with great
ability and fulness what he regarded as the most important question
raised—the existence of a suzerainty over the South African
Republic—a proposition which, he says, was now for the first
time since 1884 put forward in any British despatch ; and he
prefaces that discussion with an emphatic declaration that they
were prepared in every respect to abide by the stipulations of the
Convention of 1884.

Perhaps the most graphic presentation of the case for abolition of
suzerainty is contained in the draft of the new Convention, sent in
the letter [4] of Lord Derby, the Colonial Secretary, to the Transvaal
representatives on February 15, 1884.  It shows, for comparison,
the preambles of 1881 and 1884, the former surrounded by a black
line to which a " note " is prefixed, stating that paragraphs " within
a black line are proposed to be omitted." [5]   The preamble of 1881
was omitted ; and the new preamble bears that the Convention of
1881 shall continue in full force and effect, but only " pending the
ratification " by the Volksraad of the articles of the new Convention,
implying that after the ratification of the new one, the old shall
cease to have effect.

On the subject of arbitration Dr. Leyds argued that if, as he
contended, suzerainty did not exist, the objection on the ground of
incompatibility fell to the ground ; but that, even though suzerainty
existed, it was only, as Lord Kimberley pointed out, in reference

---

[1] I. 17.                         [2] I. 18.                                    [3] II. 7–19.
[4] South African Republic, 1884.   C 3947, p. 43.              [5] II. 12 and 26.

to certain matters specified and reserved, and it was not reserved to the British Government by either Convention to be the sole judge of the meaning of a mutual document regulating the rights of the two Governments.[1] As will appear hereafter, the question of arbitration admitted of adjustment on the principle of excluding from the office of arbiter foreigners or foreign nominees.

Upon the suzerainty parties were really even now agreed, for Lord Derby, in the above letter, to which both parties appealed, said to the Transvaal representatives :

"Your Government will be left free to govern the country without interference, and to conduct its diplomatic intercourse and shape its foreign policy, subject only to the requirement embodied in the 4th Article of the new draft, that any treaty with a foreign State shall not have effect without the approval of the Queen."

Lord Derby also, when interrogated in the House of Lords on March 17, 1884, on the meaning of the Convention of 1884, declared that, whatever it is called,

"a certain controlling power is retained when the State which exercises this suzerainty has a right to veto any negotiations[2] into which the dependent State may enter with foreign Powers."

In this view and considering that the claim, which was very doubtful in itself, was also very irritating to Transvaal susceptibilities, it is not wonderful that Sir Alfred Milner, in forwarding Dr. Leyds' reply to Mr. Chamberlain, said :[3]

"I am unable myself to see anything very material in this controversy. . . . Whether the relationship created by the Convention is properly described as ' suzerainty ' is not, in my opinion, of much importance. It is a question of etymological rather than of political interest."

On the question of arbitration Sir Alfred Milner contented himself with saying that it would be a grave error of policy to submit differences as to the meaning of the Convention to any *foreign* Power.

Mr. Chamberlain did not take the warning which Sir Alfred gave, but proceeded, in his despatch of December 15, 1898,[4] to rub in the suzerainty as based on the preamble of 1881, which, he said, "remained unchanged." To this he added the argument that the grant of internal independence was contained in the same preamble and must stand or fall with it. This, however, is the despatch in which he accepts the " substance of suzerainty " as described by Lord Kimberley; and concludes this subject by saying : " There is

---

[1] II. 17.

[2] This is not accurate. The veto is not on *negotiating* but on *concluding* an effective Treaty. See Lord Derby's letter of February 15, 1884, *supra*. The next sentence of his answer in the House of Lords is as follows: " Whatever suzerainty meant in the Convention of 1881 the condition of things which it implied still remains. Although the word is not actually employed, we have kept the substance." This is not accurate and scarcely consistent with the previous sentence, if it means more than that a measure of suzerainty remained; for obviously the amount or extent of it was very much limited.     [3] II. 6.          [4] II. 28.

thus no controversy as to the essential point in the relations between the two Governments which gives to Great Britain a position of superiority."

It is a great pity that, with so much unanimity in substance, Mr. Chamberlain should have thrown in the apple of discord in the shape of a vague claim to suzerainty, and suzerainty based on the superseded preamble of 1881. The Transvaal State Secretary in his reply[1] of May 9, 1899, while protesting that his "Government did not desire to invite or proceed with a useless controversy" on matters already discussed by both Governments, adhered to the statement in their despatch of April 16, 1898,[2] that Lord Derby regarded the preamble of 1881 as abolished. He further endeavoured to answer[3] the argument that internal independence would fall with the suzerainty by saying that the self-government of 1881 fell only to give place to the much wider absolute right of self-government at present enjoyed; and he added that that was not derived from either the Convention of 1881 or that of 1884, "but simply and solely follows from the inherent right of this Republic as a Sovereign International State." It could not be expected that this extreme view on the other side could be accepted, and of course it met with instant repudiation in Mr. Chamberlain's next despatch of July 13,[4] when it was declared unwarranted either by law or history and wholly inadmissible. The true view, however, appears to be neither that internal independence (or self-government) flowed from the superseded preamble of 1881 (as Mr. Chamberlain contended), nor from a supposed inherent right (as Mr. Reitz claimed), but from the renewed grant implied in the Convention of 1884, accompanied as it was by the continued acknowledgment of the Transvaal as a constitutional State under the new designation of the South African Republic. It was an International State, indeed, but with its sovereignty limited, being subject to the British veto on foreign treaties, a qualification which was frankly admitted. The claim to suzerainty on the one hand, and to be reckoned a Sovereign International State on the other, were each fitted to sunder the negotiating parties, and it was high time that this useless controversy should cease.

Mr. Chamberlain's repudiation, on July 13, 1899, of the Transvaal as a Sovereign International State was followed up by a brief *resumé* of its history; and at that time it looked as if diplomacy had come to an end, for the Bloemfontein Conference had already, in the beginning of June, broken up without result.

What Sir Alfred Milner proposed to President Kruger at that Conference may be shortly summarised.[5] He wished to deal first with the question of the franchise, as affording the best means of enabling the Uitlanders to protect themselves, and avoid the constant.

<hr />

[1] II. 32.   [2] II. 8.   [3] II. 32.   [4] II. 33.   [5] III. 2.

irritation that would arise from Britain dealing with internal grievances in detail.    Accordingly he proposed that the full franchise
should be conferred on every foreigner who

(a) had been resident for five years in the republic;

(b) declared his intention to reside permanently, and

(c) took an oath to obey the laws, undertake all obligations
of citizenship, and defend the independence of the country;

(d) the franchise to be confined to persons of good character,
possessing a certain amount of property or income, and

(e) some increase of the Rand seats—the number to be
adjusted.

President Kruger, on the other hand, proposed a seven years'
residence, complicated with intricate conditions.    The question of
arbitration cropped up at the Conference, but Sir Alfred would not
discuss it, and insisted that the franchise should be disposed of first.
Without committing the Government in any way, he indicated to
the President that, should a plan for submitting future questions to
an impartial tribunal, and excluding the interference of a foreigner,
be devised and suggested to him, he would lay it before the Government, and personally do what he could to assist in a satisfactory
solution, for he thought it would open a way out of many difficulties.
The Conference, which lasted nearly a week, broke up on June 5 with
a friendly feeling on both sides.

The next step was the passing, on July 20, by the Volksraad, on
the President's initiative, of a Franchise Act based on a seven years'
residence, but subject to various conditions, and adding three new
members to the Rand, making five out of thirty-one.    It was passed
with the knowledge, but without consultation with the British
Government.    But it was acknowledged by Mr. Chamberlain, in his
despatch of July 27,[1] to be an advance and improvement on what
had preceded, and he expressed the hope that it would prove a basis
for a settlement on the lines of the Bloemfontein Conference, of
which the Government approved.    This despatch is an elaborate
*resumé* of the Government's objects in its controversy with the
Transvaal, being mainly to secure for the Uitlanders immediate
enjoyment of such a share of political power as would enable them
to exercise a real influence on legislation and administration, without
swamping the old burghers.    But it is unfortunate that, though
coming immediately after admitted concessions, the despatch bristles
with the old suzerainty and the irritating and untenable contention
that the preamble of 1881 governs the Convention of 1884.
Mr. Chamberlain admitted that the Articles of 1884 are open to fair
differences of opinion, for the solution of which he was willing that
an impartial tribunal, with the foreign element excluded, should be

[1] IV. 7.

set up; but he dictatorially declared there can be no question as to the interpretation of the preamble of 1881, which governs the Articles of 1884, a proposition open to the gravest doubt.

This despatch was telegraphed to Sir Alfred Milner, but not at first communicated to the President, and was meantime followed by other telegrams[1] on July 31 and August 1, in which Mr. Chamberlain proposed that the President should appoint delegates to discuss with delegates from us the question of whether the new reforms would give immediate and substantial representation to the Uitlanders, and if not what alterations were necessary. The President here took alarm, mainly no doubt because he thought the proposal involved interference in internal administration. It might indeed wear that aspect, but not more so than the franchise discussions of the Bloemfontein Conference. The apprehension brought on the last stage of the controversy. Through his State Attorney he on August 15 communicated with Mr. Greene, the British Resident, and offered improved franchise proposals, provided the joint inquiry were not pressed. Mr. Greene's account[2] is interesting. He was sounded as to whether the Government would press for a joint inquiry if a simplified franchise law adhering to seven years' residence and increasing the number of Rand seats were conceded. Mr. Greene said that he had no idea, but the situation was most critical, and the Government, who had given pledges to the Uitlanders, were bound to press their demands, if necessary, by force; further, that the only chance was an immediate surrender to the Bloemfontein minimum. The State Attorney, after holding out ineffectually for a seven years' residence, offered the scheme (to be now noted) which Mr. Greene, without committing the Government in any way, promised to recommend for acceptance in return for waiving the proposed joint inquiry.

The scheme as embodied in Mr. Greene's telegram on August 15 and afterwards in Mr. Reitz's telegrams of August 19 and 21, both forwarded to this country, was suggested as an alternative proposal to the joint inquiry, and was as follows:[3]

1. A five years' retrospective franchise, as proposed by Sir Alfred at Bloemfontein.

2. Eight new seats in the First Volkeraad, making ten for the Rand out of thirty-six in all, and in future not below one-fourth of the total.

3. The new burghers, equally with the old, to vote for the State President and Commandant-General.

4. "This Government will always be prepared to take into consideration such friendly suggestions regarding the details of the franchise law as her Majesty's Government, through the British Agent, may wish to convey to it."

5. In putting forward these proposals the South African

Republic "assumed" (the later telegram making it "expressly conditional")—

(*a*) That the British Government would agree that the present intervention should not form a precedent for future similar action, and that in the future no interference in the internal affairs of the Republic should take place.

(*b*) That the British Government would not further insist on the assertion of the suzerainty, the controversy on the subject being allowed tacitly to drop; and

(*c*) That arbitration, from which the foreign element, other than the Orange Free State, be excluded, should be conceded as soon as the franchise scheme had become law.

(6) The Volksraad to adjourn, and the people to be consulted, so that the scheme might pass in a few weeks.

The scheme was characterised by Mr. Chamberlain as an adoption in principle of the franchise proposals of the Bloemfontein Conference; and it contained this further advance, that details suggested by the British Government should be taken into consideration.

Obviously the conditions were the most important point, and were deemed essential by those who proposed them. In view of what has since been stated on the subject, it is worth noting what Mr. Greene (without, however, committing the Government) reported on August 15 to Sir Alfred Milner, as what he had said to the State Attorney—viz.: (*a*) as regards the interference, that if, as he was assured, this was a *bonâ fide* attempt to settle the political rights of the people once for all, the Republic need not fear that the British would either wish or have cause to interfere in their internal affairs; (*b*) as regards suzerainty, that while our Government would not and could not abandon the rights which the preamble of 1881 gave them, they would have no desire to hurt Boer susceptibilities by publicly reasserting it, so long as no reason to do so was given by the Boer Government; and (*c*) as to arbitration, they were willing that we should have our own judges or lawyers, English or Colonial, to represent us, and that the president or umpire should be either English, Colonial, or Boer.

These proposals, with Mr. Greene's views thereon, were forwarded to Mr. Chamberlain on August 15, and the authentic telegrams of the President on August 23, the latter accompanied by a declaration by Mr. Reitz that the proposals were dictated by a strong desire to get the controversies between the two Governments settled and prevent a racial war, from the effects of which South Africa would not recover for many generations, if at all. It is obvious, from Mr. Greene's testimony,[1] that the Transvaal authorities were thoroughly alarmed at the attitude of the British Government, and more disposed than ever before to make terms.

[1] VI. 21.

Mr. Chamberlain's first response was not fitted to aid the objects Mr. Reitz referred to. It was sent on the evening of August 23 to Sir Alfred Milner as follows : [1] " If not already done deliver despatch of July 27 at once. Greene can explain that having been written before the last proposals, it only deals with situation as it was when sent." Accordingly this despatch, bristling with suzerainty and the preamble of 1881, was delivered that evening, in reply to new conciliatory proposals—a significant illustration of the new diplomacy! As further preparatory to the coming reply, Mr. Chamberlain held a garden party at Highbury on August 26, and sneered at the President as a " squeezed sponge," and talked of the sands running in the hour glass. Was there ever such folly ?

We now come to Mr. Chamberlain's famous reply of August 28,[2] which he has since described as a " qualified acceptance," but which was understood as a refusal of the terms. As to the substance of the scheme, the Bloemfontein proposal, Mr. Chamberlain very properly " assumed " that it should not be hampered by restrictions that would impair its effect, and that, though there was not to be a joint commission of inquiry, every facility would be given to the British agent for investigation and suggestion regarding details, before submitting a new franchise law to the Volksraad and people. No difference arose on this point.

As to the three conditions, no difficulty arose as to the (1) intervention and (3) arbitration, as is shown by a comparison of Mr. Chamberlain's reply and the rejoinder of Mr. Reitz of September 2.[3]

### INTERVENTION.

Mr. Chamberlain said :

" Her Majesty's Government hope that the fulfilment of the promises made and the just treatment of the Uitlanders in future will render unnecessary any further intervention on their behalf; but her Majesty's Government cannot, of course, debar themselves from their rights under the Conventions, nor divest themselves of the ordinary obligations of a civilised power to protect its subjects in a foreign country from injustice."

Mr. Reitz rejoined that

"this Government has neither asked nor intended that her Majesty's Government should abandon any right which it really might have on the ground either of the Convention of London 1884 or of international law to intervene for the protection of British subjects in this country."

### ARBITRATION.

Mr. Chamberlain said :

" Her Majesty's Government agree to a discussion of the form and scope of a tribunal of arbitration from which foreigners and foreign influence are excluded."

[1] V. 48.    [2] V. 49-50.    [3] V. 52.

Mr. Reitz rejoined :

" This Government is pleased to see that her Majesty's Government is ready to enter upon negotiations touching the scope and form of a Court of Arbitration."

The remaining condition regarded SUZERAINTY, on which Mr. Chamberlain said :

" Her Majesty's Government would refer the Government of the South African Republic to the second paragraph of my despatch of July 13."

That paragraph was as follows : [1]

" Her Majesty's Government . . . have no intention of continuing to discuss this question with the Government of the Republic, whose contention that the South African Republic is a Sovereign International State is not, in their opinion, warranted either by law or history, and is wholly inadmissible. They therefore confine themselves to a brief review of historical facts," &c.

The question here is whether that reply would naturally be understood by the Transvaal Government as an acceptance of their condition of August 19, " that Her Majesty's Government will not further insist on the assertion of the suzerainty, the controversy on the subject being allowed tacitly to drop." It certainly does not bear to be an acceptance. It describes the attitude of her Majesty's Government at a prior stage of the negotiations on the merits of the suzerainty or sovereignty question as one of uncompromising opposition, so much so that the British Government would not even discuss it. The despatch of July 13 was a *non possumus*. On the other hand, the standpoint of the condition of August 19 was to let each party hold his own view, but drop the unprofitable controversy. It was a strange way of accepting the condition to refer to a despatch written prior to the conditional offer, and when, for the time, negotiations were at a deadlock.

It is not wonderful, therefore, that the Transvaal Government understood the reply as a refusal ; and, accordingly, in their answer of September 2,[2] they express the deepest regret at the non-acceptance of the proposal of the five years' franchise and extended representation " with the conditions attached thereto," and consequently that the proposal had lapsed. On the condition in question Mr. Reitz, in the first place, follows suit on the merits of the controversy, saying that as regards the assertion of suzerainty its non-existence had been clearly stated in the despatch of April 16, 1898, to which they adhered ; but he goes on to say that the stipulations (conditions) attached to the franchise proposal

" *are most reasonable, and demand on the side of her Majesty's Government no abandonment of existing rights,* but solely the obtaining of the assurance

[1] II. 33.     [2] V. 52.

that her Majesty's Government would in future, as regards this Republic, simply abide by the Convention of London, 1884, and the generally recognised rules of international law."

He then refers to the reasonableness of arbitration between civilised States; and further declares that his Government could never have anticipated that the answer of her Majesty's Government to their proposal would be unfavourable, and continues to cherish the hope that the terms of this and the former communications would open the way to a solution of existing differences. Thus the Transvaal Government showed clearly that they thought Mr. Chamberlain's answer was a refusal, while at the same time they sought to explain that there was nothing in the conditions of August 19 and 21, the acceptance of which could be regarded as an abandonment by the British Government of existing rights. The tacit dropping of the controversy about suzerainty was not a dropping of the claim on either side. The acceptance of the condition as to suzerainty did not mean the acceptance by the British Government of the Boer views on suzerainty, but only the acceptance of the dropping of the controversy, both parties being agreed on the substance of the rights in conformity with the Convention of 1884. Surely at this point a solution was not far to seek; and Mr. Chamberlain ought to have explained that it was a mistake to take his reply as a refusal. But he did not, and, on the contrary, in his despatch of September 8,[1] he acquiesced in and confirmed the view that it was a refusal, based on the conditions as to future intervention and suzerainty being unacceptable to the British Government. He again repudiated the Transvaal claim to be a Sovereign International State, which is the counterpart of the suzerainty of 1881, and declared that the British Government

"are therefore" (*i.e.*, on account of that claim) "unable to consider any proposal which is made conditional *on the acceptance by her Majesty's Government of these views.*"

But clear it is that the acceptance by the British Government of the sovereignty claim, or of the non-suzerainty claim, was never made a condition of the proposals of August 19 and 21. It was only the tacit dropping of the fruitless controversy that was stipulated for. Accordingly, while in the next sentence Mr. Chamberlain makes his position abundantly clear, he makes it clearly untenable, for he says:

"It is *on this ground* that her Majesty's Government have been compelled to regard the last proposal of the Government of the South African Republic as unacceptable in the form in which it has been presented."

Was it, then, unacceptable only in form? It has been declared that nine-tenths of the substance were conceded, and he admitted that the other tenth was not worthy of a war; so that in any view we are dealing with a very small point involving very large issues.

This despatch contains more on other points, before examining which let us see what the Transvaal Government say to the closing of the door on their proposal of August.  They, on September 16, again tried to disabuse Mr. Chamberlain's mind of the notion that the conditions involved an admission of the Boer claim.  They declare [1] that it was

" in no way the object of this Government either then or now to make any needless recapitulations of its contention about its political status as an independent State [2] as defined by Convention of London, 1884, but only to try to put an end to the tension by meeting her Majesty's Government upon a proposal which it supposed "

would be acceptable to them.  They then explain that they thought the proposal was so liberal that they ran the risk of being disclaimed by the Volksraad, but were willing to incur that risk if their highly prized independence were protected by the three conditions.  It is evident that they thought the conditions of value and conducive to a peaceful settlement.

To return to Mr. Chamberlain's despatch of September 8.  He there offers to accept the franchise proposals of August 19, taken by themselves (*i.e.*, without the conditions), provided they be not rendered nugatory by cumbrous stipulations, adding that he assumed the new members of the Rand would be entitled to use their own language.  He then winds up with a veiled threat of an ultimatum, saying that if, as he most anxiously hoped would not be the case, the reply was

"negative or inconclusive, her Majesty's Government must reserve to themselves the right to reconsider the situation *de novo*, and to formulate their own proposals for a final settlement."

It was surely a strong thing to rule out the conditions which, rightly or wrongly, the Transvaal valued, and on which the parties were really at one, under threat of an ultimatum framed on different lines.  Accordingly the Transvaal, on September 16, declared that they could not make the offer of August stripped of the conditions designed to safeguard their independence, and demurred to the use of the Uitlanders' language in the Volksraad being accepted as a new condition imposed by the other side ; finally, they appealed to her Majesty's Government to abandon the idea of making new proposals more difficult for their Government, and imposing new conditions, and declared themselves satisfied to abide by the Joint Commission first proposed by Mr. Chamberlain, but withdrawn by him on September 8.

Mr. Chamberlain's final reply is contained in his despatch of

[1] VI. 11-13.

[2] Observe "sovereign" is omitted.  A State cannot be sovereign in the fullest sense under such a Convention as that of 1884.

September 22 [1] to Sir Alfred Milner, communicated to the Transvaal Government. ·In it he expresses "profound regret" at the Transvaal Government's refusal to accept what he calls his "moderate and conciliatory offer," which was to accept their August proposal shorn of its conditions—conditions which they prized, and he, as we have seen, could have accepted. He then reasserts his position as to the independence of the Republic, the subject of the first condition, on which, as shown from the despatches of August 28 and September 2, there was no difference between the parties. He does not refer to the arbitration condition, on which also parties were agreed. But he reverts to the Transvaal assertion on May 9 that it was a Sovereign International State, and again absolutely repudiates that claim; and founds on the despatch of September 8 as containing the British minimum. He then winds up by saying that the refusal to accept that proposal makes it useless further to pursue a discussion on the lines hitherto followed, and that his Government are now compelled to consider the situation afresh, and to formulate their own proposals for a final settlement of the issues created by the policy followed for many years by the Transvaal Government.

Here Mr. Chamberlain is back at the old misapprehension or fallacy that the condition of August as to suzerainty involved the acceptance by him of the Transvaal claim to sovereignty or non-suzerainty. And he expresses the same idea in so many words in another despatch of September 22,[2] complaining that

"the proposals for franchise and representation were stated to be expressly conditional on the acceptance by her Majesty's Government of these assumptions."

They were no such thing. The assumption or claim was not asked to be conceded by the British Government. It was only asked that the controversy about it should drop. This is what the condition in its terms bore, and what the Transvaal Government had since explained to be its meaning. Moreover, both parties, and particularly the Transvaal, had over and over again declared their entire adherence to the Convention of 1884, which in its 4th Article placed the Transvaal in subjection to Britain in the matter of concluding foreign treaties. Further, Mr. Chamberlain has since admitted himself out of court in this matter, for, in the House of Commons on October 19, 1899, in answer to Sir Edward Clarke, he said that the Transvaal Government

"did not ask us to admit that we were not the suzerain power, *but only that we would tacitly allow the subject to drop*, and that we had already declared our intention of doing."

There was thus in Mr. Chamberlain's mind no misunderstanding as to the meaning of the condition, and further, no objection to its

---

[1] VI. 16.    [2] VI. 17.

reasonableness. Why, then, did he not accept it, instead of ruling it out as he did by insisting on his offer, which was their offer shorn of the conditions, being accepted under threat of an ultimatum ? He says, indeed, that " we had already declared our intention " of tacitly allowing the controversy to drop, in support of which he refers to the July 13 despatch, on which comment has already been made ; to which this only need be added, that if these words were an acceptance, or of the nature of an acceptance, why did he afterwards, on September 8, hark back and say that on the ground of this condition the Transvaal proposal of August was unacceptable, and that nothing would suffice but the acceptance of the August proposal with all the conditions excluded ?

This was the final breach, for the Transvaal had, on September 16, declared that they could not give up the conditions, which they valued, and to which Mr. Chamberlain could state no tangible objection. When he penned the despatches of September 22 he must have known that he was closing the door at the most hopeful point of the negotiations, and taking a step which inevitably brought us to war. He did not invite any reply, but indicated that new proposals would be formulated by her Majesty's Government and communicated. It is thus abundantly clear that Mr. Chamberlain, and not the Transvaal Government, broke off the negotiations, and did so deliberately, without any adequate or, indeed, any stateable reason.

It is now said that war was from the beginning inevitable and that there was for long a conspiracy to subvert the British authority in South Africa.[1] It is not suggested that this (if it existed) was known when Mr. Chamberlain broke off the negotiations. Indeed, he says he was hopeful of a peaceful result till near the end, and he does not put forward this new theory as having influenced his action in the negotiations.[1] Both he and Mr. Balfour made this quite clear in their speeches in November 1899. Thus Mr. Balfour, at Dewsbury on the 28th of that month, said :

" It certainly is true that the Transvaal Government deliberately elected for war rather than make any concession about the franchise."

Mr. Chamberlain, at Leicester on November 29, refers to the " moderate propositions " we made at Bloemfontein in May, on

[1] It is not within the scope of this paper to deal with the alleged Dutch conspiracy ; but it may be here noted that George McCall Theal, LL.D.,—who is Historiographer under the Government of Cape Colony, and generally recognised as a high authority on South African history, on which he has written in five volumes—recently gave a newspaper interview, in which he said, " I have known the thoughts and aims of the Dutch through a long period. I say to you on my word of honour that I am as sure as I am sitting here that the design to oust the English from South Africa and set up a great Dutch Republic no more entered the minds of men like Kruger, Steyn, Reitz, Joubert, and Esselen, than it has occurred to Premier Laurier to oust the United States from the American continent and make of all North America a great Canadian dominion."—*Manchester Guardian*, March 5, 1900.

which Mr. Kruger might have had peace on easy terms and without threatening the independence of his country :

"But to do this, to make some advance towards just and honest government, that was precisely what he was determined not to do."

Then, after referring to the seven years' Franchise Bill of July 27, which he describes as illusory, he adds that Mr. Kruger

"was not willing to make any substantial concession ; and when he found himself faced by a Government as determined as himself, he was ready to defy its forces, and to defy them to do their worst."

This is the Government's reason for breaking off the negotiations and precipitating war, and to any one who has read the correspondence, or followed its course as traced above, these representations are a travesty of the facts. The Boer proposal of August, conceding a five years' franchise, was an improved edition of the Bloemfontein terms, for it gave one seat more in the Volksraad ; and the conditions were such as Mr. Chamberlain could accept, as he fully explained in the House of Commons on October 19.

The sequel is soon told. Nearly three weeks elapsed without any new terms being communicated. Meantime British military preparations were pushed on, including hiring of transports and calling out of reserves. It was now a condition of scarcely veiled war, and the tension was brought to an end by the ultimatum of the Transvaal Government of October 9, followed by the invasion of Natal. This may have been wise as strategy : it was fatal as policy. It made the Transvaal the aggressor, and drew the whole Empire into line to resist the attack. But it could not relieve of heavy responsibility the statesman who had broken off the negotiations and precipitated war, when diplomacy was moving hopefully to a peaceful solution.

# OUR NATIONAL IMBROGLIO.

To make pretence of dealing in any complete and exhaustive manner with the great struggle in which we are engaged is not the purpose of this paper. Where authorities differ so widely, and where, as from the nature of the case, and from its many-sidedness and complexity, they are hardly likely to see eye to eye, it may well be that a prudent reticence should obtain.

There are, however, certain general considerations which demand thought, and which, if presented with the force and precision they deserve, should result in nothing but good.

As heirs to a splendid inheritance, it may well behove Britons to duly estimate its value and to preserve it, not only inviolate, but magnified, for the ages to come. According to the different stand-points from which the estate is viewed will be its appreciation, both in regard to the trust itself and the means of its preservation. An insular position, a sturdy and enterprising people, an expanding treasury, rich argosies, mighty ironclads, heroic legions, broad acres, the roll-call of the great past that reverberates with deeds of daunt-less daring, a solid and compacted commonwealth, may all be viewed in a material and a moral aspect.

Because it is inherent in the nature of things that both should have due weight, whether in individual or in national life, this is no justification for the depreciation of either, much less for dishonour done to the more worthy. If in the infancy of races the tyranny of might is an instrument of nature to secure her ends, the very example of nature urges that to such necessity there is a limit. Moreover, a wide experience counsels man that might is the least reliable and the most treacherous of energies working in the name of right, unless it be the might of a common need and of a kind agreement.

That materialistic view of empire which on the tongue is far other, generous, just, freeing, which is moral by fits and starts and spasms, is, no matter the girdle of its defences, nor the stubborn energy of its defenders, a subterfuge and a snare. The simple notion of nationality carries with it the idea of concession, and of agreement in spite of difference, among its members ; and the pros-perity of any one nation among the Powers demands—so says the law of nature which the philosopher respects—so says the law of

Christ which others beside Christians approve—that self-surrender in which is the firmest and most continuing existence. It becomes, therefore, a question of some importance whether or not our present entanglement is due to shortcomings or overt misdemeanour in the national character. To shirk the inquiry proudly does not augur wisdom; to reject it as irrelevant is self-convicting, if not suicidal. Signs are not wanting that a materialistic view of empire is predominant, and that a premier people are occupied with inconsequential aims and ends. We have entered on the possession of a great estate, irresponsibly, as though this Great and Greater Britain were a puppet-show or panorama for eyes' delight. Philosophically this is childish; morally it is criminal. The material asset dominates the life of the people, and depresses it in the same proportion. Instead of using the vantage gained by our ancestors—grit, courage, commerce, wealth, opportunity—to become intensively great, premier in character as well as in name, the nation has gone out after some eidolon of imperialism, which behind its glamour conceals a sword, perhaps a grave.

Within the restricted borders of Great Britain the amenities of higher law and life are in abeyance. A good many are patriotic to the verge of distraction as long as dollars are to be made by it. Trade stands before morality and before man. The soldier is a valuable integer in the hour when danger threatens. Great gulfs separate classes to the hurt of all. The philosophy of government largely resolves itself into a partisan scramble. Laws are politic strokes. There is no deep, wide, solid, and enduring base of law such as consults the interests of man as man in the school of a didactic nature. Our free press has run to licence. Public life is in no sense a replica of that which is honoured as honourable in private. Great journals, professing to lead mankind and to influence them for good, are themselves overawed by money sanctions, indulging in coarse jest, unseemly taunt, unworthy irritation of Great Powers as great or greater than ourselves. Napoleon was not wholly mistaken when he declared that an empire of adamant would be broken to pieces by a free press. In such a case freedom is licence only. From whatever cause or causes we have not, as a nation, kept pace in a moral sense with increasing wealth and opportunity. Internally our condition does not warrant unlimited expansion; in other words, at heart the empire is unsound and its body politic bloated. The empire has grown, but not the mind to govern; wealth has increased, whose chief fruit is the inclination to abuse it. *Similia similibus.* The miser belikens his store, and an imposing national asset inflates the pride of the possessor, peopling the mind with images which degrade the reason through fancy's charms. To a great extent our character has been entailed together with the estate. A good deal of the pirate still rules in our blood. Behind and before we are beset by unscrupulous ambition. The imperial microbe is upon the nation, eating out its life. Instead of honouring honest growth from within, we have laid hands with indecent haste and energy upon territory without. The old British bull as a silent monitor has been spurned. Infatuation has determined a "blood-and-thunder" insistence upon what is euphoniously called our rights.

All this may have been consistent with mediæval lust and scrimmage, when law was might, science superstition, and brotherhood discredited and almost unknown. At such times it was a demerit not to slay, for that meant to be slain.

Consider man's environment to-day, his advance in science and art and luxury and theoretic truth, the parade of religion and of justice! Thrones and courts and peerless men and women constitute a glittering pageant that is a mockery if not a gracious symbol. Wealth is multiplied, and the food-stuffs of the world abound. Ecclesiasticism, gorgeous in its pretension and display, indicates, if it does not supply, what man has a right to expect. Cathedrals and minarets pointing heavenward, hierarchies and sacraments and conventions and proud ultimatum of revealed truth, suggest a brotherhood which is yet only in the air, a solid and accordant family of man which is still distracted by cruel lust. The insignia everywhere are prophetic and suggestive in vain. Man's charter is a papyrus, a document only, his rightful hope a dream.

Unfortunately mankind does not profit by the examples of history; they must go through the fire to learn. It is sentiment that rules, passion rather than reason. The true wealth of nations, it has been shown over and over again, consists of other items than surface lands and mineral strata. As the world is solid and one, so is human interest and obligation. Passion divides; reason, interpreting nature aright, determines a homogeneous unity. The meanest atom in the human family is of value to the whole; in it the whole is vitally concerned. Whether on the small scale or the large, a submerged fraction is an incubus to the commonwealth, and to the commonwealth of the world. In brief, man is the world's asset, and mind the asset of man. It is by no means strange, therefore, if modern mankind should concern itself with that most conquering and only possible imperialism which centres in human character—in the control of the passions, and in the right holy use of reason. First and foremost, let it be freely granted, man owes it to his progenitor to secure the dignity of his entail, to become the inward power which may aggrandise the empire and the race. To continue the use of instruments employed in the dark ages for the attainment of those ends is illegitimate, inasmuch as the end does not condone the means. In letter it is lawful; in spirit it is not. Ancient sanctions should be at once dishonoured when nobler come into view. That which hurtling passion once achieved yields in the advance of the ages to a more humane suasion, with the added benison of a greatly exalted humanity.    There is all the difference in the world between the self-acclaimed greatness of the tall-hatted, aggressive, imperialistic man and that reason regnant which after all is the only real man.

All this, it will be said, is anything but practical politics.    Neither is steam an engine, nor gravitation either architect or builder. Practical politics! as though it were the height of wisdom to drift into affairs anyhow, or as rude passion dictates, and to blunder through them as happens.    Mr. Herbert Spencer is the most practical politician in the world just because he is a profound theorist, adjusting the lines of social order lest disorder ensue.    If, as is evident, the complexity of any individual life is such as to demand the combined wisdom of all so as to secure its fruition, what shall be said if individuals massed in the commonwealth, with their infinite correlation and chances of an erratic life—what but that their government is no sinecure, neither to be administered by adroit partisanship nor by place-hunters and irresponsible *ad captandum* orators.    As it is, the legislature requires reconstruction; money and ambition usurp the place of character and philanthropy.    A moneyed merchant, a lawyer fired by *esprit de corps*, a member of some unscrupulous syndicate, the young scion of a noble house trying his paces, a country squire with a mind equal to the field and farm, some sauntering member of the *beau monde* may sit side by side in the senate, united by the common tie that they know little and care less about the great first principles which govern man and mind.    And so gladiatorial shows go forward, more or less rude, which serve chiefly to emphasise the hostile camps, dividing mankind, which it is their prime duty to unite.    In a word, where the spring of undefiled truth should be, chicanery and policy and empiricism abide—with results that should not be surprising.

Manifestly the nation has not yet subdued its hereditary character to the loftiest thought and aim.    It is subjective and inquisitive one day a week, objective and materialistic the rest.    As a nation we have earned the title of the Arch-Pirate, and by all the laws of international obligation an *amende honorable* is due from us in the form at least of a magnanimous self-restraint.    Quite recently a Liberal peer expressed surprise that the British nation should be the object of European suspicion and dislike.    And yet surely the long catalogue of British raids might have afforded him some light if not relief. Where are the aboriginal races that have crossed our conquering path, both in the East and the West ?    What of the buccaneers by whom we swear, who enriched our coffers with gold ?    The virgin soil of Australasia fell to our lot, it is true, by a good fortune which secured a bloodless treasure ; but of India what can be said save that her conquest was characterised by perfidy and spoliation ?    With the great West our relations, after a century of estrangement, have only just entered on a new and happier stage. On all sides wealth has been gained by stratagem, and has been again employed for further aggression as chance offered.

Our immediate concern, however, is with present conditions. The lust of power and greed of gain threaten our undoing. From a Carlyle and a Ruskin the indictment might be expected, whilst the castigation at their hands would fall lightly as from so-called poetasters and enthusiasts with a craze. Not before it is time another class of mind comes to the rescue. A distinguished man of the world, now in high command on the seas, went out of his way recently at a banquet given by a literary society to emphasise our idolatry of money. The difficulty is to get outside ourselves sufficiently to realise the grave fact. Brag, Jingoism, emblazoned monuments, invidious national songs, a coarse buffoonery, and a boasted all-sufficient isolation—all proceeding from or inalienably associated with wealth—indicate a character which is as unworthy as it is ominous for our own future and for the world's peace.

That there exists no codified law of international amenity, and obligation is of itself a misfortune. It is further to be regretted that the trend that way is only half-hearted. On the broad platform of international life a temper prevails which is a positive violation of all that rules elsewhere. The individual must be self-restrained and law-abiding, crowds and nations proceed anyhow. Municipalities and separate States are amenable to sanctions which are more and more freeing as time goes on. Where dissonant forces arise a constituted authority knows how to deal with them. Over the acrid tongue the law of libel is a restraint, and he who provokes an assault is subject to the law equally with him who commits the act. A man may think what he likes, but beyond that is dangerous ground. Bluster and threat and unseemly reviling are all controlled by statute or crushed by contempt.

In the wider sphere of international concerns a similarly drastic control is needed, lest national accord be violated by the world's great unrest. Even if it could be allowed that all the nationalities of the world were moved by the loftiest motives in all that pertains to inward development and international relation, this would be no security for the world's peace, in the absence of a framework of international law. Where every nation is largely a law unto itself, and a too exclusive self-regard inevitably determines this attitude, the causes of friction are sure to appear. A wider prospect broadens the mind, good is seen where evil only is suspected, and mutual concession is recognised to be both necessary and wise.

It is to avoid misunderstanding and to deepen reciprocal regard that a premier people should lend itself with all the singleness and energy it possesses. Pre-eminently it is incumbent on them to encourage, even at some cost, such *rapprochement* as shall, whilst giving assurance of sincerity, advance the cause at heart. That other nations are, even as we, in a low moral state as compared with what the age warrants is nothing to the purpose. If it is not just, it is magnanimous that, as the chief offender in a policy of " grab," Britain should take the lead in securing an international concordat as a warranty for the world s peace.

Presumably, in common with other Powers represented at the Hague, we took the Conference seriously, and espoused its aim kindly. If we did not, as has been alleged, then more's the pity and more's the crime. The elevation of Sir Julian Pauncefote to the Peerage for the handsome manner in which he advanced, if only a little way, the interests concerned, gives the lie emphatic to the base suggestion, unless, indeed, the nation is a lie at heart. To gauge the feeling of the country upon the question is not an easy matter, but in the light of subsequent events the real disposition of the Government would seem to have been of a proud, suspicious, and disloyal character. Even if as a nation it may be allowed that we yielded to the mood of the hour, it was neither hearty nor enduring. Plainly, an appeal to the great Powers in the event of international complications was a worthy design or it was not. And if, as is allowed, it was, then it cannot but appear that some magnanimity, and no little self-restraint, was to have been expected upon every emergency from every nation that joined hands over the issue.

What has happened since is known, and Britain excuses herself with the greater clamour perhaps because, after all, she has an inkling that to excuse is to accuse, in point of fact. The proud and rich and mighty nation, the prize-raider of earth, she who has kept the cauldron a-boiling through the ages past, and has compelled other Powers to emulate her " tricks and manners," she who could well afford to stoop to conquer and to do the *amende honorable* by an exemplary self-restraint in a crucial hour, has signally failed just when an act of self-sacrificing regard for the world's peace might ha 've brought her the undying tribute of the world's honour.

Granted all that may justly be alleged concerning Transvaal aspirations and methods—and in regard to all this the retort courteous may be made of *tu quoque*—granted the breach of conventions and the invasion of British territory, it is very questionable whether, in view of our piratical conquests everywhere, the verdict of history will be an acquittal of the Power proudly named Great Britain for her resort to the arbitrament of war.

That Britain should have been the first among the Powers to resort to the ordeal of battle after a nominal assent, at least, to the prudence and nobleness of other modes of allaying strife, is a most lamentable occurrence. Diplomacy, of course, pleads the impossibility of another instrument. But, then, diplomacy is ofttimes neither magnanimous nor human, relying on brute force when humane methods would achieve more. Condescension to an inferior in such a case is regarded as romantic, and yet if the romance had triumphed none more than the diplomat would have gloried over the result. Indisputably an appeal to the great Powers was on the cards, and might have been essayed, and with the better grace that raiding is an art in which Britain had already given instruction to the world. It was national pride that prevented, pride in our own resources, and pride of our prestige. There is little doubt that the Continental gibe would have been hurled at us, and all manner of fearsome and selfish reasons have been assigned for our retrocession from the ordeal of blood. Even so, whichever of the Powers incline the way of peace will be liable to the same attacks.

There were, however, several circumstances which might have inspired Britain with a confidence she lacked—to say nothing of the fact that, if loftier standards of human life are to be upheld in practice, some great Power will have to go out of its way to raise them. A strong inclination in the way of peace on the part of the Government would have found some assurance from the harmony which prevailed among the signatories at the Conference. Russia was represented, whose Czar is undoubtedly sincere, and would strain a point to prove it in an hour when the principle was on its trial; America, a great self-controlled and amicable republic, whose humanity in her recent struggles was most pronounced; Italy and Denmark, indubitably friends of the new gospel; Germany and France, both dependent for their prosperity on the peace of the world, and both large investors in the Transvaal. In any case, to have made the appeal to the Powers would have cleared Britain's conscience, and might have availed her purpose without loss of blood and treasure—hers and her enemy's. Certainly such a course would have disarmed suspicion, multiplied our friends, and magnified our heritage, as nothing else could.

The crucial hour has come and gone, and found our character wanting. The question that now arises is, supposing the upshot of the struggle to be all that Britain desires, what is the net gain? Will it compensate for the cost—the suffering of the field, the darkened hearts and homes, a shrunken treasury, a dishonoured national life, a re-incarnate militarism, a riotous conqueror's song? An appeal to arms does not even afford the consolation which might accrue if victory crowned the right. Invocation of supernal powers as *aide-de-camp* to either or both of the belligerents is fatuous, if not worse. It is the loudest threat, the wiliest cunning, the largest armies, the longest purse, the mightiest instruments of death that are invoked in fact, no matter how faith may pose. Whether the two win, or neither, both are losers in every way, and the great world at large.

It is not denied—it would be unworthy to do so—that British success means liberty and civilisation to black and white races alike. Nevertheless, the question will arise, Does the end justify the means? There is even a prior consideration still, Do we know what the end will be? Can we either measure or control the consequences? As is well known, the war was sprung upon the nation like an electric spark; apparently this country was as innocent of its probability as it was impotent to prevent it. Where one forecast has been fallacious and costly others may be. The sword has been unsheathed, and none can tell when it shall be restored to its scabbard. The course of events which it was possible at one time to have directed is now beyond control. What that may be in its main current, as well as in its side issues, none can conceive. Upon our own nation victory will be dearly bought if it worsens the national character—if it revives the reign of brute force, and discourages endeavour after a saner life.

Since, then, it is impossible to anticipate the consequences of the imbroglio, it is vain to invoke them as a warrant for our methods. We do not apprehend the result; we cannot claim it as a justification of the means. There are those who urge that the mines and gold-fields are the main cause of the entanglement, and this probably is so far true that but for them neither Britain nor her enemy would have set such value on the soil, whilst most assuredly the sinews of war would not have been so freely forthcoming. For the purposes of this paper the moneyed aspect may, however, be disregarded. It may even be allowed that our hands have been imbrued with blood for no other reason than that freedom and right may reign. More, it may be taken for granted that this result will follow. Nevertheless, how dissonant and disproportionate, not to say contrary, the ends and the means! In the use of such means is seen the apotheosis of coercion as a warrantable authority over mankind, and of a fatuous faith in miraculous disproportion. It is assumed that some particular nation has a mandate from the Highest to kill or cure the rest—oddly enough, to kill in order to save their lives. It is also assumed that a brutal method can achieve a humanely noble end, that between cause and consequence there is no direct relation whatever; that the child of tyrannies is freedom; that cruelty is the open Sesame to the door of life.

And yet it cannot be denied that the same ends might, and in all probability would, have been obtained by other means. The order of nature, if man would only regard it, is not of a violent kind. Nature has no passion; her moods are sane. A nation's growth, our own, calls for time and patience, for personal experience and compacted decision. Hasten slowly is a maxim taught by nature and declaimed by history. It is so easy to spend and be spent in doing that which were better left undone. Certainly the work may be spectacular and imposing—but so are the fires of hell.

The matter resolves itself into an impossible sum, which may be stated but cannot be solved. If ten thousand maimed and slaughtered men *plus* the domestic sorrows and privations entailed, added to ten thousand times ten thousand gold coins of the realm, are a fair investment for the instant enfranchisement of a few settlers in a crude and avowedly immature commonwealth, what is the fair charge for a good example to the nations by a Power which boasts itself to be eclectic and considers itself all but divine? Or again, it may be fairly asked, what, given the same premisses, is the purchase-money required for the emancipation, both of soul and body, of millions of men within our own borders whose disadvantage cries aloud for relief? To be recognised as sincere missioners abroad we might well have deserved the character at home.

Talk of "eidola tribus": our Pantheon is full of them! In spite of loud professions to the contrary, the nation adores the god of war. So fatuous is human philosophy that men regard the least competent means as efficient to achieve the greatest ends. To consolidate and extend our Empire there must inevitably be war—so runs the creed. Our fathers used the instrument, and so must we. The great of the earth are identified with war; indeed war is itself great; and so it is—a great curse, a great cross, a great obstacle to man's sublimation.

The thought will not bear thinking, and because it is passion's output. As if brotherhood, the only true annealer, were advanced by discord! As if the genius which espies solidarity could find no rational means to compass it about! As if hell were the highway to heaven!

Between cause and effect, means and end, there is, and must be, a consequential relation, the two must be congruous. A nation that aims at some lofty ideal is necessitated by a force over which it has no control to foregather some worthy means. They may not always be efficient, because judgment is erring, but they cannot be low, degrading, and immoral without reflecting on the aim in view. To make avowal of a sublime purpose and to invoke a malign instrument is self-convicting: between the two there is no accord. If, therefore, in the matter of international complications no more humane methods than war present themselves, only one conclusion is possible—that the aim is base as the means. In this the teaching of history agrees. Wars are always unjust, must be in the very nature of things to one combatant or another, and after a lapse of years are allowed to be. Wars are always inefficient, because in the end they do as much harm in one direction as good in another. Every section of the earth's surface, every member of the family of man, has its special genius and opportunity, which after its own fashion is realised. Harmony does not result from overriding tyrannies nor uniformities, and they who in any way impose them on their kind are in that same hour suffering the extreme penalty of the law themselves.

Our present embroilment teaches nothing more surely than that as a nation the appetite has overrun the stomach. The nation has grasped at more than it has been able to administer or protect. Avarice does not consort with wisdom. A genuine interest in our kindred across the seas would have inspired a competent care for their well-being. Our concern was rather with some glamour of Imperialism. The very least the country should have done, and would have done if its aims were single and lofty, was to have planted on our own soil our own people, and in such numbers as the circumstances of the case demanded, and such as our own densely peopled centres at home did warrant. A tithe of the millions now spent on war, if devoted to a well-advised system of emigration, would in all likelihood have tended to peace, and that for many reasons. That no such scheme was concerted is evidence of misrule. Evidently it is a garish Imperialism that occupies the eye of the nation, extent rather than intent, glory without cross-bearing. As is invariably the case where passion chooses, the nation has inverted the proper order of national development—producing a monstrosity rather than a well-developed and compacted body politic. At heart the Empire is unsound, and the limbs thrown out are attenuated and long. Between these there is no such vital connection as constitutes fellowship, much less unity, so that the nation verily goes a-begging for federation of what should never have been anything else but a solid whole.

It can hardly be repeated too often, the nation has never realised its assets nor its responsibilities in any one direction, and certainly not in its colonies. To acquire them is easier than to hold and develop; to be a worthy appanage they must be made so by a people who are themselves worthy. A colossal Empire without moral integrity is a name only. Its wealth may be a boon but is more likely to be a bane. For our own character's sake, and for our credit, it is well that the nation should see itself as others see us. Perhaps it will then be felt that to fan the feuds of the nations, shaking our fist in their faces, chinking our money-bags in their ears—the game isn't worth the candle.

JOHN TRIST.

# WAR AND EVOLUTION.

O EVOLUTION, what crimes are committed in thy name! Thus are we tempted to vary poor Madame Roland's death-cry uttered as, on her way to the guillotine, she passed the statue of Liberty erected by her murderers. For just as in France at the end of the eighteenth century the political idea of liberty, excellent in itself, was made an excuse for revolutionary outrages; so now, in England, at the end of the nineteenth century, in the name of that Evolution which science has made plain, some of our literary "Jingoes" are writing of war as being not simply a passing affliction, but a glorious and inevitable mode of progress, sanctioned of old and for ever by a law of nature. People such as these have heard the already trite expressions "battle of life" and "survival of the fittest"; perhaps they have read Darwin's works (which scarcely deal with Social Evolution) and have seen how and why this battle of life is fought, among animals with tooth and claw, and among uncivilised races with axe and knife; certainly they have eagerly studied the typical history telling much of military campaigns and little of social institutions; and then they hastily assume that because even among men calling themselves civilised the fierce fight with gun and bayonet has been waged in past and present times, it must and ought to be so waged throughout the future. Consequently here we find one who ventures to write that "the day of universal peace will be the day of universal death" because "war, as every student of evolution is aware, is the law of the universe," and there we find another who, lamenting the unfortunate degeneracy of some of his fellow citizens, satisfies himself and would like to satisfy others that this and other ills are the "cankers of a long peace." Periodic bloodshed is the panacea which these quacks prescribe for us, to cure our social diseases and to increase our social prosperity. Infatuated by the glamour of militarism—which has ceased to be glorious unless defensive—they overlook the truism that industrialism is the basis of our national welfare, and that the navy and army are nowadays maintained as protectors not producers.

No real student of evolution believes their reactionary dialectics. Evolution, nature's transformation-process of development, has no doubt necessitated frequent wars in the past, and does now necessitate severe economic competition; but it does not necessitate everlasting war of the military type. There is some limit to the long-drawn agony. And the idea of the battle-field perpetually taking the place of an international tribunal is more than ghastly, it is preposterous. To fancy that the merits of a private dispute can be settled by a fight, is usually held to be worthy only of schoolboys, in whose natures there often predominates the ancestral taint of that ancient trial by battle which the trial by law so very slowly superseded. And yet, to this day, when nations quarrel, most of us seem to suppose that a trial by battle on a large scale can satisfactorily decide upon a question of honour, or exactly adjust a boundary line, or correctly interpret a convention.

Let these believers in civilisation by slaughter study almost any one of the numerous works of Mr. Herbert Spencer, the philosopher of evolution, and they will realise with dismay the absurdity of their mistake. They need not be afraid that he is a sentimental idealist. On the contrary, in his prose epic, *The Synthetic Philosophy*, not content with describing in a masterly series of generalisations the fearful and wonderful evolution from nebulous homogeneity to the heterogeneity of civilised societies; not content in fact with interpreting all that is knowable of nature, with "a philosophic calm" which is almost superhuman he has tried in some degree to justify the ways of nature to men. And yet writing in favour of Arbitration he can confidently proclaim the truth, pleasant as well as scientific, that

"henceforth social progress is to be achieved not by systems of education, not by preaching of this or that religion, not by insistence on a humane creed daily repeated and daily disregarded, but only by cessation from those antagonisms which keep alive the brutal elements of human nature, and by persistence in a peaceful life which gives unchecked play to the sympathies."

In other words, he holds that war must become impossible not only, as M. Bloch has pointed out, because of the enormous loss of men and money involved, but because of the growth of those higher ethical feelings which make war unendurable.

Not indeed that he would be in the meantime a supporter of the old meek apathy or of the new reckless arrogance which have in turn been known to neglect the proper means of defence. For elsewhere he distinctly says: "There is no gainsaying the truth that while the predatory instincts continue prompting nations to rob one another, destructive agencies must be met by antagonistic destructive agencies." But though defensive war is justifiable as a last resort, offensive war, whether for expansion or for prestige, can be justified no longer.

Over and over again he has shown how the struggle for existence among nations, which ultimately leads to the survival of the "fittest," was in primitive times carried on almost entirely by military war;

has in modern times been carried on partly by military and partly by industrial war ; and must in the future, so far as civilised nations are concerned, be continued by industrial war.   In his *Principles of Sociology* he has described in detail that gradual change " from militancy to industrialism " which marks the progress of human societies from barbarism to modern civilisation.   Speaking generally, the organisation of primitive societies having been developed by stress of war, is maintained chiefly for military purposes, and only slightly serves as an improved system of obtaining the necessary food and shelter.   In the next stage of progress we find societies whose energies are about equally divided ; now wielding the weapons of war, now cultivating the arts of peace.   Finally we come to the modern civilised nations, for the most part organised for industrial competition, and keeping in the background those necessary military and naval forces which are maintained (nominally at any rate) solely for defence.   And, further, he points out that it is owing to this humanitarian development (still incomplete) that individual liberty has been successfully asserted ; that the position of women has improved, and that social sympathies have widened.

To quote Herbert Spencer's own words from a popular summary of the facts above outlined :

" Warfare among men, like warfare among animals, has had a large share in raising their organisations to a higher stage. . . . War in the slow course of things brings about a social aggregation which furthers that industrial state at variance with war : and yet nothing but war could bring about this social aggregation."

So much for the past.   As regards the present and future :

" Persistent war is at variance not only with industrial development, but also with the higher intellectual developments that aid industry and are aided by it . . . such advantages, bodily and mental, as the race derives from the discipline of war, are exceeded by the disadvantages, bodily and mental, but especially mental, which result after a certain stage of progress has been reached. . . . After this stage has been reached, the purifying process, continuing still an important one, remains to be carried on by industrial war."

Then, as a climax, follows the sarcastic remark :

" Those educated in the religion of enmity—those who during boyhood, when the instincts of the savage are dominant, have revelled in the congenial ideas which classic poems and histories yield so abundantly, are naturally blind to truths of this kind."

No doubt he did not imagine that it would be possible for the advocates of militarism to appeal for confirmation of their primitive theories not to the classics but to modern science.   Yet just this has happened.   Pleading a supposed necessity implied by evolution, men and even women are to be found who contemplate the horrors of constantly recurring military war with that relentless assurance with which he himself is wont to contemplate the lesser horrors of industrial war. For that expression " the purifying process " vividly suggests the general tone of his extremely naturalistic ethics when treating of the later form of the struggle for existence. Seldom does he show any sign of feeling that the new process is but slightly less fiendish than the old. Still, he has protested against the mistaken conclusion of a French critic who remarked that his biological method of reasoning practically amounted to a *væ miseris* as barbarous as the old *væ victis*. And while acknowledging that " the battle of life, as carried on by competition, may have a mercilessness akin to the battle of life as carried on by violence," he has advised some restraint (though merely voluntary) upon triumphant egoism.

Only in recent times, since the evolution theory has become, chiefly owing to the labours of Herbert Spencer, Darwin, and Huxley, a part of established science, have we been able to understand something of the real meaning and significance of the struggle for existence. Adaptation to environment is the law of life ; and, in fact, life has been defined by Herbert Spencer as " the continuous adjustment of internal relations to external relations." And this itself, he shows, is only an illustration of the wider truth that one phase of the universal evolution necessitated by the persistence of force is " a continual approximation to and more or less complete maintenance of a moving equilibrium."

But—and this is an important point—" the survival of the fittest " which results merely means that the men and animals successful in the struggle succeed because they happen to be best suited to their surrounding conditions, whether those conditions are simple or complex, high or low. And, further, there is no such thing as a general and continual progress going on simultaneously in all societies ; each has what we may call its " terminal excellence " which is reached sooner or later in its history.

Well, the form which the battle of life usually takes to-day, in civilised societies, is, as we have seen, an economic competition ; a competition which is waged between different nations, and between different individuals of the same nation.

This modern battle is, like the ancient battle, chiefly caused by excess of population ; and yet—such is the irony of things—if that excess did not prevail, natural selection would not have sufficient scope for carrying out its gruesome work, which, in some degree, still remains a painful necessity. Though, indeed, we are assured by the highest scientific authority that some day in the select societies, in the future of which we can only dream, adaptation, having become approximately complete, and the excess of population.

having normally ceased when no longer requisite, the martyrdom of
the "unfit" will be no more, and all men will win happiness with
greater ease.

Be that as it may, under existing circumstances, it is useless to
ignore the awkward fact, none the less true because unpleasant, that
the very *raison d'être* of the struggle for existence implies that as
among animals more are born than can find suitable food, so,
though to a lesser extent, among human beings more are born than
can find suitable work, and the resulting competition for work, and
as a climax, for wealth, rages with particular severity among the
highly educated in the restricted field of the higher professions.

Perhaps a general explanation of the present social position may
be obtained if we divide the successful and also the unsuccessful into
four classes :

Among the former we have :

(1) Those who honestly adapt themselves to their social
environment.

(2) Those who dishonestly adapt themselves to their social
environment.

(3) Those who adapt themselves to their social environment
only after that environment has been partly adapted to
them by influence or capital.

(4) Those few who having ample means have no need to adapt
themselves (in the business sense) to their social environment, since it has already been completely adapted to
them.

Among the latter we have :

(1) Those who would have proved just as suitable as some of
their more fortunate fellows, if they had had similar
opportunities.

(2) Those who are hampered by an education fashionable
instead of useful, or literary instead of technical.

(3) Those who suffer from excess of sensitiveness or lack of
self-assertion, or in whom, as in Hamlet

"The native hue of resolution
Is sicklied o'er with the pale cast of thought."

(4) Those who are afflicted with considerable physical or mental
weakness, and may be doomed to hopeless failure and  .
endless misery.

That merit does almost always win some amount of success there
can be no doubt ; but one need only read the newspapers to be painfully reminded that sometimes in modern London as in ancient
Rome, Virtue gets praise and little else.

Clearly the facts of life, as a whole, do not justify either pessimism or optimism ; and " meliorism" has been suggested as a definition of the intermediate attitude.

Granted that this is by no means the best of all possible worlds, still it does contain more happiness than misery. Happiness, in the sense of a predominance of pleasures over pains, is more or less obtained by the majority of mankind. The satisfaction of desires is their aim; and, fortunately for their content, the desires of most people are not unduly ambitious. On the other hand it is impossible to forget that too many—some unable to work, some unable to rest—can only long for most of the pleasures of life, and go on living, simply through instinct or through hope.

Anyhow, it is becoming common knowledge that natural law means something very different from our idea of justice. And, in fact, ever since man has had capacity and opportunity for contemplating things in general, attempts have been made sometimes to explain and justify, sometimes to remove or mitigate, the misery, the disease, the cruelty, and the injustice which, through the history of the world, have impaired the predominating happiness.

Some of these attempts, both old and new, deserve a short consideration.

Religion, which seems to have had its origin in the dread of ancestral ghosts, gradually gave rise to organised institutions whose main objects were propitiation, exhortation and consolation arising from and seemingly confirmed by some explanation which was offered to all (often with compulsion) and accepted by the faithful.

Now, among all the various doctrines of various theological systems, two stand out conspicuous. Always they assume the existence of an immaterial soul distinct from the material body which is its temporary dwelling-place; and nearly always they assume that each individual has, or had at some time, however remote, "free will" to do right or to do wrong. What has science to say on these essential points? After premising that we can never have *absolute* knowledge of mind, because (among other reasons) "a thing cannot at the same instant be both subject and object of thought, and yet the substance of mind must be this before it can be known," Herbert Spencer shows how mental phenomena are dependent on the brain, and "the human brain is an organised register of infinitely numerous experiences received during the evolution of life, or rather, during the evolution of that series of organisms through which the human organism has been reached." When therefore religious faith tries—if we may adapt a famous political speech—to call another world into existence to redress the balance of the present, it cannot obtain the support of science, which knows no other life than this for man. To the metaphysical upholders of the "free will" theory who, seemingly, believe in an absolute *ego* with full power to decide which of conflicting feelings shall prevail, his answer is (in brief), " All actions whatever must be determined by those psychical connections which experience has generated, either in the life of the individual, or in that general antecedent life of which the accumulated results are organised in his constitution." Clearly, then, man is not, scientifically speaking, responsible for his actions ; though for practical purposes he must, if sane, be treated as if he were responsible. The tragedy of life is surely heightened when we realise that, not " men at some time are masters of their fates," but the exact opposite is the fact, if by " fates " we mean the inherited characters and present environments, acting and reacting upon each other. Approximations to this tragic truth are, however, to be found in the Augustinian doctrine of " predestination ;" in the Buddhistic theory of " karma," signifying that man's character is an inherited compound of his soul's experiences in his previous lives ; and also in the tragedies of the Greek poets who depicted their heroes sometimes as controlled by an irresistible destiny ordained by Zeus, and sometimes as doomed to evil by the " Nemesis " sent by offended deities to avenge ancestral crime. But that theology, with its fanciful explanations, its illusory hopes and empty threats, should be waning in this scientific age will hardly cause surprise.

Most of those endeavouring to ameliorate the lot of man are now turning their attentions to sociology in general and to politics in particular. And among political systems we have Socialism, Individualism, and a working compromise between these two extremes. The chief aim of Socialism, whether " communistic " or " collective," is to abolish or, at least, to alter entirely, the present economic competition, by abolishing the individualistic landlordism and capitalism which now are its concomitants. With a certain amount of plausibility Socialists base their theories on the patent fact that the history of civilisation is largely the history of artificial legislation by the State, owing to which the aboriginal selfish propensities of citizens have been more or less controlled and bent to social ends. But though altruism, as well as egoism, is essential, egoism ought, as a rule, to predominate, and will strive to predominate whatever the form of government, whatever the industrial system. Consequently, if by carrying artificial legislation to its logical conclusion, Socialism were temporarily established, it would inevitably bring about an equality of poverty instead of the present inequality of property ; while the new democracy would become but the old tyranny " writ large." And eventually it must be ended by political reaction unless in the meantime the society had sunk to impotence or disappeared. Herbert Spencer's Individualism is exactly the reverse of the foregoing. Preferring the " natural moulding " of gradual adaptation rather than the " artificial moulding " of drastic legislation, he has repeatedly urged (without success) that the State should never interfere with individual citizens except to administer legal justice and to defend them from foreign aggression. "Justice," as he understands it, is based upon the biological law that every adult creature should receive the full advantages of its strength, and all the disadvantages of its weakness, with the limitation that, as regards human beings, each individual, while enjoying his own liberty, must respect the equal liberty of other individuals. "But," you will say, "his very limitation, his justice, is itself artificial." Exactly. He has to admit that "Nature . . . cares not for the claims of the weaker even to the extent of granting them fair play." Nay, more, he had previously admitted that "Doubtless it seems, from one point of view, unjust that the inferior should be left to suffer the evils of their own inferiority for which they are not responsible." Especially, it should be added, as those inferior in natural fitness are not *necessarily* inferior in human merit.

For all that, he will not support the idea that the State should assist its weaker citizens beyond securing for them, as for the rest, mere legal justice, that fair play, unknown to nature, without which no organised society could exist. Any further artificial help, any supplement to this meagre instalment of mercy, ought, he argues, to be left to the chance beneficence of individuals. And so, in his opinion, not only our Poor-law, but our national education, our public libraries, our public parks, our public sanitation, our factory laws, are one and all symptoms of social disease, because they are interferences with individual liberty, enforced and organised by the central or local agencies of the State.

How different from these are Huxley's views! In his Essays, which are learned without heaviness, and sad without pessimism, you seem to hear as a *leit motif* the pathos of that classic verse:

"Sunt lacrimae rerum et mentem mortalia tangunt."

As a scientist, he fearlessly interprets the laws of nature; as a humanitarian, he protests against some of the results of their mechanical mercilessness; and as a political philosopher, he considers that, since they have been somewhat modified in the past, they may be modified in the future by judicious statesmanship supported by human sympathy. The art of politics, he would have agreed, should take a middle course, avoiding alike the apathy of utter naturalism, and the fanaticism of frenzied discontent. The statesman should, as it were, steer the ship of State between the Scylla of Individualism and the Charybdis of Socialism. Huxley, of necessity, realises that to get complete and general happiness is impossible, but still does not despair of a nearer approach to that ideal end for which humanity has yearned so long. And as a means he relies largely on rational legislation prompted by the "ethical process" which is typical of developing civilisation. This "ethical process" is, he points out, somewhat akin to the "horticultural process" which selects flowers instead of weeds, and it has done much to vary for the better the effects of the "cosmic process," though, in an ultimate sense, itself a product of that "cosmic process." History shows how it has mitigated the painful inequity of the struggle for existence by improving those social conditions to which, as to their physical environments, men must somehow become adapted.

Knowing only too well that social evolution is a part of cosmic evolution, Huxley never encourages the charming fancy that nature can be literally overcome by art; but he does continually proclaim his opposition to "Administrative Nihilism," and with his last words he urges that to obtain a worthy civilisation, "that which lies before the human race is a constant struggle to maintain and improve, in opposition to the state of nature, the state of art of an organised polity."

After all, the obsolescent myth of man's "special creation," now finally confuted by science, does suggest a psychological truth. If man is, as we have seen, one among many results of a universal process of development, he is also the highest type of that development. Supreme in intellect, and supreme in emotion, he alone can criticise the pitiless laws which rule his destiny; and so, even with full consciousness that his existence is but fleeting, his forces but weak, in comparison with some other modes of the energy immanent in the universe, his views and sympathies must ever tend to be anthropocentric. That is the reason why the contrast between the human process and the cosmic process will last as long as civilisation. For civilisation clearly is, to a large extent, an artificial work; the gradual modification of physical laws by the human mind, which has itself been gradually modified by centuries of social life. And this distinction between nature and art the Germans have emphasised in describing primitive folk as "*Natur-Völker.*"

None the less, it must be admitted that while the cosmic process errs from absence of feeling, the human process is wont to err from excess of feeling, and to forget that, whether we like it or not, human and natural are ultimately one. In politics, as in religion, there always lurks the danger of the wish being father to the thought, always, too, the risk of reason being awe-struck by authority. No human hopes, no human legislation may entirely nullify the aptness of the hard saying, "Might is right," for it still expresses, though in a somewhat different sense, an ever-lasting law of life. To every nation, and to every individual, unjust, unfeeling Nature's first commandment is, "Thou shalt not be weak." Prosperity without humanity is possible; prosperity without honesty is possible; prosperity without energy (either one's own or another's) is, and always will be, impossible. All that can be done is to take care that these energies shall be devoted more and more to industrialism, less and less to militarism; and that they shall be controlled by law, persuaded by beneficence. True it is that with our highly organised societies we have long left behind primeval barbarism, that we have done much to develop Nature's pleasant gifts, and much to remedy its cruel defects; but, creatures of Nature that we are, we can never reach the Utopia of Man.

Meanwhile, though nature, in spite of man, will still crush individuals for the advancement of the race, though the struggle for existence, however modified, will still go on until, in each society, equilibrium is reached, yet there is no excuse for those who argue that war must remain the inevitable test of civilisation. Against a suggestion as absurd as it is barbarous, a deeper sympathy and a wider knowledge will join in protest.

*Pax Romana* was the aim of the military Roman Empire, *pax Humana* must be the aim of modern industrial nations; abolition of military war, mitigation of industrial war—that degree of peace humanity could gain.

C. O. OVINGTON.

# J. S. MILL'S LETTERS TO A. COMTE.[1]

THE appearance of the *Letters of John Stuart Mill to Auguste Comte* have a special interest for readers of the WESTMINSTER REVIEW, with which Mill was so closely connected, and which owed much of its early success to his support and assistance; and all English students of philosophy are under a deep obligation to M. Lévy-Bruhl for the publication and careful editing of this remarkable and interesting correspondence, and for the clear and able introduction in which he describes the relation, both personal and philosophical, between the two great thinkers. The letters of Comte to Mill were published in 1877 at the instance of the Société Positiviste, but, interesting as they are by themselves, they necessarily leave much to be desired; the letters of Mill were necessary to our complete understanding of the situation, the agreements and differences which existed between them, and the reasons why, after so close an approach, they finally diverged and took a separate path. Much of this, of course, can be gathered from Mill's *Autobiography* and from the articles he wrote for the WESTMINSTER REVIEW in 1864. But in this correspondence we get a more comprehensive view of their philosophical and personal relations, and their most intimate thoughts and confidences are revealed. How little we knew before we are reminded by M. Lévy-Bruhl, who, at the opening of his introduction, says, after quoting the passage in Mill's *Autobiography* which refers to this correspondence:

"Ces quelques mots de Mill, dans ses *Mémoires* caractérisent exactement sa correspondance avec Comte. Mais ils sont aussi fort sommaires. Comment les relations se sont-elles établies entre les deux philosophes? Quelles questions furent traitées dans cette correspondance 'active'? Et sur quels points portait la controverse qui la fit d'abord dégénérer, puis bientôt cesser? Mill a passé outre sans nous le dire."

To these interesting questions the present volume supplies a full answer, and will completely satisfy our natural curiosity. But, more than that, English readers will probably get a fresh insight into Mill's own character. Bain has correctly said that in this correspondence with Comte, Mill was unusually open. Naturally

[1] *Lettres Inédites de John Stuart Mill à Auguste Comte.* Publiées avec les réponses de Comte, et une Introduction par L. Lévy-Bruhl. Paris: Félix Alcan.

reserved, says M. Lévy-Bruhl, and little inclined to speak of himself, of his health, of his affairs, of his projects, Mill did not hesitate to open his mind to Comte as to an old friend. This departure from his constant practice would have appeared very surprising to his acquaintances if they had known of it. It is explained by the enthusiasm into which the reading of the first volumes of the *Cours de Philosophie Positive* had thrown Mill. His first letter in which he introduced himself to Comte (dated November 8, 1841) makes this quite clear. In this letter Mill expresses to Comte his sympathy and adhesion, and says that since the happy epoch when the two first volumes of the *Cours* had become known to him, he had waited for each new volume with a lively impatience, and read and re-read it with a veritable intellectual passion. In all the first part of this correspondence Mill preserves a tone of affectionate deference and even of humility; but he shows also, as M. Lévy Bruhl observes, a very firm determination not to abandon, without decisive reasons, certain opinions which were dear to him. But what strikes us at first is the force of the attraction to which he yielded in writing to Comte. His deference, however, created an erroneous impression on Comte, who thought he had secured a disciple in a man who ultimately showed himself his equal. The misunderstanding slumbered for a time; Comte believed that the adhesion of Mill was more complete than it really was. Mill accepted the positive method; Comte concluded that he accepted equally the positive philosophy in its principles and in its consequences. But little by little irreducible divergences of opinion showed themselves under the apparent identity of method and principles. Mill went as far as he could to meet Comte, and Bain says that he afterwards regretted some of the things he had written to Comte on the inequality of the sexes—he had made too many concessions. But Comte would yield nothing; he did not even imagine there was anything to yield; he would not even take into consideration, as Mill wished him to do, the ideas which were submitted to him. Comte, as we have said, at first took Mill for a disciple, but when he perceived that agreement between them was impossible, he looked upon Mill as a dissentient, not to say a heretic. Mill proposed to discuss " opinions " on certain points; but Comte had no " opinions " in the sense in which Mill used the word; he had a system, a body of doctrine, which he had constructed expressly to put an end to the flux and reflux of " opinions." As everybody knows, Comte was born in Catholicism, and he was imbued with its spirit, and ultimately assumed for himself a position of spiritual authority in succession to or in rivalry with the Catholic Church.

Mill was altogether of a different temper; he had been " born in Benthamism," which was, after all, a form of Protestantism, and his mind was naturally much more open than that of Comte; he never regarded his ideas at any time as final. As M. Lévy-Brühl generously and truly says :

" Penetrated with a religious respect for truth, and persuaded that this truth, at least in philosophical and social matters, offers a multitude of aspects of which we see only a part, his endeavour was to discover the greatest possible number of these aspects. He did not believe he had the right to sacrifice the slightest particle of truth to the beautiful logical order of a system."

The two principal questions over which the writers of this correspondence differed were psychology and the inequality of the sexes.

Mill had been brought up in the belief, which he tenaciously held, that differences in character were due to circumstances and education—environment, as we now say. That men were all born alike and all variations were acquired. Men are what they are made. Gall, towards the end of the last century, undertook to refute this doctrine, which was generally that of the French and English philosophers. He connected the innate faculties with the cerebral organs. Cabanis also had taught that psychological differences corresponded with organic differences. Comte took this for granted.

Mill promised to read Gall, and his first letter on the subject contains an amusing passage :

" I have read the six volumes of Gall with serious attention, but up till now I find myself too much embarrassed to judge his theory properly. I am to some extent persuaded that there is some truth in it, and that the elementary propensities and capacities, whatever they may be, are each attached to a particular part of the brain. But I find very great difficulties. At first you agree to the prematureness of all special localisation ; and, in effect, the proofs do not fail to show the inexactitude of those which up to the present have been attempted. I will cite myself as an example. The only thing that I know with certainty of my craniological development is that the pretended organ of constructiveness is not very pronounced in my case. A very decided phrenologist exclaimed at the moment when he saw me for the first time, ' What do you do with your constructiveness ? ' But I fail almost totally in the corresponding faculty. I am deprived of the mechanical sense, and my inaptitude for any operation which demands manual dexterity is truly prodigious."—*Letter xi.*

It is only fair to Comte to say that he did not accept Gall's theory in all its details, but only in its general principle.

The differences which the discussion on Gall indicated gradually grew deeper, though Mill continued to hope that an agreement might be arrived at. In letter xl. he wrote :

" Our disagreement on the question which you rightly characterise as the most fundamental which social speculations can present ought not to cause any disquietude on the final possibility of a sufficient convergence of opinion amongst well-informed people on purely rational bases."

The disagreement, he went on to say, only confirmed him in the opinion that the intellectual bases of static sociology were not yet sufficiently prepared. In his opinion, the foundations of social dynamics were fully constituted. But as to the statics, history no longer held the first place. What was required was a very advanced state of the science which he called "Ethology"—that is to say, the theory of the influence of diverse external circumstances, whether individual or social, on the formation of the moral and intellectual character.

This difference of opinion, following exactly the same lines, comes out in its most pronounced form on the question of the inequality of the sexes. Comte held the view that the position of woman was natural, and determined by her anatomical and physiological inferiority—the volume of the brain is less in woman than in man, she is physically weaker, and so on. But Mill retorted that the anatomical and physiological inferiority of woman is not proved. The inequality may be due to secondary causes—it may be the result of the conditions in which women have lived from time immemorial. Until all these possible causes have been taken into account, we have no right to assume that woman is not the equal of man.

This subject is discussed with some fulness in the letters which passed between Comte and Mill during the six months July to December 1843 (letters xxxii. to xlii.), when Mill declined to continue the controversy upon the point any further. Mill dealt fully and finally with the subject in the *Subjection of Woman*, but it may be interesting to gather from one of these letters (xxxv.) his views as they were freely expressed to Comte. We translate the passage freely:

"To resume our important sociological discussion, I believe I understand what you mean in comparing the organic constitution of the feminine sex to a prolonged state of infancy. I am not ignorant of what has been said on this subject by many physiologists; and I know, not only by the cellular and muscular systems, but still more by the nervous system, and very probably by the cerebral system, women are less far removed than men are from the organic character of children. This is very far from being decisive with me. If it is true, it would prove that the inferiority of children as compared with men depends on the anatomical difference of their brain, while it evidently depends for the most part, if not entirely, only on default of exercise. If one could always keep the brain of a child, while we developed its functions by education, and by a careful and regulated exercise, we should certainly not remain children, but should become men, and very superior men, offering without doubt notable deviations from the ordinary type of humanity. Equally, I do not deny that the most feminine type does present, on the average, considerable divergences from the masculine type. I do not pretend to define exactly in what these natural divergences consist, and I do not know that the time has yet come for that; but I do know that some very eminent physiologists pretend that the brain of women is smaller, consequently weaker, but more active than that of men.

According to that, women ought to be less capable of continuous and prolonged intellectual work, but able to do more in less time than men, and to do better everything which demands great promptitude of mind. They would, therefore, be less fit for science and more fit, at least by their organisation, for poetry and the practical life. It appears to me that this agrees sufficiently well with what we observe in life. But we run a danger of exaggerating the degree of actual diversity if we do not take into account the difference of education and social position; for whether women are or are not naturally inferior in capacity for prolonged intellectual effort, it is not doubtful that there is nothing in their education arranged in a manner to develop in them this capacity. While amongst men the study of science, and even that of the dead languages, certainly has this tendency."

Mill then remarks that the daily occupations of a great number of men, especially amongst the higher classes of workers, require, or at least permit, continuous intellectual work; while the great majority of women are occupied constantly with the minute cares of domestic life, which distract the mind without occupying it, and have no opportunity for intellectual work which requires either solitude or continuous attention. He further observes that men who have not been accustomed to study from their childhood rarely take to it in later life, and also that in the ordinary things of life, in which the intelligence of women is exercised as much or even more than that of men, that even the average woman generally shows more capacity than the average man.

Mill also remarks on the feminine element in the French character, and asks, notwithstanding this, what nation has produced more great philosophers or more distinguished statesmen?

In a later letter, Mill refers to the moral aspect of the question, and says that general opinion allows to women a conscience ordinarily more scrupulous than that of men; but what is conscience, he asks, if it is not the submission of the passions to the reason?

It was all in vain; Comte remained fixed in his opinions, Mill could not change his, and the discussion quickly came to an end.

The final rupture, if we may so describe it, was brought about by the well-known story of the "English subsidy." Comte being placed in financial difficulties through the loss of one of his posts at the Polytechnic School, Mill generously obtained for him a donation of 3000 francs, subscribed by Grote, Molesworth, and Raikes-Currie. Comte took it into his head that this gift, which was meant as a temporary assistance, was to be an annuity, and considered himself deeply aggrieved when Mill explained to him the true state of the case. Comte persisted, and Mill wrote a letter (lxxxi.) which seems almost unduly severe, but it was rendered necessary by the persistence—a persistence founded upon a misunderstanding—with which Comte urged his claim. After this the correspondence relaxed and finally ceased altogether.

Of the personal element in these letters there is no need to say much. They cover what may be called the tragic period of Comte's life; the separation from Madame Comte, his quarrels with the scientists, the loss of his post and part of his income, his meeting with Clotilde de Vaux, and his "irreparable loss" by her early death.

All the details of this sad time we have learned from Littré, Robinet, and Comte's correspondence with Madame de Vaux. The recollection of this period is revived by the perusal of this correspondence with Mill, and we see with how much sympathy the English thinker listened to the story of the wrongs and griefs of his French *confrère*. Mill's letters also reveal him afresh as the earnest, conscientious, open-minded thinker, whom all Englishmen, however much they may differ from him upon some points, will remember with a respect such as they render to but few for his unquestionably great intellectual and moral qualities.

WALTER LLOYD.

# MONSEIGNEUR LE DUC D'AUMALE.

IT is a strange coincidence that a century after Horace Walpole wrote his *Catalogue of Royal and Noble Authors* at Strawberry Hill, a literature-loving foreign exiled Royal family should have selected the same neighbourhood as their place of residence. During the second French Empire the members of the House of Orleans were much respected by the inhabitants for their many acts of kindness and generosity to the poor of this pleasant riverside resort, and now the bond has been further renewed by the recently married Duc d'Orléans selecting York House as his future English home. Alexander Pope, another famous resident, also seems to have anticipated their arrival in the neighbourhood when he wrote on his grotto at Twickenham :

> "Thou who shalt stop, where *Thames'* translucent wave
> Shines a broad Mirror through the shadowy Cave ;
> Where ling'ring drops from min'ral Roofs distil,
> And pointed Crystals break the sparkling Rill,
> Unpolished Gems no ray on Pride bestow,
> And latent Metals innocently glow :
> Approach.   Great Nature studiously behold !  . . .
> Let such, such only, tread this sacred Floor,
> Who dare to love their country. . . . "

It has been the destiny of nearly all the descendants of King Louis-Philippe to pass through rather stormy experiences.   The records of the early career and wanderings of the King himself read more like pages out of a *Life of Oliver Goldsmith* than one destined to sit on the throne of a great and cultured nation.   The King as a child had for governess one of the greatest literary women of the time, Madame de Genlis, and during his reign was surrounded by ministers and advisers selected from the highest ranks of literature.[1] It is, therefore, not surprising that his children should have desired

[1] "The Revolution of July 1830 established representative government in France. The men of letters instantly rose to the highest importance in the State.   At the present moment most of the persons whom we see at the head both of the Administration and of the Opposition have been Professors, Historians, Journalists, Poets. The influence of the literary class in England, during the generation which followed the Revolution, was great, but by no means so great as it has lately been in France. For, in England, the aristocracy of intellect had to contend with a powerful and deeply rooted aristocracy of a very different kind.   France has no Somersets and Shrewsburys to keep down her Addisons and Priors."—Lord Macaulay's *Life and Writings of Addison*.

to distinguish themselves in the Republic of letters. His eldest son, the unfortunate Duc d'Orléans, who was killed by an accident, wrote some interesting volumes, the *Récits de Campagnes* and *Campagnes de l'Armée d'Afrique*, 1835–1839 1 and was fortunate enough to obtain the hand of a Princess for wife, who was on intimate terms with Goethe and other luminaries of the most brilliant period of German literature. The Prince de Joinville has proved himself to be a competent writer on naval affairs, and in his old age has given to the world a delightful volume of *Vieux Souvenirs*. The Duc d'Aumale has won a deserved reputation as a historian by his *Histoire des Princes de Condé*, and was one of the most respected members of the Académie-Française. Some of King Louis-Philippe's grandchildren and great-grandchildren have also entered the charmed circle of literature. The late Comte de Paris wrote a creditable work on *La Situation des Ouvriers en Angleterre* and a *Histoire de la Guerre Civile en Amerique* in seven volumes. The Duc d'Alençon has published a description of *Luçon et Mindanao*, and Prince Henri d'Orléans, the young son of the Duc de Chartres, is undoubtedly an energetic writer, lecturer, and explorer.

The Duc d'Aumale, who was the fourth son of King Louis-Philippe and his Queen Marie-Amelie, displayed tokens of promising talents in early life, which his father cultivated with all the zeal of parental solicitude. The Duc had the good fortune to have for tutor a distinguished man of letters, Cuvillier-Fleury. The tutor was twenty-five years of age on his appointment, and his pupil only five. Cuvillier-Fleury, however, was not the first tutor of the infant prince. His parents previously, as M. Jules Claretie reminds us,[2]

"had confided his education to a man of great value, M. Damiron, who, during his lessons, spoke to the young duke, as he would have done to himself, of M. Cousin's philosophy or the new psychology. One day the philosopher plainly declared that he could not continue to give lessons to a child of five years, and the child had, for a moment, the sweet hope of not having again a professor. This illusion was of short duration. M. Trognon, the tutor of the Prince de Joinville, recommended to the future King Louis-Philippe one of his former pupils, ex-secretary of the ex-King Louis Bonaparte, and M. Cuvillier-Fleury, during twelve years, from 1827 to 1839, was attached to this young prince of whom he wished, before everything, to make a man. I can say that from the day when he approached the Duc d'Aumale, M. Cuvillier-Fleury, after having been an assiduous and vigilant master, remained, until his last hour, a faithful friend, devoted and grateful. One has not forgotten his word, eloquently remembered on his tomb, in connection with 'his best work'; and in the last years of his life, M. Cuvillier-Fleury projected a volume of confidences and souvenirs which he wished to entitle—he spoke often of it—the *Education of a Prince*."

The Duc d'Aumale soon after the death of Cuvillier-Fleury in

---

[1] Published by his sons. Avant-propos by the Comte de Paris and Introduction by the Duc de Chartres.

[2] *Discours de Réception a l'Académie-Française*, in succession to Cuvillier-Fleury.

1888 wrote for the *Journal des Debats* some "souvenirs" of his old tutor, which contains interesting reminiscences of his own childhood days.   Though Cuvillier-Fleury was greatly indebted to King Louis-Philippe for his rapid promotion in the world, he did not forget his early benefactors.  This is proved by the following anecdote related by the Duc d'Aumale :

" ' Look at those images,' he said to me when pointing out four medallions hung upon his fireside :  ' they are engraved in my heart—the Commandant Fleury, to whom I owe my existence ; Napoleon, to whom I owe my education ;  the eminent master [1] whose lessons were worth to me my triumph at the University ; your father, who confided to me the care of your education.'  I was between seven and eight years, and I cannot conceal that I felt very proud to be thus indirectly associated with the memory of the Emperor."

Cuvillier-Fleury's favourite models, the Duc informs us, were Virgil, Horace, Cicero, and Livy, and no one understood the *Conciones* better than he.  "This predilection, sufficiently exclusive, for the Latin letters was reflected in his instruction : the Greeks were not omitted, but remained in the shade."   The Duc d'Aumale also confesses :

"When I commenced to bestride a pony, Fleury conducted me sometimes to the Bois de Boulogne.  A cavalier, with an olive-coloured complexion, a slightly turned-up nose, with piercing eyes and a thin moustache (which was remarkable at the time) came and grasped my master's hand and discoursed familiarly with him, especially upon the books of the day.  Assuredly I could not understand everything said in the course of these conversations, which seemed to me long, . . . but I saw well that at the word 'romantic' the imaginations of the two interlocutors were kindled.  If by chance concord was disturbed, it was on the name of Voltaire, whom Fleury would never permit any one to meddle with.  His friend, who did not go further than Racine, would not admit that good French was written in the eighteenth century, and delighted in deriding the moderns.  Those intolerant 'classics' were then considered in painting the most rash innovators.  Eugène Delacroix finished at the time his first canvases of the work so vast, so bold, and so brilliant, which will remain one of the glories of the French school.
"Cuvillier-Fleury had, in literature, some views different than that of the painter of *l'Entrée des Croisés*, and his horizon extended early.  His preferences remained the same ; but he studied and appreciated the masterpieces of all countries, of all times, and even the present.  At an early age he made me read a large number in all styles, scrupulously reserving all which should be respected, but, in this limit, not being afraid to raise the intelligence of the child, selecting without hesitation the books, even those on the eve of publication, and with what *verve* and what purpose he commented on them !  On the ground of art he was less eclectic, remaining absolutely Italian, and especially in music.  Rossini was for him what Racine was for Delacroix."

The master's temper was not always of the sweetest, and the royal

---

[1] M. Pierrot-Deseilligny, then rector at Louis-le-Grand.

pupil confesses that they often disagreed. But it is pleasing to record that peace was soon restored.

" Careful in his dress as in his style," the Duc says, " everything that was trivial displeased him. The sight of my first clay pipe caused him a strange emotion."

It is evident that the Duc d'Aumale was early well grounded in the principles of morality, and that the master instructed his royal pupil with great diligence and perseverance. King Louis-Philippe was a model father, and Cuvillier-Fleury has related some characteristic incidents of the father's anxiety with regard to the education of his sons. The master, in after years, reminded his old pupil before an assembly of French Academicians [1] that the King often told him, when speaking of the Duc and his brothers :

" They must remain princes ; the profession is hard nowadays ; I do not wish, under the pretext of renouncing some of the advantages of their state, that they escape from its duties and dangers, but we must educate the princes as if they were not so."

Cuvillier-Fleury also said :

" The King desired that you were to be initiated not only in the knowledge of modern languages, but to the understanding, discreetly by degrees, of some of those geniuses who have illustrated it. He said of Shakespeare : ' Apart from defects, it is the great school of the human heart.' "

After leaving the hands of Cuvillier-Fleury, the Duc d'Aumale was sent by his parents to the College Henri IV., and such eminent masters as Poulain du Bossay, Duruy, and Davelny gave a last polish to what the early tutor had successfully begun. The Duc entered the army at the age of seventeen, and, after having served under his brother, the Duc d'Orléans, in the Algerian campaign of 1840-41, completed his military education at Courbevoie. He was soon again in Algeria, and conducted one of the most brilliant campaigns of the French conquest of North Africa. For his services he was made Lieutenant-General, and appointed to the command of the province of Constantine, and subsequently succeeded to the post of Governor-General of Algeria. The Duc d'Aumale was not destined to long enjoy his well-earned position, and on hearing the news of the revolution of 1848, he resigned and joined King Louis-Philippe and the French royal family in England.

The Duc d'Aumale, having laid down the sword and resigned his official duties, took up the pen. It was quite natural that his first desire was to write about those Algerian scenes which he was obliged to abandon through no fault of his own. His first volume, *Les Zouaves et les Chasseurs à pied*, is written with considerable spirit, and is not only valuable as a supplement to his elder brother's writings, but also as a source of entertainment and information to every one

---

[1] *Discours Prononcé a l'Académie-Française, en reponse au discours de reception de M. le Duc d'Aumale.* 1873.

desirous of learning something of military life in Algeria. As Lord Beaconsfield once enthusiastically remarked :[1]

"We are indebted to his (the Duc d'Aumale's) pen for those vivid pictures of the origin and character of that novel arm of modern warfare which seems to combine the discipline of Europe with the fire of the desert. In those precise and picturesque sketches of the Zouaves we must not forget that the writer observed them in the tented field, where he was encamped among the rest, and whence he led them to war and victory. The same pen has analysed in ancient Gaul one of the most remarkable campaigns of Cæsar, and I think I may say that he has treated a subject of great interest and difficulty in a spirit and a style not altogether unworthy of that consummate character, whose exploits and whose narrative of them he has analysed with an admiring but with a severe scrutiny."

The last work mentioned by Lord Beaconsfield is entitled *Alesia ; Etude sur la septième campagne de César en Gaule.* This study has been extensively quoted by French and German authors and commentators, but before its publication many of the Duc d'Aumale's admirers, including Montalembert, on being informed that he was engaged on the work, expressed some doubts that he would succeed in the difficult task. Montalembert one day said to Cuvillier-Fleury : "He will not succeed in judging well Cæsar; he is too much a Gaul."

The Duc d'Aumale during his first sojourn in England was a prominent and active member of the now defunct Philobiblon Society, which once occupied an enviable position in cultured circles. Lord Houghton (then Mr. Monckton Milnes) was the founder, and his biographer, Sir T. Wemyss Reid, gives the following concise history of its existence :

"The club was established in 1853, the number of its members being limited to thirty, and the qualification for membership being the interest taken by the candidate in the history, collection, or peculiarities of books. The members were in the habit of breakfasting together, when it was expected that such of them as possessed rare books, or other literary treasures, should bring them forth for inspection by their fellow members. The club published a number of volumes of *Transactions,* which were for the most part edited by Lord Houghton, and to which he contributed largely. In the first instance the secretaries were Mr. Sylvain Vandeweyer, the Belgian Minister in London, and Milnes; subsequently Sir William Stirling replaced Mr. Vandeweyer, though the latter continued until his death to be deeply interested in the meetings of the society. Prince Albert was for a number of years its president; afterwards the Duc d'Aumale was closely connected with it, enjoying the position of patron ; and one of its later presidents was the Duke of Albany, who held that post at the time of his death. One of Lord Houghton's last labours was the preparation of a sketch of the Duke in his character as president. It was after the death of the young prince that the society itself fell upon somewhat evil days. Most of the original members had passed away, and it was difficult to secure worthy successors to them, so that in the end it

---

[1] Speech at the Royal Literary Fund dinner of 1861.

. was resolved that the society should cease to exist. On Christmas Day, 1884, the last Christmas Day of his life, Lord Houghton penned a little valedictory notice, with which to close the last volume of the *Philobiblon Transactions.*"

That the Duc d'Aumale was not a mere "ornamental" member is proved on opening the first volume of *Transactions.* After the rules and list of members of the society, and a short " Letter of Thomas James to Lord Lumley (1599)," communicated by Sir William Stirling, the reader finds "Notes sur deux petits Bibliothèques françaises du XIV. siècle," by the Duc d'Aumale. In this kind of work he greatly excelled, and the reader at once discovers the royal author's love of books. The next contribution was of equal interest to students of French and also English history. It was entitled "Notes et documents relatif à Jean, Roi de France, et sa captivité en Angleterre." The Duc gave some interesting particulars concerning his unfortunate ancestor, who was defeated by Edward the Black Prince at the Battle of Poitiers, and after his so-called "liberation" died at the Savoy Palace in London. The work has high pretensions to eloquence and research, and reminds us of a time when publication was less frequent than now, and a single book might embody the labour of a life. The contribution "Information contre Isabelle de Limeuil—Mai–Aout 1564," is also not deficient either in value or interest. Admirers of Alexandre Dumas's novels will find much to entertain them in *Inventaire de tous les meubles du Cardinal Mazarin, dressé en 1653 et public d'apres l'original.* It is full of curious details, and presents a mass of information most lucidly arranged. The Philobiblon Society having ceased to exist, the complete set of the volumes are somewhat scarce, as only a limited number have been printed, but they are to be found in some of the public libraries of the United Kingdom. The Duc d'Aumale's name appeared on the prospectus as patron of the society for many years, and his contributions are not the least instructive of the series of *Transactions.*

Literature not only engaged the attention of the royal prince during his early sojourn in England, for he also became widely known as a collector of the fine arts. There is in existence a " Description Sommaire des Objets d'arts faissant partie des collections du Duc d'Aumale, exposés pour la visite du Fine Arts Club " at Orleans House, Twickenham, on May 21, 1862.[1] The Duc, however,

---

[1] The Duc d'Aumale's choice library was also accessible to literary men. The celebrated American author, George Ticknor, in the preface of the first edition of his *History of Spanish Literature,* says: "I owe much to the libraries of Europe, both public and private, which I visited anew in 1856 and 1857: in England, the British Museum, where Mr. Panizzi has done so much to render that vast storehouse of knowledge accessible and useful; the library at Holland House, tapestried with recollections of its accomplished founder; the precious collection of the Duc d'Aumale, at Orleans House on the Thames, . . . all of which were opened to me with a kindness which sometimes made me feel as if I might use them like my own."

modestly explained that " Ce volume n'est pas un catalogue, mais une simple liste d'objets choisis pour représenter les diverses branches d'une collection, et exposés pour une occasion speciale." The varied collection shown that day to the members of the club numbered 738 exhibits, and consisted of valuable paintings of the old Italian, Spanish, Dutch and Flemish, and French schools; works by modern French painters; miniatures; enamels; drawings of the Italian, Lombard, Venetian, Spanish, French, German, Dutch, and Flemish schools; engravings by German, Flemish, Dutch, French, and Italian masters; painted glass; mosaic work; statues and busts; manu-scripts on vellum with miniatures; autographs; rare printed books; bindings; and various other objects. The Duc d'Aumale's residence at Twickenham was also adorned with a choice selection of old portraits of French kings and princes, and a " Collection de quarante-deux portraits des Princes et Princesses de la branche royale de Bourbon, et de la branche de Condé, exécutes pour les Princes de Condé, d'après des portraits originaux. Provenant du Château de Chantilly." Another feature of interest was the " Salle de Condé." " Cette Salle," it was stated in the volume presented to the visitors, " consacrée au Grand Condé contient presqué exclusivement des objets qui se rapportent à l'histoire de ce Prince, et de sa famille." The English visitors were also no doubt gratified by the display of a picture by Sir Joshua Reynolds. It was a " Portrait de Louis-Philippe, Joseph d'Orléans, Duc d'Orléans, en costume de Colonel-Général des Hussards. C'est la réduction du portrait exécute pour le Prince de Galles et qui fut détruit en 1820 dans l'incendie de Carlton House. Il a appartenu à Lawrence, puis à M. Evans qui l'avait achetè à la vente après dècés de Lawrence." This collection, which had been much added to by its royal possessor, is now permanently housed at Chantilly.

The Duc d'Aumale was in 1861 invited to preside at the Royal Literary Fund annual dinner, and his modest address on that occasion proved that he was early in life initiated into the beauties of English literature :

" I cannot even present myself as being thoroughly acquainted with your literature; but if I know something of it, I owe it to two circumstances. The first is, that I was educated by a father who had been an exile, as I am now, who had found on these shores the same hospitable refuge, and who both knew and loved your country, your language, the great works of your literature as well, I suppose, as any foreigner ever did or can. I remember that in the earliest days of my life, when he was himself free from all political responsibility, in the happy and quiet evenings of Neuilly, he used often, after having shown to his children the engraved portraits of illustrious men, and told their deeds, or plates which commemorated the great military achievements of our countrymen, he used, I say, to take down from the shelves of the library some huge folio volume of Boydell's *Illustrated Shakespeare*, a copy which he had bought himself at the auction-room at Cheltenham, and then give us an outline of the finest compositions of your great dramatist, reciting occasionally some of the beautiful passages which had remained engraved in his wonderful memory. That was my first impression of English literature, and one which will never disappear from my mind, for it is connected with one of my earliest recollections of the best and most beloved of fathers. I grew up with the first French generations who, abandoning an old tradition, began to study foreign literatures—I mean the literatures which do not belong to the great Latin family of languages. Well, when I was a young man, the great authors of this country were understood and admired in France, and numerous translations of their works were published for the benefit of those who could not read them in the original. Shakespeare was commented on, quoted, and even imitated by some who were daring enough to try such an experiment. The walls of our picture exhibitions were covered with works of art signed by the best names, the subjects of which were borrowed from your stage, your poets, or your annals. Your novels were in all hands; and I remember, if I may be allowed another personal recollection, that being at school I concealed more than once under my desk some of the Waverley novels, and that when I was supposed to be bent upon some of those celebrated grammatical works which came from the pen of our great Port Royal scholars, and which are more admired by men than loved by boys, I was quietly reading *Ivanhoe* or *Old Mortality*. Such is our natural taste for what we call in French *le fruit défendu*. I could not answer to go correctly through all the tenses of a Greek verb; but I am sure I could even now trace the footsteps of Nigel in the streets of London, point out the spot where once stood the house of Jeannie Deans, or serve as a cicerone among the ruins of Lochleven. Since the days of Sir Walter Scott, the novels of your countrymen have continued to attract general attention abroad. *Vanity Fair, David Copperfield, Coningsby*, and *My Novel* are as much read on the Continent as the works of Georges Sand or Alexandre Dumas. On this very day the readers of a great French newspaper, after a rapid glance at the telegrams, hasten to peruse the *feuilleton*, where they will find the continuation of the *Woman in White* translated into their own language."

The Duc d'Aumale also related an incident which could not fail to make a lasting impression on his mind :

"It is the great privilege of those who are called upon to preside at these meetings that your records are open to them, and the only drawback to the great satisfaction which results from this inspection is that your chairman is not allowed to disclose what he has seen. There is only one case of timely assistance given by this society to which I may allude, because it has been already brought before the public by the very man who was interested in it. That man was Chateaubriand. It is impossible not to feel a real emotion on seeing the autograph lines in which this illustrious writer declares that without the help he had received from this institution he would have been unable to complete his work called the *Natchez*, the first which created his reputation ; so that if this society had not existed the glory of that great man would perhaps have been lost for France and for letters."

The same year that the Duc d'Aumale presided at the Royal Literary Fund dinner was also memorable for the appearance of the much debated pamphlet, *Lettre sur l'histoire de France*, addressed to Prince Napoleon. The Imperial authorities condemned the publisher and printer to fines and imprisonment, but were not able to suppress entirely its circulation. The Duc's pamphlet and challenge to Prince Napoleon created considerable sensation all over Europe, and the opinion of the English Court may be seen by consulting the last volume of Sir Theodore Martin's *Life of the Prince Consort.* A few years afterwards the printing was commenced of the ·first volumes of the monumental *Histoire des Princes de Condé,* but the copies were seized before publication. This attracted no small attention and discussion, and the case was heard more than once in the Imperial law courts. The Duc d'Aumale's actions were for a long time unsuccessful. In the interval the celebrated *Histoire de César,* by the Emperor Napoleon III., was published. Sainte-Beuve one day said to Cuvillier: "There is the book of the Emperor on sale; now is the moment to be generous. Cæsar must open the door to Condé." The publication of the Duc d'Aumale's volumes, however, was not permitted until March 1869. When the work appeared the Paris correspondent of the *Times* wrote:

" He (the Emperor) has sustained just now an internal defeat which was not worth incurring, and for which he is indebted to a deep-set, exaggerated, and rather too impulsive dread of whatever comes from the Orleans family, and also to the ill-advised zeal of a faithful but too excitable servant, M. de Persigny. You must remember that, six years ago, that ever-vigilant Minister seized, without a shadow of legal pretence, a work printed but not yet published, not even bound in volumes, *L'Histoire de la Maison de Condé.* The authorship of the Duc d'Aumale was a sufficient reason for M. de Persigny to treat the book as a kind of outlaw which has no right to be protected by any tribunal. And, indeed, if the right to legal protection against such an inroad upon literary property exists, the chance of obtaining that protection of the law was small; and not less than six years were spent in useless efforts to obtain, not the punishment of the offending officials, but the simple release of the captive book. If your readers were only of the learned profession, I could not resist the temptation of giving them an account, which they would perhaps relish, of those curious and truly French proceedings; they would see the unfortunate but persevering plaintiff sent incessantly from a civil to an administrative tribunal, and from that to another, each of them refusing to give judgment or even to enter into the merits of the case, and plainly evincing an only natural desire to get rid by any means of the disagreeable business. 'It is a suit against a public functionary,' said, or rather pleaded, the civil tribunal; 'therefore be kind enough to go to the Council of State, which is the only body empowered to accept or reject your suit'; and then the Council of State was heard politely entreating the plaintiff out of his audience: 'Your suit is nothing but a reclamation of stolen property; it is just as if your house had been taken from you by the Government without the sanction of the law or the' payment of an indemnity. That kind of thing is precisely the business of civil tribunals. Please to go there again, and do not make us uncomfortable any more.' No end seemed likely to this amusing and, at the same time, lamentable denial of justice, when the eminent counsels for the plaintiff, MM. Dufaure and Herbert, luckily thought of singling out a certain official left unprotected by the too famous Article 75 of the *Constitution de l'An VIII.* They discovered that the Director of Domains could undoubtedly be sued as the alleged receiver of the detained property. Thus, the defensive

works which so effectually protect in France the inviolability of our func-
tionaries and the most unlawful acts of the Executive were cleverly
turned ; and, having seen what the wooden horse coming through that
unprovided breach into its Troy contained, the Government decided, not
unwisely, after six years' fighting, on an immediate surrender.  Now, that
attempt to stifle, even in the quiet region of remote history, the voice of
an exiled prince, seeking the noble solace of literary work and fame, was
not only a direct offence against the law, but an unlucky trespass on good
taste and social justice.  Indeed, many living men can still remember the
unlimited tolerance which the present ruler of France found here under
the Orleans dynasty, for his writings, not only literary but political, and
not only when an exile, but even when a prisoner, after having plunged
twice into fight, defeat, and condemnation.  There was one other consideration, too, which we wonder was not remarked, or rather felt by the Emperor,
and which made the proscription of such a work more invidious still.  It
was the publication of his own *Cæsar*, and that renewed assertion of
his right of citizenship in the republic of letters.  Was it decorous to take
so much trouble to send the *History of Cæsar* triumphant through the
world, and at the same time to stop *manu militari* the publication of the
*History of Condé ?*  By allowing himself to be misled on this question by
the suspicious mind of a devoted Minister, the Emperor missed a natural
and good occasion of showing that personal kindness of disposition and
that equanimity of judgment for which he has been so often, and not
unjustly, praised."

A collection of the literature on the great Condé would fill the
shelves of a private gentleman's library, but naturally none of the
historians and biographers have had access to, or were in possession
of, material and documents so extensive as the Duc d'Aumale, who
succeeded to the rights and estates of the last prince of that house.
The spirit in which the *Histoire des Princes de Condé* was written,
the reader may gather from the following modest paragraph :

" I have not written, nor do I intend to write, an Introduction, because
I have neither a new system to propound, nor have I the right, or wish,
to put myself prominently before the reader.  I was not influenced by
party spirit when it occurred to me to profit by the numerous documents
of which, through the kindness of the last of the Condés, I had become
possessed, and to relate the lives of some of his most illustrious ancestors.
I have endeavoured to remain faithful to the motto of Montaigne, and
I think I can say, in his words, ' Cecy est une livre de bonne foy.' "

The brilliant career of the great Condé, whose victories have
been immortalised in verse by the leading poets of the reign of
Louis ·XIV., have excited so much admiration that the ordinary
student of history is quite likely to forget that some of the other
members of the princely family have also achieved distinction.   The
Duc d'Aumale described the events in the lives of the Condés with
a uniform tendency ; they rise one above another in natural succession and gradual progress to still more important and interesting
scenes.   To arrange seemingly unconnected transactions under one
great plan, and assign to each its proper place and due proportion of
attention, is, without doubt, the most trying test of a historians'

skill. In this the royal author greatly excelled, and in the execution of it in the present work he has given proof of uncommon talent. No epic poet has preserved the unity of his plot better. The great scene of action is, of course, the brilliant achievements of the Condé, where our attention is long detained. From this noble theme, however, we are frequently led, and made to contemplate other important events, in the management of which the historian has shown so much address that we always follow him without reluctance. They are all so happily introduced as never to embarrass the great outlines of the picture, and seem as so many underparts to make one complete whole.

Chantilly, the home of the Condés, which, with its majestic collection, now passes to the care of the Institute of France, is situated fifty minutes from Paris, on the Great Northern Railway main line. The beautiful domain, one of the most remarkable ornaments of France, was enriched and adorned under a long succession of wealthy noblemen, but owes most of its splendour to the Princes de Condé and the Duc d'Aumale. The old château was in existence in the reign of Charles VI., when the lordship belonged to Pierre de Orgemont, Chancellor of France. About the year 1484 it was handed over by his grandson to the noble family of Montmorency, and nearly two centuries afterwards was transferred to the Condés. It was a favourite residence of the great Condé, and there he frequently enjoyed the society of Boileau, La Fontaine, La Bruyère, Molière, Racine, and other famous literary men of that period. The place was at the time, and long afterwards, celebrated for its royal receptions. During the reign of Louis XVI. the future Emperor Paul I. of Russia, on the conclusion of a visit to the then Prince of Condé, said: "Ah, Monsieur le Duc, I would give all I possess for your superb Chantilly." "The loss would be on the side of your Imperial Highness." "No, because I would be a Bourbon and a Condé." On the death of the last Prince de Condé the estate passed into the hands of the Duc d'Aumale.

In 1853 the Government of Napoleon III. declared that the royal family of France were "incapable" of possessing property in their own country, and the magnificent estate was consequently sold by auction. It was purchased by the London bankers, Coutts & Co., and after the fall of the Empire it passed back again to its rightful owner, the Duc d'Aumale.

The royal author's volume on *Les Institutions Militaires de la France* belongs practically to the same period as the *Histoire des Princes de Condé.* The Duc d'Aumale, who greatly distinguished himself as a soldier during his early manhood days, was fully qualified to write such a work, and it attracted universal attention in European military circles. An English version was published in 1869 It was translated and annotated (with the author's consent) by Captain Ashe, of the King's Dragoon Guards. The translator, in introducing the volume to English readers, announced that he was " greatly indebted for access to some rare and useful military works of reference in French and German contained in the Prince Consort's library." Captain Ashe, however, was a faithful translator, and carefully avoided tampering with the original work. His annotations are not only interesting to English readers, but to Frenchmen who have a limited knowledge of military terms and technicalities.

The Duc d'Aumale was elected a member of the Académie Française by a large majority, in succession to Montalembert, on December 30, 1871. The new royal member, however, was only received and took his seat on April 3, 1873. Previous to his reception there was a discussion on the question whether it would be advisable to address a prince of royal blood as " Monseigneur," in accordance with his rank, or simply " Monsieur," following the tradition of the Académie Française. The Duc d'Aumale, like a true son of the republic of letters, desired to be styled like any other member, and he was called " Monsieur," probably for the first time in his life.

France was still suffering from the effects of a disastrous war, and it is a strange coincidence that at the Academy the predecessor of the new member, the new member himself, and the old tutor who was there to welcome him, all suffered from the changeable French Governments. Montalembert's father was driven into exile owing to the downfall of the old monarchy, Cuvillier-Fleury's first misfortune was the final overthrow of the first Empire, and the Duc d'Aumale was driven into exile owing to the overthrow of the monarchy of July. Here we have a perfect illustration of the saying, "One touch of nature." Montalembert's father was for some years a colonel in the English army, and on the restoration of the Bourbons was appointed secretary of the French Embassy in London. He married a Scotch lady of the name of Forbes, and their celebrated son was born in London in 1810. The Duc d'Aumale, in his *Discours de Reception* at the Académie Française, gave a picturesque description of Montalembert's childhood days in England, and also frequently alluded to the solid foundations of English institutions and the literary celebrities of this country. In fact, there is not in existence another address delivered before the members of the Academy containing so many references to English life and literature. The new royal member had only recently returned to his native land after an absence of twenty-three years, and his long residence on this side of the Channel made him a competent critic of the scenes and incidents he described.

It was during the Duc d'Aumale's second exile that the bequest of Chantilly to the Institute of France became known to the world. The Duc first communicated his determination to M. Edmond

Boucher, Senator, M. Denormandie, Senator, and M. Edmond Rousse, Academician, and that historical letter was written in England:

WOOD NORTON, *August* 29, 1886.

"MESSIEURS AND DEAR FRIENDS,—Desiring to insure the destination which, in accord with my heirs, I have given to the mansion and domain of Chantilly, I am resolved to accomplish at once a resolution which might after my death be hampered by difficulties of detail easy to smooth away in my lifetime. I have consequently invited Maître Fontana, notary at Paris, to open an envelope which contains my holograph will, dated the 3rd of June, 1884, and I have directed him to hand you a certified copy of the paragraphs of that will relating to the domain of Chantilly, as also a copy of the codicils since added connected with the same object.

"I appeal to your friendship and intelligence in order that the provisions contained in these documents may at once receive execution, subject to the usufruct, which I intend to retain, not merely in order to enjoy, if it so happens, the use and habitation, but to complete certain portions, still unfinished, of the work which I have undertaken, with a view to reduce the expenses of management, and lastly, in the interest of the parishes and the poor of the vicinity.

"I give you for this purpose the most extended powers, even that of altering any accessory provisions that may not appear to you consistent with the main object which I have in view. I beg you to take the assistance of M. Limbourg, advocate, who enjoys my confidence and is acquainted with my intentions.

"H. D'ORLEANS."

The following are the most important passages of the will referring to the bequest of the home of the Condés:

"Resolving to preserve to France the domain of Chantilly in its integrity, with its woods, lawns, waters, edifices, and all that they contain—trophies, pictures, books, artistic objects, all that collection which forms, as it were, a complete and varied monument of French art in all its branches, and the history of my country in times of glory—I have resolved to confide the care of it to an illustrious body which has done me the honour of calling me into its ranks in a twofold [1] capacity, and which, without evading the inevitable transformations of societies, escapes the spirit of faction, as well as too sudden commotions, retaining its independence amidst political fluctuations.

"I consequently give and bequeath to the Institute of France the domain of Chantilly, as it shall exist on the day of my death, with the library and other artistic and historical collections which I have formed there, the furniture, statues, trophies of arms, &c. The present bequest is made under the obligation by the legatee of preserving in all respects the character of the domain, and especially of introducing no change in the exterior or interior architecture of the mansion of Enghien and the Sylvic wing, of the tennis-court and of the three small chapels; of preserving the chapel of the mansion for its use, with the articles belonging to it, and for the artistic or other objects which it contains; of watching over the depository of the hearts of the Condés."

The revenue of the estate, according to the will, is to be devoted by the Institute of France to—

---

[1] The Duc d'Aumale was shortly afterwards elected a member of the Institute in a threefold capacity.

" (1) In keeping in a perfect state the buildings, parks, gardens, and collections. . . . (2) To the extent of which it shall determine in the acquisition of works of art of every kind, books, ancient or modern, destined to enrich or complete the collections, without being able to make any alienation by exchange or otherwise. (3) In the creation of pensions and annuities in favour of indigent men of letters and artists. (4) In the foundation of prizes intended to encourage those who devote themselves to a literary, scientific, or artistic career.

" It will take, besides, the steps necessary in order that the galleries and collections at Chantilly, under the name of the Condé Museum, shall be opened to the public at least three times a week during six months of the year, and in order that at all times students, men of letters, and artists may find there the facilities for work and research of which they may stand in need."

The gift was naturally gratefully and enthusiastically accepted by the Institute of France, and a medal, engraved by one of the members, M. Chaplain, was struck in commemoration of the event.

In 1891 the honorary degree of D.C.L. was conferred on the Duc d'Aumale by the Oxford University. On the same occasion similar degrees were bestowed on Lord Halsbury, the Right Hon. A. J. Balfour, Sir Donald Martin Stewart, Bart., Hon. Samuel James Way, Mr. Richard Claverhouse Jebb, D.Litt., and Mr. Briton Riviere, R.A. The Duc d'Aumale was the third distinguished Frenchman who was honoured with the degree of D.C.L. by the Oxford University since 1871, his predecessors being Hippolyte Taine in 1871, and M. Gaston Maspero in 1887. The Duc d'Aumale, who was one of the original members of the defunct Philobiblon Society, always took an interest in the circulation in England of rare examples of French literature, and a publication of the Roxburghe Club in 1894 bears the title of " *Le Livre et Mistère du glorieux Saint Andrien.* Publie . . . aux frais de S. A. R. Mgr. le Duc d'Aumale."

The Duc d'Aumale until a few days before his death was busy with his pen. During the last winter of his life he wrote and published an interesting work on his father entitled *Le Roi Louis Philippe et le Droit de Grâce*, 1830–1848. He was also supervising the preparation of a monumental work. A contemporary writer at the time of the Chantilly bequest remarked :

" To enumerate the artistic treasures of all kinds of which France now becomes the possessor would require, not an article, but a thick volume. These are not only priceless and of the vastest extent, but they are ordered and classified with exquisite taste, and rather for the purpose of study than of indiscriminate display."

The publication of the volume, or rather volumes, will shortly be an accomplished fact. The Duc divided the work into seven sections, each of these being in the hands of illustrious art specialists. M. Georges Duplesis, of the Académie des Beaux Arts, has charge of the engravings; M. Henri Bouchet, the Keeper at the Bibliothèque Nationale, will describe the wonderful sixteenth-century crayon drawings; and M. Leon Heuzay, of the Académie des Beaux Arts and the Académie des Inscriptions, the antiquities. The famous library will be fully described by M. Picot and by M. Leopold Delisle, of the Institute. The artistic collection is divided between M. Germain Bapst and M. A. Gruyer, of the Académie des Beaux Arts. The work will form an artistic encyclopædia, and the Duc d'Aumale had made arrangements to write an introduction to the volumes.

ANDREW DE TERNANT.

# THE RENASCENCE OF JANE AUSTEN.

AFTER considering the short, feverish, genius-filled lives of such people as Marie Bashkirtseff or Aubrey Beardsley, what a rest it is to go back to the contemplation of a peaceful, homely, healthy existence like that of Jane Austen! It is, indeed, this peaceful, homely element in her writings that gives them the place they are rightfully reclaiming in English literature.

The word "reclaiming" gives rise to an unfavourable reflection upon ourselves; for, after according a worthy position to Miss Austen's novels in the early part of the century, we certainly allowed them to drop out of sight for a while, and many men and women of forty years old are at present reading her novels for the first time because they were not fashionable in their youth, when they were being fascinated instead by Scott, Thackeray, Dickens, the Brontës, and George Eliot. Some of these men and women are asking themselves how it is that these works, which are being brought out to-day in new and popular editions, were not put into their hands at an earlier date, and an approximate answer to this question is the *raison d'être* of this paper.

Before Miss Austen's death in 1817 her works had received much valuable appreciation. We read of the Prince of Wales, afterwards George the Fourth, admiring them, and of a certain able man even making them a test of mental ability, those who read and cared for them being, in his opinion, intellectual; those who did not, unintellectual; also of such great spirits as Sir Walter Scott and George Eliot thinking most highly of them. Having been read, and very favourably noticed, it nevertheless was not strange that they should stand aside for a time while such wonderful books as the Waverley Novels came out, or while Dickens supplied the nation with new pictures of grotesque, pathetic, lovable characters from among the people, their salient qualities requiring no fine insight, no delicacy, no culture to apprehend. Then came the passionate weird writings of the Brontës, and George Eliot's masterly, all-embracing novels to seize hold of the mass of fiction readers, so that we are not surprised to know there was not a "run" upon her books, which contained no hairbreadth escapes, no complicated plot, no touching pathos, though they never ceased to be asked for and read by the more thoughtful and studious class of readers.

Within the last five-and-twenty years books and publications of all kinds have increased at such an enormous rate that people have been quite at a loss as to what, out of all the mass before them, it would be wise or interesting to read. If they join libraries and take out books at random they find unacceptable at least half the books they get. This being well known, thoughtful people—some asked, some unasked—have prepared lists of valuable books in different classes of literature for the guidance of those who care to be guided. Taking up the novels of the last twenty-five years, what a weighing, and a sifting, and a reluctant rejection there has to be! With laborious facility we recognise the amount of good writing and culture spent on glittering, evanescent trivialities, also the quantity of intensely commonplace writing, hiding, perhaps, the faint glimmer of a solid thought! Putting aside concise, apt descriptions and witty, well-sustained conversations between men and women, which charm us at the moment of reading, we have to ask ourselves, "Will this last? Is there anything in it that people will care to read fifty years hence?" Most difficult questions to answer, and yet, pleased as we are with some of these productions, we know that we must reply in the negative. We invert the question when we take up Miss Austen's books, and say, "What made them last? What in them made us call for fresh editions eighty years after?" The answer is twofold: first, Miss Austen's unerring truthfulness in picture-drawing; secondly, Anglo-Saxon patriotism.

Let us take up the patriotism first, as it may be more shortly disposed of. Patriotism! She has not said one word on the subject, she has not touched on the virtues of England, nor yet has she hinted at any particular love or admiration for her native land. No, but she has faithfully depicted the manners, and ways of life and thought of a class of English society which is said to be rapidly dying out—namely, that of the rural gentry.

Certainly families of the same rank still exist and flourish, and send forth many of the cleverest men in the nation, but they can no longer be termed rural. Towns and telegraphy and facilities for travel have obliterated the differences between town and country gentlemen; but in Miss Austen's day they were two distinct classes, and her exact, natural, and easy portrayals of the country society to which she belonged—which she unpretentiously considered as mere two-inch-wide miniatures on ivory—are now prized by us as elegantly sketched and accurate models of the rural gentry at the end of the eighteenth and beginning of the nineteenth century. Intelligent Anglo-Saxons are generally patriotic, though often unknown to themselves, and these pictures of that enviable class of people who had assured futures, and yet were without the calls and responsibilities of high rank, are pleasing to us as a nation, and equally so as individuals, as we note that human nature, with its foibles and idiosyncrasies, remains about the same whether particular classes die out or not.

Those who read in languages not their own are generally anxious to get books that will be typical of the country to which they belong. Now the Saxon can introduce Miss Austen's novels to our colonists in Australia, or to Americans, or to any foreigners with a glow of patriotism, for he knows he is presenting something entirely English, as the " country gentleman " class is a unique creation, never having had an existence anywhere except in the British Isles. The next point on patriotism finishes our subject from this side, and at the same time takes us into the domain of Miss Austen's fidelity to nature ; it is that it required the Anglo-Saxon genius, and the higher powers therein, too, to see and feel, and admire, and call for a wider spread of her thoroughly English, realistic and moral solidity. If the movement towards the recent new editions of her novels had been left to the tender mercies—or should it be flimsy criticism ?—of the pure Celt, or of the citizen of the United States of America, probably our bookshelves would not have been enriched with them, for highly as their good qualities are valued by thinkers everywhere, they are too lacking in piquancy and vivacity to appeal so warmly to the quicker, more versatile imaginations of these English-speaking peoples as they do to the Saxon himself. Yet lately, not only the everyday Saxon, the Celt, the Australian, the American, but some French are reading Jane Austen. How is it ? Well, the un-every-day Saxon has pointed out that she is worthy to be read, and somehow other nationalities have a wonderful respect for the mature, deliberately pronounced opinion of England even on literary matters. So France reads and laughs, and is well content that her gentry is not composed of Sir Thomas Bertrams nor Mr. Woodhouses, so stiff and so mournful ; the United States read, and are well pleased that the *Mayflower* carried out their fathers ; Australia reads, and wonders if " home " is still like that ; Hibernia reads, and frankly confesses that life in the wilds of Donegal or Connemara has a hundredfold more attraction for her; yet all read with pleasure, and feel the charm of the characters that Miss Austen meant to be charming. This is just where her genius lay. She depended on no sensational effect, she uses no idealistic treatment, she never works us into a weird state of expectancy as some of our most powerful authors do, but goes quietly on sketching ordinary, unimaginative — indeed, commonplace—people, until she has placed them before us so naturally and so true to themselves that we recognise them, and have to accept their annoying qualities along with their good ones, just as we do in real life, knowing only too well that " the web of our life is of a mingled yarn, good and ill together."

It is difficult to catch hold of such a difficult, impalpable thing as a ray of genius in order to put it under the analyst's microscope to show to our neighbours, and our clumsy handling and inadequate expression of the result do not always tend to make it more tangible or clearer to those who could not perceive it before the analysis. Nevertheless, we like to try—so to Miss Austen's unerring truthfulness in picture-drawing. As regards her fidelity to nature, her realism, nothing need be said; it lies before us on every page; it is in her consummate working up of very ordinary material into elegant pictures that her art lies. Truthfulness, realism—we have them in abundance from the chattering housekeeper, the talkative business man, the freed schoolmistress, the exact diarist; but how far their accounts are from being pictures! She has the inborn faculty of the artist. Given her materials, and hers were certainly very limited, she sees what to reject, what to group together, knows how to arrange them, what to place in the foreground, what in the background, where the shadows should fall, and, above all, she understands well the proportion of things. In these pictures we do not get much breadth of colour, but we get enough, joined with an accuracy and delicacy of finish, to keep out any of that cold correctness which is so repellent to things artistic.

As to Miss Austen's style, we can scarcely define its attraction, for in it we get no music, no magic, no caressing phrases; it is not trenchant; we carry away no glittering epigrams, but it is apt and spirited, and has that indefinable felicitous touch that genius alone gives. The qualities without which no sustained writing can exist— knowledge, observation, toleration, and expression—are all there, deepening and mellowing towards the end, and make a solid foundation on which to rest her easy, graceful dialogue, in which part of her art she might be said to be without a rival.

In character-painting Miss Austen's sincerity is biblical; the good and ill are inextricably mingled. How one begins by disliking Emma Woodhouse for her self-confidence, her presumption, her general superiority, and then how her solid, thrifty, Saxon common sense, her kindness, her frank acknowledgment of her failures and shortcomings, bring us round to her, and make us glad of her final happiness.

Then, what a diverting sketch is good Miss Bates, mentally a middle-aged butterfly, most lovable, most trying of grateful, bewildering old ladies, flying off, as Emma Woodhouse in a fit of momentary malice expressed it, from thanking a man at intervals all day long for his kindness in marrying her niece, to her old mother's petticoat, " not that it was such a very old petticoat either, for still it would last a great while—and, indeed, she must thankfully say that their petticoats were all very strong."

A hasty judgment is apt to decree that, notwithstanding many winning or racy traits in her girl characters, like Fanny Price's gentleness combined with strength, or like Elizabeth Bennet's *verve*, as in parrying the ill-bred inquisitiveness of Lady Catherine de Bourgh, most of them are indelicate almost to vulgarity in the way they speak of their own and their neighbours' business affairs in the matrimonial market. But it ought to be remembered that marriage was the sole profession for women then, and naturally their thoughts and speech ran in that groove, whereas they now have wider outlets in the mission field, in medicine, in university life, and in their more serious cultivation of art.

Miss Austen's clergymen are poor creatures. Three out of four are insufferable with gourmandise or conceit, and seem to have no idea whatever as to the life-work of a clergyman; and the fourth is good, but without much vigour. Whether she failed in painting them, or whether the Church was unfortunate enough to have many such specimens, apparently devoid of ideals at all, not to speak of high ones, among her servants, we can scarcely decide. Perhaps the reason lies between, for we do not think the clergy of her day were very energetic in their work; also she may not have been at her best in describing them, for often the most familiar scene is the one which we succeed least well in depicting. Her laymen, however, are excellent. Nothing can be more natural than her bluff, but gentlemanly, young sailors, her dignified, sensible heads of houses, and as for Mr. Woodhouse, the valetudinarian, his name is a household word among readers of Miss Austen.

Advice is sometimes given as to the age at which people should read certain books, the *Song of Solomon* being one of those not to be read till one has reached thirty. Probably the best time to read one of these novels is just after one has graduated, or is inflated with University honours, or is puffed up with having had some fugitive verses accepted by a high-class magazine, or has surfeited himself with *fin de siècle* stories till literary dyspepsia has set in. These things generally occur before one is very old, but there is another good time also, which is even less limited by years, namely, after one has somehow had an overdose of ethics, for Miss Austen never pointed a moral or set herself to teach. Like all true geniuses, she knew, consciously or unconsciously, that "art works for all whom it can teach," and that it delivers its own message to us. She does not assure us that the apparently most commonplace of human beings will be found interesting in some point if we only take the trouble to find it out, but nevertheless through her art we learn it, and greater things, the power of love and the beauty of self-sacrifice. Of her teaching "the rest is silence."

JANET HARPER.

# SHAKESPEARE'S GHOSTS.

IT is curious to note that Shakespeare's introduction to the Ghost as *dramatis persona* was accidental. He brought it on the stage in *Julius Cæsar*, not because he had thought out the possibilities of the character, but because he found it in the material he was adapting. Its few short speeches are transcribed almost without alteration. The apparition, which in Plutarch is the evil genius of Brutus, becomes in the play the ghost of Cæsar; but with this exception the poet is a mere copyist. Plutarch, however, supplied him not only with an incident, but with a theory. Cassius explained to Brutus that "not everything we see is real: in extreme bodily fatigue the function of the mind is perverted, and we may be deceived by the products of its imagination." Shakespeare learnt from this that sights which are seen and words which are heard may be the creation of the mind of the person who sees and hears. Guided by this theory, he seems to have studied some of those abnormal mental phenomena which depend on the possession of the mind by a dominant idea. His genius and his minute observation placed him almost, perhaps, abreast of our latter-day knowledge of the causes and conditions of these mental aberrations. Had he lived to-day he would have been an invaluable member of the Society for Psychical Research. The results of his study appeared the following year in *Hamlet* (1602), and four years later in *Macbeth*. Were every other means of fixing the dates of these three plays lost, a study of the ghost-scenes would enable us to arrange them in chronological order.

We must first ask, "What is a ghost?" There is no doubt that a person may apparently see objects and hear words which another person close by cannot see and hear. Such impressions are to be referred not to actually existing objects, but to the action of the subject's mind. Dr. Abercromby tells us of one patient who could, by directing his attention to an idea, call up to sight the appropriate image or scene, though the thing called up were an object he had never seen, but had merely imagined. When meeting a friend in the street he could not be sure whether the appearance was his friend or a spectral illusion till he had tried to touch it and had heard the voice. Goethe saw an exact counterpart of himself advancing towards him, an experience repeated by Wilkie Collins.

Sir Walter Scott relates that soon after the death of Lord Byron he read an account of the deceased poet. On stepping into the hall immediately after, he saw right before him, in a standing posture, the exact representation of his departed friend, whose recollection had been so strongly brought to his imagination. After stopping a moment to note the extraordinary resemblance, he advanced towards it and the figure gradually disappeared. Some of the cases narrated by Sir David Brewster are particularly instructive. The subject was a lady (Mrs. A.), and her hallucinations were carefully studied by her husband and Sir David. On one occasion she saw her husband as she thought, who had gone out half an hour before, standing within two feet of her in the drawing-room. She was astonished to receive no response when she spoke to him. She remembered that Sir David had told her to press one eyeball with the finger, when the impression of any real object would be doubled. She tried to apply the test, but the figure walked away and disappeared. The simple scientific experiment diverted her attention from the creation of her mind, and this, no longer being in sole possession, could not maintain itself, and was dissolved. Another hallucination took the form of her dead sister-in-law. The figure appeared in a dress which Mrs. A. had never seen, but which had been described to her by a common friend.

The ear, too, has its hallucinations. A notable case is given by Cardan, that strange sixteenth-century physician, charlatan, mathematician, astrologer, and gambler. When his son died he grieved deeply and could not sleep. When lying awake he heard, in the dark, a voice, which said, "Take the stone which is hanging round your neck, place it to your mouth, and so long as you hold it there you will not be troubled with thoughts of your son." He did so; in a moment all remembrance of his son faded from his mind and he fell asleep. The physician's mind gave him a faith-healing remedy such as he had probably often given to others. Dickens, when writing his novels, saw vividly the scenes he described and heard many of the conversations he wrote, so that he appeared to himself to write from dictation.

As Sir Walter Scott says, "There is every reason to believe that instances of this kind are frequent among persons of a certain temperament, and when such occur in the early period of society they are almost certain to be considered as real supernatural appearances." Often, no doubt, the supposed ghost would be a misinterpretation of something actually seen. A group of people might look at a moonbeam struggling through the branches of a tree and be convinced that they had seen a supernatural visitor. Scott's mind created the apparition of Lord Byron from impressions given by the hats, shawls, cloaks, and other things in the hall, and closer approach resolved the illusion into its elements. But the cases given above enable us to explain the belief that a ghost could appear to whom it pleased, while invisible and inaudible to others. In reality, the true ghost could, as a rule, appear to one person only, the one whose mind created and projected it. Only in cases of sympathetic rapport, or of partial hypnotism, could other minds share the creation and projection, and therefore see the ghost.

On cases of this kind, explained in this way, Shakespeare built up most of his later ghost work.

His first application of the theory he learnt from Plutarch was made in *Hamlet*, which appeared the year after *Julius Cæsar*. In this play there are two different ghosts, though actors represent but one. In Act I. the ghost of Hamlet's father, as it appears to Horatio, Bernardo, Marcellus, and Hamlet, is the ghost according to popular superstition. It appeared in full armour, and counterfeited his appearance during life, even to the grizzled beard. It claimed to be the veritable elder Hamlet, condemned to revisit the earth during the night, though unable to remain beyond the first cock-crow, condemned to endure horrible tortures during the day as punishment for the crimes of his life on earth until these were "burnt and purged away." When we make his acquaintance his purification was not far advanced; he revealed himself to Hamlet only to secure revenge, in accordance with the popular belief that the spirit of the murdered knew no rest till justice had overtaken the murderer. When this ghost spoke, his words were audible to all within range of hearing; his thrice-repeated adjuration, "Swear," was heard by all the four; to give Hamlet his message in private he took him to a remote part of the ground. It is quite correct and good Shakespeare to represent this ghost on the stage as visible to the audience and heard by them. They see and hear what any one of them might have seen and heard had he been present that night on the castle platform at Elsinore.

In Act III., scene 4, the case is very different. In this stormy scene between Hamlet and his mother a ghost appeared and spoke to Hamlet. His mother neither saw the ghost nor heard it, and as Hamlet stared at vacancy and conversed with nothing at all, she concluded that much excitement had made him mad. The ghost was subjective—*i.e.*, was a creation of and projection from Hamlet's mind. The mere fact that the ghost was invisible and inaudible to the only other person present might not be conclusive evidence that Shakespeare intended to indicate its subjective character. He has, however, furnished indications which require such an interpretation. Its subjective production is carefully prepared for; its entrance and its exit take place in strict accordance with the mental laws which are known to condition such hallucinations, and such an explanation takes its place in the chain of evidence bearing on the vexed question of Hamlet's insanity.

Hamlet's mental health would be profoundly disturbed by his interview with his father's spirit and by the revelation it made : his bodily health was poor ; he had sunk into almost hopeless melancholy ; he was tortured by doubts as to the degree of his mother's complicity, not prevented, but perhaps strengthened, by the Ghost's injunction, "Taint not thy mind, nor let thy soul contrive against thy mother aught." He was harassed by self-reproach on his delay in carrying out his revenge. Both body and mind were ready for the operation of a dominant idea, and this is not far to seek.

The interview with his mother took place in the evening. During the afternoon he had arranged private theatricals to represent the murder of his father. At and after the evening performance he was wildly excited. His father was the central object of thought the whole of this time. So engrossed was he in his purpose that even the death of Polonius made little impression : a contemptuous "Take thy fortune" dismissed the prying chamberlain from mind. When upbraiding his mother his excitement increased while he was comparing the two kings, till at the words, "A king of shreds and patches"—the idea of his father being in violent opposition, a change occurred which may be not inaptly compared with the flying off of water in vapour at 212° ; the excited mind projected its dominant idea and—"Enter Ghost." As in the play scene the elder Hamlet would be represented in the ordinary garb of civil life, the Ghost entered, not in armour as before, but "in his habit as he lived."

The exit of the Ghost is equally in accordance with psychological law. It is difficult to keep one's attention focused on one thing for any length of time, even on a ghost of one's own creation. Just as Mrs. A.'s ghost walked away when she began to try an experiment on it, and so withdrew her attention from the figure, this ghost walked away when Hamlet became interested in an argument with his mother as to whether they were alone or not. The least withdrawal of attention from the subjective creation is (in the writer's experience) fatal to its continuance as an apparent object of sight. When Hamlet became interested in convincing his mother the apparition vanished.

The fact that the Ghost addressed Hamlet need cause no difficulty. If the Ghost had given Hamlet information on matters with which he was unacquainted the theory here advocated would fall to the ground, but the speech merely reproduces Hamlet's two tormenting thoughts. He has reproached himself for his indecision and delay in revenging his father. "Do you not come your tardy son to chide ?" he asked. What wonder that his mind made the Ghost reply, "Do not forget; this visitation is but to whet thy almost blunted purpose" ? The latter half of the speech refers to Hamlet's mother. "Amazement on thy mother sits. O step between her and her fighting soul. Speak to her, Hamlet." Hamlet had been tortured by doubts as to whether his mother was or was not an accessory to the murder. He had just upbraided her almost brutally. In the remorse awakened by her poignant distress his mind worked in accordance with the Ghost's command to taint not his mind against his mother. The whole speech is a case of self-suggestion paralleled by the cases of Cardan and Dickens before cited.

His mother thought he was mad. Shakespeare lets us see by means of Gertrude that he had observed the phenomena of hallucination: "This is the very coinage of your brain. This bodily creation ecstasy (*i.e.*, madness) is very cunning in." The queen clearly believed that excessive grief had turned Hamlet's brain. As the scene is now played, the audience cannot realise this. They think Hamlet is justified as against his mother's accusation of madness. The effect on them is very different from that which Shakespeare intended. In this scene the audience should not see a ghost and should not hear one. There should be an interval of silence corresponding to the time necessary to speak the speech given to the Ghost—Hamlet being the while in an attitude of strained attention—and Hamlet should appear to the audience as to his mother, to address vacancy. Then the spectators would think as his mother thought, that his mind was giving way under the stress of long-continued grief, and would realise her state of mind when she said, "Alas, he's mad!"

The tests that Hamlet offers to prove his sanity—a normal pulse and an ability to reword the matter—*i.e.*, to recapitulate his speeches in the same words—are to some extent valid against the accusation of ecstasy, or madness, but are worthless in respect of the degree of aberration which conditions hallucination. Shakespeare gives one later indication of the unsettling of Hamlet's mind. On shipboard he rewrote the king's letter and sent Rosencrantz and Guildenstern, two comparatively innocent men, to execution in England. This strange weakening of moral control seems to indicate that he was on the verge of insanity, from which he was roused only by the need for instant and rapid action, which diverted his mind from things that, so thought on, led to madness.

Four years elapsed between Hamlet and Macbeth. Shakespeare appears to have been attracted by the phenomena of hallucination and to have studied the mental states leading to them, perhaps in conjunction with the physician who is introduced in the sleep-walking scene. We might not unjustly describe Macbeth as a study of the influence of a dominant idea on two minds of different temperaments, producing in one case hallucination, in the other somnambulism. In both cases the phenomena are as accurately reported as if by a scientific specialist.

There is a parallelism between the cases of Macbeth and Hamlet. Hamlet never recovered from the shock which resulted from meeting his father's spirit and hearing its horrible story. Macbeth's mental balance was disturbed by the meeting with the three witches, whose predictions let loose a flood of emotional excitement. This was not allayed by the speedy fulfilment of two of their promises. Even the sober-minded Banquo asked:

> "Have we eaten on the insane root,
> That takes the reason prisoner?"

He fell a prey to his wife's ambition and was tormented by the conflict between his longing for great place and his conscience. "What thou would'st highly," said Lady Macbeth, "that would'st thou holily: would'st not play false, and yet would'st wrongly win." He hung in miserable indecision, drawn to one side by conscience and fear, to the other by his wife's ambition. The violence of the struggle may be estimated by the reproaches and the taunts she found it necessary to address to him. No wonder that in the last waiting moments before the murder of Duncan, while Lady Macbeth was toning up her nerves with wine, Macbeth's agitated mind produced hallucination. He saw before him the appearance of the dagger he was to use. In this stage he was not completely hallucinated. He tested the reality of the appearance by trying to grasp it, and then grasped his own as a standard of comparison. When grasping his own he lost sight of the appearance for a moment. When the intense preoccupation of his mind, busy with the details of the murder, again produced the apparition, new details are added, the dagger is covered with spots of blood, and Macbeth rightly concludes:

> "It is the bloody business which informs thus to mine eyes."

This incident is correctly given on the stage; the actor tries to grasp an imaginary dagger. No one has yet proposed to suspend a real dagger in air to lend a colour to Macbeth's speech. The second hallucination scene in Act III., scene 4, is not so correctly represented. It occurred at a feast of nobles in a rude baronial hall with stools for seats. As at that time beggars often surrounded the doors, surged into the hall, and snatched pieces from the dishes which the servants carried, there is nothing improbable in the murderer's beckoning from the door to Macbeth, who learnt that Banquo lay dead with "twenty trenched gashes in his head." Lady Macbeth went to recall him to the company, to whom he returned and gave the invitation, "Good digestion wait on appetite, and health on both."

> "LENNOX: May't please your highness, sit."

The stage direction here is: "The ghost of Banquo enters and sits in Macbeth's place." Whenever the play is acted a visible ghost enters at this moment. Charles Kean arranged that a pillar should suddenly become luminous and show Banquo. When Madame Sarah Bernhardt produced the play at the Porte St. Martin in Paris, Banquo scrambled from under the table, the "twenty trenched gashes" being shown by a dab of red on the cheek. Other stage managers send Banquo through a trap-door in the floor. All this is ingenious, but it misrepresents Shakespeare. The ghost is purely subjective. No one saw it but Macbeth. The noble on the next seat thought the place empty. "You look but on a stool," said Lady Macbeth.

We can trace the causes of the appearance and disappearance of the Ghost. With his usual care, Shakespeare has given an indication of Macbeth's health. Lady Macbeth tells us he had suffered much from want of sleep. A wild jealousy of Banquo had taken possession of his agitated mind, producing strange mental and physical effects, of the nature of which we are not clearly told. "Then comes my fit again," he said, when informed of the escape of Fleance; "I had else been perfect, Whole as marble, founded as a rock." In the afternoon he arranged for the murder of Banquo, and was burning with anxiety to know the result. His anxiety is betrayed by his arranging with a third murderer unknown to the two previously sent. Shakespeare had, since the production of Hamlet, studied the dominant idea, and he is here minutely accurate in its use. For days Banquo had filled Macbeth's mind; this day it must have been all Banquo. He had just heard the news of the murder. In courtly phrase he regretted Banquo's absence: "Were the graced person of our Banquo present——" Shakespeare here rightly makes Macbeth's mind plant out on the only vacant stool, the one reserved for Banquo, the image of the murdered man. And, just as Brewster's Mrs. A. dressed one of her phantoms in a dress she had heard of but not seen, Macbeth's mind constructed the gory head of which the murderer had spoken.

The apparition disappeared because Macbeth's attention was withdrawn from it. He had to defend his courage from his wife's imputation. This tended to the dissolution of the apparition. Then, while he addressed the gradually vanishing figure, his mind became filled with other images—those of charnel-houses, graves, monuments, maws of kites, and so forth—and this withdrawal of attention necessitated the departure of the Ghost. If he could have kept his mind from returning to the subject, the spectre would not have reappeared, but his place as host compelled him to "drink the general joy of the whole table, And to our dear friend Banquo, whom we miss, Would he were here——" The Ghost very naturally re-entered. For a moment Macbeth's whole attention was given to the ghastly creation of his mind, but, as before, other images crowded in—"The rugged Russian bear," "the armed rhinoceros," "the Hyrcan tiger," "the baby of a girl"—and the Ghost again disappeared.

At the first hallucination—that of the dagger—Macbeth tested the reality by touch; at this second hallucination he was completely hallucinated, he unquestioningly accepted the reality of the appearance. In this way Shakespeare marked his mental deterioration. He was on the verge of lunacy, from which he only saved himself by breaking out into rapid action—that series of cruelties which caused him to be reputed mad, but which by engaging his attention saved him from madness.

It may be urged that the ghost as staged is more effective. It is not only less effective, but erroneously effective. A wrong impression is produced on the audience. The other persons present at the banquet saw no ghost: the audience see one. Macbeth's exclamations are to them justifiable: they cannot bring themselves into sympathy with Lady Macbeth, who reproached her husband for cowardice, or with the nobles who hurriedly departed, thinking him seriously deranged. They do not realise how great was Macbeth's mental aberration. It would be just as reasonable to represent a visible dagger in the first hallucination scene as it is to represent a visible ghost in the second. On the view here advocated, the stage directions, "The ghost of Banquo enters and sits in Macbeth's place," "Re-enter Ghost," and the corresponding "Enter Ghost," in Act III., scene 4, of *Hamlet*, are no more than hints to the actors who play Macbeth and Hamlet. They give a clue to the cause of the strange behaviour of these characters, and indicate the gestures appropriate to the circumstances.

Shakespeare's genius placed him here far in advance of the general knowledge of his age. Only custom and familiarity blind us to the wonders of these plays. They are as sensational as R. L. Stevenson's *Dr. Jekyll and Mr. Hyde*, or Hugh Conway's *Called Back*. The former revealed to the general public the strange phenomena of so-called double personality; the latter based itself on striking and little-known facts of thought transference. So in *Hamlet* and *Macbeth* Shakespeare brought before the public abnormal phenomena of mental life, hallucination and somnambulism, which the audiences of the time were not competent to understand. The staging of a visible ghost was a concession to popular ignorance. The theatrical tradition has endured to the present day, and we can but regret that it took its rise when the theatre-going public was incapable of appreciating some of the most interesting work of our greatest dramatist.

J. H. HUDSON.

# THE INFLUENCE OF THE WOMAN'S CLUB.

So gradually and slowly, during the past few years, has the woman's club made its way and enforced its claims, that it is doubtful whether those in whose lives such institutions to-day constitute a factor, any more than others to whom a club is an undefined even if occasionally a disparaged quantity of the imagination only, realise the influence which these organisations are at present exerting upon things feminine. To declare that the youngest of us is able, within a short experience, to trace a perceptible advance upon the part of women towards greater breadth of thought and liberty of action is but to propound a truism. But the fact is one by no means universally recognised that that onward impulse has been materially promoted by the clubs which have sprung into being around and upon the path of progress.

The world is made up of mediocrities. While the self-recognised exceptions to this rule individually float in a rarefied ether of their own appreciativeness, the majority of folk are struggling in a lower and thicker atmosphere, but units that go to compose an undistinguished mass. Sometimes the head of one or another may be honoured as forming an eligible spring-board whence an aspiring genius may "take off." Oftener the heads are not thus favoured. With separate personality engulphed in a seething crowd, where is to be found the opportunity for a display, even for a self-recognition, on the part of the ego? A babel of inseparably blended cries rises above the *melée*, without articulation, without discernible sense. Only by the force produced by co-operation, the harmony induced by union, can distinction and power be achieved. Here, then, in one direction is made manifest the action of the club—of the club social, political, educational, what you will—upon the world at large. Those with similar ideas own each other as comrades, join hands and raise voices, thus accomplishing expression whilst experiencing sympathy. The woman question is old. It is, indeed, probably as old, within an inappreciable moment, as the man question. Until, however, its exponents began to learn the secret of amalgamated strength it failed to impress its reality upon the world.

So much for the general aspect. With regard to the particu'ar, the importance of the club is scarcely less. Upon the existence of the London woman its effect has become very manifest. It is a more or less recognised fact that the club constitutes a refuge from many a domestic ill, affording a comforting, if but a transitory, solution even of the ever-recurrent servant problem. A luncheon party rendered impossible at home by the sudden decease of all the cook's near relatives can be adjourned to the club, and the hostess's self-esteem remain intact. An unintimate interview may be arranged with a minimum danger of subsequent encounters. Acquaintances may be kept at a distance, friendships may be drawn close by the special safeguards and opportunities of the club. Though the objection that that same easy mode of solving difficulties may react upon the attractions of the " ain fireside " is not open to refutation. The club —the woman's club, *bien entendu*—is, for the same person, the rendezvous of chosen intimates, the arena of discussion and outspoken theory, the place where opinions are formulated if not formed, self-realised if not created. It is, moreover, the resort where, on occasions, pleasure and instruction may piously be believed to walk hand in hand, as its members listen to some brilliant *jeu d'esprit*, yclept by courtesy a lecture.

Upon the provincial and country woman, too, the club is gradually tightening its grip. To say nothing of the cities which have followed metropolitan example and established clubs of their own, country membership of London clubs has rendered the intercourse of the town mouse and the country mouse a simpler and a better thing. By a morning wire to the club the frigid solitude and depressing unfamiliarity of the hotel, with its thousand apartments, is avoided. Away from home the club member is at once amongst, yet independent of, friends. She has, in fact, a second abode at her disposal, an abode which is within reach and touch of the world of intellect and of thought. The provinces fail to retain her as a provincial, so soon as the club enables her to walk as a woman of the world.

It is in comparatively small matters that the results of club life and the impulse which it exerts upon the trend of the age may, however, be best and most definitely gauged. The woman orator, for instance—that sometime legitimate target for every feeble joker, that present-day most ordinary person—from what source have the recruits to her army been drawn, upon what ground have they been drilled, except that of the club ? The debates of the Pioneer, the Sesame, the Grosvenor Crescent clubs produce consequences more often remarked than is the cause discerned. The more so since these consequences are frequently indirect, the exploitation of a gift by one woman being apt to induce the discovery of similar talents upon the part of another. The woman-smoker—why are the feminine votaries of the cigarette upon the persistent increase ? To the women's clubs, the establishments where women live their own lives, untrammelled by criticism or advice, the question should be addressed. In more than half the women's clubs of London provision has been made for the smoker.  The smoking-room may, indeed, be described as the club's heart.

The influence of women's clubs—it is wide indeed in its reach. Through its lessons women have learned to walk hand in hand, and march shoulder to shoulder, to comprehend the secrets of cohesion and partnership, of originality and organisation, with a potent efficacy that spreads and permeates.  So spreading and permeating, with an unaggressive persistence, through the joints of society's armour, the influence of the club affects the nation.  Self-assertion being dwarfed by a wider horizon of personal and relative responsibility, there becomes visible a prospect of loyal comradeship.  Intercourse between woman and woman resulting, not in sentiment, but in work, stagnation gives place to movement.  And thus are produced by emanations, impalpable but irresistible as mist, from the drawing-rooms, reading-rooms, smoking-rooms of our clubs fresh and important possibilities to strengthen and to ozonise the atmosphere encircling womanhood.

JULIA M. A. HAWKSLEY.

# CO-EDUCATION.

I HAVE read with interest Mr. Ablett's article on this subject in your January number, and, as a teacher of both sexes for upwards of eleven years, can fully endorse all his remarks.

I have no hesitation in saying that the evil he speaks of, which tends so much to enervate both the minds and bodies of the young people of our day, and to impair their powers of reproduction in after life, might be largely mitigated by co-education. It is the stolen fruit which is the sweetest, and the "don't-look-on-the-other-side" system has always the desired, and in this case disastrous, effect. The mere sex-distinction in schools is dangerous, and the mere fact of the secrecy with which sexual subjects are treated makes an imaginative child, of an inquiring turn of mind, eager to find out what all take such pains to hide. And, what is more, find out he will, oh fond and foolish parent, whatever you do. I do not believe in the "absolute ignorance" of these matters which some people profess that young girls have before marriage, any more than Mr. Ablett, and I think most medical men who are in the habit of attending any large public or private girls'-school will bear us out; and if she has learnt such things surreptitiously from low sources, such as did the girl in the tableaux in Marie Corelli's *Sorrows of Satan*, much better that she should do so in a decent manner from some pure-minded woman such as, for instance, her own mother. There is another, perhaps minor, effect, but one none the less to be avoided by co-education. The boy from whom the other sex has been religiously excluded very likely from the age of eight to eighteen, finds himself altogether out of his element when mixing with girls on his entrance into society, and the result is awkwardness or gaucherie. He does not know what subjects of conversation will interest her, nor which must be avoided as "not fit for girls to know," whilst the girl is doubtless at a similar disadvantage. Society thus ceases to have any attractions for him, and he looks elsewhere, and generally in less desirable quarters, for his amusement and information. Hence such results as the "dearth of dancing men," about which so many hostesses complain.

And now for the other side of the picture. The boy who, up to the age of nine or ten, has learnt side by side with his sisters at home, is not cruelly separated from his beloved little play-mates, but goes with them in due time to a mixed school or college, and whilst there receives sensible instruction in the duties of man, and amongst others in the glorious reproduction of a perfect species, at the close of his education is not hampered by the mysteries of the sexual question, nor with a morbid curiosity to "find out" what these are. On the contrary, familiar from the first with the other sex, with whom he has mingled through all their mutual stages of development, his chief aim will be to work hard, to get on in life, that he may soon be in a position to choose a mate, and with her share in the duties of reproduction, which should be looked upon by all as one amongst the most glorious privileges granted us by a beneficent Creator.

I cannot do better than close in the words of Dr. James Currie, in his *Common School Education :*

" It has been made a question whether pupils of different sexes should be classified together, or even received into the same school, not from any doubt of their being able to go on together with the same studies, but partly from the consideration that their studies should not be entirely the same, and mainly from some suspicion that the character and manners of each may be injuriously affected. There does not appear to be any force in either of these reasons. When the school is under judicious guidance the weak points in the character of the pupils of either sex, so far from being transferred to, are corrected by the presence of the other. The character of the boy is refined, that of the girl strengthened ; the tendency of the one to inconsiderateness and rudeness, of the other to triviality, is restrained ; the tone of manners in both is elevated. Nature sets us the example of the mingling of the sexes for mutual influence in the family circle ; and there is no reason why the good effects that flow from its constitution should not be looked for, in greater or less measure, when we imitate her example in the common school. That they may be attained in a well-governed school, experience, it is believed, attests : under any other conditions, the influence of the pupils is not to be trusted, whether the school is mixed or not. As for the minor difficulty, that the studies of the sexes must be to a certain extent different, a teacher of any skill can easily arrange to give the girls their industrial instruction without destroying the equilibrium of attainment in his classes. In mixed schools the boys and girls are generally arranged in different classes ; but there is the same propriety in mixed classes as in mixed schools, provided the pupils of different sexes form distinct parts of the class, and interchange places (where that practice is followed) among themselves alone."

HERBERT WHISKIN.

# CONTEMPORARY LITERATURE.

## SCIENCE.

THE *Annual Report of the Smithsonian Institute for* 1897 [1] contains much original matter of scientific interest. Dr. J. M. Flint's catalogue of recent foraminifera is a valuable monograph on the subject, the utility of which is much enhanced by a large number of excellent photographic illustrations. Some of the species described are new to science, and are here figured for the first time. Mr. J. D. McGuire's monograph on Pipes and Smoking Customs of the American Aborigines is full of interest, and is also well illustrated. Some of the forms of pipes are exceedingly curious, especially those from the mounds, with their curious carvings, representing birds, beasts, and even human beings. Another excellent paper is that on Arrowpoints, Spearheads, and Knives of Prehistoric Times, by Mr. T. Wilson. One of the special features of Mr. Wilson's work is the description and illustration of a number of microscopic sections of the different varieties of stone used for the manufacture of stone implements. Although the bulk of the illustrations are from the collections in the United States National Museum, yet the author has made use of other sources of information, and the result is one of the best treatises on this subject that we have yet seen. It is a pity that these valuable scientific monographs are not bound separately, so that they might find a permanent place in the libraries of naturalists. The binding of these reports is always of the poorest description, and is certainly not at all in keeping with the great scientific value of some of the papers.

Recent progress in bacteriology has not only enabled us to take efficient steps for preventing the spread of contagious diseases, but has also contributed very materially towards the effective treatment of existing cases. Even tuberculosis is beginning to yield to modern methods, and some excellent results of successful treatment have recently been recorded. In his *Consumption and Chronic Diseases,* [2] Dr. E. Densmore gives the history of a number of tuberculous patients who have been either cured or have materially

---

[1] *Annual Report of the Board of Regents of the Smithsonian Institution for 1897.* Washington. 1899.
[2] *Consumption and Chronic Diseases.* By E. Densmore. London : Swan Sonnenschein & Co.

benefited by an open-air system of treatment similar to that adopted at Nordrach. While, however, the Nordrach system necessitates residence at a sanatorium and continuous medical supervision, Dr. Densmore advocates a diet of milk and absolute rest for the patient, combined with the maximum amount of fresh air obtainable. Under these conditions the increase of weight was very marked, and with this increase a corresponding diminution in the phthisical symptoms was observed. Any improvement in the means at our disposal for combating this terrible disease must be cordially welcomed, and we trust that Dr. Densmore's results may be corroborated when the treatment which he advocates has been tried on a more extended scale.

We have received a useful little *Manual of Chemistry*,[1] by Messrs. A. P. Luff and F. J. M. Page, which is decidedly above the average of the numerous text-books on the subject which are constantly issuing from the press. Primarily intended for the use of medical students, this book may be recommended to any general student of chemistry. The information given is concise and up-to-date, and the authors have not merely been content to copy from other text-books, but have exercised a wise discretion in the selection of the matter utilised. For instance, the test for ozone, described on p. 81, is far preferable to the one usually employed, and is not liable to the sources of error familiar to all who have studied this subject. One excellent feature of the book is the reference to the antidotes in the case of poisonous substances, and even the danger of compressing acetylene is referred to. We would remind the authors that the absorbent used for ordinary dynamite is not now infusorial earth.

We have received a scientific work of great importance which is destined to arouse much attention, especially among those interested in molecular physics. In *La Constitution du Monde*,[2] the gifted authoress Madame Clémence Royer develops new atomic theories, in the light of which many physical and chemical phenomena acquire a new significance. In opposition to the generally accepted theory, Madame Royer conceives the ultimate atoms as being liquid or plastic instead of hard and incompressible. Three kinds or states of atoms are supposed to exist, namely ethereal or imponderable, material or ponderable, and vitaliferous or psychic monads. All careful students of the subject must admit that the usual atomic theories do not satisfactorily explain all observed facts, and Madame Royer does good service to science in calling attention to the anomalies and in attempting an explanation. The atoms and molecules of the various chemical elements and some of their combinations have been

[1] *A Manual of Chemistry.* By A. P. Luff and F. J. M. Page. London : Cassell and Co., Ltd. 1900.
[2] *La Constitution du Monde.* Par Madame Clémence Royer. Paris : Schleicher Frères. 1900.

submitted to a careful and exhaustive inquiry, and, in accordance with not a few other investigators, the authoress comes to the conclusion that some of the generally accepted atomic weights are not altogether correct. Gaseous, liquid, and solid bodies are considered separately at considerable length and their relations to the omnipresent ether discussed. It is somewhat startling to the physicist to be told that bodies do not attract each other; but Madame Royer not only brings much independent evidence in favour of this view, but quotes the words of Newton himself in opposition to what most of us would have considered as his own theory.

In connection with a new theory of tides some interesting data are given bearing especially upon the fluid state of the earth's centre, and atmospheric tides are also referred to at some length. The work is illustrated copiously, and numerous tables assist the reader in surveying the numerous facts adduced. All those interested in the advance of science should study this book, in which they will find much food for reflection. We congratulate Madame Royer on so successful a termination to the labour of many years.

---

## PHILOSOPHY AND THEOLOGY.

A CONCISE and connected historical sketch of philosophy in France is a valuable addition to literature and was very much wanted. This has now been supplied by Professor Lucien Lévy-Bruhl in his masterly *History of Modern Philosophy in France.*[1] With the philosophers individually we are already familiar—Descartes, Boyle, Voltaire, Condorcet, Diderot, Comte, and many more. What we learn from M. Lévy-Bruhl is their relation to one another, and the development of the leading ideas which are characteristic of French philosophy and which give it a character distinct from German, English, or Scottish.

There is no attempt at biography in this volume, which we cannot but regret, though the addition would probably have expanded the one volume into two. It is therefore entirely critical, but the criticism is that of a writer himself endowed with considerable philosophical insight, and fully competent to trace the lines of thought which distinguish the writings of several generations of the most brilliant set of thinkers the modern world has produced. Besides those we have already mentioned, we find included others

---

[1] *History of Modern Philosophy in France.* By Lucien Lévy-Bruhl. With Portraits of the leading French Philosophers. London : Kegan Paul, Trench, Trübner & Co., Ltd. 1899.

like Pascal, Rousseau, and Renan, who, though not philosophers by profession, have greatly influenced the evolution of thought in France. The volume contains no less than three-and-twenty fine portraits of the most renowned French writers, from paintings, engravings, or sculpture. The work is deserving of high praise, and will be a valuable addition to any library. The publication of this work in English is due to the enterprise of the Open Court Publishing Company (Chicago), and the admirable translation is by Miss G. Coblence, assisted, in revision, by Professor W. H. Carruth, of Kansas.

Syriac literature is prolific in New Testament Apocryphal writings, from which Mr. E. A. Wallis Budge has selected for translation, after editing the Syriac texts, *The History of the Blessed Virgin Mary and the History of the Likeness of Christ.*[1]  Much of the contents of the first is familiar to English readers in what is popularly known as the Apocryphal New Testament—"The Gospel of Thomas," "The Gospel of the Infancy," &c. There is much in the Gospel of Mary that is comparatively little known, but which will repay reading. A well-informed introduction by the editor and translator gives some account of this literature. Much of the so-called history consists of stories of the same character—accounts of miracles which were wrought by the swaddling bands of Jesus, or by the water in which He had been washed, as well as by His word and touch. The account of the death of Mary at Jerusalem is very impressive. The Apostles had gone into the four quarters of the world, and Mary prayed that she might see them before she departed. First of all, those who were living were transported by the spirit to Jerusalem ; then those who had died were called from their graves and borne in a chariot of light into the presence of the Virgin. "And then there arrived at the door of the upper chamber the chariot of the patriarchs, and our father Adam alighted therefrom and entered in and did homage to the holy woman Mary." Abraham and David followed, and the Cherubim and Seraphim, and last of all the Lord Christ himself. There are many other legends relating to the death, burial, and assumption of Mary.

The story of the "Image of Christ painted upon wood" is in the form of a letter by the Deacon Philotheus. The Jews, pretending to be Christians, persuaded a painter to paint them a picture of the crucified Christ, which, when they received it, they set up in an inner chamber and insulted it. And one of them took a spear and drove it into the side of the likeness, and "then straightway blood and water came therefrom." Many other miracles occurred, and numbers were converted. The volume is not only interesting, but

[1] *The History of the Blessed Virgin Mary and the History of the Likeness of Christ which the Jews of Tiberias made to mock at.* The Syriac Texts edited with English Translations by E. A. Wallis Budge, M.A. English Translation. London : Luzac and Co. 1899.

throws considerable light upon the character of Syriac Christianity in early days.

Mr. Joseph McCabe, after having been a priest—or at least a monk—has turned prophet, and ventures to forecast *The Religion of the Twentieth Century.*[1] Needless to say, it is Mr. McCabe's own present religion, or no-religion. That is to say, he expects it will be ethical rationalism. We cannot say we agree with him. We anticipate that, either for good or bad, old types of religion will last much longer than he prophecies. There is really nothing new in his pamphlet; the same thing was said more than a hundred years ago, and yet Christianity still survives. This has nothing to do with the desirability or otherwise of Mr. McCabe's new reformation, which is not the same as Mrs. Humphrey Ward's; we only think he is too sanguine.

A curious story of fanaticism is that related in all candour and simplicity by Mr. Eastlake in *The Oneida Community.*[2] America has produced many strange things, but none stranger than this combination of revivalism, socialism, and polyandry. The Community has been unjustly charged with encouraging free love, while in fact it only practised "communal marriage." Every woman was (or might be) the wife of every man, and every man was (or might be) the husband of every woman. But restraints were imposed which kept improper tendencies in check. No man could make advances, and he always ran the risk of the ordeal of "criticism." Confession appears to be child's play in comparison with this. Apart from this peculiarity, the community appears to have been composed of curiously simple and pious people, who have perhaps contributed to the improvement of the race; but we have our doubts. The Community is now a limited liability company, but we believe polyandry has been given up, or the shares might be sought after.

*Zion's Works—New Light on the Bible from the Coming of Shiloh, the Spirit of Truth,* 1828–1837. The proper name of "Zion," we believe, was Ward, who started a new era in 1825 or thereabouts, and was sent to Derby gaol for blasphemy very soon after. Mr. C. B. Hollingsworth appears to have so great an admiration for "Zion" that he is reprinting his works at some considerable cost. Zion Ward was a fanatic, but, like so many fanatics, he had a strain of common sense, and some of his criticisms on popular religion are sensible enough; but, on the other hand, when he set up a new religion of his own he must have been decidedly crazy. (London: John Macqueen.)

We frequently read Bishops' charges to their clergy, but have

<hr/>

[1] *The Religion of the Twentieth Century.* By Joseph McCabe. London: Watts and Co. 1899.

[2] *The Oneida Community.* A Record of an Attempt to Carry Out the Principles of Christian Unselfishness and Scientific Race Improvement. By Allan Eastlake. London: George Redway. 1900.

never read so admirable a one as that which the Bishop of Rochester, Dr. E. S. Talbot, delivered at his first visitation last year. The subject is *The Vocation and Dangers of the Church*, and Dr. Talbot says much that is very wise and very bold on the dangers of ecclesiasticism and dogmatism. (Macmillan & Co.)

We have also received from Messrs. Macmillan the first two numbers (October 1899 and January 1900) of *The Journal of Theological Studies.* The contents are largely archæological, but the magazine promises to be of great value to all who wish to keep themselves abreast of the higher theological learning.

---

## SOCIOLOGY, POLITICS, AND JURISPRUDENCE.

*Good Citizenship: A Book of Twenty-three Essays by various Authors on Social, Personal, and Economic Problems and Obligations,*[1] edited by the Rev. J. E. Hand, is explained by its sub-title. Many of the authors are well-known writers on social economic subjects, such as Mr. G. Laurence Gomme, who writes on "Municipal Government"; Mr. J. A. Hobson, who reproduces here his views on labour and capital; Dr. Rashdall, who describes the "General Functions of the State"; Miss Mona Wilson, the lady expert on the position of women in "Factories and Workshops"; Dr. Morrison, the well-known authority on "The Treatment of Criminals"; the Hon. W. P. Reeves, who is specially qualified to point out "The Nation's Duty to the Empire"; Canon Holland on "The Obligation of Civil Law"; and Miss Busk on "Women's Work on Vestries and Councils."

Other articles are by writers better known perhaps as workers in special fields of social effort. Canon Barnett gives us "The Churchman as a Citizen," and the Rev. Francis Powell "The Church and Civilisation." Mrs. R. C. Phillimore writes on "Women in Social Life," and the Ven. James Wilson on "The Progress of Morality in the Relations of Men and Women." Miss Ethel Portal describes "The Work of a Ladies' Settlement," and Dr. Fry, the successful headmaster of Berkhamstead School, discourses on "The Obligations of Social Service." Poetry and art are not neglected, and the Rev. Ronal Bayne and the Rev. A. G. B. Atkinson are responsible for two stimulating papers on those subjects.

The object of this collection is set forth by the Rev. Charles Gore in the Preface. It is intended as an appeal to Englishmen to take their citizenship more seriously. The line taken by the writers is

---

[1] *Good Citizenship: A Book of Twenty-three Essays by various Authors on Social, Personal, and Economic Problems and Obligations.* Edited by the Rev. J. E. Hand. With a Preface by the Rev. Charles Gore, M.A., D.D. London: George Allen. 1899

that which we have so long advocated in this REVIEW—viz., a mean between the extreme individualism of Mr. Herbert Spencer and the thoroughgoing scheme of State Socialism. As may be gathered from the profession of many of the writers, there is in addition an appeal to churchmen in particular, and they base their appeal upon the principles of Christian Socialism. For this side we have every respect. We fully recognise the magnitude of the influence for good of the teaching of Christ as a social reformer and a teacher of ethics, but the claim for a divine origin for those principles weakens rather than strengthens any appeal based upon them alone. To assert that there can be no morality apart from some particular religion, such as Christianity, is absurd. With this reservation we have nothing but praise for this collection of admirable papers upon the various aspects of our social organisation.

France, says Baron Mourre, in *D'ou Vient la Décadence Economique de la France,*[1] has been beaten by England and Germany—commercially, that is to say. The cause of this inferiority he considers to be the dislike of the French higher classes for commerce, manufacture, and agriculture, and their longing for positions under Government. What is the origin of this prejudice? Is it ancient or modern? To answer this question the author examines French history, noting the various effects of feudalism, the Hundred Years' War, the Revolution, &c. The temperament of his countrymen he also finds in fault. After examining causes, he turns to effects, and specially notes as consequences of this general prejudice an exaggerated State interference and a want of technical education. In the latter part of his work the author examines the causes, both in the physical condition of the countries and the temper of their peoples, of the economic progress of England and Germany. The work is well reasoned and well written, and not to be omitted by those who take an interest in the commercial development of France.

M. Georges Aubert is one of those Frenchmen who are suffering from a bad dream—a nightmare. The wealth and progress of England annoy him. He cannot help but see that his own country is a very poor second. And so he has written a book—*A Quoi Tient l'Infériorité du Commerce Français*[2]—to teach his countrymen that they may do better than openly express their detestation for "la perfide Albion" by quietly agreeing with us until "new circumstances may give place to new opinions and new combinations," meanwhile copying, "as far as their habits will allow them," our industrial and commercial methods. If any Englishman desires to read from the pages of a *soi-disant* candid friend a buffoon's burlesque of our country and character, he may try this for a start; and he will get only one satisfaction—the barefaced avowal (p. 16

[1] *D'ou Vient la Décadence Economique de la France.* Par Baron Charles Mourre. Paris : E. Plon, Nourrit et Cie.
[2] *A Quoi Tient l'Infériorité du Commerce Français.* Par Georges Aubert. Paris : Ernest Flammarion.

and others) that present French enmity to England is purely the envy of a small boy who cries what he would do if he were a man. The book, in its descriptions of English character and politics, is false, and, if taken seriously, will tend to mislead rather than to enlighten our neighbours as to our sentiments towards themselves.

*Le Marxisme et son critique Bernstein,*[1] by Herr Karl Kautsky, forms the second volume of the new series published by M. P. V. Stock under the title of "Social Research," and is a reply to the first volume of this series, *Socialisme théorique et social democratie pratique,* from the pen of Herr E. Bernstein, the well-known German sociologist. This latter work contests certain very important points of collectivism, and endeavours to prove that the new socialistic state is not so imminent as some appear to think. He arrives at the conclusion that the Socialist party must, without abandoning its ideals, unite with the Liberals in forming a strong party of social and democratic reform. This view is opposed by Herr Kautsky in the book before us. He considers such a union is incompatible with the domination of the capitalist class. The fact that both these writers are followers of Marx lends additional interest to this controversy. The translation from the German is by M. Martin-Leray.

M. Alfred Naquet, late Senator and Deputy, is responsible for the third volume of the series, entitled *Temps Futurs, Socialisme— Anarchie,*[2] whose chief interest lies in the fact that the author, formerly opposed to the principles of collectivism, now argues in their favour, and, whilst adhering to the new doctrine, does not repudiate any of those arguments with which he would once have controverted it. How the author reconciles two such opposing theories as collectivism and anarchy the reader must find out for himself. Such a pursuit appeals especially to those interested in the evolution of human thought.

The new feature in *Debrett's House of Commons and the Judicial Bench*[3] is the introduction of particulars of the Judges of both the Superior and Inferior Courts. As a work of reference for the politician and the general public it is impossible to overrate this work. For such it is necessarily invaluable. On p. 345 we notice one bad error. His Honour Judge Lushington, a Cambridge man, is assigned the degrees of B.C.L. and M.L. Cambridge, of course, has no such titles. They are LL.B. and LL.M. B.C.L. belongs to the Universities of Oxford and Durham. M.L. as a title is unknown to us.

[1] *Le Marxisme et son critique Bernstein.* Par Karl Kautsky. Traduction de M. Martin-Leray. Paris : P. V. Stock. 1900.
[2] *Temps Futurs, Socialisme—Anarchie.* Par A. Naquet. Paris : P. V. Stock. 1900.
[3] *Debrett's House of Commons and the Judicial Bench, 1900.* Illustrated with Armorial Bearings. London : Dean & Son, Ltd. 1900.

## HISTORY AND BIOGRAPHY.

A VOLUME of nearly five hundred pages entitled *Vers la Lumière*,[1] by Séverine, has been published by P. V. Stock. It deals with the Dreyfus case from a social and judicial point of view. The volume is appropriately dedicated to the memory of M. Scheurer-Kestner. The contents are of absorbing interest. The brilliant style of the author enables the reader to grasp vividly all the different stages of the great Dreyfus drama. The part played by Esterhazy in the drama is shown in the opening pages. The contrast between the trial of Esterhazy and that of Dreyfus, both of which took place in the same hall, is indicated in eloquent and impressive language. The surroundings were the same ; but the one trial was a tragedy, while the other was a farce. The details which show the rascality and the poltroonery of Esterhazy are set forth with unflinching circumstantiality, and we can scarcely feel any respect for the tribunal which exculpated such a man. The author deals ably with the Zola trial under the heading of " Les Quinze Journées de l'Affaire Zola." The closing passage is remarkable : " Cannibales, a crie Zola avec dégoût : le même mot de Voltaire, defenseur de Calas. Tandis qu'autour de lui un pacte tacite de resistance liait les âmes . . . pour ton triumphe, O Verité ! Et *pur si muove !* Et pourtant elle marche ! " Brave words, which will be echoed by every friend of truth and justice ! The proceedings in connection with " L'Affaire Dreyfus " in the Cour de Cassation, as well as the memorable trial at Rennes, cover one hundred and fifty pages of the volume. Those who wish to have an enduring impression of the course of the Dreyfus case up to its dramatic close will read *Vers la Lumière* with delight, and will find in the pages of Séverine that " nervous shudder " which genius alone can produce in presenting under a new aspect the stern facts of life.

M. Georges Clemençeau has written a new volume on the Dreyfus case which is an admirable exposition of the facts of this great *cause célèbre*.[2] M. Georges Clemençeau is well qualified to deal with this case, which has involved issues of the most momentous character. He is an able and fearless advocate, and a writer of great power. He certainly does not mince matters, and every page in his book rings true. He lashes with a pen as cutting as a rod the baseness of the malignant enemies of Dreyfus. He does not spare the miserable Esterhazy, who really is too mean a creature to be hated. As M. Clemençeau remarks, it is a matter of no consequence whether Esterhazy ends his days or not in the Ile du Diable. To quote the author's own words : " Ce que nous cherchons, c'est la vérite, et nous tenons beaucoup, plus au Jugement de l'histoire

1 *Vers la Lumière (Impressions Véenes).* Par Séverine.  Paris : P. V. Stock.
2 *Contre la Justice.*  Par Georges Clemençeau.  Paris : P. V. Stock.

qu'au châtiment matériel de tel ou tel coupable." It is manifest
that no reliance can be placed in any of Esterhazy's statements.
If he had anything to say in his own defence, he would long
since have said it when he was the person accused. It is almost
unnecessary for M. Clemençeau to emphasise this point. Another
ground for utterly discrediting the wretched man is that, if he
could justify himself, instead of boldly confronting his accusers, he
would not have placed the frontier between himself and the law.
The friends of Dreyfus must feel, as M. Clemençeau points out,
that, if Esterhazy is a liar, as appears certain, nothing is more easy
than to confound him. For instance, the truth or falsehood of
Esterhazy's statement that he wrote the "bordereau" by General
de Boisdeffre's orders could be simply tested by five minutes' con-
frontation of these two individuals. Moreover, an interview between
Esterhazy and Boisdeffre, which would have the character of
publicity, would throw a lurid light on the means by which the
acquittal of the former was secured. But this is only the fringe of
the case. M. Clemençeau goes into a critical examination of the
revision, which has been made in spite of the Chamber and the
Government. The matter cannot end there; it concerns the
interests of truth and the honour of France that full justice should
be done as between Dreyfus and his enemies. M. Clemençeau
vindicates the character of Picquart, that heroic officer who has
been subjected to so much petty persecution. The parts played
in the drama by Du Paty de Clam, the wretched suicide Henry,
Méline Freycinet, and even President Loubet, are clearly defined in
M. Clemençeau's eloquent pages. The conduct of the clerical and
military classes is subjected to a rigid analysis in one most
interesting chapter, and it is shown that the late Napoleon III. was
really the vile instrument in the hands of the clergy and the army
by which French public life was poisoned at its very source.
Indeed, the book is a lesson in political ethics, which well deserves
to be studied and taken deeply to heart. The conventional notion
that, as long as a democratic form of government prevails, the
interests of the people will be safeguarded is puerile. As
M. Clemençeau in his thoughtful preface shows, the work of the
Revolution was imperfect. The destruction of one tyrant—the
monarch—is worthless if it only gives place to another tyrant, the
mob. Of course this is no reason for taking a reactionary course.
Government "by the people and for the people" is right; but the
"master with the hundred heads" must be enlightened and must
gather knowledge and wisdom in the school of facts. The Dreyfus
case thus furnishes a criterion for the ideal of democracy. When
the clouds which surrounded this mysterious case have been cleared
away, all honest men in France will feel ashamed that under a
Republican *régime* the crime against liberty and justice committed

by persons in authority to crush one innocent man could have been perpetrated. As M. Clemençeau puts it, when that day comes, " the Dreyfusards, whether they are living or dead, will have their recompense." Then the names of Zola, Labori, and Clemençeau will be imperishably enshrined in the hearts of the people of France.

In view of the Reinach-Henry trial, M. Joseph Reinach has collected, under the title of *Tout le Crime*,[1] the series of historic studies which were originally published in the *Siècle* and in the *Grande Revue* on the *rôles* played by Esterhazy and Henry. The volume is dedicated to that great advocate, Maître Labori, who has been entrusted with the defence of M. Joseph Reinach before the Juge de la Seine. The series in the collected form must be regarded as a most careful and conscientious presentation of the facts. Moreover, the attitude taken is one of absolute impartiality. *Tout le Crime* is a historic study of one of the strangest episodes in the political life of the France of to-day. The criticism of the miserable Henry is masterly and, one might add, terrible. " Quel immense intéret a poussé cet hommes à tels crimes, à de tels périls, jusqu' à la mort ? " Let history answer !

*Le Sabre et la Loi*[2] is the title of another publication of the Librairie Stock dealing with some of the great issues raised by the Dreyfus case. In an admirable preface, M. de Pressensé unsparingly exposes the infamies of the clerico-military faction. The volume must interest every Frenchman, since every Frenchman is a soldier. The sword is necessary for the preservation of a nation's liberty as long as the present organisation of society lasts ; but justice must not be murdered by the sword. When that takes place, a national crime is committed. We are sure M. Lhermitte's work will be widely read, not only in France but in other countries.

*African Incidents*[3] is a book in which a brave English officer, Major A. B. Thruston, gives his Egyptian experiences in a simple, unaffected style, and without any desire for self-advertisement. The explanation given by the author of the genesis of the volume is the quintessence of manly simplicity. Here is what Major Thruston says : " An apology is due for this book. It is the duty of officers in my regiment to send to their annual *Chronicle* an account of their proceedings ; mine were too lengthy for the patience of the Editor, and this book is the result." General Archibald Gunter, in a short introduction, refers to Major Thruston as one who " died fearlessly and nobly as he had lived." He was murdered on October 19 by the Soudanese mutineers in Uganda. In the book

[1] *Tout le Crime.* Par Joseph Reinach. Paris : P. V. Stock.
[2] *Le Sabre et la Loi.* Par G. Lhermitte (*Le Code Rouge*). Preface par de M. Francis de Pressensé. Paris : P. V. Stock.
[3] *African Incidents · Personal Experiences in Egypt and Unyoro.* By Brevet-Major A. B. Thruston, Oxfordshire Light Infantry London : John Murray.

a most interesting narrative is given of Major Thruston's life while serving in Uganda and Unyoro between 1893 and 1896, and in the Dongola Expedition in 1896. The story is too astonishing to be summarised. Africa is the wonder-land of the world, and this volume unveils many of its mysteries.

Eton is one of the institutions of which England has reason to be proud. Mr. A. C. Benson's *Biographical History of Eton*[1] is one of the most complete accounts of this celebrated school ever written. The volume was completed as far back as 1896, but its publication was postponed by the pressure of professional work. The book has been published by Mr. Ingalton Drake of Eton. Though Mr. Benson modestly avows that the volume is "anything but a compilation," it is really a work of great learning and research. The book contains some admirable portraits, including one of Horace Walpole. The introductory sonnet is very beautiful.

---

## BELLES LETTRES.

*The Age of Johnson,*[2] by Mr. Thomas Seccombe, is an admirable specimen of the Handbooks of English Literature, edited by Professor Hales, and published by Messrs. George Bell & Sons. The chapter dealing with Dr. Johnson is luminous and critical. The comparison drawn between Johnson and Swift shows much acumen. "The juxtaposition of Johnson and Swift would," as Mr. Seccombe remarks, "be truly interesting. Assuming the soundness of Pope's well-known proposition, humanity since Shakespeare has had no properer students than these two men." Justice, too, is done in the book to the genius of Goldsmith,

The twelfth volume of the Variorum edition of *Shakespeare*[3] contains the text of "Much Ado about Nothing," reprinted from the First Folio. The preface is a most complete history of the source of the text, and cannot fail to be of absorbing interest to all students of the great dramatist. Dr. Furness shows enormous erudition as an editor, and he also proves that he possesses the critical faculty in its highest form. The light which he throws on the way in which the differences between the text of the Folio and the Quarto arose gives a special value to his researches. The Appendix gives much valuable information as to the source of the plot of the play as well as selections from English, French and German criticisms of the comedy.

[1] *Fasti : A Biographical History of Eton.* By Arthur Christopher Benson, of Eton College. Eton : R. Ingalton Drake.
[2] *The Age of Johnson.* By Thomas Seccombe. London : George Bell & Sons.
[3] A New Variorum Edition of *Shakespeare.* Edited by Horace Howard Furness, M.A. (Harv.). Vol. XII. "Much Ado about Nothing." Philadelphia : Lippincott.

*Negro Nobodies* [1] is the title of a charming volume by M. Noel de Montagnac, which forms the latest addition to the Overseas Library. It deals with the negroes of Jamaica, whom the author describes as "a people who have been, and are still, misunderstood." The dialect of the blacks of Jamaica is rather difficult to understand, but M. de Montagnac has succeeded in making it intelligible. Some of the sketches, such as "The Mistake of Samuel Uttock," are humorous, others are pathetic—perhaps this description applies most fittingly to "The Shadow of a Sin." The shrewd observation of the Jamaica negroes, somewhat tinged with cynicism, may be seen from the following extract containing the opinions of Zacche, the tailor, on women: "A woman, gentlemen, will make an affidavit that she loves you to de bottom of her soul, and really she has no more feeling for you than a croaking lizard has for a turkey cock. That is one way, and sutt'nly that is a very common way. A woman will say she don't love you in de least when all de time she is really worshipping you down to such a thing as you' smallest toe-nail. Sutt'nly, that is an extraordinary way, but it is a way all de same. When a woman is introduced to a man, she can only see his pockets then, making a note, first of all, of de size, and then whether those pockets look as if they are accustomed to carry money. Now, whether she will recognise him when she see him de second time—especially to remember his name—depends entirely upon that. Well, sutt'nly, that's another way. Supposing de man's pockets look as if they can carry something better than copper, well, then de woman becomes most awfully sweet, and give him such a fascinating conversation that de poor fellow generally forget her eye is still 'pon him pocket, and he doesn't see, sutt'nly, that very often her hand come quite close to de said pocket then." This is not exactly flattering to "the gentler sex," but perhaps there is a grain of truth in it.

It is well known that the late Matthew Arnold objected to being made the subject of a biography. We have no details of his life save those contained in the *Letters* published by his family under the editorship of Mr. G. W. E. Russell. In the volume which Professor George Saintsbury has contributed to Messrs. Blackwood and Sons' Modern English Writers Series [2] we have a record not merely of Matthew Arnold's life, but of his literary labours. Professor Saintsbury is himself a really able critic—one of the foremost of living critics—and it is only fitting that he should deal with the man whom he describes as "the master of all English critics in the latter half of the nineteenth century." He is, perhaps, over-severe on the critics of William IV.'s reign. It is true that Lockhart was too much of a theorist to be a reliable critic, but to

[1] *Negro Nobodies.* By Noel de Montagnac. (The Overseas Library.) London : T. Fisher Unwin.
[2] *Matthew Arnold.* By George Saintsbury. London : William Blackwood & Sons.

impute to Thackeray ignorance of "the very rudiments of criticism" is to be emphatically hypercritical. Professor Saintsbury appreciates the qualities in which French critics between 1830 and 1860 surpassed English critics, and he does more than justice, if possible, to Sainte-Beuve. It must be admitted that the eminent French critic's system of analysing, comparing, and making somewhat pedantic estimates of different authors is not an ideal method of criticism. Of Matthew Arnold it may be said that he was a greater critic than Sainte-Beuve because his range of vision was wider and his ideas more comprehensive. Still, even Matthew Arnold could in his *Letters* give utterance to such pettinesses as that "Thackeray was not a great writer." Professor Saintsbury shows how as a dramatic poet Arnold failed, and yet that he was a true, if not a great, poet. He discounts the crusade on Philistinism, which, however, was the outcome of a noble hatred of hypocrisy. If we are to regard this essentially modern poet and critic as having reconciled Wordsworthian enthusiasm and Byronic despair, he must certainly take rank as a great figure in the literature of the nineteenth century. This volume is a well-merited tribute to one of the least insular of Englishmen by one who is something more than a disciple of his—a true appreciator of his genius. The style of the book, too, is admirable. It is distinctly not academic, and that is one of the reasons why it commands our admiration. Professor Saintsbury is one of those rare critics who know what they are talking about. The same thing cannot be said of some of the writers in well-known English periodicals who have found fault with his style and with his methods. If to have read much and read well be a fault, Professor Saintsbury must plead guilty to it. Sometimes, in his efforts to get at "the root of the matter," he ignores the standard of fine writing which the journalistic faddists of to-day set up for themselves. But he succeeds in making his meaning clear. He teaches us the true value of criticism—and that is enough. As a proof of this, we might take two sentences in which he sums up all that can be said of Matthew Arnold by his greatest admirer, and which can scarcely be questioned by his severest judge: "What we go to Matthew Arnold for is not fact, it is not argument, it is not even learning. It is phrase, attitude, style." "He wrote, and I think he could write nothing that was not literature, in and by the fact that he was its writer." Could anything be put with more thoroughness and truth?

*Life and Happiness* [1] is a very useful and, at the same time, philosophic little book. Many of the maxims given by the author embody a true philosophy of life. With regard to the education of the young, we entirely agree with one principle strongly inculcated in these pages—never to lie to a child. The remarks

---

[1] *Life and Happiness.* By Auguste Marran. London: Kegan Paul & Co.

on " Worship " remind us of Emerson's words on the same subject. It is, indeed, true that " the most pompous ceremonies are nought but a falsehood and a lie without the purity of heart in which each of us ought to set up a true altar in honour of the Most High."

Mr. J. T. Grein has collected in a volume entitled *Dramatic Criticism*,[1] a number of articles contributed by him to *La Revue d'Art Dramatique*, *The Sunday Special*, and *To-morrow*. There is an uncompromising tone in most of these articles. Mr. Grein is convinced that the English theatre is in a " parlous state." He does not hesitate to say that England has scarcely any original dramatist at the present time, that most of the large theatres have to depend on either adaptations from the French, or on the great dramatists of the past, and that the others have to depend on the buffooneries of the musical comedy or the crocodile tears of the melodrama. His criticism of particular plays is vigorous and straightforward. He shows how, owing to the misinterpretation of Mr. J. Comyns Carr, that beautiful play of Maeterlinck, *Pelleas and Melisande*, has been made ridiculous on the English stage. " One has no right," Mr. Grein points out, " to treat so lightly the work of one who is as earnest an artist as ever lived, and, in spite of his early celebrity, a model of modesty into the bargain. Laughter is a poor but easy weapon, for from the sublime to the ridiculous there is but one step." The article on " Sudermann in English " is appreciative. The family in *Magda* are described as " a perfect picture of Teutonic Philistinism." According to Mr. Grein, *Magda* failed at the Lyceum because " it came at the wrong moment." An eloquent plea is made in the volume for the revival of the one-act play. The book is dedicated to Mr. George Bernard Shaw.

The January part of the *Oxford English Dictionary* [2] is a double section containing 1864 main words, 588 combinations explained under these, and 578 subordinate entries. The words range from *glass-coach* to *graded*. This portion of the Dictionary includes three of the most important words of the Teutonic vocabulary—*go*, *God*, and *good*. The word " God " covers three pages, and several pages are devoted to words formed from it. The etymological notes in the section are sometimes in conflict with commonly received opinions— *e.g.*, *goal*, which is supposed to be from the French *gaule*, is traced to the Welsh *gâl*.

*Rêve de Printemps*,[3] by Madame Adrienne Cambry, is a very fascinating novel. It is the story of a charming young girl, who, becoming foolishly enamoured of a clever but unscrupulous painter, is deceived by him. She awakens from her dream of love to find the reality hard and bitter, but she is consoled in her grief by Pierre

---

[1] *Dramatic Criticism.* By J. T. Grein. London : John Long.
[2] *A New English Dictionary on Historical Principles.* (Vol. IV. F–G GLASS-COACH— GRADED). By Henry Bradley, Hon. M.A.
[3] *Rêve de Printemps.* Par Adrienne Cambry. Paris : Librairie Plon.

Bernier, a faithful friend who clings to her devotedly. There is also a short story entitled *Jeu de Prince* in the volume, which is full of human interest.

A very good edition of the *Prometheus Vinctus*[1] of Æschylus has been brought out by Mr. W. B. Clive in the University Tutorial Series. The text is very clearly printed, and the notes reflect credit on the scholarship of Messrs. Plaistowe and Mills.

When a story is both unconventional and forcible, it has the quality unhappily so lacking in the fiction of the day—distinction. This much must be said of *The Fate-Spinner*,[2] by Lawrence Alma Tadema, whose work as a poet is also very remarkable. The subject of the story is the unhappy marriage of Ginevra Lady Musgrove. The way in which Lord Musgrove's affections flow naturally to Althea, in spite of his strong desire to be loyal to his wife, is admirably depicted. The tragic ending is not quite inevitable, and has therefore a certain touch of artificiality about it. But, taken altogether, this book is far above the average of latterday fiction.

---

## POETRY.

*The Prince*,[3] by Adolphus Alfred Jack, is a very ambitious effort in dramatic composition. The scene of the drama is Italy in the fourteenth century. The play is powerful, though some of the ideas embodied in it savour of artificial sentimentality. It is to be feared that it will not make a good acting play.

---

## ART.

THE new edition of Madame Albana's enthusiastic study of Correggio[4] is chiefly noteworthy for the biographical essay concerning the author's personality and ideas by her close friend and disciple, M. Edouard Schuré, whose book of supraliminal philosophy, *Les Grands Initiés*, owed so much to her inspiration. Margherita Albana's life, like her spirit, reflected heterogeneous influences

[1] *Æschylus: Prometheus Vinctus.* Edited by F. G. Plaistowe, M.A. London, and F. R. Mills, M.A. Oxon. London : W. B. Clive.
[2] *The Fate-Spinner.* By Lawrence Alma Tadema. London : E. B. Mortlock, 39 Victoria Street, Westminster.
[3] *The Prince.* A Play. By Adolphus Alfred Jack. London : Macmillan & Co.
[4] *Marguerite Albana—Le Corrège ; Sa Vie et son Œuvre.* With Biographical Essay by Edouard Schuré. Paris : Perrin et Cie. 1900.

which are possible to few. A Greek girl of Corfu, she was adopted by her relative, the English Governor of the Ionian Isles, and taken by him, first to India and then to Italy, where she married an inconsiderable painter and began that career of the Liberal lady with a *salon* which was peculiar to the period of gestation of United Italy. Her philosophy, or better, her religion, largely centred in certain great general ideas which have guided humanity until now, and which Goethe and Cousin taught the world to personify by spelling them with capital letters. These abstractions ended by taking on lofty spiritual forms, of which M. Schuré is an eloquent exponent. As a philosophy, it is perhaps belated in the present monopoly of Positive Science, and it is too early for the Psychical future. It is none the less interesting, especially as it is here associated with personalities not yet forgotten, of whom the biographer speaks with unconscious frankness. As to the criticism concerning Correggio and Italian art in general, it is quite as frankly not technical, although a good knowledge of the various works of the Master may be had agreeably from its fairly complete pages. It belongs in sum to the school of Taine, whose thought also travelled ever in ideas very general and not bound by the minute details of art. The book, as a whole, should certainly be more interesting to intelligent readers than any mere work on art could be by itself.

Mr. Rushforth's *Carlo Crivelli* [1] deserves the praise accorded to the previous volumes of Bell's series of " Great Masters in Painting and Sculpture." The illustrations are even better than before, perhaps owing to the peculiar decorative character of the Master's work. Crivelli, for many reasons, is *simpatico* to the general public, in spite of orthodox criticism having made little of him in the literature which guides the public in its art sympathies. The text is easy reading and instructive, while the apparatus— Catalogue of Works, &c.—is most excellent. But what is to be thought of the inscription given (page 92) as appearing on the painting of *The Virgin in Ecstasy* (it is really an *Immaculate Conception*)—" Karoli Chrivelli Veneti Militis pinsit 1492 " ? Crivelli's Latin was amiably irregular in spelling, but never elsewhere in grammar to this extent.

[1] *Carlo Crivelli.* By G. McNeil Rushforth, M.A. ("Great Masters in Painting and Sculpture.") London : George Bell & Sons. 1900.

THE

# WESTMINSTER REVIEW.

Vol. CLIII. No. 5.—May 1900.

## THE PROBLEM IN SOUTH AFRICA.

### BOER *V.* BRITON.

### III.

Mr. Bryce considers that the events between 1877 and 1881 described in the last paper, next to those of the Great Trek, are the most important in the internal history of South Africa. Without in any way attempting to minimise their material effect upon the present political situation, it may well be doubted whether subsequent events have not an even more important bearing.

Had the Transvaal Government observed the letter and spirit of their undertakings much of the recent history of South Africa would never have been written. The ink of the Convention of 1881 was scarcely dry before the Boers commenced extending the boundaries which had been mutually agreed upon. The establishment of the two petty republics, Stellaland and Goshen, were a deliberate attempt to cut off Great Britain from the northern regions in which it was already interested, whilst on the south-east the seizure of a large slice of Zululand was only part of a design to extend the boundaries of the Republic to the sea. Whilst acknowledging the seizure of the latter district, and finding it more expedient to cede Swaziland, where the Boers had acquired large concessions from the Swazi chief, the British Government effectually put a stop to all further encroachments, and by 1894 the Republic was strictly confined to its own borders.

In spite of these flagrant breaches of the Convention, some of which occurred before 1884, the English Government were generous enough to consent to cut down the provisions relating to their control of the foreign policy of the Republic by substituting Article 4 of the new Convention for Article 2 of the Convention of 1881, by which the Republic was bound to

"conclude no treaty with any state or nation other than the Orange Free State, nor with any native tribe to the eastward or westward of the Republic"

without the approval of the Queen. In view of recent events, it would have been wiser to have omitted even this exception of the Free State, since we should then have known the nature of the treaty between the latter and the Transvaal. It is difficult to see the motive on our part to consent to this exception. To any commercial treaty between the two Republics we should have taken no objection, but a defensive and offensive alliance would have been another matter. An offensive treaty, such as it appears to be, could only have been directed against our power.[1]

There seems to be little doubt that in the contemplation of both parties the words "all civil rights," in Article 2 of the 1881 Convention, reproduced in Article 7 of the London Convention, were intended to cover the right of the franchise.

In August 1881 the Transvaal Government made the following declaration :

"To all inhabitants without exception we promise the protection of the law and all the privileges attendant thereon."

By the law of 1876 the qualification for full burgher privileges had been the possession of landed property *or* residence for one year.

Six months later the Law of 1882 enacted that aliens could only become naturalised and enfranchised after five years' residence. Now, the Transvaal law, the Romano-Dutch law, is based upon the civil law of Rome, under which the Roman citizen was entitled to the rights of *commercium, connubium,* and *suffragium.* Upon these facts it seems highly probable that the franchise was included in the words "civil rights," and, if so, then the Law of 1882 was a breach of the Convention of 1881.

In any case Mr. Chamberlain would appear to be correct in styling it "a violation of the *status quo* as it was present to her Majesty's ministers at the time the Convention was negotiated." Since, however, the number of loyalists left in the Transvaal at this period did not exceed some 2000, the matter is not of paramount importance, but having through carelessness, omitted to define the phrase "civil rights" in 1881 the Government should have been the more sedulous in protecting the rights of newcomers which

[1] This treaty, concluded in March 1897, is reproduced by M. Georges Aubert at page 281 of *Le Transvaal et l'Angleterre.*

were defined in Article 14—a mere reproduction of Article 26 of the Pretoria Convention. In this there is not a word about the franchise and, accordingly, under the Convention Great Britain had no *locus standi* whatever in objecting to the successive franchise laws which so narrowed the privilege as to render it practically unobtainable. Moreover, the franchise grievance did not end here. The first proof of qualification was the entry of the claimant's name in the books of the Field Cornet. In nine cases out of ten this official took the registration fees and omitted to enter the name, being thus able to put the money into his own pocket. In the remaining tenth the records were either " lost " when likely to prove embarrassing or so imperfectly kept as to be useless. The concession of the Second Volksraad in 1890 may be dismissed from consideration. As Mr. Bryce truly points out, it was little better than a sham, being, in fact, created only as a tub to throw to the Uitlander whale.[1]

Most writers are agreed that the Transvaal Government has grossly violated its engagements relating to the natives.

" The treatment of the natives of the Transvaal," said Mr. Chamberlain recently, "has been disgraceful ; it has been brutal ; it has been unworthy of a civilised power."

This language would appear to be not a whit too strong. By Article 19 (1) the native was to be free to " buy and otherwise acquire land under certain conditions." The " conditions " are that the land must be bought and held in trust for him by the Native Location Commission.

According to Mr. Bovill, no native will avail himself of this privilege, which invariably means the loss of his property. By fines for supposed offences the superintendent of the Native Location eventually forces the unhappy native to surrender his land. If he wishes to buy outside the Native Reserve, the purchase must be made in the name of some white man, naturally a somewhat dangerous process. By sub-section (2) a commission to mark out native locations was to be appointed. This has been partially carried out by allotting certain locations in the north-east of the Transvaal which, however, says Mr. Bovill, are insufficient for a growing population, especially as, under the Transvaal law, more than five families cannot be settled on one Boer farm. Why a Boer farm of 6000 acres, of which only twenty to thirty acres are in cultivation, should be thus limited seems incomprehensible.

Access to the courts by the natives is provided by sub-section (3). At first there was no appeal from the Summary Jurisdiction of the Landdrost or Field Cornet, but upon pressure by England appeals to the High Court were allowed. So much does the native suffer from the Summary Justice, so-called, of the Landdrost or Field-Cornet, says Mr. Bovill, that few such appeals are made. The

[1] *Impressions of South Africa,* p. 412.

native has a very poor opinion of the High Court. The cases of the chieftainess, Toeremetsjani, and other natives against Commandant Cronjé, the hero of the Potchefstroom siege, of Doornkop and of Paardeburg, cited by Mr. Fitzpatrick, prove that this opinion is well founded. Not but what justice was done by the Court (the judge being Dr. Jorissen, who heard the case fairly and gave judgment for the plaintiffs), for Cronjé was cast in damages and costs. The latter were defrayed by an obliging State, and the former are unpaid to this day. And yet a more crushing *exposé* of miscarriage of justice was never made. Upon the mere written complaint of a Boer, Cronjé, as Superintendent-General of the natives, convicted Toeremetsjani without, according to the judge, a tittle of evidence, declaring that as he read the charge to her he "could see by her demeanour that she was guilty!" He also sentenced thirteen Indunas as instigators of the alleged crime without any evidence whatever beyond the fact that they were members of the same tribe. He told them they might appeal, but as they were flogged out of hand this right of appeal would not appear to have been of much value. Appeals *in formâ pauperis* were formerly allowable, but as soon as advantage was taken of this privilege by the natives the Volksraad was petitioned and a law immediately passed forbidding the judges to give such leave of appeal.

By sub-section (4) the natives are to be

"allowed to move freely within the country or to leave it for any legal purpose, under a pass system."

An ordinary pass system under which the natives may be under some sort of governmental supervision is, of course, necessary in all countries like South Africa, but a more iniquitous system than the one devised and developed in the Transvaal never existed. It is simply a system of official corruption and oppression, a means by which half-paid policemen and magistrates eke out their salaries, with the full knowledge and acquiescence of the State. Full details are given by Mr. Bovill [1] and Mr. Fox Bourne [2], the latter of whom, however, points out that the original Pass Law was enacted in 1880 "under the administration of the Transvaal as a British province," and that, in consequence, the British Government when requisitioned in 1891, refused to interfere.

It will be remembered that by Article 8 "no slavery or apprenticeship partaking of slavery" is to be tolerated. As one instance of the habitual disregard of this provision may be given the case of Malaboch, whose tribe was crushed and the survivors distributed among burghers willing to pay £3 a year for the services of each family. Although many in this position are treated with a measure

---

[1] *Natives under the Transvaal Flag*, pp. 21–31.
[2] *Blacks and Whites in South Africa*, pp. 68–70.

-of kindness, all the natives are more or less in the condition of bondmen. They rank rather with the dogs and cattle than even as subordinate members of the household.

By Article 9 of the Grondwet,

"the people shall not permit any equality of coloured persons with white inhabitants, neither in the Church nor in the State."

This law is rigidly applied. The status of a native is practically that of a slave. He cannot own real property; no marriage, civil or ecclesiastic, is recognised; his access to the civil courts in any suit against a Boer is a mere farce. As Mr. Bovill rightly says,

"It appears inconceivable that a Government making any pretence of being a civilised power, at the end of the nineteenth century, should be so completely ignorant of the most elementary principles of good government for such a large number of its subjects."

These oppressive laws are directly due to the Boer demand for forced labour, and to their inordinate land hunger. Mr. Fox Bourne's charge that much the same acts of oppression are committed in Matabeleland and Mashonaland, at the Kimberley diamond mines, and the Johannesburg gold mines, if true, perhaps explains why the British Government has failed to effectually protest against these breaches of the London Convention.

By the discovery of gold the situation in the Transvaal became entirely changed.

In 1882 the Moodies Gold Fields had been allotted to Mr. Moodie, Surveyor-General, in lieu of salary, and this was followed by the opening up of De Kaap, Witwatersrand, and other fields. It was during Mr. Kruger's visit to London in 1884 for the purpose of negotiating the London Convention that the Lydenburg fields came to the front. Baron Grant was largely interested in these and anxious to obtain from the President some assurance of protection for the miners. It is stated by Mr. Fitzpatrick that Mr. Kruger and his fellow delegate, after some weeks' stay at the Albemarle Hotel, found themselves in the uncomfortable position of being unable to pay their hotel bill. Upon Baron Grant providing the wherewithal, Mr. Kruger, on behalf of the Republic, published in the London papers a cordial invitation and promise of rights and protection to all comers—an invitation which would appear to meet the argument that he never asked people to enter the country, and that consequently he was entitled to treat them as he pleased.

The great rush of newcomers took place, however, in 1886 by the discovery of the wonderful Sheba Reef at Barberton, quickly followed by that of the conglomerate formation in the Johannesburg district.

At Barberton political agitation soon commenced, at first only for local requirements, such as roads and bridges, mining regulations and remission of certain taxes, but eventually the Transvaal Republican Union was formed with similar aims to those of the National Union constituted subsequently in 1892 at Johannesburg.

It has been too much assumed by the average Liberal that the Transvaal is a Republic in fact as well as in name. Admiration for the Boer love of the democratic principles of political independence and liberty of the subject has been to a large extent improperly bestowed. The average Boer cares nothing for political institutions. Liberty to him means principally to do what he likes, to live out of sight of his neighbour's chimney stacks, to treat the natives as he pleases, and to pay no taxes. Colonel T. A. Le Mesurier relates how upon one occasion a Boer was expressing his feelings rather warmly to an official: "But why do you object to the British Government?" inquired the official. "I object to any Government. I don't want to be governed," replied the Boer.[1] When a Boer talks about "independence," he really means "licence." This is his ideal, and this is what he is now fighting for. Politics for the leading Boers simply meant a struggle between a few families for the hegemony, and when one state arose the struggle continued between Kruger and his faction, the Dopper party, consisting of the stricter religious and Conservative section, and Joubert, with the so-called Progressive party, which disapproved of the corrupt and oppressive rule of the former, but was scarcely imbued with any even rudimentary ideas of progressive principles. In fact, the Republic became a close oligarchy eventually dominated by one personality—Oom Paul Kruger.

It is impossible here to do more than indicate roughly the acknowledged grievances of the Uitlanders, and the conduct of the Transvaal Government. It is perfectly true that these people went there of their own free will, and they did so to further their own pecuniary ends. At first, indeed, they only came as birds of passage, and it was only when the deep-level beds were discovered that they contemplated a more permanent residence. It is true, as was only natural, that in a mining population, many were not desirable citizens, but the franchise was not originally a privilege desired, the demand for it only arose as a means to an end, when all other means had failed. If Mr. Kruger's rule had been honest, and the moderate reforms deemed necessary in all civilised societies had been granted, events would have been very different. But it is impossible to come to any other conclusion than that the Transvaal Government has been the most corrupt, the most oppressive, the most deliberately retrograde, in short, the most iniquitous to which any body of free men has ever been subject in modern times. In

[1] T. A. Le Mesurier, WESTMINSTER REVIEW vol. cxlv. p. 432.

his eminently judicial survey of Transvaal politics, Mr. Bryce scarcely does justice to this aspect of the case. He describes how the President resisted every reform, "not merely out of personal ambition, but out of honest national feeling." I confess that at one time I shared this view. As a Liberal, of course, I entirely disapproved of his retrograde policy, but I saw no such evidence as to convict him of personal dishonesty and political corruption, and I approached my present task with distinct sympathy for Mr. Kruger's position. I believed him to be personally honest, if wrong-headed. The national sentiment no doubt was bitterly opposed to British rule, and the average Boer, perhaps, identified the Uitlanders with the British Government. Kruger himself was not likely to make this mistake, however strong his national sentiment might genuinely be. If he represented this sentiment, he did so only to play upon it in order to retain his own power. His last appeal to the people was always the threat of the loss of their cherished independence, which was in no wise endangered by the Uitlander reform movement. What would have been endangered, if the franchise had been extended, and if the Uitlanders had availed themselves of it, was the Presidency of Paul Kruger.

In addition to raising the franchise qualification the constituencies were jerrymandered by disfranchising various towns whose enlightened thought Mr. Kruger feared might conflict with his "national policy." Gross political abuse as this was, it was done openly, but the manner in which Mr. Kruger secured his re-election as President in 1893 would be considered disreputable by the shadiest politician of a third-rate South American Republic.

In the Presidential election there are two stages: the first is the election of the members of the Volksraad; the second, the election of the President. General Joubert was Kruger's opponent and the two parties were nearly equally balanced. By taking exception to the validity of the election of some of Joubert's supporters, Kruger not only prevented them from taking their seats, but ensured the presence of the old members whom they had defeated at the polls. These objections were frivolous in the extreme and were eventually overruled; but in the meantime Mr. Kruger, with admirable gravity and not without, we cannot help thinking, a twinkle in his eye, said: "The law provides that all objections must be heard in the Volksraad and that, pending that decision, the old member shall retain his seat, and before all things we must support the law." Was there ever more unblushing hypocrisy? We shall see later how much respect Mr. Kruger paid to the law.

The same tactics were pursued in the Presidential election. Although Joubert was undoubtedly elected by a very considerable majority, says Mr. FitzPatrick, the result was announced as, Kruger, 7881; Joubert, 7009.

" Outside the Transvaal," says Mr. Fitzpatrick, " Mr. Kruger has the reputation of being free from the taint of corruption from which so many of his colleagues suffer." [1]

Allowing to the full the natural bias which Mr. FitzPatrick must needs feel (he was the secretary of the National Union and suffered imprisonment with the Reform leaders), upon the undisputed evidence adduced by him it is impossible to acquit President Kruger of political corruption of the most degrading type known to politicians. It was not mere corruption for the purpose of attaining political ends, which, under some circumstances, may be excused, but it was flagrant corruption for the mere sordid purpose of putting money into his own pocket or into those of his relations and hangers-on.

There is no evidence against Mr. Kruger, as there is against his colleagues and his officials, of the receipt of direct bribery. For this he may have been too honest. He certainly was too circumspect and wary. Some may see no corruption in the head of the State borrowing large sums from the Treasury at less than half the current rate of interest, or in persuading the Raad to sanction the expenditure of some £10,000 in private improvements upon his own estate. But, if Mr. Kruger is acquitted of personal corruption, there is ample evidence that he has consistently and persistently connived at corruption in his nearest kinsmen, friends, and political adherents.

It is said that corruption is correlative with corrupters. I am not speaking here so much of mere bribery. The Reform leaders, who, as we now know, set aside a large sum annually for electioneering purposes, must be condemned even more severely than the recipients of their bribes, if the money was so spent. I am alluding to the system of concessions by which Mr. Kruger made money for himself, his family, and his followers. In the case of the Vaal River water supply concession, the vote of the Executive Council, says Mr. FitzPatrick, was " hawked " about by Mr. Kruger's son-in-law. The dynamite monopoly is another instance of political corruption which has received the direct support of Mr. Kruger. Here, again, Mr. J. M. A. Wolmarans, a member of the Executive, has been publicly charged with receiving a commission amounting to £10,000 *per annum* for his vote for the renewal of the concession.

Another scandalous concession which has received the strenuous support of the President, in spite of repeated exposure, was that of the Netherlands Railway Company, which was run by a small group of Hollander and German capitalists, and which has drawn within its net the whole finances of the State. By the trust-deed, which was prepared by Dr. Leyds, who is said to act on behalf of the concessionaires, the Hollander group secured seventy-six votes for its

[1] *Transvaal from Within*, p. 85.

subscription of less than one-third of the capital. The German group, which subscribed rather more than one-third, acquired thirty votes, whilst to the Republic, which provided the remaining portion, was assigned only six votes. This precious document was approved by Dr. Leyds in his other capacity as legal adviser to the Government.

The promotion of this company and the construction of the line formed one huge job. If the evil had stopped here it might have been more endurable, but by the imposition of preferential rates and high Customs dues (which latter the company controlled as a guarantee for their interest) this private corporation was able to throttle and hamper the whole trade of the country in its own interests.

In order to force the traffic to the Delagoa Bay Railway the company imposed prohibitive rates upon the fifty miles section between Johannesburg and their terminus on the Vaal River, where the Cape-Colony-Free-State line connects. In addition, obnoxious regulations were made, with the deliberate object of blocking the line and causing delay in delivery. The traders met this by off-loading at the Vaal River and transporting their goods by waggons across the drifts. Mr. Kruger replied by closing the drifts to over-sea traffic. This resulted in such a storm of indignation from the Dutch and English alike in Cape Colony and the Free State, together with an ultimatum from Mr. Chamberlain, that the President "climbed down" and the drifts were opened. Mr. F. H. Hatch, the well-known mining engineer, writing to the *Times* in 1897, states that this company, with a capital of £1,166,000, makes a profit, over and above its working expenses and guaranteed interest, of £1,133,000.[1]

The Selati Railway concession, granted in 1890 to Mr. Vorster, a member of the Raad, is another instance of notorious jobbery of a similar character. It was obtained by wholesale bribery of the members of the Raad, and, upon its exposure two years later, Mr. Kruger declared that he saw no harm in members receiving presents. Dr. Leyds, as State Attorney, should have protected his Government from these swindles, which were apparently discovered without any difficulty by his successor, an uneducated Boer.

For his share in these transactions we must not be too hard upon President Kruger. He was but a victim to his environment, which, for a truly religious man, must have been a most painful position! After all, it is not long ago since a small group of noble lords in the Upper Chamber demanded, as a solatium to their natural feelings, a sum of £10,000 from the promoters of the London and Birmingham Railway (now the London and North-Western Railway Company) to ensure the passing of their Bill through Parliament. The demand

[1] *Times* June 28, 1897.

was indignantly refused.   The Bill was thrown out by the House
of Lords.   Perhaps this was a mere coincidence, and not a case of
natural cause and effect ; but, anyway, the promoters changed their
tactics, there were no more refusals of such reasonable requests,
the Bill was passed triumphantly the following year—at a price;
again, perhaps, a mere coincidence.

As in those days the classes robbed the masses, so to-day the
Boers rob the Uitlanders.   What hypocrites those God-fearing Boers
must be !   Our forefathers were no less pious, but they did not
allow their piety to interfere with their business.   They did not
regard themselves as hypocrites but as good men of business, looking
after their own interests.   We manage things differently now.
Company-promoting swindles on a vast scale, extensive stock-jobbing
frauds, scandalous secret commissions, provided they are not
detected, are regarded as " good business."

We may well ask wherein lies the much vaunted commercial morality
of the nineteenth century to that of the seventeenth, in which the
Boer still lives and has his being.   But we can, at any rate, claim
that not one of our public men, so far as we know, ever abused his
political position as a minister of the Crown by making money out of it.

These concession scandals, however, may be regarded rather as
offences against the State than as personal grievances of the Uitlanders, since it was the State that was directly defrauded.   But as
the Uitlanders provided nine-tenths of the revenue they were
indirectly concerned, and were entitled to complain at the misappli-
cation of their money.   It is doubtful, however, if the majority felt
or even recognised the evil, since the effect would not be visible upon
wages and salaries.   Upon the price of food-stuffs and household
effects of course it was more apparent, although even here high
wages and salaries would tend to obscure the issue.   The Dynamite
Monopoly and the prohibitive railway rates affected directly only
the mine owners—a comparatively small class.

I have always maintained, upon the principle that the mineral
wealth is the property of the people of the country where it is
situated, that the Republic is morally and legally entitled to place
what impositions it pleases upon the right to work the mines, provided the revenue thus obtained is applied in the honest administration of the State and for the benefit of its people.   That the ample
revenue of the Republic has been grossly misapplied is beyond
dispute.   Of its application for the benefit of the people as a whole
I can find no evidence.

" With all their immense revenue," says Mrs. Lionel Phillips, " they
have never attempted a single public work except under extreme coercion,
and then always with a view to the enrichment of some Dutch or German
concessionnaire." [1]

[1] *Some South African Recollections*, p. 60.

Of the onerous nature of the burdens upon the mining industry the Government is convicted out of its own mouth. In 1897 the Industrial Commission of Inquiry was appointed, consisting of Messrs. Schalk W. Burger, member of the Executive Council (Chairman), J. S. Smit, Government Railway Commissioner; Christian Joubert, Minister of Mines; Schmitz-Dumont, Acting State Mining Engineer; and J. F. De Beer, First Special Judicial Commissioner. Mr. Thomas Hugo, the General Manager of the National Bank, was added as financial adviser; and Messrs. Edmond Brochon, A. Brakhan, and J. M. Pierce as advisory members. To this advisory committee the Commission, with the sanction of the Government, appointed Messrs. James Hay and George Albu as representatives of the mining industry. Of Mr. Kruger's motives for consenting to this Commission it is impossible to speak with any certainty. It may be that he was convinced that the alleged grievances were purely imaginary, or it may be that he thought the evidence would throw the blame upon the capitalists. If Mr. Reitz's attack upon the capitalists in any way represents the President's views, the latter alternative is the more probable. Lastly, he may have thought that his influence was sufficiently powerful to prevent any verdict antagonistic to the Republic. His subsequent conduct, however, in dealing with the Report would appear to be consistent with either of the two latter alternatives.

The evidence taken on oath is of a voluminous, minute, and overwhelming character. The report is the impartial result of a painstaking and careful investigation, based entirely upon the evidence submitted, and forms the unanimous verdict of Transvaal officials of high position, and as such becomes the most formidable indictment which could be found against the Government. It, however, cuts both ways. Whilst severely condemning the Government, it proves the existence of a body of men even amongst the official circle honestly desirous of effecting real measures of reform. This very materially weakens Mr. Fitzpatrick's view that there was no real progressive Boer party. This evidence and report, together with a valuable appendix, have been published by the Witwatersrand Chamber of Mines in a volume of some 750 pages, indispensable in forming a correct estimate of the industrial grievances in the Transvaal.[1]

In order to show the magnitude of the interests involved, the Commission reported that out of 183 mines within the State 79 produced gold to the value of £8,603,831 during the year 1896.

[1] *Evidence and Report of the Industrial Commission of Inquiry.* With an Appendix containing the Letter of the Chamber of Mines to the Commission, the Principal Laws of the Republic affecting the Mining Industry, &c. Compiled and published by the Witwatersrand Chamber of Mines, Johannesburg, S.A.R. Johannesburg: *Times* Printing and Publishing Works, 1897. This volume can be obtained in this country from Messrs. A. Barsdorf & Co., Wool Exchange, Coleman St., London, E.C.

Of this number, 25 only declared dividends to the amount of £1,718,781. The Commissioners might have added that the amount of gold still to be won in the Johannesburg district alone was estimated by Mr. F. H. Hatch in 1894 at the enormous sum of £700,000,000.

Of the non-paying dividend mines some are in a state of development and equipment, others are temporarily closed down, whilst many are only just covering the cost of production. How to reduce this cost of production was the problem to which the Commission addressed itself, having arrived at the conclusion that the principal reason of the mining depression was the high cost of production.

The Commission found that under existing conditions 100 mines would have to close down, causing an annual decrease in circulation of £12,000,000, and that to avoid such calamity,

"it was the duty of the Government to co-operate with the mining industry and to devise means in order to make it possible for lower-grade mines to work at a profit and generally to lighten the burdens of the mining industry."

This recommendation is enforced by the remark that,

" The mining industry must be held as the financial basis, support, and mainstay of the State ;"

which supports the view taken by Capt. Younghusband that the Government, whilst

" nervous lest the mining industry should outgrow their capacity to control it, have no deliberate policy of strangling it, as they have not yet entirely forgotten what the revenue of the country was before the opening of the mines, and have no wish to see it again drop from £5,000,000 to £75,000." [1]

The Commissioners give precedence in their report to the question of labour, which they state is the most vital one for the mines, since its cost amounts to from 50 to 60 per cent. of the production cost. With regard to white labour all [possible measures for reduction of the high cost of living at the mines are urged. The wages of miners, although higher than elsewhere, are not, taking into consideration this cost of living, considered excessive. In fact, there is no margin over necessary expenditure,

" and consequently it cannot be expected that white labourers will establish their permanent abode in this Republic unless conditions are made by which their position will be ameliorated."

Until such conditions are attained

" it would be almost impossible to reduce the wages of white labourers and they would strongly recommend that, as far as possible, necessaries of life

---

[1] Capt. F. Younghusband, *South Africa of To-Day,* p. 57. London : Macmillan and Co. 1898.

should be imported free of duty and conveyed to the miners as cheaply as possible."

Native labour is responsible for 23 per cent. of the cost of pro-- duction as compared with 30 per cent. of white labour. Owing to the want of adequate protection for natives travelling from a distance,. the heavy cost of their transport, the want of suitable compounds *en route* and the impossibility of enforcing contracts with them in con- sequence of the defective Pass Laws, the supply fell far below the demand. This was still further aggravated by the drunkenness which prevailed amongst the natives. In some cases as much as 40 per cent. of the black labour was incapacitated by drink. This state of things consequently necessitated the employment of a far larger number than would otherwise have been required.

In addition to economic disorganisation at the mines, armed police were frequently called in to quell disturbances caused by the drunken quarrels of the natives. The maladministration of the Liquor Laws· was principally to blame for this last state of affairs. Although by the Law of 1881, no native during employment could obtain drink without a permit, this provision (which was almost purely illusory), was rendered wholly nugatory by the Law of 1891, which allowed unemployed natives to obtain one drink at any canteen without a permit. By the Law of 1896 the sale of liquor to natives was totally prohibited. We shall see hereafter how far this law was operative. To return to the Commission, the Commissioners reported that the Liquor Law of 1896 was not properly carried out, and that the mining industry had real grievances in connection therewith,. owing to the illicit sale of strong drink to the natives at the mines..

" The evidence given on this point proves that a miserable state. of affairs. exists and a much stronger application of the law is required."

In Johannesburg, according to the test of population by the Law of 1896, the maximum of licences was eighty-eight. As a fact 438 had been granted.

Police supervision existed only in name. Illicit sales were openly carried on in collusion with "the under-paid officials." Closely associated with the maladministration of the Liquor Law was that of the Gold Law. It appears from the evidence that gold thefts were carried on with impunity, and amounted to 10 per cent. of the out- put, equivalent to £750,000 per annum. The Commissioners reported that the administration must be faulty, since only a very few instances are known of the crime being detected and punished.

The Commission also recommended a more stringent application of the Pass Law ; the constitution of a Local Board in Johannes- burg ; the reduction of railway rates by 25 per cent., and in the case of coal by even more ; and the abolition of all import duties on food-stuffs, "as at the present moment it is impossible to supply the population of the Republic from the products of local agriculture."

Concessions meet with the entire disapproval of the Commissioners.

"Concessions through which the industrial prosperity of the country is hampered, and which will always remain a source of irritation and dissatisfaction."

Explosives were 10 per cent. of the cost of production, these comprising dynamite fuse and detonators, dynamite being 95 per cent. of the whole.

At this period the consumption of dynamite was about 250,000 cases, at an average price of 85s. per case. It was proved to the satisfaction of the Commission that if imported from Europe it could, but for the monopoly of the South African Explosives Company, be delivered on the Rand at 40s. per case. As the Commissioners pointed out, this profit of 45s. only benefited the State to the extent of the royalty of 5s., the rest going to enrich individuals for the most part resident in Europe. They demanded the immediate removal of this tax of £500,000 on the staple industry of the country. This monopoly had received the support of the President upon the ground of the desirability of fostering industries within the State, but this argument is swept away by the Commissioners showing that the factory was merely a depôt where the imported manufactured article was manipulated, to a slight extent, to lend colour to Mr. Kruger's theory, and that, owing to lack of raw material, it was almost impossible to establish a *bonâ fide* industry in the Transvaal. Cancellation of the monopoly was strongly urged.

In the forefront of their report the Commissioners ungrudgingly admit that by the honest administration of the managers, by the introduction of the latest machinery and appliances, by the greatest perfection of method and process known to science, and by the devotion, energy, and knowledge displayed, the working expenses have been reduced to a minimum, and that it remained with the Government to assist the industry by the removal of burdens and hindrances.

What, then, were the direct personal grievances of the Uitlanders prior to the Raid? The chief perhaps was the education question. Bitter opposition has always been offered to any system of public education involving the use of the English language. This refusal amounted to the practical exclusion of the Uitlanders' children from the public schools, where all instruction is given in the Taal dialect, after a child has been three years in the school. Accordingly the Uitlanders opened schools of their own, supported by voluntary subscriptions, under an Educational Council. In 1895 a delusive measure was introduced by the Government, under which a school might earn a capitation grant of £4, provided 50 per cent.

of the children passed the standard in the Dutch language. Even
when this grant was earned, the teachers found it insufficient to
meet expenses, and consequently the measure became a dead letter.
Out of the £63,000 provided for the public schools it has been
estimated that £650 only has been expended on the Uitlanders'
children, or, in other words, whilst the Uitlander received 1s. 10d.,
the expenditure on the Dutch child was £8 6s. 1d. Thus, the Uitlander, who pays nine-tenths of the £63,000, receives practically no
value for his money, and in addition has to pay for his own
voluntary schools, which the Transvaal Superintendent-General of
Education suggested in his report should be suppressed.

Up to the time of the Raid the agitation for reforms had been
conducted by the National Union upon strictly constitutional lines,
and so far as can be seen there is not the slightest justification for
the measures restricting the liberty of the subject which were
passed prior to that lamentable affair.

The first of these was the Press Law of 1893, by which any mere
expression of disapproval, even in a newspaper, of any action of the
Government may become a criminal offence.

By the Election Law, which shortly followed, it was also criminal
to form committees or to take any action in elections, such as are
usually regarded as the ordinary legitimate business of electioneering.
We know now from Mr. Lionel Phillip's letter to Mr. Beit that the
National Union subscribed £10,000 per annum in securing the
return of Progressive candidates to the Raad, but there is no
evidence that this sum was expended in any but a legitimate way.
Mr. Reitz in his haste asserts that this was spent in corrupting that
incorruptible assembly, the First Raad. Unsupported by any
evidence, this assertion must be dismissed.

Under the Public Meetings Act any assembly of more than seven
persons might be dispersed at the discretion of a policeman. This
must have been imported ready made from Germany, where, in order
to put down Social Democracy, a policeman is empowered to closure
any meeting, even in a private house, of more than seven persons
by simply putting on his helmet.

Another grievance, perhaps largely sentimental, but none the less
keenly felt, was the law that no alien could sit on a jury. Thus the
fundamental safeguard of most Europeans, that of being tried by
their peers, is denied to the Uitlanders. Apart from the notorious
Edgar case, there appears to be no evidence of any actual miscarriage
of justice, although, no doubt, Uitlanders may have submitted to
injustice rather than risk the verdict of a Boer jury. In ordinary
civil cases I think we may give the Boers credit for dealing fairly
with the parties upon the evidence; but in criminal cases, or in
civil suits where political or racial appeals might be made, the
verdict of a Boer jury might well be open to suspicion, and the

unwillingness of the Uitlander to subject himself to the risk of a partisan verdict can readily be appreciated.

Apart from this particular grievance, there was little sense of security in civil actions since decisions of the High Court in favour of the Uitlander plaintiffs in suits against the State were frequently overridden by the Government. In fact the Goverment, in some cases, went even further by passing measures of a retrospective nature, depriving intending suitors of their legal claims against the State. These measures were usually rushed through the Raad in defiance of the provisions of the Grondwet stipulating for certain periods of time for notice and publication of any proposed legislation. These violations form good examples of Mr. Kruger's tender solicitude for the law and the constitution.

Up to 1895 the National Union comprised few of the wealthy mine and land owners, but in that year all constitutional agitation having proved fruitless, the leading capitalists of the Rand joined the movement. The contemptuous rejection of the franchise petition, signed by nearly 40,000 persons, amidst the laughter of the Volksraad and of the slightest redress of grievances, had convinced the whole community that any reform by peaceable means at Mr. Kruger's hands was out of the question. This view was strengthened by the proposed expenditure of £250,000 upon fortifications at Pretoria, and of £100,000 upon a fort commanding Johannesburg, and by large orders given for Krupp guns and for Maxims. All these were subsequently executed in due course. It is impossible to say with which party originated the idea of using force.

Mr. Lionel Phillips, writing early in the year, said,

" The Government is rotten and we must have reform ; the alternative is revolution or English interference."

On July 5 he wrote, " We don't want a row," and went on to suggest the raising of £10,000 to £15,000 " to improve the Volksraad." A month later, he writes, " if this plan fails, the only alternative is force." About this time Mr. Rhodes came to Pretoria, and openly fell out with Mr. Kruger over the Railway Union scheme. From that moment he gave up all hope of effecting anything through the President.

"He was absolutely hopeless and irreconciliable. There were ten more years of mischief in him," said Mr. Rhodes grimly ; " we cannot wait till he disappears; South Africa is developing too rapidly. Something must be done to place the control of the Transvaal in the hands of a more progressive ruler than Oom Paul."[1]

This was followed by an agreement between Mr. Rhodes and Mr. Beit to share the financial responsibilities of any action which might become necessary. Mr. Beit reported the result of his

---

[1] *The Scandal of the South African Commission*, p. 16.

interview to Mr. Phillips and Mr. Charles Leonard, and since all agreed that a revolution was only a question of time, it was decided that Johannesburg must be prepared to defend itself, and that a force should be ready on the border to render assistance if required. I am inclined to think that the President contemplated the use of force before any attempt to arm Johannesburg had been made by the Reformers, but, at any rate, from his reply to Mr. Leonard's manifesto of Boxing Day, " Their rights, yes, they'll get them— over my dead body," it is clear that before any overt act had been taken the President had determined to resist all demands for reform by force.

Several questions here present themselves, which must be left for future consideration. First, Was an armed insurrection inevitable? Secondly, Was it justifiable under all the circumstances? Thirdly, Was it capable of success? And lastly, How far was the English Government entitled to interfere in the dispute?

HUGH H. L. BELLOT.

*(To be continued.)*

# FOR HONOUR! FOR FATHERLAND!

## TO THE MEN OF ENGLAND.

"Men of England, wherefore plough
For the lords who lay you low;
Wherefore weave with toil and care
The rich robes your tyrants wear?

"Wherefore, bees of England, forge
Many a weapon, chain and scourge,
That these stingless drones may spoil
The forced produce of your toil?

"Sow seed—but let no tyrant reap;
Find wealth—let no impostor heap;
Weave robes—let not the idle wear;
Forge arms in your defence to bear."
—SHELLEY.

"FOR Honour! for Fatherland!" should be the battle-cry of all true democrats at the forthcoming General Election; for, whether it come, as many predict, within a month or two, or whether the Government see fit to postpone their appeal to the country till next year, the issues at stake at that election will be the honour and the liberty of our native land.

The honour of our land is at stake, because the present Government have not hesitated to make this country, in the trenchant phrase of John Burns, "the janissary of the Jews," "a pirate empire," the cat's-paw of Rhodes, Beit, Werhner, Eckstein, Neumann, Joel, and "patriots" with patronymics more strange and outlandish still.

In her contribution to the *Times* on the siege of Kimberley, the Hon. Mrs. Rochefort Maguire says, "It is hardly an exaggeration to say that Kimberley is De Beers and De Beers Mr. Rhodes"; while Mr. Rhodes claims to be "the embodiment of English ideas."

"They hate you more than they hate England," said Julian Ralph, the Yankee correspondent of the *Daily Mail*. "Because they see in me the embodiment of English ideas," replied Mr. Rhodes.

If these propositions be true, it logically follows that Kimberley —monopoly-ridden Kimberley— Kimberley with its black "compound" slaves and its white serfs—is "the embodiment of English ideas."

Kimberley is De Beers and De Beers Mr. Rhodes. Mr. Rhodes is "the embodiment of English ideas." Therefore Kimberley is "the embodiment of English ideas." So runs the syllogism.

And the mischief of it is that there is only too much of truth in the empire-wrecker's boast. Mr. Rhodes stands for exploitation, and so in a large measure does the British Empire.

Look at Ireland, overtaxed to the tune of upwards of £2,500,000 a year! Ireland, where, since the Act of Union, as Mr. John Redmond stated in the House of Commons the other day, the burden of taxation has been doubled while that of England has been diminished! Ireland, where, in the same period, the population has fallen over a million and her paupers have increased in numbers from 295,000 to 536,000; whereas, while the population of England has increased, her pauperism has diminished by one-half!

Look at Egypt, where, to safeguard the interests of the bondholders, England crushed a people struggling to free themselves from an iniquitous despotism!

Look at India, drained by this country to the extent of £30,000,000 a year! India, where millions that ought to be spent on canals and irrigation works are spent on military roads and railways, on frontier wars, and on useless and ofttimes worse than useless Anglo-Indian officials! India, where some 5,000,000 people—a population larger than that of Ireland—are, thanks largely, if not wholly, to our misrule, now suffering from famine! India, whose appeal to this country passes practically unheeded because John Bull is too busily engaged in stamping out, in the interests of the gold-hunters, two small republics in South Africa!

Kimberley, possible under British rule, is impossible under Boer rule; and it is to substitute British for Boer rule, and thus render it possible for Mr. Rhodes to make of Johannesburg a second Kimberley, that this piratical war has been engineered.

Small wonder that, seeing in Cecil Rhodes "the embodiment of English ideas," the Continental peoples, whatever may be the attitude of their Governments, hate and despise this country. "Oderint dum metuant" ("Let them hate provided they fear") may be the motto of the Jingoes, but wise men will bear in mind that, as Mr. Hugh Price Hughes said in his anti-Jingo days:

"It is all very well to talk of our fleet, but we cannot defy the moral sentiment of the human race."

The freedom of our country is at stake, because this Government is a Government of Exploiters, and cares only for the interests of the exploiters. Witness the doles to favoured classes and the record of the Government with regard to Old-age Pensions, low-flash oil, automatic couplings, the London Water Purchase Bill, &c.! It is a Landlord Government, and your landlord is your exploiter *par excellence*—a drone reaping where he has not sown and gathering where he has not strawed.

If at the next election the workers of England—for it is their votes that will decide the issue—return to power the present Government, then, indeed, will they forge for themselves "many a weapon, chain, and scourge"; and right bitterly will they repent it.

Lord Salisbury could hardly again undertake the cares of office. Even were he willing to do so, his state of health would scarce permit it. In that event, whether he became Premier or not, the reins of power would be, even more than they are to-day, in the hands of the Right Hon. Joseph Chamberlain; and whereas Salisbury has chastised with whips, Chamberlain would chastise with scorpions. His Brummagem diplomacy would to a certainty embroil us with one or more of the Continental Powers, and thus to the slavery of landlordism would be added the slavery of militarism—of conscription.

It were well, then, that those of the workers who have been misled by the false reports of a Chartered Press should cast off their Jingo madness and look present facts and future probabilities fairly and squarely in the face.

There is only too much of truth in Mr. Rhodes's boast that he is "the embodiment of English ideas." With the present Government in power, and in view of the outrages against the right of free speech, one might almost be tempted to say in despair that he spoke the truth, the whole truth, and nothing but the truth. But that is not the case. The very attempt to put down free speech shows that at heart the Jingoes realise that their cause is a bad one, and that they fear, if truth be allowed free utterance, the eyes of the democracy will be opened, and the people will resent the misrepresentations and the lies by means of which the nation has been jockeyed into this criminal war.

In addition to John Burns, such men as Joseph Arch, M.P., Henry Broadhurst, M.P., Thomas Burt, M.P., C. Fenwick, M.P., F. Maddison, M.P., Benjamin Pickard, M.P., W. C. Steadman, M.P., Keir Hardy, Pete Curran, J. R. Macdonald, George N. Barnes, and other well-known labour leaders, have most strongly condemned this war. In a circular headed "Labour Leaders and the War"[1]—a circular that ought to be carefully studied by every worker in the United Kingdom—they expose the fallacy that "the war against the Boers is being waged on behalf of justice and freedom for industrious Britons." They stigmatise the war as "a war waged by

---

[1] Copies may be had free for distribution from Mr. W. Randal Cremer, 11 Lincoln's Inn Fields, London, W.C.; from the office of the *Morning Leader*, Stonecutter Street, London, E.C.; and from the Birmingham Auxiliary of the South African Conciliation Committee, 121, Colmore Row, Birmingham.

capitalists with the object of gaining greater profits through cheap
'nigger labour.'" This they prove, as follows, out of the mouths
of the "capitalists" themselves :

"A meeting of the Consolidated Gold Fields Company of South Africa
was held at the Cannon Street Hotel, London, November 14, 1899, and is
fully reported in the *Financial News* of November 21. Lord Harris, the
Chairman, stated that upon the working capital of £2,147,000 the profit
for the year had been £1,006,000! But this enormous profit does not
satisfy these people. They want more, and they mean to have more.

"Mr. John Hays Hammond, Engineer of the Company, said in his
speech that he estimated that after the war they would increase their
profit to £2,199,000. So this single company stands to make over a million
a year profit by the war. This is the real reason why war was inevitable.
Do not think that this means a splendid opening for British labour ; it
means nothing of the kind. The plan is to apply as little British labour
as possible, and to reduce the wages of native labour to the smallest
pittance. These men do not conceal it. Mr. Hammond said: 'There
ought to be no difficulty in obtaining 80,000 Kaffirs to work the mines.'
Where does the British working man come in ? Mr. Hammond further
said : 'With a good Government there should be an abundance of labour,
and with an abundance of labour there will be no difficulty in cutting down
wages, because it is preposterous to pay a Kaffir the present wages. He
would be quite as well satisfied—in fact, he would work longer—if you
gave him half the amount.'

"British working men under such circumstances would not work at all.
But these South African capitalists mean to have a Government which
shall

### "EXPLOIT THE 'NIGGERS' IN THEIR INTEREST.

"The tax-collector is to be the crimp of the gold-mongers. Mr. C. D.
Rudd, a director of the Company, said : 'If they could only get one-half
the natives to work three months of the year it would work wonders. They
should try some cogent form of inducement or practically compel the native,
through taxation or in some other way, to contribute his quota to the good
of the community, and to a certain extent he would then have to work.'

"There can be no mistake as to Mr. Rudd's meaning, for he went on to
say : 'They might fairly call upon the native to contribute to the Government in kind or in cash.' That means that the Government is to impose
on the natives taxes which they cannot pay, and that the Company is to
collect the tax in the form of labour. It is only slavery under another
name. . . . As long ago as 1894 Mr. Rhodes made a speech in which he
said that 'if they could make these people work they would reduce the
rate of labour in the country.' Thus Rhodes and his fellow conspirators
intend to teach the natives 'the dignity of labour' by reducing them to a
condition of practical slavery.

### "No WHITE MAN NEED APPLY !

"Earl Grey, in addressing the Chartered Company's shareholders
(reported in *Times*, December 15), said : 'We must dismiss from our
minds any idea of developing our mines with white labour. . . . It is
obvious that the black labour of the aboriginal inhabitants of South Africa
must be our first line of defence. . . . An incentive to labour must be
provided, and it can only be provided by imposition of taxation. I look
forward to the imposition of a hut-tax of £1 per hut in conformity with the
practice that prevails in Basutoland, and I also hope that we may, " with
the permission of the Imperial authorities," be able to establish a labour-

tax which those able-bodied natives should be required to pay who are unable to show a certificate of four months' work. I may add that the directors are already making inquiries on their own account as to the possibility of obtaining "Asiatic" labour.'

"At the same meeting the Duke of Abercorn said that her Majesty's Government will, in the settlement following the war, 'neither wish *nor be able to disregard* the sentiments of their loyal supporters in South Africa.'

### "WHY WE REFUSED ARBITRATION.

"With such damning evidence as to the real objects of those who promoted the war, it will be easily understood why Mr. Chamberlain to please the millionaires refused the repeated offers of President Kruger to submit any matters in dispute to arbitration. We had a very weak case, and a body of arbitrators would speedily have found that out. Away, then, with the delusion that this war is waged in order to open up new territory to British colonists. The capitalists, who bought up or hired the Press both in South Africa and in England to clamour for war, are largely Jews and foreigners. The cry which they raised about the Outlanders' grievances, the arming of the Boers, a Dutch conspiracy, &c., were mere pretexts to deceive you. The enormous sums which they made out of the Rhodesian Diamond Mines emboldened them in their efforts to become absolute masters of the Transvaal Gold Mines also. They have all along wanted war to double their profits by cheap forced native labour. This is now proved out of the mouths of the capitalists themselves. And for this despicable object the British people have to pay untold millions, and British blood already is poured out like water on South African soil!"

Would that the workers in this country could be brought to realise the truth of all this. The present Government would then have a very short shrift indeed, especially if the labour leaders and the labour members would give as strong a lead on domestic questions as they have given in regard to the war.

As is pointed out in the circular, the Boers, though they might well be excused if they failed to do so, distinguish between the guilty authors of the war and the unfortunate dupes and victims serving at the front:

"The Rev. Reginald Collins, one of our army chaplains, who was engaged for three days burying our dead within the Boer lines, says: 'The Boers, great numbers of them, as they inspected the ghastly piles of our dead, cried, "Good God, what a sight!" "I wish politicians could see their handiwork!" "We hate this war." "It is not our war; it is a war of the millionaires!" "What enmity have we with these poor fellows?" "Would that Chamberlain, Rhodes, and the millionaires could see these graves!" "We hate all war; we want to go back to our homes and farms, to sow our seed and reap our fields." "Good God, when will it end!"'"

And a *Daily News* correspondent bears witness to the same truth. Captured at Rensburg, he wrote to President Steyn, asking him to set him free, on the ground that he was a non-combatant. He says:

"The President met me, and treated me very courteously, and explained to me that it was not his wish nor the desire of his colleagues to hamper me in any way in regard to my work. 'What we want more than anything else,' remarked the President,\' is that the world shall know the truth, and nothing but the truth, in reference to this most unhappy war, and we will not needlessly place obstruction in your way in your search for facts; if we can by any means place you in the British lines we will do so.' . . . He introduced me to a couple of gentlemen whose names are very dear to the Free Staters, viz., Messrs. Fraser and Fischer, and whilst our interview lasted nothing was talked of but the war, and it struck me very forcibly that not one of these men had any hatred in their hearts towards the British people. 'This,' said the President, 'is not a war between us and the British people on any question of principle; it is a war forced upon us by a band of capitalistic adventurers, who have hoodwinked the British public, and dragged them into an unholy, an unjust struggle, with a people whose only desire was to live at peace with all men. We do not hate your nation; we do not hate your soldiers, though they fight against us; but we do hate and despise the men who have brought a cruel war upon us for their own evil ends, whilst they try to cloak their designs in a mantle of righteousness and liberty.' I may not have given the exact words of the President, as I am writing from memory; but I think I have given his exact sentiments; and if I am any judge of human nature, the love of his country is the love of his life."

Surely the British people will prove worthy of such trust. Surely they will not allow so brave, yet so gentle and courteous, a foe, as the Boers have over and over again proved themselves, to be ground into the dust to further the sordid schemes of those who, had they their way, would enslave " blacks " and whites alike?

At present, indeed, the prospect looks anything but hopeful. The National Liberal Federation which, under Mr. Gladstone's leadership, some twenty years ago, fought with such sterling courage the forlorn hope against the Jingoes over the Eastern Question, rallied the party and swept the country, has now fallen on evil times, and, instead of striking out boldly for right and justice, seems concerned only to " preserve the unity of the party." The Nottingham Conference records a number of pious opinions with regard to domestic politics, and passes a resolution on the war so vague and indefinite, so platitudinarian and latitudinarian, that it receives at once the support of Sir Edward Grey, who regards the war as just and necessary and holds that, unless the Liberal party becomes Imperialist, it is doomed; and that of Dr. Spence Watson, who strongly condemns the war as both unjust and unnecessary— who, in his presidential speech, said that to " the old Liberals, of whom he was proud to be one, . . . the very word ' Imperial ' was hateful, because it told of that which throughout all history had been most opposed to Liberalism. . . . Could it be expected that those who had heard such men as Kossuth and Garibaldi would adopt this word Imperialism with satisfaction? "—who roundly declared that " if they were only to succeed by swallowing their principles and trampling upon their watchwords, then God give them failure! "

By what irony of fate was it that Sir Edward Grey was
allowed to take the place of Sir Henry Campbell-Bannerman, who
holds that the points at issue " were not worth the bones of a single
grenadier ? "

How came it, also, that in his letter to the Conference Sir Henry
Campbell-Bannerman contented himself with crying " Peace, peace,"
where there was no peace, with inculcating unity where there was not,
where there could not be, where there ought not to have been,
unity ?   Could he not, or dared he not, give the party a straight
lead upon this war and upon the settlement that must follow it?
Had he no inspiring word to write with regard to domestic problems
—with regard to the housing problem, which he has told us " is the
land question," and, speaking of which he has asked, " While these
things be, can we say that the heart of the Empire is
sound ? "

If not wilful, the blindness of the Liberal " leaders " is at least
.phenomenal.   In spite of his protestations about swallowing
principles and trampling watchwords under foot, Dr. Spence
Watson, by agreeing to the " wishy-washy " resolution submitted,
promptly proceeded to do both ; and the " leaders," all of them,
fail to see that, so long as they refuse to pledge themselves clearly
and definitely to do *what they can do if they will*, all vague
speeches and vague resolutions about domestic reform are absolutely
worthless.

Said Dr. Watson in the speech above referred to :

" In the meantime, while they differed about the war, let them remember
how many of the great domestic questions to which they had set their
hands were yet unsettled.   That most vital of all social questions—the
Temperance question—was already ripe for solution, and there was that
other question, which lay at the bottom of all questions—the abolition of
the veto of the House of Lords."

Temperance reform is all very well, but it can be blocked, and
certainly will be blocked, by the House of Lords.   And, again, it is
not true, as we have pointed out over and over again, to say that
the abolition of the veto of the House of Lords lies at the bottom of
all questions.   " The House of Lords blocks the way "—*except for
Budget reforms*.   And these, therefore, the Liberal party, if returned
to power, *can carry, if they will*.   Land reform to a large extent
underlies temperance reform.   Says the *Westminster Gazette* of
March 3 last :

" While the Prince of Wales was opening the Boundary Street area of
the new County Council dwellings in Shoreditch on Saturday, the Arch-
bishop of Canterbury was presiding over a special conference of Metropolitan relieving officers, convened by the National Temperance League.
The particular object of the conference was to obtain evidence from

the Poor-Law Officers as to the relationship of drink and total abstinence to the public work in which they are engaged. A consensus of opinion showed that 90 per cent. of the inmates of workhouses are there through drunkenness, either personal or relative. The great panacea put forth by the officers was the 'solution of the housing problem,' the present condition of so-called home-life being held accountable for much of the drunkenness prevailing."

And the late Miss Frances Willard, than whom there could be no more earnest, no more hard-working, temperance reformer, held that poverty was the, cause of drink, rather than drink the cause of poverty; that land monopoly was the root cause of poverty, and that the true remedy was the taxation of land values.

The taxation of land values can be included in the Budget, and can, therefore, be carried in the teeth of the House of Lords.

This war and the land question are test questions. On them those who are not with us are against us; and the sooner they take their stand by Salisbury, Chamberlain, Rhodes, and Co., the better for the honesty of public life, and the better for the Liberal party. To attempt to retain within the party both those who are for and those who are against the war, both those who are for and those who are against land reform is but to stultify and to wreck the party. Unity attained by the sacrifice of principle is not strength. Most emphatically is it true in these matters that "he who would save his life shall lose it, and he who would lose his life for right's sake shall save it." The Liberal party, hopeless as its prospects may seem, has everything to gain and nothing to lose by being unswervingly true to principle.

Until the Liberal party takes a firm stand upon such fundamental questions of principle—until it takes the straight line upon this war and upon the land question, it is false to the democracy of this country and false to the humanity.

If the "leaders" of the party refuse to take this stand, then it is the duty of those of the rank and file who realise what ought to be done to take that straight line regardless of consequences, but confident that their cause is just and that sooner or later right shall prevail.

Asked how it was that Daniel came forth unharmed from the lion's den, an American boy replied, "Because Daniel was three parts grit and the rest backbone." To all true Liberals the next General Election bids fair to be a veritable lion's den, but if they have got the grit and the backbone they need not fear the result. The truth regarding this war needs only to be fearlessly told, the hollowness of the perfervid "patriotism" of the present Government of Parasites needs only to be fearlessly exposed, to result in a victory for the Party of Progress as sweeping as unexpected.

Surely there is sufficient grit in the Nonconformists—"the backbone of the Liberal party "—to see the thing through? Surely the great co-operative organisations and the great trades-union organisations, numbering respectively 1,500,000 and 1,250,000 members, will not, without a struggle, see this Government of Exploiters once more returned to power! Surely, for British honour and for British liberties, they will make a worthy stand!

They have both the money power and the voting power; and if they choose to exercise them—if they dare to rise to the occasion— they can readily turn out, bag and baggage, this "the strongest Government of modern times."

Assuming that the General Election takes place next year, a levy of one penny per week per member of the trades-unionist, the co-operative, or the Nonconformist bodies—let alone such a levy upon the members of all three of them—would in that time raise an ample fund for electioneering purposes. And in case of emergency a levy of sixpence or one shilling per member, supplemented by generous contributions from strike funds and reserve funds, would amply supply the war-chest, and enable the men of England to rid themselves of the exploiters and to secure that for the future the arms they forge shall, as the present war has shown may very safely be done, be strictly reserved for defence, and for defence alone.

Mr. Stead, who is so exercised in mind about the possibilities of a war with France, who, as a result of his recent visit to Paris, is

"more than ever convinced that, while no sane or responsible person in France wills a war with England, the state of public feeling on both sides of the Channel is so exasperated that no one can feel any security that war may not break out before Christmas,"

should turn his attention to the organising of a campaign on these lines. It would prove a much surer safeguard than "an experimental mobilisation round London at Whitsuntide of the whole volunteer force of the country," and than an "Apostolate of Peace, (so) that at the forthcoming Exhibition at Paris the world should know what trades unions, co-operative societies, democrats, and Christian Socialists have to say about war and war establishments."

Mr. Chamberlain is the great danger, and to get rid of him we must get rid of the present Government.

The workers of this country, we repeat, can undoubtedly, if they choose, if they dare to rise to the occasion, turn out this Government bag and baggage. They can, if they choose, as we have shown again and again, secure by means of the Budget, and in despite of the "House of Landlords," the freeing of this country from the grip of the land-monopolist and obtain such great, immediate, and far-reaching benefits as Payment of Members and of Election

Expenses, the Abolition of the Breakfast-table Duties, and Old-age Pensions.    And, moreover, they can, if they dare, stop this unholy war, and, by securing in South Africa a just and a generous settlement, give the lie direct to the arch-exploiter's boast that he——he, of all men!——is " the embodiment of English ideas."

If they fail to do so, upon them will rest the bloodguiltiness ; upon them and upon their children will fall the consequences.

# THOUGHTS ON THE WAR.

## BY A MAN OF PEACE.

The existence of war in the world has ever been a puzzle to the optimist. "One murder makes a villain, millions a hero," wrote Bishop Porteous, and voted in favour of war with France. "The lines were not intended for the *present* war," he explained. It is always so. In the abstract war is always indefensible and unjustifiable, a crime against humanity and civilisation, a remnant of barbarism, and absolutely inconclusive as to the merits of the dispute. Yet for the particular war which, at any particular time, we happen to be engaged in there is always, and usually on both sides, some justification, some special strong reason, some great principle to be upheld, which makes it, or makes it appear, a duty and a virtue instead of a crime. I can claim no exemption from the working of this strange mental phenomenon. I have spoken, in season and out of season, of war as the most heinous of national crimes, followed, as it always is, by great national calamities. Nineteen hundred years has not yet taught the first lesson of the Christian evangelist, ἐπὶ γῆς εἰρήνη. I have stereotyped, with approval, words I once heard spoken by a native of the Scandinavian peninsula. "I know," he said, "whatever may be the duties of Great Powers in the abstract, that Sweden is happier now than when her lightest word affected the destinies of Europe." That such might be the future fate of England has seemed almost a desideratum. Our foreign policy is a great expense to us. We have to pay dearly for being a Great Power. The first step towards the amelioration of our widespread social distress would be the removal of taxes for war and its accessories. Our colonies, perhaps, when strong enough and large enough to stand alone, will sever themselves, and we shall put no obstacles in their path. It is a lovely picture. England an Arcadia, with no power, no influence, no foreign policy, no taxes, and nothing to occupy the attention of our paternal (or grandmaternal) Government, but to legislate for the universal happiness of its confiding people! Meanwhile, before this consummation arrives, many things must happen. At the present time we find ourselves encumbered with an empire extending over a large portion of the civilised world. This we look upon as a blessing or a curse according to our individual political opinions ; but, in any case, there it is, and it carries with it certain duties of a more or less (generally more) onerous character. If, too, we assume that our colonies in the future may wish to be independent, we have to remember that at the present time they are *not* independent and do *not* wish to sever themselves, but elect to remain a part of the British Empire.

The first thought that comes to a man of peace in this crisis is the question, " Are we, in this our day, this nineteenth (or twentieth) century, in the actual presence of that *rara avis in terris*, that supposed extinct species, a just war ? " Can any war be so ? Can our nation, which has destroyed the duello microbe by the light and air of reason and humanity, suffer the greater, the more unreasonable, the more inhuman custom to continue ? It is, perhaps, incontrovertible that the logician, in his study, might put together a series of conditions by the combination of which war would become a duty instead of a crime. Is it possible that this combination has actually arisen ? Doubtful as it seemed to be during the negotiations, events which have taken place since the war began almost suggest the astounding conclusion that it has. It is difficult, it is painful, to make such an admission in view of so great an evil, yet it is still more difficult to counsel inaction in reply to the calls of humanity, and callous disregard when the cry of the oppressed enters into the ears and heart of a great nation.

The question of our non-preparedness for the war does not enter into that of its justice. If it shows anything in this matter it shows that we were making for peace, and had the courage of our convictions : that we could not bring ourselves to believe seriously in anything but a peaceable solution of our disputes with civilised peoples : that, strong in the conviction of the justice of our own cause, we could not but believe that a plain unvarnished statement of the case would bring the same conviction to others. So we may pass over the now notorious fact that we were absolutely unprepared ; that the man in the street has long been telling us that the two South African Republics were armed to the teeth, were versed in all the modern requirements of war, hated the English, and *meant* to fight us. Such seemed to be the opinion of every man, woman and child, or at least nine-tenths of them, *outside* the War Office and the army. Within the War Office it was different. Such statements were looked upon with contempt. The Intelligence (?) Department (puzzle, find the Intelligence) was differently informed. The Army reflected the—Department. " Matters were much exaggerated. It would be a mere walk over." The astounding thing to us now is, not that the Government and the War Office, as has been admitted in Parliament, knew no more than the man in the street, but that they did not know so much. This supineness, this wilful ignorance, this determination not to receive information even when it was pressed upon them, may show many things: it may show the need of an entire overhauling and reformation of our system of Government and our methods of Departmental procedure, but it does not show that the war was premeditated, or even intended, by the representatives of the country. On the contrary, it shows that nothing was further from their thoughts than to go to war at the bidding of anybody. The Boer ultimatum was a surprise to the whole world except to those initiated in the Boer preparations, and to none more so than to our responsible rulers, whom for the moment, at a most difficult stage of the negotiations, it relieved of a great weight of anxiety and trouble. Their efforts for peace had failed: there was nothing for it but to accept the challenge with all their imperfections and lack of preparation on their heads; but the terrible responsibility of having to declare war on a small nation, an event which it is conceivable that a combination of circumstances might have forced upon them, was removed at a stroke.

That they had still enough to answer for later events have shown, but these events have proved more clearly than anything else could have done that, while from the very beginning of the negotiations, and, indeed, for many years before, the two Republics had determined to wage war upon us sooner or later, and had made the most continuous and far-sighted preparations for it, it had hardly upon our side been looked upon even as a possible contingency.

The first question that occurs to a man of peace is, " What are we fighting for ? " Is there any great principle at stake so important that it overrides for the time the moral law, renders wholesale murder justifiable, and makes it a duty, instead of a crime, for a Christian nation to sacrifice the lives of thousands, both friends and foes, by the overwhelming necessities of the end in view ? Does the end ever justify the means ? From the standpoint of the Jesuits, no doubt, it does. But among the Reformed Churches is not the dictum, " Let us do evil that good may come," always held to be accursed ? Personally, I can hardly bring myself to believe, as an abstract contention, that war can ever be justified. Yet, the world being constituted as it is, what, it may well be asked, is the duty of a great nation when the cry of the distressed, the wail of its unhappy countrymen suffering under the tyranny of the oppressor, comes before it, and when it has at last come to pass that the sword is the only weapon that remains to remedy the evil ?

Not only have the Republics been employed for many years past in preparing their material resources, but they have been at the same time disseminating throughout the civilised world carefully worded statements in order to justify their cause and make the worse appear the better reason. So cleverly were these statements put together that most European countries seem to have been influenced by them, and even many in our own land, not excepting, I may say, the present writer, were led away by the sophistries they contained to look upon the Boer cause as practically a just and defensible one.

The war began and the bubble exploded. The pathetic picture of the pious Boer studying his Bible, longing for peace and a pastoral life, and only taking up arms to defend his independence against a powerful and grasping oppressor, is shown to be a myth. So, too, is the widely diffused statement that the English Government, at the bidding of a few millionaires (and, of course, bribed by them), were calculatingly making for war in order to raise or depress, as might happen, the price of certain securities, thereby giving said millionaires an opportunity of effecting a series of extensive operations in bears or bulls. The only wonder now is that such statements have ever had a moment's consideration. Yet so potent was the hypnotic influence they exerted that most of the countries of Europe do not appear to have recovered from it, and there are even a few small groups of Englishmen who seem to be still under its spell. The magnificently appointed Boer preparations, now patent to the whole world, the enormous sums extorted from the owners and workers of the mines by a nearly bankrupt State, by means of which these preparations have been carried out, secret service paid for, and even traitors, it has been said, subsidised, show on which side the money-making has been chiefly going on.

We need have no special sympathy with the cynical " Empire-maker " who, it would seem, repudiated his agent as soon as his plan had failed, nor with the agent himself, who thought to accomplish with a few hundred men a task which is taxing the strength of the whole British army, and who might say with the Earl of Strafford (adapted), "Put not your trust in Empire-makers"; for if he did not meet a similar fate, it was due to the courtesy of Mr. Kruger rather than to his own foresight or wisdom.

To say that the Raid was a crime and a blunder hardly expresses it. It played into the hands of our enemies. It enabled them to increase their preparations, and with less secrecy than before, while it prevented us from continuing our own. It disposed foreign nations in their favour, thus gaining for them the most valuable assistance both in brains and munitions, and set the whole world against us. It was an interlude, and a fortunate one for them. But to say that it was in any sense the *cause* of their preparations or of their animosity is to ignore facts. Their preparations had already been going on for years. We were on the verge of war when the Raid took place, and but for this it would have occurred sooner, and their preparations would have been less complete. It gave them their trump card.

Others, again, would have us believe that we are waging war

merely from a feeling of revenge; and this, forsooth, is assumed even by Mr. Herbert Spencer, because a few irresponsible persons called out, "Remember Majuba!" Such a cry was, no doubt, a painful shock to all sensible and right-minded people, showing, as it did, the abiding influence somewhere of the most evil and senseless of passions. But to represent it as embodying in any sense the national feeling is a vile libel on our countrymen, and shows as great a lack of the relative value of things as does the feeling which it condemns—that, namely, which magnifies an unfortunate skirmish occurring twenty years ago into a national disaster. It is hardly conceivable that any reasonable person, not to say any responsible Government, would plunge the country into all the horrors of war merely to commemorate a half-forgotten episode of ancient history.

But there is yet another theory: a favourite one with our enemies abroad, and not unfrequently adopted by our candid friends at home. We are accused of going to war for the extension of our Empire, for the mere glory or greed of possessing territory, which we make every pretext for acquiring; and because our masterful feelings cannot brook the existence of two independent republics in close contiguity to one of our colonies. This theory, so stated, hardly needs refutation; yet it is constantly assumed as if it were an incontrovertible axiom.

If there is any truth in one of these accusations, if we are fighting to deprive others of freedom, to assist speculators, to gratify the evil passion of revenge, rankling long after a fair fight, or to follow out an abstract idea of Imperial extension, I, for one, and doubtless many others—indeed, all who feel the responsibility of our situation—would say it is not worth the sacrifice of a single life.

What, then, are we fighting for? That, if successful, we shall somewhat extend British influence, there can be no doubt; nor is it impossible that speculators may endeavour to fill their pockets by forecasting the issue of the war. I have no doubt that many of the sons of Abraham are even now repeating, so far as modern surroundings will allow, the operations of a well-known member of the family at the battle of Waterloo. They are ready to take advantage of any disturbing influence which affects the money market, but to accuse them of the atrocious crime of bringing about a war for this especial purpose is another matter. I am not aware that any one accused Nathan Rothschild of inducing the Government of the day to wage war against the French because he profited by it. That a feeling of revenge may arise in some undisciplined minds when war has been declared is possible, but we can hardly accuse a responsible Government, consisting of educated and honourable men, of allowing it to influence their action.

In the first place, we are fighting against a universal danger to civilisation. The existence in South Africa of two large military despotisms, armed to the teeth, with conscription carried out to a degree almost unprecedented among civilised nations, is a standing menace to the world. The other nations of South Africa are European colonies, living at peace, and maintaining only small armies for protection against native incursions. They are chiefly Belgian, British, German, and Portuguese. In each case the colonial army is sufficient for the internal maintenance of order, but not for the repulsion of foreign invaders. In their midst are these two powerfully armed States, which, had not the neighbouring countries been colonies possessing the moral support of home armies, would long ere this have swallowed up with ease the whole of the South African continent. In fact, if the work is not carried out by us now, it will inevitably have to be taken up by some other European country or countries later on, and the conditions will be still more unfavourable.

The worst horrors of war culminate in the conscription. Who doubts it should read *Le Conscrit* of MM. Erckmann-Chatrian. War in any case is bad enough, but surely it is shorn of half its horrors when its victims are not unwilling subjects, torn from their homes, but volunteers longing to go to the front. It has been said that one volunteer is worth three pressed men. Be it ours to prove it. Surely, with the large numbers still clamouring to serve, and still being refused, there can be little need of conscription, which damps enthusiasm instead of encouraging it. It is all very well to say it is a slur on the English people to suggest that they would oppose conscription, but is it not better to encourage the enthusiasm of volunteers? As it is, we are fighting the fight of voluntary service as against conscription; and in this respect we are fighting on behalf of many of our foes, who have been cruelly commandeered against their will. It would be a strange commentary on the war if it ended by our adopting the system of our enemies. Compulsory drill, however, to increase the efficiency of those who chose to offer themselves when the necessity arose, would not be conscription. Nor would general rifle practice.

Conscription covers, practically, the greater part of the whole question. It was conscription which, in the first place, appears to have stood in the way of the Uitlanders obtaining the franchise. They were offered both or neither, and may naturally have foreseen the possibility of fighting against their own country. But for this we should never have heard those heart-breaking accounts, whether true or false, of Englishmen shot in cold blood for refusing to do so. Of this there is at present no confirmation; but, if true, we may still assume that they had accepted letters of naturalisation, and with them the liability to serve in the army, which would give the Act, perhaps, some show of legality. Indeed, it would probably be the same in any country where conscription exists. I know one case of an Englishman serving with the Boers.  He was compelled to swear on the Testament that he would fight in a *bonâ fide* manner against the English, and do his best to help his adopted country. He *believed* he would have been shot had he refused.  Whether the threat would have been carried out I cannot say.  I presume he also was a naturalised South African Republican.  If the British arms should be ultimately successful, a very large proportion of those now fighting against us, whether Boer or British, will bless the day that delivered them from an intolerable tyranny, and enabled them to live under the freedom of British rule.

We are fighting, too, for equality.  In all parts of the British Empire—and no amount of platform sophistry will alter the fact—white races have practically equal rights, which in the South African Republic they have not.

Corruption in the Government of the Republic has been denied. We may have our shortcomings at home; but our rulers do not raise colossal fortunes in a few years like those of South American (and South African?) Republics by exploiting foreigners; nor do we raise vast sums out of all proportion to our population by taxing mine-owners and workers to an extent which practically amounts to confiscation of their mines.

Of the anti-English policy, President Kruger is the exponent.  It is by no means universal, and probably at one time hardly preponderant; but it has been cultivated and fostered by his genius (doubtless with some ulterior object) until we have come to be looked upon as the wickedest race on earth.  We have been told that President Kruger is a simple-minded (not to put too fine a point on it) fool.  We see no sign of it.  He is more the type (mentally, not physically) of our great opponent of a hundred years ago, and he has many points which Napoleon had not.  In physical strength and skill he is his superior, possibly in courage.  He has, up to date, shown an unfailing degree of the prudence and foresight which Napoleon, on certain occasions, lacked.  He possesses, too, religious feelings, sincere perhaps, though we believe wrongly directed, and, conceivably, faith in the justice of his cause, while his private character is unimpeached.  Upon the whole, he is the preferable character, though, none the less—perhaps, indeed, for that very reason, given equal resources—a more formidable foe.  We had not, when we fought Napoleon, the same advantage in numbers that we have now.

And not only are we fighting against the oppression of our fellow subjects in discharge of that responsibility of Empire which makes it our duty to protect from injustice any single one of our countrymen wherever residing; we are fighting, too, against slavery, as, in the sixties, the Northern States of America fought against the Southern.  Then it was not only on the continent of Europe, but in Great Britain itself, that sympathy went out to the slave-owners. Yet now slavery is abolished, and no one doubts the justice of the victor's cause. So it is now. We have not been sinless in our treatment of the native races. But no one who knows the history of the Dutch Republics can deny, and certainly the natives themselves will not be disposed to deny, that the black as well as the white races will enjoy greater freedom and happiness under British rule than they do now under that of the Boers.

Peace is much to be desired; but we fear it can now only come by the supremacy, gained, unfortunately, by the sword, of one of two races. Prophecies are at present at a discount. We have had many of them of late, and they have been falsified with quite remarkable unanimity. It may, however, be permitted to forecast two possible and opposite contingencies, one to hope for, another to fear. It is well to provide an understudy, in case of unforeseen factors in the issue of events.

As a nation, we have faith, almost to a man, in the justice of our cause, in the patriotism, spirit and determination of our men, in the skill and genius of their commanders. What Wellington was to us ninety years ago, Roberts is now. Mistakes have been made, and may be made again, and there are difficulties to be surmounted; but the end will come. Britain will be triumphant, peace will be secured, military armaments will be diminished, European races will live in harmony together, and justice, freedom, and good government will reign throughout South Africa.

But there is the other alternative. We shall be driven into the sea, and our colonies will become things of the past. Boer influence will prevail, and a vast military despotism, enslaving the natives and crushing the foreign element in its midst, will dominate the continent of Africa. And then, later on in the century, this great Republic will find itself pitted against the combined forces of Germany, France, Portugal, and Belgium, while a small island in the North-west of Europe, once the centre of a vast empire on which the sun never used to set, will, from afar, contemplate the struggle, musing with philosophic calm over its own former greatness.

J. Foster Palmer.

# SOME ISSUES OF THE TRANSVAAL WAR.

THE Transvaal—the war, and after—is a subject on which, to employ the language of Sophocles, as translated by an English poet who was capable of doing the classic tragedian no injustice, you come

"To many ways in the wanderings of careful thought."

The merits of our present military system and its defects, the future of a territorial domain exceeding the limits of the conquests of Alexander the Great, constitution-building, impending reforms and changes, going to the very root of our national character, are some only of the larger issues that are calling for a solution at no distant date. A member of the present Unionist Government has said that in politics it is the unexpected which happens. It is true in a very signal degree of the outbreak of belligerent operations in South Africa that it was unexpected. A Great Personage, long associated with South African affairs, and who has since, like Lord Chesterfield in 1745, raised one of the corps of Light Horse, is known to have declared on the very eve of the Reitz ultimatum that he did not believe in the outbreak of hostilities. The Government are, perhaps, not to be blamed so much for not foreseeing war, but such *laches* is rather excusable than justifiable—*gouverner, c'est prévoir*. No one has yet written a vindication of Lord North because Benjamin Franklin was always protesting that the American colonies were not aiming at independence. History, whether ancient or modern, is the science of facts, not of opinions or protestations. Facts have demonstrated that one at least of the South African Republics was aiming at war, at least as much as it was aiming at anything; for decision of character is not among the characteristics of President Kruger, remarkable as his personality as now it is known undoubtedly must be. Dissimulation and artifice are qualities that will be as surely identified with President Kruger as they have long been with Oliver Cromwell, or, for the matter of that, with Charles I. All this has made for much of the success which has undoubtedly attended President Kruger in peace as in war—success which in war is only just deserting him. Artifice in negotiation and diplomacy—even a new diplomacy—is cunning in action, and authority has declared that cunning is the most valuable quality in war. It is *chercher le poil aux œufs* to discuss whether President Kruger seizes the occasion or is an occasionalist only, to borrow the famous simile of Edmund Burke. It is evident that since the time of the Raid President Kruger has been waiting for something to turn up, like King Didier and Mr. Micawber. It cannot be doubted that this something was that England should find an entanglement of a more serious character than that she recently experienced at Ladysmith, and nearer home. But all the evidence runs that President Kruger, like all Transvaalers, does not love foreign countries more than England, he only hates them less. He would have been well content if "the fearful signs of coming war" had burst over the Fashoda incident, the Venezuela arbitration. But it is contrary to what is known of the Boer character that he would have welcomed, before the outbreak of hostilities, intervention or arbitration, even coming from Germany. The conclusion is induced that President Kruger is an occasionalist, far too much of a rural President to be a magnificent server of the occasion. He might have succeeded better if he had been. As a President of a South American, not of a South African, Republic he might have succeeded as it is. When all has been said that can be said of Boer exclusiveness, it would not probably surpass that of the Jesuit President of Paraguay, who excluded all strangers from the territorial limits of the State, with more or less success, for nearly thirty years. In Sir Alfred Milner a magnificent political altruism is just as obvious as political egotism is in President Kruger. In the former we equally recognise great decision of character, such as Mr. Lecky identifies with Pitt the younger. No comparison can indeed be drawn between Sir Alfred Milner and President Kruger. Macaulay disclaimed comparison between Napoleon and Cromwell on intellectual grounds, and such a protest is much more likely to be endorsed in the case of Sir Alfred Milner and President Kruger. But for all that, Cromwell was a much more successful man than Napoleon on the whole. Even students of Pitt in this country do not claim that he was a successful man. It cannot be said of any man who died in the year of Austerlitz that he died happy. The great and conspicuous qualities which have identified William Pitt with the glory of our race and the grace of our language did not avail him to avert the legions of Napoleon or to prevent the burdening of his own country with a colossal debt and a legacy of many evil days. Even the warmest admirers of Sir Alfred Milner— even those who are best qualified to appreciate the great endowments of intellect and decision of character that he possesses—may well be appalled at the difficulties of the environment that the High Commissioner is called upon to surmount and overcome. The "clean slate," of which so much was said, may prove a Danaic gift. The necessary inference is that, from that expression, Great Britain will impose a new constitution for a complete federation of South Africa. But if there is one thing in which the Anglo-Saxon race have excelled less than in another, it is constitution-building. Historians invite us to admire the mediæval constitution, perhaps in view of the failures of Pitt and Gladstone in constitution-building. Lord Salisbury, adopting a family, but not a party precedent, is so far acting out of the usual *rôle* that he complains bitterly of the defect of the English Constitution. When we find Mr. John Morley, in his *Life of Burke*, observing that the British Constitution, for some decades after Burke's death, was one of the most mischievous systems that human nature was ever asked to endure, the man in the street feels, at all events, in subconsciousness, that there has been no infringement of consistency. But when stern and unbending Tories like the Premier take to denouncing the constitution, a worse effect is produced than by the blatant announcements of Boer victories. Lord Salisbury, who finds it convenient to quote from Macaulay, should remember of all persons the lengthy quotation from Burke that the Whig historian made in his *Review of Hallam's Constitutional History*. Constitution-building for the last century has flowed from one source—the written constitutions of the French Revolution. Alone of the nations of Western Europe, Great Britain, together with such unimportant exceptions as the Grand Duchy of Mecklenberg, the republics of Monaco and Val d'Andorra has no written fundamental law. It fairly follows that she ought not to impose written constitutions on her own colonies. But if not, what is the meaning of "the free slate" of Mr. Chamberlain? Are the Government going to revert, on the other hand, to Pitt's Union policy, and purchase the existing franchises of Africa with the money of the British taxpayer? In politics it is the unexpected which happens; but at first blush one would be inclined to predict that they would not get the money. Pitt's purchase of the Irish Parliament is a much more obsolete policy than his lavish expenditure on Secret Service, which we know on the best authority is now discredited. The free slate bids fair to remain a *tabula rasa*, though this must be very disappointing to those of Sir Alfred Milner's admirers who would like to see him engaged on a task that confessedly proved too great for the combined abilities of a Mirabeau, Siéyès, and Clavière.

But of what avail are Paardeberg, and the relief of Ladysmith, if these military triumphs are deprived of any political consummation, and therefore significance? It must be said of South Africa to-day, at the close of the nineteenth century, what was said of France in Year III.—there death is *vomie à grands flots*. The whole country is one continued scene of blood and slaughter. Are we wading through blood to a resumption of right, as Curran once finely said? Or is it all to be in vain? We ought to be, if we are not, on the eve of a great constitution-building in South Africa.  But as yet authority has given no sign, though nothing would have so effectually answered the threat of Republican annexation as the promulgation of a colonial federation by the High Commissioner.

One of the Georges remarked of two Ministers, one of whom was Pitt, that while Pitt would not act the other could not.  The man in the street, who seems, according to Mr. Balfour, to assume the place of a Great Personage in the Georgian epoch, can hardly fail to notice the features of vacillation and pusillanimity in the political action of the Government.  Their military action assuredly can never procure admiration.  The country, we are told, is behind the Government ; it is a *crambe repetita*, as the London daily press is insisting.  This may be so.  Yet it is curious to note that Great Britain, now, in the plethora of her power, appealed to by all the leading voices of the day to act as if for her existence, has actually made a voluntary response which falls greatly short of the effort made by the England of George III. on the receipt of the news of Burgoyne's surrender at Saratoga.  And this is so, measured not by a relative but by an absolute standard.  The war fund of 1778 was greater by more than half a million, the number of regiments raised exceeded greatly any total that can be reliably formed of the various regiments of Light Horse and the City of London Imperial Volunteers.  In 1778 regiments were raised not only by the Corporation of the City of London but also by those of other great towns.  This is all the more significant, because the division of feeling in the country at the time of the War of Independence is an historical fact, and one fully realised at the time.  It does not seem logical, on this parallel, to assume the popularity of the present war.  Whether, however, the present Ministry correctly interpreted the signs of the day and the voice of the constituencies in declaring war is an affair of the past.  Events like the relief of Ladysmith and Kimberley, and the victory of Paardeberg are decisive events that constitute fundamental facts as certainly as " the stricken field " of Omdurman.  The question is, what is to come ?  This question can only be postponed, and not averted, by the prolongation of the war.  Military men, who now contend that an indefinite duration of the war is the leading probability, before the outbreak of hostilities urged that the war would be over in a fortnight.  If the war is to be prolonged, it can only assume the character of a guerilla war.  Sir William Napier points out that, according to the object lesson afforded by the Spaniards in the Peninsular War, guerilla operations can never be decisive.  The capture of Fernando del Figueras was the only event of importance that the Somatenes and Miguelets contributed to in the whole war, and it had no determining influence.

The political problem awaiting our statesmen, among whom, no doubt, will be Lord Roberts, is at this hour of much more importance than the military problem, in the absence of the improbable event of intervention. That the last contingency may arise is, of course, not impossible. Prince Bismarck declared on one occasion that Africa would be the grave of English power, and, in his last speech in the German Reichstag, declared that the Oriental crisis was due in "1899 or a little later." If these predictions arrive we should be tottering to our fall, but not in Africa alone. If, however, these vaticinations, like those of Lord Rosebery and Lord Kimberley, are to be dismissed as too "lugubrious," we shall, in any event, be faced with a political problem in South Africa none graver than which can ever have distracted the counsels of a British Cabinet. Our military successes, present or impending, will not help us any more than the fall of Charlestown or "the stricken field" of Eutaw Springs at the close of the War of Independence served to retain America under the British flag.

It is curious to note how adverse a conjunction of circumstances awaits us. Even in the sphere of law, where comparative equality might be looked for, this awaits us. The Cape rebel of to-day will complain, like the Irish rebel of 1798, that he is tried by harsher laws of treason than, as a subject of the Crown, he ought to be. The Irish rebel of 1798, who contended through his counsel that he ought only to be condemned on the evidence of two witnesses, as would have been the case if he had been tried in England, had hardly as much ground of complaint against legal anomaly as the Cape rebel of to-day, who will find his charge involves forfeiture, though that has been abolished nearly thirty years in this country. It would be safe to say that the full severity of the law will operate in the one case as it did in the other, only to aggravate the passions of the hour and lay the seeds of dissension and agitation in the not far distant future. Only too true is it to say that Great Britain will in South Africa have another Ireland on her hands. In this age, unlike that of Chatham, "the patriots" are in power and not in Opposition. The greatest writer on patriotism in the English language, Bolingbroke, was not only out of office at the time, but was prevented by law from taking his seat in the House of Lords. St. John declared that "civil fury" had no place in his vision of patriotism, or that, if it had, the monster is there

> " Centum vinctus ahenis
> Post tergum nodis, fremit horridus ore cruento."

The fact that our Empire, in South Africa at all events, is distracted by internecine strife ought not to prevent us from playing the good part of pacification and reform, which alone can make in this country, or in any other, a united people.

N. W. SIBLEY, B.A., LL.M.

# OUR SOUTH AFRICAN COLONISTS:
## THEIR ULTIMATE ATTITUDE.

It is proposed to trace out here what would appear to be a hidden danger to the British Empire of the most serious description, arising indirectly from those very measures which we are now taking with a view to preserving and extending that Empire!

Surely by now we ought to realise that to lay clearly before Englishmen the possible dangers before them and all their probable remoter consequences, so far from being "pro-Boer" is, rightly considered, the highest and truest form of patriotism, as manifestly it is only by boldly facing such dangers in time, that our leaders can by any possibility forestall them, or, if they are inevitable, minimise their extent.

The number of complications and indirect consequences, some of them likely and some certain, to arise from the South African war, is almost legion. At the present junction the more passionate nature of our sentiments, having worn off, it is possible to draw attention to some of these consequences; whilst Mr. Balfour's confession of ineptitude and Sir. M. W. Ridley's confession of pitiful ignorance in regard to this question, and the Ministerial statement that the "man in the street" knows as much as Cabinet Ministers, would seem to make it the imperative duty of the former to scent out for himself all further dangers that may lie ahead, in order that our leaders may be prevented from learning of their existence only by the time-honoured plan of flattening their noses up against them in a state of total unpreparedness.

It will be necessary, first, to deal with South Africa itself, and then to consider how the effects of the consequences of the South African war must, and will, spread and influence all our other colonies in turn.

In dealing with South Africa it is here proposed to consider the question from an entirely new standpoint, one which, so far, has been totally overlooked by the whole of our Press, i.e., *from the ultimate point of view of the English colonist.* To arrive at some understanding of what that view, in the nature of things, must ultimately be, it will be necessary to deal in detail with various factors making for dissatisfaction and finally disaffection.

From the tone of our Press one would imagine that the English colonist loved his dusky brother, and was in the habit of treating him in the manner desired by the Aborigines Protection Society. Let us, however, dismiss this cant from our minds, and remember that *our* ideas of how the blacks should be treated are the ideas of fireside philanthropists, totally unacquainted with that same dusky brother, and far removed from the contemplation and effects of his "little ways," and, moreover, whose business and pockets are in no way affected by his position or treatment. To take a humorous illustration, if, as is stated by a correspondent in the *Morning Post* a short time ago, the Boers are "dirty, loathsome blackguards of brutal Boer beasts," then, in heaven's name, what must the black be? But, to return to common sense, if we will trouble to revive some of our latent impressions gained from descriptions of the savage races given by travellers, we must, in our inner consciousness, admit that the Englishman in the Cape, who is in daily contact with him and employs him to do his work, is likely to have ideas on the subject strikingly at variance with our own. And it is a fact that the Home Government exercises a controlling hand over the colonies in regard to the treatment of the native races, a subject which, of all others, affects the colonists most vitally. If any one is not convinced by this reasoning, let him discuss the subject with some colonist, preferably with one of the gentler sex, assuming in that discussion the *rôle* of the Aborigines Protection Society, and it may be safely predicted that the tone of voice and the facial expression even more than the words uttered, will be for him quite a revelation.

It is by no means a secret to those who have followed South African affairs, that many an act of the Home Government has met with anything but the unqualified approval of the colonies. As to this occasional misgovernment, lack of statesmanship—call it what you will—there is a clear and irrefutable demonstration. Was the policy of Mr. Gladstone's Government in 1881 a just and sound policy—then how pitifully incompetent that of the present Government. Is Lord Salisbury's policy a just and sound one now—then how pitifully incompetent that of Mr. Gladstone!

Our own views are narrowed by party feeling; we are quite satisfied if we can say that any particular piece of bungling was the work of those rascals—the opposite political party; but to the colonies it is the simple issue of incompetent home control, their feelings are by no means calmed by the thought that it was the action of this or that party.

The question of the concomitant evils of war is a large one, and certain to breed much discontent. Far removed from the scene of actual hostilities, the worst *we* have to fear (setting aside the feelings of the families of the killed and wounded) is heavy taxes, and the indirect damage to trade arising therefrom.    For the English colonist, however, it is a very different matter.

Some considerable time back the official figures of the Cape Colony railways showed a very marked falling off (trusting entirely to memory, it was something like 20 per cent.).    A little consideration will show how very serious a matter this is for the colonists; decreased profits for the sounder merchants, practical bankruptcy for many of the weaker ones, and the loss of employment amongst the inferior descriptions of employees, are only among the more direct consequences.    That falling off in trade must by now be much greater.    There is in addition the increased price of the necessities of life, which means the virtual reduction of the incomes of all classes by a very perceptible percentage, a description of loss which could hardly be, and most assuredly will never be, compensated for by the Mother Country.    But, perhaps, most serious of all are the direct losses to some of the inhabitants of those parts of the colonies which have been invaded—actual destruction of property and the total cessation of business, in addition to more or less serious damage to health caused by mental and nervous strain.

At present these evils are being suffered more or less heroically, although the well-informed have even now indications of a disposition to murmur.    As time progresses, and more pronouncedly when the war is over and the shouts of victory have died away, the present faint murmurs will develop into a sound of greater portent.

The disproportion between the price we pay and that paid by our colonists must, in the nature of things, force itself on their attention, and their train of thought will follow these lines :

" After all, this was not *our* war; we did not want the franchise in the Transvaal ; neither did we stand in urgent need of extension of territory—there is enough, and more than enough, room in the colony for us and ours.    Why, then, have we been squeezed between the two combatants, and broken on the wheel ? "    This will be a very heavy item to the debit of England's account.

It may be safely predicted that when the war is terminated (even presuming that we succeed in completely crushing the Boer forces) it will be impossible for England to attempt to deprive the Boers of civic rights ; such an attempt would be altogether too open a confession of the " unctuousness " of our " equal rights " " rectitude." (Have Englishmen, who so profoundly believe in Mr. Rhodes's whole-souled devotion to the Mother Country, forgotten that charming description of us which he uttered?)    And it may further be safely predicted that nothing short of absolute deprivation of such rights will content the English colonists—indeed, any other policy will raise the keenest and fiercest resentment against England.    Months ago already the Natal Press was clamorously advocating this course ;

but, completely absorbed in gazing rapturously at each kharki-clad
volunteer, we are totally blind to such trifles as the passage of the
straws in the air that indicate to the observant mind the coming of
a hurricane.

(By the way, the mention of the word "kharki" suggests some
curious speculations; a cynic might be excused for believing that
the prevalent ignorance of the meaning of that word has lent no
little support to the war fever—a word so mysterious that the newspapers have not even yet adopted a uniform spelling of it, conjures
up in the popular mind vague visions of glory and something
fearfully military! Suppose it had been translated and a certain
famous line had run thus, "A gentleman in mud (colour) going
South!" The effect would have been as electrical as that produced
by the actual wording, but perhaps in another sense.)

The enormous strengthening of militarism in this country by the
present war and by the vast increase of the number of men under
arms, must presently be reflected in the conduct of our Government,
which will assume a more military and dictatorial character in every
department. Here at home we are growing so accustomed to
socialistic legislation and governmental dictation that that autocratic
tendency will certainly for a time meet with but feeble opposition;
but in the colonies, where the assertion of individual liberty is still
the prevailing note, the autocratic tendency which will mark the
home Government's dealings with them, will meet with sudden and
vehement opposition.

This state of affairs will be arrived at sooner in South Africa than
elsewhere, for this reason : autocratic action will, as a matter of fact,
be really necessary for some time to come, even assuming a speedy
and victorious termination of the campaign ; firstly, because this is
always necessary in districts which have been recently engaged in
hostilities, and more especially because the majority of the population are Dutch who, conspiracy or no conspiracy, must be in *sympathy*
with their own race ; and it would be quite impossible to use such
discrimination that the Dutch alone felt the military heel.

Before the present universal outburst of patriotism there were
many English colonists whose opinion of the British soldier was
curiously similar to that held by the Boers, the only difference was
the language in which it was expressed: to the Boer he was a
"verdomde rooinek"; to the colonist, a "damned redcoat." Nay,
when the causes for that opinion are considered, it would appear but
logical and reasonable to assume that that opinion was very widespread, if not universal. The writer has heard these reasons set
forth almost identically in the following words by colonists unknown
to one another: "You send out your redcoats to put things right;
they come here, swagger about as though they were the lords of
creation, and then muddle things up completely ; what it takes

them months to effect in their thousands we can do in weeks in our hundreds." The bungling that has almost invariably characterised our South African wars, compared to the efficiency of the small bodies of local volunteers, has, it must be admitted, but naturally created this opinion. Moreover, unfortunately so far, the actual effective work done by our troops in this war is not calculated to inspire any one with great opinions of their efficiency.

There are slight indications which go to show that there is already considerable danger of this old hostility to the English troops reviving. The stories of the resignation of colonial volunteer officers on account of the domineering conduct of the English officers, and of the strained relations between Colonel Kekewich and Mr. Rhodes, are very painful reading. The root causes of these frictions are not far to seek. Our ideas of good breeding have as a most essential factor great outward respect for, and deference to, the feelings and fads of others, but the colonial mind runs on the more robust lines of paying little deference to any one. Without going into the question of the respective virtues and vices of these two systems of training, it can be perfectly understood how the English officer, meeting for the first time with this peculiar spirit, and misunderstanding it, may assume a frigid reserve, which in its turn is interpreted as an assumption of " damned superiority."

We may anticipate the day when Gould will produce another cartoon on the lines of " Such a Surprise," depicting Mr. Chamberlain showing an item of South African news to the Secretary for War, and ejaculating, " Fancy, Lansdowne! they actually don't like our soldiers ! "

There is now being created in South Africa a quite considerable army of colonists, the existence of which will automatically give the colonists a greater sense of their importance and independence, and this must, of course, materially aggravate those frictions already referred to. The existence of an army that has done good work is always apt to foster a sense of self-sufficiency, whether towards foreign powers, suzerain powers, or mother countries.

The chief occupation of the warrior in all times and all countries, after fighting, has always been love. Bearing this fact in mind (for it is a fact), while we need not necessarily anticipate that this little weakness will produce any alteration in the loyalty of the woman-folk of the colonies, it is but reasonable to assume that the effect, in the course of time, on the male colonists will be very unfortunate; and this without taking into account the effect of the isolated acts of actual blackguardism and crime that must occur where tens of thousands of troops are fighting, an effect that will be enormously out of proportion to the actual causes themselves.

The fact is that the presence of an army from the Mother Country in any free English colony must always be fraught with more or-less danger. The effect produced by a quite small garrison is negligeable, but when the number of troops becomes large the resulting frictions are always liable to become serious.

It is now known that we will have, all told, in South Africa, about 193,000 men for the crushing of the two Republics. Two conclusions must present themselves to the colonists from this fact :

The first, that the protection from foreign aggression (which is the main object for which the colonies remain attached to the Mother Country) afforded by such soldiers is not of much account ; this is an illogical conclusion, for their relative want of success against the Boer and Boer methods in no way militates against their efficiency for warding off foreign interference, but it is of the simple and apparently just description that is sure to appeal to the popular mind.

Secondly, that if such immense forces are required for that purpose, then at least 450,000 men would be necessary to crush the British colonies should they desire to secede. The population of the two Republics is supposed to be something like 297,350, and this number included the Uitlanders ; while Cape Colony and Natal have a population of about 500,000. Neither Germany nor France (the only countries that could even entertain the idea of attempting to subdue the colonies) could dare to send that number of men abroad, for very evident reasons affecting them nearer home. But, apart from those reasons, there is the actual physical difficulty. The greatest maritime power in the world has required four months to send out 130,000 or so, that would mean a twelvemonth at least to send 450,000 men ; and these men could be destroyed piecemeal as they arrived, for they would not be able to land at friendly ports and collect into considerable bodies before advancing as we have done, but would have to fight even to gain a landing.

All these influences and conclusions working on the colonial mind must, in the natural order of things, revive the idea (which always lies dormant at the back of every English colonist's mind) that independence has much to be said in its favour, and that perhaps the necessity and virtue of loyalty to the old country has been greatly overestimated.

To emphasise this we must remember that the foundation of all loyalty and patriotism is, necessarily, a lively sense of the advantages derived from belonging to any particular race or country—and once it is demonstrated that the imagined advantages do not exist—but that, on the contrary, a subordinate position is being occupied to no good purpose, and at the cost of manifold sentimental and solid disadvantages, that loyalty is bound to perish.

The loyalty of the colonies of a race famed for its spirit of independence, must always be a delicate plant, and must require careful nurturing. This statement is borne out by the fact that in our rela-

-tions with our colonies it is our general principle to deal with them in gloved hands. The Mother Country maintains an enormous navy and large army for the protection of the whole Empire—a very large part of the expense being necessary on account of the colonies —to which the colonies (excepting to an infinitesimal extent) do not contribute—although the individual colonist is more capable of bearing taxation than the individual Englishman. The colonies are permitted to tax our goods, whilst we admit theirs free.

The relationship of mother and offspring being thus much more strikingly followed out than is usually noticed, the offspring regarding the parent as a bountiful providence from which all things are to be received, and so soon as the parent has nothing more to give, but needs assistance from the offspring, she will be regarded as an old nuisance, and will be relegated to a back place.

The views set forth here are in no way intended in a disparaging spirit to anybody or anything; they have been developed simply from an effort to trace out how the ordinary everyday workings of human feelings and instincts must ultimately affect the history of our Empire.

In a serious attempt to foresee coming events it is surely quite useless to take the enthusiast's point of view; the commonplace view is the more reliable one. An illustration of what is here meant may be obtained by a little introspection. Does anybody really believe that any of even the most ardent "patriots" of the hour will henceforth tell the Income Tax Commissioners the truth, the whole truth, and nothing but the truth? Assuredly not. That being so, is it common sense to make our calculations for the future on the assumption that *others* are going to allow their patriotism to stand in the way of their material interests?

Carried away by the enthusiasm born of the thumping of the war drum, we will not readily admit that the causes here set forth could breed disaffection in the hearts of the English colonists, but for guidance on that point let us review the causes of the American revolt. The American colonies suffered under no real grievances whatever; the duties imposed upon them originally were ethically absolutely just: they amounted to £100,000 a year, and were imposed to contribute towards the expense of a war undertaken partly in their interests. These duties were removed, and the fresh taxes that caused the actual outbreak were estimated only to yield £40,000 a year. The grievance was a purely sentimental one: "No taxation without representation;" and our persistence in the matter was curiously enough wrapped up with the determination to demonstrate on principle our "absolute supremacy."

Against this trifling grievance let us recapitulate those of our South African colonies: the hampering of South African trade by interference in regard to the control of their methods of treating the native races; the terrible damage to life and property, loss of occupation, &c., caused by the war—a war brought on by our lack of statesmanship and aggravated by incompetent management; the great revival of race hatred, which in many ways deducts from the ease and pleasantness of life and indirectly affects trade; the sentimental grievances and isolated acts of actual blackguardism caused by the presence of our army; the old memories of sundry vetoes placed upon desires and schemes of the colonists; and the tendency to a domineering form of government born of the revived militarism.

In the face of this comparison can it be denied that, the first causes having as a matter of history produced revolt and secession, the second are infinitely more than enough to produce identical results?

The question then arises, at what period is this spirit likely to develop into action? In all probability nothing definite will happen during the continuance of hostilities; in various directions there will be indications of smouldering embers, that is all; these will be allowed to pass unheeded, the individuals here and there who venture to draw attention to them will be scorned as fools or pessimists. The moment of danger will be when the bulk of our troops are withdrawn, leaving behind them only garrisons just sufficient to maintain the public peace. Then, when a master hand has matured his plans and fed the flames of discontent, all that will be necessary will be the investment of the small garrisons, which will finally have to suffer a bloodless defeat in the form of surrender to starvation—and a declaration of independence. A reply to such a declaration in the form of force would, for the reasons given, be obviously utterly hopeless, and the old country would have to accept the dismemberment of the Empire in impotent rage.

As to the master hand, where is he to be found? We have not far to seek; we will find him in the person of Mr. Cecil Rhodes. To those whose admiration of this remarkable man tends to idolisation such an assertion will seem little short of sacrilege; such a view is, however, short-sighted and unreasonable. It is Mr. Rhodes's very greatness that marks him out for the work. We in our patriotic conceit imagine that it must be the highest of all joys and the utmost limit of ambition, even for the most remarkable men, to be our servants or superior vassals. But if we recall the history of all times, what more familiar character is there than the subject who, having risen to a great position, chafes at the restraints of the established order, and either assumes the reins of power directly, if his sphere of action lies immediately under the head of the Empire, or, if it is in an outlying part of the Empire, severs the connection and founds an independent community. Cromwell, originally fighting to limit the power of the rulers, finally became the ruler himself. Washington, originally only endeavouring to remove a more or less sentimental grievance, finally tore off a portion of the Empire and founded an independent community. The Napoleons, originally dutiful servants of the State, finally became masters and Emperors. But why continue quoting instances; they are legion—'tis but the natural order of creation. Human nature will never brook control when it feels and knows its own power to be master. The only check to this tendency is when circumstances do not offer a ripe soil to work upon; given the occasion and the man, and the result is a foregone conclusion.

Remembering the incapacity, absent-mindedness—call it what you will—of our control in South Africa, let us ask ourselves what man, having lofty and vast schemes of empire, would not chafe at that control, and burn to cast it off.

Mr. Rhodes is a great man; but that has ceased to be matter for gratulation for us, and has become a danger. He holds a position absolutely unique for the great work of gathering together the smouldering embers that lie strewn about unobserved, and carefully fanning them into an irresistible flame. Rhodes's very greatness is our threatening danger.

May we not say that, having used Mr. Chamberlain as a tool by which to obtain the present war, Mr. Rhodes will now throw him aside and work out South Africa's future single-handed; or, to give a new application to phrases of recent fame, having wiped out the old South African problems, he will cast aside this "squeezed sponge," and himself work out the new problems on the "clean slate"?

The independence of South Africa might take the form of two groups of federated states—the first the Transvaal and Orange Free State; the second the English colonies. But more probably it would take the form of one group only, comprising the whole of the Dutch and English territories. This latter idea will at the first blush appear nonsensical—the idea of an alliance between Rhodes and the Dutch will appear the very quintessence of absurdity. There are, however, considerations that give the matter a very different aspect. The English in Cape Colony are largely outnumbered by the Boers, and so long as equal voting rights continue to exist there may now be said to be practically no chance of the English party ever obtaining a majority in Parliament; this will constitute a galling yoke to the English. (The idea of equal rights combined with English supremacy is of course the most absurd paradox that has ever been propounded by Ministers in a fix.) On the other hand, it is evident that the English of Cape Colony could never hope to subjugate the Dutch.

Federation would open up an outlet from this *impasse* which, whilst satisfying the Dutch and no less satisfying the English, would offer the Transvaal and Orange Free State an absolute guarantee against any further danger from Mr. Rhodes.

Cape Colony would be divided into two separate states, a southern band of territory running round the coast, which contains all the large towns and a great majority of English; and a northern internal region, populated almost exclusively by Dutch. Under such an arrangement, the vast majority of the English and Dutch would have their own government, whilst the fact of small minorities remaining in *both* states, would be a guarantee for their each receiving absolutely fair and equal treatment. Whilst, in addition, this arrangement, giving a predominance to the Dutch and Boer States, would constitute the Boers' guarantee against all further interference; and the Imperial factor being removed, there would remain no conceivable object whatsoever for the fantastic idea of attempting to drive the English *colony* into the sea—a colony that would be totally powerless to attempt any sort of effective aggression whatever against the Boer and Dutch peoples.

Mr. Rhodes is the man who did more than any other to remove race prejudices and make the government of South Africa run smoothly. He can still be the greatest force to accomplish that end, and whilst at present the Boers must naturally be consumed with the desire for revenge, yet as the master-hand for carrying out such a scheme as the above which would guarantee the Boers against any further trouble from him, there is every reason to believe that a man of President Kruger's remarkable powers and astuteness could not only master his feelings in regard to old scores, but even receive him with open arms.

One can imagine this chain of reasoning calling forth the exclamations "Exaggeration," "Fantastic," and truly those words are happily applied. But what more fantastic than the humble colonial George Washington bidding defiance to England, and sending her about her business? What more fantastic than the obscure Corsican lieutenant as Emperor of France and Master of Europe, than the youth Alexander sighing for more worlds to conquer? Fantastic exaggeration, indeed; but the common attribute of remarkable figures in history.

So excellent is our government in the great majority of cases that we are apt, in our pride of Empire, to assume that any arrangement independent of us could not possibly be good, but a consideration of the scheme outlined above will show that it seems to offer a solution of all *real* South African difficulties (that is from the point of view of the permanent inhabitants of South Africa) so excellent as to render it extremely doubtful whether any equally good could be devised under our dominion—and may, therefore, well give us reason to pause and reflect in our headlong course.

We now come to the question, How will these events eventually affect our other colonies?

The factors are, of course, the same as those in South Africa. The feeling of responsibility and independence born of the possession of a body of troops who have given a good account of themselves in the field; the knowledge that the Mother Country's protection is needless, born of their close observance of events in South Africa, and their perfect schooling in the art of defending a country with a sparse population against a great military power; these are the seeds of dismemberment that are being planted, and the forcing house necessary to make them sprout will be the autocratic tone of our Government, born of revived militarism. . Added to this there is the great influence of example—if South Africa can stand on its own legs, then why not we? And the possibility having been demonstrated there will be no lack of colonial statesmen willing to gain laurels by posing as deliverers, and with this end in view nothing will be easier than for them to manufacture any number of grievances in order to work up public feeling.

Let statesmen among us (if there be any worthy of that name—which may well be doubted) take warning of the great dangers ahead, cease to confine their range of vision to the single issue of crushing the Boer, and in a spirit of the truest patriotism endeavour to gain a masterly grasp of this vast subject—only permitting that particular item of it to occupy a justly proportioned space, lest, in our ostrich-like pursuance of a policy which we have allowed ourselves to be dragged into, but which no one among us would have deliberately adopted if he had foreseen a tithe of the dangers, we by our very efforts to maintain and enlarge that Empire of which we are so justly proud, bring upon ourselves the Nemesis of Dismemberment.

A. W. LIVESEY.

# THE TWENTIETH-CENTURY NOVEL

## A CRITICAL DIALOGUE.

SCENE: THE DORIC CLUB.

SPEAKERS: REDMOND O'NEILL, *an Irishman in London addicted to Realism.* MARK TILLOTSON, *an Englishman who has written several popular novels.*

REDMOND: In my opinion, the twentieth-century novel will not be fiction, but a stern record of facts. It will unveil men's, and women's, inner history. It will be a perfectly unconventional description of the mental and physical evolution of human beings.

MARK: Not a bit of it! We are really growing more artificial every day. Modern inventions have made us less dependent on nature. We don't want to be natural. We don't care a straw about other people's "inner history." The novels that the next generation will read will be artificial novels.

REDMOND: Like Richardson's *Sir Charles Grandison*, you mean.

MARK: No; I don't mean anything like *Sir Charles Grandison*. The works of Mr. Wells are more like the sort of fiction that will please our grandchildren. Why should not the novelist write a "thrilling" story suggested by the possibilities of electricity?

REDMOND: I would not call such a story a *novel* at all. *Peter Wilkins and his Flying Bride* would be up-to-date, in your sense, for it presents us with a description of a flying woman.

MARK: In the future it is possible flying women may exist.

REDMOND: God forbid! That would be a thousand times worse than the lady-bicyclist.

MARK: You are rather unprogressive for a realist, O'Neill. Do you want to go back to the days when women were content to stay at home and do knitting or embroidery?

REDMOND: The women who "did knitting or embroidery" were incomparably more charming, more lovable, more womanly, in the best sense of the word, than your "new women," who, to use Edgar Allan Poe's words, are "neither men nor women, neither beast nor human."

MARK: You are rather severe on the cult inaugurated by my friend Sarah Grand. After all, her ideal of woman is a high one.

Her Evadne declares that the man she marries must be " a Christlike man."

REDMOND: What insufferable cant! A Christlike man, if there be such a thing in modern life, would not marry Sarah Grand's priggish and ridiculous heroine. The real Christ associated with " publicans and sinners," and the one woman to whom, next to His mother, He paid most attention was Mary Magdalene—a female whom Mrs. Grundy and her votaries would specify as " a creature."

MARK: I am afraid your Christianity is not orthodox.

REDMOND: Neither is that of Tolstoy.

MARK: Oh! Tolstoy has created a peculiar Christ to suit his own fads.

REDMOND: Every man forms his own estimate of Christ. For my part, I don't profess to be " a good Christian "—or even " a respectable member of society."

MARK: Have you any religion at all ?

REDMOND: Yes; I am like the Master of Arts in Oliver Wendell Holmes's *Poet at the Breakfast-Table*—the only religion that could ever contain me is " the human religion."

MARK: Pooh! That is cant, too, just as much as the platitudes of Silas Hocking and the Nonconformist school of fiction.

REDMOND: Well, we were talking not of religion, but of the novel. *Revenons à nous moutons !*

MARK: I thought Irishmen were always irrelevant. However, you studied law and were called to the *Irish* Bar, so you must know something about " relevancy " and " questions at issue."

REDMOND: The question at issue now is—What sort of novels will be read in the twentieth century ?

MARK: Perhaps the best answer would be, all sorts of novels— novels realistic and novels romantic, novels scientific and novels artistic, novels political and novels polemical, novels spiritualistic and novels pornographic, sex novels and sexless novels, historical novels and unhistorical novels, novels of the boudoir and novels of the gutter. So, you see, every scribbler who is able to write any kind of decent fiction will get a chance.

REDMOND: Your list reminds me of Polonius's catalogue of plays. I don't agree with you as to the catholicity and comprehensiveness of twentieth-century readers' tastes. My idea is that naturalism, as defined by Zola, will culminate in the production of works photographing the most minute details in the lives of the most insignificant human beings.

MARK: If that be so, the novel of the future will be confoundedly dull.

REDMOND: Not at all. The motto of every novelist worth his salt should be: *Homo sum ; nihil humani.*

MARK : For heaven's sake, don't quote a dead language! I've heard that unhappy quotation before !

REDMOND : Make it the text of your next novel.

MARK : Certainly not! That learned bore, the late Professor Ebers—of course, he was a German and could not help being a pedant—made it the title of one of his dullest books.   I will write English or nothing.   I will try, too, in my next novel to delineate fairly the aristocratic side of English life, and to show that ours is the finest aristocracy in the world.

REDMOND : Don't expect me to agree with that statement.   It is is worthy of a fellow countryman of Theodore Hook and Thackeray. The author of the *Book of Snobs* was himself a thorough snob. Having regard to his caddish criticism of poor Bulwer Lytton, I would be even inclined to say worse things of him.

MARK (*rather warmly*) : Let Thackeray rest in his grave!   He was a great Englishman, and one of the aristocracy of talent. Unlike Dickens, and unlike Lord Lytton, he knew how to portray an English gentleman.   As to latter-day snobbism, it is mainly confined to Ireland, so far as the British Isles are concerned, and to the United States.

REDMOND : You are wrong.   The snob, from an ethnological point of view, had his birthplace in England.   He emigrated to America and has returned to his native land a worse snob than ever. Imperialism is a bad form of snobbery, and Rudyard Kipling is popular in England because he is an Imperialistic snob, with a touch of the Hooligan.

MARK : I disagree with you.   He is a fine fellow.   His short stories are splendid, and his verses are the best ever written of their kind.

REDMOND : *De gustibus non est disputandum.*

MARK (*angrily*) : Good God !   Will you stop quoting Latin !   It sets my teeth on edge.

REDMOND (*laughing sarcastically*) : I am glad, at any rate, you recognise the fact that it *is* Latin.   In this age of decadence, even professional novelists are infected with the snobbery of ignorance. Only one living novelist can write decent English—George Meredith. Even Thomas Hardy over and over again uses that barbarous word " scientist."

MARK : Ridiculous purism !

REDMOND : By no means.   The purity of a language is as sacred a thing as the chastity of a woman.   Flaubert knew this, and, there-fore, his works have enriched the French language.   And I agree with what the best French critics say—that, as long as the French language remains uncorrupted the heart of France will be sound.

MARK (*with a sneer*) : The heart of France !   It is rotten to the core !   What about the Dreyfus case ?

REDMOND : Let us not discuss it ! We were talking about the twentieth-century novel. I hope it will not be a mere childish fable, like *Jack the Giant-Killer.* It should be as minute as a *procès-verbal* and as instantaneously impressive as a photograph. It should possess the verisimilitude of Defoe, the scientific exactitude of Flaubert and Zola, and the masculine plain-speaking of Maupassant.

MARK : What pedantry you talk, O'Neill! Is Ireland going to realise your conception of the typical twentieth-century novel ?

REDMOND : Who knows ? Sterne was an Irishman.

MARK : He was born there by accident.

REDMOND : Oh! every man's birthplace is an accident. Shakespeare was a Celt, though he was born on English soil.

MARK : I emphatically deny that Shakespeare was a Celt.

REDMOND : Well, at any rate, he wrote good English. And I hope the twentieth-century novel will be written in good English.

D. F. HANNIGAN.

# THE CENTENARY OF COWPER.

IN this age the crowd of literature is so thronged that little but the names of our first writers of an earlier age are kept green, whilst their works for the most part lie undusted and unopened on the library shelf. Milton is too prolix, Spenser too discursive; to study them one must plead an idle illness. Shakespeare still lives supreme, but these associates of the bay wreath are like fountains lost in the thicket, out of reach to all save the honest and hardy explorer. Like sharer of their fate is the author of *The Task,* whose centenary we should at this time be celebrating.

But unhonoured save by the carving of his own works, and a eulogy written by a contemporary friend, William Cowper lives before us to-day after a lapse of a hundred years. His writings are not largely read, perhaps because he is unequal in quality and hyper-sentimental, a contrast to the tribute he paid himself to the verse of Johnson in 1785, which he characterised as being "grave, masculine, and strong." By a peculiar irony we are most closely in touch with him in an epic that is least responsive to his own mood. All, at one time or another, have read and laughed over the story of John Gilpin, racing on his mad career with the broken flagons at his belt and wig left far behind. The very humour contained therein would convert the Puritan or Paedo-Baptist, and all have fondled in their youth—and are we ashamed to add also in their manhood?—the inimitable sketches drawn by Mr. Caldecott that immortalised the incident. The sketch itself owed its birth to a happy chance. The wild gallop was not a myth, though Cowper himself was not an eye-witness of the occurrence. He had listened attentively to a lady's tale, and had been amused. By way of return he composed the incident in verse as he lay thinking at night, and delivered it in writing to her on the following morning. To such fortunate accidents the poet owed many a theme. He was a keen annotator rather than an original thinker. He would have borrowed an expression from Chaucer and called himself an artist in words of things he actually saw; he did not often enter into the half-shut library of imagination. He is an historian in verse rather than a sportsman in allegory, and, without approaching the author of the *Canterbury Tales* in colour or in style, there existed between them a quaint likeness. Cowper was the half-shadow of Chaucer. Both were men of a retiring disposition and of abstract thought. Neither cared for the world around them, a land of loose morality, and yet, though they held aloof, they described the frolics and careless laxity of their age with magnetic vividness and a piquant touch. It pleased them to condemn, and they pronounced their censure with merciless chiding. There was no lack of material, social history bears record of the truth and justice of their imputations, but it is curious to find two writers so different in diction aiming at a single object to sweep clean a nation's garner of thoughtless passion. There was the desire on the part of both to check the prevailing wantonness and profligacy of the times, to raise the Church to a higher level, and to teach the laws of religion. It was on that account that Chaucer aimed his fiercest attack against those sturdy indolent beggars, the friars; and Cowper plunged his weapon to its farthest point into the flesh of the clergy,

> " Loose in morals and in manners vain,
> In conversation frivolous, and in dress extreme."

This rebuke was the more direct because he follows immediately with an exordium of their befitting behaviour. " I venerate the man," he writes in the second book of *The Task,* " whose heart is warm, whose hands are pure, whose doctrine and whose life coincident exhibit lucid proof that he is honest in the sacred cause."

His best friends—men like the Rev. J. Newton—were clergymen, a factor which, in its sharp contrast, seems to have made the poet even more virulent against a much abused class of men, who " slip into the rostrum, pronounce a text, cry hem! read what they never wrote—just fifteen minutes—and stare and strut theatric practis'd in a glass."

Cowper refers, in an amusing allusion to a subject that provoked a passing storm in the House of Commons in July last, namely, to the trouble and friction incurred in the collection of tithes. He describes how the farmers congregate on pay-day, are made at home, and requested to sit down to a heavy dinner and to drink a bowl of punch. But this substantial hospitality none of them enjoy, because all are conscious that the meal is preliminary to the settlement, and all are calculating how far they can cheat the parson of his due by making the early frost or the late hail an excuse for lightening their levy. But, failing in these artifices,

> " Quoth one, a rarer man than you, in pulpit none shall hear,
> But yet, methinks, to tell you true, you sell it plagu'y dear."

Then, with a play upon words, the poet moralises in conclusion,

> "Oh, why are farmers made so coarse or clergy made so fine ! "

The cause of this high aim to treat religious topics with a hyper-

bolic seriousness, of this pessimism of all things existent was due
to a morbid sensibility on the part of Cowper. A prey to a diseased
mind, life became to him more and more of a misery, a sentence of
atonement, which all had to suffer. He was subject to fits of
melancholia, a lenient phrase for temporary insanity. There was
always a creeping fear that his malady would return. He fretted
over his own exaggerated wickedness, whilst he spent his time, to
quote from one of his own letters, "in forecasting the fashion of
uncertain evils." Had he been a man in sound physical health, his
fatal brooding would have been overpowered by a robust vitality.
In his early days he was of a boisterous and *débonnaire* nature, and
his comrades, who used to live with him in the Temple, where all
learnt to idle, must have wondered at the change in his temperament. He might have shone as a legal luminary, perhaps as a
Bailey Court wit, but it is doubtful whether he would have ever
spent much of his time in London. He had little love for the
metropolis. He saw it resplendent with riches but contaminated
with vices; by taste and wealth proclaimed the fairest capital of all
the world, by riot and incontinence the worst. He pauses over
London's advantages, over her possessions wherein are kept the
treasures of Reynolds and Bacon; where, also, can be heard the
eloquence of Chatham; where philosophy has become so perfect
that the dark spots in the burning sun can be recounted; where an
atom can be measured or an earth girded; where there is a mart so
rich, so throng'd, so drain'd, and so supplied. But this

"Queen of cities is not to consider herself irreproachable. She is not so
fair but that she can be free of a charge of slackness in discipline, and more
prompt to avenge than to prevent the breach of law, that she is rigid in
denouncing death on petty robbers, and indulges life and liberty, and ofttimes honour too, to peculators of the public gold. That thieves at home
must hang, but he that puts into his over-gorg'd and bloated purse the
wealth of Indian provinces escapes."

In many of his arguments Cowper was the forerunner of other
thinkers. He was a philanthropist in verse, a solitary preacher,
who shrunk in horror from the ill order of society. The ease with
which men used to be hanged was worse than a scandal, but the
poet remained unheard, and no other advocate plagiarised his cause
before another thirty years, whether it was to plead for greater
sincerity amongst the clergy, greater equity in the administration of
justice, or greater humanity in the abolition of slavery. Not until
the sentence of death became so abnormal and constant was the
penalty for smaller crimes commuted to transportation. Equally
glaring was the reverse picture, in which the English nabobs passed
scatheless through the clutches of the law, and were able to amass
their wealth through a measure of fraud which none concerned
themselves to investigate. The public was not the brother's keeper

of those natives who suffered in silence between the shores of India. Cowper may have depicted their means of becoming rich too darkly, but he could not have been accused of libel, for all knew, as well as saw, how the penniless son of good birth would sail for the Indian Ocean, and, after a few years voluntary exile, would return with an income far beyond his proper salary. The military and naval professions were in those days, even as they stand now, rich in honour rather than gold. The clergy were in the same pecuniary embarrassment, except those, as Cowper avers, who formed a servile friendship with politicians in hope of preferment.

Cowper was aware that his tirades would be of little practical avail, but it rested his conscience to speak, even if none would hear. He had lived as those whom he now vilified. He had been ignorant of a future world and had obscured its image in the fierce voluptuous glare of the existing condition of society. He grew at last dissatisfied with himself, but he was puzzled at his own unhappiness. After much thought and anxious brooding his sensitive disposition unravelled the cause of his distress. This failing he has described in his *Table Talk*, which is a confession rather than a source of information, as was Selden's. He began to realise that he had lived without God. He was not at once "converted," for in drifting away from the riotous pleasures of mischief he felt himself in the outset moving more and more alone, a wanderer in search of the unattainable. He did not, however, sink to that miserable plight of despair such as afflicted so pitiably John Bunyan, who, according to Macaulay, became so frenzied that he was prompted by a maniacal impulse to pray to the trees around him, to a broomstick, or even to the parish bull.

The paralysis of emotion was identical, but Cowper was saved in his hypochondria by good chance, for whilst he was in this frame of mind he went to stay in the country. The quiet had a calming effect upon him, and the Bible was a new revelation which influenced him perceptibly, until he felt it a moral duty to teach to others, however modestly, what he had so laboriously striven to discover for himself. At the close of his first poem he ends with this confession:

> "I am no preacher, let this hint suffice—
> The Cross once seen, is death to every vice;
> Else He that hung there suffered all His pain,
> Bled, groan'd and agonis'd, and died in vain."

He discerned that nature had not formed all men in the same crucible. He recognised that some were led away by their own knowledge (be it observed that he would scarcely have used the word "wisdom" here, a word to which he gave a strictly spiritual meaning). He perceived that some were vainglorious apostates, others unlucky searchers in obscurity, and that heretics purposely

went astray to earn by their eccentricity a reputation short-lived.
Still faithful to rhyme, the poet speaks of them in the following
strain :

> "Thus men go wrong with an ingenious skill,
> Bend the straight rule to their own crooked will,
> And with a clear and shining lamp supplied,
> First put it out, then take it for their guide,
> Halting on crutches of unequal size
> One leg by truth supported, one by lies."

His hatred of such men, his biased intolerance, was no doubt
made more extravagant through his frail health, and his retiring
disposition helped to accentuate the morbid feeling.

If we choose to contrast another William, namely, William Morris,
we shall see how little of sympathy there was between these two
writers. The author of *News from Nowhere* was active, a hard
worker, an ideal thinker, muscular, and industrious ; the framer of
*The Task* was depressed, moody, an eremite to the world at large,
and a pessimist. Morris looked with contempt upon the man who
could not compose an epic at his seat at the tapestry loom, where
he might find music in the noise of the shuttle and harmony in the
harsh voices and loud laughter of those around. But Cowper hied
away from this pandemonium and sought the idyllic field, where
imagination was not murdered by distraction, where he could seek
the shade

> "With eager step and carelessly arrayed,"

where success in rhyme could depend upon the snowy robe of winter,
the summer heat, or where fruits and perfumes could transport the
glowing bard.

It is not, then, a matter for surprise that he should refer so
frequently to all the phases of varying nature, should have praised
so constantly her unalloyed freshness, and should have condemned
that artificial mockery of country scene which was springing up in
the suburbs of every town, where people drank in clouds of dust and
called it country air. At the same time, Cowper shows no striking
vigour in his descriptive passages. There is no manly fondness for
the frowning cliffs with their wrecking waves. He prefers, rather,
the earth brought under subjection, the garden, with its neatly
trimmed hedges and well-mown lawn. Such scenes own their
pretty attractiveness, but are without any inspiring grandeur. But
the poet loved to moon along the paths of the rectory where he lived.

> "Strength may wield the pond'rous spade,
> May turn the clod and wheel the compost home;
> But elegance, chief grace the garden shows,
> And most attractive is the fair result
> Of thought, the creature of a polished mind."

None will begrudge the writer his half-acre of Paradise, and none will be disinclined to agree with the sharp reprimand he gives to the spendthrift that wastes his substance and saves himself from ruin by selling his estates :

"He that saw his patrimonial timber cast its leaf, sells the last scantling and transfers the price to some shrewd sharper, ere it buds again. Estates are landscapes, gazed upon a while, then advertised and auctioneered away."

The green verdure of the country is Cowper's sacred carpet, and every one who in this busy map of life offends by abusing it or by overlooking it commits an unpardonable offence in the eyes of the poet. The shepherd-boy receives short shrift, because he is blind to the beauty around him. Even the politician meets with greater grace, because he recuperates his exhausted energies by sauntering into the village smithy and chats with the forger on important nothings. This temporary change leads Cowper to condone his many faults, but he knows that the statesman is only half-tamed, that the passion for politics is uppermost in his mind as an ineradicable flaw, and that he will before long blame his indolence and observe :

"Though late, 'tis criminal to leave a sinking state,
Flies to the levee, and, received with grace,
Kneels, kisses hands, and shines again in place."

Apart from the pardon the poet grants to the politician because he has paid an awkward court to the delights of the country, this last passage reveals what skill Cowper could attain in giving a word-picture such as this one of a statesman being received back into royal favour. He could always use his power of expression to advantage.

Cowper was not usually so lenient in his character sketches. As has been said of Burns, Cowper is a "superb satirist," and he is the more virile when he can ordain the future position of a class on the *Index Expurgatorius*, inscribed there in indelible ink. The retired tradesman, next to his enemy the clergyman, was subjected to the most pungent criticism. Such a man was content to live half a mile out of town, and to pretend that it was country,

"With its suburban villas, highwayside retreats,
That dread the encroachment of our growing streets.
Tight boxes, neatly sashed, and in a blaze
With all a July sun's collected rays."

Almost less love has he for the sanctimonious dame who sails to church to display her dress, a foible which the poet would never for a moment pardon, for attention to "fortune's velvet altar" he conjectured implied the beggaring of husbands. But they, too, are not quit of the vice of extravagance, for in one of his satirical flings at society in general Cowper urges,

> "We sacrifice to dress till household joys and comforts cease,
> Dress drains our cellar dry, and keeps our larder lean; puts out
> Our fires; introduces hunger, frost, and woe."

The sophist and the fool, the rich and the poor, are all alike subject to his flagellations. The rich man is an idler, the student a slave to atheism, even those who engaged in a course of physical research, and for whom it might have been supposed that the poet would have maintained some lurking partiality. But he treats them with his usual brusqueness in the following account:

> "Some drill and bore the solid earth, and from the strata there extract a register, by which we learn, that He who made it, and revealed its date to Moses, was mistaken in its age."

He continues to add to this sentence one even more bitter by remarking that

> " God never meant that man should scale the heavens by strides of human wisdom,"

as though the study of chemistry was in all its science of no greater profit than alchemy. A Davy and a Faraday were not born soon enough to check Cowper in his gross ignorance of the secrets of science.

The poet was easily irritated, and it was whilst his emotions were roughly rubbed that he wrote an unfair judgment against Voltaire. The Frenchman's reputation would have been greatly prejudiced had Cowper's *Truth* been the only record of one whose pamphlets so largely influenced the events that sounded the tocsin of the French Revolution. Because Voltaire was a freethinker in religion, because he spoke lightly of the Bible, no redeeming trait could be expected of him. In no other instance has Cowper been so literally vindictive, in no other does he strike so hard or so ably. Thus he writes of the French fomenter:

> "The path to bliss abounds with many a snare;
> Learning is one, and wit, however rare,
> The Frenchman first in literary fame
> (Mention him if you please, Voltaire?—The same),
> With spirit, genius, eloquence supplied,
> Lived long, wrote much, laughed heartily and died.
> The scripture was his jest-book whence he drew
> *Bons mots* to gall the Christian and the Jew.
> An infidel in health, but what when sick?
> Oh, then a text would touch him to the quick.
> View him in Paris in his last career;
> Surrounding throngs the demi-god revere;

Exalted in his pedestal of pride,
And fumed with frankincense on every side,
He begs their flattery with his latest breath,
And smother'd in't at last, is praised to death."

To make this calumny still more suggestive, Cowper immediately
follows with a picture of a different nature, in such a scene that
would have been worthy of George Morland in his purer moods.
He describes yon cottager, who sits content outside her cottage door
playing with her bobbins, with her heart as light as her pocket.
When narrating such a homely trait of life, Cowper speaks with a
kindly and earnest sincerity. His acid contempt of man is drawn
back out of sight, as the claws of a purring puss, when he revels in
the incidents that gave him daily pleasure. In the following
passage he is almost like the Baptist himself, preaching of the
Saviour and warning the world that receives Him not. In the
third line of *Expostulation* he exclaims :

"When He that ruled them with a shepherd's rod,
In form a man, in dignity a God,
Came, not expected in that humble guise,
To sift, and search them with unerring eyes,
He found, concealed beneath a fair outside,
The filth of rottenness and worm of pride,
Their piety, a system of deceit,
Scripture employed to sanctify the cheat."

But, were we to ignore the fact that the poet showed the grasp of
a counsel dealing with a ticklish case when interested in more
serious subjects, we should unfairly confine ourselves to the least
incisive accomplishments of Cowper, of that man whose gentle
disposition so fascinated the people of the Buckinghamshire town of
Olney that he was always addressed by them as " Sir " Cowper.

Education was a theme in which he considered he could rank as
an exponent. We may differ from him in his views, but it is at
least only fair to note that he gives good reasons in his *Tirocinium*
for his objection to the training of youth at schools. He could not
properly have understood boys ; he was misled by their faults of
mischief, but he was worthily anxious to see England's sons launched
out into the world from sound slips.

Supervision at school has become undeniably more thorough in
recent years, so that Cowper would have maintained a more sober
attitude in regard to our modern educational centres. He gives us
his picture of a son who is taught to pray at home twice in the day
as a pledge for a consistent life. He continues his description of
how the same lad checks this golden rule the moment he goes to
school. There he is crammed

"With mythological stuff,
But with sound religion sparingly enough."

If a parent wishes his son to be extravagant, a dunce, lascivious, or headstrong, he has only to train him with a mob of boys. But, whatever the success in scholastic life, Cowper could never have been prevailed upon to commend our present Public School system. He was averse to the disparity of ages; he considered that the management of tiros of eighteen was difficult and their punishment obscene. The poet was horrified at the schoolboy's hero-worship, for the stout, tall captain's freaks demoralise the minor heroes who view him with envious eyes. The best praise that Cowper can give to these establishments is that they may have some corrective influence over the sturdy and strong.

College life follows school, but it is only a step from the cauldron of pitch into the flames, for there is now no regard for ordinances. A boy may, by chance, turn out well. If so, the pedagogue with complacent air will take half the credit; but all vicious habits acquired by the pupil will have been contracted through his own fault. So in answer to this the poet urges every father to be his son's own teacher, maintaining that it is an absurdity to resign into a stranger's hand a task as much within his own command

> "That God and nature and your interest, too,
> Seem with one voice to delegate to you."

No schoolboy cares to leave home, but compulsion thus exercised makes him callous. It also weakens, in Cowper's estimation, his affection for his father when he returns for his holidays, the natural effect of love by absence being chilled into respect. The error of sending boys to school is the more grave, because the masters make no effort to kindle amongst the boys, whilst under their tutelage, the proper enthusiasm for home. They are satisfied if they feed a pupil's intellect with store of syntax, but with little more. They dismiss their cares when they dismiss their flock, and, machines themselves, they are governed by a clock. With all due respect to the poet's learned opinion, we feel that under his system Britain would never have expanded as an empire as it has through its men inured to pluck at school, and that the public character which draws its chief colour from a social education would have been, had his principles been rigidly adopted, of an anæmic and maudlin type. Moreover, Cowper seemed to overlook the fact that but few parents are scholars in more than pretence, and that even the cleverest of them could rarely find the time to implant the same knowledge in the minds of their sons. Life nowadays is a game of wage-earning, not of collecting wisdom.

Kingship, rather than tuition, finds Cowper's ideas on more substantial ground. He commences to remark that great princes have great playthings:

" Some hew mountains into men, some build human wonders mountains high,
Some sought by pyramids and mausolean pomp, short-liv'd themselves t' immortalise their bones,
Some seek diversion in the tented field, and make the sorrows of
  mankind their sport.
But war's a game, which, were their subjects wise, kings would
  not play at.
Nations would do well t' extort their truncheons from the puny
  hands of heroes."

With his mind upon war he fears the tyrant, yet he acknowledges
that peace is no safer in the hands of a people, since violence can
never longer sleep than human passions please. Passion incited
Cain to take his fatal step, which was expiated by the Deluge, but
left unquenched the seeds of murder in the breast of man. In
passion Tubal was born, and as he grew he invented the sword and
the falchion, instruments for attack. So he fed the sense of individual property. The idea expanded, and others became covetous,
men jealous of the returns from the agricultural industry of those
who toiled. The result of this was an open quarrel, a combat
without system :

" Thus war began on earth, these fought for spoil, and those in
  self-defence."

The poet then traces an inchoate kingship, how one came

" Eminent above the rest, for strength, for stratagem, for courage,
  or for all,
And was chosen leader him they served in war, and him in peace,
For sake of warlike deeds reverenced no less."

At length he is made king, whilst those who have set him up as a
ruler sweat in his service until his caprice becomes the soul that
animates them all—a thousand, ten thousand, lives is an easy
reckoning for purchase of his renown :

" Thus kings were first invented, and thus kings were burnished
  into heroes,
Became the arbiters of this terraqueous swamp. Storks among
  frogs that have but croaked and died."

So servilely did the people obey him, so greatly did his authority
wax, that he became a " despot absolute,"

" The only freeman of his land."

It is a little difficult to speculate how much licence Cowper would
have granted to a king of his own choice, whether he would have
permitted him to be more influential than a mere praetor. We have
seen that he would have sanctioned no Stuart to a seat on the
throne without ordering his instant removal ; yet it seems a little

hard that he should have imposed a ban of suspicion upon even the most virtuous in his estimation. His praise, in the following context, is spoilt by a left-handed compliment, just as if he were to place his Majesty as sentry over the Treasury box, but had taken the precaution to empty it in the first place as security. Such are his lukewarm benedictions :

" We love the king who loves the law, respects his bounds, and reigns content within them: him we serve freely with delight, who leaves us free, but, recollecting still that he is man, we trust him not too far.—He is ours to administer, to guard, t' adorn the State, but not to warp or change it.—Our love is principle, and had its root in reason, is judicious, manly, free."

This may appear to be a frank expression of loyalty, but it might fairly be the spur to revolution, for its vagueness binds the sovereign with fetters of doubt. The reason for Cowper's blundering epitome is fairly obvious. In his desire to uphold the sacredness of freedom he is a little puzzled when he is called to account for the existence of a monarch. The royal figure is a peg too much in the dovetailing of the Constitution. Liberty unalloyed is his fetish, without which every State is in a condition of raw imperfection. But even in England, the best of all countries, this essential quality is a ball in the cup of dishonesty, for

"Th' age of virtuous politics is past, and we are deep in that of cold
    pretence."

Patriots are grown too shrewd to be sincere and we too wise to trust them. The loudest disclaimers of liberty are slaves to lust-provoking derision,

" For when was public virtue to be found when private was not ? "

Human nature fails, and Cowper renders it purposely the more impotent that he may add an extra victory to Providence. Liberty will rise uppermost, spite of persecution, fraud, oppression, and prisons which have no power to bind " the liberty of the heart" derived from heaven, bought with His blood who gave it to mankind and sealed it with the same token.

After studying this line of views, it will create no surprise to find that Cowper was bitterly hostile to slavery, predecessor, as we may fairly call him, to Wilberforce. After speaking of trade as the girdle of the globe, he falls into one of his lugubrious moods, and exclaims,

" But ah! what wish can prosper, or what prayer,
    For merchants rich in cargoes o' despair,
    Who drive a loathsome traffic, gage and span,
    And buy the muscles and the bones of man."

Again, in *The Negro's Complaint*, he urges

> " That skins may differ, but affection dwells in white and black the
> same."

Cowper moves also in another field, apart from the paths of potential actualities into the grove of abstract meditations. He differentiates between the science of Wisdom and Knowledge, and in his *Hope and Charity* he stencils such qualities by rendering most prominent their demerits or foibles, as though he were passing judgment on

> "The freakish humours of the present time,"

rather than finding them fit subjects for idyllic fantasies. He knows his sternness, for he informs us later that he does not mean to clothe in sable every social scene, and give good company a face severe. In his wide-sweeping sentences he condemns books that are not seldom talismans and spells, by which the magic art of shrewder wits holds an unthinking multitude enthralled. How trite is his further rebuke, when he adds that the readers are attracted by the title, hoodwinked, are infatuated with the style, and through labyrinths and wilds of error are led by a truce entranced. Others read because too weak to bear

> "Th' insupportable fatigue of thought."

Could anything be more apposite to the actual facts of the present day, or more or directly written ? This attack finds its cousin-german in a sentence recorded of M. D'Argenson, who described an omnivorous reader as one who swallowed, without pause or choice, the total grist unsifted, *husks and all*.

In some respects Cowper reaches the acme of his individuality in his *Conversation*. There he shows himself an epigrammatist unsurpassed. He throws his flashes of light on the ordinary play-goer of a day's life. They seem to cower under his investigation ; they disliked being found out to be little better worth than mario-nettes, but they cannot hide their foibles from this penetrating searcher. He makes but a passing allusion to each, but with rapier dexterity he has formed an impression which is true, characteristic, and animated. In this close atmosphere we see a group of men drawing their pipes and discussing politics, but there is one amongst them who rants and emphasises his arguments by banging his fist upon the table, for ·

> "A noisy man is always in the right."

The next scene might be in a club-room, where men of no pro-fession, men of no ideas, lounge and loiter and call upon the waiter to bring them the latest editions. These are men to whom we can apply the following judgment:

> " Of all ambitions man may entertain,
> The worst that can invade a sickly brain,
> Is that which angles hourly for surprise,
> And baits his hook with prodigies and lies."

In a similar little circle there are others who love to discuss their past, or the prevalent popular illnesses. Others, again, blame the weather, but

> "That theme exhausted, a wide chasm ensues,
> Filled up at last with interesting news,
> Who danced with whom, and who are like to wed,
> And who is hanged and who is brought to bed."

This sally about " interesting news " is essentially Cowper's in his happiest vein, and its genuine but quiet humour is the more piquant because it is so remarkably true to life. In this, at least, society of to-day is redolent of the fashion that inspired at the close of the eighteenth century a circle that prided itself on much mannerism but little thought. At the same time one is inclined to shrug one's shoulders and ask if the poet would not compel all those who would think themselves wise to resign themselves to a mute life. The only occasion on which he finds a good word for conversation is when he concludes with a picture of the disciples on their return from Emmaus. He grows impassioned. He has left slip the sneering style, and becomes seriously in earnest in lines of which all who read will remark their singular force:

> "Now theirs was converse such as it behoves man to maintain, and
> such as God approves;
> Their views were indistinct and dim, but yet successful being
> aimed at Him,
> Christ and His character their only scope, their object, and their
> subject, and their hope."

These lines are but one more tribute to his favourite theme, that of a life modelled from a Christian exemplar. Had Cowper but lived to-day he would have laboured hard, as Mr. Stead himself did, to attain an international peace, either in the Hague or out of it. With one final quotation from *Charity* must we bring this sketch to a close:

> " The statesman skilled in projects dark and deep, might burn his
> useless Machiavel and sleep,
> His budget often filled yet always poor, might swing at ease
> behind his study door,
> No longer prey upon our annual rents, or scare the nation with
> its big contents:
> Disbanded legions freely might depart, and slaying man would
> cease to be an art."

We cannot but admire a man who, subject to a lifelong illness that inflicted with frequent recurrence an intense mental agony, fought persistently against his weaknesses—at times their master, at times a victim to their influence. Still he did not flinch even under this torture, but held his pen and pressed it to write in a cause which was distinctly unpopular. Cowper was pre-eminently a poet of feelings; he may have been melancholy, but he pointed out to his readers how they were themselves subjects of emotion. He owed a debt to Providence, and he rebuked the people for their follies. In doing so he was regardless of his own fame and of their opprobrium. He gave them tolerable advice, and strove to awaken them from their apathy to a sense of their duty towards their neighbours.

First of poets, since the days of Milton, to champion the sacredness of religion, he was the forerunner of a new school that disliked the political satires of the disciples of Pope, and aimed at borrowing for their lines of song from the simple beauties of a perfect nature.

# PEPYS AND HIS WIFE.

ELIZABETH ST. MITCHELL was married in 1655, at the age of fifteen, to Samuel Pepys, author of the immortal Diary. He was then a young man of twenty-four, who had been educated at Magdalen College, Cambridge, but had no means of livelihood. The rash young couple were offered shelter by Pepys's kinsman (first cousin, one remove), Sir Edward Montagu, afterwards Earl of Sandwich, who gave them a small room in his house, and used his influence later on with King Charles II. to procure for Pepys the important post of Clerk of the Acts of the Navy Board.

Mrs. Pepys, although born in England, was brought up principally in France. Her father, a Frenchman of good family, had been disinherited by his father for turning Huguenot, and remained a poor, unsuccessful man, "full of whimsies," or fads, all his days. His daughter Elizabeth was a very intelligent, quick-witted girl, who possessed a fair share of the artistic capacity of her French compatriots. "I find she can do anything with her hands," Pepys wrote of her when he had her taught to play the flageolet. Her critical husband took great pleasure in developing his wife's mind and talents, and was charmed when she became proficient in painting and instrumental music. "She is apt beyond imagination," he said of her when he first began to teach her music.

She was very good looking we know from her portrait by Hales, still in existence, and from the entries in the Diary of her husband. For instance, on July 10, 1660, Pepys wrote of a grand wedding at Goring House, the site now of Buckingham Palace: "Amongst all the beauties there, my wife was thought the greatest." And again on November 22 of the same year, when describing some Court doings, he wrote: "The Princess Henrietta is very pretty, but much below my expectation. But my wife, standing near her, with two or three black patches on, and well dressed, did seem to me much the handsomer of the two." Mrs. Pepys stood just behind the Queen's chair in the circle, and Pepys in the crowd.

Mrs. Pepys was very sensitive, and had a highly strung, nervous organisation. Pepys wrote on August 29, 1660, and the entry gives a queer little insight into middle-class life at that time: "After we were all a-bed, the wench (which lies in our chamber) called us to listen of a sudden, which put my wife into such a fright that she shook every joint of her, and a long time that I could not get her out of it."

Pepys's personal relations with his wife were, as a rule, extremely cordial, and he lived with her on terms of great affection, when the discordant element of jealousy happened to be absent. He was madly in love with her when he married her we know from his statement in the Diary of February 27, 1667, *à propos* of his visit with his wife, and her "woman," Deb Willet, to the King's play-house. *The Virgin Martyr*, a tragedy by Messenger and Decker, was performed, which he found

"mighty pleasant, and finely acted by Becke Marshall. But," he wrote, "that which pleased me beyond anything in the whole world was the wind musique when the angel comes down, which is so sweet that it ravished me, and indeed, in a word, did wrap up my soul so that it made me really sick, just as I have formerly been when in love with my wife, that neither then nor all the evening going home, and at home, I was able to think of anything, but remained all night transported, so as I could not believe that any musique hath that real command over the soul of a man as this did upon me: and makes me resolve to practise wind musique, and to make my wife do the like."

This is a curious example of the power of music upon the emotions.

Pepys's two ruling passionate pleasures were women and music. He loved both equally well, and could dispense with neither.

His was a curiously complex nature — painstaking, methodical, sensible, practical; in some respects commonplace and *bourgeois*, yet intensely emotional and artistic. He had a profound admiration for beauty in every form, not only of "the human form divine," but for art, of which he was a discerning critic; for music, in which he was a proficient; for culture and grace. He was highly educated, well read, and appreciative of every branch of knowledge. He had a sincere admiration for virtue and morality—in others—but he was unable to control his own passions for any length of time. He deplored, and at length remonstrated with his patron and friend, Lord Sandwich, for his connection with a "slut at Chelsea," yet all the way through the ten years' entries in his Diary there are constant allusions to his own amours and "freedom" with "sluts" of every kind and degree. During the whole time he faithfully records his affection for his wife, how content he is with her, and how well they got on together as a rule. But Pepys was unfit for monogamic marriage, as it was impossible for him to be faithful to one woman.

Mrs. Pepys was always more or less superficially jealous of her amorous husband, and of his attentions to attractive ladies, notably Mrs. Pierce, the Court Surgeon's wife, and Mrs. Knipp, the lively and accomplished actress, but she never seemed to have suspected him of absolute unfaithfulness to her until the year she died.

It is to be regretted the poor young woman did not go down to the grave happily ignorant of her husband's immorality! Pepys always had the decency—or hypocrisy—to conceal this side of his character from his wife and his associates, to whom he posed as the grave, sober man of affairs, and certainly a more conscientious, thorough man of business and able public official never existed than the Clerk of the Acts, later on to be Secretary to the Admiralty. It never appears, in the most candid and truth-telling autobiography ever written, that his colleagues knew of his amours. Once he mentioned he was greatly vexed that Creed, a Navy official, had seen his "dalliance" with an innkeeper's wife in a cherry-orchard, and that is the only allusion of the kind. By taste, he strongly disliked immodest women, although he was for ever trying to overcome their moral scruples and make them what he deprecated. When he was resisted, as in the case of pretty Betty Mitchell, who dumbly sidled up to her young husband for protection when Pepys tried to take hold of her hand in the dark, and who would not see him alone, so great was his familiarity, he failed to understand it or to attribute it to right motives, but said, "Betty grows shy or silly," and made no doubt if he had sufficient opportunity he would be able to overcome her scruples, as he had done with Bagwell's wife, a young woman whom he acknowledged to be "modest," but whom he tempted and corrupted.

What makes Pepys's immoralities peculiarly odious is that he was "the great man" to many of his *inamoratas*, whom they dare not offend for fear of injuring their husbands' or kinsmen's prospects in life. He took advantage most shamefully of his position with Mrs. Bagwell, Mrs. Daniell, and other women and girls in his employ, but, above all, his deliberate corruption of the youthful Deb Willet, his wife's sweet and innocent companion, whose friends were only too pleased to have the girl reside in a family of such high standing as Pepys's, was infamous.

When Pepys died, a doctor of divinity, Dr. George Hickes, sang his praises in the following words: "I never attended any sick or dying person that died with so much Christian greatness of mind," &c., "and I doubt not but he is now a very blessed spirit."

After this eulogium, the cynical may well say, "The only moral man is he who is not found out."

It must be remembered posterity would never have known anything about his *affaires de cœur* if he had not written it all down, and forgotten to burn it.

Mrs. Pepys sincerely loved her fascinating husband, and was faithful to him, although she seems to have had one or two fancies which were highly disquieting to her jealous lord. Coming in contact, as Pepys's wife, with men in high official or Court life, who regarded "gallantry" as an attribute of manliness to be boasted of rather than concealed, and being undeniably beautiful, she attracted the attentions of many men. When she found out her husband's misconduct with Deb Willet, and bitterly punished him with what he said he hated, an "unquiet" home, she cast in his teeth her own virtuous conduct in resisting the advances of the great Earl of Sandwich, and of his son, Lord Hinchingbroke, whose attentions to her made his "lady" unhappy; of Captain Ferrers and several others, all of which her husband did not deny. In the thick of his own infidelities, he was furiously jealous of his wife on the smallest provocation, or no provocation whatever. He remarked at once when any one, great or small, took any notice of her. "The Duke of York did mightily eye my wife," he said on the first occasion of their riding in "Hide Park" in their own coach. He became jealous of all personal attentions to her, save in one case, that of Armiger, whom he found at his house inviting Mrs. Pepys to go to a play, "and like a fool would be courting her, but he is an ass," Pepys said with supreme contempt. He hardly ever allowed her to go out by herself, and compelled her to lead a very dull life at home. So dull was she that she begged him to let her have a companion, or "woman," as he always termed her. He wrote, "I see I must keep somebody for company's sake to my wife, for I am ashamed she should live as she do." So, after much jangling and counting the cost, for Pepys was nearly always mean with his wife, although generous to others, he agreed to let her have a companion. But these companions from first to last were "a perpetual thorn in the flesh" to poor Mrs. Pepys from her husband's amatory temperament. Being young herself, she liked to have a young person with her, but Pepys's house was an utterly impossible one for any pretty, respectable girl. Even the mere description of the good looks of one companion, *before he saw her,* so inflamed his mind that he could not sleep previously to her arrival for thinking of her beauty, and at his office it distracted his thoughts and attention from his business. Jealous scenes between husband and wife took place from the outset. The companion was frequently changed because of Pepys's attentions. Yet, in spite of all Mrs. Pepys saw, she never seemed perfectly to realise the real danger and thoughtless wickedness of having attractive, innocent young girls exposed to the temptations of such an unscrupulous sensualist as Pepys, until she caught him embracing Deb Willet, when she was struck speechless with amazement. The scenes which followed were intensely painful. Mrs. Pepys made herself ill, and was nearly frantic with grief. Pepys depicts her sufferings and outraged feelings in the most graphic language, and his own tears and regrets. He made no end of virtuous resolutions, and never kept a single one.

The Diary ended soon after this, and Mrs. Pepys died a few months later, so nothing more is known of the inner life of this extraordinary man, who died "in the odour of sanctity," full of years and honours.

One of the most amusing and interesting episodes in the Diary is Pepys's account of his jealousy of Pembleton, Mrs. Pepys's dancing-master. To enliven her exceptionally dull life at a certain period, Pepys agreed to let her learn to dance. He was always pleased to see her occupied at home, either with music, painting, card-playing, sewing, "making marmalett of quinces"—in fact anything—provided she stopped at home. So the dancing lessons began, but in a very short time Pepys got angry with her for "minding nothing but the dancing-master, having him come twice a day, which is folly." From this time forth, until the lessons came to an abrupt termination a few weeks later, Pepys was possessed with "devilish jealousy," which caused "a very hell" in his mind, and made him so ill that he could neither eat, sleep, nor attend to his business. There does not seem to have been much cause for all "this deadly folly"—his own words for his jealousy. Mrs. Pepys was young—only twenty-three—she delighted to dance, and got a little excited about it. Pembleton, "a pretty, neat, black (*i.e.*, dark) man," doubtless made himself agreeable to his attractive pupil. He dined once with her, and on one occasion gave her a lesson when no one was in the house. Pepys came from his office, close by, to pry, and found him there. He then became so full of "damned jealousy" that he could not contain himself. He walked up and down in his own chamber for hours in the most miserable state of excitement. Mrs. Pepys came and begged him to tell her what was the matter, but he "construes it to be impudence." He went to bed, but could not sleep. At last, towards morning, he confessed what ailed him. He taxed his wife with indiscretion, but this she denied, and said it was merely his "old disease of jealousy." He made her cry, and then fondly caressed her, and made up the quarrel. After this, Mrs. Pepys told Pembleton not to come to the house when her husband was out, of which Pepys was much ashamed, but would rather have it so than allow him to come. Pembleton was then invited to supper, and Pepys made himself extremely agreeable (and he could be very charming when he pleased), for fear Pembleton should tell people of his jealousy. He was much provoked to see that his wife had told the dancing-master the whole truth of the matter, but was greatly relieved at the same time. The dancing lessons then ended. But so powerfully had Pembleton affected Pepys's feelings, that for months afterwards the mere sight of him in church, either looking at Mrs. Pepys or not, so agitated him that it put him into "a great sweat," as he elegantly terms it; and even the sight of a gentleman, who resembled the dancing-master, walking in "Hide Park," threw poor Pepys into the same distressing state of heat and whirl of emotion, as the real Pembleton himself. Yet, immediately following on this, besides outdoor amours, he was immensely taken with his wife's companion, Ashwell, "a witty girl," he called her, so that he said he was not as fond of his wife as he ought to be, and so cannot blame her for being in an ill-humour with him.

After the Pembleton affair, the two did not get on as well together as of old. They squabbled about the smallest thing, even as to whether Sir William Penn's "footboy" was good looking or not. Another day they "jangled mightily about her cushions in worsted that she had made the year before." He cursed the time he ever let her have a "woman" and dancing lessons, and wrote, "She has got such an opinion of my being jealous, and her mind is so devilishly taken off her business, and she finds other sweets besides pleasing of me, and so makes her that she begins not at all to take pleasure in me, or study to please me as heretofore. But I must have patience."

Mrs. Pepys was no doubt feeling the reaction after the excitement of the dancing and its outcome. But Pepys hoped, as they really had great affection for each other, that after forgetting their late differences, and being absent awhile from one another, they would agree together as well as ever.

So he sent her and her "woman" to his father's at Brampton. He saw them off, kissed his wife many times, and Ashwell once, and was delighted, such was his jealousy, to see that in the coach there were only women and one parson !

Mrs. Pepys seems to have gone away in an irritable and discontented state of mind, and while at Brampton quarrelled with old Mr. and Mrs. Pepys, their son John, and the girl Ashwell, with whom she came to blows. On her return home John Pepys came to his brother Samuel to complain of her, but Pepys very sensibly declined to listen to him, and told him that if he and his father and mother were wise they would all keep in with her, "for," said he, "she deserves to be pleased, considering the manner of life I keep her to." He was greatly annoyed, though, when his wife taxed him "with keeping the house all in dirt" (after alterations), "in order to find her employment to keep her within, and from minding her pleasure, in which, though I am sorry to see she minds, it is true enough in a great degree," he said.

He then bought pretty things for her chamber, and to occupy her mind, began to teach her arithmetic and the globes. "And," said he, "I hope with great pleasure I shall bring her to understand many fine things." He also spent £12 on clothes for her, and £55 on himself. It must be remembered in extenuation of this startling disproportion, that Pepys had constantly to go to Court to see the

King and the Duke of York, who was Lord High Admiral of England, about Navy matters, and that it would never have done for him to dress meanly.

After settling down, the two seemed to be very happy again, and Pepys frequently mentioned the fact. " I enjoy great pleasure in her company, and learning of arithmetique." And again he wrote : " To dinner with my wife, very pleasant and pleased with one another's company, and in our general enjoyment one of another, better, we think, than most other couples do."

Mrs. Pepys was a delicate woman who suffered from frequent attacks of indisposition. Pepys was always most sympathetic and kind to her at such times. He had his meals by her bedside and " comforted her and pitied her," and showed some of the most lovable traits in his character. Once, while riding to Brampton, she was taken very ill, and on alighting at an inn at Buntingford she became so pale that Pepys was " in great horror, thinking she would have died, and having," he said, " a great tryall of my true love and passion for her."

Yet he was occasionally very rough, and even cruel to her. Twice, when she spoke crossly to him, he pulled her by the nose, and hurt her so much that the poor thing cried.

On another occasion when they were in bed, owing to some remissness on the part of one of the servants about which Pepys complained, Mrs. Pepys made a cutting remark, which so exasperated him that he struck her violently in the face, giving her a black eye. She cried out, and was in great pain, " but yet her spirit was such," he said admiringly, " as to endeavour to bite and scratch me. But I coying " (caressing with the hand), " made her leave crying, and sent for butter and parsley, and friends presently one with another, and I up, vexed at my heart to think at what I had done, for she was forced to lay a poultice or something to her eye all day, and is black, and the people of the house observed it." However, Mrs. Pepys was too forgiving to bear malice, for the same day he stated " her eye is very bad, but she is in a very good temper to me." She was unable to go out for a fortnight, and when Pepys went to a dinner party at Sir William Batten's at Christmas time, she stopped at home, and played games with her servants.

Although docile and amiable enough as a rule, she could show temper on occasion, and it then generally ended in her husband giving way to her. Nothing annoyed her more than his meanness about her clothes. Once Lady Sandwich remonstrated with him about this, and made him ashamed of himself.

On one occasion the two fell out desperately because he would not allow her to have " a laced dress," but said she should merely have a plain one. Upon this, " she flounced away " in a manner which highly incensed him, and he retired to his office. Mrs. Pepys dressed herself to go to Lady Sandwich's, but could not resist going into her husband's office *en route* to give him a piece of her mind. But Pepys's words are too rich to paraphrase. "She by-and-by in a rage follows me, and coming to me tells me in a spiteful manner, like a vixen, and with a look full of rancour that she would buy a new dress and lace it, and make me pay for it, and then let me burn it if I would, after she had done it, and so went away in a fury."

Pepys was "cruelly vexed" at this, but Mrs. Pepys got her "laced dress," and he admired her in it immensely.

Just before she died in 1669, at the early age of twenty-nine, he repented of his meanness to her, and agreed to allow her £30 a year (a substantial sum in those days) for dress, to her very great delight. He also gave her a handsome pearl necklace, and other good jewels "which pleased her mightily."

One curious fact must be mentioned about the Diary, namely, that in all the daily entries extending over ten years, Pepys invariably speaks of Mrs. Pepys as "my wife"; never once by her Christian name. He sometimes repeated the words "my wife" three or four times in one sentence.

Pepys's constant and open admiration of pretty Mrs. Pierce, who, he said, had a lovely complexion, the best he ever saw "on any woman, young or old, or child either," and also of Mrs. Knipp, the merry, sparkling actress, who sang his songs to him (most insidious of flatteries!) and played little jokes upon him, such as pulling his hair (periwig) when she sat behind him unnoticed in the pit of the theatre, caused Mrs. Pepys much disquietude, and once she was extremely rude to the two ladies when they came to call upon her. Mrs. Knipp arrived first, and on hearing of this, Pepys left his office, which was in another part of the same building—the Navy Office—and went home to see her. "I sat and talked with her," he remarked,

"I very pleasant with her, but perceive my wife hath no great pleasure in her being here, she not being pleased with my kindness to her. However, we talked and sang, and were very pleasant. By and by comes Mr. Pierce and his wife. And here we talked and were pleasant, and my wife in a chagrin humour, she not being pleased with my kindness to either of them, and by and by she fell into some silly discourse wherein I checked her, which made her mighty offensive to Mrs. Pierce, which did displease me, but I would make no words, but put the discourse by as much as I could (it being about a report that my wife said was made of herself, and meant by Mrs. Pierce that she was grown a gallant, when she had but a few suits of clothes these two or three years, and a great deal of that silly discourse), and by and by Mrs. Pierce did tell her that such discourses should not trouble her, for there went as bad on other people, and particularly of herself at this end of the town, meaning my wife, that she was crooked, which was quite false, which my wife had the wit not to acknow-

ledge herself to be the speaker of, though she has said it twenty times.
But by this means we had little pleasure in their visit. However, Knipp
and I sang, and then I offered them to carry them home and to take
my wife with me, but she would not go : so I with them, leaving my wife
in a very ill-humour, and very slighting to them, which vexed me. However, I would not be removed from my civility to them, but sent for a
coach and went with them, and in our way, Knipp saying that she came
out of doors without a dinner to us, I took them to old Fish Streete, to the
very house and woman where I kept my wedding dinner, where I never was
since, and then I did give them a jole of salmon, and what else was to be had.
And here we talked of the ill-humour of my wife, which I did excuse as
much as I could, and they seemed to admit of it, and did both confess they
wondered at it, but from thence to other discourse. I set them both at
home, Knipp at her house, her husband being at the door ; and glad she was
to be found to have stayed out so long with me and Mrs. Pierce, and none
else ; and Mrs. Pierce at her house, and am mightily pleased with the
discretion of her during the simplicity and offensiveness of my wife's
discourse this afternoon. So home, and there find my wife mightily out of
order, and reproaching of Mrs. Pierce and Knipp as wenches and I know not
what. But I did give her no words to offend her, and so to bed without
any good looks or words to or from my wife."

Poor Mrs. Pepys might well feel exasperated at her husband's
excessive "kindness" to the two fascinating ladies. The next day
she was very angry with her "woman" Mercer, who, she said, must
have told Mrs. Pierce that she (Mrs. Pepys) had said Mrs. Pierce
was "crooked." But Pepys's conscience told him the real cause of
all the anger. "She is jealous of my kindness to her."

Yet in the very same paragraph in which he noted this he acknowledged that he was all aflame with jealousy because he met Mrs.
Pepys walking in the street with Mr. Batelier. "But Lord !" he
exclaimed, "to see how soon I could conceive evil fears and thoughts
concerning them."

Needless to say, after the stormy little interview between the
three ladies, "relations were strained" for some months, but eventually matters were patched up, and visiting between the families began
again. This would not have been the case as regards Mrs. Knipp if
Mrs. Pepys could have foreseen the jaunts and pleasure trips the
lively actress and Pepys were to take together the next time
Mrs. Pepys went into the country, and all that transpired between
them.

During the great plague Pepys stuck manfully to his business,
although he was about the only public official who did not flee from
the stricken city. For safety he sent his wife and servants to Woolwich. On one occasion, when the plague was dying out, Mrs. Pepys
paid him a surprise visit to see if Mrs. Knipp were with him, but
fortunately for all concerned, the actress did not go and see him till
the next day !

Pepys was inclined to be jealous of a Mr. Sheres, who was evidently an accomplished man of refined tastes, an excellent draughts-

man, and something of a poet, which appealed to Mrs. Pepys's imagination. Pepys said his judgment told him "there was no hurt" in the friendship on either side, but yet, so jealous was his nature, he was troubled by it, for his wife so delighted to talk to Mr. Sheres. He was annoyed, too, because Mrs. Pepys was "mighty careful to have a handsome dinner for him"; for although he saw no reason to be troubled at it, and Mr. Sheres was "a very civil and worthy man, yet," he said jealously, "it do seem to imply some little neglect of me." Mr. Sheres lent Mrs. Pepys books, and offered to teach her perspective, but this was too hard for her. Pepys was greatly relieved when Mr. Sheres had to go back to his appointment at Tangier, though it "troubled" Mrs. Pepys "mightily"; so much so that she was out of humour all the evening of his departure, and so restless and sleepless at night "that," Pepys said, "I was forced to take her and hug her to put her to rest."

Perhaps it was fortunate for all parties that Mr. Sheres's profession took him back to Tangier in the early days of so interesting a friendship!

The Diary ended suddenly and sadly.

Mrs. Pepys had her eyes rudely opened to her husband's infidelity, and was made miserable for a time by the revelation. Pepys's eyesight became very bad, and he feared he was going blind. (This was not the case.) The King gave him permission to absent himself for a lengthy period from his duties, and expressed much sympathy with him, as did his ever-staunch friend and patron the Duke of York, who had an immense respect for Pepys's ability and conscientious discharge of his duties in Navy matters. So Pepys and his wife went for some months on the Continent, where, let us hope, and in all probability, they were happy together, for, be it remembered, that in spite of his unfaithfulness to her, Pepys was deeply attached to his "comely" wife.

A short time after they returned to London in 1669, Mrs. Pepys died of a fever in the prime of her beauty and youth. Pepys erected a handsome and costly monument to her memory in St. Olave's, Hart Street; and when he died, many years later, his body was brought to rest beside her.

He never married again, and it was as well.

That Pepys had great powers of attraction for women is evident, but his male friends seemed equally attached to him. The stately Mr. Evelyn, in his Diary, wrote that Pepys was "immensely beloved, hospitable, generous, learned in many things, skill'd in music, a very great cherisher of learned men of whom he had the conversation," &c. "For forty years" (he was) "so much my particular friend that Mr. Jackson" (Pepys's nephew and heir, and ancestor of the Pepys-Cockerell family) "sent me compleat mourning."

The obsequies were magnificent. Pepys died at Clapham at the residence—" a very noble and sweet place "—of his friend of forty years' standing, formerly his clerk, Mr. William Hewer, whom he appointed executor.

" This great man who died so greatly," as Dr. Hickes said of him was buried at St. Olave's Church on June 5, 1703, at nine o'clock night, in a vault just beneath the monument of the young wife h had loved with a fond but not exclusive passion.

MARIANNE DALE.

# DIARY JOTTINGS IN ALASKA.

AT one time Alaska conveyed the idea of an indefinite tract of ice and snow, wrapped in fog and darkness, and devoted only to the walrus and the polar bear, or at best it was thought of as produce-ground of the exquisite furs which adorn beauty. Recent discoveries in the Klondyke, at Atlin, at Cape Nòme and in other districts have materially changed our primary conception of the country, and now gold, barbaric gold, is the vision conjured up by the name. There is, however, another side to Alaska which will, in the future, attract to it more steady and lasting riches than the most prolific mines—the extreme grandeur of its coast fiord and glacier scenery, which is unexcelled by any country in the world. . This fact is beginning to be appreciated by Western and even Eastern Americans, who will come in increasing numbers every summer and make of it a transatlantic Norway,

Seattle, Tacoma and Port Townsend, rising and opulent cities on the shores of forest-girdled Puget Sound, are ports whence the steamers of the Pacific Navigation Company convey intending passengers to the Alaskan waters. A journey of nearly a thousand miles by rail from San Francisco, through the stately forest and mountain scenery of California, Oregon and Washington, brought us to Tacoma, where the *City of Topeka* lay at anchor. A glance at the passengers showed us how times were changed since the Alaskan trip was merely one of health or amusement; stalwart miners, prospectors, and treasure-seekers were well *en evidence*. Lawyers and doctors from the Eastern and Western States, with their families, and a few of undefined occupation, on pleasure bent, constituted the upper class on the steamer. It was evening when we weighed anchor, and slowly we swept down the Sound, leaving Tacoma with its fine buildings and lofty aspirations in the distance. A gorgeous sunset invested the sea in the richest hues of Burgundy, and afar snowy Mount Rainier, in its pride of 10,000 feet, blushed like one huge red rose, whilst the serrated peaks of the Olympian range stood out in gold against the evening sky. By degrees the glory grew dim, the sea changed to a cobalt blue, and Mount Rainier faded to the ghastly paleness of a corpse. A unique feature of the Alaskan voyage is the absence of rough water. During the thousand miles to Skaguay, our farthest point north, we travel between chains of islands and the mainland, over lake-like seas, where *mal de mer* becomes impossible. During the night we passed Port Townsend, and all the next day steamed between British Columbia and Vancouver Island. The scenery was typical of that encountered during the entire voyage ; mountains on either side densely clothed, from base to summit, in fir and pine, with here and there a snow-covered peak breaking the uniformity of green. The roots of the trees actually dangled in the water, so narrow was the dividing-line between the commencement of vegetation and the sea. In the wide gulf of Georgia we saw several shoals of whales spouting and gambolling, and soon we entered the Seymour Narrows beset with dangerous whirlpools, where the water seethed like a caldron, and soon our own ship was violently swung about by the force of the tides. The fact that several vessels were wrecked here added a spice of adventure to the passage, and to complete the impression we were informed that the neighbouring woods teemed with bears and eagles.

The next morning we passed through the forty-mile break in the continuity of our protecting island-chains, and felt the long swell of the Pacific. Alaska is pre-eminently a country of mirages, and in the afternoon we witnessed a striking one that looked exactly like a railway embankment and bridge. Small rocks, in place of becoming smaller by distance, grew larger, till they seemed almost mountains on the horizon. All this day we passed fir-clad rocky islands, and toward evening traversed the Finlayson Channel, between perpendicular mountain walls, over 3000 feet high, diversified frequently by great cataracts rolling down their sides into the sea. Next morning we passed the celebrated boundary of Alaska, 54° 40′ N. L., and soon reached the flat and woody Mary Island, where our captain went on shore in his gig for custom-house formalities. The island contains only one building, and the life in the winter season must be most forlorn. We continued our voyage over the same tranquil waters, and under English skies, where white banks of cloud rested our eyes, weary of the eternal blue of California. There is a charm, too, in the vaporous atmosphere, which lends grandeur to the mountains by robing them partly in mist, and leaving something on the landscape for imagination to fill in, not as in the South, where every scenic feature stands out as clear cut as an intaglio.

In the afternoon we reached Ketchican, a mining and fishing village, consisting of about thirty wooden houses, situated on a semi-circular bay, with a lovely background of forest-clad hills and snowy mountains. There was also a pretty river, where the salmon were so abundant as to realise an American's description, " more fish than water." The bay, too, is continually agitated by the finny tribes to a degree that excites attention even in northern waters. The pier had been destroyed by the Pacific steamship *Alki* on the preceding voyage, and consequently we were unable to land as the transit in boats would take too long for such a brief stay. Like Mohammed at Damascus we probably profited by this circumstance, and enjoyed the picturesqueness at a distance without the smells and squalor of a too near approach.

Leaving Ketchican, we passed through winding and placid channels till, towards ten o'clock in the evening, we saw a magnificent range of snowy mountains, and on the shore at their feet lay Fort Wrangell, the first important stopping-place on the Alaskan voyage. The situation of the town is superb, the town itself melancholy to the last degree. Its wooden houses are in decay and the wooden platforms which serve as sidewalks are broken and dangerous to the wayfarers. Nearly eighty years ago, when Alaska belonged to the Russians, Baron Wrangell had a fort erected here to repel the incursions of the Hudson's Bay Company; and in 1861, when gold mines were discovered at Cassiar, in British Columbia, Fort Wrangell, being the nearest port to the Stikine River, rapidly advanced in prosperity. Too soon, however, the mines were exhausted, the town gradually decayed till it reached its present position. What makes Fort Wrangell interesting to the traveller are the totem poles of the Alaskan Indians, over half a dozen of which can still be seen here, out of many hundreds which were burned or removed to museums. The totem pole is really the genealogical tree of a particular family, and the fact of having one enhances the owner's status considerably. On the pole, which often costs the Indians as much as £200, are carved various animals—generally whales, bears, birds, or fish—and these emblems are not merely on the totems, but also on the canoes and clothing of the family. The totem pole is not infrequently eighty feet high. Members of the same badge cannot intermarry. A whale cannot marry a whale, nor a salmon a salmon. There are several curio-shops at Fort Wrangell, and, as may be imagined, there is much business doing on the arrival of the passenger steamers. We found, however, a better choice of objects and more reasonable prices at Sitka, the Alaskan capital. Garnets, of rather inferior quality, are obtained by the Stikine River, and an interesting curio of Fort Wrangell is a block of slate studded with them as thickly as "raisins in a plum-pudding." The traveller generally makes his first acquaintance with the Alaskan baskets at these shops. They are made by the Indian women from the root of the hemlock, and are so closely woven that they can hold water. They are stained various colours, notably green, red, and yellow. Excellent native dyes used to take the place of the present flaring aniline. Connoisseurs can easily distinguish the workmanship of the different Indian tribes, and some baskets fetch much higher prices than others; for instance, those wrought by a tribe numerically small are more valuable than the product of a populous tribe. There are

also miniature totem poles for sale, now always wooden, because
the slate of which they were formerly made is no longer imported
from Canada.

Leaving Fort Wrangell at midnight, we arrived at Juneau at
five o'clock the next afternoon, passing *en route* scenery similar to
yesterday's, with some additional glaciers thrown in.    Juneau is
almost forced into the sea by precipitous mountains, which rise to
a height of 3000 feet, so much so that a large portion of it is built
on piles, giving it the appearance of a primeval lake-dwelling.    In
other respects, however, it looks eminently up-to-date, having
electric lights, a small theatre, two newspapers, two hotels, and
numerous fine shops.    The "lions" of Juneau are two Indian
villages, one at either end of the town.    The total number of the
aboriginal inhabitants of Alaska hardly amounts to thirty thousand—
a fact rather surprising in a territory that is as large as one-sixth of
the entire United States.    They are divided into Esquimaux, who, of
course, inhabit the Far North, and who are much the most populous
section; the Aleuts, who occupy the Aleutian Islands, the Atha-
pascans, who dwell in the interior; and the Thlinkets.    The last-
named are the only Indians one encounters on this voyage,.
inhabiting, as they do, the south-eastern portion of the country.
Formerly they used to wear many interesting, if rather disfiguring,
ornaments, such as nose-rings and labrets; now, under the influence
of the civilising missionaries, they have discarded them; they wear
American clothes, talk an uncertain English, and, from the tourist's
point of view, have become comparatively uninteresting.    In our
visit to the Auk Indian village—a tribe of the Thlinkets—we passed
a brawling stream, celebrated for the earliest gold discoveries in
Alaska being made by its banks.    The Auks occupied about
thirty wooden houses, and seemed anything but cleanly in their
habits.    We saw large quantities of fish hanging up drying to
form provision for the coming winter.    Several canoes were carefully
beached and covered with clothes to prevent their being warped by
the sun.    In all parts of Alaska we observed that the Indians took
the same care of their canoes, for they recognise their importance,
not only as a means of locomotion, but as enabling them to capture
the fish, which forms their staple diet.    The canoes, or "dug-outs,"
are formed of one tree, and are often large enough to contain forty
people!    The Alaskans, like all North American Indians, perish of
consumption when they begin to assume the ways of civilisation;.
and a poor, attenuated girl in the village reminded us of their sad
destiny.    She was of a yellowish tint, wore the ordinary American
clothes, and had absolutely no ornaments.    There was a small Indian
graveyard adjacent to the village.    The dead were interred in metal
boxes, which were exposed to view, being merely surrounded by a
slight wooden fence.

Returning to the steamer, we noticed the graves of several Irish-men, workers in the neighbouring Treadwell mine, who reposed peacefully by the side of Italians and Portuguese. The vegetation of the mountains around Juneau is of the most dazzling green, eclipsing even the Emerald Isle, the reason being the abundant moisture caused by the proximity of the Japanese stream; a fact accounting also for the comparatively warm climate of Juneau, which, though situated so far north, is more temperate than New York, and the thermometer very seldom falls below zero.

On Douglas Island, opposite Juneau, and only a few hundred yards distant, is situated the Treadwell, supposed to be the largest gold quartz mine in the world. Steam launches ply frequently between it and Juneau, and our passengers availed themselves of them to make the visit. On the island, and a few minutes' walk from the mine, is quite a considerable town, with numerous shops exclusively devoted to the miners. The Treadwell is unique in being situated actually beside the sea, a matter of no small import-ance in procuring water inexpensively for the working. This fact and low wages account for the mine being profitable, for the ore is of very poor grade, though in almost inexhaustible quantities. The labourers' wages range from $3.00 a day with keep, in the case of whites, and from $2.00 without keep for the Indians. The vein is said to be 400 feet in width, and the mine has paid for many years large and steady dividends. After the ore is quarried it falls through ore-shoots into little waggons in the tunnels below, and "is moved through all the processes by gravity." There are 880 stamps grinding night and day, stopping only on Christmas and on the Fourth of July. The traveller sees the mine under the greatest possible difficulties, there being no one to show him around or to give him any explanations; furthermore, he is exposed to the risk of falling fragments from the blasting, and to be seriously injured or killed by the ore-laden trains which dash continually through the obscure tunnels. Surely it would not imperil the financial position of the Treadwell mine to allow two or three workmen an afternoon off once or twice a week, during the summer tourist season, to act as guides, charging, if necessary, a small fee, which everybody would gladly pay. It would, undoubtedly, be an act of humanity as well as courtesy, on the part of the proprietors.

We departed from Juneau late at night, and next morning on going on deck, found everything foggy and obscure, owing to the smoke of numerous forest fires. We steamed through the beautiful Lynn Channel, for hours having on either side almost perpendicular mountains sparsely wooded and wild and savage in the extreme; falling torrents, glaciers, and snowy peaks added sublimity to the landscape. Lynn Channel divides into several branches, those on the left and middle terminating in the Chil*kat* and Chil*koot* Rivers respectively, whilst that on the right extends to Skaguay, and at the latter place our vessel touched. Here was our farthest point north- wards, and was nearly in latitude 59°. Skaguay may be called a baby city, being only about two years in existence. New sites and new streets are being marked out daily, so it affords the traveller a good idea of the rapidity with which an American town springs into- existence. It is, however, essentially a place for supplying miners' outfits, and in curio shops or sights has nothing of interest. As terminus of the White Pass Railway leading to Klondyke, and being situated near the Atlin mines, Skaguay seems to have a future of considerable brightness, and without doubt many people will make fortunes there by judicious real estate investments at the present time. The town rejoices in steam-laundries, electric-lighting, good confectioners and greengrocers, pineapples even being available, as everything is shipped from Seattle and Tacoma. We now enjoyed the most charming experience of our journey, the excursion to the summit of the White Pass, at an altitude of nearly 3000 feet and a distance of twenty-two miles. The railway proceeds still further, to Lake Bennett—forty-five miles from Skaguay—whence steamers convey the traveller by the Yukon River to Dawson City, a journey of 600 miles.

Leaving Skaguay, the train ascended continually, turning and twisting up the mountains, and, below us, the Skaguay River boiled over its rocky bed. Sometimes we could see five or six loops of the line, which we had already traversed, beneath us, and above us several more that we had yet to pass. There were numerous tunnels, and we travelled over trestle-work several stories high, reminding one of a house of cards in its instability. Leaning from the carriage window we could distinctly hear the creak, creak of the timbers, whilst 200 feet below rose enormous savage-looking boulders from the bed of the stream. Gold mines were of frequent occur- rence along the Skaguay. At the station known as the " Summit " our excursion terminated. The view extended over range on range of bare hills, with little else to relieve the landscape. There are several encampments here, and the Stars and Stripes and the Union Jack float quietly side by side. On the return journey we saw a magnificent forest fire, and the bright red flame shot in fiery pillars into the clear air, extending on both sides of the line, so that we were obliged to enjoy the unusual experience of dashing right through its midst. We were also to have " accidents by flood," for the swelling of the torrents by recent rains had carried away parts of two bridges, and at one time it looked as if we would not be able to get over, and so lose our steamer. Fortunately, an hour's delay enabled the workmen to patch the bridge up sufficiently well for us to cross in a very tentative way. The line was constructed in great haste and, many people affirm, none too securely. It was British capital and British industry that surmounted the terrible White Pass, where even now the numerous skeletons of horses attest the difficulty and danger of the way. Late in the evening we returned to the *City of Topeka* and the next morning were steaming up "Glacier Bay," which is so-called from the large number of glaciers that fringe its mountain shores. The water was full of icebergs, and our vessel required the most careful navigation. Nothing could be more beautiful than the exquisite blues and tender greens of those huge ice-masses, with their summits of driven snow, and flocks of all kinds of aquatic birds wheeling and hovering around them. On both sides of the bay were bare and bleak mountains, and as we advanced we obtained a good view of the celebrated Mount Crillon, which exceeds Mount Blanc in altitude, reaching 15,900 feet—and adjacent towered Mount La Perouse, 11,300 feet, and Mount Fairweather, 15,500 feet. Having regard to their height, expectation is sadly disappointed, for, being distant upward of sixty miles, and many other mountains interposing, they distinctly fail to be impressive. The grand feature of the Alaskan excursion—the Muir Glacier, the largest in the known world—was now visible at the head of the bay. It was named after Professor Muir, of California, who first explored it some twenty years ago. It is about thirty-five miles long, by a width of one and three-quarter miles in its front portion, to fifteen miles further back. It rises from 100 to 250 feet above the surface of the sea, and extends under it at least three times as far. It has receded enormously, and every year is growing smaller, a proof, it is alleged, that the climate of Alaska is growing milder, owing to the shifting of the Japanese current. We landed in small boats, but, before leaving the ship, the name of each passenger was taken, and marked off on our return, so that none might be left behind. Arriving on the sandy shore we found Alpine stocks in a small cavity, of the existence of which we had been apprised. Armed with these we proceeded by a good path towards the Muir, obtaining views of its bold and towering front, and its kaleidoscopic range of tints. Great icebergs, detached from the glacier, were thrown on the beach, and many of the passengers mounted them and had their photos taken with arctic surroundings. Every few moments great blocks of ice fell from the Muir, plunging into the sea with a noise like thunder. Our vessel, on the preceding voyage, was in danger on account of approaching too near the glacier. An unusually gigantic boulder of ice fell, raising a wave over sixty feet high, on which the steamer hung balanced for what seemed an age, and then the great mass of ice rose very near, but fortunately clear of, the vessel, and everybody drew a breath of relief, conscious of avoiding a great danger. Since then the captains are very chary of a too close approach. The line of high tide all along the beach was marked by myriads of tiny dead shrimps, and the numerous rounded stones attested the continuous glacier action.

After our departure from the Muir the *Topeka* steered between Admiralty and Chicago Islands during several hours, and when we arrived at Killisnoo, at nine o'clock in the evening, there was still plenty of daylight to see all of interest. The making of herring-oil is the great industry of Killisnoo, and consequently the odours are generally none of the pleasantest; but, the day of our landing being Sunday, the temporary respite in the working greatly benefited the atmosphere. We saw numerous groups of pretty and clean-looking Indian women, wearing over their shoulders gaudy blankets of green and yellow, and, in marked contrast, plain black shawls on their heads. They were vending various curios, notably silver bracelets made out of dollars, reindeer moccasins, Esquimaux dolls clad in furs, and pretty models of the Alaskan canoes. We visited the house of "Jake," the Indian chief, who is almost an historical character, being hostage for the good behaviour of his tribe in 1869, when it was in a rather bellicose condition. He is said to be very amusing and courteous to visitors, but when we saw him, deep sleep, induced possibly by too liberal use of fire-water, made him oblivious to all but Morpheus. We saw his photo, taken in San Francisco— for "Jake" is a travelled man—and also some military uniforms which on occasion it pleases him to assume.

We woke next morning to find everything foggy, a circumstance none of the pleasantest, as we had to traverse Peril Strait, whose boiling waters and suggestive name indicated its shipwrecking qualities. Accustomed as we were to fir-clad shores, we were astonished at the density of the wooding, for, as we steered by one lofty island after another, even from the very sea to the topmost summits there seemed to be but impenetrable masses of trees. The cloudy skies, the cool temperature, and the brilliantly green vegetation reminded one of the British Isles. By ten o'clock we entered the magnificent Bay of Sitka, covered with hundreds of rocky islets.

Sitka is situated on the side of Baranof Island that faces the Pacific, and hence it is protected only by a few rocks from the full swell of the ocean. Sitka, the capital of Alaska, and beyond question the most interesting and beautiful town in that territory, extends with its few hundred houses along the bay. On the right of the landing wharf is the site of Baranof Castle, where the luxurious Russian Governors held almost royal sway before Alaska was purchased by the United States. Nothing now remains of it but a few charred remains, as it was accidentally burned down a few years ago. The most conspicuous building is the Greek church, with its green spire and dome. Formerly in a neglected and semi-ruinous condition, it has recently been tastefully repaired and painted, and the interior, of blue and white with the rich ornaments, is almost imposing. The altar is divided from the rest of the church by richly gilt brass doors, with inlaid figures of the four apostles in silver. There are several pictures on the walls, donated by the different Russian Governors and nobles ; for instance, a good *Annun-ciation*, and a *Baptism of our Lord ;* but the gem of the collection, and perhaps the finest picture in America, is the *Madonna*, the sweetness and beauty of whose face are inimitable. The body of the figure is in exquisitely chased silver. It is much to be deplored that so great a work of art should be left in this frail wooden building, exposed to the continual danger of fire, more especially as in the vicinity of the town forest conflagrations are of frequent occurrence during the summer. Sitka has an excellent museum of Alaskan curios, such as Indian canoes, quaint musical instruments, totem poles, bows and arrows, and ornaments. In the town proper there are a hotel, a newspaper office, and numerous curio shops. Furs can be procured for most reasonable prices here, and in one of these shops we were fortunate enough to find a genuine Chilkat blanket, *the* curio *par excellence* of Alaska, made from goat's hair, and now very rare. Other interesting objects are wooden frog-shaped card-receivers, the frog being a totemic sign held in great reverence by the Indians. An amusing lawsuit is in progress *à propos* of this. A Yakatat tribe had had the frog as its exclusive coat of arms, or totem, for many years, when, to its horror, another tribe declared its intention of assuming it, and appointed a certain day for the ceremony of erecting a totem pole. The indignant Yakatats applied to a United States lawyer for, and obtained, an injunction to restrain the audacious tribe from infringing on their rights. About this time the chief of the sued tribe died, really of pneumonia, but the Indians persisted that it was of a broken heart for not being allowed to use the frog emblem. Ridiculous' as all this may seem, it is, perhaps, not more so than the heraldic preten-sions of more civilised nations.

In the outskirts of the town were numerous pretty villas, some of them to be let for the summer months, for foreigners not infre-quently spend July and August here, where they can revel in grand scenery and enjoy phenomenal fishing in the bay. About a mile further on is the beautiful Indian River. Clear and sparkling, it flows through a large and charming park, which has been well compared to a jungle in the luxuriance of its vegetation. Lying around, where they fell, are huge cedars, over a hundred feet long and of enormous thickness, and growing out of them large trees. The devil's club, with leaves like a magnified sycamore's, is most noticeable in the park. The intense moisture and heat arising from the vicinity of the Japanese current make the place a veritable forcing-house. Returning to the steamer, we encountered frequent groups of Indians, clean and well-behaved, but civilised out of all interest by the missionaries. In the early days the white lived with the native women in undisguised concubinage, but the United States authorities gave these Lotharios the choice of wedding their dusky inamoratas or going to prison. Most of the men chose the matrimonial fetters, saying that in obedience and unselfishness the Indian women far excelled their more civilised white sisters. The Presbyterian Mission at Sitka performs much useful work, and has above a hundred Indian pupils at its school. The course extends over five years, and includes the teaching of different trades, besides the English language and the three R's. In fact, in the matter of education the aborigines fare better than the white population, for in this respect the Government at Washington has paid scant attention to its distant northern territory. Now, however, the rapid growth of the people incident on the mining discoveries has compelled attention, and remedial legislation will not be long in bettering the condition of all.

With Sitka the Alaskan trip is practically concluded, as no new port is touched at on the return voyage. We stop again at Fort Wrangell and at Juneau long enough to make our final purchases, and to enlarge our first impressions. From the former port to Seattle the passengers employ themselves writing up their diaries and gleaning information from the numerous Klondykers who have joined the ship on their return from Dawson City. We hear many tales of adventure and endurance which, though told in a "plain, unvarnished" manner, speak more strongly to the imagination than more ambitious narratives. Thus rapidly passed the days, till early one morning the cry, "Seattle!" tells us that one delightful episode in our life is closed—the Alaskan voyage is over.

R. W. W. CRYAN.

# CAPACITY IN MEN AND WOMEN.

THIS much vexed question has been treated often and variously by many writers and speakers in modern times; hence no apology is needed for considering it in this article from perhaps a wider stand-point than it is usually accorded.

There are a few well-known axioms, forming planks in the Liberal political propaganda of the hour, which hardly need, one would think, reiteration at this stage of thought. I allude to those which herald the endeavour to give the capacity of women scope in political fields, under the idea that taxation and representation should go together, since " taxation without representation is tyranny " !

Were it not that some minds are too jealously narrow to recognise that such truth—indeed, most truth—applies all round, there would be no need for the Woman's Movement, or any other movement, to enforce particular sides of it. But until that happy time shall have arrived when justice shall reign ubiquitously over human affairs, both writers and speakers will be required to pull down the screens which prejudice is for ever putting up against certain sides of truth, in order to show that the community at large is simply darkened detrimentally by the shadows such screens throw.

How strange it must seem to the denizens of higher spheres, if such there be, that upon the earth endless friction and ages of struggle go to evolve the popular reception of such simple tenets of justice as would give rights and possibilities as freely to women as to men, position as cordially and fervently to the dark-coloured as to the white races, religious liberty as gladly to the Catholic as to the Protestant !

And were all the women of England unanimously to rebel from Imperial taxation to-morrow, they would practically evince their capacity to grasp the well-worn political axiom already alluded to, and yet surprise many men who entirely ignore or deny, while making that very valid quotation in their own interests, the appli-cation of it to which women have an equally legitimate right.

Yet, though "a fair field and no favour" for the exercise of capacity by either sex, is a fit and natural subject for political agita-tion, it is by no means merely the political aspect of this question with which we would here deal.

The sphere wherein human capacity works must necessarily be as wide as the world is, and as varied as are the talents every item of mankind possesses. It is, therefore, to this wider human aspect of the matter to which attention may most profitably be directed.

In what does the capacity found in men and women differ? Where is it alike?

How far does it divide the sexes? Where unite them?

Are there mental capacities and faculties which exclusively belong to men from which women are exempt, and *vice versâ?* Or is it merely physical capacity which invariably differentiates the sexes?

And does this difference in physique and constitutional capacity constitute an inequality or a bond of union between men and women?

These are the questions which meet us at the threshold of this subject.

A definition of capacity, however, let us first have—" The power of containing a certain quantity," and again, " ability," according to the dictionary.

Yes, it is aptitude for work—mental, manual, or physical. And often, it may be asserted from observation, the mental or manual capacity or skill is inherited *by the son from the mother, by the daughter from the father.*

In substantiation of which it is usually admitted that most men of genius have had remarkable mothers; and it is well known that women of genius have been fathered by remarkable men.

Yet how variedly, in what multitudinous and different degrees, does custom react upon the natural endowments of all of us!

And still the ordinary talker may be heard readily assigning monopoly of brain power to men, artistic faculty to women; vicious ways to men, virtuous and domestic callings to women; manual labour out of doors exclusively to men, the lighter spheres of usefulness indoors to women!

It may here be stated, in spite of current ideas to the contrary, that the person who would limit and prescribe the capacity of women to fit his own ideas, or a local custom, is in danger of being confuted if he lift his eyes where we would have him lift them—to the contemplation of facts as they lie open for inspection in history and human experience.

If mental capacity and talents are characteristically divided between men and women, they will be found so divided—masculinely and femininely—universally; for the division of sex is universal and invariable. If physical capacity alone differentiates the sexes, it will also be found so to differentiate them universally.

Universality must be the test of such an assertion as this, since the divisor, as well as the characteristic of sex, must, without doubt, be both as universal and invariable as sex itself is; and that is as consistently constant as the extension of the human race itself.

Let us consider secular history, both primitive and civilised, aɪ a religious history, both mythical and sacred, with regard to th matter; remembering that whichever is the true idea will have t be proved true, up to the hilt, through every nationality all over the globe, from country to country, continent to continent, through every generation and many an age; because the difference between the sexes must be just as universal as sex itself is, and that has remained intact from pole to pole, from ancient to modern times.

Turning to the testimony of secular history, as gleaned from its primitive stages first, what says this?

Many writers, including notably of late years Karl Pearson, in his *Ethic of Free Thought*, record the capacity of women to nucleate society in mother-love and its concomitant, maternal energy. The matriarchal age, a historical although a recondite fact, attests that home and agriculture were founded in woman's efforts by the tribal mothers of the children whose fathers were not so distinguishable as they ought to have been—not distinguishable enough, at all events, to be relied upon for help in parental duty. Hence the mother not only bore, but also provided for, her child, and land and name were inherited through the mother; instances of this being still extant in tribal life. In the insect world there is a striking parallel to the matriarchal capacity in every ant-hill, its wonderful order and industry being instigated, founded, and sustained by maternal energy.

Among the aborigines of South Australia there are many customs witnessing to the equal capacity shown by woman in primitive stages of society, where legal and foreign affairs are open to her influence.

If war be imminent, a council of women meets and squats in a ring near the council of men; and it is in the event of the unanimity of the decisions of both councils that action is determined upon. Indeed, only after the women, as trusted ambassadors, have failed in their friendly expedition to effect peace does war break out.

(A valuable hint here for civilisation to follow!)

Again, in the horrible occurrences of treacherous murder which disgrace tribal life it is the woman's instinct—the wife or mother of the murdered man—which is consulted in the interests of justice and taken as the guide to revenge.

But, leaving this embryo stage of capacity in social organisation, let us glance at the record of the working capacity of women held by civilisation.

Noticeable among the civilisations which have left deep impress upon history, are the Indian, the Egyptian, the European, and, lastly, the American.

What have women been capable of doing in these different civilisations that comprise a period existent as long as civilisation itself w—longer, indeed, than the 5000 years usually ascribed to it—for some of the bas-reliefs of the Egyptian pyramids are supposed to be 10,000 years old, and some of the old Vedic hymns are ascribed to the year 12,000 B.C.

To begin near at hand and work backwards; in America they are bringing up families and going into businesses, preaching from pulpits, teaching in schools, entering successfully the legal, medical, literary, and dramatic professions.

They are nursing in hospitals, working as matrons in prisons, and in every direction striving for means to live amid a rampant competitive struggle for existence.

Yet, remarkable though it may seem—the prejudice which has fallen before women's capacity to befriend, and to act as colleague with, and to companion man, in the workaday world, still obstructs her entrance to work and privilege in political fields.

Many of the American States, Kansas and Wyoming excepted, have done less for the political enfranchisement of their women than England, Australia, or New Zealand, and the American Republic is notoriously corrupt. Is it in consequence of this?

In Wyoming, however, a territory as large as the British Isles put together, the Bench, the ballot, and all the civil offices have, for over twenty years, redounded to the indisputable capacity of women to judge, to vote, and to advocate—using those terms technically—as well, if not better than men can do.

Still in our own country, England, what strange limits we find yet extant with regard to popular conceptions of women's capacity! A woman, the Queen, holding the highest and most exacting office in the land, and women still excluded from the Bench, Parliament, and, as a rule, the pulpit and public dinners!

Still are we told that the fragility of a woman's physique " unfits " her for the higher and more remunerative professions, while the obvious fact that it always has enabled her to cope single-handed with the world's drudgery escapes comment!

It is indeed a superfine and curious sense of justice, which, working on this plea, ousts her from wealthy positions and well paid public offices, while it keeps her standing for twelve hours per diem in shops, mills, or at the pit's brow, and at nail-making!

And so strangely askew is the popular esteem of modesty among some English people to this day, that a woman's capability to take part in public platform work on behalf of morality or municipal needs, will cause a shudder, in those who cling with affection to the memory of a Jenny Lind or a Mrs. Siddons! Beautiful, womanly women these, without doubt, we all admit; yet they stepped into the most conspicuous publicity possible! " Ah! but then," says this strange judgment, " only to minister to the world's amusement and æsthetic pleasure." It is most undoubtedly this same twitch in the modesty idea, which considers it "indecent" for a woman to 's in a faculties in the law courts as barrister or judge—in the serv..rove her own sex even—while it yet tolerates or welcomes her there in <sub>se</sub> prisoner's dock or the witness-box; often making of her isolati.<sub>g</sub> in the latter position a convenient butt for most compromising ana undeserved innuendoes.

What strikes the unbiased student of capacity in sex as unfair in all this is, *not* the fact that women must appear in public to answer for and to the frailties of human nature, but that, when there, they are never judged by their peers—*i.e.*, their own sex! A position which, in regard to themselves, Englishmen denounce as intolerable. And it is intolerable and illogical, with the object-lesson which Wyoming affords well in view!

In support of the slight to women's governmental powers which England in this particular, with its queenly exception, still presents, it has been urged that "women cannot fight, therefore they shall not govern."

"Upon the capacity to fight rests the stability of nations," says this argument.

"Women do not risk their lives in national defence, therefore they shall not be allowed a voice in Imperial affairs."

Strange reasoning and still stranger deduction!

The first assertion that women cannot fight is untrue to the facts of history. Joan d'Arc, who conducted the war of 1429 in France in person, is by no means the only woman who has excelled in military talent. The Chinese have a brilliant example also; another appeared chronicled in the newspapers the other day in modern warfare, the Greco-Turkish War; women are found among the Boer sharpshooters, and in both hemispheres distinct historical reference is found in many countries to the Amazons or women warriors.

Scandinavia, too, had its "shield maidens"; and in Lord Byron's Journal, distinguished for accuracy of fact, we find allusions to the share women bore in the guerilla warfare entailed by the Greek struggle for independence, which occurred at the beginning of this (the nineteenth) century; their ability and courage therein he warmly commended, while admiring the beauty of those he came across who were engaged in making roads! And in the Irish agrarian agitation of contemporary notice, the same share has fallen to women—even the share of physical struggle; as it has also in the great commercial crises of the day, the strikes between labour and capital.

Indeed, however much force may be deprecated as a moral arbiter: it is as inevitably mixed up with certain stages of human development, as are the talents of women, which continually have and will take therein a valiant part.

—long is it true, apart from these considerations, that women do not risk their lives" in national defence?

Motherhood is itself the confutation of this statement. Only by the risking of women's lives daily in the interests of population can the army be manned, and the ravages of war recouped.

It is woman, then, *à priori* who has a right to a voice in the expenditure of life in war.

"But," the reader may here interpose, "you seem to be forgetting the capacity of man!"

By no means; yet since his is so seldom disputed, there is not the same need to assert his. Happy, indeed, has man been all these centuries, compared with his helpmeet and sister, for his talent to do anything he chose to do has seldom been questioned! No bitter opposition on the score of sex have his claims to work received; but rather warm approbation!

Yet, in turning from the belligerent to the peaceful arts, in our cosmopolitan survey, we may here and at once release him from the delusion popularly cherished in England, that he cannot sew!

The very position peculiar to the convenient plying of the needle is characteristically male, and announces the masculine profession of sewing! For undoubtedly, though the tailor of *The Arabian Nights* may be fictitious, the tailor of Regent Street is an actual and mundane fact.

Sailors, too, are deft with the needle; and though it is well known that most of the sewing—especially the beautiful Church embroideries met with in England—are the work of women, done the boudoir or in the cloister, or the school of art; it is equally certain that most of the beautiful embroidery of India is the work of men.

Nursing, cooking, and housework are supposed to be beyond masculine capacity in England, and generally fall to feminine hands; but in France man proves daily that he can both cook and clean; and in India, also, he spends much of his time in domestic work.

Field work in England is done chiefly by men. In France, Italy, and Sicily, parts of Turkey and India, however, it is successfully carried on by women. There was a time in Italy—how strange it seems to read of it now!—when the following of the Fine Arts was restricted to "women, children, and tradesmen!" Yet Dante and Michael Angelo, of noble birth, arose there, in spite of this idiosyncratic national thought. In our own country, all the studios and art-galleries bear witness to the artistic talent found both in men and women.

But to drop again from the Fine Arts to drudgery, it is a common idea among English people, that there is something peculiarly appropriate to women in the wash-tub; and that it really needs the special fragility of the feminine sex to stand for long hours over this in a damp cellar or laundry. Yet the statutes of ancient India prove clearly, that washing was considered a masculine calling in those days, for a penalty is there meted out to the *washerman* who mixes in his work the wearing apparel of different persons. Moreover, the washerman exists in India to this day!

Athletic exercises have been monopolised in some countries by boys and men; but modern education is beginning to acknowledge that which Plato and the maidens of Sparta knew long ago—that the physiques of women and girls are also capable of these.

How just was the Spartan conception of women's talent to manage estates may be gathered from the fact that at one time it was calculated that half the land of the State was held in their own right by the women of Sparta; those mothers whose proverbial dictate for courage in times of war to their sons was—" With your shield or upon it."

In the brightest epoch of Egyptian civilisation—about 2000 B.C.— women were known to be capable of much that modern European prejudice would still prevent them from doing. Not only did they succeed in the dynasty to the regal office, when that entailed the strictest regulation and publicity of life—even to asceticism in food, and initiated occultism—but they, as a matter of course, also filled sacerdotal offices. Women of the highest rank led the religious services in person as priestesses, when religious ceremonies were elaborated to the highest degree, and most popularly revered. And—wonder of wonders—in Egypt at that bright epoch, it was taken for granted that women were entitled to be present at public dinners!

Now there awaits religious history for our examination. What evidence does it yield to this issue?

If we exclude modern orthodoxy here as well as elsewhere, the value and variety of feminine capacity transpires. Refer where one may, in mythology or the faiths of Eastern or Western peoples, and still have deity and the attribute to deity been personified as feminine.

In India we find such testimony as this—in the ancient Vedic hymns, and not as an isolated example—" With my invocation I celebrate the thought of the Father, and that mighty sovereign power of the Mother, the prolific parents have made all creatures."

In Egypt a *goddess*—Isis—was worshipped as *the sovereign source of all other deities!*

It is also remarkable that the most importantly cognising functions ascribed to the deified power by the faiths of the Greeks and Egyptians were conceived as feminine.

The Fates—*i.e.*, the regulators of human destiny—the moulders of that obstinate and rebellious material, human nature, to spirituality—were personified as feminine; and supremacy of *wisdom* was represented by the Egyptian *goddess* Neith, and the Grecian *goddess* Minerva.

How powerful, too, was the goddess Tregg in Scandinavian theology. And to a Norse goddess, Syne, was ascribed by faith that great task—the defence of truth in courts of law!

Coming to Christian times, how many thousands of Roman Catholics have worshipped a woman, as the Virgin Mother of God! (Whether this be strictly in accordance with the tenets of their religion or not!)

And in Genesis, how mysterious, yet clear, is the allusion to duplexity of sex capacity ascribed to the Biblical idea of the Deity (chapter i. verse 27): "So God created man in his own image, *in the image of God created he him, male and female created he them.*"

This verse sums up in an epitome, that which heathen mythology strove after variously, the idea that Deity combines in essence all the capacity that man in the aggregate—*i.e.*, as consisting of both the sexes—ever can hope to evince, and, of course, infinitely more! But the obvious inference is unmistakable. Unless both man and woman be taken together to represent "man"—or mankind— mankind cannot hope to "image" or mirror forth the Divine! Again we have this idea enforced (chapter v. verse 2) in the words: "Male and female created he them, and blessed *them*, and called *their name Adam.*

Then where does the Adam and Eve history come in *after* this clear and prior statement with regard to the prior creation of woman? Hence it must have been wrongly used as typifying an unequal and subsequent creation of woman; but probably may have reference, as many believe, to a later development of *spirituality*, as taken from the *material man*—*i.e.*, Adam, or mankind in the aggregate.

Our survey of secular history and religious history, then, clearly proves, that men and women are not divided by different mental or working powers, but ever, glancing at human nature as a whole, we find, capable of undertaking the same work, the *identical tasks*, bearing and sharing similar burdens all the world over; the man doing in this country what the woman does in that, the various kinds of toil entailed by living.

Are, then, men and women alike? is the inquiry abruptly forced.

By no means, of course, comes the inevitable reply. Although so capable of holding much in common, there is always a difference between them which nothing eradicates, modifies, or alters; and this difference alone unswervingly meets the test of universality which it should meet, being maintained the same through every variety of race, from age to age, from continent to continent—the physical, functional and constitutional difference which does separate men and women, and which both characterises and differentiates the sexes!

This alone gives to man the important function of fatherhood, to woman the honourable career of motherhood, and all that these constitutionally entail. And no legislative measures need be taken for the continuity of motherhood, since Nature herself is the guarantor for the stability of that. And the physical delicacy it entails upon some women—either at certain periods of their lives or during the greater part of them—again need not be legislated against, for weakness is inevitably its own deterrent.

Rather than beat women back from useful careers because of the physical strain caused by the mothering of each generation, rather than oust them from the ballot and representation in political life, it would be fairer to grant them that added consideration which true courtesy always accords the more heavily handicapped everywhere, and which would be as sound politically as it is graceful and just socially.

For ever, though fallen under the same frailties or raised by the same aspirations, the difference which really does exist between men and women will remain intact: uninterfered with by any provincial distribution of work, making them separate yet inseparable, united, the joint propagators of that divine mystery, life.

And around this, the ever-recurring wonder, this potency of parentage, cluster all the tender reasons that always induce the one sex to defer to the other—the man to become the protector of the woman, the woman to become trustful of the man.

And, again, it may here be emphasised that these natural instincts are too deeply engrained, set, and guarded by Nature ever to be upset by any arrangement or re-arrangement of the grooves of work.

Experience proves that children are born in spite of the toil of the mills, the fields, the pit's brow. We may safely conjecture that the world would not become depopulated if the higher and more remunerative professions and Parliament were accessible to the talent of contemporary Englishwomen.

Talent and capacity being non-sexual, we never need fear to unsex woman by giving free scope to all her faculties. Hence it is useless for the hasty harbingers of shallow maxims to ascribe to nature that which is merely artificial; hopeless for them to set down a national custom as a cosmopolitan fact; utterly illogical to argue for universal theory by provincial thought!

For the experience of life and history ever baffles such short-sighted and incompetent theorising, by producing in different quarters of the globe evidence with which it may be destroyed.

And this evidence affords indisputable proof that, taken as a whole, the two great halves of the human race are equal; equal in value—as proved by the necessity of the existence of both to effect continuity of existence; equal in capacity—as proved by a survey of the facts of history; and, drawn and united together by a difference which is calculated to cement their interests completely in parentage.

Any Englishman, therefore, who would prescribe or restrict woman's work in mental fields, is no wit wiser than the Chinaman who cramps her feet!

It were well to remind such a one in parting, that progress is of universal extraction, and bound to make international advance; hence if he, or any other man in this small island, would arrogate to himself command of its tide, like Canute's flatterers of old, he but exposes his own vanity and impotence!

"Thus far shalt thou go and no further" is the Divine decree; and the full tide of woman's capable advancement shall ebb no more at man's command than did the sea of old.

EFFIE JOHNSON.

# REVENUE WITHOUT TAXATION.

(*Unrevised.*)

THE Chancellor of the Exchequer, it is said, has been making inquiry in Lombard Street, as to what plan the financialists there think should be adopted by him in order to raise the necessary amount of money to meet the enormous expenditure which is being incurred in connection with the war in South Africa. It seems to be estimated that from about fifty to one hundred millions of extra money may be required to be provided for this year.

This is a big bill, but it must be met either by taxes or by borrowing and adding to the National Debt in some way or other. Having given much attention to finance and banking for many years while engaged in a commercial office in my early days, and afterwards engaged as a commercial traveller and wholesale merchant, I had the very best opportunities of becoming acquainted with monetary and commercial matters in all their bearings, and more particularly regarding our banking and currency system, which has been very much discussed in my time in a Chamber of Commerce with which I was connected for many years. I was also appointed a member of the Central Committee of the Associated Chambers when the Bank Acts came on for discussion. There was then a deputation appointed to wait upon Sir Stafford Northcote, with a view to recommend the appointment of a committee to inquire into the working of the Bank Acts and their reform. The late Mr. Sampson Lloyd, banker, took the lead at that meeting, it was arranged by him who were to speak, but one gentleman from Bristol went out of the way and said that the Scotch banks should not be allowed to issue £1 notes, seeing there were no £1 notes allowed in England; I ventured to reply it would be better to introduce £1 notes into England than to take them away from Scotland, as the notes were as good as gold. A Committee of the House of Commons was therefore appointed to inquire into the banking question, but Mr. Goschen was so strongly against any reform in the banking and currency system of this country that no reform was got.

The *Bankers' Magazine* for February has an article on the question, "Should the Peel Act be Modified?" written by Mr. Hermann Schmidt. This shows that the bankers are themselves now seeing that Peel's Bank Act is a great hindrance to good banking, and a bar on their business. In short, what is now felt about the present English banking system is that it is quite out of keeping with the present free-trade times.

On the present occasion, the Chancellor of the Exchequer having to raise so much money to meet the expenses of the present war, a complete change in the British monetary system is called for, so as to allow every facility for furnishing funds to carry on the different departments of the Government until an honourable peace is arrived at. The nation is now brought to face this big bill of £100,000,000 or so, therefore I venture to write this article with the view of throwing out a few hints to help the Chancellor of the Exchequer to find an easy way to get " over the stile."

It may seem to some parties to be a Utopian idea to suppose that a national revenue can be obtained without laying on taxation; but there is a great precedent for doing so, for the United States of America have already adopted this plan and found it to be an admirable arrangement for raising money *gratis*. It was adopted by the United States in 1862 when they were engaged in war (as Britain now is), and this is a great recommendation for us to adopt the same system to supply our financial necessity. A banker in Buffalo at that crisis recommended the United States Government to issue national notes from the Treasury on the security of the national credit to supply a circulating medium of money for that country. The issue of £75,000,000 was authorised by Congress, and these notes, in different denominations, immediately went into circulation and carried on the trade of the States *without gold at all* (as that metal was at a high premium) down till 1878, when gold had fallen to its old level.

Then, but not till then, gold payments were resumed in the States.

Since writing the foregoing part of the article, the *Economist* for February 24 has come to hand, which contains a communication from its New York correspondent clearing up the connection between the American money market and the money market of London, and showing the good advantage of having an *expansive* as well as a sound national currency. From that

" It appears that the total volume of money in circulation on February 1, 1900, was $2,003,149,355 (£400,620,871) an increase compared with last year on the basis of population (77,116,000 on February 1). The calculation *per capita* is $25.98 or nearly £5 5s. per head. When comparisons are extended over a longer period, however, one gets the best idea of the great increase in circulation; the volume of money in circulation on January 1879 was only $816,266,721 (£163,253,345), while on February 1, 1900, it was almost two and one-half times as large. The expansion of the circulation has more than kept pace with the growth of the population, for while the population may be estimated at about one and a half times what it was in 1879 the money in circulation in the United States now is nearly two and a half times larger."

There is an example for Great Britain. Money is now only 2 to $2\frac{1}{2}$ per cent. in New York.

That was just what Mr. Pitt did in 1798, when gold, during our war with France, rose to so high a premium that a guinea was worth about 25s. He recommended the suspension of gold payments and the adoption of the legal note currency, which continued to be the currency of Britain down till 1821. This is worth remembering by our bankers, for Pitt was a sounder financier than Peel, and if Peel had not spoilt Pitt's excellent monetary and free-trade system by violently contracting the circulation of legalised Bank of England notes there would have been fewer financial crises in the country than there have been, and trade and commerce would have gone on quite freely both at home and abroad; for when the Corn Laws were enacted in 1816, the Bank Act, making gold coin, and *not* Bank of England notes, the standard of value, was passed at the same time. This was understood to have been done to make the rents of farms payable to the landlords in gold at the premium prices, which was altogether a selfish action of the Lords of that period. Gold payments should not have been resumed until gold fell to its old level, as was done in the United States under similar circumstances.

The error of the Bank Acts was that the price of gold was fixed at £3 17s. 9d. to *buy* at and £3 17s. 10½d. to *sell* at at all times. The proper principle to have followed should have been, as Adam Smith and Mr. Pitt proved, to allow gold to rise and fall in price according to demand and supply as with other metals. The way we are now dealing with the Bank of England is ruinous with regard to gold. It is, in a manner, bound to pay too much for gold bullion when it is *plentiful*, and to sell it too cheap when that metal is scarce. It ought to be bought and sold for market prices according to supply and demand, and this would not disturb the money market and the Bank rate so much as it does. The Bank seems at length to have discovered that it can *lower* the buying-price for gold, as it has intimated that it will only buy certain kinds of gold at reduced prices. Now, if it can make a small reduction, it can also make a large reduction; and, if so, why should it not reduce its buying price for Johannesburg gold and so put an end to the war directly. For there is no doubt the Transvaal war would collapse. if Britain ceased to buy the gold at the present inflated price.

Free trade in gold and in banking is urgently required. The old contracted and monopolist system of doing banking business in London is getting out of date. There is far less *discounting* of bills in trade than there used to be. Mercantile business is now more generally carried on upon *cash terms* of payment than on credit. Accounts are more generally paid in cash by bank notes or "bank cheques." Thus bank cheques and bank notes are superseding the use of gold coin. It is said that in London almost all the business payments are made in this manner. The drying-up of the supply of bills has driven the bankers to do more business in advances to customers on cash credit accounts and advances on overdrafts than formerly. This more liberal system is better for the banks as well as for their customers. It is found that as banks increase their advances to their customers the deposits increase in the banks. This much is to be said for liberal banking. But banks are not yet liberal enough. The banks ought to turn the deposits lodged in the banks to the very best account to *serve their customers*, as the deposits belong to the public. At the same time, all banks should be allowed to issue their own notes if they lodged Consols with the Treasury to cover their note issues, and then obtain a licence from the Treasury for a corresponding issue of notes, and be subject to Treasury inspection.

This brings me back to the idea I set out with, namely, to show *how to raise revenue without taxation* and to meet the expenses of the present war in the easiest manner. Having seen how the same financial business is carried on in the great Treasury Bank of the United States it seems to me to be a very simple thing to adopt something like the same economical system by the British Government. I was shown through the Treasury in Washington by an official there who explained the way money matters were managed there and the circulation of notes kept up. I was particularly interested in the process of printing the National notes. These notes are put through fourteen processes of printing so that they are almost impossible to be forged, and are as safe as our sovereign. The public have full confidence in them, and they are the common circulating medium in that country. It is a great saving to the States to use paper money instead of gold. If Great Britain would adopt paper-money, as it did in former times, particularly in Pitt's time, when Bank of England notes were made *legal tenders* in England, and continued to be so down till 1821, this would be a great saving for this country.

It is estimated that there is about £90,000,000 of gold coin in England, Scotland, and Ireland, including what is in the banks and in circulation. This money would be worth 2½ per cent. per annum to invest in Consols. If this large amount of gold coin were to be gathered in and thereafter superseded by an authorised issue of 10s. and £1 notes from a National Treasury to take the place of the sovereign and half-sovereign coins just as required, *that change would soon save as much money as would meet even the heavy expenses of the war* without making the country feel this plan of raising money to be a burden. On the contrary, it is more than likely that this proposed plan, if adopted, would be found to be a great public boon, as a great expansion of the currency and a freer competition in banking would be obtained and is wanted. The Treasury Bank would act as the great National Bank in London with branches all over the three kingdoms, and take in deposits from all parties, allowing such interest for these deposits as would be found to be reasonable ; and, on the other hand, lend out and make advances to all parties, large and small, on satisfactory securities at reasonable rates. In that way the whole accumulated and lying money of the country could be put into active use in different businesses and industries instead of letting so much remain dormant as now. The olden mode of close banking is now, fortunately, getting out of date, and bankers are growing liberal to their customers, and even giving them cash credits and overdrafts pretty freely since they are finding so few bills passing. This is as it ought to be, as merchants have to give credit to their customers, without security, generally, so might bankers, the more so as they are *paid for giving credit.* I have been informed by commercial travellers that it is quite a common practice in Birmingham and the Midlands for the banks there to give very good credits and accommodation to tradesmen to enable them to carry on business with, and these banks are prospering more than the old banks.

There is a great deal of banking business done in the regular way which is as safe as can be, the doubtful cases are comparatively few and easily watched. There used to be too much strictness with some old-fashioned bankers, which injured the trade of the place. Bad bankers sometimes keep down a town or a district, while good bankers can raise up trade where they see fit. Competition will cure this. The popularising of banking and the spread of the circulating medium in this country will make the manufactures and other branches of industry—even farmers and market gardeners—turn out an immense quantity more goods and stuffs than they are now doing, provided they are properly supplied with the *needful.*

This needful money is just what the Treasury Banks would supply. If we had a proper system of supplying good, *honest* workmen, however poor, with money to help them to work out their own independence—see what the " people's banks " have done for the Continental people—there would be no room for " the Gordon class of money-lenders " to " take in " people here as they do.

There are millions of money gathered into our savings banks, but by their trustees sunk with the Commissioners of the National Debt, for which only 2½ per cent. is allowed. This is treating the thrifty, industrious classes very shamefully, for the savings bank trustees could invest the savings to much better advantage if they would study to get the best investment to be had for the money. I have had experience in this way. In 1875 I was a trustee of a savings bank, and some of us trustees thought we could do better than send the whole deposits to the National Debt Commissioners; so we started an auxiliary bank along with the old one, and allowed the depositors to lodge their money either with the old bank or the new one.

We gave one-half per cent. more for interest in the new bank, which we registered as a limited company with a large enough subscribed capital, callable but little needed. Both banks have done very well, but the companies' bank has done best: it has now got a large amount of deposits—about £100,000 in a town of 24,000 inhabitants, and it is making a profit on its capital of nearly 20 per cent., giving 10 per cent. dividend to the shareholders, and carrying the balance to a guarantee fund. This shows that there is great room in the country for improving the savings-bank system. I have seen and know how much better the savings banks are carried on in the United States and in Germany, and would strongly recommend the improvement of the banks here, so as to make the savings already gathered in and lying locked up and idle to be made available for the raising of the working classes by their own industry and thrift to help one another on. The co-operative stores are not good enough. Banks to gather in and lend out money to *work* upon would be better.

> "To catch Dame Fortune's golden smile
> Assiduously wait upon her,
> And gather gear by every wile
> That's justified by honour!
> Not for to hide it in a hedge,
> Nor for a train attendant,
> But for the glorious privilege
> Of being independent!"

THE LATE ROBERT EWEN.

# CONTEMPORARY LITERATURE.

## PHILOSOPHY AND THEOLOGY.

WE believe it was of Dr. J. H. Stirling that it was said that he is the only man living who understands Hegel; whether this is correct or not, we feel pretty certain that Dr. Stirling is the only man who understands Dr. Stirling. For metaphysical subtleties his new volume *What is Thought?*[1] is clearly entitled to the prize. We have spent a great deal of time over it, and our " general conclusion so far " is that we are no wiser than before. The aim of philosophy as expounded in this work, Dr. Stirling tells us, is the " explanation of the universe." But the universe is still unexplained—" so far." Science, says our author, has failed. " Metaphysicians, with a similar purpose, may not have done perfectly or even well; but have they not done better? " If they have, it is a matter for regret that they are not more intelligible. Still we have met with metaphysicians that are more intelligible than Dr. Stirling. Kant, Schelling, and Hegel afford much material for discussion in these pages. We gather that Kant is becoming obsolete, and that Schelling confounded Leibnitz with Descartes; but Hegel appears to be sound —" so far." The question "What is thought?" is still unanswered, for how can thought be the absolute, the first? Can there be a thinking subject without a thinkable object? But the Ego is at once a double, subject and object of thought: is the Ego, therefore, the *first?* We must refer our readers with a taste for metaphysics to Dr. Stirling for an answer.

" How philosophers misunderstand one another " might be the title of a neat pamphlet by Dr. Paul Carus, really entitled *Kant and Spencer.*[2] " Auguste Comte," says Dr. Carus, " denounced Kant as an antiquated metaphysician, and Herbert Spencer looked upon him as the champion of mediævalism and dogmatism." The truth is, says the defender of the founder of the critical philosophy, that neither of them knew anything about Kant. However, as Mr. Spencer discredits Dr. Carus's knowledge of Kant, they appear to

---

[1] *What is Thought?* Or the Problem of Philosophy by way of a General Conclusion so far. By James Hutchison Stirling, LL.D. Edinburgh: T. & T. Clark. 1900.
[2] *Kant and Spencer.* By Dr. Paul Carus. Chicago: The Open Court Publishing Company. London: Kegan Paul Trench & Co.

be on equal terms. Mr. Spencer appears to be well advised in refusing to prolong a fruitless controversy.

Leaving metaphysics, we get on more solid and fruitful ground, in a volume entitled *Ethics and Religion*,[1] a series of essays or addresses by Sir J. Seeley, Dr. Felix Adler, Mr. W. M. Salter, Professor H. Sidgwick, Professor G. Von Gizycki, Dr. Bosanquet, Mr. Leslie Stephen, Dr. Stanton Coit, and Professor Muirhead. The volume is edited by the Society of Ethical Propagandists. This is a book we can recommend; the level maintained by the various writers is so uniformly high that it would be invidious to select any particular essay for special commendation. The spirit of the essays is by no means antagonistic to religion, but popular theology is occasionally treated to criticism.

Mr. J. M. Robertson's attitude towards religion is so well known and well defined that it is unnecessary to describe it. The present volume[2] consists of reviews and articles which appear to have been previously published. Professor H. Drummond, Mr. Lang, Mr. Balfour, and Mr. Gladstone come in for some trenchant criticisms, to which it is only fair to say they lay themselves open, and give Mr. Robertson an easy victory. Mr. Robertson is very caustic in his treatment of Mr. Saintsbury, and goes to the indefensible length of charging every one who defends opinions with which he does not agree with doing so for "economic" reasons. Mr. Robertson should abstain from imputing unworthy motives.

It does not need much talent to criticise "Evangelical" theology, so that Mr. C. P. Gasquoine in his *Scientific Theology*[3] had an easy task. It is nevertheless ably done. The direct object of the criticism is a sermon or essay by Dr. T. P. Forsyth which was read at the Congregational Conference at Boston, U.S.A., and was afterwards printed in the *Contemporary Review*. We believe that Dr. Forsyth is regarded as a leading light amongst the Congregationalists, and that this address is described as "epoch-making." If this is really the case, it speaks very little for the intelligence of the Congregationalists. Mr. Gasquoine's criticism is as just as it is forcible.

There is a freshness about Mr. Gould's *Will Women Help?*[4] that makes it attractive. The relation of women to religion and free thought has not received the attention it deserves; women have always played a great part in promoting religious movements, though they have originated few. Whether they will assist Mr. Gould in liberating modern thought from theological bonds remains to be seen, but they should read his appeal. The chapter on the attitude of the Bible towards women is a striking one. The Bible,

---

[1] *Ethics and Religion.* London : Swan Sonnenschein & Co.
[2] *Studies in Religious Fallacy.* By J. M. Robertson. London : Watts & Co.
[3] *Scientific Theology : a Reply to Popular "Evangelicalism."* By C. P. Gasquoine. London : Watts & Co.
[4] *Will Women Help?* By F. J. Gould. London : Watts & Co.

as he says, is a purely masculine production, though we understand that Harnack has recently put forward the theory that a woman (Prisca) wrote the Epistle to the Hebrews. We are glad to see that Mr. Gould acquits St. Paul of writing the absurd passage beginning, "I permit not a woman to teach." The rationalists have no such prejudice, but it is still strong amongst Christians.

Our own sympathies are distinctly on the side of religion, and, *pace* Mr. Robertson, not from "economic" motives; "it is therefore with regret that we have to confess that the only two theological books before us are really inferior to the rationalistic ones in point of intellect. This, however, is purely accidental. The first is by a lady—*Old Testament Types and Teaching*,[1] by H. W. Smith. This a well-written and a very good book of its kind, but it is not profound. The writer finds matter for the edification of Christians in the books of the Old Testament by reading into them meanings which neither the historian nor the critic can find there. It is in a sense devout, and therefore deserving of respect, but more we cannot say for it.

The last book on our list is to the last degree irrational. It is entitled *To the End of Time, a Prophetic Work*,[2] by Albert Mitchell. The author no doubt is a sensible man, but we think many an inmate of a lunatic asylum could have done as well. What is a prophetic work? Judging by this it is a jumble of the Bible—Abraham, Daniel, Nebuchadnezzar, the Czar of Russia, the Prime Minister of England, the Ottoman Empire, the Millennium, the Lake of Fire, mysterious dates, bad grammar and worse spelling—mix all these up together, and any one can make a book like the one before us.

---

## SOCIOLOGY, POLITICS, AND JURISPRUDENCE.

IT is now nearly twelve years since the first volume of the *Dictionary of Political Economy*[3] appeared. Vol. III. now before us brings this stupendous work to its triumphant conclusion. We say "stupendous" advisedly, not on account of the bulk, for three volumes of 750 pages apiece is a mere nothing as dictionaries go nowadays, but by reason of the vast field of knowledge traversed. Moreover, although somewhat similar works have been published in France,

---

[1] *Old Testament Types and Teaching.* By Hannah Whitall Smith. London: James Nisbet & Co.
[2] *To the End of Time.* By Albert Mitchell. London: H. R. Allenson.
[3] *Dictionary of Political Economy.* Edited by R. H. Inglis Palgrave, F.R.S. Vol. III.—N-Z. London: Macmillan & Co. Ltd. New York: The Macmillan Company. 1899.

Germany, the United States, and even in this country, none of them have undertaken what is attempted here. It would, of course, be easy to pick holes in a work of this description. This article, it may be alleged, is not exhaustively treated, another contains information known to every fourth-form Public School boy. " Better," says the editor, Mr. Inglis Palgrave, "that fifty should consider an explanation superfluous than that one should find a difficulty unsolved." Absolute fulness of treatment in such a work is, of course, impossible, but the want has been to a large extent met by an admirable system of cross-references. Perhaps the most valuable feature is the bibliography attached to each subject. The student who wishes to pursue his investigation is here referred to the best authorities. To the barrister, next to knowledge of the law, his most valuable stock-in-trade is knowledge where to find it. Another useful feature is the biographies of less known writers, whose monographs are sometimes of greater value than the great works of better known men.

Not only is the historical method employed, but also the mathematical. In connection with the latter the use of diagrams is explained, as well as the graphic method. As a practical application of these latter we refer the reader to the article on Pole-graphy.

Lastly, and certainly not the least valuable feature, are the accounts, under distinct heads, of the labours of the principal writers, and the characteristics of the different schools of economic thought throughout the civilised world.

In the list of contributors will be found almost all the best known writers on social science, both in this country and in the United States, together with some leading names from the Continent.

With such writers it would be strange, indeed, if the quality of the articles was not of a very high order. It is true that here and there an article is below the average. For instance, the article on Betterment in vol. i. is distinctly biased, misleading, and generally ill informed. But such cases are extremly rare. Even Mr. Palgrave cannot be omniscient, but in this work he has attained such omniscience as is humanly possible. We can give no higher praise than to say that the *Dictionary* is indispensable to the student of Economics, and would instil the minds of the average politician and journalist with some sound economic doctrines, of which they are so sadly in need.

*Taxation of Land Values and The Single Tax,*[1] by Professor Smart, of Glasgow University, is a very timely production. As an intro-

1 *Taxation of Land Values and the Single Tax.* By William Smart, LL.D., and Adam Smith Professor of Political Economy in the University of Glasgow. Glasgow : James Maclehose & Sons, Publishers to the University. 1900.

duction, Professor Smart deals with the theory of taxation in his terse and lucid manner, showing how it is based on the two principles of benefit received and ability to pay. In his treatment of the taxation of land values he examines in detail two definite proposals for such taxation—the one emanating from the London County Council and the other from the Corporation of Glasgow. Of the former Professor Smart gives the *pros* and *cons* with eminent impartiality, and clearly distinguishes the fundamental differences between the two proposals. In the former the ground-owner, at the termination of the lease, resumes possession, with all the accretion of material placed upon the land, together with such increased site value as may have accrued; in the latter the ground-owner grants a perpetual lease at a fixed fee or rent, and consequently, except there were failure in paying the rent, he can never re-enter into possession. So far as he is concerned, there is no "increased increment" for him. Professor Smart follows the majority of the economists who recently gave evidence upon this subject before the Commission on Local Taxation, who were unable, even when favourable to the principle, to offer any suggestions for giving practical effect to taxation of land values.

To the single tax Professor Smart is even more hostile. His objection that land does not stand alone in gaining unearned increment is by itself no argument against taxing such unearned increment when proved. The question of "unearned decrement," he says, is never considered. Independently of those objections he, urges others which demand serious attention. As a popular exposition of an exceedingly difficult subject this treatise could scarcely be bettered.

Those who are interested in the *Italo-Columbian Dispute*[1] will find the particulars duly and impartially set forth by M. Paul Bureau. The matter is commonly known as *The Cerruti Affair*, and the case is of extreme value inasmuch as it deals with the status of aliens according to International Law. It is also valuable as showing the defects in the present procedure of International Arbitration, and in view of the recent decision in the Delagoa Bay Railway Arbitration we can the more readily sympathise with Columbia in her misfortune. The story and its moral are clearly told by M. Bureau, and the fact that he is a Frenchman and a recognised jurist lends greater weight to his conclusions.

[1] *The Italo-Columbian Dispute (The Cerruti Affair).* The Status of Aliens according to International Public Law and the Defects in the Present Procedure of International Arbitration. By Paul Bureau. Paris: Arthur Rousseau. 1899.

## VOYAGES AND TRAVELS.

To open a book like *Tasmanian Rivers, Lakes, and Flowers*,[1] by
Mr. A. S. Murray, fills one with vain regrets that we were not born
in the other hemisphere. With a March east wind piercing one's
clothes as if they were paper, one longs for the balmy air of the
Garden Island. The beautiful sketches by the author fill one with
admiration mixed with a sad feeling that we shall never see a tenth
of Nature's most lovely masterpieces. However, on reading further
we become more reconciled to our English climate, for Mr. Murray
describes a fishing expedition, when the weather was extremely
cold and bleak. Clad as they were in stout waterproofs, they
fairly shivered under storms of sleet and hail. In chapter v.
we have a description of the convict system, the horrors of which
seem sadly out of place amidst the beautiful scenery depicted by
Mr. Murray's brush. This is relieved, however, by an account of
the Huon River, accompanied by a charming little sketch of "The
Huon Belle," a lovely stretch of water with blue mountains in the
background. Particulars of the trout-fishing here and elsewhere in
Tasmanian rivers will be of much interest to followers of the gentle
sport. Students of zoology are also not forgotten, and lovers of
flowers will find a monograph on the wild flowers of the Garden
Island. This volume is the work of an artist, and appeals specially
to the artistic mind, yet it will be welcomed by the general public
of Australasia as reviving pleasant memories, and by those here who
are not so fortunate as to have visited the originals of this series of
plates, as affording some conception of the reality of Nature's handiwork in our distant possessions.

---

## HISTORY AND BIOGRAPHY.

Mr. Harold E. Gorst has written a very interesting book on Lord
Beaconsfield.[2] The facts of the Conservative statesman's life are set
forth fairly, but the attempt to show that Beaconsfield was actuated
by unselfish motives in many of his actions, which were manifestly
the outcome of a time-serving and unscrupulous character, has
utterly failed. If there were no other reason for regarding the
worship of brute force, now known as Imperialism, with disgust and

1 *Tasmanian Rivers, Lakes, and Flowers.* By A. S. Murray. With Facsimile Reproductions in Colours of Numerous Sketches by the Author. Australia : George
Robertson & Co. London : H. Virtue & Co. Ltd. 1900.
2 *The Earl of Beaconsfield.* By Harold E. Gorst. (Victoria Era Series.) London :
Blackie & Son.

abhorrence, it would be the fact that it was originally the inv. way, of a cunning Jewish politician, who, while he talked about rs greatness of England, had no real claim to be considered n Englishman at all. When Carlyle said, "How long will John B de permit this absurd monkey to dance on his stomach?" he o ry expressed the indignation of all honest Englishmen at the succ n of a man who, though possessed of much superficial cleverness, wa from a philosophic point of view, shallow, ridiculous, and false. Mr. Gorst has made a vain endeavour to prove that Disraeli—the name by which in his fighting-days he was known—must get the credit of having organised and educated the Tory party. In reality he was not a sincere Conservative at all. He made use of the Con-servative party as a stepping-stone to power, and he demoralised the nation by teaching it that British patriotism consisted in trampling on the rights of every other nation. When the question is asked about Lord Beaconsfield—as Mr. Gorst does ask it in his closing chapter—What has he done for posterity? the true answer is, nothing, save, in the language of George Eliot, to "lower the moral currency." The Imperialism which has in our own day exhibited itself in the horrible war in South Africa is the bastard creation of Disraelian political jugglery. Let his memory bear the infamy of having propagated the vile opinions which have betrayed England into that war—a war destructive of England's honour, and placing her amongst the deadly enemies of humanity and civilisation.

Much has been written about Ruskin, and perhaps by this time the public may be trusted to form a correct estimate of his influence on art and thought. Still, it is desirable to have the life and work of this great writer and teacher presented in a compendious form, so that after a brief perusal even the young reader may be able to know what John Ruskin was. Mr. M. H. Spielmann has done this admirably, and we earnestly recommend his work[1] to all lovers of art. The little volume has been charmingly brought out by Messrs. Cassell & Co.

Scotland is justly proud of Sir David Wilkie, and we hail with satisfaction the publication of a biography of the great painter in the "Famous Scots Series."[2] The book is written by Mr. Edward Rivington, who properly describes Wilkie as a "Son of the Manse." In the criticism of the painter's work the author points out that it is mainly objective. It is, in fact, not the highest art; but it is true, as Mr. Rivington says, that "so long as human nature is constituted as it is, so long as the heart has passions, and humanity remains the one great subject of all-absorbing interest to man, so

---

[1] *John Ruskin: a Sketch of His Life, His Work, and His Opinions.* With Personal Reminiscences. By M. H. Spielmann. London: Cassell & Co.
[2] *Sir David Wilkie and the Scots School of Painters.* By Edward Rivington. Edinburgh and London: Oliphant, Anderson & Ferrier.

ill there be a place in art for such works as those of Sir
nd Wilkie."

To The name of George Buchanan[1] has been imperishably associated
Mr.th that of John Milton. He was not, like Milton, a great poet,
in it he was just as doughty a champion of political and religious
cloterty. On the day when Lord William Russell was beheaded, the
Gaolitical writings of Buchanan and Milton were publicly burned by
a decree of the University of Oxford. If the two writers had been
living at the time they would probably have been burned, or, at
least, hanged themselves. Instead, their works were outraged by a
learned University. Such is the irony of history. The life of
George Buchanan contributed to the " Famous Scots Series " by
the late Dr. Robert Wallace, M.P., with a supplemental chapter by
Mr. J. Campbell Smith, does justice to a great Scotsman. The
book is an admirable picture of Scottish life and thought at the
period when George Buchanan lived.

*Notes from a Diary,*[2] by Sir Mountstuart E. Grant-Duff, is a
delightful book. The writer is a man of wide observation and
exquisite culture. He has travelled in the East, and his eyes and
ears as well as his mind and heart have been open to the impressions
and the inspiration of that mysterious, wonderful world which may
be regarded as the incarnation of man's past and the cradle of all
religions. The descriptions of various scenes in Palestine are very
vivid, indeed quite photographic. Sir Mountstuart Grant-Duff has,
apparently, no weakness for Judaism. He does not regret the disappearance of the Temple. He prefers "the delicious Mosque of
Omar." No doubt, Mohammedanism is less repulsive to refined
tastes than the Jewish ritual and the Jewish ideal, which to some
people appears nothing better than an ugly sort of theocratic
materialism. We have in the book some interesting pictures of
Italy. Interspersed through the two volumes we find some noteworthy anecdotes of celebrities. Two stories about Lord Beaconsfield make one almost forgive that so-called statesman. When asked
what he thought about John Stuart Mill, he replied : " Oh ! a
political finishing governess ! " This sapient judgment was based
on Mill's somewhat professorial manner in the House of Commons.
When the late Mr. Roebuck complained that Disraeli had left his
camp, the ex-Radical Israelite politician cleverly remarked : "I did
not know that the honourable gentleman had a camp ; I thought
that he was the solitary sentinel of a deserted fortress." But wit
is no substitute for want of principle and utter unscrupulousness.

A *Life of D. L. Moody,*[3] by W. R. Moody and A. P. Fitt, will

[1] *George Buchanan.* By Robert Wallace. Compiled by J. Campbell Smith.
Edinburgh and London : Oliphant, Anderson & Ferrier.
[2] *Notes from a Diary* (1886-88). By the Right Hon. Sir Mountstuart E. Grant-
Duff, G.C.S.I. In Two Vols. London : John Murray.
[3] *Life of D. L. Moody.* By W. R. Moody and A. P. Fitt. Introduction by the
Rev. F. B. Meyers. London : Morgan & Scott.

just now be read with deep interest. Mr. Moody was, in his way, an excellent man. He was, to use the words of the Rev. F. B. Meyers in his admirable preface, " one of the most influential factors " in the " character and life-work of many men." His earnestness made even educated persons forget his gross ignorance of Biblical history and his incapacity to speak even plain English properly. But in this critical age illiterate apostles will not suffice, and the class to which Mr. Moody belonged is necessarily fast dying out. The facts of Mr. Moody's remarkable life are clearly and succinctly set forth in these pages.

*Malay Magic,*[1] is a book teeming with curious and almost incredible facts. Mr. W. W. Skeat is deeply learned in Malay folklore, and he had the opportunity of practically studying the subject during several years spent in the Malay Peninsula. Many of the superstitions of the Malays are extraordinary, especially those connected with weapons of war. Divination and the black art flourish amongst them quite as much as they did in Europe in mediæval times. Amongst the legends of the Malays which finds a counterpart in Occidental folklore is that of the Man in the Moon. A hunchback is said to be always making a fishing-line which is never completed owing to its being gnawed by a rat.

*The Matriculation History of England,*[2] by Mr. C. S. Fearenside, M.A. Oxon., is a book which students will find exceedingly useful. It is one of the well-prepared volumes in the University Tutorial Series. The book deals with English history from the days of Early Britain down to the close of the reign of William III. In dealing with the subject, Mr. Fearenside has had regard to proportion with respect to the various historic periods, the general trend of events, and the importance of letting the learner work out historic problems for himself.

Madame Edgar Quinet has done a real service to literature by the publication of the correspondence of Michelet and Quinet.[3] Though the work only contains a portion of the letters, the book is in reality more than mere correspondence—it is the biography of two great men united by a lifelong friendship. The work has been prepared in view of the centenary of Michelet, perhaps in many respects the greatest of modern historians. Madame Quinet shares in her husband's admiration of Michelet, and she has paid a well-deserved tribute to the memory of both men.

The extraordinary historic episode of the Diamond Necklace which has furnished Dumas the elder with materials for one of his most fascinating romances, has been subjected to an impartial analysis in

---

[1] *Malay Magic.* By W. W. Skeat. London : Macmillan & Co.
[2] *The Matriculation History of England.* By C. S. Fearenside, M.A. Oxon. London : W. B. Clive.
[3] *Cinquante Ans d'Amitié (Michelet-Quinet).* Par Madame Edgar Quinet. Paris : Armand Colin et Cie.

*Marie Antoinette and the Diamond Necklace from another Point of View*, by F. de Albini.[1] The work presents Marie Antoinette in the light of a mistress in the art of dissimulation. At the same time, she is shown to have really played a very different part in the transaction from that attributed to her by Dumas père.

Mr. Henry Smetham's *History of Strood* is a most valuable work from the standpoint of local history and archæology. Mr. Smetham has taken the utmost pains in collecting his materials, and the work has been with him a labour of love.

*Sketches : Prose and Rhyme*,[2] by Henry Smetham, will be read with interest by those who admire naturalness. The verses ·in the volume have the great merit of appealing to the purely human view of life. The prose sketches, without possessing any exceptional literary merit, are charming on account of their simplicity and innocent realism.

Deep interest will be taken in Prince Bojdar Karageorgewitch's work, *Notes sur l'Inde*.[3] The volume gives us a most picturesque and at the same time accurate account of the India of to-day. The author had, before starting for India, sought for books in which he could find all the necessary information about that marvellous country. He was advised to read a huge volume of a serious character, presenting, in a statistical form, a view of the progress of India year after year under the Anglo-Indian administration. The book appears to have been a glorification of English rule in India. In reality it proved disappointing. The plague has not been banished from India. The miseries of the natives have not been removed by the benevolent sway of England. The Indian famine is at this moment a thing of which we hear only too much. Prince Bojdar Karageorgewitch was naturally a little bored by a record of monotonous orderliness. He conceived India as an immense country parcelled out in regular squares, over which careful officials presided. It was when he came to read two very different works—Judith Gautier's *Conquête du Paradis* and Jean Lahor's *Histoire de la Littérature Hindoue*—that he began to realise the romance, the mystery, and the beauty of the true India. His own book reproduces in a most interesting form all the wonders of India of which he was an eye-witness. His description of Bombay is exceedingly fascinating. He makes the reader see, at least with the mind's eye, the *bizarre* figures of fakirs, Mongols, Parsees, and Hindoo women which one meets every day in this land of marvels. At Mazagoon, one of the "faubourgs" of Bombay, he saw a Parsee wedding. It was like a transformation scene, with its display of white lanterns, flowers,

[1] *Marie Antoinette and the Diamond Necklace from another Point of View.* By F. de Albini. London : Swan Sonnenschein.
[2] *Sketches: Prose and Rhyme.* By Henry Smetham. London : G. Whiting & Co.
[3] *Notes sur l'Inde.* Par Prince Bojdar Karageorgewitch. Avec 30 illustrations. Paris : Calmann Levy.

dancing girls, and mystical ceremonial. The guests were all clad in long white tunics. The bridegroom, also in white, with a collar adorned with orchids, lilies, and jessamines around his neck, must have been a remarkable figure. The high priest—the "Grand Dastour"—arrayed in white, with a turban of white muslin on his head, added to the extraordinary picturesqueness of the scene. The wedding presents were borne by women on heavy dishes to the steps in front of the house. The bride's mother advanced to meet them, and, making three circles with her hands, cast from them rice, and then sugar, sweetmeats, and a cocoa-nut, and every time she did so a black boy, nearly naked, darted forward, picked them up, and vanished. The singing of a hymn and the casting of handfuls of rice by the priest preceded the marriage ceremony. Such are some of the features of the wedding minutely and beautifully described in the pages of this charming volume. The description of a dance by nautch girls is very vivid, and reminds us of the "cancan." Side by side with such pictures we have a description of Bombay, the "city of mourning," where the deserted streets and the closed hotels showed how the terrors of the plague can overpower ordinary minds in the India of to-day as they did in the England of Charles II.'s reign. The chapters on Trichinopoly, Kandy, Benares, Agra, and Delhi are all full of interest. The author rightly points out the good side of the Hindoo caste system, which respects merit and distinction, and the barbarism of the English view, which puts a common British soldier on a higher level than a Brahman. Those who desire to learn the truth about India should read Prince Kara-georgewitch's book.

*La Vie Privée d'Autrefois*[1] is a very valuable book. It is drawn from a collection of original documents published in 1749 under the title of *Causes Amusantes et Connues.* The features of social life shown by these documents bear some resemblance to the life of France to-day. But it is improbable that nowadays any lady of rank would sacrifice her reputation as a woman to break the legal bond of marriage which united her to a man supposed by her father to be of inferior rank. This, however, actually happened in the case of Madame de Coligny, who, though the wife of M. de la Rivière, publicly declared herself his mistress to please her father, le Sieur de Bussy. The story of the ambassador, M. Jean-Jacques de Mesmes, who was cheated by the mercenary *danseuse*, Demoiselle Prevost, is also a remarkable revelation. Such things happen to-day, but in a very different fashion. The volume is made additionally interesting by the illustrations.

[1] *La Vie Privée d'Autrefois* (*La Vie de Paris sous Louis XV.*) Par Alfred Franklin. Paris : Librairie Plon.

## BELLES LETTRES.

*Logan's Loyalty*,[1] by Sarah Tytler, is a very readable, though rather commonplace, novel. There is very little characterisation in the book, but in these days of silly fiction the novel must take a certain rank. It has the merit of being a well-told story in which the incidents are not altogether improbable.

*The Fountain of Siena*[2] is a little book apparently written for the purpose of showing that the late John Ruskin had no sympathy with the Church of Rome as a creed, and that he hated usury, or rather the Jews, who are—at least, many of them—usurers. This may be true; but poor Ruskin was, in spite of his genius, a weak mortal, and it was scarcely necessary to write a book to satisfy us that at heart he was neither a Catholic nor a hater of Jews. Philosophers know that there is not much real difference between Judaism and Catholicity.

The edition of the *De Bigis of Isocrates*,[3] by Mr. W. J. Woodhouse, will be found exceedingly useful by students. The masterly introduction gives a vivid account of Isocrates and his work. The incidental sketch of Alcibiades, that brilliant and much misunderstood young Greek—a kind of Athenian Charles James Fox—is interesting. The notes are short but comprehensive.

In the same series we find an admirable edition of the *Eratosthenes* and the *Agoratus* of Lysias.[4] The editors, Messrs. J. Thompson, M.A., and T. R. Mills, M.A., have done their work excellently. Lysias was the great master among the Athenian orators of the plain style. Though far inferior in eloquence to Demosthenes, he had some advantages over the great king of Greek orators. His language is like that of everyday life, and could be easily understood by even the least educated Athenian citizen. The Introduction gives a good account of the orator and his style. The notes will be of great assistance to the student.

*The Bishop's Secret*[5] is a very readable story, though its unreality will revolt those who are not satisfied with mere sensationalism. Mr. Fergus Hume revels in murders and mysteries. He writes apparently for those who like the gruesome and the bewildering. Life, however, is not made up of such things ; and, while it must be acknowledged that the author of *The Mystery of a Hansom Cab* is entitled to a place amongst writers of fiction, it is certainly not a high place.

*The Harvesters*,[6] by J. S. Fletcher, reads like an unhappy

[1] *Logan's Loyalty*. By Sarah Tytler. London : John Long.
[2] *The Fountain of Siena*. An Episode in the Life of John Ruskin. London : S. W. Partridge & Co.
[3] *Isocrates : De Bigis*. Edited by W. J. Woodhouse, M.A. Oxon. London : W. B. Oliver.
[4] *Lysias : Eratosthenes and Agoratus*. Text and Notes. Edited by J. Thompson, M.A. Camb., and T. R. Mills, M.A. Oxon. London : W. B. Clive.
[5] *The Bishop's Secret*. By Fergus Hume. London : John Long.
[6] *The Harvesters*. By J. S. Fletcher. London : John Long.

imitation of some of Thomas Hardy's earlier novels. English country life is tolerably well depicted in the novel, but the character of the Irish labourer, Larry Desmond, is most unreal. No Irish peasant says "nay" or "ain't." There is some cleverness in the book, and the plot is ingenious. The fault is chiefly in the characterisation, which cannot be pronounced successful.

The fame of the great Polish novelist, Henryk Sienkiewicz, has travelled far and wide. His novel, *In the New Promised Land,*[1] which has been admirably translated into English by S. C. de Soissons, is a masterpiece. It is simple in construction, but full of keen observation of life. The story of the poor Polish peasant Lorenz Toporek and his daughter Mary is most pathetic. Their sufferings in New York recall the experiences of many poor Irish peasants whose sufferings, alas! have never found a chronicler, for the plain reason that Ireland has not as yet produced a novelist with the genius of Sienkiewicz. The book will be read, we are sure, with delight by millions.

The eighth volume of the fine edition of the works of Jonathan Swift, published by Messrs. George Bell & Sons, contains Swift's greatest work, *Gulliver's Travels.*[2] The Introduction is appreciative, and shows Swift's real motives in the composition of his masterpiece. The book is clearly and beautifully printed.

Few French novelists of the day can boast of a more finished style than M. Edouard Rod. His position as a critic and as a writer of fiction entitles him to a high place in contemporary French literature. His latest novel, *Au Milieu du Chemin,*[3] though not exactly a masterpiece, is a book which appeals to all advanced mind. The plot is very simple. Paul Clarencé, a successful dramatist, is startled to find that a young girl, who committed suicide, had, at the moment of her death, one of his plays under her pillow. He is interviewed on the subject by a reporter, to whom he confesses that he regarded himself as partly to blame for the girl's sad fate. A kindly, or perhaps partly morbid, impulse leads him to call at the house of mourning. There he discovers that the girl's lover was his friend Laurier, an artist, who was married. The unfortunate artist is crushed by the catastrophe, and confesses to Clarencé that but for wife and child he would follow the poor girl to the grave. Clarencé, who had himself contracted a free alliance with Madame Claudine Breant, a lady separated from her husband, is deeply moved by this tragic history. He reconsiders his whole position as a writer, and his moral responsibility for any evil wrought by his works. He consults his mistress, who ridicules his views, and advises him to seek change of air in the country, from which, as an ambitious

[1] *In the New Promised Land.* By Henryk Sienkiewicz. Translated by S. C. de Soissons. London : Jarrold & Sons.

[2] *The Prose Works of Jonathan Swift, D.D.* Edited by Temple Scott. With a Biographical Introduction by the Right Hon. E. H. Lecky, M.P. London : George Bell & Sons.

[3] *Au Milieu du Chemin.* Par Edouard Rod. Paris : Biblithoèque Charpentier.

peasant, he had come up to Paris some twenty years before. The artist Laurier also leaves Paris to visit the rustic home of his ancestors. The effect of the change is different on the two men. Clarencé comes to recognise that there is a solace in the calm and settled life of the country. He writes enthusiastic letters to Claudine in praise of rural life; Laurier sinks into despair, and, though pardoned by his wife, gradually becomes insane. The picture of his mental degeneration is terribly realistic. Clarencé proposes to buy an estate in the country, to marry Claudine, and to found a family. At first she refuses on the ground that his change of mood shows his love is waning. Moreover, she has, owing to her unhappy domestic experiences, conceived a hatred of marriage as an institution. Eventually, however, she yields, simply because she cannot bear to lose her lover. She feels that marriage will lessen their passion, but, as she can only hold him in this way, she puts aside her prejudices. This book recalls the late Grant Allen's novel, *The Woman Who Did;* but it must be confessed that M. Edouard Rod has imparted to his work a tone of reality which is absent from Grant Allen's somewhat unfortunate experiment in advanced fiction. The question as to the moral responsibility of authors is not settled in the book. It is a problem that would have puzzled Goethe himself. M. Edouard Rod must be congratulated on having written a most interesting and original novel.

M. Jules Verne has given us another of his interesting "Voyages Extraordinaires" entitled *Le Testament d'un Excentrique.*[1] The idea of the plot is very novel, the scene being laid in America, and will enchant all young readers.

We have received the *Memoires d'une Idealiste,* by Malevida de Meysenberg. Want of space prevents our reviewing it in this number.

The Librairie Plon is publishing a work *Paris de 1800 à 1900.* Nothing of the kind had yet been attempted. It reconstitutes very vividly the life of Parisians, not only month by month, but day by day, during the last hundred years. Each part covers a period of five years; the work will be complete in twenty parts. The value of the text, contributed by about fifty academicians, artists, and savants, is trebled by beautiful and very numerous illustrations (4000) of medals, furniture, engravings, and portraits of most of the well-known people of the time, photographed from private collections and museums. Our readers would do well to subscribe to this work, the price of which is very moderate, as it is of the highest interest to amateurs as well as artists. We shall continue to notice the forthcoming parts as they appear.

---

[1] *Testament d'un Excentrique.* Par Jules Verne. Paris: Hetzel et Cie.
[2] *Paris de 1800 à 1900.* Edited by Charles Simond. Parts 1 to 5. Paris: Librairie Plon.

THE

# WESTMINSTER REVIEW.

## VOL. CLIII. No. 6.—JUNE 1900.

## THE RIGHT HON. JACOB BRIGHT.

IT is sometimes said that gratitude is all but unknown in the political
world, and that, save in a few exceptional instances, the modest and
retiring men, those who live for their fellow men and never covet
the applause of the multitude, are soon forgotten. But it is not
always so; and when in the early part of last November the newspapers announced that Mr. Jacob Bright had gone to his rest, full
of years and honour, the testimony of men of all parties, the sympathetic memoirs of journals representing widely different opinions,
were unanimous in their appreciation of his honesty and unselfish
devotion. And though for more than five years Mr. Bright had
lived in retirement, taking only the very slightest part in public
affairs, the recollection of his services was so vivid in the memory of
those who had known him, and the influence of his character and
conduct was still so strong, that in the North of England, at least,
it was generally admitted that his part in public life was admirably
summarised by the following words of a distinguished writer:
"On the whole, it may perhaps be said with no unpardonable
exaggeration, that the stormy stage of politics, so full of striking
talents and remarkable men, has seldom presented to us among its
many varieties of personal worth a character more deserving of
respect than that of Jacob Bright."

It was perhaps inevitable that, from his entrance into the parliamentary arena, comparisons should be made between Mr. Jacob Bright
and his elder brother, and that these should be revived in newspaper
comments after his death. His relationship to the foremost orator of
the day and one of the most illustrious statesmen of the century
was at once an advantage and a difficulty to the younger
brother. A brother of John Bright could not but be noticed

when he came before the public, and to fall short of the great man in any respect might have been supposed to mean failure. Some have said, indeed, that Mr. Jacob Bright would have been a more successful politician had he borne any other name ; but this is unquestionably a mistake, and it is not too much to say that, had his ambition been more personal and the honour of men his aim in life, he might easily have made his family name instrumental to these objects.

The two men had, indeed, many qualities in common—courage, firmness, and perhaps an occasional unwillingness to see two sides of a question in which he was deeply interested, were conspicuous in both ; but no greater proof of Mr. Jacob Bright's distinctive individuality could be offered than the fact that he played so prominent a part in public life under the influence of more than a few aspirations with which his brother did not sympathise.

In private life Mr. Jacob Bright was one of the most kindly and generous of men, one of the truest, most trusted, and loyal of friends, taking his pleasure in the society of his family and friends, in pictures and sculpture, in the glories of nature on land and water, and in the reading of the best authors. But while the charm of Mr. Bright's personality, the happy combination of dignity, simplicity and sincerity, endeared him to the inner circle of his private friends, the influence he exercised on his political supporters and on the Liberal party in the manufacturing district of South Lancashire was almost entirely due to the public confidence in his integrity and the unselfishness of his aims and objects. Every one knew that he had no private ends to serve. He never studied the arts of popularity and never attempted to win the favour of the multitude by meretricious means. Flattery was unknown to him, and he would rather have lost a vote than have it by pandering to the prejudices of the ignorant ; and it is surely a healthy and hopeful sign of the times that a politician so high-minded and so disinterested should have been so much honoured and respected. For it may be confidently said, that though during the greater part of his life Mr. Jacob Bright was of a minority, and not infrequently of a very small minority, no one ever questioned either the purity of his motives or the strength of his convictions.

Jacob Bright was born at Rochdale in 1821. He was the fourth of five brothers, of whom John, born ten years earlier, was the eldest. Their father, Jacob Bright, was a successful manufacturer and a member of the Society of Friends, and the home surroundings of the boy were of the most fortunate. The example of his father led him to the practice of considering the welfare of his workpeople, and the refinement of a happy home, blessed by the privilege of domestic happiness, permanently influenced his character and aspirations. Rochdale, though a manufacturing town, has still romantic surroundings; but the neighbourhood was much more beautiful seventy years ago than it is now, and, while still a child, Mr. Bright acquired the intense love of nature, which continued with him through life. He was educated at the York Friends' School, and to the instruction he received there he mainly owed the fine command of vigorous and lucid English which stood him in such good stead in his public life. Here, too, he was introduced to a knowledge of Byron, who never ceased to be his favourite poet. Byron, indeed, had no place in the school course, but one of the teachers was a passionate admirer of the poems, and he introduced their beauties to his young pupil in the quieter recesses of the playground when the other boys were actively engaged in pursuits of a different kind. To the end of his days Byron was a constant delight to Mr. Jacob Bright, his speeches frequently including quotations from the poet; he would occasionally recite favourite passages in his country walks, and during his last long and painful illness the recollection of them would soothe him in the still hours of sleepless nights. And it was with peculiar pleasure that he made the acquaintance in comparatively recent years of Lord Byron's granddaughter, to whom the expression of his keen appreciation of the poet's works was very gratifying. Mr. Bright's business career began at a comparatively early age, and he was little more than a boy when he established and taught classes of his father's workpeople. But all the time he was being unconsciously prepared for his future career. In his childhood the Reform agitation was influencing the whole of South Lancashire; his father and brothers were deeply interested in the movement, and every town and village was familiar with the cry, "The Bill, the whole Bill, and nothing but the Bill." Nor should it be forgotten in considering the influence of his family in the development of his character that Mr. Bright owed much to the exceptional intelligence and devotion of his sisters, all of whom were active in the cause of everything that made for progress—and of whom Mrs. Duncan Maclaren is still living. His brother John's earliest political activity was displayed a few years later in the agitation that led to the abolition of Church rates, and these and other political movements sensibly influenced the boy's character. He was greatly interested some years later in the work of the Anti-Corn Law League, and this led to his first introduction to Mr. Cobden, for whom his admiration, which might almost be called veneration, never ceased. Jacob Bright, indeed, was one of the most loyal of Richard Cobden's disciples, and when Cobden in later years became member for Rochdale, the election was specially gratifying to John and Jacob Bright.

Mr. Bright was married in 1855 to Miss Ursula Mellor, who became and remained throughout his life a helpmeet in an exceptionally close and intimate sense. Mrs. Bright shared his aspirations, his sympathies with the less fortunate of their fellow creatures, and his passionate love of justice, and no sketch of the career of Jacob Bright would be complete which took no note of his keen domestic instincts.    He was most happy in his home, and only those who saw him there could understand the close relation between his private life and his public career.    From the early days of his married life he was frequently visited by men distinguished in politics, literature and art, and it may almost be said, of all sorts and conditions, of all sects and parties ; but he never ceased to be a student, and he collected a remarkably fine library. Before his marriage he had made a long tour in America and several visits to the Continent ; he never, moreover, lost his delight in foreign travel, and frequently made the tour of Europe with his wife and family.    Mr. Jacob Bright's earliest public work in national politics was connected with the formation of the Lancashire Public School Association, a society founded in Manchester in which Mr. Cobden took great interest.    The proposals then made were in advance of the time, but they certainly paved the way for the reforms carried out in Mr. Forster's Act of 1870.    Mr. Bright continued to take active interest in the problem of National Elementary Education, and the policy he advocated in 1847 was defended at a later period in the House of Commons and on many public platforms.    He was prominently concerned in the movement that secured for Rochdale its Charter of Incorporation in 1856, and he was the first mayor of his native town.    Like his brother he opposed the Crimean War and the miserable Chinese War that followed it.    His first public political speech in Manchester was in the afternoon of the Parliamentary Election of 1857, at which Messrs. John Bright and Milner Gibson were rejected.    At the gathering of the friends of the defeated candidates the speeches had not been cheerful, but when Jacob Bright, who was then known to only a few present, stood up, his words came as a revelation to the meeting, and his courage and confidence in the future did much to revive the hopes of the party. In 1865 he himself accepted an invitation to contest Manchester as one of the Liberal candidates, but the party was divided, and Mr. Edward James, a man of less advanced views, defeated Mr. Bright and Mr. Abel Heywood.    On the death of Mr. James in 1867, however, Mr. Bright was again invited to stand, and he defeated Mr. Alderman Bennett by a very large majority.    At the General Election of 1868 Manchester had become a Three-cornered Constituency, and Mr. Bright was again returned, as one of two Liberal members. In 1874, however, he was defeated, Mr. W. R. Callender taking his place ; but when the new member died in 1876, Mr. Bright was again elected by an enormous majority over his Conservative opponent, Mr. (now Sir) F. S. Powell.    In 1880, the last election by the undivided constituency of Manchester, Mr. Bright, with his colleague, Mr. Slagg, was again triumphantly returned. When the City of Manchester was divided into six constituencies, and Mr. Bright selected the South-Western division, his fortunes as a candidate were again varied. At the General Election of 1885, consequent on the desertion of the Irish voter, whose cause he had so long championed, he was defeated by Lord Frederick Hamilton; but after the Dissolution in the following year this decision was reversed, as he defeated his former opponent, and he was again elected in 1892, when he was opposed by Mr. Alfred Hopkinson. This was Mr. Jacob Bright's last Parliament, as after the Dissolution of 1895 he was compelled by increasing infirmities to retire from public life.

It will be seen that his career as a member of Parliament extended, with a few short intervals, over nearly thirty years, during a period of wonderful political, social, and commercial activity; one that saw momentous changes in our constitutional system, and something like a revolution in the relations between Ireland and Great Britain. And it is not too much to say that in all the movements that made for reform Mr. Jacob Bright was a consistently active participator. He lived, indeed, to see the Statute-book extended by more than a few Acts based on opinions he had persistently defended for many years.

In 1885 Mrs. Bright published a selection from her husband's speeches delivered between 1869 and 1884, and though these addresses illustrate the variety of his range of thought and the extent of his research, they only inadequately display the extent of his political activity. They do, however, give an admirable idea of the speaker's luminous and vigorous style, in which there is never the slightest trace of obscurity or confusion of idea; and in reading them it is easy to understand a remark once made by Mr. Gladstone: "When I first heard Mr. Jacob Bright speak in the House of Commons I had at once the assurance that the gift of eloquence had not been granted to only one member of his family."

It would be impossible within the compass of an article like this to give even a complete outline of Mr. Bright's political life, or an adequate idea of the influence he exercised; and perhaps because he was more prominently associated with a few subjects, his successful advocacy of many others may have been forgotten. The weak and the oppressed, both in public and private life, at home or abroad, never appealed to him in vain; because a cause in which he was interested was unpopular, or because its arguments were ridiculed, he never hesitated to defend it. He once said: "I am told I have too many crotchets, but I venture to call them convictions;" and he lived to see many of the opinions which the more timorous deemed extreme become the creeds of party leaders. The right of women to vote was treated with ridicule when Mr. Jacob

Bright first proclaimed it, and the right of wives to own property was denounced as dangerous. And possibly many of the women who now exercise the franchise at elections for Town Councils, County Councils, School Boards, Boards of Guardians, and other municipal bodies forget how much they owe to Mr. Jacob Bright, without whose efforts those rights might have been long postponed. When Mr. Gladstone's Government brought in their Coercion Bill he was one of a small minority who resisted it to the utmost of their power, but he lived to see Coercion opposed by the whole of the Liberal party. His early views on education were deemed Utopian, but they were adopted in later times by Cabinet Ministers. He did not, however, support measures on these subjects more cordially than the successive extensions of the Parliamentary franchise, reforms in the licensing laws, commercial freedom, resistance to any sort of slavery, and arbitration. Some of the speeches on Ireland might be studied with advantage just now, and we cannot resist a quotation from one of them delivered in Manchester twenty years ago :

"Queen Victoria once visited this country, and a happy visit it appears to have been. It is a pity it was not renewed. I should like to have seen the Sovereign with a great palace in one of the most beautiful parts of Ireland. I should like to have seen her spending as much time annually in Ireland as in Scotland. I would not expect too much from such influence, but I would expect something, and all in the right direction. England in that case would have known more of Ireland; there would have been probably fewer Irish absentee landowners; it would have been the fashion to visit that country; thousands of tourists would have visited it who have never been there; a kinder feeling between the two countries might have grown out of it, and at least a great deal of mutual knowledge."

But Mr. Bright's work as a practical reformer was not restricted to his political career. As a Governor of Owens College he did more than a little to obtain for it the measure of State aid which it now receives, and he rendered valuable assistance to the movement that secured the Charter of the Victoria University. Few members of Parliament were so ready and willing to assist his constituents in the furtherance of useful work, and this whether they were of his own party or otherwise, and no personal trouble was too great for him when his services were needed. Mr. Bright, moreover, was the first of the local members who openly advocated the construction of the Manchester Ship Canal, and his zealous devotion to the enterprise had much to do with its ultimate success. He never, however, took up any question lightly, and his support of the Canal is a case in point; he read all that could be said either for the scheme or against it, but having convinced himself that the work would be an immense commercial benefit to Manchester and the district he never ceased to help in the herculean task of overcoming the opposition to it. Another illustration of his firmness under the influence of strong convictions, based on careful inquiry, was seen in his opposition to the proposed treaty which would have given up both banks of the river Congo to Portugal, and his powerful speech in the House of Commons against the treaty was in all probability instrumental in defeating the proposal.]

One of the secrets of Mr. Jacob Bright's success as a public man was the confidence of all who knew him in his disinterestedness, to which we have already referred. He never thought of his own aggrandisement, he never sought any personal honours, and Lord Rosebery's proposal to make him a Privy Councillor came to him as a complete surprise, and it was well said of him: "He was a supremely honest man. He had in view no private ends. His sole aim was the furtherance of the interests of the country. He served his constituents with a fidelity which cannot be surpassed. His voice was always ready to denounce an unrighteous or uphold a righteous cause."

Then he was not only fair in controversy, never indulging in personalities, but rancour or anything like an approach to vindictiveness were entirely foreign to his nature. When on the polling day of the 1885 election he was told that he would be defeated and that the Irish were deserting him, he replied with perfect equanimity, "Are they? Well, if they are, I think I may say I shall never desert the Irish." And when his defeat was officially announced and it was known that this was entirely due to the Irish vote being cast for the Tory candidate in the belief that the Tories would go further in the direction of Home Rule than the Liberals, Mr. Bright said "that he had not a single word to say against the Irish, but that he could quite understand and appreciate their action."

These incidents are distinctly characteristic of the man, but the quality they display is not too common to make reference to them superfluous. It would be easy to extend these reminiscences, this catalogue of the disinterested services of a faithful citizen and of the merits and virtues of a high-minded and kind-hearted man; but perhaps sufficient has been said to warrant the opinion that, "taking him all round, such men are rare."

His health broke down seriously soon after he retired from public life, but he bore his grievous afflictions with patience and resignation. Everything was done to mitigate them indeed, and the story of the devotion of his wife and daughter, if it could be told, would be overwhelmingly pathetic. He passed two or three winters on the French Riviera, and though walking exercise was out of the question, he drove out regularly and thoroughly enjoyed the glorious scenery of that enchanting region, enjoying on one occasion a pleasant visit from Mr. Gladstone at Cannes.

He spent the warmer months of the summers on the Thames, or at Aix-les-Bains, or at Leysin in Switzerland, and up to within a short time of his death, on November 8 last, he found delight in cruising up and down the river in his electric launch. He never lost his interest in public affairs, and was always happy to see his old friends, who, even when his physical frame was at its feeblest, were often surprised at the liveliness of his conversation, at the brightness of his fancy and the sagacity of his thoughts. His long illness came to a peaceful end at Nun's Acre, Goring, by the shores of the great river he had loved so well, and as we have said, the announcement that he had "crossed the bar" was heard with general and revering interest.

In the course of the previous year a bust of Mr. Jacob Bright had been offered to the City of Manchester, and at the ceremony of the unveiling and its acceptance by the Lord Mayor, speeches in grateful recognition of Mr. Bright's services and patriotism, and in appreciation of his noble and dignified personal character, were delivered by some of his old friends.

Yet another gathering of the friends of Mr. Bright was reported in the *Manchester Guardian* of November 14. This took place at Nun's Acre, where the last marks of respect were paid before the ashes of the departed. The cremation had taken place a few days previously at Woking, but no public gathering could have been conveniently summoned then. From the newspaper report we quote the following :

"Nun's Acre the house is called, and the sweet reposeful name is justified by the surroundings. Over the pine hills beyond the house the last rosy streaks of sunshine were lingering across the sky, and the scent of the heath roots and the pine hung sharp in the air. Over the porch still clung the late clematis and the winter roses. On the other side at the foot of a gently sloping lawn was the sparkling river. All struck with the astonishing beauty of the place rejoiced that propitious fates had ordained that the 'happy warrior' after a strenuous career had here passed a serene old age."

The memory of the high-minded and unselfish men who have laboured long and successfully to make the lot of the less fortunate of their fellow countrymen more happy, to see justice prevail in the national counsels and goodwill extend over the earth, are surely worth preserving—and among such fine patriots the Right Hon. Jacob Bright assuredly has a place.

# THE DANGER OF EMPIRE.

WHILE decentralisation or expansion is admittedly the political necessity of the age, Parliament remains to-day similar in its constitution to its primary state. That is to say, the machinery which in the reign of Charles II. sufficed to govern a home population of 7,000,000 and to protect a dependent population of about the same number, is now expected to govern a home population of 40,000,000, and to protect a dependent population (including Egypt) of 300,000,000.

If Liberals hesitate to throw up their caps as high as the Unionist or Conservative proletariat when fresh extensions of Imperial responsibilities are secured by diplomatic triumph or feat of arms, this hesitation is chiefly due to the doubt as to whether the Government machinery can fairly bear the strain without neglect of the interests of the inhabitants of the British Isles.

We are all conscious that things are not as they should be with the great majority of the population of the richest country in the world.

We know that the elementary education of the people (excepting, perhaps, the people of Scotland) is inferior to that of several actively competing countries, and that our competition will soon become hopeless unless almost revolutionary changes are introduced into our technical teaching. We feel that the country could readily afford by one bold stroke to place these matters once and for all upon a satisfactory basis. Yet Parliament proceeds by diffident tinkering in this all-important branch of legislation.

The man in the street would inform the intelligent foreigner that this is due to conflicting class interests, which equally retard any bold reform of the sanitary conditions of the country.

If an inquisitive stranger were to ask the average member of Parliament why, at the end of the century, millions of our rural folk live under circumstances of overcrowding which would disgrace any London slum and drink daily pond-water which a Londoner would not wash his doorstep with, the reply would doubtless be that agricultural depression has relegated such matters to the background, and that Parliament has been occupied in diminishing rather than adding to the burdens of the farmer.

The fact is, however, indisputable that the healthy condition of the people is as much the concern of the whole nation as their elementary and technical education, and that it is the function of Government so to regulate the incidence of taxation that the burden shall fall on shoulders able to bear it.

It is a lamentable fact that the great political prizes are not to be won by the pursuit of domestic reforms.

Parliament is an Imperial machine, and it is the mastery of the facts which make for Empire which most adorns the mental equipment of the statesman who would lead.

Compare the House of Commons on a night when the Cape, Egypt, or China is to the fore with another when some domestic topic, however important to the welfare of the nation, is on the *tapis*, and who shall doubt that we are an Imperial race?

It is as if a sudden substitution of a popular melodrama for a concert of sedate music were effected at a transpontine theatre. If, in the case of the tamer entertainment, the pit were even a quarter full, its occupants would be listless and weary.

In Switzerland and New Zealand, where foreign politics do not vitiate the legislative palate, domestic legislation keeps well up in step with the needs of the people.

So exciting have become the conditions of parliamentary life nowadays, that it may well be doubted whether, if Free Trade had been delayed for discussion till now, its Cobden would not have been confronted with a count-out.

In France, a progressive income-tax has come well within the domain of practical politics, and in England sliding-scale death duties make in the same direction; yet it is doubtful whether, if a large majority of voters were convinced of the desirability of such a sweeping reform, the time and temper of Parliament would be accommodated to its calm and deliberate discussion.

Private members complain that their Bills stand no chance of discussion, and yet there is frequently a count-out on their own particular night.

A huge mass of legislative *pabulum*, which men of all parties are prepared to swallow, and much of which has been fully dressed in Committee, lies yearly hopelessly neglected by the jaded appetite of Parliament.

Any Prime Minister, not overburdened with Imperial duties, would naturally tabulate such non-contentious reforms and afford them legislative opportunity, but a not overburdened Prime Minister is a feature of the far past, and opportunism necessarily shoulders out opportunity.

Lawyers and laymen are agreed that the law should be codified. This is no party question, and the ability and expense are at command; yet the pace of the nation is too fast and its pulse is too feverish for sane reflection upon such a momentous issue.

The tendency in Imperial extension and consequent patriotic

excitement is to render pallid domestic problems, especially such as excite no party passion.

Parliament is a community of fighting men, and measures which promise no tussle, and which are free from the hurtling of half-bricks, extort neither enthusiasm nor interest.

The secret is here. To rise to eminence in the County Council, an appreciation of the needs of the people is essential; to shine as a light at Saint Stephen's, expert knowledge of the factors in the game of the nation, among other nations, is the one thing needful. Acres and cows, pensions and pure beer may serve to tickle the ears of the groundlings, but it is when Venezuela or Fashoda, the Trans-vaal or Persia, are heatedly declaimed upon from the provincial platform, to the accompaniment of the fancied clash of steel or boom of cannon in the air, that the illiterate realise what dangers they escape by their ignorance, and what a fortunate thing it is to have men clever enough to represent them at Westminster.

The national disease is thus as prevalent among the people as among their representatives.

Little Englanders, in the face of any wave of national excitement, are jeered at, even on Liberal platforms, in remote rural districts, and may vainly protest that they would like to see a few repairs effected in our home garments before we further rend our hearts abroad.

The farmer hopes, year after year, to see some legislative check put upon inland rates of freight, which hopelessly handicap his produce in competition with foreign imported food; but his eyes, perforce, glisten under the heated oratory of his member, who thunders on his wonderstruck mind that not only the future pros-perity, but the very existence of the country depend upon new markets, and that the nation's operations throughout Africa and in China are in a direct line of interest with the bucolic breeches-pocket.

A member who could or would talk only to his constituents, at any of their local meetings, of domestic reforms would be voted a terribly dull kind of bore. Popular contests of sport generally wind up with fireworks; and are not politics of the nature of sport among an essentially sporting people?

Delve deep into the heart of the Little Englander, and it will probably be found that he is almost as proud as the common jingo of the extent and power of the British Empire, but that he seeks to love the people which compose the nation even better than the nation itself.

Will they continue to spurn him for this perfidy? It is to be feared that they will, in spite of spreading political intelligence; and there are few among us who would wish to watch the field-nights at Westminster on foreign crises pale into insignificance through the waning of popular sympathy with Empire.

The remedy lies close at hand. Let Parliament remain the Imperial engine. But, let us consider the ways of the County Council, and learn the methods of peaceful legislation.

The County Councils have infused into multitudes of men, previously dormant in public affairs, the most remarkable revival of public spirit which has ever dominated the middle classes.

Here no international issues are at stake; even the sacred word "markets" (unless referring to the local ones) is never mentioned within those walls. Here, in succession to the local vestryman, who nodded over the parish accounts, as a preliminary to adjournment to the welcome of the tavern fireside, has started up the new legislator.

The intellectual merchant, who finds his successful business an insufficient object for his active brains; the ambitious barrister, who has a hobby for Local Government law; the unsuccessful aspirant for parliamentary honours, fondly hoping to convince Dives of the power to his hand; the hitherto idle rich, and even the struggling professional man, have yielded to the fascination of the government of their fellows.

Bumble may well rub his eyes, for in the old vestry days water and gas and insanitary areas were subjects for alternate wrangling and yawning, relieved by an occasional job.

To-day, working-class dwellings, waterworks purchase, and "betterment" are political cries, fraught with a measure of indescribable enthusiasm and big with the issues of fate.

It was the reproach of the middle-class in England that, while in Germany and France local public affairs were administered by men of both means and education, in England they were in the hands of the greengrocer and his fellows.

The key to this riddle was discovered when the School Board was first established. The areas of public interest had hitherto been too small.

A school committee, dealing with a single school, naturally commended itself to the village tradesman, but a Board, controlling fifty schools and questions of policy and matters affecting the welfare of whole blocks of the rising generation, at once appealed to the higher intelligence, and there was a surprising rush for the honour of a seat in an assembly occupied directly in building up the greatness of England from the very foundations.

Areas were then extended in other directions of local government, and the rush of candidates continues to such an extent that there are ten capable men who would like, without remuneration, to serve their country to every one who is doing so.

And here surely lies the solution of the Imperial question.

It must be an anomaly that, while there is a large floating surplus of legislative capacity throughout the country, the 670 men at

Westminster exhibit the spectacle of mountains of legislative work neglected through a choked-up and paralysed machinery.

Home Rule is a term hateful to many from its association of political rancour, but the principle of decentralisation, or expansion, has lately been strikingly recognised by the present Government in Ireland, and every such movement, allied with the palpable deadlock at St. Stephen's, brings nearer the day when the legislative and administrative ability, so plentiful throughout the country, and so strikingly exemplified in the case of School Boards and County Councils, will be organised and brought into the general service of the people.

The service of the people by the people must be the cry of the future, and equally in the interests of both Liberal and Conservative principles.

The extension and consolidation of Local Government have at least taught this fact, that Imperialism is not the only sentiment which can excite the most fervent enthusiasm in the minds of Englishmen; but that duty, in far more homely guise, has claimed, and will still claim, their highest abilities and most unselfish patriotism.

Sit on the safety-valve, insist on the immaculate nature of the British Constitution, continue to throw the whole burden of government on Queen, Lords, and Commons, and the inevitable will follow. Many members of Parliament now confess that they regret they ever stood and sat. Ardent reformers in the House speak with despair of progress in any given direction, while County Councillors are cheerful and jubilant, and, if anything else, a trifle alarmed at the speed of their vehicle.

The danger of Empire is that its claims will oust the just rights of the citizens at home unless government itself grows with the Empire.

Fresh markets will increase the wealth of the few and the employment of the many, but the ignorance of the mass of the people will still remain a menace at home and a byword abroad; the sanitary conditions of our towns and villages will still acidulate the satire of the pessimist; railways will still compete in dividends to the ruin of the producer; financial reform will air itself in the futility of academic discussion, and the law itself will remain as much the terror and enigma of the layman as the happy hunting-ground of the lawyer.

Home Rule for England, Ireland, Wales, and Scotland is merely a catchword. Local Parliaments must come, in relief of stagnation, but the grouping of the constituencies must be viewed from the necessities of circumstance rather than from any sentimental or so-called national standpoint.

The areas which should be covered for all purposes of domestic legislation by any one Parliament should be regulated by industrial peculiarities or agricultural conditions. There are few parts of the kingdom more different than North Wales and South Wales, while there is probably far more sympathy and community of interests between the inhabitants of Montgomery and Salop than between those of Cardiff and Carnarvon.

No country in the world has to deal with anything like similar conditions.

Russia has the next largest colonial population, but it is exclusively Asiatic, and the method of government is military and monotonous in formality ; and while the foreign policy of Russia excites the admiration of the world, the condition of her people could not serve us for a model, even if any comparison were.possible between an autocracy and a royal republic.

Should the American Empire ever rival the British, the system of separate State government, extant in the United States, will be found an incalculable aid to imperial control.

The States of America, no doubt, owed their origin of area to racial, pastoral, or industrial conditions, and were not subject to the circumscription of any "melancholy ocean." Why Ulster and Munster, which are antipathetic, both racially and industrially, should be forced under the same local Parliament has taken the eloquence of a Grattan and the strangely honest sophistry of a Gladstone to commend.

The British nation, like the foot of a Chinese girl, can only resist growth in method of government at the expense of becoming wholly crippled.

That an Empire with a population of 300,000,000 needs a different machinery of government to the same Empire with 15,000,000 seems an almost self-evident proposition.

Let us see to it that the reform is not delayed till we fall behind in the race of nations.

Excess of raw material in the legislative mill is the mother of opportunism.

Legislation, such as that required by backward technical education, is shelved session after session, owing to other more exciting or more party-satisfying claims.

Panic is born of accumulating statistics of national discomfiture, and some Bill is rushed through Parliament, with or without the aid of the closure, which is conspicuous by its carelessness in detail and in its remedial inconsequence.

Meanwhile, there is not a member of Parliament who could not name a score of reforms which are essential, in various directions, and with which it would be impossible for either Party to disagree, but which are hopeless of attainment under present conditions.

That local Parliaments must come is the opinion of most political students since Parnell riveted the public gaze on a force more powerful than steam or electricity—obstruction, *vis inertiæ*.

It is true that this force no longer controls political situations, but it flashed a search-light on the incompetence of Parliament and disclosed the humiliating spectacle of Ministers continually kept out of bed, idle and yawning, at ridiculous hours of the morning, by methods previously associated with pantomime rather than Parliament.

Members no longer sit up all night, at the behest of any piper, to so melancholy a dance, but the speed is almost as slow as when they got no sleep.

To Parnell is due the nation's gratitude for showing it the ludicrous incapacity of its brobdingnagian machine.

The areas for local Parliaments and the classes of legislation which shall be committed to their care are questions for deliberation.

Once established, they will afford opportunities for experimental and initiatory legislation which are out of the question in an Imperial Parliament, while it may be hoped that they will be less susceptible to appeals for class bribes.

Recent events indicate the possible ultimate inclusion of colonial representatives in Imperial Government; and the relegation of " Gas and Water politics " to local legislatures is a pre-condition to any workable scheme of federation.

Let us fortify ourselves with the reflection that no human institution is final ; and even the British Constitution, which, according to Mr. Podsnap, came to us direct from the hand of Providence, must march with the times.

F. A. A. Rowland.

# THE PROBLEM IN SOUTH AFRICA.

## BOER *V.* BRITON.

## IV.

THE last instalment brought us to the plan of campaign of the Reform leaders and to the consideration of the following questions: First, was an armed insurrection inevitable? Secondly, was it justifiable under all the circumstances? Thirdly, was it capable of success? And lastly, how far was the English Government entitled to interfere in the dispute?

It is necessarily impossible to dogmatise on the inevitable. In human affairs all sorts of contingencies may arise and entirely change the course of events. Granted a body of men determined rather to fight than submit to certain conditions, and a Government equally determined to maintain those conditions, the result may be said to be a foregone conclusion. In the present case it seems certain that the President had determined not only not to make any concessions to the Uitlanders, but to resist by force any attempt to extort redress by constitutional means or otherwise. He intended to keep the Uitlanders in a state of subjection by a display of overwhelming force. Four years before the Raid the Government selected the site for the gaol in the favourite residential quarter of Johannesburg. Upon protest being made to the President, he replied, "That he did not care about] the convenience. He was going to build the gaol there because some day the town would be troublesome and he would want to convert the gaol into a fort and put guns there before that time came."

On the other hand, serious as the personal grievances undoubtedly were, they were not such as usually impel men to sacrifice their lives to redress. As Mr. Bryce says, "Life, religion, property, personal freedom were not at stake." Yet, at the same time, Mr. Lionel Phillips more correctly hit off the situation when he declared, in his speech of November 1895,

"that it is a mistake to imagine that this much-maligned community, which consists, anyhow, of a majority of men born of freemen, will consent indefinitely to remain subordinate to the minority in this country, and that they will for ever allow their lives, property, and liberty to be subject to its arbitrary will." [1]

The Uitlanders were composed of three classes—the capitalists, the middle class, traders, professional men, engineers, and the like, and the working men. The middle class was represented by the National Union, which up to the middle of 1895 had conducted the agitation, when it was joined by the capitalists, who subsequently directed the whole movement.

The National Union certainly intended to fight to a finish whenever a favourable opportunity occurred, but whether it would have carried the bulk of its supporters with it is an open question. The capitalists, at first at any rate, having made up their minds that a revolution was inevitable, only proposed to make such a display of force as to extort terms from Mr. Kruger. Later, part of the plan of campaign became offensive by the proposed seizure of the arsenal at Pretoria. The unknown factor was the attitude of the working men, upon whose co-operation rested the success of the movement. The leaders expected to rouse them by their eloquence when the time was ripe. As a matter of fact, the majority proved themselves willing and anxious to fight, but it was an accident which roused them at that particular moment. The news that Jameson had crossed the border and was marching to their assistance, that arms were being served out, and that a Boer commandant had been ordered to ride through Johannesburg and crush the rising compelled them to take sides. Many, indeed, including most of the Cornish miners, left the country amid the jeers of the spectators :

"Up to now," writes Captain Younghusband, " it may be said with certainty that the majority had not wished to fight. . . . For weeks past, and especially after the issue of the manifesto, letters had been written to the newspapers denouncing in the strongest terms the folly of attempting to take up arms against the Government. Some had gone so far as to say that, if any should attempt to do so, they would forcibly oppose. Organisations even had been formed for this express purpose ; yet, when the move was made, when arms were actually taken up, every one, with hardly an exception, joined in." [2]

The great mass of the people, he says, were not at that time discontented, and, strongest proof of all, he states that "the leaders, on comparing notes, found they had only three or four hundred men on whom they could depend." [3]

An armed conflict, then, was not inevitable. It was only possible provided the working classes, who were not seething with discontent, could be induced to co-operate. As I have said, the monetary grievances did not appreciably affect the average Uit-

[1] *South African Recollections*, p. 65.
[2] *South Africa of To-Day*, p. 77.
[3] *South Africa of To-Day*, p. 70.

lander. "The ordinary miner, the business employé, and the clerks were all getting very high wages," as Captain Younghusband rightly points out. The high cost of living, concessions, and other of the main grievances did not consciously affect the majority, although doubtless the better educated amongst them fully appreciated the situation. One sentiment, however, was held unanimously. All were keenly aware of the position of inferiority in which they stood. The official Boer, at any rate, took no pains to conceal his contempt for the Uitlander. Galling as this was, it was not in itself a sufficient cause for a revolution; carefully worked upon, it might have become so.

"What are the circumstances," asks Mr. Bryce, "which justify insurrection? Some cases are too clear for argument. Obviously any subject of a bloodthirsty tyrant, ruling without or against law, is justified in taking up arms. . . . On the other hand, it is clear that subjects of a constitutional Government, conducted in accordance with law, do wrong and must be punished if they take arms, even when they have grievances to redress. Here, however, was a case which seemed to lie between the extreme instances. The Uitlanders, it need hardly be said, did not concern themselves with nice distinctions. In the interior of South Africa Governments and constitutions were in a rudimentary stage; nor had the habit of obeying them been fully formed. So many non-legal things had been done in a high-handed way and so many raids into native territories had been made by the Boers themselves that the sort of respect for legality which Europeans feel was still imperfectly developed in all sections of the population. Those of the Reformers, however, who sought to justify their plans argued that the Boer Government was an oligarchy which overtaxed its subjects and yet refused them those benefits which a civilised Government is bound to give. It was a Government of a small and ignorant minority, and, since they believed it to be corrupt as well as incompetent, it inspired no respect. Peaceful agitation had proved useless. Did not the sacred principle of no taxation without representation which had been held to justify the American Revolution justify those who had been patient so long in trying to remove their grievances by force, of course with as little effusion of blood as possible?" [1]

The case for the Uitlanders on this point could not have been stated more fairly. A revolution which succeeds ceases to be a revolution. Mr. W. T. Stead takes precisely the same view:

"The right of appeal to Revolution, that *ultima ratio* of oppressed populations, is indestructible, and may always rightfully be exercised when two conditions are present: first, that the sufferings and grievances of the oppressed population are sufficiently real to convince them that life were well risked in order to remove them; secondly, that they have a reasonable prospect of success." [2]

Mr. Stead, however, refuses to believe in the reality of these grievances:

"They were not weighty enough to drive the Uitlanders themselves to risk their lives in a desperate struggle." [3]

[1] *Impressions of South Africa*, p. 425.
[2] *The Scandal of the South African Commission*, p. 6.      [3] *Ibid.* p. 7.

Was there such a prospect of success? Under the circumstances Mr. Bryce thinks not. A movement conducted by three groups of persons at three places distant from one another—Johannesburg, Pitsani, and Cape Town—to which he should have added a fourth group in London, rendered concerted action extremely difficult. It was the London group which wrecked the whole scheme.

The Jameson raid was no part of the Jameson plan. It was carried out against the express orders of the Reform leaders and of Mr. Rhodes himself, who afterwards declared " it had upset his apple-cart." The original plan was for Johannesburg to rise and for a force of 1500 men to be stationed on the border to come in and defend the town if necessary. But for Jameson's criminal and blundering attempt to rush the movement, I have little hesitation in coming to the conclusion that the Reform movement would have largely succeeded. Captain Younghusband alone of all the writers explains the situation. Many Dutchmen even in the Transvaal, to say nothing of those in the rest of South Africa, thought the Government were going too far. The Government could not have counted on the support of the Boers as a whole in suppressing any spontaneous rising in Johannesburg, for many were openly saying that if the President was obstinate enough to set the fire alight, he might put it out himself.

" Indeed," he declares, " when orders were sent to the districts to mobilise, one district, not having heard that it was in order to resist an outside invasion, but thinking it was merely to suppress an outbreak in Johannesburg, flatly refused to obey the summons. It was only when they were informed that the object was to defend their country from a foreign invasion that they obeyed." [1]

Moreover, it seems highly probable from a consideration of the events of the crisis at Johannesburg, that in spite of the Jameson Raid the movement would have proved largely successful.

The Leonard manifesto stood upon three planks: (1) The maintenance of the Republic; (2) The securing of equal rights; and (3) The redress of grievances. It demanded (1) the establishment of the Republic as a true Republic; (2) a constitution framed by representatives of the people as a whole; (3) an equitable franchise law and fair representation; (4) equality of the Dutch and English languages; (5) responsibility to the legislature of the heads of the great departments; (6) removal of religious disabilities; (7) independence of the courts of justice, with adequate and secured remuneration of the judges; (8) liberal and comprehensive education; (9) efficient civil service, with adequate provision for pay and pension; (10) free trade in South African products.

The President commenced to climb down by removing on Satur-

[1] *South Africa of To-Day,* pp. 70–71.

day, December 27, the special duties on foodstuffs. On the 30th Dr. Jameson crossed the border, in spite of the special message which reached him on the previous day from the Reform leaders. The Reform Committee immediately came into existence and placed the town in a state of defence, the Boer police quietly effacing themselves. Unfortunately for the Committee less than 3000 rifles had come to hand, and they had only a few maxims. No less than 20,000 men volunteered for service and demanded arms. The Boers, however, were ignorant of the true position, and fully believed Johannesburg had 20,000 men under arms. There is no doubt the Government was thoroughly frightened. Negotiations took place. Delegates from the Executive Council met the Committee at Johannesburg and requested that a deputation should be sent to Pretoria to meet a Commission to be appointed by the Government with a view to a peaceful settlement and the redress of grievances, the delegates stating that the Government were anxious to remove the causes of discontent, and that Johannesburg would get practically all that was demanded in the manifesto.

The result of the conference with the Commission was that as the High Commissioner, Sir Hercules Robinson, had offered his services as mediator, the Government had accepted them. Pending his arrival there was to be an armistice. The grievances would be earnestly considered. With this result the deputation returned perfectly satisfied. Unfortunately Sir Hercules took no steps to ascertain the terms upon which Dr. Jameson had surrendered. He accepted the statement that the surrender was unconditional. He persuaded the Uitlanders to give up their arms as the only means whereby the lives of Dr. Jameson and his men could be spared, stating that the disarmament of Johannesburg was a *sine quâ non* to the renewal of further negotiations, and assuring them that their grievances should be considered and righted. The Reform leaders loyal to the last to the misguided Jameson who had so cruelly betrayed them, with great difficulty damped down the insurrection and left themselves to the mercy of the Government.

Even after Jameson's frightful blunder Mrs. Phillips contends that the Uitlanders had the game practically in their own hands, and only lost it owing to the action of the High Commissioner.[1]

Captain Younghusband, however, considers that there was great probability of Dr. Jameson and men being shot if the leaders had held out.[2] I think he is mistaken. The President, by a breach of good faith, would at once have forfeited all public sympathy. I think he is also mistaken in his view that the Boers would have made any real attack on Johannesburg, which they believed to be defended by 20,000 rifles with maxims and guns. Recent events

---

[1] *South African Recollections,* p. 103.
[2] *South Africa of To-Day,* p. 89.

have proved the inability of the Boers to capture the towns even weakly defended. Moreover, the trick by which Mr. Kruger obtained the surrender proves that he had no longing to try conclusions with Johannesburg. At the best it might have been a long business which would have given occasion for English intervention.

All is fair in love or war, but the fact remains that Mr. Kruger won the winning trick either by *suggestio falsi* or *suppressio veri*. The moralist, at any rate, cannot acquit Oom Paul of dishonourable conduct. I should be sorry to think that an English, French, or German Commander of any standing would have been capable of similar action in this case.

A subsidiary question here arises whether the movement was wise or expedient. Why not have waited? The Uitlanders were rapidly increasing in numbers. The President was an old man, with whom would have died his peculiar personal influence. His probable successor would have been General Joubert, an honest man of wider views. Mr. Kruger was gradually losing his ascendency even with the Boer of his own generation, whilst the young Boer was growing up freed from many of the prejudices and superstitions of his fathers. It was only the Jameson Raid which welded the Boers into one nation to repel foreign invasion.

Mr. Bryce suggests two reasons without, however, placing much value on them. First, it was believed that the Government was entering into secret relations with Germany. Secondly, it was feared that an independent English Republic might emerge, spreading Republican feeling in our colonies.[1] Neither of these reasons would appeal to the average Johannesburgher, although there is some truth in the first. Of the second contingency I find no evidence at all. On the contrary the Reform leaders raised the Transvaal flag at the first opportunity after strenuously rejecting any other. Mr. Bryce assigns as the more obvious cause the natural impatience of men unable to obtain redress and tired of inaction. This, no doubt, constituted a large element. But the real reason to my mind is to be found in the President's obvious determination to keep down Johannesburg by force, evidenced by the vote for fortifications and war material, and by his threat that they would only get their rights over his dead body. His favourite simile of the tortoise which must first put out its head before you strike, and his steady refusal of all reform clearly show his determination to strike hard when the opportunity occurred, and settle the business once for all. The Reform leaders felt that if they waited much longer it would be too late, and I think they were right. Unfortunately for them Dr. Jameson rushed them and the revolution [went off at half-cock.

[1] *Impressions of South Africa*, p. 430.

Lastly, how far was the English Government entitled to interfere in the dispute ?

The Jameson Raid must be carefully distinguished from the Jameson plan or plan of campaign. The Uitlanders calculated upon a comparatively bloodless rising involving the overthrow of the Kruger *régime*, the intervention of the High Commissioner and a popular vote which would transfer the control of the government to the Progressive party. They were to receive moral support by the presence on the frontier of a body of Rhodesian Police under Dr. Jameson. But this force was not to cross the border except under extreme circumstances. This was the plan of campaign.

The distance from the Rhodesian frontier rendered any assistance in that quarter out of the question. Accordingly, Mr. Rhodes had secured from Lord Ripon the promise of the transfer of the Bechuanaland Protectorate. With the change in the English Ministry the same request was made to Mr. Chamberlain by Dr. Harris, the emissary of Mr. Rhodes. Dr. Harris was proceeding to explain the real reason for the transfer when Mr. Chamberlain interrupted him, and said : " I do not want to hear any confidential information ; I am here in my official capacity." Dr. Harris stated in his evidence

" That he had in his mind something which Mr. Rhodes told him, that he made no explicit statement to that effect but that he referred to the unrest at Johannesburg and added a guarded allusion to the desirability of there being a police force near the border."

Mr. Chamberlain admits the statement as to the " unrest at Johannesburg," and does not deny the " guarded allusion," but says

" If such an allusion was ever made I did not understand it, at all events as referring to anything which has subsequently taken place. I desire to say in the most explicit manner, that I had not then and that I never had any knowledge or, until I think it was the day before the actual raid took place, the slightest suspicion of anything in the nature of a hostile or armed invasion of the Transvaal."

This evidence cuts both ways. It is evidence that Mr. Chamberlain was innocent of complicity in the Raid, but it also proves that he had cognisance of the plan.

Shortly after this incident occurred the struggle over the drifts and the guarantee of half the costs of a probable war by the Cape Ministry. Mr. Rhodes, foiled over the Protectorate, devised another expedient which would serve the same purpose. Eventually, Mr. Chamberlain, as a *quid pro quo* for the guarantee, conceded a strip of territory running the whole length of the Transvaal frontier on the ostensible pretext of constructing a railway, a transfer which carried with it that of the police. In view of Mr. Chamberlain's evidence, cited above, to say nothing of all the probabilities of the case, it is impossible to believe that he was ignorant of the purpose for which this territory was to be used— viz., to provide a vantage point for an armed force, in case the High Commissioner should require assistance after the rising. If Mr. Chamberlain was not cognisant of this part of the Jameson plan, he failed to exhibit that acuteness with which he is usually credited. But his worst enemy would hardly accuse him of complicity in the actual Raid.

It was the expansion of the Jameson Plan which destroyed the whole movement. This consisted of two parts. One was the attempt to carry out the rising under the British flag. The other was the invasion by Dr. Jameson. Both originated in London. Pressure from some influential person or persons was brought to bear on Mr. Rhodes to accept the first. The Reform leaders, believing Mr. Rhodes to be yielding, declared they would have nothing more to do with the matter unless Mr. Rhodes repudiated the British flag policy. Satisfactory assurances were given to Mr. Leonard at Cape Town by the latter.

" Who alone in London," asks Mr. Stead, "was strong enough to compel Mr. Rhodes to run so terrible and, as the result proved, so fatal a risk? Whose support was so indispensable as to force Mr. Rhodes against his better judgment to waver on the flag question? There was one man in London and only one man who was in such a position, and by a very significant coincidence this very man was in close, intimate, and constant intercourse with the group from which emanated the cablegrams that put pressure upon Mr. Rhodes."

" It may not have been Mr. Chamberlain," continues Mr. Stead, " but if not who was it? In the engineering of the revolutionary campaign the introduction of the flag was the one fatal mistake which was made; and it is evident that pressure was brought to bear on Mr. Rhodes in that direction by his emissaries, who had been in communication with Mr. Chamberlain. That at least is clear and although it may not carry us far, it at least leaves considerable suspicion whether the failure does not lie at the door of the inconsiderate and headstrong Imperialism which over-reached itself by grasping too eagerly the fruits of revolution."

And there the suspicion must lie until the suppressed cablegrams are disclosed. Mr. Stead's further argument that this was the only method by which Mr. Chamberlain could have secured the control of the movement seems not so well founded. Through the High Commissioner, with the Jameson force at his back in Johannes-burg, Mr. Chamberlain might have been in a position to dictate terms.

Dr. Jameson's head was doubtless filled with the British-flag policy, and it only needed Miss Shaw's " Hurry up " telegram to Mr. Rhodes to start the Raid. The telegram was as follows:

"Held an interview with Secretary Transvaal, left here on Saturday for Hague, Berlin, Paris, fear in negotiation with these parties. Chamberlain sound in case of interference European Powers but have special reason to believe wishes you must do it immediately."

Asked for her " special reason," Miss Shaw assigns a remark of Mr. Fairfield—a remark declared by him to be merely casual without any ulterior signification—

"Well, if the Johannesburg burghers are going to rise, it is to be hoped they will do it soon."

Mistaken or not, it is clear that Dr. Jameson was convinced that it was Mr. Chamberlain's wish that he should " go in " at once, and " go in " under the British flag.

Assuming Mr. Chamberlain to be *particeps criminis* in the Jameson Plan, how far is his conduct justified? From the point of view of international law of course a constitutional Minister is not warranted in conniving at a revolutionary conspiracy, even where his own countrymen are concerned. If, in addition to this, he was also the author of the British-flag policy, then he committed not only a constitutional but a political blunder of the gravest character. So far as the Jameson Plan is concerned, I agree with Mr. Stead that his conduct does not call for any severe censure from the moralist. Had Mr. Chamberlain frankly confessed his share in the Jameson Plan, and invited investigation, he would have lost little in public estimation. Instead every obstacle to prevent the elucidation of the truth was raised. Cablegrams which were vital to the inquiry were allowed to be destroyed, the production of others still in existence was refused, witnesses who came prepared with important evidence were dismissed unquestioned, or stopped whenever they approached the real point—in fact, the whole inquiry was a farce, and intended to be a farce. The South African Committee was appointed, not to elicit the truth, but to conceal it. One or two questions in cross-examination of Mr. Chamberlain would quickly have revealed how far he was committed. Nothing of this kind took place. On the contrary, Mr. Rhodes was made the scape-goat, and Mr. Chamberlain squared accounts by presenting that gentleman with a certificate of honour in the House of Commons, after having previously signed the report accusing Mr. Rhodes of lying and of acting with bad faith, not only to the Imperial Government but to his colleagues and subordinates, by inducing the latter to believe that the Colonial Office was a consenting party to the conspiracy.[1] The participation of Mr. Rhodes in the movement was of course constitutionally utterly unwarranted, but apart from his indecision on the flag question, I see no reason for severe moral censure. And indeed, holding the Colonial Secretary in his pocket, as undoubtedly he did, his conduct may be described as magnanimous. Another prominent

[1] W. T. Stead, *The Scandal of the South African Committee.* Mr. Stead's analysis of the evidence is a masterly and convincing piece of work.

actor was far from displaying the latter virtue. The notorious "women and children" letter had lain in Dr. Jameson's pocket for two months before he wired it to Miss Shaw for publication in the *Times*, filling in the appropriate date as if just received from Johannesburg. Its publication was at one and the same time a gross breach of faith to the Reform leaders and a scandalous fraud upon the public. Dr. Jameson's charge of cowardice against the Johannesburghers for not coming out to his assistance utterly breaks down. This charge he obstinately maintained until its repudiation was reluctantly dragged out of him before the Committee. Whatever else the Reform leaders may have been they were no cowards. They loyally stood by Dr. Jameson to the point of offering their persons as security. He had betrayed them, and, by forcing their hands, had betrayed the movement, and yet they never uttered a word against him. Dr. Jameson was the popular hero of the day. Now the truth is known, his reputation is irretrievably ruined.

It is obvious, and, indeed, it has been an open secret in political circles that both before and after the change of Ministry in 1895 the Colonial Office was cognisant of the movement in Johannesburg. In fact ignorance would have been in the highest degree culpable. We expect the Colonial Office to know a little more of the business entrusted to it than "the man in the street." In carrying out that part of the Jameson plan which consisted in the mediation of the High Commissioner and the presence of an armed force on the border to prevent excesses on the part of the Boers against the lives and property of British subjects the English Government would have been amply justified.

But to take active participation in a conspiracy which had for its object the overthrow of the Republic under the Union Jack was another matter altogether. Upon a review of all the circumstances of the case it is impossible to acquit Mr. Chamberlain of complicity. His own conduct throughout the investigation, the methods adopted by the Committee, the omission of obvious inquiries, the impotent and inclusive findings, and even the constitution of the Committee are all open to the gravest suspicion. Sir William Harcourt's recent explanation would appear to be utterly inadequate. His fear that if the Committee did not report then it might not be re-appointed the following session seems groundless in the face of the fact that up to that date it had signally failed to achieve the object for which it had been constituted. Its report added nothing of any value to what was already common knowledge. Innocent or guilty Mr. Chamberlain then forged a weapon which, in Mr. Kruger's hand, has since proved invaluable. Doomed to failure as such a scheme was, supported by the information of the London group, it could only have presented itself to Mr. Chamberlain as a short cut through the South African imbroglio.

In the drifts ultimatum Mr. Chamberlain had acted splendidly. His action was firm, prompt, and circumspect. Mr. Kruger was prodigal of breaches of the Convention. He was even then contemplating a breach of the clause relating to equal taxation by passing a measure for the taxation of farms. But apart from those technicalities Mr. Chamberlain would have been justified in bringing pressure to bear upon the Boer Executive in many other directions. As Mr. Gladstone once aptly said:

"Wherever your subjects go, if they are in pursuit of objects not unlawful, you are under a moral obligation to afford them all the protection that is in your power."

I do not propose to enter upon the circumstances immediately surrounding the arrest and trial of the Reform Committee. The story is graphically told in all its details by Mr. Fitzpatrick, Mrs. Lionel Phillips, and Mrs. Hays Hammond. The chief evidence against the Reform leaders was the "women and children" letter found in Dr. Jameson's wallet. As Mrs. Hammond remarks, one would have thought that any one not utterly selfish would have swallowed such a compromising document if no other means of destruction were possible. Against the rest of the Committee the only evidence connecting them with the movement was a list of the members voluntarily given to the Transvaal Commission during the negotiations. There is thus some ground for the charge of treachery urged by the prisoners. The trial itself forms a good illustration of the Boer idea of the administration of justice. The whole thing was cut and dried. Although there was a jury the verdict and sentences were settled days before. The trial was a mere farce, presided over by Judge Gregorowski, imported from the Free State for the occasion, whose behaviour was such that he was hooted in the streets on his return to Bloemfontein.

Of the treatment of the prisoners in gaol one cannot speak without intense disgust. It is urged on behalf of the Boers that they did not appreciate the fact that the prisoners were not accustomed to rough it like themselves. It was not a question of roughing it. It was a case of maintaining existence under loathsome and insanitary conditions of the worst description. To this state of things was added the petty tyranny of a brutal, ill-conditioned gaoler whose reputation for refined cruelty will not suffer by comparison with any recorded in history. Du Plessis—for such is his name—is a near relative of the President, and in spite of repeated exposures by his superiors, not only retained his position, but has since been promoted. His answer to one of the Reformers gives away the case of alleged ignorance.

"Not one of you," he said, "would be alive a month if the rules were enforced. No white man could stand them: indeed, if the rules were properly enforced, not even a nigger could stand them."

For an adequate consideration those rules were sometimes relaxed, since much as Du Plessis loved cruelty for its own sake, he loved gold more. This inhuman wretch was one of Mr. Kruger's favourite officials.

In the long-drawn-out commutation of the sentences the President thought to obtain much kudos for his magnanimous conduct. But he overshot the mark. It was described throughout South Africa as "magnanimity by inches," and characterised as a game of "cat and mouse."

The deputation of over 200 mayors settled the business so far as the bulk of the prisoners was concerned. They were released on payment of a fine of £2000 each before the deputation was granted an interview with His Honour. Then followed negotiations for the commutation of the sentence of fifteen years' penal servitude upon the leaders, itself a commutation of the death penalty. To impose a fine would be an offence against God since it would be taking blood-money, but to accept an offer of so much cash down upon the understanding that the sentence would be remitted would be an entirely different transaction, which could not possibly offend the susceptibilities of the most pious Boer. It was, moreover, suggested that the money would be devoted to some charitable purpose. And so the bargain was struck at £25,000 apiece. Nothing has since been heard of any charity in connection with this transaction. It is a pity Mr. Reitz has not furnished an explanation on this point.

Of the sufferings of the prisoners and of themselves Mrs. Phillips and Mrs. Hammond write somewhat hysterically. If people go in for revolutions they must not expect much mercy if unsuccessful. Mrs. Phillips hardly appreciates the answer made by Mrs. Kruger to one of the lady app'icants for her intercession.

"Yes," she said, "I will do all I can for you. I am very sorry for you all, although I know that none of you thought of me that night when we heard that Jameson had crossed the border and we were afraid the President would have to go out and fight."[1]

Mr. Kruger emerged from the events of 1895_96 with £212,000, the fines from the Reformers, £50,000 worth of stores from Johannesburg, together with rifles and maxims. To this must be added a claim of £677,938 3s. 3d. for the costs of the Raid and £1,000,000 for "moral and intellectual damages." A very natural demand for "particulars" of these costs meeting with no satisfactory response, there the claim rests to this day.

Besides these pecuniary advantages, Mr. Kruger's power had become so consolidated as to be irresistible in the Transvaal. The Uitlanders were at his mercy, precluded under pain of banishment from either directly or indirectly meddling in the internal or external

---

[1] *South African Recollections*, p. 170.

politics of the Republic, and deserted, in spite of their promises, by the English Government.

Here was a grand opportunity for Mr. Kruger to display those virtues with which he is credited by his admirers. As a mere matter of policy it would have paid. By moderate reforms and the grant of some representation in the Government he might have established his power upon a sound and honourable basis.

Upon an examination of the events subsequent to the Raid it will be found that Mr. Kruger preferred to sacrifice the real interests of his country to those of himself and his immediate circle.

Two of the Reformers, Messrs. Sampson and Davies, had elected to serve their time rather than petition for their release. Two notorious gold-thieves were caught *flagrante delicto* by the officials of the City and Suburban Gold-mine Company and handed over to the authorities. They openly boasted that nothing would happen, as "they had made it all right." A few days later one escaped; the other was convicted and sentenced to six months' imprisonment. This penalty was regarded as entirely inadequate, the judge himself commenting adversely upon a law which tended to screen the prisoner. There was not a single mitigating circumstance, and yet Mr. Kruger, whilst retaining in gaol Messrs. Sampson and Davies, remitted three-fourths of the term and discharged the gold-thief unconditionally.

In 1897 occurred the High Court scandal. This arose out of the case of Brown *v.* the State. The Witfontein farm having been proclaimed a public digging, the plaintiff amongst others had, in spite of a subsequent illegal notice withdrawing the proclamation, pegged out his claim. The Government, realising their false position, rushed a measure through the Volksraad absolving the State from all liability. Chief-Justice Kotzé declared this law unconstitutional and gave judgment for Brown.

The President thereupon introduced and carried Law 1 of 1897, whereby he was empowered to exact assurances from the judges that they would respect all resolutions of the Volksraad as having the force of law and declare themselves not entitled to test the validity of a law by its agreement or conflict with the Constitution, and, in the event of their failure to comply, to dismiss them summarily.

The judges protested in a body, and Sir Henry de Villiers came up from Cape Colony as mediator. A compromise was arrived at. Pending the introduction of a measure promised by Mr. Kruger, safeguarding the independence of the courts, the judges agreed not to exercise the testing right. Nothing having been done, in February 1898 Mr. Kotzé charged the President with failure to redeem his promise. The latter promptly dismissed the Chief-Justice, who had completed twenty years of faithful service, without compensation or pension, and appointed Mr. Gregorowski in his place, who had previously stated that no honourable man could possibly sit on the Transvaal Bench so long as Law 1 remained in force. Mr. Kruger further vindicated his reputation for truth by denying that he had made any such promise as alleged to Sir Henry de Villiers or any one else. Not even Mr. Reitz attempts to defend this law of 1897. In fact, he discreetly avoids all mention of it. Mr. Hobson likewise omits to say anything of this gross violation of the Constitution.

That the independence of the judiciary is absolutely vital to the well-being of every State is a mere truism. Unquestionably this was a distinct breach of Article 14 of the London Convention. The Law of 1897, passed in defiance of the Grondwet, is itself invalid. It actually deprived several aliens of their undoubted rights of property, and it is the instrument by which, upon a mere snatch vote in the Raad, any inhabitant may be deprived of his existing rights in respect of his person, property, or business.

The second case in which this law was applied was the Pretoria Waterworks Company. Full details are given by Mr. Fitzpatrick, and it must suffice to say here that by a gross breach of faith the Government, under the provisions of this law, was enabled to expropriate the company at more than 25 per cent. discount.

The Report of the Industrial Commission was presented to the Government on July 27, 1897, and was laid before the Volksraad, with a request for the appointment of a Committee to act with the Government in carrying into effect the recommendations of the Commission. Here was a golden opportunity for Mr. Kruger to have silenced his enemies for ever by promoting the reforms advised by his own officials. What happened? In the Volksraad the President violently denounced the Report, charged Mr. Schalk Burger, the Chairman, with being a traitor for signing such a report, and finally obtained the appointment of a small committee composed chiefly of men already concerned in the scandals exposed by the Commission, to report on the Report of this very Commission!

Mr. Reitz sets out the bald heads of some of the recommendations, carefully omitting all reference to the concessions denounced, with the exception of the dynamite monopoly. He then endeavours to show that they have all been carried out.

He contends that there was no chance of contesting the dynamite concession in the law courts; he talks about the "solemnity of contracts;" states that the mining industry was naturally eager for cancellation even without adequate compensation, and "willing to wound but yet afraid to strike," winds up with the following charming insinuation:

"People, however, knew that the Messrs. Chamberlain were interested in the English ammunition and dynamite house of Kynoch, but they hesitate to assume that the Colonial Secretary was actuated in his Transvaal policy by considerations of private financial interests."

Mr. Kruger and Mr. Wolmarans defended and saved the monopoly. This action was obviously not in the interests of the State,
on the contrary, the interests of the State were sacrificed when the
small reduction of 10s. a case was made by reducing the tax of 10s.
to 5s., making the net reduction, so far as the company was concerned, only 5s., the State losing the other 5s. What was their
motive ? Mr. Wolmarans was a member of the State Executive,
but he was also one of the directors of the company. It was found
that 22,500 shares stood in the name of Dr. Gobert, and were given
" for services rendered." It is alleged that Dr. Gobert is only
another name for Mr. Kruger.

If one had to choose between those two allegations of personal
interest, the probabilities certainly point to the truth of the latter.

But it is not by such methods that Mr. Reitz can establish his case.

So far from cancellation being legally impossible the preponderance
of legal opinion was in its favour. Not only the Industrial Commission, but the Volksraad Dynamite Commission urged the cancellation, whilst the former reported that judging from the published
accounts of the company it was not clear that the Government had
received the 20 per cent. of the surplus profit secured to it under the
contract.

Mr. J. A. Hobson, whilst admitting the blackness of the whole
business, seems to me to go out of his way in his attempt to
minimise its gravity. He seeks to show that if the concession were
abolished, Nobel or the Dynamite Trust might form a ring, and the
last position of the mines would be worse than the first.[1]

Upon this very point the Industrial Commission report that they
" are of opinion that effective free trade will be in no wise jeopardised
by the existence of any ' ring ' or combination for sale of explosives
in Europe."

Mr. Hobson contends further that the price of dynamite cannot
be regarded as an intolerable burden on the mining industry.
Here, again, he is in conflict with the Industrial Commission and a
whole army of mining experts. The profits for the years 1897 and
1898, upon imported dynamite, were estimated by the Volksraad
Dynamite Commission at £580,000. To maintain that a large and
increasing sum like this, which benefits the State not one penny,
quite apart from the high price of the home-manufactured articles.
is not a most serious injury to the mining industry is absurd.
These were not profits upon manufacture, but upon a monopoly.
Mr. Hobson also maintains that from the standpoint of the Uitlanders the grievance was of no serious magnitude. But since the
interests of the Uitlanders are so intimately bound up with those of
the mining industry, it is difficult to accept this view.

---

[1] *The War in South Africa : its Causes and Effects.* By J. A. Hobson. Second edition.
London : James Nisbet & Co., Ltd. 1900. Pp. 88-95.

There is much to be said for his argument that the bucolic statesmen of the Transvaal were not fitted to cope with the astute foreign financiers. But the Industrial Commissioners proved themselves fully qualified to deal with many intricate questions. There were many in the Volksraad who were ready and willing to back up their recommendations. But when it came to a conflict with Mr. Kruger and his faction they were always worsted. The President made every question a racial one, and blood proved thicker than water. There is every excuse for commercial ignorance; there is none for corruption. The assumption that Mr. Kruger and his astute Hollander and German henchmen were incapable of fathoming the mysteries of the Dynamite monopoly, for instance, is too absurd. The simplest farmer could not fail to understand and appreciate the recommendation of the Industrial Commission.

Mr. Reitz states that the Netherland Railway Tariff was lowered in accordance with the recommendations of the Industrial Commission, and the duties on nearly all necessaries abolished, making a loss to the State of about £700,000 for the year 1898–9. Mr. Hobson gives the same figures.[1]  Mr. Fitzpatrick admits an inconsiderable reduction in the tariff, but says that the Volksraad Committee, whilst adopting those recommendations, stipulated that in order that the State Revenue should not suffer, the duty upon other articles of consumption should be increased so as to rather more than counterbalance the loss.

If Mr. Reitz is correct then two of the grievances disappear; if Mr. Fitzpatrick this is only another instance of Boer slimness.

Finally Mr. Reitz states that the administration of the Liquor, Pass and Gold Laws has been so improved that " evidences of dissatisfaction have disappeared." As conclusive proof of this he cites two resolutions passed August 17, 1899, by a Congress of the Chamber of Mines, the Chamber of Commerce, and the Mines Managers Association, viz. :

" 1. This combined meeting . . . desires to express once more its decided approval of the present Liquor Law, and is of opinion that prohibition is not only beneficial to the natives in their own interests, but is absolutely necessary for the mining industry, with a view of maintaining the efficiency of labour.
" 2. This meeting wishes to express its appreciation of the efforts made to suppress the illicit liquor trade by the Detective Department of this Republic since it has been placed under the administration of the State Attorney, and is of opinion that the success which has crowned these efforts disproves the contention that the Liquor Law is impracticable."

But no one except, perhaps, those interested in the Native Liquor Trade ever doubted the admirable provisions of the Liquor Law.

---

[1] *The War in South Africa*, p. 278.  Upon the freed articles there is still an *ad valorem* duty of 7½ per cent., but even so, says Mr. Hobson, the tariff is far more liberal than in Cape Colony.

It was purely a question of administration, and owing to the representations of the mine-owners and merchants, Mr. Smuts, an able and rising young barrister, was appointed, in July 1899, State Attorney. Under his administration a wonderful improvement took place, which was inflicting a heavy blow upon the interests of the traders in native liquor. These traders, who formed one of the most powerful and wealthy bodies in the Transvaal, immediately commenced to intrigue with the Volksraad, and secured, no doubt by corrupt methods, the introduction of an amending measure, upon the ground that the present Liquor Law was unworkable. This produced the public meeting which took place and passed the resolutions above-mentioned. The debate which then took place shows that the object of the meeting was to prove that the Liquor Law was not unworkable, and to prevent any change in the Law.[1]

This illicit trade with natives was equally obnoxious to the respectable liquor merchants whose business lay with the whiter, and whose interests were affected by the sale of inferior liquors such as were supplied to the natives, and they accordingly combined with the mine-owners in the movement. This struggle has been continuous, first one party and then the other obtaining the advantage.

In their letter to the Industrial Commission the Witwatersrand Chamber of Mines state that on the prohibition Law of 1897 coming into force, for the first month there was an almost total disappearance of drunkenness, but that illicit selling soon became again rampant, and the state of things worse than ever.[2]

This law Mr. Kruger denounced as "immoral" since by restricting the sale of liquor a number of honest people were deprived of their means of livelihood. The President, by the way, is a total abstainer.

The land-tax of £20 upon every farm, proposed in 1895, was made law in July 1899. This measure provided for the exemption of any owner who personally resided upon his farm, and consequently became a special tax upon the Uitlanders who, as members of corporations, companies, associations, or partnerships, held interests in land but did not reside upon it. This law is clearly a breach of Article 14 of the London Convention forbidding special taxation, and was so held by our own law officers of the Crown. Whether there is any connection between this measure and the remission of the 5s. dynamite duty there is no evidence, but assuming the State had to make good its loss in this respect it appears to be probable.

The year 1899 was also remarkable for the negotiations between some of the leading capitalists and the Government for moderate reform. The matters to be settled were the Press agitation, the

---

[1] *The Star*, Johannesburg, August 19, 1899.
[2] *Industrial Commission of Enquiry*, p. 472.

coolie question, the dynamite monopoly, a State loan, the severance from the South African League, the appointment of a State financier and a State auditor, taxation of mines, valuation of bewaarplaatsen, and the franchise. Whilst these negotiations were in progress, Mr. Kruger made two determined efforts to rush the confirmation of the dynamite monopoly through the Raad. The first proposal was for the fifteen years' extension; the second, for the condonation of all breaches of the concession and for compensation upon the expiry of the concession. In the correspondence published by Mr. Fitzpatrick, Mr. Reitz, as State Secretary, declared that the President was prepared to expropriate the company after the term of the concession upon the basis of an expired concession.[1]

It is clear that in these negotiations Mr. Kruger was endeavouring to detach the mine-owners from the general body of Uitlanders, and it is to the credit of these capitalists that they refused to secure their own advantage by the sacrifice of the general interests.

The rinderpest plague in 1897 gave occasion for "the donkeys and mealies scandal," and the grant of the sham municipality to Johannesburg to "the sewerage scandal," for full particulars of which I must refer to Mr. FitzPatrick's book.[2] Other scandals there were, such as the Eloff location transaction, in which Mr. Eloff, son-in-law of the President, was enabled to pocket £25,000. This gentleman, says Mr. Fitzpatrick, enjoys the unsavoury reputation of being interested in every swindle which is worth being in in the Transvaal. I certainly know of one company-promoting swindle of his which came within my own professional experience.

About this time the Selati Railway case came before the courts, and a complete list of the bribes given to twenty-one out of twenty-eight members of the Raad, with names and items, was pleaded by the company. Mr. Hobson severely condemns Mr. Fitzpatrick for accepting this list as evidence, which, of course, it is not. But Mr. Hobson forgets that the President, when defending the concession in the Raad, stated publicly that he saw no harm in members receiving presents.

The case has recently been fixed for hearing on June 13, before the Supreme Court at Brussels, and the defendant company has pleaded a further list of bribes, consisting of large sums of cash and shares, including one of £1000 to Mrs. Kruger. The President is alleged to have received £4000 in cash and 20,000 shares. It remains to be seen how far these allegations will be proved. But as such charges, if unfounded, only recoil with greater force upon those who make them one is almost bound to assume their truth.

The enormous Civil List must also be noticed. For 1899, official salaries amounted to £1,216,394, a sum largely in excess of legitimate requirements. As a glaring instance of the recent exercise of

1 *The Transvaal from Within,* pp. 345–360.    2 *Ibid.* pp. 321–324.

nepotism may be mentioned Mr. Kruger's recent appointment
the High Court Bench of Mr. Kock, a young man of twenty-fo
years of age.

The importance of the Edgar case, the Lombaard incident, an
the Amphitheatre occurrence have, I think, been greatly exa
and Mr. Chamberlain was ill-advised in attaching undue value
what were, at the best, extremely controversial questions, incapab
of proving any general course of official despotism. Even
true, they proved nothing. Such cases occur in every ci
community.

Of the legislation since the Raid may be mentioned the
Law of 1896, the Alien Expulsion Law, and the Alien Im
Law. By the first the President was empowered to suppress
newspaper which might be considered to contain dangerous
to the peace of the Republic. This law was used for the sup
of the *Critic* and the *Star*, and, according to Mr. Hobson, con
no more oppressive powers than are contained and have been enfor
within the last few years in the English law. "In Ireland and
India, during recent years, many prosecutions have been institu
for offences which were venial as compared with those habitually
committed by the Johannesburg Press." [1]

Mr. Hobson gives some examples from the latter which, he says
cannot be read without wonder at the apathy of a Governmen
which could tolerate such an abuse. Mr. Hobson appears to m
singularly unfortunate in his examples, which the most susceptibl
Government would not deign to notice. It is true, however, that
articles of violent and intemperate language and untruthful and
misleading character have emanated from this Press, but they can
easily be matched, if not surpassed, by those appearing in the
Krugerite Press.

By the two latter laws any foreigner who should by act or word
take any step dangerous to the public peace may be expelled with
appeal to the courts, and any person unable to prove means
self-support may be prohibited from entering the country.
these laws are infringements of Article 14 of the London Conve
tion. The former, upon protest from the Colonial Office,
amended and finally repealed.

Mr. Hobson attempts half-heartedly to defend such laws with the
plea that there are similar laws upon the statute-book in England,
which when quoted sound like terrible restrictions upon liberty. Of
course there are, but no one dreams of enforcing them. They are
rightly regarded as obsolete. But these Transvaal laws were passed
only yesterday, and we can only assume were passed with the object
of being applied when deemed necessary by the Government.

There is no cloud without a silver lining, even in the Transvaal,

[1] *The War in South Africa*, p. 59.

and Mr. Fitzpatrick has painted his picture too black. He complains that the monopoly of colour is not of his making, but was in the nature of the facts.[1]

Neither he nor Mr. Reitz mentions the improvement in the education question, which, as I have indicated, constituted one of the most serious of the grievances. This has been reserved for Mr. Hobson, who cites a letter dated August 22, 1899, to the *Transvaal Leader*, in which the writer, Mr. Hugh J. Evans, states that four State schools in which English is the sole medium of instruction were opened in the years 1897-8, and eight in which English is the medium for English children, and Dutch for Dutch children, were opened in the years 1897-9. Particulars of each are given. He also gives the names of six English schools which are not State schools but subsidised schools.[2] None of these, however, appear to be in Johannesburg, but they show that Mr. Kruger's violent opposition to the English language as the medium of instruction has not been allowed to prevail universally.

Upon an impartial review of all the circumstances during this period it will be found that a few reforms were effected. Some were real and substantial, others of little value, and others, again, wholly illusory, and merely made to order.

To all of them alike Mr. Kruger offered the most violent hostility. But whilst the condition of the Uitlanders in some directions was undoubtedly ameliorated, yet in others it was equally without dispute worsened. The loss of its independence by the judicial bench is by itself an enormous aggravation of their position, since their persons, liberty, and property are subject to the caprice of the Volksraad, an assembly which, if not corrupt, as we have every reason to believe, is at any rate undeniably incompetent to transact the business which is placed before it—an assembly, moreover, which is dominated by Paul Kruger, the most unscrupulous statesman of modern times. If we are to believe Mr. Hobson, "the evil genius of Transvaal politics has been Dr. Leyds." The notion of an unqualified Dutch political supremacy, with a complete dominance of Dutch language and ideas, which this imported Hollander sought to impress upon Transvaal politics and administration, has been a chief source of such Uitlander grievances as possess a real foundation.[3]

"One might almost go so far," he adds elsewhere, "as to say that had there been no Dr. Leyds there would have been no Transvaal crisis to-day."[4]

I am the last to deny the evil influence of Dr. Leyds and his compatriots upon Boer policy and administration, but Mr. Kruger, not Dr. Leyds, is the evil genius of the Transvaal. Dr. Leyds was

[1] *The Transvaal from Within*, p. 361.  [2] *The War in South Africa*, pp. 37–39.
[3] *Ibid.* p. 74.  [4] *Ibid.* p.74.

a mere tool in his hands. The methods may have been Dr. Leyds':
the policy was assuredly Mr. Kruger's. Ten years ago Dr. Leyds
was sufficiently indiscreet to commit to writing his estimate of the
President. In a letter to a friend with whom he afterwards quarrelled he described the President as an ignorant, narrow-minded,
pig-headed, and irascible old Boer, whom he could twist round his
little finger. Upon the publication of this pleasing description, the
President, in spite of the opposition of his colleagues, who had also
formed the subjects of Dr. Leyds' caustic pen, retained the latter in
office, carefully explaining to him, however, that he would keep him
there just so long as it suited his convenience.[1]

Apart from this story, for the truth of which I cannot vouch,
Mr. Kruger is much too strong a man to be the tool of any one.
He, and he alone, must be held responsible for the policy of the
Transvaal Government. The question of the responsibility for the
outbreak of hostilities must be left for future consideration.

HUGH H. L. BELLOT.

[1] *The Transvaal from Within*, p. 107.

(*To be continued.*)

# A PLEA FOR AN HONOURABLE PEACE:

## WITH A FEW WORDS ABOUT MAGNANIMITY.

AN honourable peace! What is that? In the minds of most
Englishmen, judging from the newspapers and the political talk
of the hour, it seems as though an honourable peace can come only
with the dishonouring or the crushing of our opponents. It is the
purpose of this article to plead for a peace which will be honourable
to all men, Dutch and English alike, who have the welfare of South
Africa at heart.

The one dominant fact to be borne in mind in determining
a settlement is the obvious and commonplace truism that after the
war both races, English and Dutch, must continue to live together.
Nay, not only to live together—that is possible even under conditions of anarchy and rebellion—but to live together in such ways
and under such conditions of social and political life as will tend to
produce mutual respect, harmony, good-will, and those civic and
political virtues which will make for a stable, a well ordered, and a
progressive Commonwealth.

Before proceeding to sketch the lines of such a settlement as will
promote this end, let me say a word or two about that much-abused
word " magnanimity." Not that I intend to advocate magnanimity
here. The temper of both parties is against it, and I wish at
present to confine myself to what I conceive to be strict equity. But
I wish also to enter a firm and strong protest against the contempt
which has been thrown upon this great word. Magnanimity, in the
fullest and highest sense, has never yet been tried. If I can prove
this, then I shall not only do something towards rescuing the word
from the contempt which has been poured upon it, I shall also, at the
same time, be preparing the minds of the readers of this article, not
perhaps, for exercising magnanimity, but for approaching this grave
South African problem according to those principles of equity a
departure from which, more or less on both sides, has brought South
Africa to its present lamentable condition.

First, then, as to magnanimity. We have it on the authority of
the Earl of Kimberley and the late Duke of Argyll, both members of
the Gladstone Cabinet at the time of the Majuba disaster and the
ensuing peace, that no magnanimity was intended. (By the way

many people seem to think that all our South African racial troubl
date from the time of Majuba. It would be far truer to say th
they date from the time of the unwise annexation of the Transv
by Disraeli in contravention of what should be recognised as one c
the first principles of international morality—that no civilise
country should be annexed by another without the consent of a larg
majority of the permanent and settled inhabitants of that country
The policy of the Gladstone Cabinet was dictated by pruden
a desire not to alienate Dutch feeling in South Africa, and,
negotiations having been opened, a desire to avoid what would hav
appeared to be a war of revenge for a very minor reverse. By wha
ever fine word these motives may be dignified they certainly canno
be labelled with the word "magnanimity."

But apart from this I venture to say that under the then circum
stances a policy of magnanimity was almost impossible. What
magnanimity? Let us take an illustration. Suppose two pas
sengers, a big man and a little man, on board a steamer have
quarrel and begin to fight. During the first round the little m
loses his footing and tumbles overboard, whereupon the big m
immediately jumps in to his assistance, and succeeds in bringing h
safely on board again. That we should call magnanimity. B
suppose instead that the little man by a fluke succeeded in throwi
his opponent on the first round. Then the friends of the big m
intervene and persuade him not to continue the fight, pointing o
that the little man has a certain amount of right on his side, th
there has been a misunderstanding between the two, and that the b
man can easily crush the little one if he likes, but that to d
so would be to stoop to the mean and low policy of revenge, b
which, if he adopts it, he will alienate many of his own friend
The big man adopts this view of the matter, and voluntarily with
draws from the fight. Then some of the big man's friends begin
taunt the little man. They tell him that he owes his existence
the big man's magnanimity, that he must be very careful or the b
man will renew the fight and crush him; that they, the friends
the big man, have a flag called the "Union Jack" which they w
run up over the little man's head, despite all he can say or do, an
that he is a mean, dirty, ignorant, cowardly, stupid fellow, whom i
will be a pleasure to some of the big man's friends to wipe out c
existence. The little man retorts in like terms, and says that he wi
fight till death before he will allow his flag to be hauled down an
the big man's put in its place. Now I need not say anything abou
the rightness or wrongness of all this—it may have been inevitabl
in the circumstances in which the respective parties were placed, bu
I do most strongly resent the assumption that magnanimity, even
the narrowest sense of the word, has been allowed free or fair pla
I trust that my fellow ministers, also, will do all on their

to undermine that assumption. For we are face to face with this amazing moral phenomenon : that the people of England and South Africa are virtually being told that one of the finest human feelings— magnanimity, great-heartedness, noble–spiritedness—is of no account, and that nations should rule their policy according to the barbarous method of uncivilised ages :

> " The simple rule, the good old plan,
> That they should take who have the power
> And they should keep who can."

Indeed, this doctrine is sometimes openly avowed. " The Boers acquired the country from the natives, why should not we acquire it from them ? " it is said. As though Germany or any other State would have the right to take Cape Colony, Australia, or Canada, had she the power to do so !

Inasmuch, however, as magnanimity, owing to the temper of the times, is out of the question, let us consider the problem from the point of view of equity. Here again, opinions will vary just as widely as conceptions of justice vary in different individuals. To some, a settlement after the war is over will seem a comparatively easy matter. Hoist up the British flag at Pretoria and Bloemfontein, and declare the two Republics British Colonies, and the thing is done. But, as a matter of fact, easy, patent-pill remedies are of all things to be viewed with suspicion and distrust. Only the most delicate and tactful handling of the many matters in dispute, and an entire avoidance of Lanyon-like methods of government, will pave the way for a return of those feelings of mutual amity and respect between British and Dutch—if, indeed, this be now possible—by which alone a united South Africa can be built up. Whether the two Republics should be annexed and proclaimed as British Colonies I will leave for discussion later on. Possibly the statesmen and the peoples of the Transvaal and the Orange Free State would prefer such a course to a settlement which, while professing to grant them autonomy, would really rob them of the substance of their independence and leave them only the shadow. What I wish to do now is to dwell on one or two essential principles which will make for a return of cordial relationships between the two peoples, and then, in the light of these principles, to discuss the question whether an honourable peace and settlement can be established on the basis of them.

First, then, I take it that there will be no great difficulty about such questions as more effective municipal government for Johannesburg, greater facilities for a more efficient English education, and equal electoral rights. But in interpreting the meaning of " equal rights " we must take care that we are not deluded by a phrase. The most violent extremist would see the injustice of assuming that the political "rights" of the money-maker or the fortune-seeker, who confessedly goes to spend only a few years in the country and get all he can out of it, are equal to the "rights" of the permanent and life-long settler who makes the country his home. To assume that the political rights of the two are equal would be to place a most dangerous power in the hands of the former, who, on such questions as taxation, might use his power merely for the furtherance of his own interests, rather than for the permanent well-being of the State. Still, no great difficulty need be anticipated here. Even before the war the Transvaal was willing to grant a five years' franchise, and, whatever happens, some such restrictive principle must be established in order to weed out the adventurer from the genuine colonist. It must be remembered that the British naturalisation law necessitates a residential qualification of a little over five years, and unless Great Britain alters her naturalisation laws, which she is not likely to do, the non-British Uitlanders in the Transvaal—if it is proclaimed a British Colony—will be in worse case as regards the franchise than they would have been under the Transvaal Government if President Kruger's latest offer had been accepted. Apart from this, however, we may, I presume, take it for granted that between the permanent settlers in a country, to whatever nationality they may belong, there should be no invidious distinctions made. The independence of the Republics—if it is to be maintained—could be safe-guarded under such a principle by declaring a three-fourths majority necessary to any alteration in the fundamental constitution, if such alteration were likely to affect their independence prejudicially.

But the question of greatest importance in this matter—of far greater importance than any question about franchise—is the question of the Gold Mines. By common consent it is the "geological accident" which placed these enormous goldfields in the land across the Vaal which has caused the whole trouble, and our first business is to take care that this cause of trouble shall not endanger the future political peace either of the Transvaal or of South Africa. It is quite certain that any settlement which would place the permanent and settled population of the soil—the agricultural and pastoral interests—in subservience to the necessarily impermanent, and, to some extent, unsettled mining and speculative interests, could not long endure, however strongly backed such a settlement might be by military power. And indeed, I do not think that the British Government would intentionally countenance any such arrangement. Hence the necessity for some settlement of this matter which will work for the future welfare of the whole of South Africa rather than for the enrichment of a few, and the consequent antagonism of the varying interests which make up our social, industrial, and political life. Such a settlement may be found in the principle which has received the approval of some of the greatest political economists of our time—*i e.*, that the mineral wealth of a country should be placed under public control and utilised for the benefit of the whole of the people of that country. The application of such a principle is surrounded with great difficulties in an old country, where the diverse, and multitudinous, and complex interests involved require the most delicate handling and adjustment. But it is by no means so difficult in a new country, where a new situation has been created by war, and where the application of such a principle must of necessity be confined, in its initial stages at any rate, to the particular class of mineral wealth which is the root cause of the war. Hence, I venture to suggest that the whole of the gold mines of the Transvaal should be placed under the control of a Mining Commission, composed of representatives from all the States of South Africa, including, of course, the Transvaal and the Orange Free State, Rhodesia to come in as soon as it becomes a Crown or self-governing colony. Whatever powers might be given to such a body in respect to the regulation of labour in the mines, its business should be financial—*i.e.*, it would be charged with the power to tax the profits—the profits, not the output—of all gold mines in the Transvaal, the tax to rise gradually in proportion to the amount of profit made, falling lightly on the poorer mines and more heavily on the richer ones.[1] The profits of this tax might be allocated somewhat as follows, though, of course, details would be arranged at the time of the constitution of the Commission; what I am contending for now is the essential principle : First, the payment of an annual sum towards the extinction of the war debt ; secondly, the payment of an annual sum for a given number of years to the Transvaal Government—a sum based on its past revenue from the mines—as compensation for the taking over of the mines by the Commission ; thirdly, the division of the remainder of the proceeds of the tax, and of the first-named quota as soon as the war debt is extinguished, amongst the various South African States represented on the Commission, in proportion to their respective populations.

Let us see what advantages would follow from such a settlement. First, there is the obvious advantage that the mineral wealth of South Africa would be more largely used for the development of the country instead of for purposes of private gain. It must be obvious to the meanest intelligence and the most undeveloped conscience that to allow a country to be depleted of its richest mineral resources without receiving some adequate return is opposed to the dictates both of justice and of common sense. South Africa is waiting, with bare lands as it were, to be developed. Railways, irrigation,

---

[1] The same principle might, of course, be applied to all the mines—gold and diamond—in South Africa. But the opposition of the vested interests would be too great to overcome at present. The war creates a new situation which must be dealt with at once.

improved methods of agriculture and horticulture, education—all these the country is just hungering for. How long are we to allow this vast mineral wealth to be used for the building of palaces in England, or for the amassing of private fortunes by foreign speculators who, through their wealth and influence, bring the disturbing element of foreign complications into our political life?

Again, the moral advantages of such a policy would be even greater than the material advantages. The demoralising influence of the presence of enormous quantities of gold, the excitement, the greed, the speculation to which it gives rise—all this is more than sufficiently attested by the experience of every mining country in the world to need illustration. But it is demoralising in a much wider and deeper sense. The control which individuals or small companies of men have obtained over large portions of this mineral wealth places a most dangerous power in the hands of a few to the detriment of the community as a whole. We talk about democracy, but how can democracy have free play where power becomes concentrated in the hands of a few. I make no personal allusions—I am simply stating what must be obvious to every one as the natural outcome of social and economic forces when working under a given set of circumstances. The example of the United States will occur to every one. The old aristocracy had great traditions and a fine sense of honour, but the new aristocracy has no traditions, and its sense of honour is largely moulded by the influences of the Stock Exchange. Public life under such circumstances is degrading. The Church, the Press, Commerce, political parties, even social life itself, have become infected with a nameless something which may be termed either patronage or corruption, and which oftentimes passes imperceptibly from the one into the other. Public life, I say, cannot be healthy under such circumstances, and any measure which limits the aggregation of huge fortunes in private hands, especially where such fortunes are made, not by individual agency or talent employed in the public service, but by the skilful and speculative manipulation of the resources of a nation—any such measure should be welcomed as one necessary for the purification of political life and the true development of the State.

So obvious, then, and so numerous are the material and moral advantages of the policy I have suggested that I can hardly conceive of any disinterested opposition to it. The only question that remains is, is it practical? That there are difficulties in the way is obvious, but I do not think the difficulties are of such a nature as to be insurmountable. The present is certainly a most opportune time for the initiation of such a policy. War creates a new situation. We break, to a certain extent, with the past. Hence the necessity for placing things on a just footing. There would, of course, have to be a very careful consideration of the claims of existing share-

holders in imposing taxes on the profits of old mines, but the owners
of new mines would be given to understand that the whole of their
profits above the maximum fixed would be regarded as the property
of the Commission, *i.e.*, of the virtually but loosely federated States.
The principle is no new one.  It was advocated by John Stuart
Mill with regard to the unearned increment of land.  It is in force,
in partial measure, in various States in Europe with regard to such
minerals as iron, lead, tin, and coal.  In Rhodesia 50 per cent. of
the profits of mining operations goes to the Chartered Company.
Why, then, should not a similar principle be introduced for the
benefit of the whole of South Africa?  It is peculiarly fitting that
such a principle should be applied to gold mines.  For gold, being
the medium of exchange, should naturally be made subordinate to
the interests of the community as a whole; its further use, outside
art, being mainly for the gratification of those instincts which are a
survival of the barbaric nature—the instincts of personal adornment
and display.

This then, the collective control of the mines in the interests of
the whole of South Africa, being made one of the chief of the
terms of settlement, what shall be said respecting our future policy
as to the war?  Shall we go on with the grim determination of
" putting the thing through " and ending the Republics, with all
the sacrifice of life, and the deep and interminable bitterness
which that would involve: or shall we state our terms of peace, *i.e.*,
generally speaking, equal rights, collective control of mines, and a
recognition of the independence of the Republics.  In the present
state of the public mind it is almost hopeless to ask for a dispas-
sionate consideration of this question.  I am afraid that the majority
of Englishmen in Cape Colony are very strongly in favour of the
former course.  Still, I do not despair of getting the more sober-
minded of my English readers to consider the very weighty objections which seems to me to lie against such a policy.  There is no
doubt that it would delay, indefinitely, the return of peace.  It
would probably mean military Government for a long time to come.
And it would leave behind it generations of most bitter racial hatred,
with, probably, an attempt to re-establish the Republics as soon as
military Government was withdrawn.  Is such a peace desirable?
Could it be called peace in the true sense of the word?  Is it a
wise policy for Great Britain to hold her colonies by force instead
of by the free consent of the governed?

But there is a weightier objection still, for which I would ask
the consideration of the most passionate of my critics.  To prolong
the war will cost us, say, the lives of thousands of men.  Have we,
sitting amid the comfort of our own homes, the right to ask this
sacrifice of our fellow men for the mere sake of gratifying a
passionate desire for dominance?  Have we the right to demand

that so many wives shall be made widows, so many more parents bereft of children, so many children rendered fatherless, as the case may be? Only the very sternest necessity would justify such a course of action, and if that necessity does not exist, then we should stand guilty of the most brutal form of selfishness— demanding the sacrifice of human life and the blighting and darkening of thousands of other lives for the gratification of the blind passions of revenge and race-dominance. It will be said, I know, that the necessity does exist—that it exists in the fact that a recurrence of the present fearful catastrophe must be effectually prevented in future. But such an answer obviously assumes the very point in dispute. Is it likely that the keeping of a whole people in military subjection in a wild and sparsely populated country will allay racial animosity and the spirit of revolt? Let us remember that these men are not merely the Dutch, who beat back the might and power of Spain: they are also the descendants of those Huguenots with whom our own English blood is mingled. Would not the British flag at Pretoria be to them the symbol of a foreign despotism? How should we Englishmen, and especially we Yorkshire men, regard such a symbol, say in Leeds, Bradford, Halifax, or York? Should we not deem it our duty to fight against it to our latest breath? Or, again, do we wish to include in the British Empire any civilised people that does not wish to come in? Would it not be far better if the British flag could fly alongside the Transvaal flag at Pretoria by a friendly federal arrangement, thus giving free play to the national aspirations of both peoples? And probably the Commission, the establishment of which I have suggested, would form the beginning of such a federal arrangement. After every quarrel there is a method of settlement by which both parties may be prevailed upon to shake hands and live as friends. It is that method we must find and adopt. And I am afraid that we shall not find it if, either embittered by the soreness of temporary defeat or inflamed by the passion of victory, we proceed on the assumption that the only right settlement is to be found in the crushing of our antagonists, or in holding them permanently in subjection.[1] Again, I ask, should we Englishmen sit down under such a settlement if we were the defeated party? Where all is so dark for the future let us order our policy by the light of that ancient and sacred rule of doing unto others as we would have others do unto us.

The outlook for the future is dark indeed, and if we are to have something more than a mere semblance of peace the two peoples will have to show far more patience and forbearance to each other

---

[1] Even now, men—and not Dutchmen only—are bitterly announcing that their future political ideal must be a United States of South Africa as free from British control as is the United States of America.

than they have hitherto done.  I notice that even fair-minded papers like the *Spectator* are assuming that England is wholly in the right and the Boers wholly in the wrong.  So long as that attitude of mind prevails, the elements which make for peace are absent.  There is wrong on both sides and there is right on both sides; the evil and the good in both peoples have become inextricably commingled, and, for the time, evil, in the shape of passion and hatred, has got the upper hand.  Let us try to put aside all pride, vain-glory, greed, animosity, and lust for power, and approach the problem of the solution of our difficulties in a nobler and fairer temper, striving to remedy the wrong on both sides and to be generously just towards each other.  We are too apt to think that these great calamities come by divine appointment, forgetting our own share in the making of them.  We cry to God and bow before His will, as though He were the author of all our misery and our sorrow.  But is it not ourselves that we should arraign at the bar of the divine tribunal?  Is it not our own selfishness, our own injustice, our own readiness to believe evil of each other that has plunged us into this great calamity and brought upon us the purifying retribution which must ever follow our own misdoing?  We worship at the feet of the Master, but the spirit of the Christ " drifts back into the eternal silence," sorrowing at the faithlessness of his own brethren.  Can we gather together in the thought of that spirit and say that we have always been true to its behests?  Can we say that we have always striven to carry out our Master's rule of conduct in our individual, our social, and our political life?  Let us forsake the path upon which we have blindly entered.  Let us abandon our hatred, our falsehood, our injustice, our selfishness, our lust for the splendour of wealth and the pride of power, and enter upon that nobler heritage of heroic purpose and ideal achievement which life is ever holding out before us.  Again we may see our country blessed by the white-winged Angel of Peace.  Again we may see a great people knit together by a million cords of love, of friendship, of mutual respect and gratitude, uprearing that beautiful fabric of our common life, of which we ourselves may perceive a dim vision when we faithfully and conscientiously pray, " Thy kingdom come on earth."  Again we may see that people animated and inspired, not by the fret and fever of ignoble speculation or the vain desire for material wealth, but by the meditations which exalt, the ideals which ennoble, the aims which consecrate, and the endeavours which redeem the life of man.  Then will the sunlit graves of our fathers and our brothers, and the sacred memories which the thought of them revives, rekindle our spiritual energies, not to the bitterness of racial hatred and the misery of social dissension, but to the nobler rivalries of sympathetic effort, the refining ministry of art, the broadening and uplifting influence of literature, the informing and civilising gifts of scientific achievement, the exalting and purifying power of religious aspiration and love, until there arise in South Africa a nation and a commonwealth as fearless as it is large-hearted, as equitable as it is courageous, and so strong in its desires and endeavours for the enlightenment and progress of its people as to be a beacon-light of advancing civilisation to the peoples of the southern hemisphere of the world and an inspiration to the generations which are to come.

RAMSDEN BALMFORTH.

# WHY IS BRITAIN HATED?

THE saying "that griefs shared are divided, and joys shared are multiplied," applies to nations no less than to individuals. And although either of the two acts referred to is likelier to be genuine when professed by the individual than when one nation professes to share with another its griefs or its joys, yet even this latter kind of profession is by no means devoid of encouragement or of consolation.

With reference to the situation now existing in South Africa, we apprehend that there is no period in the career of the British Empire when the knowledge that we possess the sympathy of the other Great Powers would have been more welcome than the present. But alas! instead of their sympathy we are deafened by the noises of their hostility—an hostility, too, not incapable, unfortunately, of the direst developments. As to the causes producing the present eruption of international enmity, doubtless the inequality of the combatants forms an important part. Without stopping to inquire too closely, or perhaps without inquiring at all, the spectacle of the greatest Empire in the world in battle array against two diminutive Republics has been deemed by the judgment of our critics a sufficient reason for deciding against the stronger of the belligerents, and by their feeling, a reason for raining upon the bully their most stinging invectives. But in the endeavour to credit these nations with cherishing for the weak that profound compassion whose indignation has been resounding in the utterances of the international Press, we confess to being seized with a violent attack of scepticism; and so, without dismissing the sentiment of compassion from the present display of passion, we pass on to search for other factors; in the scrutiny we discover this other, viz., commercial jealousy. This same spirit that moved us to pass the Navigation Laws in the seventeenth century, with the object of dealing out a blow to the commercial supremacy of the Dutch, is certainly causing other nations to look to-day with unfriendly eye upon our commercial supremacy. Jealousy is not, however, the true merit of our commercial supremacy, hence we can deplore only its manifestation, not its cause. But there is still another ingredient that we are to name, to which we believe the hatred of the British Empire is mainly due. It is our "Imperialism," or our committal to the policy of *expanding indefinitely*. The following are a few facts that are presented from a study of the Empire. Approximately, the British Empire covers an area of 11,111,467 square miles; that is to say, it covers one-fourth of the surface of the globe. It contains a population of nearly 400,000,000 souls, or less than one-third of the inhabitants of the world. Of the enormous territory represented by the figures here quoted, and that embraces some of the choicest spots of our earth, it would be found on examination that Canada, for example, which is twenty-nine times the size of England and Wales, and that Australia, which is forty-two times the size, have in the aggregate a population of one person to the square mile. It would be found also concerning our West African Empire, that the absence of railways for opening up the country, and the lack of scientific knowledge among the inhabitants for turning its illimitable resources to the best account, place the possibilities of that region, commercially, at the embryonic stage, while the future of South Africa, in its commercial aspect, is at the dawn only of its capabilities. These features being all more or less applicable to our foreign possessions, one powerful impression which we think the facts just stated convey is, that the development of the British Empire has hardly yet begun.

Turning our thoughts for a moment away from the Empire, we behold certain nations who, in colonial acquisition and commercial evolution, are yet in their youth. But with the ardour and ambition of youth, these nations are looking forward to securing in both of these fields places of eminence. In their attempt, however, to find possessions in the three-fourths of the land that is unappropriated by the stronger races, and among the two-thirds of the peoples left by Great Britain outside the pale of her jurisdiction, these nations find themselves jostled, outbidden, and handicapped by this very nation, whose possessions are already so large and so little used, in the pursuit of her policy of indefinite expansion. On every side the young tradesman finds himself hemmed in by an old, rich, powerful, and aggressive firm, that threatens to follow him into every new field.

But it is this element, in my opinion—*indefinite expansion*—that gives activity to the volcano of international hatred of Britain. It is contended that unless the nation continues to expand she shall be unable to maintain her place in the world as a Great Power. We do not deny that progress is associated with expansion, but admitting the association one must also admit, that in proportion as the Empire expands, in that same proportion the risks of its maintenance increase; so that, in the stupendous size now reached, the gain, incident to further expansion, would, we believe, be out of all relation to the greater risks that such expansion would involve. Conscription, that now floats about the political horizon like a mirage, and that is occasioning divergent views among politicians, would no longer leave room for doubt as to the necessity for employing it, were continuous expansion to be our future policy. But while we do not deny the association of progress with the expansion of the Empire, we deny that such an association is found with expansion alone. And we affirm that the greatest progress that the Empire is capable of making may be reached by what seems to us to be the alternative policy of continuous expansion, that is, *development*. For taking the present rates of imports and of exports of the Empire as our standard, it would be found upon computation that by a small increase of population in the regions that are sparsely peopled, that by the opening up of inaccessible places, and that by imparting proper instructions to the inhabitants of the countries that are newly opened up, we should create such a demand in our colonies and dependencies for our products, as well as create in them supplies for our demand, as would tax to their utmost extent both our exporting and our importing powers. But while this alternative policy, development, is capable at least of yielding as much profit as indefinite expansion, unlike indefinite expansion it is attended with the smallest amount of risk possible. It is the policy, in my judgment, that would transform the enmity of Europe towards Britain into friendship. If the attacks made upon this nation by the world's Press during the present war, and if the jubilation shown in our misfortunes are among the most unpleasant incidents that we have felt, they have not been the most dangerous. What have been fraught with greater danger to us than these hostile criticisms are the volunteers that have been flocking to the Boers' standard from other countries —auxiliaries whose aid the loopholes of international law have made possible, and antipathy to this country has made practicable. Had these nations been better disposed towards this country, how differently they might have acted, and how different might have been the earlier course of the war. The auxiliaries that the Boers have been able to command illustrate the ineffectiveness of the most plausible neutrality, and prove that the best neutrality is that which is founded on friendship. And friendship with Europe is within the competence of no other European nation, and of no other nation in the world save America, to possess and to enjoy, to the extent of Great Britain. So near the continent of Europe, yet free by her insular position from those dangers and incidents that lurk about the frontiers of other European countries, by her powerful fleet, her splendid commerce, and her great wealth, if it were known to the other nations that Britain has withdrawn from competing with the rest of Europe for the remaining three-fourths of the globe that are unappropriated by the white races, that she is resolutely confined to developing her great possessions, such a policy and such a knowledge would, we believe, go a far way towards securing to Britain the friendship of these nations; so that instead of being suspected and hated, she would be respected and trusted, causing thereby the most powerful reason for the growth of armaments to be removed.       Theophilus E. S. Scholes, M.D.

# THE BOER.

## BY ONE WHO KNOWS HIM.

PEOPLE who describe the Boer generally contrive to get hold of the lowest and worst specimens that they can find and describe them as typical of the whole race. Tant Sannie, in Miss Schreiner's *Story of an African Farm*, is about as much a type of a Dutchwoman as Mrs. Gamp is a specimen of English womanhood. There are Tant Sannies in Africa and there are Mrs. Gamps in England, but it is an injustice to consider either a type of her race.

Among the Boers there are good and bad, coarse and refined, educated and ignorant, precisely as one finds elsewhere; the only difference being that the extremes met with in England are not seen in a large pastoral country like South Africa, where there are few large towns to foster extreme culture or breed excessive vice.

The Boers are often described as being rude and inhospitable to strangers. The writer has, however, found them quite the opposite. He has travelled in many countries, and nowhere has he met with such kind-hearted, open hospitality. When the war commenced, and the Free Staters crossed into the Colesburg district, national feeling ran very high, yet the writer, a Briton and a stranger living amongst a purely Dutch population, has never ·from that day to this had reason to complain of ill-treatment or abuse from his Dutch neighbours. Except in one instance, when a rebel about to join the Boer commando was a little off-hand, the writer received nothing but the rough, hearty courtesy of the veldt from the local Boers, whose sympathies naturally were quite opposed to his own.

This tolerant spirit is not to be found everywhere. On the border the Boer is a fine, manly fellow, rough in his ways according to European standards, but kind-hearted and tolerant to those from whom he receives kindness and tolerance. He has enough of the leaven of civilisation to make him an agreeable companion, but otherwise he is essentially a man of the veldt, and his whole life is bound up in his farm, with an occasional turn at politics. He is a dead shot, a good rider, and has a perfect knowledge of the country he lives in, and he requires nothing more than his horse, his rifle and bandolier, and a piece of biltong (dried meat) in his pocket, to be ready for any campaign that may be forthcoming. Intermingled with these sturdy Afrikanders is a type of cowardly windbags, to whose efforts the racial hostility of Africa may be largely attributed. The nearer one gets to Capetown and the larger towns the more numerous become these contemptible creatures, who, vastly inferior to the up-country Boer, are the most clamorous in boasting of the Majuba and other disasters to the British army; defeats which, without the sturdier man of the veldt, could never have taken place.

When one reads in the papers of the "disaffected border-districts," one should remember that the presence of the Boer commando alone would account for this disaffection. The real seats of rebellion should be placed four hundred miles to the south-west.

However, this is not a political article, but is intended to describe that type of Boer best known to the writer—the Boer of the veldt, whose fathers pioneered the land he farms, and who is the best and truest type of his race.

If the people of England in general are deceived as to the Boers' rudeness and inhospitality, the possessors of the Nonconformist conscience are equally deceived as to their morality. The writer has often been amused by reading speeches by Little Englanders lauding the "pastoral simplicity" and religious fervour of the Boers.

As a matter of fact, the Boer nature is not simple. It is distinctly complicated, and has as many sides as a hexagon. Most people are so.

That the Boer is frequently religiously fervent is a fact, but in these days it is generally admitted that mere lip religion is no religion.

In business the Boer is much the same as other people, neither better nor worse, though, on the whole commercial integrity is not at a premium in Africa. In his social life, however, there is a side to the Boer's nature that would puzzle his European admirers to account for. His ideas on morality are distinctly vague, and it is a regrettable fact that must be admitted by any one who has lived among the Boers, that impurity of speech and conduct is far too common among the younger members of the community, and extends even to the boys and girls not yet out of the schoolroom. Nor is this "freedom" peculiar to any one class. It may be less openly displayed by the higher class Boers, but it is there nevertheless, as any one living among them can testify.

So little check has religion upon these evil habits, that it is frequently made the cloak for all manner of abuses.

Many true and well attested anecdotes, quite unfit for publication, could be quoted in support of this strange intermingling of religion and immorality. Nor are such offences thought much of in Africa. People convicted of such indiscretions seldom lose caste in the eyes of their associates.

One of the most curious features of South African life is the almost socialistic lack of class distinction among the farmers.

Imagine yourself seated at breakfast with a well educated and refined Dutchman and his wife. They are speaking English at table for your benefit, and there is a goodly spread of porridge, venison, boiled eggs, rich good coffee, and " green mealies."

But for the latter, and a certain scantiness of furniture in the room, you might almost fancy yourself in a country house in England.

Then the scene changes. Enter a dirty, unshaven, unwashed son of the veldt, in a shirt and trousers that have not been removed for weeks, a pair of ragged veldschoens, and an old slouch hat. He hardly deigns to remove the latter, as, preceded by an odour of dirt and stale tobacco, he marches round the table, giving a limp and filthy hand to every one in turn and grunting " More " (Good morning). After shaking hands, he seats himself on the settee, pipe in mouth and hat on head, and, if you understand Dutch well enough, you will possibly hear him hold forth on the symptoms of one of his oxen that is sick, going into horrible details that make you thrust your plate from you untouched.

Yet this creature, a little lower than an English tramp, is an Afrikander, and as such considers himself as good as Mr. Schreiner or President Steyn, and a good deal better than any " verdomde rooinek " that ever came out of England.

The writer once had the pleasure of staying a few days with some of these low Dutch. He cannot speak highly enough of their rough but kindly hospitality, and they did all in their power to make him comfortable, but one dinner deserves description, giving, as it does, an idea of the manners and customs of these people.

The man was away, working on the farm, so, there being no family, the writer dined alone with the " vrouw." She entertained him during meals with a full and clear account of how she suffered from her liver, describing all the symptoms with quite unnecessary details, and especially urging the fact that her affected organ prevented her wearing stays. Having at last convinced him of her unhealthy condition, she proceeded to pick her teeth with her fork, while the writer went on with his meal.

Being blessed with a good appetite, he presently asked for some more meat. The fork was instantly withdrawn from the region of the lady's back teeth, plunged into a dainty tit-bit, and held across the table to the horrified recorder of this anecdote. He being hungry, and moreover careful not to offend the prejudices of the Dutch, took the meat and, with an effort, devoured it.

Perhaps no characteristic of the Boer is so distasteful to the Briton as his boasted superiority. When the unkempt visitor at the breakfast-table before mentioned remarks, casually, that one Boer is worth ten, twenty, or fifty British soldiers, the most philosophical " Little Englander " could hardly avoid rising in his wrath and breaking things.

It is not said with an air of braggadacio.  It is not shouted with the vehemence of one who would convince himself as well as others.  It is said with an air of conviction as one states a simple and uncontrovertible fact, a law of nature.

Education is at a discount among the farms.  For one man who has passed the Fifth Standard (Cape Colony) there are a dozen who have not, and the Fifth Standard of Africa would not be thought far advanced for an English boy of twelve.  The grossest ignorance prevails as to the world outside South Africa.  One farmer informed the writer that there were three great Powers in Europe—England, Holland, and Germany.  France and Russia were two other countries he had heard of, and these, he concluded, belonged to one of the great Powers aforesaid.  On being asked if he had never heard of America and Australia he opined that they *might* be in Africa, but rather fancied they were simply a couple of islands in the sea.

A young fellow of twenty was once asked how large he thought the sun was.  He glanced gingerly at the glowing orb and replied, " Just about as big as a cart-wheel."

Now, there are people in every country whose education ranges no further than this, but the peculiar feature in this instance consists of the fact that no shame is attached to lack of education, nor is ignorance confined to any one class, and the man who can neither read nor write may be a wealthy and influential farmer, who is considered quite fit to dine with the Prime Minister, or lead his neighbours in political matters.

Talking of dining, the table manners of the raw Boers sometimes approach the sublime.  One or two true anecdotes will amply prove this statement.

A young Boer seated himself at table in a hotel at Bloemfontein, and proceeded to eat his porridge with a knife and fork.  A friend of his remarked, " That is not the way to eat porridge, Schalk. What's your spoon for ? "

" Don't try and humbug me," replied Schalk in his most dignified air.  " *I* know how to eat at table.  I have had meals at hotels before."  And he resumed his knife and fork.  Whether he had been deceived by some practical joker, or whether he merely wished to brazen the matter out, never transpired.

On another occasion a young Boer was served with a cup of hot coffee, as is the custom during meals at African hotels.  The coffee, being too hot to drink in the ordinary way, he lapped it up with his teaspoon.  A friend of his said : " Don't drink your coffee like that. It isn't polite."

" Certainly not," put in the young man's father, in reproachful tones.  " What is your saucer for ? "

And, by way of adding example to precept, the worthy old "Oom" poured his coffee into his saucer and drank therefrom with audible avidity.

At home these two would have sat down to meals in their shirt-sleeves, placed their elbows on the table, eaten with knife, fork, or fingers, according to fancy or convenience, and drunk in the manner that pleased them best.

In those social customs which are peculiarly their own the raw Boers are very particular. Thus, an elderly man or woman is always called, respectively, "Oom" (uncle) or "Tante" (aunt), and in speaking to them young people must use the pronoun "jy" (you) as little as possible. For instance, a young man addressing an old one will say: "Oom, will Oom outspan Oom's cart and come in?" To say: "Will *you* outspan *your* cart," &c., would, under the circumstances, be considered the height of ill-breeding.

The handshake is another important factor in African etiquette. To come into a room and not to shake hands with every one in it, whether you know them or not, would have as bad an effect in Africa as the contrary would in England.

A curious instance of the conditions under which this custom is adhered to occurred during the present war at a spot in the Colesburg district not far from the residence of the writer.

A Lancer patrol was racing away from some Boers when the horses of three of the former got stuck in a muddy river-bed; they were cut off and had to surrender. The leader of the Boers, an old man, went up to the soldiers and shook hands with the two first, who responded willingly enough. The third soldier, who was much older than the other two, possibly a dignified sergeant, would not give his hand; whereon the old Boer, placing one hand on the Lancer's shoulder and peering anxiously into his face, said in broken English: "Are you very much cross?"

As regards the brutality and ignorance of some Boers enough has been said by other writers. Mr. Rider Haggard's description of the "Unicorn" and his ill favoured companion in *Jess*, gives two very fair specimens of this class. But the writer of this article, although he admits and deplores the fact that such specimens do occur in some districts pretty frequently among the Boers, can assure the tolerant British reader that such are no more to be considered types of their race than the Hooligans are types of ours. Good and bad occur in all races, and if a certain coarse type is apt to occur more frequently in Africa than elsewhere, we may safely attribute it to the rough, half-civilised condition of the country, and its lack of refining influences. In our big towns where there is far less excuse for it, we find a type of brutality infinitely worse than anything Africa can bring forth, and a man might walk from Buluwayo to Cape Town with far less chance of molestation from his fellow man than would be the case if he went by night through the paved and lighted streets of civilised London. The one part of Africa which is more dangerous than an English slum, and which our traveller would do well to avoid, would, strange to say, be that triumph of civilisation, Johannesburg. Whether he falls into the hands of an Uitlauder robber or a Transvaal zarp, he is to be pitied by all lovers of law and order. Far better for him to avoid the towns and trust himself to the tender mercies of the rough men of the veldt, who, in nine cases out of ten, open their doors to the dusty wayfarer as readily as they will shoot him who comes with armed force against them.

JULIAN JENKINS.

# CONSCRIPTION.

THE advocates of conscription, or of compulsory drill, have most unaccountably and unfortunately quite ignored one awkward little circumstance, for giving prominence to which the present time is eminently suitable.

I understand that young men would have to prepare for serving their country in arms when occasion required. I believe no exceptions, save such as bribery could effect, would be made among the able-bodied selected—that is to say, a young man would not be asked whether his countrymen ordinarily treat him justly, or whether he is happy in the lines appointed for the achievement of his livelihood; nor would any account be taken of the little interest he may have in keeping English soil unviolated by foes.

There are thousands of sober and industrious young men whose lives, between twenty and thirty, may be likened to frozen wastes, upon which their country has never shown the faintest inclination to throw a sunbeam. If a young man has no influential connections, every effort he may make to win a most moderate competence is treated with implacable and snobbish disdain by those to whom he offers his services. He is treated like the organ-grinder in a well-known cartoon. He must not hope for recognition before thirty. Witness the numerous advertisements of educated men of high references who repeatedly offer their services merely for board. First-class Oxford men have been obliged to sell lucifers as a consequence of relying upon journalism.

I do not here plead with national duty on behalf of the educated unemployed. I am too sad and too wise ever to have any hope of seeing the waters of kindliness flow from that barren rock; but I strike it that its flinty reverberation may be heard far and wide.

Moreover, I insist upon knowing what the country has ever done for the average young man, and how he can possibly be called for service. Is he to fight for a hearth upon which snow has drifted? Our country tells us "to eat grass!" For my part, I do not consider myself an Englishman. I was, indeed, born in England, I learned her tongue, and my name is English; but I deny that any further ties subsist between England and the thousands of young men I refer to. I am ashamed of my nationality.

This is no nation of loving brothers; it is a nation where the weak are trodden down by the strong in the furious struggle for existence, and the Englishman, with Mammon and Law for his postillions, drives over the mangled hearts of those whom he should have loved. It is a nation of wealth-seekers, when it ought to have been a nation of livelihood-seekers and mutual supporters. This is the cardinal mischief. But, for all this, one must admire the masterly skill with which the influential have shed upon the noisome vapour arising from their habitation a rainbow radiance which seems capable of luring thousands to their graves, merely that those who send them may preserve their purses. I mean the delusion of national glory.

The barbarity of the Boers is not worse than the Mammon-worship of Englishmen, nor has the ambition of Napoleons caused greater misery. It is a catastrophe without grandeur to redeem it. I do not deny that compulsory service, such as my friends suggest, may not be desirable, if it will not be necessary presently to keep the Empire intact; but, under the circumstances I mention, ordinary conscription must ever be a monstrous injustice. It is said that injustice is repaid with terrible compound interest, and to-day there are thousands of scathed hearts who would hail the dissolution of the British Empire as they would that of a vast pile of ice, snow, and mud. Yes, England is no brother, but a cruel stepdame, to her children. Perhaps the existence of these discontents is questioned; but are their attempts at utterance *never* suppressed? And is it well to stifle a volcano? We have knowledge and that should make us formidable.

I challenge any one to contradict a single assertion, or to combat one inference, I have made.

A SUPPLIANT OF NEMESIS.

# WHY NOT A PREMIUM-TAX?

THE anxiously-awaited Budget is a thing of the past. If not a particularly brilliant effort, it has, at all events, not disappointed the expectation that the financial genius of the Treasury would prove unequal to the task of devising new methods of raising revenue, and that in consequence the Chancellor of the Exchequer would fall back on the hackneyed system of raising the income-tax and adding to the duty on beer, spirits, tea, and tobacco. It is as humdrum a Budget as could well be imagined; the money had to be obtained, and obtained it has been by the simple expedient of increasing existing taxation in place of, as it seems to us, the more equitable method of imposing altogether new taxation.

It appears to us that this rough-and-ready, certainly easy, method of making ends meet cannot be defended unless it can be clearly shown that no source of revenue that ought to be, and that might be, laid under contribution has been overlooked or disregarded by the Treasury.

That this cannot be shown is only less notorious than the fact that at a time like the present we cannot afford to overlook or to disregard possible sources of revenue. Those upon whom added taxation has recently been laid grumble at it; they will, in all probability, have fresh reason to grumble when the Budget of 1901 is brought forward, unless in the meantime new sources of revenue be sought after by the Treasury.

The spectre of lean financial years casts its shadow before. Revenue on the basis of existing taxation will not always flow as abundantly into the coffers of the Treasury as it does in this the flood-tide of our prosperity. On the other hand, there is the practical certainty of largely increased expenditure on both Services during the next few years.

For these reasons, it seems to us that one of the most important questions of the moment is : What can we fairly tax that at present escapes taxation ?

It will be generally conceded that there are many commodities that might be taxed ; it will not, however, be so generally conceded that they *ought* to be taxed. That is why a Chancellor of the Exchequer never proposes *new taxation*, as opposed to *increased taxation*, if he can avoid doing so.

There is, however, one tax that might be levied—we believe it would be pretty generally conceded, fairly levied—that, so far as we are aware, has not been previously advocated.

We refer to what, for want of a better designation, we shall term " a premium-tax."

By this term we mean a separate assessment (altogether apart from and in addition to income-tax) on unearned increment in stocks and shares.

Such increment most commonly accrues :

    (a) From genuine investment ;

    (b) From selling allotments for special settlement ;

    (c) From speculation in time-bargains ;

    (d) From purchasing stocks or shares for a temporary " lock-up," as distinct from buying for investment.

Under existing conditions, profit accruing from each and all of these operations escapes taxation unless such profit be included in the operator's income-tax return.

It is the object of this article to propose that, so far as is possible, such profits should no longer remain untaxed. We say " so far as is possible," because in the case of profits accruing from operation " A " we do not see clearly how the profits of the investor, *unless when he happens to be an allottee or a purchaser for special settlement,* could readily be ascertained and assessed. In the other cases we fail to see any insuperable difficulty.

We believe that in every case the imposition of such a tax would not only be fair, but that continued exemption from taxation is absolutely indefensible !

In order to test this assertion we shall briefly examine each operation separately.

First, as regards genuine investment. Any one looking over the daily stock and share list must be struck by the fact that many quoted stocks and shares stand at a more or less high premium, some of them at a premium of as much as several hundreds per cent. It is obvious that any one fortunate enough to have obtained an allotment at par in a concern the stock of which stands at 50 per cent. premium was uncommonly lucky. Assuming him to have sold none of his holding up to date, the fortunate person—whom we shall style " X."—who obtained an allotment of fifty £10 ordinary shares in such a company would to-day find his original investment of £500 worth £750, and himself, in all probability, in receipt of an annual income of from £30 to £40.

On the other hand, let us suppose that his neighbour " Y." at the same time invested *savings* to the value of £500 in 3 per cent. Corporation stock, yielding a gross income of £15 per annum.

What is the contribution of these two respectively to the revenue in respect of capital increased on the one hand by sheer good fortune, on the other hand by the self-denial which savings always more or less represent?

" X." pays nothing; " Y." pays income-tax on the interest of his savings to the extent of 15s. per annum—*i.e.* 1s. in the £ on a gross income of £15.

This is surely indefensible?

It is our contention that " X.'s " premium on his investment should be taxed *annually* at the rate of 10s. per cent., also that if at any time he sell the amount allotted to him he should be liable to pay premium-tax at the rate of £5 per cent. on the realised premium. But, it will be objected, on what principle do you propose that, while the interest on " Y.'s " savings only pays income-tax at the rate of 1s. in the £, or a little more than one-eighth per cent. on the amount invested, no less than one-half per cent. per annum is to be paid by " X." on what you style his " unearned increment"? We reply : Because it *is* unearned increment, and because the fact that his stock stands at so high a premium shows that he is in receipt of so high a return on his original investment that he can well afford to pay it, and ought to be thankful to be in a position to be called upon to do so.

Moreover, when it is remembered that " X.'s " capital, by no exertion on his part, has increased itself by £250, while " Y.'s " has remained practically stationary, it cannot, we submit, be contended that it would be unfair that the amount of " X.'s " liability to the State should be substantially increased.

The foregoing argument applies with almost equal force to the case of an investor who, not having succeeded in obtaining an allotment of shares in a new issue, purchases them for Special Settlement. His profit on his investment may not quite equal that of an original allottee, but, as every one is aware, shares are sold for special settlement by weak holders at a comparatively low premium which, if the company be a sound one, in no way represents their intrinsic value, and falls far short of the level to which they may subsequently be expected to attain.

As regards operation " B "—*i.e.* applying for and obtaining an allotment, and then selling the shares for special settlement—it cannot, so far as we can see, be urged that there would be any injustice were the operator, or " Stag " as he is called on the Stock Exchange, made to pay a percentage, say, of £5 per cent. on the premium obtained by him over and above the issue price of his allotment. The man who gets an allotment only to sell again as soon as he can at a premium is, if he can only do so a few times a year, in the position of receiving an income, by the frequent investment of quite a trifling amount of capital, far in excess of what he could obtain were he to put the money into a security yielding, say, £4 per cent. per annum.

In how many cases does the "Stag" consider his gains as income? How often does he make any return in his annual declaration to the Income-tax authorities? We shrewdly suspect that he seldom does anything of the kind, rather preferring to consider that he has increased his capital. True, he has done so, but so, too, has the man who saves a portion of his income and invests the amount of his savings. But the Income-tax Commissioners do not on that account let him off payment of income-tax on the amount thus saved!

Operations "C" and "D" are so closely akin that they may be considered together. "D" is the operation of the man who does not object, and can afford, to "lock-up" his money in stocks that promise a pretty certain rise in a rather uncertain future; "C" that of the man who does not care to stand out of his money for too long a time, and prefers to buy and carry over stocks which promise to rise within a comparatively short period; it is, of course, also the operation of the man who, going on the other tack, sells what he has not got in the expectation of an early and remunerative fall in value. The aim in each case is, however, identical—viz. making money by means of "differences." One distinction may be noted—viz. that the man who "locks-up" stock does pay Government stamp on transfer at the rate of 10s. per cent. on value of his purchase; the speculator in time-bargains pays nothing.

The operation we have styled "D" may be considered as, perhaps, the safest of all forms of speculation. It is, however, a luxury in which the wealthy alone can indulge. The man of small means has no available funds, and must, therefore, stand to one side. Nevertheless, on an investment of a similar amount he will, in all probability, contribute the more of the two to the Revenue. To illustrate : "Y.," the man of small means, invests £500 in 3 per cent. Corporation stock and pays income-tax amounting to 15s. per annum; "X.," the wealthy man, taking advantage of a temporary depreciation, buys 500 mining shares at £1 per share, which he holds for six months, and then sells, on confidence being re-established, at 30s. per share, thus making a profit of £250. Generally speaking, he will prefer to call this an increase of capital, and will pay no income-tax thereon. Consequently he contributes *nothing* to the Revenue.

Can this in any way be justified?

The operation which we have styled "C" is, of course, the commonest form of speculation. It is also the one of all others which, in our opinion, ought to be the subject of taxation. It is at present absolutely exempt from taxation, unless one dignifies the 1s stamp on contract notes by such an appellation.

It is an undoubted fact that a bold and well-informed "Bull" or "Bear" can realise large profits on his operations without paying anything whatever to the Revenue, he, too, being shrewd enough to consider such as increased capital, and omitting to make any return in respect thereof to the Income-tax authorities. He is thus on a better footing than the ordinary investor. In illustration : " Y.," the investor, buys, let us say, £1000, nominal, Mexican Central 4 per cent. bonds, from which he derives an annual income of £40, on which he pays income-tax amounting in the aggregate to £2 ; " X.," the speculator, buys £1000, nominal, of the same stock, and, it may be, within a week closes the operation at 4 per cent. advance, thus realising a profit of £40, on which he pays nothing in the way of taxation. Can it be fairly contended that there is nothing unjust in a system of taxation which makes sure of income-tax being paid by " Y.," but takes no step to ensure that at least its equivalent is paid by " X." ?

We have already pointed out that, even as compared with the speculative operator who buys for a "lock-up," the speculator in time-bargains is unduly favoured, inasmuch as the former pays stamp-duty at the time of making his purchase, a remark which also applies to the ordinary investor other than the lucky recipient of an allotment letter.

Why should the investor pay stamp-duty and the speculator in time-bargains go free ?

Before further discussing the proposed premium-tax, we desire to point out the necessity of putting the four operations, A, B, C, and D, previously referred to, on a similar footing, so as to bring about the disappearance of the anomaly that, whereas purchasers for special settlement (operation " A ") and purchasers for a temporary "lock-up" (operation " D ") pay stamp-duty on transfer of one-half of 1 per cent. on actual value, allottees (operations " A " and " B ") and speculators in time-bargains (operation " C ") pay nothing of the kind.

This could easily be done—(1st) as regards allottees, by requiring that no certificate be issued to an allottee without having legibly stamped across it the words " Allottee's Certificate," also that within a fortnight of being issued said certificate must be stamped at Somerset House with a stamp of the value of 10*s.* per cent. on par value of stock or shares mentioned therein ; also by laying down that no " allottee's certificate " be held to be a " good delivery " on the Stock Exchange if not stamped as aforesaid. (2nd) As regards speculation in time-bargains, by requiring that, where a purchase is made either to close a " Bear " operation or on buying for a rise, the broker should, in the first instance, send his client a contract note (stamped, as at present, with a 1*s.* stamp), showing amount payable by client in respect of stamp-duty at the rate of 10*s.* per cent. on actual value, payment of said amount to become due at once (N B. In order to protect the broker from being out of pocket in respect of heavy stamp payments); and on receipt of client's cheque for the amount, the broker to have a second contract note stamped at Somerset House, and thereafter to forward same to his client. (N.B. The first contract note to be considered operative and binding only in conjunction with the second, stamped as stated.)

In this way ordinary investors, allottees, and speculators in time-bargains would be put on an equal footing as regards payment of stamp-duty. Nor would such an alteration prove unprofitable to the Treasury. Apart altogether from the immense sum that would annually be realised from stamp-duty on time-bargains, a very considerable sum would accrue from the imposition of a similar duty on allotments. During the second half of 1899—*i.e.* six months ending December 31—capital was created to the extent of £48,712,060. Stamp-duty, levied and collected as we have suggested, would on this amount have totalled no less a sum than £243,560!

To return to the proposed premium-tax.

How, it may be asked, is this to be collected? Is it practicable to do so?

That it is practicable admits, we think, of no doubt. A better application of the tax and a simpler method of collection could doubtless be devised; the following is, however, one way in which it might be carried out:

### 1. Allottees and Purchasers for Special Settlement.

At the end of each company's financial year, and before distribution of final dividend, the company secretary to deduct from the amount payable to allottees a sum equal to 10s. per cent. *on the premium* at which the holding of said allottee stood at the date of closing the company's transfer-books, the same procedure to be applicable to all registered in the company's books as having acquired their holdings at the special settlement, with this slight difference—that they, having bought at a figure presumably slightly over par, be entitled to a deduction from the premium at which stocks stand, of, say, 5 per cent. To illustrate : the ordinary stock of a company stands at £150, or at a premium of £50 per cent. The allottee would pay 10s. per cent. on £50, or 5s. ; a purchaser for special settlement would pay 10s. per cent. on £45, or 4s. 6d.

The company secretary would, as in the case of income-tax, account for same to the Revenue authorities.

In addition, we would propose that, on a sale by either allottee or purchaser for special settlement, stamp-duty should be levied at the rate of £5 per cent. on the premium actually realised by such sale. Allottees' certificates bearing, as we have suggested, Government stamps, would be at once distinguishable by the selling broker, and we would suggest that certificates issued to purchasers for special settlement might have the words " Special Settlement " legibly stamped across them, so as also to be readily distinguished by the broker, whose duty it would be in either case to debit his client with the amount of stamp-duty payable, and to have stamps to the amount affixed at Somerset House on the transfer, which would thus bear *two* stamps—one paid, as at present, by purchaser's broker, the other by seller's broker.

### 2. SALES FOR SPECIAL SETTLEMENT.

We would suggest that the procedure should, in the case of allottees who sell for special settlement, be precisely similar : viz. stamp-duty at 10s. per cent. to be affixed to certificate, and £5 per cent. duty levied on realised premiums—*i.e.* difference between allotment value and sale value. Stamps on sale to be similarly affixed on transfer.

### 3. BUYING FOR A "LOCK-UP."

In order to distinguish between ordinary investment and one made merely for a speculation it would be necessary to fix a period within which, if stocks or shares were purchased and disposed of, the operation would fairly come under the above definition. We would suggest that this period might be fixed at twelve months, it being unlikely that any one buying for a "lock-up" would calculate on chances likely to be influenced by events happening any further ahead than that length of time. On a sale taking place, we would suggest that the procedure might be as follows: The company's secretary, on receipt of certificate from vendor's broker, to notify said broker (who would already be aware from date on certificate that the transaction was one liable to Government duty) the price at which stock had been bought, he being able to ascertain this by a reference to the transfer-book. The broker, if transaction showed a profit, to debit vendor with stamp-duty at the rate of £5 per cent. on such profit, and to cause transfer to be stamped at Somerset House.

Any one who has any idea of the very large "buying-for-a-lock-up" business that is transacted on the Stock Exchange in respect of mining shares will appreciate the large source of revenue that the imposition of such a tax would prove to the Treasury.

### 4. SPECULATION IN TIME-BARGAINS.

In respect of profits derived from such speculation, we would similarly advocate the imposition of "premium-tax" at the rate of £5 per cent., were it not that it would prove a very difficult matter to ascertain these profits. To do so, and also to calculate stamp-duty thereon, would add very greatly to the responsibility of stock-brokers and throw much additional work on their staff.

Nevertheless, such profits ought not to go untaxed. We would suggest that, in lieu of premium-tax being levied on profits, it should be levied on speculative purchases at the rate of 5s. per cent. on actual value of stocks and shares purchased; the procedure of the broker to be precisely the same adopted by him to ensure payment of the one-half per cent. stamp-duty which we advocated should be exacted from speculative operators, so as to put them on no better a footing than ordinary investors—viz., contract note to be sent in first instance, showing stamp-duty payable; amount of said duty to be remitted at once by client to broker, who would then have a duplicate contract note stamped to the amount at Somerset House and send on same to client.

Stamp-duty and premium-tax together would thus amount to three-quarters of 1 per cent. on all purchases in connection with which no stock changed hands.

But, it will be urged, every speculation is not profitable, yet you propose to tax all speculative transactions! It is true; but, on the other hand, it may be urged that, if a speculator should feel disgusted at having had to pay premium-tax on a losing transaction, he could console himself by the reflection that on other transactions which showed a greater profit than 5 per cent. he was better off than if premium-tax had been levied at the rate of £5 per cent. on actual profits made.

In passing, and lest it should be imagined that by suggesting a tax on purchases and not on sales of stock we are leaving speculation for a fall untaxed, we would point out that this is not so, inasmuch as in order to close a speculative sale it is at some time or other necessary *to buy*. Of course the proposed tax could equally well be levied at one-eighth per cent. on purchase and one-eighth per cent. on sale contract notes, but it seems simpler to levy the full one-quarter per cent. on the former.

Doubtless a Chancellor of the Exchequer proposing such a tax would meet with strenuous opposition from the members of the Stock Exchange. He would be told that its imposition would restrict business and do great injury to their interests. Possibly it might do so for a short time, but only for a very short time. The man who wishes to speculate, and who thinks he sees his way to make money by doing so, will not for long be deterred from tempting fortune by a mere 15s. per cent. against him. The Chancellor of the Exchequer who paid attention to any such remonstrance would be foolish indeed. Nor would he have the right to do so.

Why should he consider the stockbroker more than the brewer? A tax of a shilling per barrel on beer affects profits and depreciates the value of a brewer's property; but the Treasury takes no account of that. Stockbrokers have a profitable business as well as brewers; if the latter have to put up with taxation which certainly affects their profits, why should the former grumble at taxation which may possibly, though rather improbably, interfere with theirs?

And if, as the result of such taxation, speculation on the Stock Exchange did to any extent decline, would it be an unmixed evil? If the impecunious speculator—who alone would pause to consider payment of stamp-duty and premium-tax—were to withdraw from the game, would it not be an unmixed blessing?

What is wanted at the present time is a more liberal interpretation of the term "income." Dividends, interest on bonds and mortgages, rents, trade profits, professional earnings, &c., are not the only items that deserve to come under that definition. Everything that *comes in*, that tends to make a man richer than he was before, ought to be, though at present it is not, classed in the category.

The plea that the imposition of such a tax as we have spoken of would impair the value of the property of allottees and of purchasers for special settlement will not hold water for a moment, inasmuch as the tax being personal to such a class of investor, and not in any way to the shares, the market value of same would be quite unaffected, would-be purchasers being well aware that the investment on changing hands would be no longer subject to premium-tax. Nor could it be said that a tax on "time-bargains" and on "lock-up" profits was an unwarrantable interference with the rights of the individual. Taxation of all kinds constitutes an interference with the rights of the individual. Why should the rights of one be respected more highly than the rights of another?

It is evident that, by allowing the operations we have referred to to escape taxation, the Treasury allows an immense annual sum to slip through its fingers.

The stamp-duty on transfer of stocks and shares amounted in the financial year 1898–99 (the figures for 1899–1900 are not yet obtainable) to over £1,498,000 sterling. Stamp-duty is at the rate of 10*s.* per cent., so, too, is the stockbroker's commission to cover the operation of sale and re-investment. But does any one imagine that £1,498,000 is all that is earned on the Stock Exchange by brokers? If so, looking to the immense number of brokers both in the provinces and on the London Stock Exchange, the annual earnings of each firm, after deducting expenses, would in that case be poor indeed. It is speculation that keeps the Stock Exchange going, and that speculative business is greatly in excess of investment is plainly shown by the much lower rate of commission charged by brokers in respect of it; a reduction, in fact, on taking a quantity. We do not think it would be an excessive estimate to put the volume of speculative business at from four to five times that of investment business. If this be so, it is at once obvious what it would mean to the Treasury if premium-tax on unearned increment in stocks and shares and stamp-duty on allotments and speculative transactions were imposed by the Chancellor of the Exchequer.

As we have already pointed out, stamp-duty, at the rate of 10s. per cent., on transfer of stocks and shares—*i.e.*, on investment business—amounted in 1898 to £1,498,000. Assuming speculative business to be four times that of investment business, it is clear that stamp-duty at 10s. per cent., plus premium-tax at 5s. per cent., would yield an annual revenue of just under £9,000,000 sterling, in addition to which the best part of another £1,000,000 sterling might be reckoned on as the annual receipt from stamp-duty and premium-tax imposed in the other directions we have indicated.

Ten millions sterling per annum is worth thinking about! If there is no insuperable difficulty in the way of enforcing and collecting the imposts we have referred to—and we claim to have shown that there is no such difficulty—what argument can be urged at the Treasury against making an endeavour to put them in operation? Stamp-duty is paid on transfer of stock: why not on allotments and speculative transactions? Income-tax is paid on savings and on the interest of these savings when invested: why not on premiums resulting from lucky investments and fortunate speculations?

JAMES DOUGLAS HOLMS.

# LIBERAL POLICY:

## THE LAND QUESTION.

THE heavy war-cloud has for the moment overshadowed all other questions. But this cannot long continue. We have pretty well reached the limits of possible "expansion." Anything further we shall find at once too dangerous and too costly.

Disraeli in 1874, when the publicans and parsons had combined to give him a majority, made haste to cover over the beer-barrel with the red flag of Jingoism. Salisbury has been but a hesitating disciple of the great political conjurer; yet a short time before his party was a second time returned by "the trade" with a sweeping majority he pointed in somewhat vague, yet very intelligible language, towards "expansion," as it is now termed, as the source from which he expected to secure national prosperity. In this he may have been quite sincere, though it is open to suspicion that his main motive was to defer, if not strangle, political, social, and economic reforms, and draw a red herring across the trail of the Tory fox.

But, however that may be, we have had enough of Jingoism and expansion. We have had frontier wars in India, to pay for which, though they were for purely Imperial purposes, the natives have been grievously taxed, till they have no reserve left to meet a time of famine. We have annexed vast tracts of Western Africa, and when they have turned out utterly unprofitable have imposed a hut-tax to pay for the expense of governing them, with the result that we have provoked revolts which we have put down with fresh military expeditions. We have "avenged Gordon" in a fashicn which that humane warrior would scarcely have approved, and have opened out large tracts of Africa for exploitation by mining specu-lators and stockjobbers, English and foreign, Jew and Gentile, by the slaughter—would not massacre be the appropriate word?—of thousands of Matabele and Mashonas. But so far we have done these things "on the cheap," so far as present cost to ourselves is concerned. But at last we have stirred up a hornet's nest, have sustained considerable loss in men as well as in money, and roused the jealousy or hatred of the principal nations of Europe.

It is time that we should retrace our steps as far as that is possible, that we should pursue the old Liberal policy of Peace, Retrenchment, and Reform; should leave off extending and seek to consolidate and develop our Empire, cultivate a good understanding with all other Powers all the world over, and set them an example of internal improvement that shall convince them that peaceful development is the surest path to national prosperity.

The utterances of the present Liberal leader are very satisfactory so far as they go, and probably portend more than they have definitely expressed. They embrace three leading ideas—first, justice and considerate treatment to all our dependencies, and coupled with this, peaceful relations with foreign Powers; secondly, Temperance reform on the basis of Lord Peel's Report, a substantial measure of progress, though by no means a permanent or completely satisfactory settlement of the question; and thirdly, a recognition that the housing question is a branch of the land question, with an implied pledge to deal with this question.

Here, then, we have the promise of a return from a career of wild adventure, reckless injustice, and shame, to a manly, honest, prudent, and beneficent policy.

Of all the problems that confront us that of South Africa is the one of most immediate interest, and one of the most difficult. We have to reconcile the Boers, to maintain the rights of the English settlers, and to protect the natives. And the question is as to the way or the best way of combining these three objects. To solve this question fully will require special study and special knowledge. Here we can only touch lightly on one or two main points. The autonomy of the two republics should be preserved, without, however, the power of making treaties with foreign States, or making military preparations. Secondly, the Chartered Company should be abolished and their territory formed into a British Protectorate, guarded by a certain number of native troops under properly chosen British officers. Possibly the colonies, with the two republics, might be included in a Customs' union. And I think the gold and diamond mines should be taxed to compensate those who have suffered by the war, to pay some portion of its expense, and after that to defray the expenses of government in the republics, colonies, and Protectorate. But South Africa at present is chiefly important as the half-way house to India. Indeed it has been for this reason that we have been so anxious to retain it.

India has for more than a century, for good or evil, chiefly the latter, been the key to our foreign and much of our home policy. Yet we have neglected the main thing necessary—the governing India for India's benefit, and so gaining the confidence and good-will of its people. On the contrary, we have impoverished it to the verge of bankruptcy, and what is worse, inability to stand up against a season of drought, by a costly administration and a series of wars. We must remember that India does not exist for the benefit of Haileybury, nor for our military caste, nor yet to give training and experience, such as it is, to our soldiers.

Nor yet does it exist for the benefit of Manchester. Yet it would be a better customer to Manchester if we had not acted the part of a vampire towards it.

But how are we to come to the rescue of India ? how are we to reduce its crushing burden of taxation ? We must have a less expensive army in it, and a less expensive administration. And then we can do something to aid it by revising our own system of taxation, and still more by other economic reforms, especially those connected with the LAND QUESTION. We come back, then, to this point— *Internal Development* v. *External Expansion.*

## THE LAND QUESTION.

Free Trade gave us cheap food, and so enlarged our home as well as our foreign market, and thus became the chief source of the prosperity which followed, and of that which we now enjoy. But this prosperity has been greatly diminished by various causes, but chiefly by the rise in rents. Therefore our greatest economic need now is cheap dwellings, with cheap shops, warehouses, and factories.

Cheap dwellings will, as cheap food did, give a margin to those who now have none, a margin which will enable them to save for the future and spend more widely in the present. There will thus be a greater production and a greater distribution of wealth, and these two will react upon and intensify each other, producing an indefinite increase of prosperity.

But we want not simply cheaper houses, but better ones. It is a great scandal that, not only in large towns but in small ones, and even where land, except for building purposes, is of very little value, houses are huddled together with no front gardens, or the merest apology for them, and with the merest bit of yard at the back, where there is no room for children to play about; so that for recreation they are driven into the streets, where the streets are sufficiently quiet for their purpose. Dirt, demoralisation, and drunkenness are the natural fruits of this huddling of houses and people together.

But there is another branch of the land question, that relating to agriculture.

As in the housing question, the perversity and stinginess of the landed class is the source of many and grievous evils, so in regard to agriculture their greed is the cause of poverty and bad trade, besides being a check on improved cultivation. For how shall a farmer venture any great outlay on his land, when the first result of all his improvements will be an increase of his rent?

From the state both of town and country, from overcrowded dwellings and poverty-stricken country districts where labourers "subsist" on starvation wages, it is evident that landlords have too great power and that they have greatly abused it.

What, then, shall we do to bring prosperity to our agricultural classes and health and comfort to our town dwellers, aye, and to our villagers too?

Various solutions of the land question are offered, some of which are sufficiently drastic, not to say revolutionary. Some go in for land nationalisation by the very simple process of complete and instant confiscation. Others, for gradual confiscation by the "single tax;" while others would be satisfied with a more or less heavy tax on land values—that is, on the value of the sites apart from improvements. Others, and I confess that I belong to this number, adhere to John Stuart Mill's principle that the unearned increment in the value of land should belong to the public. But this rule can scarcely be made retrospective; we must start from present values.

As to the other schemes, confiscation would no doubt give the State an immense revenue; and one question is, how it would be spent? But we need not go into this, as the scheme is as impracticable as it is undesirable. Economic changes should be gradual and attended with a social and moral uplifting; otherwise they might do more injury to the classes deprived of their possessions than they would confer benefit on those beneath.

But this objection does not apply, or not so strongly, to the next scheme, that of the single tax. Still it contemplates "levelling down," the gradual confiscation of landed possessions. But if the change is not very gradual, there will still be too rapid a levelling down and much social disturbance; and if it is very gradual, it will be long before it is very effective. Besides, the opposition to it will be of the most desperate and determined character; for the landed aristocracy will naturally fight with all the weapons at their command against extinction.

There remains, then, to apply J. S. Mill's principle in some form or other. It might be combined with a tax on the land of 10 per cent., the landlord to value the land himself. A tax of this amount on the estimated annual value would be sufficient. Then, when any portion of the land was wanted for building, parks, gardens, recreation grounds, or any other public object, municipalities or other local authorities should have power to take the land at, say, forty years' purchase, or by paying its annual value to the landlord.

It should be an advantage to have houses built and owned by public bodies, since all large owners can get repairs executed more cheaply and expeditiously than small owners. Besides, we want to get rid of jerry-building and to have a fair allowance of garden-ground to each house. For the sole advantage of increased wealth, besides the power of saving for a "rainy day," is in elevating the standard of living. Without this, increased wages are of no avail.

But what if a capitalist wants to erect a factory, or a body of men to build a church? Let the local authority be used as an intermediary, charging some slight fee. Let the capitalist bring the purchase-money, or the congregation produce sufficient securities; then the local authority can take the land and hand it over to the parties in question under mortgage, or in full possession if all expenses are paid at the outset.

Even to such a scheme as this there would be much opposition. Yet the landholders may be glad to compound for the weakness of their title by a moderate tax. The weakness of their title, I say, for there is no such thing in this country as private *property* in land; the Sovereign—that is, the State—is the supreme landlord, the landholders are but tenants who have practically usurped the rights both of their sub-tenants and of the State, and for this usurpation they are liable to be called to account. They received the land conditionally on the performance of certain services. They have shifted their burdens on others, while they have increased the tax on their sub-tenants. The tax I say, for rent is a tax, though, unlike other taxes, it is paid to private persons for their own sole profit, and is fixed arbitrarily, at the will of the landlord mainly (though there are certain limits to his power of extortion other than his will). "Private contract" is a mere fallacy, and Ricardo's *Economic Rent* is another.

In any case, landed property does not bear its fair share of taxation. This is a point which must be insisted on. Nor can it be made to bear that or any appreciable share of taxation, except by "the single tax," by some such scheme as I have suggested, or by strictly limiting rents. And landlords, when hard pressed, will probably prefer to escape the "single tax," which spells confiscation sooner or later. They will prefer a tolerable, and, in fact, an easy compromise, rather than lose everything.

And on the other side, the benefit from the plan I have sketched would be more immediate than from the single tax. And, which is no small matter, there would be no great levelling or pulling down as a preliminary to building up a completely new Socialist fabric. Well, we are all Socialists, more or less; but there is Socialism and Socialism. The less destruction and the less hazardous our attempts at construction the better. We want steady progress, not revolution.

But we shall have to reckon with leaseholders as well as free-holders. There are some of these, large owners of slum property, that have no claim on our sympathy or consideration. But there are also numbers of small property owners who are likely to suffer serious loss by the very necessary process of cheapening and improving the houses of the people. They may be relieved, however, by the remission of taxation on house-property. Besides the local authorities may be directed to devote the profits from their new buildings, in the first instance, to acquiring, at reasonable rates be it understood, and clearing away slum property. This and other improvements will prevent a too rapid fall of rents, while, on the other hand, the people will get a direct benefit in improved dwellings, and an indirect one in the great activity of the building trades, which, of course, will benefit all others.

I have spoken of a tax on land of 2s. in the pound. But that may be taken as the average or normal amount. Small holdings might pay much less, and large estates much more, especially those town estates which have become so valuable by leases falling in. These as well as slum property should pay extra rates, as well as taxes, so as to lighten the cost of clearances and other improvements.

But there is another difficulty to be faced. Besides freeholders and leaseholders there are Building Societies. How shall we safeguard their interests or make the change more tolerable to them ?

Instead of giving the local authorities power immediately on the passing of the Act to take what land they want, a period of two or three years should intervene, during which these societies, as well as private owners, might wind up their affairs or do the best they could for themselves except by letting it on building leases. During this time the local authorities might take land for building, by private agreement, from these societies in the first instance, and afterwards from individual owners. Such a measure would bridge over this difficulty.

Besides the local authorities, a central and national one should have the power of purchase, as a check which in some cases might be necessary against the under-valuation of estates, while the amount of the tax would be a check to over-valuation.

### AGRICULTURAL LAND.

But the Housing problem, though perhaps the most important part, is not the whole of the land question. J. S. Mill's principle is not applicable to agricultural land, for the mischief here is, that though not often what is called rack-rented in this country, the rents are still much too high. The proof of this is that farmers' profits are very precarious, and labourers' wages much too low. And what is required is to give the farmer fair security for the fruits of his labour and a free hand in dealing with his land, so that he may make the best of it, both for himself and the country ; and at the same time be able to pay fair wages to his labourers. For the best way to benefit the main body of this class is to put their employers in a condition to pay them better.

We should take it as a maxim that in *the first instance* THE LAND SHOULD SUPPORT IN COMFORT THOSE WHO TILL IT, and that *the landlord's share should simply* COME OUT OF THE SURPLUS.

This is by no means the case now. How can we bring it about?

Again, we shall have much opposition to encounter, but with a little educating we ought to have the main body of the agriculturists at our back. In fact, as regards political engineering, we should no doubt gain more power, or gain it more quickly, on this branch of the subject than on the other.

But as to our mode of action. Shall we have the three F.'s as in Ireland? Or what?

In spite of the Land courts, rents in Ireland are not, in general, nearly low enough. And, without reasonable rents, security of tenure is not of much use. Besides the Tenant Right system is not so well adapted to the English as to the Irish mind. But, as before said, "Free Contract" is an utter fallacy. For how many years did the farming class hold to the land while their capital was gradually wasting away? Meanwhile the landlords were getting more than the net produce of the soil. And for a long period, with but few exceptions, no reduction was made as long as the farmer held to the land; though when he was thoroughly beaten and had to give it up, the rent was perforce reduced for a newcomer.

Farmers who had been on their land many years, and were, perhaps, born on it, did not like to give it up until actually forced to do so. Besides they could seldom hope to better themselves very much by a move, especially as the move would entail more or less loss, through being forced to sell their stock below its value, or keep it at considerable expense till they could find another farm. So then, added to sentiment and the natural hesitation to move, there is a positive present loss of all improvements that have been made, and probably another considerable one in the loss on stock. In order to equalise conditions the tenant should be allowed the full value of all improvements, and the landlord also be compelled to take over the stock, or any part of it, that the tenant did not wish to keep. Or there should be substantial compensation for disturbance.

It may be urged that this would be too favourable to the tenant, and that under such arrangements rents would fall lower and lower. But, in any case, the landlord could retain the land in his own hands if he could not make more of it by letting. And as to the stock, he could use it or part with it to the next tenant. With such arrangements rents would soon fall to their normal level, to the great benefit of farmers, labourers and all the tradesmen they deal with. Of course there would be some little drawback to this, but nothing serious. Landlords would not have quite so much to spend, but they would not be ruined. They would not suffer as the farmers have done. They would probably keep fewer servants, and some West End houses might stand empty for a short time; not for long. Nor would capable servitors be long without employment, in the general increase of prosperity. The landlords themselves would be none the worse for living rather more economically, and the army would be the better for the officers having to follow suit, and lavish expenditure becoming a mark not of gentility but snobbery.

It is by no means necessary that land should be at once nationalised or municipalised. This will doubtless come in course of time. Changes should be made gradually, according as circumstances render them necessary or desirable. But it might be well that landlords should be able to call on the State to purchase their lands under certain conditions, of course not at too high a valuation.

But what we have to get rid of are exorbitant rents both in town and country, slums, land speculation, and fictitious or artificial values.

One point has been missed. Certain offensive trades should be banished from the great towns. If, for instance, the London County Council acquired some estate in Essex for the tanneries now at Bermondsey (allowing a certain period for the erection of new premises and the abandonment of the old), the terrible pressure on that part of London and the excessive rents would be sensibly mitigated.

But as regards the whole question of the land, some such solution as I have shadowed forth would speedily remove the worst evils of the present system, and as has already been said, would bring in a period of prosperity, which we look for in vain from the hazardous policy of expansion, land-grabbing, and gold-hunting. After all, little England, though not the whole of the Empire, is its head and heart. Increase our trade and the production of commodities, as a proper settlement of the land question would increase them, and that heart can perform its functions properly, and send streams of wealth to all portions of the Empire, which are now neglected or even oppressed and starved. External Expansion has reached its utmost limits; it is now time to see what can be done by Internal Development. And for this development the first object that requires our attention is the Land Question.

We have two roads before us, one leading to prosperity and peace, the other to war upon war, risk upon risk, and eventual ruin. Which shall we take?

J. M. K.

# CROZIER'S SCALE.

BEFORE we handle the Scale [1] it will be convenient to at once dispose of what Mr. Beattie Crozier calls "the belief in the existence of mind in our fellow man"; it occupies the second place in the order of the rather formidable six beliefs below,[2] which Mr. Crozier pontifically fulminates and decrees as a sort of necessary congenital truth that we imbibe with our mother's milk, or otherwise acquire later by a kind of illative or hocus-pocus legerdemain which is rather unintelligible. Whatever may be meant by this, he is guilty of the trick of wilfully misusing terms ambiguously, and so misleading his readers by neglecting the useful practice of definition.

Scientific belief is, of course, quite of a different order from religious, sentimental, or poetic belief, and Mr. Crozier ought to know it by this time, if he does not, before he sets out to instruct other people. The first, fourth, fifth, and sixth of this list in order are indirectly and practically refuted elsewhere,[3] and the third will be discussed now immediately after the second.

How we arrive at "the belief in the existence of mind in our fellow man" is as follows: Having determined by experience the existence of mind within ourselves, we apply our knowledge of the same to our fellow creatures by analogy, an inference from the known to the unknown,[4] although the result of this inference is practically acquired, or rather assumed, unconsciously and spontaneously by intercourse between ourselves and fellow creatures through a common existence together. This belief, as distinct from that resting upon mere poetic fancy or superstitious imagination, enjoys a veritable foundation of credence in experience, a.though this experience may never become the subject of conscious thought nor of direct investigation.

As to the "superiority of mind over matter" and our belief in it: mind's power over matter (the environment and the mind's

---

[1] Crozier's *Inner Life*.
[2] 1st. Belief in existence of world outside ourselves.
   2ndly.  ,,   in existence of mind in our fellow man.
   3rdly.  ,,   in superiority of mind over matter.
   4thly.  ,,   in persistence of force.
   5thly.  ,,   in co-existence of attraction and repulsion.
   6thly.  ,,   in scientific causation.
[3] See "Space and Time," in WESTMINSTER REVIEW, December 1899.
[4] As Ami Boue arrived at the knowledge of the geology of Asia. Both these applications of analogy seem to be legitimate.

container, the body) increases up to a certain limit; for instance,
over cold, heat, disease; and this power is gained not only by flat
resistance and exercise of the will in direct opposition, but by adroit
investigation, manipulation, and capture of nature's processes, and
by turning them to its own purposes—meeting it half-way, in fact.
Mind's power over itself and management of its own thoughts is
gained with much difficulty, and is best furthered by close and constant attention to the maintenance and increase of its influence
over matter exterior to itself, its own container, the body, inclusive.
If the mind's origin is material,[1] recollecting how matter tends to
run to excess (vice, base appetites), the hard-earned victory, after a
desperate struggle, of the finer nervous matter of the brain over
the ordinary matter [2] seems to us not only to satisfy the keen sense
for sport and fair-play, but also the panting demand for the ideal.
And this victory is only gained by a resolute attitude and the adoption of tactics which, if pursued definitely and continuously (science),
results in real benefits and utilities to human nature and civilisation.
The power of a transcendental mind to subdue the baser appetites
and passions of a material body is supposed to confer upon the
favoured substance a superiority.   But as the forces in the battle
between mind and matter are from the beginning supposed to be
crushingly unequal and the latter is admittedly handicapped, while
the humiliation is but small to the vanquished, the superiority leaves
little to the victor to boast of.   On the other hand, the ideal of a
deserved superiority of the mind's finer though weaker stuff over
the body's coarser material is instinct with the thrust, the counter-
thrust, and glow of combat, and, even from an art point of view, is
far more attractive and imaginative than the vague lifelessness of
the platonic alternative.

Apart, however, from this hard struggle between the human mind
and matter and the slow advance of the control over the influence
of the first on the second, mind, whether its source be supernatural
or the contrary, is inferior, in a general sense, to force, which is
dubbed blind because we are not acquainted with its real nature.
Mind's subordinate position in the cosmos is most conspicuous to
the sober eye of examination from its very late arrival in this cosmos
and its humble *rôle* during the vast panorama of many geological
life-systems and zoological species.   Mind, for instance, in spite of
the efforts of the new psychology, will also continue to possess a
very poor knowledge of itself and of its own operations, and it is
admittedly unequal to attaining possession of a scientific instrument

[1] The dependence of mind and consciousness upon brain and nerve matter favours
this origin.

[2] As to Mr. Crozier's notion that nervous matter does not differ from any other
matter, even an outsider has only to glance at the illustrations, or rather engravings,
in such a work as Klein's *Histology* (ed. of 1891), to be satisfied with the difference
between the morphology and superficial appearance of nerve-fibre from that of
striped muscular-fibre or connective-tissue.

for the discovery of any rules for the interpretation and provision of the class of phenomena which are entirely within its own province and more especially connected with its own nature ; these are the acts of man derived from their thoughts—such as the collections of theories and facts, which politics, sociology, and history do their best for, which is not much. The irrational (to us) evolution of political, sociological, and historical phenomena sets at defiance the feeble efforts of mind to wrest its secret, and we are still unwarned and practically impotent, not only before and during the event of a fearful cataclysm, such as the French Revolution, but in the presence of the ordinary march of historical events.

Ontology, we know, is as dead as a coffin-nail, although we feel, however, confident that if any discovery was possible in this region, acutely conscious as we are of the irrationality, perverseness, and habitual uncanniness of the ups and downs of social evolution, we should not be surprised to find a first cause behind it all who luxuriated in an intellectual endowment quite unlike that of man— in fact, the very antipodes of it.

Now, as regards the latest *minimum réchauffé* of Platonism, it appears to us that its contriver has mistaken the effect of a highly complex moral and intellectual condition with a superior altruistic standard, the outcome of an immense evolution in time, for an always -existing-from-the-beginning-of-things-permanent quality, essence, or substance in the mind, the so-called Scale. This Scale is supposed, in its *rôle* of father-confessor and adviser at a pinch, to be independent of the rest of the mind and the general movement of evolution, which latter is otherwise accepted as an explanation of the growth and course of things both mental and material.

Suppose we for the moment accept this miraculous critical *corner* of the mind as not subject to the vagaries and chances of evolution submitted to by the rest of the mind, then are we further bound to accept its position of latency and, therefore, impotence in the mental systems of a Fuegian or an Andaman ? Was the corner caught napping, and did it nod with " its knowledge of what is high or low," its fixed rating " of what is good or bad," before the sensual outbursts of a Solomon's wisdom or a Jacob's ethics, or did it, ostrich- like, thrust its critical neck sandways ? Or were " the material and social condition of the time " too much for it ? Did the " World of Nature and Human Life " (observe the trick of capitals), which is here to represent " a spiritual reality," whatever that may mean, and " which also exists for our guidance," come to loggerheads with their dear paradoxical ally ?

Concerning the intellectual debt we owe to Bacon[1] and the so-

---

[1] "It is quite a mistake to suppose that Lord Bacon really understood the inductive logic by which Galileo, about the same time as Sir Isaac Newton, &c., succeeded in detecting the chief laws of nature. Not only was Lord Bacon unable to make any real discoveries by his own method of inquiry, when he tried to do so,

called poetic-thinkers, Shakespeare, Dante, Newman, Carlyle, and Emerson, &c., for whose benefit, apparently, the Scale is inflicted upon us, we cannot repeat too often that the human mind without method is like a fishing-smack without chart or rudder. Men of extraordinary mental grasp and insight—genius, in fact—may in a haphazard way with such a craft net up from the ocean of the unknown a scanty catch amid whole rubbish-heaps of sand and sea-weed, but they will assuredly miss and pass by whole tracts with shoals of fish. Rare guesses at truth they are—and the dazzle of the hits blinds us to the overwhelming number of the failures. Still we not ungratefully store up these scattered insights, as capital suggestive grist for our intelligence mills in moral and social instruction, but we take our final stand upon the firm and lasting foundation of the inductive system (inductive logic or the logic of science) which has so often brought us into port with bountiful reward.[1]

This last rather foolhardy attempt, amid mumbling and cackling of "metaphysick" apes and geese to set up transcendentalism once more upon the philosophic pedestal, will have its day and run its full course until a successor from a similar mint arises to take its place, when *it* will also vanish into oblivion, for we fear that for a long, long time yet to come, some one amongst us will be engaged in shooting at this *a priori* folly as it flies.

HORACE SEAL.

but he could not see the truth of the excellent discoveries in astronomy and magnetism, which Copernicus and Gilbert had made known a little time before."—Jevon's *Primer of Logic*, p. 77. Also "Bacon, in short, in the practice of induction did not advance an inch beyond Aristotle. Rather he retrograded, inasmuch as he failed to draw so clear a line between the respective spheres of Inductive collection of facts and 'Explanation.'"—Minto's *Logic*, p. 252.

1 And to which we owe our scientific belief in beliefs 4, 5, 6.

# WOMAN IN THE ANCIENT WORLD.

AMONG the primitive nations of the world woman was commonly regarded as a chattel or slave—a creature existing and originally created merely to minister to the wants of man. The Egyptians alone treated her with respect and consideration.

In Ancient Egypt monogamy was practised, although it was not enjoined by law. There is no evidence of the existence of a marriage ceremony, but the marriage contract secured to the wife certain rights, one of which was that of complete control over her husband, who promised to yield her implicit obedience! Nearness of relationship was no barrier to wedlock, the union of brother with sister being quite common.

Women, both married and unmarried, participated with the men in all the pleasures of social intercourse. They took part in the public festivals, shared in banquets, drove out in their chariots, and made pleasure excursions on the Nile. At banquets the guests were entertained chiefly with music and dancing. Singing was also an esteemed accomplishment, and the more solid part of their education must have been attended to, as women often held important offices in the priesthood. They presided at birth and officiated as mourners at death and burial.

Ladies of rank occupied their spare moments in embroidery and in the cultivation of flowers, of which they were passionately fond, and which were lavishly used on all festive occasions. Women of the humbler classes were employed in spinning, and in the rural districts in tending cattle and sheep, and in carrying water—the heavier employments being left to the men.

This halcyon state of affairs lasted only during the days of Egypt's greatness; during the period of her decline her daughters were fearfully downtrodden and degraded. The hardest manual labour was assigned to them, and they suffered cruel punishments for the crimes of their fathers, husbands, or brothers, as the case might be. Sometimes they were publicly beaten with sticks, at others thrown into dungeons or sent to work at the mines, where the miseries they endured were so great that, as the old historian tells us, they longed for death as far preferable to life.

In Babylonia, and also in Persia, woman was a mere chattel of man. She had no rights, and was supposed to have no feelings.

Assyrian maidens had no voice in the disposal of themselves in marriage. Those of marriageable age were once a year collected and brought together into one place, there to be sold to the highest bidders. The most beautiful were offered for sale first, and these were eagerly competed for by the wealthy men of the community desirous of marrying. With the money obtained for the beauties the plain and deformed ones were dowered, so that they, too, might obtain husbands, they being given to the men who offered to take the smallest sums. Each purchaser was obliged to give security for the due fulfilment of the marriage contract—marriage being a condition of purchase—and for the public acknowledgment of his newly acquired wife. If a pair found on coming together that they could not live amicably the husband could return his purchase and receive back his money, but the wife who repudiated her husband was condemned to be drowned. Womanly purity was discountenanced by the Babylonians, and woman's life was held in light esteem. During a period of revolt thousands of women were massacred by their own nearest relatives, merely to save the provisions which otherwise they would have required.

In Ancient Greece the position of woman varied in the different eras and in the different states. In the renowned State of Sparta women were regarded as instruments for the production of strong, robust citizens for the State, and great care was taken that they should be well developed physically. They were from their earliest youth allowed the utmost liberty, and were exercised in running, wrestling, and boxing, accomplishments which they displayed in the public games at the theatre. Scantily clad, so as to allow perfect freedom of motion, and crowned with flowers, they also took part in the religious ceremonies, and sang and danced at the national festivals. On ordinary, as on festive occasions, the dress of the Spartan women was of the simplest description. A woollen robe loose at one side, and fastening with clasps over the shoulder, was the attire of maidens, whilst married women wore also an upper garment and a veil. The wearing of embroidery, gold, and precious stones was restricted to prostitutes.

When they married, which, according to Plutarch, was not till they had arrived at maturity, they were always well dowered. We are told by the same writer that the Spartan bride was dressed "in man's clothes," and had her hair "cut close to the skin." Her troth was plighted, not to her husband, but to the State, and patriotism seems to have been a leading sentiment in her bosom. For some time after her marriage the wife continued to reside with her parents, seeing her husband but occasionally, by stealth, and disguised in masculine apparel. Specially beautiful women were allowed to have several husbands, and so lightly was the marriage tie regarded that a man could, if he chose, give away his wife without any legal process whatever. Indeed, it was considered rather a meritorious action for him to do so. Heiresses were at the disposal of the king, who, without consulting either themselves or their parents, bestowed them upon the poorest citizens, that the wealth of the nation might be equally distributed among all classes.

During the frequent absences of their warlike lords the Spartan women had entire control of their households and their affairs. So much power did they enjoy in comparison with other women of the time, that a foreign lady on one occasion said to Gorgo, the wife of Leonidas, "You of Lacedæmon are the only women in the world that rule the men," whereat the Spartan quickly retorted, "We are the only women that bring forth men."

In other parts of Greece women led lives of strict seclusion. They seem to have scarcely been allowed to leave their own apartments, which were always situated in the back, and commonly in the upper part of the house, so as to ensure the utmost privacy. Young girls had to ask permission to go from one part of the house to another, and the reputation of a newly married woman was in danger if she were seen out of doors. When she became a mother she enjoyed a little more freedom, though only during her husband's pleasure, for those of a jealous temperament kept their wives in close confinement. By the laws of Solon women were prohibited from leaving home with more than three changes of clothing and a certain allowance of provisions, or a basket of more than a cubit's length. Neither were they permitted to appear in the streets at night, save in a chariot and preceded by torch-bearers. It is said that those strict laws were framed in order to check the depravity of the daughters of Athens, but it was not only to the peregrinations of women that the laws of the great Athenian extended, but to all the details of daily life, including even eating and drinking.

The ordinary employments of women, apart from their domestic duties, were spinning, weaving, embroidery, and other kinds of needlework. Instruction in these mechanical arts seems to have been all the education they received—all that was considered necessary or fitting for them. "She is the best woman," says Thucydides, "of whom least is said either of good or evil."

An orphan heiress was compelled by law to marry her next-of-kin, in order to keep the property in the family. When, however, she had married prior to the death of her father, she could, at his decease, be taken from her husband and given to her relative along with her estate, the bond of wedlock, as in Sparta, being somewhat loosely regarded and quite easily dissolved.

As in Sparta, too, a man could give away his wife either for a time, or permanently as he desired. It was by no means the most depraved or the meanest of mankind who exercised this strange privilege, Socrates and Pericles being amongst the number.

During the golden age of Athens, when the ashes of her illustrious law-giver had long been at rest in his native isle (for Solon was an Athenian but by adoption), the daughters of the classic city enjoyed more freedom than they had done in earlier days. Husbands when they went from home often took their wives along with them, but from a moral point of view it was not always the best of society into which they were thus introduced. The house of the celebrated Aspasia, the mistress of Pericles, was a favourite resort of even the wisest and highest cultured of the citizens of Athens. This remarkable woman was noted, not only for her beauty, but for her talents, and for the elevation to which she had attained in learning. The unfortunate class to which she belonged was then the only class of women in Athens that enjoyed freedom and culture. Whether from a desire to heighten their charms by means of a knowledge of " divine philosophy," or from a genuine love of learning, many of them frequented the schools and the company of philosophers and studied mathematics and other sciences. Their personal beauty often made them the chosen models of painters and sculptors, and the themes of licentious poets, and, as we have already said, Aspasia, who was at their head, wielded such a powerful influence over even their best and wisest men that they resorted to her house as to a lecture-room, accompanied by their wives. They evidently wished the latter to profit by the learned and brilliant conversation of the gifted courtesan, who at least had taught them that the life of ignorance and seclusion to which they doomed their women was that which was least calculated to develop their mental powers and render them congenial companions. The corrupt condition of society, however, may be inferred from the fact that such women occupied a prominent, almost a leading position in it, and, indeed, at this period, the golden age of Grecian art and literature, learning, luxury, and vice were equally dominant in " the eyes and light of Greece," as her panegyrists called Athens.

" In the brave days of old " the Roman patriarch could, with the sanction of the law, throw his daughter into a dungeon, deprive her of food, lash her with the scourge, sell her as a slave, or slay her with the sword. When she married, her husband assumed over her the same power. She could, like the Grecian woman, inherit either the whole or a part of her father's estate, but whatever property she possessed, or whatever right of inheritance, was at marriage passed over to her husband. She could be divorced for drinking wine, or even for having in her possession the keys of any place in which it was kept. A wife could, however, be divorced almost at pleasure, provided that her dowry was returned along with her. For a considerable period a woman was forbidden by law to wear a garment of various colours, to have personal ornaments weighing more than half an ounce of gold, and to drive in a chariot within a mile of the city. In those early days the women were employed in cooking, spinning, weaving, and sewing.

When the Romans became rich in the usual way, by plundering their neighbours, the laws relative to woman's dress and recreation were repealed; the domestic duties were relegated to slaves, and the Roman matron blossomed into a lady of fashion.

There were " blue-stockings " as well as " belles," however, amongst the ladies of ancient Rome. The speech of Hortensia against the unjust taxation of women, delivered before the three assassins who governed Rome during the second triumvirate, is mentioned admiringly by Cicero, and her courage must have been as great as her eloquence since no man could be found to undertake the perilous task. In another of Italia's cities it is evident that the " new woman " was in existence at a very early date. One of the inscriptions found amongst the ruins of Pompeii shows that women were put forward by women as candidates for seats on the board of magistrates, but whether successful or not in gaining the coveted office is not recorded. Honoured, however, above all other women were the vestals, to whose care was committed the sacred relics upon which the safety of the city was supposed to depend. Often they were the custodians of wills and other important documents, and enjoyed many privileges denied to ordinary mortals.

The usual accomplishments of the Roman maiden were music and dancing. During the Empire, however, ladies were skilled in fencing, boxing, and wrestling, and often appeared in the amphitheatre as competitors for the prize. They appeared there more frequently, however, as spectators of the bloody gladiatorial combats in which unfortunate slaves, unhappy captives, or not less unhappy criminals were butchered to make a Roman holiday. Cruelty, gluttony, and even drunkenness had become prominent traits in the character of the Roman lady of those latter days, and those ugly vices are apt to obscure the virtues of the simple matrons, the pure-minded Lucretias of early Rome.

Among the ancient Germanic tribes women were regarded with peculiar reverence, and were commonly treated as the equals, sometimes as the superiors, of men. They were believed to be recipients of messages from the gods, and, like the rhapsodists of Greece, they were the repositories of the unwritten history of the race, the reciters of the poems in which were commemorated the stories of the tribal heroes. The " wise women," who were carefully set apart from the rest, were believed to be endowed with the power of lifting the veil of the future and learning the decrees of fate, and so were often consulted as oracles. Others were supposed to be gifted with supernatural powers, because of their allegiance to malignant divinities. The daughters of kings and princes were often priestesses, but what were their official duties it is difficult to say. We are told by

Tacitus that the priests settled disputes, awarded and inflicted punishments, and attended the armies to battle.

Both sexes were remarkable for their conjugal fidelity, monogamy being practised except in the case of royalty, the possession of more than one wife being a purely regal privilege. The marriage ceremony in those primitive times was exceedingly simple, consisting chiefly of the interchange of presents in the presence of the friends assembled for the feast. Says Tacitus, " To the husband the wife gives no dowry, but the husband to the wife." The present of the bride, he continues, " consisted of oxen, horses, and arms to intimate to her that she was to share in the toils and dangers of her husband as well as in his pleasures." This it was customary for her to do, for the wife of the ancient German was her husband's companion and counsellor in time of peace and his comrade in time of war.

Of the male sex, he says, " those who are bravest and most warlike amongst them never do any work, or mind any business, but, when they are not engaged in war or hunting, spend their whole time in loitering and feasting, committing the management of their houses, lands, and all their affairs to their women, old men, and children." This custom, which to the Roman seemed so strange and so contemptible, was doubtless but a relic of the earlier mother age, when woman was not the dependent of, but the teacher and ruler of man. Students of German mythology claim that from woman proceeded agriculture, medicine, tradition, and family life— from man, warfare and hunting. Long before the father had become a member of the family group, the mother reigned supreme in the den, teaching to her children the knowledge she had acquired in her efforts to provide for herself and offspring. For a long period such property as there was descended through the mother, and the management of the houses, lands, and all the affairs pertaining to them was in all likelihood due, not to the indolence of the men, but to the fact that woman had not entirely given place to man as head of the household.

The social customs which prevailed among the ancient Britons were in many respects similar to those of Germany. Both Germans and Britons lived in the semi-promiscuous fashion which seems to have led the Romans to form such a low estimate of their morals. Their houses consisted of but one apartment, which was shared by men, women, and children, who during the night rested on one continuous bed of rushes. This mode of life must have seemed exceedingly barbarous to the civilised, luxurious Romans, but that the wives of the Britons were held in common, as is stated by Julius Cæsar, is, we consider, extremely doubtful. The treatment of Cartismandna, the adulterous queen of the Brigantes, whom her indignant subjects obliged to vacate the throne in favour of her injured husband, tends to induce the belief that they did not so lightly look upon the marriage bond, and that monogamy was practised by all classes of society. In Wales, however wedlock was by no means indissoluble. There a man could divorce his wife upon very slight pretext, and a wife could separate from her husband for such a slight cause as a disagreeable breath. By the laws of Hoel Dda, who was a prince of that country in the tenth century, a man was allowed to give his wife three blows with a stick upon any part of the body except the head if she committed adultery, if she squandered his means, if she pulled his beard or "called him opprobrious names," but if the beating were more severe or for any more trifling reason he was fined.

It is difficult to determine what was the exact status of woman in every part of Britain in that olden time. By the law of regal succession a British king was succeeded by his daughter or by his widow, if he left no son. It was in this way that the famous Boadicea became Queen of the Iceni.

In the ordinary ranks of life a man's property was at his death divided equally among his sons. What share was apportioned to his daughters is not quite clear. Among the Saxons on the Continent it was customary for the daughters to receive a smaller share than their brothers. In like manner the laws of Wales in the tenth century decreed that a daughter receive but half as much as falls to her brother of their father's inheritance. There is, however, a law of King Canute, from which it appears that sons and daughters were made equal, as they may have been in even earlier times.

Although the British woman was in many cases legally recognised as the equal of man, she was by no means considered fit to be her own guardian, but during her whole life was in the care of one of the opposite sex. Whilst unmarried she was, of course, under the control of her father. At his death her brother took his place, or, if she had none, her nearest male relative. The women who had no relations fell to the guardianship of the king. A married woman was under the legal control of her husband, provided that she had been married with the consent of her previous guardian, whose authority could not be taken from him without his consent. His compliance was usually gained by means of ample presents, sometimes so ample that it became necessary to pass a law fixing the amount for people of all ranks. The value of the presents varied not only according to the rank, but according to the condition of the woman, only half as much being paid in the case of a widow as was paid for a maiden of the same rank. The man who married without the consent of his bride's guardian had no legal authority over his wife nor any of her possessions, and had to suffer various severe penalties for his crime (*mundbreach*), for such it was reckoned.

Marriage was celebrated with a great deal of festivity, although the ceremony was, like that of the Germans, of the simplest description. Among the guests were included all relatives within the third degree. Each guest was expected to give a present to the bride and bridegroom, and the latter also received a present from the guardian of the bride. This "faderfium" was all the dowry which the husband received with his wife. On the morning after the marriage the bridegroom had to retaliate by presenting a valuable gift to his wife. This "morgaengife" (morning gift) became her own separate property, to which she had exclusive right.

The ancient British woman appears to have been as fond of dress as were her Continental sisters, the women of Gaul. Boadicea is described by Dio as wearing a short tunic of thick woollen cloth, over which was a long mantle reaching nearly to the ground. Massive gold ornaments were worn by both sexes, the gold chains of Caractacus and of Boadicea being thought worthy of special mention by the Roman historians. Luxuriant tresses were also esteemed "a thing of beauty," and the golden hair of the ill-fated Queen of the Iceni is said to have floated far down over her armour when engaged in battle. Indeed, it is evident, from all that we can learn of the women of the remote past, that they did not differ so widely from the women of the present day as the lapse of time would lead us to expect, and that, apart from outward circumstances, they were women "in all things like as we are."

ELIZABETH STITCHELL DIACK.

# THE LATE DUCHESS OF TECK.

## A PARVUM IN MULTO BIOGRAPHY.

THE story of the life of Mary Adelaide, Duchess of Teck, as edited
by Mr. Kinloch Cooke, and published by Mr. Murray, is a very
disappointing piece of biographical work.  The princess was a fine
example of a patriotic, public-spirited Englishwoman, who performed
with fidelity the duties of her position and spent her leisure hours
in philanthropic activities.  For the limitations on her generosity
imposed by a scanty purse she found compensation in the sacrifice
of her ease and the employment of her time in the service of the
unfortunate, and her warm-hearted devotion stirred the sympathies
and exacted the aid of many who came within the sphere of her
influence.  Thus she became, as all good people are, the cause of
goodness in others, and this in an especial degree on account of her
exalted station.  The history of a life fulfilling so conspicuously the
obligation of nobility was well worth writing as an exemplar to
others of high degree and a stimulus and encouragement to women
of all classes.

But what does Mr. Cooke give us?  Not a succinct account of her
character and her work, but two massive volumes of petty detail and
small talk.  What time she rose, who came to lunch, where she
drove in the afternoon, who were her neighbours at dinner, what
games they played in the evening, when she went to bed—hundreds
of pages are filled with the record of such facts as these.  The
Duchess, like the industrious and intelligent woman she was,
recorded in a journal, and in letters to her friends, her daily doings
for many years, and these documents were naturally placed at the
disposal of her biographer ; and such is the use he has made of
them.  He tells us in his preface that

"Her late Royal Highness was present at almost every State ceremony
that has taken place during the last fifty years, and generally noted down
the people she met and some account of the proceedings she witnessed. . . .
Princess Mary saw most of the crowned heads of Europe, as well as the
distinguished diplomatists, artists, and littérateurs of the latter half of the
nineteenth century."

After a prelude like this one expects to find in the course of the
800 pages some contributions to the history of the century, some

light upon the careers and characters of the personages with whom she was brought in contact, perhaps a little of the secret history of Courts and Cabinets ; but of such things the biography is almost completely bare. There is scarcely a page which will be of the slightest value to the historian of the century.

It cannot be that the princess associated so long with the makers of history and never learnt anything worth recording, nor is it reasonable to suppose that she refrained from setting down anything beyond what is either notorious or of no public value. In nearly every page of the diary and letters we find leaders denoting a hiatus, and though probably many of these indicate the omission of trivialities it is beyond doubt that other suppressed passages relate to matters of public interest which the hypersensitive editor has thought it well to delete. For example, writing on March 7, 1868, the Princess says :

"London is fast filling, and engagements are thickening. People wonder and speculate as to whether or no the D'Israeli Government will last. I confess the new Premier in the room of dear Lord Derby seems strange. . . . We hear good accounts of my sister from Strelitz."

Does this mean the omission of some piquant fact or Court opinion about Disraeli at the moment of his apotheosis ? Again, the record that the Princess sat between two Cabinet Ministers at dinner will be followed by the irritating dots, and one cannot help inferring that an interesting piece of political gossip is struck out. The anxiety not to insert a word that might hurt the feelings of any one is sometimes carried to the point of absurdity. In 1861, after a visit to the House of Lords, the diary records : "As we took our places, Lord —— was mumbling the last words of his speech." It is, of course, of no consequence who the noble lord was, but the omission of his name forty years afterwards, because he is described as mumbling, is an example of the lopsided view Mr. Cooke takes of his duty as a biographer. Why give the passage at all if the name could not be mentioned ?

It may be said that the purpose was to narrate the life of Princess Mary, and not to make a contribution to political history. If that was so, why give us all this pudding with the plums picked out ? The life of the Princess might have been written much more effectively in a quarter the space. In such a form it might have been widely read and served a useful purpose. But even from this point of view the work is weak and incomplete. It is surely a feature of interest in the career of the Princess that she delayed until the age of thirty-two to make choice of a husband, a most unusual thing for royalty, but no explanation is attempted. It is well known that she had many suitors, but the book contains the barest reference to the fact.

There is reason to believe that political consequences of some gravity followed from an attempt of Lord Palmerston to marry the princess to Prince Jerome Napoleon (Plon Plon), and it is known that the Queen, while strongly objecting to the proposition, referred the question to the princess herself; but the biography says not a word of this. One passage in a letter to a friend, written in 1854, may refer to a current rumour of these negotiations; but one cannot tell, for the value of the extract is lost by the insertion of a dash, which one would think to be superfluous at this time of day :

" Pray accept my best thanks for your kind letter, and the hope, or rather wish, you cherish of seeing me one day Empress of ———, but I honestly confess I am *too* fond of my English home ever to resign it for any other."

The passage was doubtless worth giving, but it was surely needless to omit the nation of which the lady thought the princess a possible empress.

But, whatever the sins of omission, the chief fault of the work is the insertion of masses of superfluity. Here are a few examples. Writing to a friend in 1852, her nineteenth year, the Princess says :

" Finding you are coming to town for a day, I write to know whether there is any possibility of our meeting, and, if so, when and where? Now in my own head I settled that it would do charmingly if you were to come to Gloucester House on Tuesday evening, as there will most likely be a party there; a little hint to Aunt Mary on the subject, and your invitation would be sent to Prince's Gate immediately, and if you could come at half-past nine o'clock we should be able to have a nice chat ere people began to arrive. But would this suit you? is the question. Think it over well, as I fear it is the only chance we have of meeting, for it is rather a busy week with us, what with the Drawing Room and all; and as we shall be in town Monday morning it would not be very convenient to come up either of the following days early."

What possible interest this can have had, even at the time it was written, for any being upon earth except the recipient it is difficult to perceive, and to print such letters after the lapse of half a century seems the acme of absurdity. Turning, almost at random, to a date forty-five years later, I notice this thrilling paragraph in a letter from the princess to one of her sons, relating to a visit to Belford Hall, Northumberland :

" I have taken the centre bedroom upstairs, a three-windowed, large, roomy, comfortable apartment, with a view over a grassy slope planted with clumps of trees *à distance*, and single ones most judiciously dotted about— just what I should like to see in Richmond Park. Papa has the room next me. There is a nice bathroom through Fell's room, immediately opposite Papa's, which is a great comfort. Algie and Graham have charm_ ing rooms on the same floor—Nurse Smith occupying a room between them."

And so forth—just the information an affectionate son would like to have, no doubt; but mothers are writing letters like this every day, and the princess herself would probably have been the last to suppose that the little household arrangements were of importance to any but themselves.

The journal is even less suitable for extended publication than the letters ; and if, as I have suggested, we are given the pudding without the plums, the result can scarcely do justice to the princess as a diarist. That she entertained any idea of subsequent publication may be doubted, but this doubt involves no reflection on the discretion of the family in placing the journal in the hands of the biographer. A careful and judicious use of it was essential to the fulfilment of his task. Whether these adjectives are applicable to the performance or not the reader may judge from two or three extracts :

"*February* 12, 1852, Sunday.—We went to the Chapel Royal, and afterwards I walked with Mamma and Knese in Hyde Park to see the vulgar *monde* [an expression very uncharacteristic of the Princess] ; then paid Aunt Mary a long visit. On our way home we walked up Piccadilly. Tea, and I read till six in my own room ; when I went .to Mamma and found her deep in converse with poor Madame de Brunnow, who was much affected on taking leave."

"*January* 2, 1856.—After a late breakfast I read with Mamma and walked till one o'clock, when Mr. Walbaum read with us till 2.45 and again for an hour after luncheon. We then had a visit from the Lavradios, and I read till it was time to dress for our dinner-party of twelve *personnes*— the Oxholms, Hochschilds, Count Colloredo, Karolyi (*père et fils*), Chotek, and Trautmansdorf. Conversed all the evening."

"*April* 18, 1870.—I was hindered in my dressing by having for a while to mind the chicks, the nursery being thrown into great commotion by the arrival of Ellen's [a nurse] sister with the sad news of the sudden death of their father. I sent her off at once to her poor mother, and then proceeded to dress, breakfasting *vers la fin de ma toilette* in bedroom. . . . The chicks departed for Chiswick at 4.30. Francis [Duke of Teck] and I drove over to Coombe, where we dug up primrose roots for our garden."

"*May* 17, 1870.—At four o'clock I started with Ella and the whole family (*two* in double perambulators, pushed by *two* nurses, and *one* in Girdie's arms) for the paddock at the foot of our hill, into which Henry Sawyer let us. Here we sat and sauntered about picking cowslips for an hour or more. Home about six, baby crowing all the way; and after packing up my goods and chattels for Kensington, I went to the nursery to take leave of the chicks before driving with Ella to town, where I found a telegram from Francis, announcing his return for next morning."

There are scores of pages with no better claim to publicity than these extracts—just the unpolished daily jottings of a busy lady. On one page, relating to a visit to Belvoir, we read : " We took a glimpse *en passant* at the dear gallery "; " Lord Granby took us to see the dear Duke "; " We took leave of our dear hostess "; " We reached Kew about eight, where dear Knese, *tout à fait rajeuni*, received us." And two or three pages farther: "We rushed to a window to see the *dear* Coldstreams go by," and afterwards "dressed for a grand and charmingly first-rate Ball at dear Apsley House." A lady who found everything so dear must have been dear herself, and perhaps, if these passages were to be given at all, it would have been a pity to omit the iteration; but it is apparent that the princess never looked upon her diary as a contribution to history or to literature.

The fact is that, notwithstanding the omissions—the nature and extent of which can only be conjectured—there is sufficient in these volumes to have made a book of 200 or 300 pages of real interest and value. The excellent closing chapter, describing the princess's charitable and philanthropic work, would have made a good ground-work, and colour and picturesqueness would have been given to the story by a few of the private notes and episodes. For instance, it seems quite worth while to know that the Queen liked a game of battledore and shuttlecock when past forty years of age. During a visit to Windsor Castle, in October 1855, the princess was sent for by the Queen to play this game with her; and again, in January 1861:

" I went to the Queen's room to sit to her Majesty, and after luncheon, as it rained, I again sat for the completion of the portrait, and then played at battledore and shuttlecock with the Queen in the corridor."

Her Majesty at this time had been two years a grandmother, and the record is of interest as showing how she retained her youthful spirit until the death of the Prince Consort in the following December.

The gift of a knife to Princess Mary's eldest son by Lord Beaconsfield is another little incident which throws light upon a great character. This is the note sent by the Prime Minister to Prince Adolphus in 1877, on the boy's ninth birthday:

"2, WHITEHALL GARDENS, *August* 13, 1877.
" MY DEAR LITTLE PRINCE,—As this is your birthday, I send you a knife, because at your age that was the kind of thing I liked to have. When you are a man I will send you a sword.
" Your friend, BEACONSFIELD."

The fond mother sent a charming letter of thanks, and Prince Adolphus, who is now Duke of Teck and serving with the army in South Africa, wrote as follows:

" KENSINGTON PALACE, *August* 17, 1877.
" DEAR LORD BEACONSFIELD,—I thank you very much for the beautiful knife you sent me, as well as for your nice letter. It was very kind of you to remember my birthday. I only wish I could be sure of keeping the knife *ever* as a remembrance of you.
"You are very good to promise me a sword when I am a man, and I can promise you in return I will try not to disgrace the giver; but use it

like a true Briton ! Please to accept the enclosed, and believe me, dear Lord Beaconsfield, ever your grateful little friend,

"ADOLPHUS OF TECK."

Princess Mary was a tolerably keen Conservative and was a politician from an early age. Before her fifteenth birthday she wrote regarding her brother-in-law's little principality of Mecklenburg-Strelitz :

"What a pity it is for Lord Palmerston to meddle with it, or to make as great a mess of it as he has done of all the other places he has kindly interfered with, to the great detriment of the monarchical government and to the advantage of the Radical party."

Which shows that the Court opinion of Palmerston was cordially endorsed at Cambridge Cottage.

In point of mere readableness, perhaps, the tit-bit of the book is a sketch of some characteristics of the Duke of Cambridge, Princess Mary's father, who was a worthy son of pious, blunt, honest George III. The Duke, in his old age, was a conspicuous figure at the parish church of Kew, where long before (in the sapient language of a Vestry resolution passed in 1805) the King and his family had "graciously condescended to attend Divine Service " :

"The Duke was a strong Churchman, and, in his simple way, very religious, but, as a friend of his Royal Highness used to say, 'his religion sometimes took rather an unconventional form.' He would frequently make audible remarks when the service was in progress. On one occasion, after the clergyman had repeated the usual exhortation, 'Let us pray,' the Duke was heard to reply, 'By all means.' Another time he startled those near him by saying, 'Shawms, shawms! What are they?' During a very dry summer the vicar read the prayer for rain; at the close the Duke joined fervently in the 'Amen,' adding, in exactly the same tone of voice, 'but we sha'n't get it till the wind changes.' One Sunday, during the reading of the offertory sentences, when the words 'Behold the half of my goods I give to the poor' were read, his Royal Highness astonished his fellow-worshippers by exclaiming, 'No, I can't do that; a half is too much for any man, but I have no objection to a tenth.' Again, on hearing the text, 'For we brought nothing into this world, neither may we carry anything out,' he ejaculated, 'True, true; too many calls upon us for that.' The Duke at times expressed himself in a forcible manner. After hearing an eloquent preacher at the Temple Church, he observed to his friend, Sir Frederick Thesiger (afterwards Lord Chelmsford), as they were walking up the street together, 'That was a d——d good sermon,' a criticism which in no way implied irreverence, much less profanity."

Mr. Cooke's *magnum opus* will doubtless have a good circulation among the hundreds of people whose families and connections are mentioned in association with the Princess, but it is quite unsuitable for the general reader, and one can only hope that in due course we may have a life of Princess Mary in such a form that it will go far and wide and help her good works to blossom in the dust.

JAMES SYKES.

# THE FINAL SEAT OF AUTHORITY.

## A REPLY TO "THE NEW EVANGELICALISM."

THOUGHTFUL men and women seeking for proof of the existence of God are met with three alternative answers ; they anchor their faith to miraculous revelation, they find satisfaction in an innate "consciousness" of His existence, or they deduce Him from a rational observation of phenomena. The doctrine of miraculous revelation is not only unscientific, for a reason that will be indicated shortly, but to many thoughtful students must appear inadequate and even repulsive. On the other hand the mere "consciousness" of the existence of God, which brings peace of mind to some, will seem to others, determined to think the matter out, insufficient data upon which to base any assumption of such existence, for, upon similar grounds, it would be equally justifiable to assert that fairies and imps really exist, because we can conceive such a possibility ! Far be it from me, however, to question the existence of any à priori basis in the human mind. But whether we accept the advanced theory of Leibniz that knowledge, like matter, is indestructible, and that every mind simply develops into activity all the potency within it, a doctrine which no evolutionist can consistently hold, or merely content ourselves with the conception of à priori knowlege as an heirloom, capable of enhancement as it passes through our hands to be handed on to our successors, the existence of that fundamental consciousness itself cannot be logically regarded as an essential proof of the reality of our conceptions, although having proved the reality of a fact by more scientific means we are justified in regarding our "innate consciousness" of it as valuable corroboration.[1] It is not until we reach the age at which rational deduction from the observation of phenomena becomes possible that a *scientific* conception of God becomes possible. The child-mind is incapable of mastering the

---

[1] Mr. Arthur Balfour, in his *Foundations of Belief*, rejecting the old-fashioned theory that "innate ideas" are true because they were implanted in us by God, retains the conclusion that "there must be a God to justify our confidence in innate ideas." The point is ingeniously put, but the reality of conceptions admittedly imaginary can be logically proved by similar means, and if it be true that fairies do not exist in spite of the child's confidence in his innate conception of them, how are we justified, merely upon this ground, in assuming the existence of God?

problems that trouble us in later life as to the meaning of Infinitude and the nature of Superhumanity, and in order to bring God within infantile mental focus it appears impossible to avoid resenting Him as a kind of glorified man. It is when, with growing years and developed intellect, we look out upon the world and ask the meaning of it all that the ordered system of phenomena begins to demand a First Cause and an Ultimate Authority in order to complete the only rational explanation of the harmonious activity of nature.[1]

Having dispensed with the theory of "innate ideas" we are left with miraculous revelation and rational deduction as alternative paths to the ultimate explanation of things.

There are many good souls, who, either from moral fear or intellectual incapacity, never get beyond the anthropomorphic stage in their theological conceptions, and, although the old idea that science and religion are essentially antagonistic is now held, in its crudest form, only by the less intellectual adherents of the Christian faith, the germ of the fallacy continues to live in the insistence, still urged by cultured exponents of the most modern phases of "evangelicalism," of the pre-eminent position of "grace" among the forces of salvation. Not content with these ample natural resources, upon which scientists rely in the evolution of the human mind and the formation of human character, modern evangelicalism seeks its authority and regenerative power in the halo of supernatural mysticism which Christianity has thrown around the Cross. The aim of Christian "evangelicalism" from the time of Paul, who was its first exponent, down to the present day has been to alienate the philosophy of Jesus from the realms of reason and science, and to surround his life and teachings with an atmosphere of miracle, more or less irrational. "The forms of humanism," according to the new evangelicalism, "are the æsthetic (or literary) and the philanthropic, and each by itself threatens the evangelical note. Each would detach love and pity from the moral conditions of sin, and, therefore, from grace. Each would naturalise Christ's love, and, while enhancing its charm, would reduce its miracle. Each would make religion but the spiritualised man, natural affection etherealised. But to love your enemy and forgive your revilers is a totally new and supernatural affection. It is not a natural affection educated, cultured and refined. Our note is neither culture nor is it character as the result of culture——even of religious

---

[1] The naturalistic theory that phenomenal activity is self-caused and is controlled by the accidental convenience of the moment leaves us without an adequate explanation of the "uniformity of nature" and the obvious law of natural adaptability. If each atom acts, without the influence of an ultimate design, upon purely individualistic principles the only explanation of the ordered system of phenomena is that it is due to a fluke, or rather a series of flukes, a solution which makes a greater draft upon credulity than is demanded by the theory of "miraculous interference."

culture. It is the change made by grace as an act of forgiveness, and not as a system of consecration."[1] The new evangelicalism "must insist on the miraculous nature of the Christian life," and, although God is never spoken of as a person in the whole of the New Testament, it finds its inspiration to seek the final seat of Authority in the Cross in the assumption that "there is an absolute person and His act" beyond the pale of criticism.

But the most elementary logician, if he be at all acquainted with the rudiments of philosophy, will at once detect a paradox in such a sweeping premise. What is "an absolute person"? The Absolute must inevitably be the Unconditioned, the Inconceivable, the Infinite; but the very idea of person suggests finity and relativity. The conception of a person is strictly within the pale of criticism, because it is capable of analysis; therefore, unless the phrase is a meaningless contradiction of terms, evangelicalism is seeking for a final authority within the realms of the finite. The explanation of the forces of nature, physical and moral, the seat of the controlling Power of the Universe, the Supreme Creator and Cause behind all phenomena and effects is, we are asked to believe, concentrated in an historic incident in the life of one of its planets!

What says experience? How far can we grasp an idea of the Supreme Authority from the result of observation? The careful study of physical nature from the lowest mineral form to the highest development of animalism, in man, at once suggests the idea of a central law of control operating upon phenomena from a central point. If there be no such authority behind the activity of phenomena how can we reasonably explain the regularity with which nature acts? How comes it that the stars do not fall, that the seasons are never erratic in their course, and that we do not tumble off the globe on which we walk? Surely, for some other cause than chance nature's laws are never broken; her works never go wrong. Look at the humblest plant-life and you observe a spirit of unconscious utilitarianism actuating all vegetable growth, obedient to a law of obligation to some Central Authority. The plant-life is controlled by tendencies calculated to achieve reproduction; the lower animals act upon instincts of self-preservation for the benefit of the species (*i.e.*, for their continuity of existence), and man, so far as his animalism goes, does likewise. When we pass from the physical sphere, where submission may be regarded as almost, if not quite, compulsory, to the moral sphere, where it is voluntary the same law is found, by experience, to be operative.[2]

---

[1] *The Cross as the Final Seat of Authority.* By Dr. P. T. Forsyth.—*Contemporary Review* for October.

[2] It is probable that Determinists will object to the idea of moral submission being regarded as voluntary. While it may be readily admitted that all psychological activity is controlled by influences, either of environment, heredity, or circumstance, at the same time I venture to suggest that the force of such influences can be regulated at will, else, the sensations of indignation and admiration become amiable but

Just as the plant, in order to reproduce its life must obey the law of obligation, so the moral being, in order to safeguard his moral life, must lose it in subjection to the law of moral obligation, an attitude we call self-sacrifice. So far as our experience goes, then, we are conscious of the existence of a Central Authority, which holds the Universe in order and regulates phenomena (physical and moral) by the operation of the law of obligation and submission to itself.

Bearing this result of experience in mind, let us apply the test of reason to the assumption that the Final Authority is *in* phenomena and not beyond it. It follows logically from our observation of the universality of the law of obligation that to break the law is to lessen the force of the Central Authority; therefore nature, in her own interests, does not break her own laws. The complete regularity with which nature acts is the fundamental fact of which naturalists (both scientific and philosophic) are most conscious, and it is by means of that very regularity that the Central Authority exerts its infinite power, and enforces the conception of its existence upon our observant conscience. Yet "Evangelical" Christianity invites us to believe that the most unique revelation of the existence of the Final Authority was brought about by an infringement of the laws of nature, and was enforced upon the consciousness of man by an action antagonistic alike to experience and the reasonable realisation of a super-phenomenal Power! Reason applied to the result of observation compels the belief that the Central and Final Authority lies in a Power which can command the submission of phenomena, and is therefore outside phenomena; for even if it were possible to conceive the idea of one phenomenon commanding the submission of all other phenomena, upon what data could we rely to determine which phenomena were superior, and which inferior? But if the Supreme Authority be outside phenomena, as apparently it must be, it is obvious that no such finite phenomenal conceptions as personality or historic incident can be reasonably regarded as Final or Central, since an act and a person are themselves not the Creator, but creatures, not the Cause but effects. To talk therefore of a creature being a Creator, and of a revelation

irrational attributes. It is difficult to believe that such instinctive sensations as those which lead to blame and praise are, contrary to all other instincts, irrational; and we are, therefore, led to believe that while it is unreasonable to laud or censure a man for the existence of external influences operating upon his moral actions, it is not unreasonable to pass judgment upon him for exerting or not exerting that subtle power, of which we are none the less conscious because we cannot entirely explain its presence, that enables him to regulate the force of these influences. It has been urged that the moral sense by rendering itself irresponsive to a certain influence, can by degrees, abolish the existence of that influence, and that, thus, even the *existence* of influences are subject to the will of man. But even if it be granted that an influence can be abolished at will the result will merely be to throw moral conduct back on to residuary alternatives, and, unless *every* influence (including environment and heredity) is abolished, which is inconceivable, absolute freedom of determination is impossible. At the same time, however, the most advanced Determinist can hardly deny that the forces of influence are comparatively subject to volition.

(*i.e.*, an effect) being a Cause is contrary to all possible logical conclusion. Deprived by the criticism of experience and reason of the possibility of the miraculous, " Evangelical " Christianity is left with a Final Authority that consists of nothing more than an historical act, neither absolute, because it is conceivable, nor final, because it is finite.

How far modern Christian ethics, as held by the self-styled " Evangelical " Churches, have departed from the basis adopted by Jesus himself will be realised most fully when we apply the teachings of the great Master to the principles of the universal law of obligation. " The whole theology of Jesus," says Renan, " was God conceived directly as Father." The human race, dependent upon and subject to a final authority, as children are dependent upon and subject to the father of a family, is a system of philosophy based upon the scientific knowledge gainable by observation and a poetical interpretation of the law of moral obligation. The doctrine of the vital necessity of submission as the only end to salvation has never had a truer exponent than the author of the golden rule, which John Stuart Mill claimed as the ideal of utilitarian ethics and the great need of the present day is a fuller realisation of Jesus as a philosopher and the emphasis of his life-work, both in precept and in example, as a scientific rather than a miraculous basis of regenerative ethics. The law of the relationship of humanity to the Infinite elaborated in the parables is as sound science as the less æsthetic though, in their degree, not less truthful agnosticism of Darwin and Spencer, and the philosophy of the Sermon on the Mount is unrivalled in the realm of modern intellectuality. Jesus may have been a dreamer, he certainly was a poet, but, above all, he was a philosopher, and if the great scientists of the world and the leading modern philosophers are found outside the Churches, it is not because they dissent from the philosophy of Jesus, but rather because they desire to maintain the purity of its meaning and the intensity of its appeal, not to blind faith (mistaken by many for religion), but to the rational experience of men. The doctrine of self-sacrifice as a means to the higher life, to the perfect communion between man and God, needs no miracle to render it appreciable by the human intellect ; nor is it conceivable that its force would be augmented by the violation of the law which proves its necessity. Salvation therefore becomes a matter, not of the intervention of supernaturalism, rendering a man a helpless plaything in the hands of a God with partialities, and wicked enough to bring men into the world for the sardonic purpose of damning them, but a science, a natural evolution, attainable at will by the efforts of the moral faculties of mankind. Man, in fact, according to the philosophy of Jesus, is practically his own saviour ; the attainment of his highest ideal is within his reach and the " kingdom of heaven " is at his hand.

It is doubtful whether the purely scientific nature of the philo-. sophy of Jesus was ever understood by his contemporaries and his immediate followers as it is beginning to be understood to-day. The great teacher was so far ahead of his day that it has taken almost two thousand years for us to overtake him in the intellectual race, but modern scientific research, far from damaging the philosophy of Jesus, is more and more firmly establishing its claims to our rational attention. It is small wonder, therefore, that Paul, the inventor (so far as scriptural record goes) of "Evangelicalism," with all his fine qualities and many high ideals, hopelessly failed to catch the real meaning of his Master's doctrines. When we pass from Jesus to Paul we cross the bridge that spans the gulf between science and assumption. With Paul there is initiated a totally new scheme of salvation, and in nothing is this more strikingly illustrated than in the introduction of the word "grace"; that word which has been the stumbling-block of Christian ecclesiastics for centuries and is still the hindrance to a rational acceptance of the pure and lofty naturalism of the philosophy of Jesus. Jesus has nothing to say about "grace"; it is outside his philosophic vocabulary and antagonistic to his theory of life and its potentiality and purpose. So far as the new Evangelicalism claims to base its ethics upon the "miraculous nature of the Christian life" it admits that Paul, and not Jesus, is the source of its inspiration, and it is the development of the Pauline doctrine of "grace" that has found a logical outcome in the horrors of the Westminster Confession and the Thirty-nine Articles. True, the Westminster Confession is practically a dead letter, its crude theology having disappeared in the light of a more cultured and sympathetic Evangelicalism, while it is but a small band of earnest though irrational Churchmen who still fondly cling to the essential importance of the Articles of Faith; but we are face to face with a renewed activity on the part of a powerful section of "orthodox" Christianity in the direction of an attempt to divorce religion from the sphere of reason and to consign it to the unscientific arena of "faith." The old idea that science and religion are mutually destructive cannot be said to be totally eradicated until it is recognised that religion to be real must be scientific, and that scientific truth is the only correct criterion of the value of religion, for it is obvious that that which binds man (and all other natural subjects) to the Central Authority, if man realise its existence at all, must be an object of his consciousness; he must be able to give it its place in the order of phenomena, and thus it must come within the realm of science.[1]

The persistent misrepresentation of Pauline doctrines as Christian

[1] Mr. Herbert Spencer's theory that science and religion are mutually exclusive terms appears to me to be due to a confusion between "religion" (regarded as a scientific fact) and "faith" (regarded as an intellectual attempt to conceive the unknown).

on the part of modern evangelicalism is responsible for many difficulties which the simple scientific acceptance of the philosophy of
Jesus would immediately dispel. In the first place we too often
use loose expressions and lax language in speaking of God. It is
significant that Jesus travelled no further along the road of metaphysics than to postulate that God is Spirit; he made no attempt
to define the nature of the Supreme Authority, remaining content to
symbolise His relation to humanity as of a Father to his dependent
children, not only the Creator, but the Final Authority. Evangelicalism is more ambitious, for it has renewed the anthropomorphic
ideas of the ancient Hebrews. God is regarded as " personal," and
the essence is dragged down to the level of the symbol. The
anthropomorphic conception of God is responsible for the attribution
to the Infinite of the passions and conditions of the finite. God is
spoken of as " thinking," " desiring," " loving," " being angry," and
" forgiving "! It would be quite as reasonable, however, to invest
the Infinite with vicious, as well as virtuous, attributes, since man
(whose moods are borrowed for the purpose) is also prone to evil.
But the utter irrationality of applying relative attributes to an
Absolute Essence makes it supremely necessary that care should be
taken in defining what we mean by " goodness," " sin," and " forgiveness." A philosophic interpretation of these terms will probably
clear away the difficulty which many thoughtful men find in accepting
the philosophy of Jesus as scientific rather than miraculous. When
men object that the rational conception of Christianity fails to make
adequate, if any, provision for forgiveness of sins they forget that
they are unconsciously conceiving the relation of God to man as that
of man to man. They cannot struggle free from the anthropomorphic idea. To determine the reality of goodness and evil we
have to penetrate to motive, and to motive alone can moral judgment
be applied. In seeking the attributes of the Supreme Authority
we are therefore compelled, as far as possible, to seek the divine
motives on which Authority acts, and observation of phenomena
leads us to the conclusion that a desire for improvement both in
physical and moral activity is at the bottom of the Authorised law
of obligation. Hence, we may logically conclude that all that tends
to physical and moral evolution is *good*, and all that tends to impede
that growth is *evil*, the wilful production of which is *sin*. The Final
Authority may be regarded as that " power outside ourselves that
makes for righteousness," and he who fights against physical or
moral progress, either in the individual or the race, may be regarded
as a sinner, not from a merely sentimental, but from a scientific
point of view. Can he who commits a sin be forgiven? Let us
face the question philosophically. Conscious of the fact that an
infringement of the laws of the Central Authority cannot fail to
impede the progress of phenomena as designed by the Supreme

Cause, and unable to discover any natural force capable of calling back the irrevocable, "evangelical" philosophers have resorted to the expediency of introducing the miraculous, and have decided that the only agency possible for effecting forgiveness is supernaturalism. This is a hasty conclusion that will not bear examination. The act of forgiveness, as humanly understood, is the treatment of an injurer by the injured in such a manner as to leave out of the reckoning all thought of the injury inflicted. When we forgive our neighbour we regard him as if he had never done us a wrong, but the wrong remains, and the impression of that wrong, although we refuse to allow it to influence our conduct and sentiments, has left an indelible mark upon our experience, and, consequently, upon the course of our moral development. It is on the part of the injured and not of the injurer that the continuity of sentiment and conduct is required to constitute forgiveness, and, as the law of obligation is not strengthened or relaxed owing to our obedience or disobedience of its dictates, the conditions of forgiveness are here found resting on a scientific basis, and the employment of miracle is proved superfluous.

In speaking of God's "love" we are misled by similar thought-less use of expressions. One of the cardinal dogmas of "Evangelical" Christianity is insistence upon the love of God for man. But to speak of God loving is, once more, supposing God to be, not the Creator, but a creature; not the Cause of sensibility but the subject of its effect! What do we mean by love as felt by man for man? Love is that feeling for a fellow being which prompts us to desire his happiness, even at the sacrifice of our own. But love is a feeling, a sensation, and it is irrational to attribute to the First Cause a sensation—that is, an effect—because if the First Cause is subject to an effect, either there must be a cause beyond the Supreme Cause begetting that effect (which is impossible), or the First Cause is subject to its own causation, which is an equally illogical conclusion; or, finally, the God of Evangelical Christianity is not the First Cause, but something inferior to the First Cause, a conclusion the Evangelicals are hardly likely to be willing to accept, although it is their only other alter-native. We must beware, then, of attributing to the First Cause conditions which are effects dependent upon final causation, and remember that in regarding God as being angry or loving we are reducing the Creator in conception to the level of a creature, and attributing conditions to the Unconditioned. But while we cannot reasonably think of God as loving we may be justified in regarding Him as more than the subject of effect, as Cause itself, the Cause of love, and it is for the very reason that He is the Cause of love that it is impossible that He should be subject to its effect. God does not love; God *is* love.

Evangelicalism is responsible for much; not least for the crude and immoral doctrine that the object of a good life is to gain reward and to avoid punishment. But virtue needs no miracle to justify its worth; salvation is not bestowed by means of supernaturalism, it is the possible outcome of man's endeavours to obey the natural law of obligation, and in the universal recognition of this law, which binds phenomena in submission to the Supreme Authority, we find a scientific foundation of theological belief, and a system of ethics which, while providing for the noblest ideals of conduct, is built, not upon the shifting sands of speculation and assumption, but upon the bedrock of valid evidence and sound reasoning.

C. Penrhyn Gasquoine.

# CONTEMPORARY LITERATURE.

## SCIENCE.

THE success of the Nordrach open-air treatment of consumption has given rise to many imitations in this country, and efforts have been made to obtain the advantages of that treatment for those who are unable to leave their homes and occupations. Dr. J. J. S. Lucas, in his little work, *Nordrach at Home*,[1] has developed a system under which the patient is prescribed a maximum amount of fresh air, together with a strict but generous diet. The fresh air seems to be an indispensable aid to any successful treatment of tubercular disease ; but, with regard to the diet prescribed, we think a little more accuracy would have been desirable. For instance, the patient is told that he is consuming 8oz. of carbon and ½oz. of nitrogen when he eats a breakfast of which some of the items are : "Two rashers of bacon and two eggs (or chop, steak, or fish)." This is an affectation of accuracy which can only mislead the reader.

Considering the important part that glass plays in our daily life, it is surprising how little is known among the general public about its manufacture and working. Popular books on the subject have been scarce, and the factories themselves are usually in inaccessible neighbourhoods and are generally hot, dusty places that offer few attractions to the tourist. Now, however, even the man in the street can obtain full insight into the mysteries of glass-blowing by the perusal of a compact and instructive little work by Mr. P. N. Hasluck.[2] As the editor of *Work*, Mr. Hasluck has had excellent opportunities of collecting information, and of these he has availed himself to the fullest extent. The various operations of glass-blowing are fully described and illustrated, and there are interesting chapters on grinding specula, and on turning, chipping, and grinding glass generally. Even the drilling and riveting of glass and earthenware are fully described, and altogether the work is replete with valuable hints. When another edition becomes necessary, we would suggest that the illustrations of Liebig and Geissler's potash bulbs, on pages 60 and 61, be inverted, which will bring them into their correct position.

[1] *Nordrach at Home.* By J. J. S. Lucas. Bristol : J. W. Arrowsmith.
[2] *Glass Working.* By P. N. Hasluck. London, Paris, New York, and Melbourne : Cassell & Co., Ltd. 1899.

Another useful little text-book, and one dealing with a subject of general interest at the present moment, is Mr. S. R. Bottone's *Wireless Telegraphy.*[1] Although wireless telegraphy was really the first method of transmitting electrical signals, yet it has only recently been revived in a practical form, and its advocates do not hesitate to declare that it will in time supersede the transmission of messages through wires and cables. The modern resuscitation of wireless telegraphy is due to various advances in electrical science, and not to any particular invention. Among those whose labours have contributed most to the progress which has been made in this subject Mr. Bottone rightly mentions Hertz, Branly, and Lodge. The author's descriptions of the various pieces of apparatus are clear and free from unnecessary technicalities, and the general reader may, by the perusal of this work, acquire a very complete knowledge of the principles underlying wireless telegraphy and the apparatus now in use.

One of the great advantages of Darwin's work has been the largely increased interest taken in biological questions and the sifting of evidence, either in favour of or against the Darwinian theory of the survival of the fittest. Most of the facts ascertained since Darwin's death have undoubtedly been in favour of his views; but some do not so easily fit in with the theory propounded in the *Origin of Species*, and these, of course, are seized upon with avidity by the opponents of evolution. Most of those who think they can detect some instances that do not agree with the mass of facts collected and sifted by Darwin promptly rush into print, and thus secure whatever celebrity may be obtained by contradicting so great a naturalist. The consequence is that anti-Darwinian literature has attained a bulk out of all proportion to the value of its contents, and the supply shows no signs of abatement. We have received a work on *Darwin and Darwinism,*[2] in which the author dilates at very great length upon certain observations which do not, in his opinion, agree with some of Darwin's statements. It is not a difficult matter to criticise a book such as the *Origin of Species* in the light of the experience gained and the facts observed in the number of years which hav elapsed since the publication of that work, and we think Mr. Alex ander might have stated his case very fully in about one-tenth o the number of pages of which his book consists. The style of th author may be gauged from this reference to the *Origin of Specie* which has been rightly considered by high authorities as one of th best hundred books: "This confessedly incomplete, erroneous, an self-contradictory book." Of Darwin himself we are told that h "had a most insular mind, with small capacities of real independen

[1] *Wireless Telegraphy and Hertzian Waves.* By S. R. Bottone. London: Whittake and Co. 1900.
[2] *Darwin and Darwinism.* By P. Y. Alexander. London: John Bale, Sons an Danielson, Ltd. 1899.

thought, yet had little or no capacity for assimilating that of others, and, indeed, wrapped up in his own pursuits and conceptions, failed to read and to study where he ought to have done so." Mr. Alexander does not even hesitate to impute the most unworthy motives to one who was notoriously unselfish in character and always ready to assist others. He says: "It would have been more to his honour if he had brought his earlier books into line before going on to manufacture more. But then, you see, the books went on *selling —as they were, as they were."* We may safely predict that this will not be the case with the book before us, for, beyond a few original observations on birds, there is very little of scientific value in it.

## PHILOSOPHY AND THEOLOGY.

DR. HARALD HÖFFDING has accomplished something like a miracle: he has written *A History of Modern Philosophy*[1] which may be described as fascinating. It is much more than instructive and interesting, at least we have found it so; we have read it with positive pleasure. The reason for this is not far to seek. Dr. Höffding does not treat philosophy as a mere matter of abstract thinking having no relation to science, history, or persons; on the contrary, he attaches especial value to the personal factor and to the relation to empirical science, and gives the first place to the raising of problems rather than to their solution. The comparative method, which has been used with so much success in the treatment of religion, is here adopted in the treatment of philosophy. The history of philosophy, as Dr. Höffding says, is the history of the attempts which have been made by individual thinkers to discuss the ultimate problems of knowledge and life. The form in which these problems present themselves to modern thinkers is determined by modern natural science, while the solutions attempted have been affected by the personality of the philosopher. "There are thoughts which can only spring up on a particular psychological soil." It is the recognition of this truth, too commonly overlooked both in religion and philosophy, which gives originality to Dr. Höffding's work. Philosophers succeed one another, but not in an unrelated and disconnected order: a disciple uses the intellectual apparatus provided by his predecessor, and yet many arrive at very different conclusions; but without the first the second would never have appeared. Political and religious differences, as well as new scientific knowledge, will also affect the conclusions reached. So

[1] *A History of Modern Philosophy.* A Sketch of the History of Philosophy from the close of the Renaissance to our own day. By Dr. Harald Höffding. Translated from the German edition by B. E. Meyer. Two vols. London and New York: Macmillan and Co. 1900.

that in discussing a philosophical theory it is necessary to take into account all the circumstances in which it arose. This is what Dr. Höffding does with so much success, and gives us not only philosophies but living pictures of the philosophers.

Dr. Höffding rightly begins the history of modern philosophy with the Renaissance, which was a transition from the theological to the natural way of regarding the universe. Free thought took the place of theological thought; human nature asserted the rights of which ecclesiasticism had so long deprived it, and the intellect rejoiced in a freedom and expansion such as it had never known before: in a word, modern science and modern philosophy were born. Dr. Höffding regards the earliest contribution to the philosophy of the Renaissance as being Pomponazzi's little treatise, *De Immortalitate Animi*, because it declares the author's intention of discussing the question by the light of natural reason and independent of all authority. Humanism or "the discovery of man," as our author calls it, came first, and then came the new conception of the world to which Copernicus has given his name; this, indeed, may be regarded as the starting-point of modern thought. It changed everything, truth for truth's sake became the object of search, and Giordano Bruno was its martyr; Kepler, Galileo, and Francis Bacon carried on the great work, and they were followed by the philosophers Descartes, Gassendi, Hobbes, Spinoza, and Leibniz. One gratifying feature in Dr. Höffding's book is the justice he does to the English thinkers Locke, Newton, Hume, Adam Smith, Hartley, and especially John Stuart Mill. A large amount of space is necessarily devoted to the French philosophers of the eighteenth century, who developed English philosophy on lines of their own; to the critical philosophy, Romanticism, and Positivism. But all through fresh light is thrown upon each development by Dr. Höffding's psychological method, and the insight it gives him into the workings of the human mind. Nothing escapes him. The work done in merely gathering the material for these volumes must have been prodigious; more than sixty English writers alone are referred to, the life and works of the principal of whom are treated at considerable length. Italy, France, and Germany are treated in the same exhaustive manner. We have tried to convey to our readers some idea of the contents of this welcome contribution to the history of modern philosophy, but we are quite unable to convey a full impression of the masterly manner in which it is done; it should be read by every one who takes the slightest interest in the higher departments of human thought; it will interest every educated reader as well as serve as an invaluable guide to those who are making philosophy a special study. The translator is to be congratulated on the spirited English in which the work is presented to English readers.

## MEDICAL.

So much sickly sentiment has been spent on nursing and nurses that it is well the public should learn that there are many black sheep in the much-lauded flock. Mr. Gant, whose noble ideas of perfect womanhood illustrate his previous works, has had great experience of nurses in both hospital and private practice. It is therefore well that he should undertake to expose the malpractices of the few who disgrace the general body. This he has done in a series of stories of sham nurses[1] drawn from life. Like many of his professional brethren, he has had to deplore the existence of the mock nurses who prey on the reputation of the real. The titles he gives to some of these show the necessity of his exposure—*e g*, " Satan in Petticoats," the " Husband Hunters," the " Breach of Promise Nurse," and so on. Most of the stories appeared last year in the *Medical Press and Circular*, and provoked some indignant remonstrances from correspondents, who seemed to think every self-styled nurse impeccable. Mr. Gant is one of the warmest supporters of nurses as a class, and this very book is written in their interest.

He would purify their ranks and register all those who have been properly trained and whose conduct is satisfactory. Registration is just now a popular cry. We are told that a plumber ought to be registered before being allowed to stop a leaking waterpipe. The spectacle-makers have lately obtained authority to register, and the consequence is a new danger to the public, for some of them are posing as qualified to give advice as to defects of sight, about which they know as much as other mechanics. The registration of nurses cannot improve their training or character, and would certainly include for a long time a number of incompetent persons and a few of the mock class exposed by Mr. Gant. The truth is that nurses have been too much pampered ; consequently they are apt to forget their proper position and first duty—obedience. The perfect nurse is a servant of the patient and the doctor—a skilled servant called in for special assistance. The nurse who disobeys or thwarts the doctor deserves the same condemnation as the soldier who so treats his officer. Yet it is to be feared that a spirit of insubordination too often spoils the work of even a devoted nurse. As to the fraudulent persons who trade on the good repute of the true nurse, Mr. Gant's book is a useful warning.

[1] *Mock Nurses of the Latest Fashion.* By Frederick James Gant, F.R.C.S., &c. London : Baillière, Tindall & Co. 1900.

## SOCIOLOGY, POLITICS, AND JURISPRUDENCE.

WE gladly welcome the second edition of Mr. Charles Waldstein's powerful vindication of the Jews, entitled *The Jewish Question.*[1] To the original work published anonymously Mr. Waldstein has added an introductory chapter dealing with the latest Jewish movements, viz., the Dreyfus case, the spread of anti-Semitism in Austria, and the Zionist movement among the Jews themselves. Paradoxical as it may seem, Mr. Waldstein boldly declares there is no Jewish Question. A study of the Dreyfus case certainly prepared us for this curious state of affairs, so far as France was concerned. It soon became evident as the mysteries of that case were solved that anti-Semitism in France was but a cloak for other designs by the anti-Dreyfusites. But until we read Mr. Waldstein's convincing treatise we have never understood the Jewish Question as a whole. We have waded through long-winded articles upon anti-Semitism in the *Nineteenth Century* and other magazines without any other result than utter mystification and loss of temper.

Just as there is no true Semitic party, so there is no true anti-Semitic party. The nearest approach to the former, says Mr. Waldstein, is the union of all civilised nations in protesting against the iniquitous Dreyfus verdict. In France anti-Semitism is identical with Clericalism, *alias* anti-Protestantism, and Nationalism, *alias* Chauvinism. In Austria it is identifying itself with the Catholic, Clerical, and Conservative parties. In Germany it is associated with the Agrarians and Conservatives, having previously been mainly Socialistic.

But this book is not merely political, it is also largely historical, and deals sympathetically with the large part played by Jews in the social and economic life of European nations.

Many people, no doubt, will be surprised to learn how large a share the Jews have taken in the various intellectual movements throughout Europe, and the sooner they possess themselves of this valuable contribution to the history of the development of human knowledge the better. The Jews are not all Isaac Gordons.

*Law without Lawyers: An Epitome of the Laws of England for Practical Use,*[2] by Two Barristers-at-Law, approaches as nearly those ideal times when the wicked shall cease from troubling as any such handbook we have seen. It forms an attempt, as the authors tell us, of enabling the layman to solve for himself without recourse to professional assistance, " those legal doubts and difficulties that are continually arising in everyday life." But so long as there are laws

---

[1] *The Jewish Question and the Mission of the Jews.* By Charles Waldstein. Second edition. With a Chapter dealing with the Dreyfus case, Zionism, &c., and an Appendix. London : Gay & Bird. 1899.

[2] *Law without Lawyers : An Epitome of the Laws of England for Practical Use.* By Two Barristers-at-Law. London : John Murray. 1900.

so long will there be lawyers to interpret them.  Unfortunately the English law does not consist of clear commands and prohibitions which have only to be stated to be understood.  There are so many qualifications, so many exceptions to the simplest proposition, that a trained mind becomes absolutely necessary.  Moreover, the average man has not that judicial mind which is required in the elucidation of the technical language in which legal ideas are necessarily expressed.  People who rely upon their own natural instinct upon even the apparently simplest legal problem will often find to their cost that it would have been far cheaper to have taken professional advice.  There is no truer saying than that the man who acts as his own lawyer has a fool for his client.  Even experienced lawyers are chary of acting for themselves.

Nevertheless, with the aid of such a book as the present covering most of the ground over which the average man may have to travel, he ought to avoid many of the pitfalls of the law.  To compress into one volume of 700 pages the whole of the English law is obviously impossible, but the authors have been eminently successful in giving the main outlines of those rights and liabilities affecting the ordinary citizen.  For the purpose of solving those knotty points of the law with which it is the business of the expert to deal the book is useless, but in giving a clear general idea of a man's position of, for example, an executor, a husband, or parent it could scarcely be bettered.  On the other hand there are serious omissions. For instance, there is not a word about the law relating to the Stock Exchange or to money-lenders, the law of which is at least of equal value to the average man as the law of merchant shipping, copyright or patents.  However, as it is the book is a marvel of cheap production.  In producing 700 pages of accurate information well printed on good paper and handsomely bound for 6s, Mr. Murray has distinctly rivalled the new American Press.

The war continues to produce the usual crop of books, good, bad, and indifferent.  Any history properly so-called is, of course, out of the question till long after the close of the war.  "For such a work," writes Mr. Spenser Wilkinson in his Preface to *Lessons of The War* [1] "must be based upon a close study of the military correspondence of the generals, and upon the best records to be had of the doings of both sides.  Nor can the tactical lessons of a war be fully set forth until detailed and authoritative accounts of the battles are accessible."

The modern man, however, apparently prefers to have his war-history by instalments, each brought up to date as closely as possible.  He does not ask for niceties of strategy.  He merely wants

---

[1] *Lessons of the War.* Being Comments from Week to Week to the Relief of Lady-smith. By Spenser Wilkinson. Westminster: Archibald Constable & Co. Philadelphia: J. B. Lippincott Company. 1900.

a rough idea of how affairs in the field are going, and from that form his own conclusions for the moment.

Mr. Wilkinson's contribution consists of the republication of a series of weekly papers to *The London Letter* consisting of critical reviews of the operations of the moment. Such reviews, even though to some extent ephemeral, yet have a certain permanent value. Mr. Wilkinson is a well-recognised military critic, and although we cannot agree with all his political opinions his indictment of the Government for their invertebrate policy in the conduct of the war is well founded. Another criticism equally well founded is that directed against the present system of entrusting the administration of war to an incompetent politician. When the nation discovers its danger, he says it will no longer tolerate the practice of choosing a Secretary of State for War for his ignorance of the subject.

*Towards Pretoria,*[1] by Mr. Julian Ralph, Special War Correspondent to the *Daily Mail,* is an entirely different work, consisting mainly of his personal experiences before the war and with Lord Methuen's force. A short historical introduction of little value is followed by a defence of Sir Alfred Milner, a graphic picture of Cape Town, with a few well-known Boer stories, a page or two on the climate and the Kaffirs, a chapter on Natal and Ladysmith, of which the English newspaper reader probably knows more about the campaign in that quarter than Mr. Ralph, form so much padding to an otherwise most interesting book.

In his description of the Modder River campaign Mr. Ralph does not offer much criticism. Modern weapons and explosives have, he says, entirely changed modern warfare. Nor does he offer anything further to our knowledge of the Maaghersfontein disaster. His *forte* lies in describing the incidents of the fight and the nature of the country. His obvious Boer hatred, natural enough, no doubt, under the circumstances, disqualifies him from speaking with authority upon the Boer character. When we say that he has the gift of making us picture to ourselves the scenes he lightly sketches, we can give him no higher praise. The appendices contain some useful documents and tables of facts.

*The Transvaal in War and Peace,*[2] by Mr. Neville Edwards, should meet with a large and ready sale. It is not remarkable, it is true, for historical accuracy or for any very deep views or political insight, but it contains a bright and chatty account of the various places in which interest is at present centred throughout South Africa. As an instance of Mr. Edwards' historical

1 *Towards Pretoria.* A Record of the War between Briton and Boer to the hoisting of the British Flag at Bloemfontein. By Julian Ralph. With Historical Foreword, Appendices and Map. London : O. Arthur Pearson, Ltd. 1900.
2 *The Transvaal in War and Peace.* By Neville Edwards. With numerous Illustrations. London : H. Virtue & Co., Ltd. 1900.

inaccuracy, we may mention the statement that Kruger and Joubert took office under the English Government after the annexation in 1877. Joubert was the one honest Boer who stoutly refused any connection with the Government. There are extremely interesting descriptions of the principal towns and of their life and customs, together with plenty of good stories of Dutch and English inhabitants alike.

Mr. Edwards' criticisms upon the War Office and our officers in the field are very much to the point. The War Office is incorrigible, and we have not the patience to deal with it. We naturally shrink from attacking our officers, but when disasters are directly attributable to their self-conceit we feel bound to speak. As Mr. Edwards says, when colonials who know what they are talking about offer their advice to English officers, they are only snubbed. To take one instance out of many. The disaster of Isandula would never have occurred if colonial advice had not been utterly disregarded. Mr. Edwards is very optimistic of the future of the Transvaal after the war, believing that agriculture and mining will open employment for our emigrants. This may be doubted so far as agriculture is concerned.

The most remarkable feature of the book is the wealth of the illustration. Every place of interest or likely to be of interest is here reproduced, and every regiment, we imagine, is represented. Many of the photographs are by the author himself, and are exceedingly good, quite equal to any of the professional ones.

*The Boer in Peace and War,*[1] by Mr. Arthur M. Mann, as its title implies, deals principally with the Boer characteristics, and confirms the popular opinion of our present antagonist. It is a bird's-eye view, and may be read comfortably in an hour, but it is worth reading.

*To Modder River with Methuen,*[2] by the well-known War Correspondent Mr. Alfred Kinnear, will also take but a short time in the reading. It is a story which will do something to modify assumptions hitherto hastily made. It tells of exhausting victories, long marches with insufficient food, bad water, and terrible disasters. It tells of wrong tactics, and hints at insubordination among the commanding officers, but it also seeks to do justice to a general who laboured from deficient resources, and to correct the impression of a campaign "shelled with blunders." Mr. Kinnear tells the same tale of colonial offers of aid and advice. Both were declined by the Imperial authorities with freezing politeness. When will our Jacks-in-office learn the elements of the business they profess to conduct?

[1] *The Boer in Peace and War.* By Arthur M. Mann. With Sixteen Illustrations London : John Long. 1900.
[2] *To Modder River with Methuen.* Briton, Boer, and Battleness. By Alfred Kinnear. Bristol : J. W. Arrowsmith. London : Simpkin, Marshall, Hamilton, Kent and Co., Ltd.

## VOYAGES AND TRAVELS.

IT may be remembered that it was in 1895 that the French Expeditionary Corps occupied Antananarivo, and received the submission of the Hovas. This volume[1] is a detailed account of the measures taken to combat the rebellion which broke out in the following year, and of the gradual pacification of the entire island of Madagascar during that and the three following years. The task of solidifying French authority in the island was entrusted to General Gallieni, who had already made himself famous by his successful campaigns in Suakin and the Soudan: all civil and military authority was placed in his hands. In accounting for the rapid and decisive results which followed upon the General's administration, the author sums up the rules which he followed thus: Unity of action and direction in each district; the largest possible initiative left to subordinate commanders in the choice of executive methods; progressive and methodical occupation, each step forward being supported by the establishment of military posts and bases, and later on by armed native colonies; the employment of force in those cases only where pacific measures had failed. This work is something more than a popular account of warlike operations; specialists will find in the latter part of the volume much information upon the working of the different arms of the service, and upon the feeding and lodging of an army. There are some excellent coloured maps and sketches which enable the reader to follow the occupation step by step, while numerous photographs of the places and peoples of the island much enhance the value of the book from the popular point of view. It is a record of a colonial effort of which France may be in every way justly proud.

---

## HISTORY AND BIOGRAPHY.

THE war in South Africa makes the important work just published by Messrs. Smith, Elder & Co., *The Life and Times of Sir John Charles Molteno*,[2] exceptionally interesting. The book is not merely a biography of the first Premier of Cape Colony, but a history of responsible government at the Cape of Lord Carnarvon's Federation Policy and of Sir Bartle Frere's High Commissionership of South Africa. Mr. P. A. Molteno has devoted great care to the work, and,

1 *La Pacification de Madagascar (Operations d'Octobre 1896 à Mars 1899)*. *Ouvrage Rédigé d'apres les Archives de l'Etat-Major du Corps d'Occupation*. Par F. Hellot, Capitaine du Génie. Paris : R. Chapelot et Cie. 1900.
2 *The Life and Times of Sir John Charles Molteno, K.C.M.G.* By P. A. Molteno, M.A., LL.M. London : Smith, Elder & Co.

as the text was completed before the outbreak of the war, there is not even the shadow of an excuse for charging the author with partisanship. The late Sir John C. Molteno had a very remarkable career. He was born three months before the final cession of the Cape of Good Hope to England, and one year before the battle of Waterloo. His father was a Catholic, and was in the Home Civil Service at Somerset House. At an early age he got an appointment which induced him to proceed to the Cape. He was only seventeen at the time, and was destined to play an important part in the history of the colony. His attachment to the country of his adoption enhances the value of the evidence furnished by his experiences as to the real state of affairs in South Africa. After a hard struggle he succeeded in making a fortune by industry, enterprise, and perseverance. When the Kaffir War broke out in 1846 he volunteered as a burgher, and was elected assistant-commandant by his fellow burghers. This war was in many respects a disastrous one, but it taught Molteno something about fighting, and also showed him the futility of attempting to set South African affairs right by brute force. After the war he sat in the first Cape Parliament, and his career is a proof of the capacity of Englishmen for self-government. One of his first useful acts as a practical politician was to initiate legislation for the improvement of the law as to master and servant in the colony. To his efforts was also due the establishment of responsible Government in Cape Colony. During the *régime* of Lord Carnarvon, Mr. Molteno strenuously fought for popular rights. The views of such a man on the entire South African Question must be regarded as of the most weighty character. In the circumstances which led the Dutch to set out on the Great Trek ending in the foundation of the Transvaal Republic and the Orange Free State, England, as Mr. P. A. Molteno remarks, "appeared a harsh and unjust stepmother. The name of Downing Street had become a name of opprobrium and reproach throughout the Cape Colony." Can we wonder that it was more detested still amongst the Dutch farmers? In his manly stand against the aggressive action of Lord Carnarvon and Mr. Froude the subject of this admirable biography proved himself a true statesman. He showed that he fully realised the value of political liberty to a young colony, and he fought doggedly for his principles. Such a man may not appeal to the spirit of Imperialistic rapine, like Mr. Cecil Rhodes, but when the future history of South Africa comes to be written we shall find its pioneers and patriots amongst the Moltenos, and not amongst the Rhodeses!

The volume on *British America*[1] in "The British Empire Series" is full of valuable information. Most people know something about Canada, but Jamaica is to some extent a *terra incognita*. The

---

[1] *British America.* With Two Maps. (British Empire Series, vol. iii.) London: Kegan Paul, Trench, Trübner & Co., Ltd.

account of Nova Scotia, by Mr. James S. Macdonald, gives a glowing description of that much-favoured colony. The volume also contains an admirable review of Canadian literature by Sir J. G. Bourinot.

*Souvenirs Inédits sur Napoléon*[1] contains some very interesting reminiscences from the "Notes" of Senator Gross, Municipal Councillor of Leipzig, from 1807 to 1815. The Senator had several conversations with Napoleon, in which the latter showed himself not merely a man of action, but a shrewd and practical-minded person. Indeed, it is evident that, if he had not been a great commander, *le petit caporal* would have made a successful merchant.

Few more absorbing autobiographies have ever been written than *Mémoires d'une Idéaliste*,[2] by Malwida von Meysenbug. We gather from the preface to the book, by M. Gabriel Monad, that Malwida von Meysenbug was a descendant of a French Huguenot family which had taken refuge in Hesse, and had become German by marriage, and received from the Elector William I. of Hesse-Cassel the title of Baron von Meysenbug. We may trace her French origin in the simplicity of her style as well as in her democratic antagonism to the conservative traditions amidst which she was reared. The life of Fraulein von Meysenbug was full of interest owing to her utter freedom from conventionality. She was, in the noblest sense of the word, an emancipated woman. Brought up in a Lutheran family with conservative views, she liberated her mind at an early age from the code in which it was sought to cramp her nature. Her development in the direction of advanced liberal ideas was due partly to her love for Theodore Althaus—unhappily ill requited—and partly to her innate love of independence. Even when her dream of happiness had ended in disappointment, and when her own family had become bitterly hostile to her, she bravely faced the world, earned her bread, and never for one moment swerved from her high principles. During her sojourn in England she met a number of distinguished refugees, including Kossuth, Mazzini, Orsini, Herzen, Ledru-Rollin, Louis Blanc, Karl Schurz, and Kinkel. We find in her Memoirs admirable portraits of these noble and generous spirits who placed love of country and of humanity before all personal or selfish considerations. It was in the household of the great Russian writer, Alexander Herzen, that she contracted the strongest attachment. She undertook the education of the daughters of this illustrious exile, and in 1862 she accompanied one of Herzen's daughters, Olga, to Italy, where she has resided ever since. The charm of the narrative in which this accomplished woman tells the story of her life can only be appreciated by those who read it. Her intensely sympathetic character reveals itself on every page. We

[1] *Souvenirs Inédits sur Napoléon.* D'après le Journal du Senateur Gross. Par Capitaine Veling. Paris : R. Chapelot et Cie.
[2] *Mémoires d'une Idéaliste.* Par Malwida de Meysenburg. Préface par Gabriel Monod. Paris : Librairie Fischbachen.

see it in her pathetic account of the death of the lover who deserted her, and whom she subsequently nursed, when even the members of his own family left him to die alone. We see it in her references to the unfortunate Frenchman, Barthélemy, who was executed in 1855 for a mysterious murder, the real motive for which was never made clear. We see it in her enthusiastic praise of that great-souled Englishwoman, Emilie Reeve. We see it, too, in her passionate admiration of the Polish patriot, Stanislas Worcell, who certainly was a man "out of ten thousand," though that may not have been the opinion of the average Anglo-Saxon. Her impressions of Mazzini cannot fail to interest the admirers of that gifted and heroic man. On the question of education she has much to say. She disapproves of what is called "religious" education, but she suggests that children should be taught to reverence the heroes and the leaders of their race. It is gratifying to learn that now, in her eighty-third year, Malwida von Meysenbug remains faithful to the aspirations of her youth.

In a volume entitled *Trois Femmes de la Révolution* [1] M. Léopold Lacour has given us accurate portraits of three interesting personalities—Olympe de Gouges, Théroigne de Méricourt, and Rose Lacombe. The materials from which the author derived his minute knowledge of the lives of those extraordinary women are either unpublished documents or the testimony of contemporaries. The book will be read with intense interest by all who desire to know the truth about the Revolution and the chief actors in that great historic drama. M. Léopold Lacour does justice to the noble side of the women who espoused the cause of their own sex during the wild fever of the Revolution. Olympe de Gouges, whose sympathies were to some extent with the *ancien régime*, directly championed the rights of women to citizenship as well as to that common justice which in her day was not accorded to them as human beings. She is rightly credited with having been one of the first pioneers of feminism—a glory which she shares with Mary Wollstonecraft.

The portion of the volume devoted to Théroigne de Méricourt clears up many of the obscurities which have surrounded that strange woman's life. In spite of her faults, Théroigne was a true patriot, and it is easy to conceive that, when the Revolution was at its height, she was worshipped as a popular idol. In our cold-blooded days we can scarcely realise the enthusiasm and wild emotion of a people rejoicing over their new-found liberty. The account of Théroigne de Méricourt's insanity gives some very painful details, which cannot fail to excite pity for a woman who, in spite of her frailties, loved France "not wisely but too well." Perhaps the study of Rose Lacombe is the most important of the three from a purely historical point of view. The association of

1 *Trois Femmes de la Révolution.* Par Léopold Lacour. Paris : Librairie Plon.

La Citoyenne Lacombe with the famous club of " Républicaines Révolutionnaires," which struck terror into the heart of Robespierre, imparts an additional interest to her biography, and entitles her to the honour of having given a great impetus to the Woman Movement in the early stages of its history. Altogether this volume is a splendid example of the psychological and realistic method of dealing with historical questions, and we anticipate for M. Léopold Lacour's work a brilliant and enduring success.

---

## BELLES LETTRES.

*A Man of His Age* [1] must be acknowledged to possess one great merit which few historical novels exhibit—dramatic verisimilitude. Mr. Hamilton Drummond thoroughly understands the period with which he deals, and in the narrative of Blaise de Bernauld he gives us a most vivid picture of France in the days of Coligny. The incidents follow one another in rapid succession, and every scene in the story is presented to us as if we saw the whole thing happening before our eyes. In many respects this book is superior to anything that Mr. Stanley Weyman has written. The characters are splendidly limned. The brave but villainous Denis la Hake is a real personality—a marvellous portrait of a type of man for whom the world has to-day no counterpart. The glimpses which Mr. Drummond gives us of Jeanne D'Albret and Henri of Navarre are deeply interesting. Perhaps the only defects in the story are the solecisms into which the author is occasionally betrayed. Surely Blaise de Bernault would never have spoken of the " ipsissima verba" of a letter? Neither would he have used the expression " hysteria " with reference to an angry mob. But there are spots on the sun; and, when all has been said, it must be candidly admitted that *A Man of His Age* is a work of a very high order indeed.

*His 'Prentice Hand* [2] is apparently a study of the feminine mind under the influence of religious faddism. Ethel Vivian is scarcely a lifelike person, but there is much cleverness in the narrative, and the author, Mr. Sydney Phelps, has the art of making everything come right in the end. The novel is worth reading, but it is desirable that Mr. Phelps should try to gather his materials for his next work from observation of actual life.

*The Experiment of Dr. Nevil* [3] is one of those fantasti cattempts to construct a story out of a scientific phantasmagoria of which we have had only too many specimens of late. The idea of this somewhat ridiculous tale is that the brain-tissue of a man who has been executed for murder may be removed into the brain of another man

[1] *A Man of His Age.* By Hamilton Drummond. London : Ward, Lock & Co.
[2] *His 'Prentice Hand.* By Sydney Phelp. London : John Long.
[3] *The Experiment of Dr. Nevil.* By Emeric Hulme-Beaman. London : John Long

suffering from the effects of an accident, with the result that the latter regains the use of his faculties but is, for a time at least, endowed with the murderer's personality. The part played by Lord Carsdale is, of course, physiologically and psychologically impossible. The author, however, displays much ingenuity in working out his extravagant plot. Mr. Hulme-Beaman possesses decided talent, though he shows very little discretion in his selection of a subject. Even the late Robert Louis Stevenson, or even Mr. Wells, could not lend to the plot of this book an aspect of vraisemblance. No wonder, then, that Mr. Hulme-Beaman has failed to do so!

*All Fools,*[1] by Marmaduke Pickthall—is the author's aristocratic name an assumed one?—may fairly be described as "excellent fooling." The characters in the book are all puppets created for the purpose of making the reader laugh. It must be confessed that some fun is really evolved out of Blackstone, Brown-Geegee, the bulldog, Mr. Lee-Stretton, and Miss Woodward. The same result would, however, have been produced by a Punch and Judy entertainment. The production of such books as *All Fools* is one of the literary crimes for which the late Charles Dickens, that most artificial of humorists, has to answer.

*The House of Hardale,*[2] by Rose Perkins, is a well-written but most unconvincing novel. The subject, too, is trite. We have read only too often about the practical-minded father and the scapegrace son. But, indeed, there is so much new fiction that we can scarcely wonder at the lack of novelty in a great number of our latterday novels.

*The Angel of Chance*[3] is scarcely equal to *The Sport of Circumstance,* by the same author. It might be described as a wateringplace romance. The opening scene in which the hero and heroine meet while bathing is awkwardly managed, to say the least of it. How differently a French novelist would deal with such an incident! The story ends happily, and in spite of the author's apparent wish to appear unconventional, the novel shows a painful effort to avoid offending Mrs. Grundy.

*A Fighter in Khaki*[4] is an "up-to-date" novel. Of course it deals with the war in South Africa. Presumably "Ralph Rodd" is a fictitious name. Judging from this specimen, we cannot predict for the author a brilliant literary career.

Anything written by Count Lyof Tolstoy must arrest public attention. He is one of the great spirits of the century. In *Résurrection*[5] he has dealt with Russian prisons with terrible power. The book has been admirably translated into French by M. T. de

[1] *All Fools.* By Marmaduke Pickthall. London : Swan Sonnenschein & Co.
[2] *The House of Hardale.* By Rose Perkins. [3] *The Angel of Chance.* By G. Chatterton. [4] *A Fighter in Khaki.* By Ralph Rodd. London : John L G.
[5] *Résurrection.* Par Comte Léon Tolstoy. Traduit par M. T. de Wyzema. o
Perrin et Cie. Paris :

Wyzema. The character of Nekludov is an extraordinary study, and in his portrait of the fallen woman Maslova, Tolstoy exhibits an almost Balzacian power. The fault of the book is its didacticism—a fault from which none of Tolstoy's works are quite free.

The readers of THE WESTMINSTER REVIEW may remember some articles which appeared in it from the pen of Thomas E. Mayne. This promising young Irish writer has, we regret to find, been cut off before his powers had full time to mature. A neat volume of short stories by the late Mr. Mayne, with the attractive title of *The Heart o' the Peat*,[1] has been recently published. Of these tales it must be said that they are all " racy of the soil "—all true pictures of Irish life. There is about most of them an undertone of sadness, peculiar to writers who die young. A handsome copy of Mr. Mayne's book was presented to Queen Victoria on her arrival in Ireland.

An excellent translation of the Second Book of *Herodotus* [2] has been published in the University Tutorial Series by Mr. W. B. Clive. The translation is the work of Mr. J. F. Stout, B.A. Camb. At the end of the volume some test-papers on the text are given.

*Storyology* [3] is the unhappy title of a very readable and amusing volume by Mr. Benjamin Taylor. The author discusses such odd subjects as " The Devil's Candle " and " Davy Jones's Locker." We are surprised to find that " Davy Jones " may be traced to the Hindoo Deva or the Welsh Taffy, but sailors are often learned folk, and strange things " happen at sea."

M. Paul Bourget's *Drames de Famille* [4] have all the distinction of that gifted writer's style. Each of the stories in the volume has a distinct interest both from a dramatic and a psychological point of view. *L'Echcance* is, perhaps, the least dramatic narrative in the book. The conversion of a practical-minded and successful young physician into a monk owing to the dishonest conduct of his parents is an event scarcely in accordance with our preconceived ideas of human nature. *Le Luxe des Autres* is a very powerful story of modern Parisian life. The character of Mme. le Prieux, that cold-hearted fashionable beauty, is a splendid study—perhaps one of the most marvellous to be found in any of M. Paul Bourget's works. Of the shorter stories in the book *Résurrection* is the best. It is, indeed, an exquisitely beautiful idyl of child-life. The author of *Crime d'Amour* has certainly, by this charming volume, sustained his high reputation as one of the finest contemporary French writers.

Miss Isabelle Kaiser is at present the most popular Swiss poet. Her style is marked not only by cultured imagination, but the most

[1] *The Heart o' the Peat.* By Thomas E. Mayne. London : Simpkin, Marshall & Co. Belfast : W. Erskine Mayne.
[2] *Herodotus.* Book II. Translation by J. F. Stout, B.A. Camb. London: W. B. Clive.        [3] *Storyology.* By Benjamin Taylor. London : Elliot Stock.
[4] *Drames de Famille.* Par Paul Bourget. Paris : Librairie Plon.

exquisite feeling and tenderness, added to a true spirit of Christianity, are some of the many rare qualities which characterise it. She writes French and German with equal facility and with an astonishing command of language. Since the great poet, Heinrich Heine, no author has written in such a masterly way in those two languages. She has just published two new novels—*Our Father*,[1] the present book, and *Hero*—which will be read with avidity by all English people who have visited the Lake of Lucerne, but of this we will speak on some future occasion. *Our Father* is a study of morals ; the end it has in view is to show that amongst those who deviate from the right path very few do so from natural inclination, but are more generally driven to it by the various circumstances or evil influences to which they are exposed. It is an ingenious idea to have given to each chapter the title of one of the eight petitions of which the "Pater" is composed without in any way disconnecting them. The author shows the possibility of redeeming those unhappy beings by pity, pardon, and prayer, however deep the abyss into which they have fallen. It suffices to meet with some good influence which would teach more by example than by words ; making them first to· respect themselves, in order to be respected by others. The apostle who, however humble his sphere, undertakes such a mission towards his fellow creatures, is worthy of the Christ. The unfortunate would never be repulsed by him, and he would deprive himself of everything for his neighbour. Why are such men so rare ? Full of evangelical charity, *Our Father* is an interesting, real, breathing romance, that we should like to see translated into English.

---

## ART.

THE convenient, well-written, and well-illustrated works of Mr. Lewis F. Day on Ornament and its application in the various decorative arts promise to form a series like those of M. Henry Havard in French. The latest volume (5*s.*, with 78 full-page plates from photographs, and 28 illustrations in text) devotes over 250 pages to *Art in Needlework*.[2] The book has been composed with the co-operation of Miss Mary Buckle, whose name appears on the title-page, and who is chiefly responsible for the technical part, leaving design and ornament to Mr. Day. A practical embroiderer must have been needed to disentangle all the ornamental stitches which the authors explain ; for their theme—embroidery as distinct from tapestry and lace—brings up constantly " stitch and stuff with reference to their use in ornament." In the illustration of samplers, the back is given too, so that the practical

[1] *Notre Père qui êtes aux Cieux.* Par Isabelle Kaiser. Paris : Perrin et Cie.
[2] *Art in Needlework.* A Book about Embroidery. By Lewis F. Day and Mary Buckle. London : B. T. Batsford. 1900.

needlewoman will be as satisfied as the artist; there are even parts which "should be read needle-and-thread in hand—or skipped." After a general chapter on embroidery and embroidery stitches, there are eighteen more on the various stitches in particular—herring-bone, Oriental, darning, couched gold, and all the rest. The eleven final chapters deal with outline and shading, figure embroidery, Church work, design and materials, and general advice. The examples chosen for illustration represent impartially the needlework of all nations and ages, from the East to Western Ind, from Egypt and Coptic embroidery, and the Syon cope of mediæval England to modern darning designed by William Morris. And there is a very good index.

A new volume is to hand from Bell's Cathedral Series, of which many numbers have been noticed here during the past two years. The method adopted from the beginning is consistently followed out. There is a history of the fabric, with a description of the exterior and interior, followed by a history of the Episcopal See of which it is the seat (*cathedra*). The volume on *Saint Paul's*[1] adds to this an account of the old buildings, which is full of interest. It is not only the general details which make the importance of this series; the particulars given are sufficient to guide on his way the artist and the historian, while the careful sightseer finds step by step the explanation of each part. The illustrations are well chosen, and the views of Old Saint Paul's are of unusual interest. The author says, by the way, of the cathedral treasures destroyed and sold under Edward VI. in the heat of reform: "Elaborate gold and silver embroidered work found its way to Spanish cathedrals, and up to a short time ago was reported to be still there." Any tourist can be shown at Tarragona, for a single example, what are said to be altar ornaments of Henry VIII. of England; a competent student of art-history might do worse than take time to report on these relics of our mediæval art.

No one will dispute Mr. Selwyn Brinton's competence to treat historically of Italian Painters; and the excellent methods adopted by Messrs. Bell for their series of Great Masters in Painting and Sculpture give a peculiar value to his volume on *Correggio*.[2] For all but the most detailed study it is a veritable handbook to the art and literature of the subject. In the notes on the "Virtue" and "Vice" of the Louvre collection (they are in the Hall of Drawings, and not among the paintings) Morelli's views are exaggerated (see English edition, p. 313, where genuineness of these "originals" is left undoubted).

[1] *Saint Paul's.* By the Rev. Arthur Dimock, M.A. (Bell's Cathedral Series.) London : George Bell & Sons. 1900.
[2] *Correggio.* By Selwyn Brinton, M.A. London : George Bell & Sons. 1900.

# INDEX.